# ROTHMANS SNOOKER YEARBOOK 1990-91

Editor: Janice Hale

ROTHMANS
Queen Anne Press

A QUEEN ANNE PRESS BOOK



First published in Great Britain in 1990 by
Queen Anne Press, a division of
Macdonald & Co (Publishers) Ltd
Orbit House
1 New Fetter Lane
London EC4A 1AR

A member of Maxwell Macmillan Pergamon Publishing Corporation

*Front cover photograph*: Dean Reynolds (David Muscroft)

*Back cover photograph*: Steve Davis and Dean Reynolds at the Rothmans Grand Prix 1989 (David Muscroft)

*Black and white photographs*: Eric Whitehead



British Library Cataloguing in Publication Data

Rothmans snooker yearbook. — 1990–91—
1. Snooker — Serials
794.7′35′05

ISBN 0-356-19102-8

Typeset by SB Datagraphics, Colchester, Essex

Printed and bound in Great Britain by BPCC Hazell Books Ltd, Aylesbury, Buckinghamshire

# CONTENTS

## ACKNOWLEDGEMENTS

The editor would like to thank the following for their assistance in compiling this book:
Clive Everton, editor of *Snooker Scene* magazine
Julie Kane, whose statistical research has been invaluable

## A VERY SPECIAL SNOOKER WEEK

**Bob Holmes, snooker correspondent of the *London Evening Standard***

Sociologists and tabloid news hounds may disagree but the rule that snooker players must keep at least one foot on the ground during play is, with the odd memorable exception, a practice maintained well beyond the television lights.

Unlike certain cosseted upstarts in other spheres, superstars of the green baize seldom stray far from their roots: mornings after major triumphs are often 'celebrated' with a few quiet frames at the local club where fine tuning for the next tournament will resume before the same unsung sage.

Anyone still to be convinced of such down-to-earth qualities should make the annual pilgrimage to the Pro-Am extravaganza at Prestatyn at the end of May. For here among the barrack-room accommodation blocks and cafeteria catering on the north Wales coast, the mighty meet the merely ordinary, and the humble amateur may grasp a once-in-a-lifetime chance to slay his hero.

For the stars it can be the ultimate hiding to nothing: play brilliantly and you still face humiliation with the handicap system, while even victory may not pay the bar bill. Yet many of those who do not qualify for a holiday voucher keep coming back for more.

There are countless similar centres dotted about the coast and there are other Pro-Ams, but in snooker there is only one 'Pontins'. The eagerly-awaited potting orgy overlooking the Irish Sea was once a commercial twinkle in the eye of Fred Pontin, who sought imaginative schemes to fill his chalets. He whispered it to Ted Lowe who understood the grass roots of the game and the upshot was an overnight institution.

The secret was that the concept appealed as much to the club player seeking a moment of glory as it did to the household name looking for a respite from it. And its reputation was further enhanced last season when newly-crowned world champion Stephen Hendry declared: 'I wouldn't miss it for anything.'

Most 21-year-old millionaires would probably prefer Club Med but Hendry, who is closing on the Mansells and Faldos as British sport's biggest earner, dutifully spent three nights in a chalet 'which', said an official, 'was just like all the rest', to pocket a less-than-princely £2,700. And if that is not testimony enough to the place's peculiar magnetism, just before his first match the normally icicle-veined Scot admitted: 'I was shakin' like a leaf.'

Hendry controlled his 'tremor' sufficiently to account for Joe Johnson, James Wattana and then Mike Hallett in the final — for a title which pleased him no end. 'This may not be the most important event on the calendar but it's important to keep in the winning habit,' said the former Star of the Future whom many old Pontins hands first remember as a cherubic 12-year-old who could barely reach over the table.

Spotting similarly-talented tots is always a major part of Pontins week and if this time it was a disappointment that none notched a century with a dummy in his mouth, the disdain which certain gnarled 12-year-olds displayed for old codgers in their twenties was something to behold. The notion that a certain worldly wisdom is required to find your way around the table was well and truly laid to rest by mere infants. Butter may not yet melt in their mouths but with a cue in their hands they boast back-street cunning by the lorry-load and it was mainly old lags who were crying into their beers.

Leading the charge of the little brigade was Liverpool's Paul Wythe, 13, who put out Ireland's Paddy Browne early on in the Pro-Am, while the most entertaining final was appropriately the junior showdown between winner Chris Scanlon, 15, and Mark Williams, 14.

Holiday centres are of course renowned for looking after youngsters and, although the 'Baby Crying in Chalet' sign was switched off in the ballroom, old fogies might have felt officials were going too far when they communicated by means of . . . a baby-talker. But this is how referees on the top floor notify tournament director John Williams, seated below, that tables are free whereupon another hopeful pair are despatched to the conveyor belt, confirming the impression that this really is the Dagenham of snooker.

In 1990 some 1300 matches were played and all were presided over by Williams's unique blend of military precision and matey banter. But, and this is another Pontins tradition, players scored for themselves on spot and plain boards with the patrolling refs hardly being called upon.

Immortality at Pontins may come in many guises: for the good club player it is a clash with a well-known pro but for the lesser light it might just be the winning of a sub-section which is pinned to the wall and perused like a BR timetable on a busy night at Waterloo. Lovingly called 'your sheet', this hand-written fragment of the draw has its share of cancellations, too, as hopes are dashed on the hard best-of-three frames format.

But it is the pros, both invited and uninvited, who are really on a hiding to nothing with the obligatory surrender of 21- and 16-point starts respectively. The young and upwardly-mobile likes of Nigel Bond, Gary Wilkinson and David Roe were to be seen upstairs in the 18-table room that was a veritable Hackney Marshes of the Baize, while older hands like Cliff Wilson and Eugene Hughes fared little better in the more select confines of the ballroom.

Hughes it was who, arriving four minutes late after customs had delayed him on his return from the Dutch Open, captured the true Pontins spirit by gracefully accepting his ejection from the draw but pleading to play in the losers' Plate. But he had no luck there, either, losing to Spencer Dunn, a humble Division II player from the Stourbridge League, who also removed Nick Terry and Andrew Cairns. Liverpool's Tony Rampello, 18, ran out the eventual winner, having included Darren Morgan and James Wattana among his scalps.

Wise-cracking Cliff Wilson, who had earlier observed that 'today's youngsters look as if they're going for open-heart surgery', also came a cropper, as did 17 other pros who had not wanted to miss the week's time-honoured blend of bonhomie and banter.

But perhaps the biggest casualty was the fellow who, having leapt out of a first-floor window to escape an irate husband, turned up on crutches only to lose when his pal, to whom he had entrusted his cue, could not be prised from the bookies.

The event's most celebrated loser had always been regarded as London's Roger Brown, who took a decade to show his face after his epoch-making defeat by Agnes Davies in 1976. To be fair, it was not just because she was a woman but that she had played him with her arm in plaster. . . .

Also back but not in action was 76-year-old Louis Ward who still dresses up in a green baize suit complete with 'a table' embroidered on his top hat. More Ascot than Pontins, perhaps, but the same can hardly be said of his shirt — autographed by some 120 players, including a 13-year-old Jimmy White. 'A real ragamuffin' was how the Whirlwind came across in those days and he and Tony Meo were inseparable. Steve Davis was described as 'ordinary when he came and with long red hair halfway down his back', and it was Doug Mountjoy who made the biggest impact when he won the Pro-Am and turned in his job.

With tables of the highest quality and corridor talk of check side and the cut of the pockets, it is an ideal baptism for an aspiring pro and not hard to see why every self-respecting club in the land sends a minibus. Dress is jeans and tee-shirt until the finals and no one remembers this better than Jimmy Chambers, the modest Midlander who surprised himself and his valet by reaching the Open final in 1985. After safely negotiating the afternoon session against John Parrott in a lounge suit, Chambers dashed to nearby Rhyl to get properly attired for the evening. Dinner suit duly hired, he arrived back in his chalet to discover that the shirt looked as if it had only just emerged from a mangle. Resourceful to the last, he ironed it with a Pontins kettle of boiling water — and won the title.

A great leveller, Pontins maintains its FA Cup-style traditions and tales: it is nothing to see fish sellers wander in off the street and offer a player a pound of cod, while under the table a child could be playing with a toy and his anxious mum run on to grab him. As one old Pontins hand said, 'It must be the only tournament in't world where a kid can ask for your autograph and then give you a good hiding.'

## THE MANAGEMENT

### Bruce Beckett, snooker correspondent of the Press Association

Barry Hearn was once quoted as saying: 'He who manages the world champion controls snooker.' While that may be stretching the point, there is certainly a degree of truth in the statement. Just as Steve Davis governed on the green baize during the 1980s, so his manager, Hearn, called the shots off the table.

Player power gave Hearn the management muscle to become the most influential figure in the politics of the game. It also gave him a seat on the board of the World Professional Billiards and Snooker Association and even when he temporarily resigned as a director in 1987, due to 'a potential clash of interests', he still had a major say in the future plans for snooker.

Hearn, a qualified chartered accountant, became interested in snooker in 1973 when he walked into the Lucania Snooker Hall in Romford and decided to buy the chain of 16 clubs. A few years later he met Davis, the player who provided the son of a Dagenham bus driver with his ticket into the world of professional snooker. When Davis captured the first of his six world titles in 1981, there was Hearn at his side.

The rest, as they say, is history. On 1 June 1982, Hearn sold his chain of Lucania Snooker Centres to Rileys for £3.1 million, created Matchroom Ltd and launched 'the most exclusive club in snooker'. Five years later, with his stable now housing seven thoroughbreds, Matchroom pulled off the 'Grand Slam', completing a clean sweep of the major tournaments in the 1986–87 season and topping the £1 million in prize money.

Hearn has always been unashamedly elitist. He is now one of the wealthiest and best-known figures in British sport. But while some may regard him as *nouveau riche*, he remains a man whom it is hard to dislike. 'Money has ceased to be important,' he says. 'Financially, I have moved up, but socially I haven't. Socially, I am more at home with snooker punters and boxers than business people.'

His promotional interests in boxing now take up a great deal of Hearn's life. Yet he insists snooker is just as important to him today as it was when he first set out on the road to fame and fortune with Davis. Wise-cracking Welshman Cliff Wilson once said: 'I hope Barry doesn't go out of snooker because the only other job he would want is God's; and that will take a bit of getting.' But while Matchroom supremo Hearn is still a leading light in the corridors of snooker power, he no longer has things all his own way.

Just as Hearn rose to prominence through Davis, so shrewd Scottish businessman Ian Doyle has emerged on the scene via Stephen Hendry. As with Hendry deposing Davis as world champion and world number one last season, one could argue that the balance of power has shifted significantly in Doyle's direction. While Hearn's once mighty Matchroom team was weakened by the departure of Dennis Taylor, Willie Thorne and Neal Foulds during the summer, Doyle's Cuemasters squad goes from strength to strength. Hearn admits: 'I think it's true to say Matchroom is becoming more of a promotions company than a management company.' Doyle, in contrast, is always on the lookout for new talent and is prepared to make an investment in the future, as he demonstrated by signing players like Darren Morgan and Nigel Bond.

Doyle, like Hearn, trained to become a chartered accountant. 'I didn't complete the course because I was offered a chance to work for a private limited company, getting some practical and commercial experience,' he explains. 'I was offered a position on the selling side at the age of 20 and, by the time I was 23, I was general manager of a division of that company.'

Three years later, Doyle set up his own business, distributing building materials and hardware. From there, he expanded into the leisure industry and property development. He owns the John Spencer Snooker Centre in Stirling and it was there that he first set eyes on Hendry, who just happened to be drawn against his son, Lee, in a junior league match. 'He glided around the table like a ballet dancer,' recalls Doyle. Doyle is more than just a manager to Hendry, whose parents are divorced. He is a father-figure who provided him with stability at a time 'when he thought his whole world had been turned upside down by his mum and dad splitting up'.

Doyle, for whom snooker management has become a full-time job, is a strict disciplinarian — as Cuemasters man Mike Hallett has discovered. Hallett, who admits he has a taste for the good life, had his social activities curtailed when Doyle confiscated his credit cards! In Hallett's case, Doyle was not just a father-figure but headmaster and bank manager as well. 'I have very definite ideas on how players should act and behave as professionals,' says Doyle, like Hearn, a board member of the WPBSA. 'If you don't have discipline, you have nothing. When I first started in the management game, I had to look very closely at professional snooker. Steve Davis stood out — he was a man apart.'

Doyle and Hearn have had their clashes in the past. Doyle, while perhaps not so high-profile as Hearn, nevertheless strikes a hard bargain.

While players hold the key to a manager's stature in snooker, it is not all plain sailing. Howard Kruger attempted to take on Hearn and Matchroom through his Framework operation but fell by the wayside. It will be interesting to see how Mark McCormack's International Management Group fare in snooker after their success in so many other sporting fields, notably golf and tennis. They have signed up several players, including Dean Reynolds, from Kruger and invested in the future with Ken Doherty and Peter Ebdon.

Some players do not fit into a team set-up. John Parrott split with Cuemasters in January 1990, with Doyle blaming the break-up on an 'unworkable relationship' with Parrott's personal manager, Phil Miller. Miller's response was: 'Doyle has continually tried to disrupt my relationship with John but, as you can see, he has failed.'

Midlander Steve James, who captured his first major title by winning the Mercantile Classic last season, has found he functions best under the guidance of another disciplinarian, Ramsay McLellan.

However, most players on the circuit at least have a travelling companion, someone to do the many miles of motoring from one tournament to the next, or simply a shoulder to cry on. Davis is usually accompanied by his father, Bill. Geoff Foulds paces the floor while his son, Neal, plays the matches. A friend or father can provide companionship, a manager financial security, but snooker remains very much an individual game.

# EDITOR'S REVIEW OF THE SEASON

**Janice Hale**

Stephen Hendry superseded the 1972 vintage Alex Higgins as the youngest champion and took over top place in the world rankings from Steve Davis by beating Jimmy White 18–12 in the final of a glorious Embassy World Championship at the Crucible Theatre, Sheffield. At six hours, three minutes for 30 frames, this extraordinary final was completed at an average of barely 12 minutes a frame. The standard of break-building and potting on both sides was of the highest quality but White's safety play fell away, particularly on the second day. So deeply had Hendry psyched himself up for the match that he appeared eerily cool in the aftermath of victory. 'I was determined to win and confident I could do it,' he said.

The match of the championship was undoubtedly White's 16–14 semi-final win over Davis, the defending and six-times champion who had dominated the 1980s to a degree to which it seems inconceivable anyone can ever dominate the game again. White won seven of the eight frames in the penultimate session to lead 13–9, but even then it was close.

For most of the season, Hendry had looked sharp and confident. He won three other ranking titles, the Asian Open (in Bangkok), the Dubai Classic and Stormseal UK Open, plus the Regal Scottish Masters and the Benson and Hedges Masters. In Bangkok, Hendry beat James Wattana 9–6 in the final. The 20-year-old Thai, in his first professional season, created such interest in his native country that even the main television evening news was delayed so that his match could be televised live. A few weeks later, he reached the semi-finals of the Rothmans Grand Prix but fell away slightly as the season progressed even though Thailand continued to take live satellite coverage of some of his matches.

In the Dubai final, Hendry trounced Doug Mountjoy 9–2 and the UK final provided a significant win over Davis, who was attempting to win the title for the seventh time. Hendry prevailed 16–12 and beat Davis again, 6–3, in the semi-finals of the European Open in Lyon, France, before losing 10–6 to John Parrott in the final.

Three players won ranking events for the first time. Mike Hallett captured the Hong Kong Open (which started life as the Australian Open before force of circumstance brought about a change of continent and title) by beating New Zealand's only professional, Dene

O'Kane, 9–8. Steve James, who rose from 16th to 9th in the rankings during the season, beat Davis 6–4 in the semi-finals and Warren King 10–6 to win the Mercantile Classic; and French Canadian Bob Chaperon beat Alex Higgins 10–8 in the final of the Pearl Assurance British Open after both Davis and Hendry had lost in early rounds.

The other two ranking titles had, in early season, been Davis's. He beat Hendry 9–4 in the final of the BCE International — which for the first time was not televised — and followed this with victory in the Rothmans Grand Prix by whitewashing Dean Reynolds 10–0, the third time he had won by a whitewash in a major final. Although he struggled painfully in mid-season and ended it not as world champion and as number two in the rankings, it is far too soon to make any judgement along the lines that he is a spent force. He is still only 33 and has the experience and knowledge to work out just why his game was not honed to its sharpest as the season wore on. He is only two points behind Hendry in the world rankings, remarkable in that during the two seasons over which they are calculated he did not compete in four events. Hendry played in all 18.

The season produced snooker's most notorious grudge match. The emotional build-up to it began at the British Car Rental World Cup in Bournemouth when Alex Higgins, in an incredible outburst, said to his Northern Ireland captain, Dennis Taylor: 'I'm from the Shankhill, you're from Coalisland. The next time you're in Northern Ireland, I'll have you shot.' They met in the next tournament, in the quarter-finals of the Benson and Hedges Irish Masters at Goffs sale ring in Kill, Co. Kildare. The standard of play was not up to much but in the highly charged atmosphere, made the more intense by the cockpit of an arena and the packed house of mostly Irish, it was surprising that it was up to anything at all. It was an evening when only the result mattered. Taylor won 5–2.

Already the subject of disciplinary action over his outburst at Bournemouth, Higgins was to get himself into deeper water still at the World Championship. After losing in the first round to Steve James, he was on his way to the press conference when he punched the press officer. He proceeded to utter a slurred monologue, venting his spleen about just about everything and everyone. More disciplinary action followed. Gavin Lightman QC, acting as the WPBSA's one-man disciplinary tribunal, suspended Higgins from WPBSA tournaments until after the 1991 Embassy World Championship, docked him 25 ranking points and ordered the Irishman to pay £5,000 towards the costs of the hearing.

After the Lord Mayor's Show at the Crucible Theatre, Sheffield, there came what it is hoped will be the last of one of snooker's more unfeeling rituals — the lowest ranked professionals playing off for their full professional tickets against ten amateurs. Amongst the professionals last season was Fred Davis, 76, world champion eight times. He lost 10–5 to Jason Prince at which point the capacity crowd of 100 gave him a standing ovation. So, too, did the players in the practice room who laid down their cues as Davis, limping with arthritis, walked through to go to a press conference where, admitting to 'a sense of relief', he announced his retirement from snooker. He will, however, continue to play billiards.

During the summer it was hoped that proposals would be accepted by the membership of the WPBSA that would make snooker open, ending the indignity of such occasions and giving everyone the chance to see if they have the ability to find the gold at the end of the rainbow professional snooker has now created.

## EDITOR'S NOTE

Because of the volume of statistics which modern snooker is constantly creating, the *Rothmans Snooker Yearbook* has had to limit to a certain extent which items are included under the various sections.

To qualify for inclusion in the 'Players' section, matches must have been played in a bona fide tournament with at least four competitors and be of the best of nine frames or more.

The 'Circuit' section is more comprehensive in that we have tended to record at least the result of the final in events where either the earlier rounds consisted of an insufficient number of frames or were played on a round robin basis.

# RANKING LIST

As both the number of professionals and the number of tournaments have increased, the game's governing body, the World Professional Billiards and Snooker Association, have had to devise some form of ranking list, not only to quantify the standings of the players but also to enable them to seed tournaments.

The ranking list is drawn up at the end of each season and is based on performances over the past two seasons in events which are designated ranking tournaments.

To qualify for ranking status, a tournament must be open to all 128 tournament members of the WPBSA with any vacancies in the field going, in order of merit, to non-tournament professionals (except for the World Championship which is open to all snooker members of the WPBSA). Altogether, eighteen events were taken into account for the list which was compiled immediately after the 1990 World Championship. There were eight in the 1988–89 season and ten in 1989–90. In 1988–89 they were: Fidelity International, Rothmans Grand Prix, Canadian Masters, Tennents UK Open, Mercantile Credit Classic, European Open, Anglian British Open and Embassy World Championship. In 1989–90 the Hong Kong and Asian Opens were added to the list and the slot filled by the Canadian Masters was instead occupied by the Dubai Classic.

When seedings are decided for each tournament, the defending titleholder is automatically seeded one with the world champion, if he is not the defending titleholder, two. The remaining seeds are then taken, in order, from the ranking list.

To separate players who tie on ranking points, merit points, 'A' points and 'frames won' in the first round have also been introduced to the system which also favours performances in the immediate preceding season.

Players seeded 1–16 are exempt until the last 32 of the World Championship but in the other events, players seeded 1–32 are exempt only until the last 64.

The various points are awarded as follows. World Championship: winner – 10 ranking points; runner-up – 8 ranking points; losing semi-finalists – 6 ranking points; losing quarter-finalists – 4 ranking points; losers in last 16 – 2 ranking points; losers in last 32 – 1 ranking point (if qualifier), 2 merit points (if exempt); losers in last qualifying round – 2 merit points; losers in 2nd preliminary round – 1 merit point; losers in 3rd preliminary round – 1 'A' point; losers in 1st preliminary round: number of frames won. Other ranking events: winner – 6 ranking points; runner-up – 5 ranking points; losing semi-finalists – 4 ranking points; losing quarter-finalists – 3 ranking points; fifth round losers – 2 ranking points; fourth round losers – 1 ranking point; third round losers – 1 merit point; second round losers – 1 'A' point; first round losers: number of frames won.

# WORLD RANKING LIST 1990

| *Figure in brackets denotes previous year's ranking* | | *1988–89* | | | | *1989–90* | | | | *Total* | | | |
|---|---|---|---|---|---|---|---|---|---|---|---|---|---|
| | | *Ranking Points* | *Merit Points* | *A Points* | *Frames* | *Ranking Points* | *Merit Points* | *A Points* | *Frames* | *Ranking Points* | *Merit Points* | *A Points* | *Frames* |
| 1(3) | Stephen Hendry | 25 | — | — | — | 44 | 1 | — | — | 69 | 1 | — | — |
| 2(1) | Steve Davis | 34 | 1 | — | — | 33 | — | — | — | 67 | 1 | — | — |
| 3(2) | John Parrott | 28 | 1 | — | — | 26 | 1 | — | — | 54 | 2 | — | — |
| 4(4) | Jimmy White | 24 | 1 | — | — | 24 | 1 | — | — | 48 | 2 | — | — |
| 5(10) | Doug Mountjoy | 22 | — | — | — | 19 | 3 | — | — | 41 | 3 | — | — |
| 6(5) | Terry Griffiths | 21 | 2 | — | — | 15 | 3 | — | — | 36 | 5 | — | — |
| 7(6) | Mike Hallett | 19 | 2 | — | — | 16 | 2 | — | — | 35 | 4 | — | — |
| 8(15) | Dean Reynolds | 18 | — | — | — | 16 | 2 | — | — | 34 | 2 | — | — |
| 9(16) | Steve James | 10 | 2 | — | — | 22 | 2 | — | — | 32 | 4 | — | — |
| 10(8) | Dennis Taylor | 16 | 1 | — | — | 13 | 4 | — | — | 29 | 5 | — | — |
| 11(9) | Willie Thorne | 15 | 1 | — | — | 13 | 2 | — | — | 28 | 3 | — | — |

| | | | | | | | | | | | | | |
|---|---|---|---|---|---|---|---|---|---|---|---|---|---|
| 12(17) | Martin Clark | 11 | 4 | — | — | 16 | 2 | — | — | 27 | 6 | — | — |
| 13(20) | Neal Foulds | 7 | 4 | — | — | 18 | 1 | — | — | 25 | 5 | — | — |
| 14(24) | Alex Higgins | 9 | 4 | — | — | 16 | 1 | — | — | 25 | 5 | — | — |
| 15(13) | John Virgo | 13 | 1 | — | — | 12 | 3 | — | — | 25 | 4 | — | — |
| 16(14) | Tony Meo | 17 | 3 | — | — | 7 | 3 | — | — | 24 | 6 | — | — |
| 17(35) | Alain Robidoux | 8 | 4 | 1 | — | 15 | 0 | 2 | — | 23 | 4 | 3 | — |
| 18(11) | Joe Johnson | 14 | 2 | — | — | 9 | 6 | — | — | 23 | 8 | — | — |
| 19(7) | Cliff Thorburn | 15 | 2 | — | — | 7 | 5 | — | — | 22 | 7 | — | — |
| 20(39) | Gary Wilkinson | 4 | 3 | 1 | — | 17 | 2 | — | — | 21 | 5 | 1 | — |
| 21(19) | Steve Newbury | 7 | 3 | — | — | 14 | 3 | — | — | 21 | 6 | — | — |
| 22(12) | Tony Knowles | 8 | 4 | — | — | 13 | 4 | — | — | 21 | 8 | — | — |
| 23(31) | Wayne Jones | 8 | 4 | 1 | — | 11 | 2 | — | — | 19 | 6 | 1 | — |
| 24(28) | Dene O'Kane | 6 | 2 | — | — | 12 | 5 | — | — | 18 | 7 | — | — |
| 25(25) | Peter Francisco | 4 | 7 | — | — | 12 | 4 | — | — | 16 | 11 | — | — |
| 26(29) | Robert Chaperon | 5 | 4 | — | — | 11 | 5 | — | — | 16 | 9 | — | — |
| 27(23) | Silvino Francisco | 6 | 4 | — | — | 10 | 6 | — | — | 16 | 10 | — | — |
| 28(21) | Barry West | 9 | 5 | — | — | 7 | 6 | — | — | 16 | 11 | — | — |
| 29(18) | Cliff Wilson | 9 | 3 | — | — | 7 | 5 | — | — | 16 | 8 | — | — |
| 30(36) | Danny Fowler | 5 | 5 | — | — | 10 | 5 | 1 | — | 15 | 10 | 1 | — |
| 31(30) | Tony Drago | 4 | 5 | — | — | 10 | 3 | 1 | — | 14 | 8 | 1 | — |
| 32(22) | Eddie Charlton | 7 | 4 | — | — | 7 | 4 | — | — | 14 | 8 | — | — |
| 33(–) | James Wattana | — | — | — | — | 12 | 3 | 3 | — | 12 | 3 | 3 | — |

| *Figure in brackets denotes previous year's ranking* | *1988–89* | | | | *1989–90* | | | | *Total* | | | |
|---|---|---|---|---|---|---|---|---|---|---|---|---|
| | *Ranking Points* | *Merit Points* | *A Points* | *Frames* | *Ranking Points* | *Merit Points* | *A Points* | *Frames* | *Ranking Points* | *Merit Points* | *A Points* | *Frames* |
| 34(47) Mark Bennett | 4 | 2 | 3 | — | 8 | 4 | 1 | — | 12 | 6 | 4 | — |
| 35(27) Eugene Hughes | 7 | 2 | — | — | 5 | 7 | — | — | 12 | 9 | — | — |
| 36(62) Tony Jones | 0 | 7 | 2 | — | 11 | 1 | 3 | — | 11 | 8 | 5 | — |
| 37(26) David Roe | 6 | 4 | — | — | 5 | 7 | — | — | 11 | 11 | — | — |
| 38(32) Rex Williams | 7 | 5 | — | — | 4 | 7 | — | — | 11 | 12 | — | — |
| 39(–) Nigel Bond | — | — | — | — | 10 | 4 | 2 | 4 | 10 | 4 | 2 | 4 |
| 40(55) Warren King | 2 | 4 | 3 | — | 8 | 3 | 3 | — | 10 | 7 | 6 | — |
| 41(53) Darren Morgan | 3 | 0 | 4 | 3 | 7 | 5 | 2 | — | 10 | 5 | 6 | 3 |
| 42(43) Steve Duggan | 6 | 2 | 1 | — | 4 | 4 | 3 | — | 10 | 6 | 4 | — |
| 43(–) Brian Morgan | — | — | — | — | 8 | 2 | 1 | 7 | 8 | 2 | 1 | 7 |
| 44(41) Tony Chappel | 4 | 4 | 1 | — | 4 | 4 | 3 | — | 8 | 8 | 4 | — |
| 45(33) David Taylor | 6 | 6 | — | — | 2 | 5 | 3 | — | 8 | 11 | 3 | — |
| 46(65) Les Dodd | 1 | 8 | — | — | 6 | 3 | 2 | 5 | 7 | 11 | 2 | 5 |
| 47(70) Robert Marshall | 1 | 1 | 3 | 12 | 6 | 4 | 2 | 5 | 7 | 5 | 5 | 17 |

| | | | | | | | | | | | | | |
|---|---|---|---|---|---|---|---|---|---|---|---|---|---|
| 48(42) | John Campbell | 3 | 3 | 3 | — | 4 | 3 | 4 | — | 7 | 6 | 7 | — |
| 49(48) | Colin Roscoe | 3 | 1 | 2 | 10 | 4 | 3 | 5 | — | 7 | 4 | 7 | 10 |
| 50(58) | Jack McLaughlin | 2 | 5 | 2 | — | 4 | 6 | 2 | — | 6 | 11 | 4 | — |
| 51(59) | Ian Graham | 2 | 3 | 2 | 10 | 4 | 6 | 3 | — | 6 | 9 | 5 | 10 |
| 52(46) | Nigel Gilbert | 4 | 6 | 1 | — | 2 | 2 | 6 | — | 6 | 8 | 7 | — |
| 53(37) | Jim Wych | 5 | 4 | 2 | — | 1 | 6 | 1 | — | 6 | 10 | 3 | — |
| 54(44) | Paddy Browne | 5 | 2 | 3 | — | 1 | 5 | 4 | — | 6 | 7 | 7 | — |
| 55(–) | Brady Gollan | — | — | — | — | 5 | 2 | 2 | 6 | 5 | 2 | 2 | 6 |
| 56(38) | John Spencer | 4 | 5 | — | — | 1 | 6 | 3 | — | 5 | 11 | 3 | — |
| 57(45) | Murdo Macleod | 4 | 3 | 1 | — | 1 | 5 | 4 | — | 5 | 8 | 5 | — |
| 58(34) | Steve Longworth | 5 | 5 | — | — | 0 | 4 | 6 | — | 5 | 9 | 6 | — |
| 59(60) | Jim Chambers | 1 | 2 | 4 | 2 | 3 | 6 | 2 | — | 4 | 8 | 6 | 2 |
| 60(52) | Mark Johnston-Allen | 3 | 2 | 4 | — | 1 | 8 | 2 | — | 4 | 10 | 6 | — |
| 61(99) | Mark Rowing | 0 | 2 | 2 | 5 | 3 | 3 | 2 | 12 | 3 | 5 | 4 | 17 |
| 62(69) | Craig Edwards | 1 | 2 | 3 | 5 | 2 | 2 | 2 | 11 | 3 | 4 | 5 | 16 |
| 63(40) | Joe O'Boye | 2 | 4 | 2 | — | 1 | 4 | 5 | — | 3 | 8 | 7 | — |
| 64(79) | Brian Rowswell | 0 | 3 | 3 | 6 | 2 | 2 | 3 | 8 | 2 | 5 | 6 | 14 |

65(–) Nick Dyson 2-2-4-11; 66(104) Jason Smith 2-2-10-18; 67(82) Paul Gibson 2-1-4-11; 68(130) Joe Grech 2-0-1-0; 69(50) Kirk Stevens 2-7-9--; 70(61) Roger Bales 2-4-12--; 71(71) Tony Wilson 2-3-7-23; 72(68) Marcel Gauvreau 2-2-13-3; 73(49) Ray Edmonds 2-8-9--; 74(54) Ray Reardon 2-5-5--; 75(63) Dave Gilbert 1-9-9--; 76(57) Tommy Murphy 1-9-8--; 77(90) Mick Price 1-8-5-13; 78(85) Bill Oliver 1-5-6-26; 79(80) Paul Medati 1-4-4-32; 80 (76) Martin

Smith 1-4-8-17; 81(–) Andrew Cairns 1-3-3-8; 82(86) Mario Morra 1-3-8-13; 83(–) Barry Pinches 1-2-4-7; 84(–) Ian Brumby 1-2-3-14; 85(67) Jon Wright 1-8-7-8; 86(66) John Rea 1-7-5-19; 87(72) Nick Terry 1-6-7-8; 88(51) Graham Cripsey 1-5-12--; 89(73) George Scott 1-1-1-26; 90(74) Anthony Harris 1-0-9-37; 91(56) Dave Martin 0-10-8--; 92(98) Steve Campbell 0-7-7-22; 93(93) Bob Harris 0-6-5-13; 94(94) Eddie Sinclair 0-6-5-33; 95(78) Graham Miles 0-6-6-18; 96(75) Ken Owers 0-6-6-14; 97(81) Pat Houlihan 0-5-10-6; 98(–) Stephen Murphy 0-4-2-12; 99(64) Mick Fisher 0-4-14--; 100(77) Robby Foldvari 0-4-5-37; 101(107) Steve Meakin 0-3-5-29; 102(114) Paul Watchorn 0-2-6-32; 103(92) Ian Williamson 0-2-10-22; 104(101) Tony Kearney 0-2-8-19; 105(96) Eric Lawlor 0-2-8-22; 106(105) François Ellis 0-2-5-29; 107(87) Malcolm Bradley 0-2-10-27; 108(91) Glen Wilkinson 0-2-5-25; 109(–) Duncan Campbell 0-1-7-4; 110(112) Matt Gibson 0-1-7-31; 111(83) Vic Harris 0-1-7-23; 112(116) Gino Rigitano 0-1-6-35; 113(113) Robbie Grace 0-1-6-30; 114(84) Jim Donnelly 0-1-3-45; 115(103) Jimmy Van Rensberg 0-1-3-39; 116(106) Jack Fitzmaurice 0-1-8-23; 117(95) John Dunning 0-1-8-28; 118(100) Terry Whitthread 0-1-6-14; 119(88) Jim Bear 0-1-5-32; 120(102) Mike Darrington 0-1-5-32; 121(109) Dessie Sheehan 0-1-4-41; 122(108) Dennis Hughes 0-1-3-25; 123(110) Mike Watterson 0-1-3-32; 124(111) Paul Thornley 0-1-0-19; 125(97) Mark Wildman 0-0-7-32; 126(119) Billy Kelly 0-0-7-11; 127(115) Jim Meadowcroft 0-0-6-21; 128(89) Fred Davis 0-0-5-32; 129(118) Geoff Foulds 0-0-5-29; 130(120) Greg Jenkins 0-0-3-24; 131(117) Jack Rea 0-0-2-38; 132(122) Bernie Mikkelsen 0-0-2-20; 133(121) Ian Black 0-0-2-10; 134(132) Clive Everton 0-0-1-3; 135(128) Derek Mienie 0-0-1-20; 136(123) Patsy Fagan 0-0-1-13; 137(124) Pascal Burke 0-0-1-12; 138(129) Jim Rempe 0-0-1-12; 139(125) Dave Chalmers 0-0-0-10; 140(126) Ian Anderson 0-0-0-7; 141(134) Bernard Bennett 0-0-0-4; 142(131) Derek Heaton 0-0-0-3.

*Those ranked 119 and below are non-tournament members of the WPBSA as are also Joe Caggianello, Lou Condo, Bert Demarco, Mannie Francisco, Sam Frangie, James Giannaros, David Greaves, John Hargreaves, Mike Hines, Frank Jonik, Eddie McLaughlin, Steve Mizerak, Paddy Morgan, Maurice Parkin, Vic Potasznyk, Gerry Watson and Bill Werbeniuk.*

# MONEY LIST 1989–90

The *'Ranking'* column takes into account nine ranking events played in the 1989–90 season. These were: the Hong Kong Open, Asian Open, BCE International, Rothmans Grand Prix, Dubai Classic, Stormseal UK Open, Mercantile Credit Classic, Pearl British Open and European Open. The tenth, the Embassy World Championship, is shown separately. *'Sanctioned'* takes into account the New Zealand Masters, Regal Scottish Masters, Everest World Matchplay, Benson and Hedges Masters, Senator Welsh Championship, British Car Rental World Cup and the Benson and Hedges Irish Masters. There were numerous other events played during the season but so numerous and various were they that this list comprises only major tournaments regarded as being part of the main circuit.

| | *Ranking* | *Sanctioned* | *World* | *Breaks* | *Total (£)* |
|---|---|---|---|---|---|
| 1 S. Hendry | 242,296.25 | 138,230.00 | 120,000.00 | 18,000.00 | 518,526.25 |
| 2 S. Davis | 193,625.00 | 79,000.00 | 36,000.00 | 13,375.00 | 322,000.00 |
| 3 J. White | 45,125.00 | 142,750.00 | 72,000.00 | 11,000.00 | 270,875.00 |
| 4 J. Parrott | 83,561.24 | 100,576.00 | 36,000.00 | 21,500.00 | 241,637.24 |
| 5 S. James | 109,531.24 | 7,000.00 | 9,000.00 | 2,500.00 | 128,031.24 |
| 6 T. Griffiths | 47,415.24 | 51,900.00 | 18,000.00 | — | 117,315.24 |
| 7 R. Chaperon | 91,249.99 | 16,000.00 | 4,000.00 | — | 111,249.99 |
| 8 D. Reynolds | 66,915.25 | 25,000.00 | 9,000.00 | — | 100,915.25 |
| 9 A. Higgins | 70,798.87 | 23,500.00 | 5,000.00 | — | 99,298.87 |
| 10 D. Mountjoy | 56,062.50 | 32,000.00 | 9,000.00 | — | 97,062.50 |
| 11 M. Hallett | 67,368.27 | 18,826.00 | 9,000.00 | 1,000.00 | 96,194.27 |
| 12 Dennis Taylor | 35,031.25 | 54,576.00 | 5,000.00 | — | 94,607.25 |
| 13 W. Thorne | 27,593.12 | 39,576.00 | 9,000.00 | 2,960.00 | 79,129.12 |
| 14 A. Robidoux | 42,375.00 | 16,000.00 | 5,000.00 | 6,000.00 | 69,375.00 |
| 15 Gary Wilkinson | 60,030.62 | — | 5,000.00 | — | 65,030.62 |
| 16 J. Wattana | 53,321.50 | 7,000.00 | 4,000.00 | — | 64,321.50 |
| 17 C. Thorburn | 14,186.87 | 31,750.00 | 18,000.00 | — | 63,936.87 |
| 18 D. O'Kane | 46,921.24 | 6,076.00 | 4,000.00 | 2,500.00 | 59,497.24 |
| 19 J. Johnson | 29,571.50 | 20,700.00 | 5,000.00 | 3,500.00 | 58,771.50 |
| 20 T. Knowles | 31,687.50 | 18,000.00 | 9,000.00 | — | 58,687.50 |
| 21 N. Foulds | 37,328.12 | — | 18,000.00 | — | 55,328.12 |
| 22 W. King | 47,515.62 | 5,000.00 | 400.00 | — | 52,915.62 |
| 23 D. Fowler | 41,202.50 | — | 5,000.00 | — | 46,202.50 |
| 24 M. Clark | 40,953.12 | — | 4,000.00 | — | 44,953.12 |
| 25 J. Virgo | 27,545.62 | 7,000.00 | 9,000.00 | — | 43,545.62 |
| 26 S. Francisco | 36,483.74 | 3,000.00 | 4,000.00 | — | 43,483.74 |
| 27 S. Newbury | 37,500.00 | 900.00 | 5,000.00 | — | 43,400.00 |
| 28 D. Morgan | 12,040.24 | 10,500.00 | 18,000.00 | 1,200.00 | 41,740.24 |
| 29 T. Meo | 18,055.67 | 12,000.00 | 9,000.00 | — | 39,055.67 |
| 30 W. Jones | 29,233.74 | 2,750.00 | 5,000.00 | — | 36,983.74 |
| 31 P. Francisco | 29,281.24 | — | 5,000.00 | — | 34,281.24 |
| 32 T. Drago | 23,727.44 | 3,000.00 | 5,000.00 | — | 31,727.44 |
| 33 N. Bond | 27,390.62 | — | 4,000.00 | — | 31,390.62 |
| 34 M. Bennett | 25,165.24 | 900.00 | 5,000.00 | — | 31,065.24 |
| 35 R. Marshall | 28,250.00 | — | 2,062.50 | — | 30,312.50 |
| 36 C. Wilson | 20,358.24 | 3,900.00 | 5,000.00 | — | 29,258.24 |
| 37 E. Charlton | 19,014.99 | 5,000.00 | 5,000.00 | — | 29,014.99 |
| 38 E. Hughes | 18,017.62 | 5,000.00 | 4,000.00 | — | 27,017.62 |
| 39 T. Jones | 25,687.50 | — | 400.00 | — | 26,087.50 |
| 40 B. West | 20,796.24 | — | 4,000.00 | — | 24,796.24 |
| 41 B. Morgan | 21,875.00 | — | 2,062.50 | — | 23,937.50 |
| 42 D. Roe | 18,358.74 | — | 4,000.00 | — | 22,358.74 |
| 43 L. Dodd | 19,765.62 | — | 2,062.50 | — | 21,828.12 |
| 44 R. Williams | 16,821.49 | — | 4,000.00 | — | 20,821.49 |
| 45 J. Campbell | 11,562.49 | 5,000.00 | 4,000.00 | — | 20,562.49 |
| 46 T. Chappel | 11,452.50 | 2,750.00 | 5,000.00 | 1,000.00 | 20,202.50 |
| 47 T. Murphy | 7,571.50 | 10,000.00 | 400.00 | 1,500.00 | 19,471.50 |
| 48 B. Gollan | 13,515.00 | — | 5,000.00 | — | 18,515.00 |
| 49 I. Graham | 13,265.00 | — | 4,000.00 | — | 17,265.00 |
| 50 J. Chambers | 12,455.12 | — | 4,000.00 | — | 16,455.12 |

| | *Ranking* | *Sanctioned* | *World* | *Breaks* | *Total (£)* |
|---|---|---|---|---|---|
| 51 S. Duggan | 14,696.49 | — | 400.00 | — | 15,096.49 |
| 52 J. McLaughlin | 14,562.49 | — | 400.00 | — | 14,962.49 |
| 53 P. Browne | 6,884.00 | 5,000.00 | 2,062.50 | — | 13,946.50 |
| 54 M. Macleod | 6,821.50 | 4,500.00 | 2,062.50 | — | 13,384.00 |
| 55 M. Johnston-Allen | 9,171.24 | — | 4,000.00 | — | 13,171.24 |
| 56 C. Roscoe | 11,843.74 | 900.00 | 400.00 | — | 13,143.74 |
| 57 N. Gilbert | 4,577.49 | — | 5,000.00 | 3,000.00 | 12,577.49 |
| 58 M. Rowing | 10,384.00 | — | 2,062.50 | — | 12,446.50 |
| 59 David Taylor | 10,296.25 | — | 400.00 | — | 10,696.25 |
| 60 J. Wych | 8,858.74 | — | 400.00 | 1,000.00 | 10,258.74 |
| 61 John Rea | 1,000.00 | 6,750.00 | 2,062.50 | — | 9,812.50 |
| 62 J. Spencer | 7,390.00 | — | 2,062.50 | — | 9,452.50 |
| 63 M. Price | 5,250.00 | — | 4,000.00 | — | 9,250.00 |
| 64 B. Rowswell | 8,953.12 | — | 250.00 | — | 9,203.12 |
| 65 D. Gilbert | 6,281.24 | — | 2,062.50 | — | 8,343.74 |
| 66 S. Campbell | 3,781.24 | — | 4,000.00 | — | 7,781.24 |
| 67 T. Wilson | 3,634.00 | — | 4,000.00 | — | 7,634.00 |
| 68 N. Terry | 5,702.50 | — | 400.00 | 1,000.00 | 7,102.50 |
| 69 J. O'Boye | 6,250.00 | — | 400.00 | — | 6,650.00 |
| 70 J. Smith | 6,125.00 | — | 250.00 | — | 6,375.00 |
| 71 N. Dyson | 5,937.50 | — | 400.00 | — | 6,337.50 |
| 72 T. Kearney | 875.00 | 5,000.00 | 400.00 | — | 6,275.00 |
| 73 P. Gibson | 5,750.00 | — | 250.00 | — | 6,000.00 |
| 74 C. Edwards | 5,562.50 | — | 400.00 | — | 5,962.50 |
| 75 B. Oliver | 5,671.24 | — | 250.00 | — | 5,921.24 |
| 76 K. Stevens | 5,515.00 | — | 400.00 | — | 5,915.00 |
| 77 E. Sinclair | 5,483.74 | — | 400.00 | — | 5,883.74 |
| 78 S. Longworth | 5,421.24 | — | 400.00 | — | 5,821.24 |
| 79 A. Cairns | 3,750.00 | — | 2,062.50 | — | 5,812.50 |
| 80 J. Wright | 5,327.50 | — | 250.00 | — | 5,577.50 |
| 81 R. Bales | 5,077.50 | — | 400.00 | — | 5,477.50 |
| 82 R. Edmonds | 3,343.74 | — | 2,062.50 | — | 5,406.24 |
| 83 S. Murphy | 4,983.74 | — | 250.00 | — | 5,233.74 |
| 84 B. Harris | 4,827.50 | — | 400.00 | — | 5,227.50 |
| 85 B. Pinches | 3,000.00 | — | 2,062.50 | — | 5,062.50 |
| 86 G. Miles | 2,640.00 | — | 2,062.50 | — | 4,702.50 |
| 87 I. Brumby | 4,281.25 | — | 400.00 | — | 4,681.25 |
| 88 P. Medati | 4,250.00 | — | 250.00 | — | 4,500.00 |
| 89 M. Morra | 3,890.62 | — | 400.00 | — | 4,290.62 |
| 90 J. Grech | 3,750.00 | — | — | — | 3,750.00 |
| 91 S. Meakin | 3,281.24 | — | 250.00 | — | 3,531.24 |
| 92 P. Houlihan | 1,375.00 | — | 2,062.50 | — | 3,437.50 |
| 93 M. Gauvreau | 3,000.00 | — | 400.00 | — | 3,400.00 |
| 94 P. Watchorn | 1,312.50 | — | 2,062.50 | — | 3,375.00 |
| 95 G. Cripsey | 2,031.24 | — | 400.00 | — | 2,431.24 |
| 96 D. Martin | 2,000.00 | — | 400.00 | — | 2,400.00 |
| 97 M. Smith | 1,937.50 | — | 400.00 | — | 2,337.50 |
| 98 J. Donnelly | 1,640.00 | — | 250.00 | — | 1,890.00 |
| 99 V. Harris | 1,531.24 | — | 250.00 | — | 1,781.24 |
| 100 M. Fisher | 1,375.00 | — | 400.00 | — | 1,775.00 |

101 R. Reardon £1,300; 102 R. Foldvari £1,250; 103 I. Williamson £1,125; 104 G. Rigitano £900, K. Owers £900, E. Lawlor £900, R. Grace £900, D. Campbell £900; 109 G. Scott £750, M. Gibson £750, F. Ellis £750; 112 J. Van Rensberg £500; 113 J. Bear £400; 114 M. Bradley £250, M. Darrington £250, F. Davis £250, J. Dunning £250, J. Fitzmaurice £250, A. Harris £250, D. Hughes £250, Jack Rea £250, D. Sheehan £250, M. Watterson £250, T. Whitthread £250, M. Wildman £250, Glen Wilkinson £250, G. Jenkins £250, P. Thornley £250, D. Mienie £250.

# THE PLAYERS

(WS) = *World Series. Figure in brackets denotes previous season's ranking.*

## ROGER BALES (England)

**Born** 15.8.48. **Turned professional** 1984. **World ranking** 71 (61).

| | | | | |
|---|---|---|---|---|
| **1984** | v Sheehan | 5-2 | Qualifying | Jameson International |
| | v Murphy | 5-4 | Qualifying | Jameson International |
| | v Fisher | 5-3 | Qualifying | Jameson International |
| | v Reynolds | 4-5 | Qualifying | Jameson International |
| | v Higgins | 1-5 | 1st round | Rothmans Grand Prix |
| | v Chalmers | 9-2 | Qualifying | Coral UK Open |
| | v E. McLaughlin | 9-4 | Qualifying | Coral UK Open |
| | v Gauvreau | 8-9 | Qualifying | Coral UK Open |
| **1985** | v Bennett | 5-1 | Qualifying | Mercantile Credit Classic |
| | v Kelly | 5-3 | Qualifying | Mercantile Credit Classic |
| | v Virgo | 1-5 | Qualifying | Mercantile Credit Classic |
| | v Dodd | 3-9 | Qualifying | Tolly Cobbold English Championship |
| | v Black | 6-4 | Qualifying | Dulux British Open |
| | v Higgins | 3-6 | 1st round | Dulux British Open |
| | v Chaperon | 7-10 | Qualifying | Embassy World Championship |
| | v Drago | 5-2 | 1st round | Goya Matchroom Trophy |
| | v Edmonds | 5-0 | 2nd round | Goya Matchroom Trophy |
| | v S. Davis | 2-5 | 3rd round | Goya Matchroom Trophy |
| | v Smith | 5-1 | 1st round | Rothmans Grand Prix |
| | v Fisher | 5-3 | 2nd round | Rothmans Grand Prix |
| | v Wilson | 1-5 | 3rd round | Rothmans Grand Prix |
| | v Simngam | 2-9 | 1st round | Coral UK Open |
| **1986** | v Parkin | 5-0 | 1st round | Mercantile Credit Classic |
| | v Fowler | 4-5 | 2nd round | Mercantile Credit Classic |
| | v V. Harris | 9-7 | 2nd round | Tolly Cobbold English Championship |
| | v Knowles | 4-9 | 3rd round | Tolly Cobbold English Championship |
| | v Parkin | 5-1 | 1st round | Dulux British Open |
| | v Dunning | *wo* | 2nd round | Dulux British Open |
| | v Dennis Taylor | 5-4 | 3rd round | Dulux British Open |
| | v Williams | 4-5 | 4th round | Dulux British Open |
| | v Gilbert | 7-10 | Qualifying | Embassy World Championship |
| | v F. Davis | 5-4 | 2nd round | BCE International |
| | v Stevens | 5-3 | 3rd round | BCE International |
| | v Wilson | 1-5 | 4th round | BCE International |
| | v F. Davis | 4-5 | 2nd round | Rothmans Grand Prix |
| | v Cripsey | 6-9 | 2nd round | Tennents UK Open |
| **1987** | v Murphy | 2-5 | 2nd round | Mercantile Credit Classic |
| | v Owers | 5-6 | 2nd round | Tolly Ales English Championship |
| | v Gauvreau | 0-5 | 2nd round | Dulux British Open |
| | v Spencer | 3-10 | Qualifying | Embassy World Championship |
| | v John Rea | 2-5 | 2nd round | Fidelity International |
| | v Anderson | 5-1 | 2nd round | Rothmans Grand Prix |
| | v J. Campbell | 5-3 | 3rd round | Rothmans Grand Prix |
| | v Thorne | 2-5 | 4th round | Rothmans Grand Prix |
| | v Dunning | 8-9 | 2nd round | Tennents UK Open |
| **1988** | v John Rea | 0-5 | 2nd round | Mercantile Credit Classic |
| | v D. Gilbert | 2-6 | 2nd round | English Championship |
| | v Gary Wilkinson | 1-5 | 2nd round | MIM Britannia British Open |
| | v Miles | 7-10 | Qualifying | Embassy World Championship |
| | v John Rea | 2-5 | 2nd round | Fidelity International |

| | | | | |
|---|---|---|---|---|
| | v S. Campbell | 2-5 | 2nd round | Canadian Masters |
| | v Robidoux | 4-9 | 2nd round | Tennents UK Open |
| **1989** | v J. Smith | 1-5 | 2nd round | Mercantile Credit Classic |
| | v Chambers | 1-5 | 2nd round | European Open |
| | v Medati | 3-5 | 2nd round | English Championship |
| | v Fitzmaurice | 5-1 | 2nd round | Anglian British Open |
| | v Newbury | 5-3 | 3rd round | Anglian British Open |
| | v Hallett | 0-5 | 4th round | Anglian British Open |
| | v Glen Wilkinson | 1-10 | Qualifying | Embassy World Championship |
| | v S. Campbell | 5-2 | 2nd round | Hong Kong Open |
| | v Mountjoy | 0-5 | 3rd round | Hong Kong Open |
| | v Miles | 4-5 | 2nd round | 555 Asian Open |
| | v S. Campbell | 5-3 | 2nd round | BCE International |
| | v Roe | 5-4 | 3rd round | BCE International |
| | v Robidoux | 1-5 | 4th round | BCE International |
| | v S. Campbell | 2-5 | 2nd round | Rothmans Grand Prix |
| | v M. Gibson | 5-4 | 2nd round | Dubai Classic |
| | v Roe | 3-5 | 3rd round | Dubai Classic |
| | v Price | 2-6 | 2nd round | Stormseal UK Open |
| **1990** | v B. Morgan | 2-5 | 2nd round | Mercantile Credit Classic |
| | v Gauvreau | 5-1 | 2nd round | Pearl Assurance British Open |
| | v Meo | 2-5 | 3rd round | Pearl Assurance British Open |
| | v Kearney | 5-3 | 2nd round | European Open |
| | v S. Davis | 2-5 | 3rd round | European Open |
| | v Miles | 7-10 | Qualifying | Embassy World Championship |

## JIM BEAR (Canada)

**Born** 21.1.40. **Turned professional** 1983. **World ranking** 119 (88).

| | | | | |
|---|---|---|---|---|
| **1983** | v Morra | 9-8 | 2nd round | Canadian Championship |
| | v John Bear | 9-5 | Quarter-final | Canadian Championship |
| | v Stevens | 8-9 | Semi-final | Canadian Championship |
| **1985** | v Caggianello | 4-5 | 1st round | Canadian Championship |
| | v Houlihan | 5-2 | 1st round | Goya Matchroom Trophy |
| | v Donnelly | 5-2 | 2nd round | Goya Matchroom Trophy |
| | v Johnson | 1-5 | 3rd round | Goya Matchroom Trophy |
| | v Kearney | 3-5 | 1st round | Rothmans Grand Prix |
| | v Demarco | 9-1 | 1st round | Coral UK Open |
| | v Watterson | 9-0 | 2nd round | Coral UK Open |
| **1986** | v Kearney | 0-5 | 1st round | Mercantile Credit Classic |
| | v O'Boye | 1-5 | 1st round | Dulux British Open |
| | v Burke | 10-8 | Qualifying | Embassy World Championship |
| | v Gauvreau | 5-10 | Qualifying | Embassy World Championship |
| | v Chaperon | 3-6 | 1st round | Canadian Championship |
| | v Watchorn | 5-1 | 1st round | BCE International |
| | v Duggan | 4-5 | 2nd round | BCE International |
| | v B. Bennett | 5-2 | 1st round | Rothmans Grand Prix |
| | v Fowler | 5-2 | 2nd round | Rothmans Grand Prix |
| | v Williams | 2-5 | 3rd round | Rothmans Grand Prix |
| | v Everton | 9-1 | 1st round | Tennents UK Open |
| | v Edmonds | 6-9 | 2nd round | Tennents UK Open |
| **1987** | v Jack Rea | 10-5 | Qualifying | Embassy World Championship |
| | v Gauvreau | 5-10 | Qualifying | Embassy World Championship |
| | v Mikkelsen | 6-0 | 1st round | Canadian Championship |
| | v Wych | 6-4 | Quarter-final | Canadian Championship |
| | v Stevens | 7-2 | Semi-final | Canadian Championship |
| | v Thorburn | 4-8 | Final | Canadian Championship |
| | v Clark | 2-5 | 1st round | Fidelity International |
| | v Greaves | 5-0 | 1st round | Rothmans Grand Prix |
| | v B. Harris | 5-3 | 2nd round | Rothmans Grand Prix |

| | | | | |
|---|---|---|---|---|
| | v Thorne | 1-5 | 3rd round | Rothmans Grand Prix |
| | v Chalmers | 9-5 | 1st round | Tennents UK Open |
| | v B. Harris | 9-4 | 2nd round | Tennents UK Open |
| | v Johnson | 5-9 | 3rd round | Tennents UK Open |
| **1988** | v J. Smith | 5-3 | 1st round | Mercantile Credit Classic |
| | v Scott | 3-5 | 2nd round | Mercantile Credit Classic |
| | v A. Harris | 5-2 | 1st round | MIM Britannia British Open |
| | v Houlihan | 5-0 | 2nd round | MIM Britannia British Open |
| | v S. Francisco | 0-5 | 3rd round | MIM Britannia British Open |
| | v Mienie | 10-4 | Qualifying | Embassy World Championship |
| | v G. Foulds | 10-2 | Qualifying | Embassy World Championship |
| | v F. Davis | 4-10 | Qualifying | Embassy World Championship |
| | v Caggianello | 3-6 | 1st round | BCE Canadian Championship |
| | v Heaton | 5-1 | 1st round | Fidelity International |
| | v Edmonds | 1-5 | 2nd round | Fidelity International |
| | v Jenkins | 4-5 | 1st round | Rothmans Grand Prix |
| | v Ellis | 7-9 | 1st round | Tennents UK Open |
| **1989** | v A. Harris | 3-5 | 1st round | Mercantile Credit Classic |
| | v Kelly | 0-5 | 1st round | European Open |
| | v Jack Rea | 5-4 | 1st round | Anglian British Open |
| | v Martin | 5-2 | 2nd round | Anglian British Open |
| | v Drago | 2-5 | 3rd round | Anglian British Open |
| | v Edwards | 7-10 | Qualifying | Embassy World Championship |
| | v Jack Rea | 6-0 | 1st round | Stormseal UK Open |
| | v M. Bennett | 5-6 | 2nd round | Stormseal UK Open |
| **1990** | v Rowing | 3-5 | 1st round | Mercantile Credit Classic |
| | v J. Smith | 5-4 | 1st round | Pearl Assurance British Open |
| | v T. Murphy | 2-5 | 2nd round | Pearl Assurance British Open |
| | v Cairns | 4-5 | 1st round | European Open |
| | v Fitzmaurice | 10-5 | Qualifying | Embassy World Championship |
| | v Chambers | 3-10 | Qualifying | Embassy World Championship |

## MARK BENNETT (Wales)

**Born** 23.9.63. **Turned professional** 1986. **World ranking** 34 (47).

| | | | | |
|---|---|---|---|---|
| **1986** | v Smith | 5-4 | 1st round | BCE International |
| | v Browne | 5-1 | 2nd round | BCE International |
| | v Virgo | 1-5 | 3rd round | BCE International |
| | v Watterson | 5-1 | 1st round | Rothmans Grand Prix |
| | v O'Kane | 5-2 | 2nd round | Rothmans Grand Prix |
| | v Macleod | 5-1 | 3rd round | Rothmans Grand Prix |
| | v Browne | 0-5 | 4th round | Rothmans Grand Prix |
| | v Sheehan | 8-9 | 1st round | Tennents UK Open |
| **1987** | v Sheehan | 5-3 | 1st round | Mercantile Credit Classic |
| | v Black | 5-3 | 2nd round | Mercantile Credit Classic |
| | v Virgo | 3-5 | 3rd round | Mercantile Credit Classic |
| | v W. Jones | 3-6 | 1st round | Matchroom Welsh Championship |
| | v Morra | 4-5 | 1st round | Dulux British Open |
| | v Hargreaves | 10-6 | Qualifying | Embassy World Championship |
| | v Mikkelsen | 10-4 | Qualifying | Embassy World Championship |
| | v W. Jones | 10-3 | Qualifying | Embassy World Championship |
| | v Werbeniuk | 10-8 | Qualifying | Embassy World Championship |
| | v Dennis Taylor | 4-10 | 1st round | Embassy World Championship |
| | v Chalmers | 5-0 | 2nd round | Fidelity International |
| | v White | 3-5 | 3rd round | Fidelity International |
| | v Medati | 5-4 | 2nd round | Rothmans Grand Prix |
| | v Hendry | 1-5 | 3rd round | Rothmans Grand Prix |
| | v V. Harris | 7-9 | 2nd round | Tennents UK Open |
| **1988** | v G. Miles | 5-1 | 2nd round | Mercantile Credit Classic |
| | v Stevens | 5-2 | 3rd round | Mercantile Credit Classic |

| | | | | |
|---|---|---|---|---|
| | v Clark | 2-5 | 4th round | Mercantile Credit Classic |
| | v Everton | 6-0 | 1st round | Welsh Championship |
| | v Mountjoy | 3-6 | Quarter-final | Welsh Championship |
| | v Morra | 2-5 | 2nd round | MIM Britannia British Open |
| | v Rigitano | 10-4 | Qualifying | Embassy World Championship |
| | v Wych | 10-5 | Qualifying | Embassy World Championship |
| | v Stevens | 7-10 | Qualifying | Embassy World Championship |
| | v Marshall | 5-1 | 2nd round | Fidelity International |
| | v Newbury | 0-5 | 3rd round | Fidelity International |
| | v Watterson | 3-5 | 2nd round | Rothmans Grand Prix |
| | v John Rea | 5-4 | 2nd round | BCE Canadian Masters |
| | v E. Hughes | 5-2 | 3rd round | BCE Canadian Masters |
| | v White | 3-5 | 4th round | BCE Canadian Masters |
| | v V. Harris | 9-7 | 2nd round | Tennents UK Open |
| | v David Taylor | 9-4 | 3rd round | Tennents UK Open |
| | v White | 9-6 | 4th round | Tennents UK Open |
| | v West | 4-9 | 5th round | Tennents UK Open |
| **1989** | v Terry | 3-5 | 2nd round | Mercantile Credit Classic |
| | v F. Davis | 5-2 | 2nd round | European Open |
| | v Drago | 5-1 | 3rd round | European Open |
| | v J. Campbell | 3-5 | 4th round | European Open |
| | v Roscoe | 6-3 | 1st round | Senator Welsh Championship |
| | v C. Wilson | 6-1 | Quarter-final | Senator Welsh Championship |
| | v Mountjoy | 5-9 | Semi-final | Senator Welsh Championship |
| | v J. Smith | 5-4 | 2nd round | Anglian British Open |
| | v Meo | 1-5 | 3rd round | Anglian British Open |
| | v Price | 9-10 | Qualifying | Embassy World Championship |
| | v Pinches | 2-5 | 2nd round | Hong Kong Open |
| | v Morra | 5-1 | 2nd round | 555 Asian Open |
| | v James | 3-5 | 3rd round | 555 Asian Open |
| | v Terry | 5-4 | 2nd round | BCE International |
| | v Meo | 5-2 | 3rd round | BCE International |
| | v N. Foulds | 2-5 | 4th round | BCE International |
| | v Medati | 5-2 | 2nd round | Rothmans Grand Prix |
| | v E. Hughes | 2-5 | 3rd round | Rothmans Grand Prix |
| | v Rigitano | 5-2 | 2nd round | Dubai Classic |
| | v O'Kane | 2-5 | 3rd round | Dubai Classic |
| | v Bear | 6-5 | 2nd round | Stormseal UK Open |
| | v E. Hughes | 9-3 | 3rd round | Stormseal UK Open |
| | v Stevens | 9-2 | 4th round | Stormseal UK Open |
| | v P. Francisco | 9-3 | 5th round | Stormseal UK Open |
| | v Hendry | 2-9 | Quarter-final | Stormseal UK Open |
| **1990** | v Rigitano | 5-2 | 2nd round | Mercantile Credit Classic |
| | v Dennis Taylor | 2-5 | 3rd round | Mercantile Credit Classic |
| | v Reardon | 2-6 | 1st round | Senator Welsh Championship |
| | v V. Harris | 5-0 | 2nd round | Pearl Assurance British Open |
| | v Thorne | 5-1 | 3rd round | Pearl Assurance British Open |
| | v Higgins | 2-5 | 4th round | Pearl Assurance British Open |
| | v M. Smith | 5-3 | 2nd round | European Open |
| | v Griffiths | 5-2 | 3rd round | European Open |
| | v S. Francisco | 5-3 | 4th round | European Open |
| | v N. Foulds | 2-5 | 5th round | European Open |
| | v Lawlor | 10-3 | Qualifying | Embassy World Championship |
| | v Macleod | 10-1 | Qualifying | Embassy World Championship |
| | v Williams | 10-9 | Qualifying | Embassy World Championship |
| | v Parrott | 9-10 | 1st round | Embassy World Championship |

## NIGEL BOND (England)

**Born** 15.11.65. **Turned professional** 1989. **World ranking** 39.

| | | | | |
|---|---|---|---|---|
| **1989** | v Glen Wilkinson | 5-1 | 1st round | Hong Kong Open |

| | | | | |
|---|---|---|---|---|
| | v D. Morgan | 5-2 | 2nd round | Hong Kong Open |
| | v N. Foulds | 2-5 | 3rd round | Hong Kong Open |
| | v Edwards | 4-5 | 1st round | 555 Asian Open |
| | v Browne | 5-0 | 2nd round | BCE International |
| | v Thorburn | 5-4 | 3rd round | BCE International |
| | v S. Francisco | 5-3 | 4th round | BCE International |
| | v James | 5-0 | 5th round | BCE International |
| | v Parrott | 5-2 | Quarter-final | BCE International |
| | v Hendry | 5-6 | Semi-final | BCE International |
| | v Scott | 5-0 | 1st round | Rothmans Grand Prix |
| | v Chappel | 5-2 | 2nd round | Rothmans Grand Prix |
| | v Chaperon | 5-4 | 3rd round | Rothmans Grand Prix |
| | v Hendry | 1-5 | 4th round | Rothmans Grand Prix |
| | v Owers | 5-1 | 1st round | Dubai Classic |
| | v Murphy | 5-0 | 2nd round | Dubai Classic |
| | v Johnson | 5-3 | 3rd round | Dubai Classic |
| | v Robidoux | 5-4 | 4th round | Dubai Classic |
| | v P. Francisco | 4-5 | 5th round | Dubai Classic |
| | v Sinclair | 6-5 | 1st round | Stormseal UK Open |
| | v Macleod | 6-3 | 2nd round | Stormseal UK Open |
| | v White | 3-9 | 3rd round | Stormseal UK Open |
| **1990** | v Glen Wilkinson | 5-2 | 1st round | Mercantile Credit Classic |
| | v Roscoe | 4-5 | 2nd round | Mercantile Credit Classic |
| | v Rowswell | 5-3 | 1st round | Pearl Assurance British Open |
| | v Chappel | 4-5 | 2nd round | Pearl Assurance British Open |
| | v Dunning | 5-0 | 1st round | European Open |
| | v Fisher | 5-2 | 2nd round | European Open |
| | v Drago | 5-2 | 3rd round | European Open |
| | v Reynolds | 5-4 | 4th round | European Open |
| | v J. Campbell | 5-4 | 5th round | European Open |
| | v Parrott | 3-5 | Quarter-final | European Open |
| | v Werbeniuk | 10-1 | Qualifying | Embassy World Championship |
| | v Rowswell | 10-1 | Qualifying | Embassy World Championship |
| | v T. Jones | 10-2 | Qualifying | Embassy World Championship |
| | v Watchorn | 10-2 | Qualifying | Embassy World Championship |
| | v Newbury | 6-10 | Qualifying | Embassy World Championship |

## MALCOLM BRADLEY (England)

**Born** 8.7.48. **Turned professional** 1984. **World ranking** 107 (87).

| | | | | |
|---|---|---|---|---|
| **1984** | v Darrington | 5-3 | Qualifying | Jameson International |
| | v Jack Rea | 5-2 | Qualifying | Jameson International |
| | v Morra | 3-5 | Qualifying | Jameson International |
| | v Jonik | 5-1 | Qualifying | Rothmans Grand Prix |
| | v Virgo | 0-5 | 1st round | Rothmans Grand Prix |
| | v V. Harris | 9-8 | Qualifying | Coral UK Open |
| | v Kelly | 9-6 | Qualifying | Coral UK Open |
| | v Meadowcroft | 9-7 | Qualifying | Coral UK Open |
| | v Hallett | 8-9 | Qualifying | Coral UK Open |
| **1985** | v Browne | 3-5 | Qualifying | Mercantile Credit Classic |
| | v Williamson | 9-8 | Qualifying | Tolly Cobbold English Championship |
| | v Knowles | 8-9 | Qualifying | Tolly Cobbold English Championship |
| | v Morra | 6-2 | Qualifying | Dulux British Open |
| | v David Taylor | 6-3 | 1st round | Dulux British Open |
| | v Fowler | 5-4 | 2nd round | Dulux British Open |
| | v S. Davis | 2-5 | 3rd round | Dulux British Open |
| | v Mienie | 10-4 | Qualifying | Embassy World Championship |
| | v Mikkelsen | 10-9 | Qualifying | Embassy World Championship |
| | v Wych | 7-10 | Qualifying | Embassy World Championship |
| | v John Rea | 5-1 | 2nd round | Goya Matchroom Trophy |
| | v Hallett | 5-4 | 3rd round | Goya Matchroom Trophy |

| | | | | |
|---|---|---|---|---|
| | v Johnson | 2-5 | 4th round | Goya Matchroom Trophy |
| | v Gibson | 4-5 | 2nd round | Rothmans Grand Prix |
| | v Jenkins | 9-3 | 2nd round | Coral UK Open |
| | v White | 4-9 | 1st round | Coral UK Open |
| **1986** | v Oliver | 5-3 | 2nd round | Mercantile Credit Classic |
| | v N. Foulds | 3-5 | 3rd round | Mercantile Credit Classic |
| | v Gilbert | 9-5 | 2nd round | Tolly Cobbold English Championship |
| | v S. Davis | 3-9 | 3rd round | Tolly Cobbold English Championship |
| | v Jack Rea | 5-1 | 2nd round | Dulux British Open |
| | v Higgins | 3-5 | 3rd round | Dulux British Open |
| | v Gilbert | 7-10 | Qualifying | Embassy World Championship |
| | v Wilkinson | 5-4 | 2nd round | BCE International |
| | v Wych | 2-5 | 3rd round | BCE International |
| | v Wright | 0-5 | 2nd round | Rothmans Grand Prix |
| | v Meadowcroft | 9-2 | 2nd round | Tennents UK Open |
| | v Parrott | 4-9 | 3rd round | Tennents UK Open |
| **1987** | v Rowswell | 5-4 | 2nd round | Mercantile Credit Classic |
| | v David Taylor | 5-1 | 3rd round | Mercantile Credit Classic |
| | v White | 0-5 | 4th round | Mercantile Credit Classic |
| | v D. Gilbert | 6-3 | 2nd round | Tolly Ales English Championship |
| | v Fowler | 3-6 | 3rd round | Tolly Ales English Championship |
| | v O'Boye | 1-5 | 2nd round | Dulux British Open |
| | v Rowswell | 10-6 | Qualifying | Embassy World Championship |
| | v O'Boye | 10-7 | Qualifying | Embassy World Championship |
| | v Wych | 7-10 | Qualifying | Embassy World Championship |
| | v J. Smith | 5-1 | 2nd round | Fidelity International |
| | v Dennis Taylor | 0-5 | 3rd round | Fidelity International |
| | v John Rea | 1-5 | 2nd round | Rothmans Grand Prix |
| | v Watchorn | 5-9 | 2nd round | Tennents UK Open |
| **1988** | v Everton | 5-2 | 2nd round | Mercantile Credit Classic |
| | v Thorne | 1-5 | 3rd round | Mercantile Credit Classic |
| | v Lawlor | 5-6 | 2nd round | English Championship |
| | v Williamson | 3-5 | 2nd round | MIM Britannia British Open |
| | v Williamson | 10-9 | Qualifying | Embassy World Championship |
| | v Werbeniuk | 8-10 | Qualifying | Embassy World Championship |
| | v Sheehan | 4-5 | 1st round | Fidelity International |
| | v Rowing | 5-3 | 1st round | Rothmans Grand Prix |
| | v Murphy | 5-3 | 2nd round | Rothmans Grand Prix |
| | v Johnson | 2-5 | 3rd round | Rothmans Grand Prix |
| | v Meakin | 5-0 | 1st round | BCE Canadian Masters |
| | v Browne | 2-5 | 2nd round | BCE Canadian Masters |
| | v T. Wilson | 9-7 | 1st round | Tennents UK Open |
| | v J. McLaughlin | 3-9 | 2nd round | Tennents UK Open |
| **1989** | v Fagan | 5-3 | 1st round | Mercantile Credit Classic |
| | v T. Jones | 5-4 | 2nd round | Mercantile Credit Classic |
| | v Newbury | 3-5 | 3rd round | Mercantile Credit Classic |
| | v Rempe | 5-4 | 1st round | European Open |
| | v O'Boye | 3-5 | 2nd round | European Open |
| | v Chambers | 5-2 | 1st round | English Championship |
| | v D. Gilbert | 4-5 | 2nd round | English Championship |
| | v Everton | 5-0 | 1st round | Anglian British Open |
| | v Cripsey | 4-5 | 2nd round | Anglian British Open |
| | v Thornley | 7-10 | Qualifying | Embassy World Championship |
| | v Meadowcroft | 2-5 | 1st round | Hong Kong Open |
| | v Jack Rea | 5-2 | 1st round | 555 Asian Open |
| | v O'Boye | 3-5 | 2nd round | 555 Asian Open |
| | v G. Foulds | 5-1 | 1st round | BCE International |
| | v Robidoux | 2-5 | 2nd round | BCE International |
| | v Rowing | 4-5 | 1st round | Rothmans Grand Prix |
| | v Dyson | 5-4 | 1st round | Dubai Classic |
| | v Gauvreau | 4-5 | 2nd round | Dubai Classic |
| | v Grace | 4-6 | 1st round | Stormseal UK Open |
| **1990** | v Fitzmaurice | 5-4 | 1st round | Mercantile Credit Classic |

| | | | | |
|---|---|---|---|---|
| | v N. Gilbert | 1-5 | 2nd round | Mercantile Credit Classic |
| | v Grace | 5-1 | 1st round | Pearl Assurance British Open |
| | v Browne | 2-5 | 2nd round | Pearl Assurance British Open |
| | v Graham | 0-5 | 2nd round | European Open |
| | v Dyson | 6-10 | Qualifying | Embassy World Championship |

## **PADDY BROWNE** (Republic of Ireland)

**Born** 1.4.65. **Turned professional** 1983. **World ranking** 54 (44).

| | | | | |
|---|---|---|---|---|
| **1983** | v Murphy | 2-5 | Qualifying | Professional Players Tournament |
| **1984** | v Duggan | 10-9 | Qualifying | Embassy World Championship |
| | v Roscoe | 10-4 | Qualifying | Embassy World Championship |
| | v Sinclair | 1-10 | Qualifying | Embassy World Championship |
| | v John Rea | 5-2 | Qualifying | Jameson International |
| | v Black | 4-5 | Qualifying | Jameson International |
| | v Duggan | 2-5 | Qualifying | Rothmans Grand Prix |
| | v G. Foulds | 9-5 | Qualifying | Coral UK Open |
| | v King | 5-9 | Qualifying | Coral UK Open |
| **1985** | v Bradley | 5-3 | Qualifying | Mercantile Credit Classic |
| | v Everton | 5-0 | Qualifying | Mercantile Credit Classic |
| | v Miles | 5-3 | Qualifying | Mercantile Credit Classic |
| | v White | 2-5 | 1st round | Mercantile Credit Classic |
| | v Newbury | 0-6 | Qualifying | Dulux British Open |
| | v Murphy | 3-6 | Qualifying | Irish Championship |
| | v Anderson | 10-5 | Qualifying | Embassy World Championship |
| | v Morra | 6-10 | Qualifying | Embassy World Championship |
| | v B. Harris | 3-5 | 2nd round | Goya Matchroom Trophy |
| | v B. Harris | 3-5 | 2nd round | Rothmans Grand Prix |
| | v Chalmers | 9-4 | 2nd round | Coral UK Open |
| | v Thorne | 6-9 | 3rd round | Coral UK Open |
| **1986** | v Everton | 5-0 | 2nd round | Mercantile Credit Classic |
| | v Wilson | 5-3 | 3rd round | Mercantile Credit Classic |
| | v Gauvreau | 3-5 | 4th round | Mercantile Credit Classic |
| | v Hendry | 5-0 | 2nd round | Dulux British Open |
| | v Spencer | 5-0 | 3rd round | Dulux British Open |
| | v Charlton | 1-5 | 4th round | Dulux British Open |
| | v Hendry | 9-10 | Qualifying | Embassy World Championship |
| | v Burke | 4-5 | 1st round | Strongbow Irish Championship |
| | v M. Bennett | 1-5 | 2nd round | BCE International |
| | v Sheehan | 5-4 | 2nd round | Rothmans Grand Prix |
| | v Johnson | 5-2 | 3rd round | Rothmans Grand Prix |
| | v M. Bennett | 5-0 | 4th round | Rothmans Grand Prix |
| | v Hendry | 3-5 | 5th round | Rothmans Grand Prix |
| | v Williamson | 4-9 | 2nd round | Tennents UK Open |
| **1987** | v Dunning | 5-1 | 2nd round | Mercantile Credit Classic |
| | v J. Campbell | 2-5 | 3rd round | Mercantile Credit Classic |
| | v Rigitano | 4-5 | 2nd round | Dulux British Open |
| | v Wright | 6-10 | Qualifying | Embassy World Championship |
| | v Jack Rea | 5-3 | 1st round | Matchroom Irish Championship |
| | v Burke | 6-2 | Quarter-final | Matchroom Irish Championship |
| | v Dennis Taylor | 1-6 | Semi-final | Matchroom Irish Championship |
| | v Roscoe | 2-5 | 2nd round | Fidelity International |
| | v Meadowcroft | 3-5 | 2nd round | Rothmans Grand Prix |
| | v M. Smith | 4-9 | 2nd round | Tennents UK Open |
| **1988** | v M. Smith | 1-5 | 2nd round | Mercantile Credit Classic |
| | v Jack Rea | 5-0 | 1st round | Irish Championship |
| | v Murphy | 6-5 | Quarter-final | Irish Championship |
| | v Dennis Taylor | 5-6 | Semi-final | Irish Championship |
| | v Chalmers | 5-2 | 2nd round | MIM Britannia British Open |
| | v Martin | 5-4 | 3rd round | MIM Britannia British Open |
| | v O'Kane | 2-5 | 4th round | MIM Britannia British Open |

| | | | | |
|---|---|---|---|---|
| | v Kelly | 10-8 | Qualifying | Embassy World Championship |
| | v James | 1-10 | Qualifying | Embassy World Championship |
| | v T. Wilson | 3-5 | 2nd round | Fidelity International |
| | v Johnston-Allen | 2-5 | 2nd round | Rothmans Grand Prix |
| | v Bradley | 5-2 | 2nd round | BCE Canadian Masters |
| | v Longworth | 4-5 | 3rd round | BCE Canadian Masters |
| | v Kearney | 6-9 | 2nd round | Tennents UK Open |
| **1989** | v Williamson | 5-3 | 2nd round | Mercantile Credit Classic |
| | v Hallett | 5-2 | 3rd round | Mercantile Credit Classic |
| | v James | 5-4 | 4th round | Mercantile Credit Classic |
| | v Chappel | 5-1 | 5th round | Mercantile Credit Classic |
| | v Mountjoy | 3-5 | Quarter-final | Mercantile Credit Classic |
| | v J. Smith | 5-4 | 2nd round | European Open |
| | v Reynolds | *wo* | 3rd round | European Open |
| | v Hallett | 4-5 | 4th round | European Open |
| | v Sheehan | 5-2 | 1st round | Irish Championship |
| | v Murphy | 5-3 | Quarter-final | Irish Championship |
| | v J. McLaughlin | 3-6 | Semi-final | Irish Championship |
| | v Sinclair | 5-3 | 2nd round | Anglian British Open |
| | v Thorburn | 0-5 | 3rd round | Anglian British Open |
| | v Meakin | 10-9 | Qualifying | Embassy World Championship |
| | v Macleod | 10-6 | Qualifying | Embassy World Championship |
| | v Longworth | 10-0 | Qualifying | Embassy World Championship |
| | v Thorne | 5-10 | 1st round | Embassy World Championship |
| | v M. Gibson | 3-5 | 2nd round | Hong Kong Open |
| | v Wright | 5-3 | 2nd round | 555 Asian Open |
| | v Thorne | 4-5 | 3rd round | 555 Asian Open |
| | v Bond | 0-5 | 2nd round | BCE International |
| | v S. Murphy | 3-5 | 2nd round | Rothmans Grand Prix |
| | v M. Smith | 5-1 | 2nd round | Dubai Classic |
| | v Fowler | 4-5 | 3rd round | Dubai Classic |
| | v Oliver | 6-2 | 2nd round | Stormseal UK Open |
| | v C. Wilson | 7-9 | 3rd round | Stormseal UK Open |
| **1990** | v B. Harris | 3-5 | 2nd round | Mercantile Credit Classic |
| | v Bradley | 5-2 | 2nd round | Pearl Assurance British Open |
| | v Virgo | 5-1 | 3rd round | Pearl Assurance British Open |
| | v Clark | 2-5 | 4th round | Pearl Assurance British Open |
| | v Kelly | 5-4 | 2nd round | European Open |
| | v Thorne | 3-5 | 3rd round | European Open |
| | v Brumby | 10-6 | Qualifying | Embassy World Championship |
| | v Johnston-Allen | 2-10 | Qualifying | Embassy World Championship |

## IAN BRUMBY (England)

**Born** 17.9.64. **Turned professional** 1989. **World ranking** 84.

| | | | | |
|---|---|---|---|---|
| **1989** | v Miles | 5-3 | 1st round | Hong Kong Open |
| | v Murphy | 5-0 | 2nd round | Hong Kong Open |
| | v Thorne | 3-5 | 3rd round | Hong Kong Open |
| | v Marshall | 4-5 | 1st round | 555 Asian Open |
| | v Owers | 5-4 | 1st round | BCE International |
| | v Spencer | 5-1 | 2nd round | BCE International |
| | v Charlton | 4-5 | 3rd round | BCE International |
| | v Bear | *wo* | 1st round | Rothmans Grand Prix |
| | v Edmonds | 2-5 | 2nd round | Rothmans Grand Prix |
| | v S. Campbell | 5-4 | 1st round | Dubai Classic |
| | v Scott | 4-5 | 2nd round | Dubai Classic |
| | v Lawlor | 5-6 | 1st round | Stormseal UK Open |
| **1990** | v Lawlor | 5-4 | 1st round | Mercantile Credit Classic |
| | v Spencer | 5-1 | 2nd round | Mercantile Credit Classic |
| | v White | *wo* | 3rd round | Mercantile Credit Classic |

| | | | | |
|---|---|---|---|---|
| | v S. Francisco | 0-5 | 4th round | Mercantile Credit Classic |
| | v Glen Wilkinson | 4-5 | 1st round | Pearl Assurance British Open |
| | v Demarco | 10-6 | Qualifying | Embassy World Championship |
| | v F. Davis | 10-6 | Qualifying | Embassy World Championship |
| | v Browne | 6-10 | Qualifying | Embassy World Championship |

## ANDREW CAIRNS (England)

**Born** 12.7.68. **Turned professional** 1989. **World ranking** 81.

| | | | | |
|---|---|---|---|---|
| **1989** | v Rowswell | 3-5 | 1st round | Hong Kong Open |
| | v Houlihan | 5-0 | 1st round | 555 Asian Open |
| | v Longworth | 5-1 | 2nd round | 555 Asian Open |
| | v Griffiths | 2-5 | 3rd round | 555 Asian Open |
| | v Foldvari | 5-4 | 1st round | BCE International |
| | v David Taylor | 5-4 | 2nd round | BCE International |
| | v O'Kane | 5-2 | 3rd round | BCE International |
| | v Knowles | 2-5 | 4th round | BCE International |
| | v Morra | 4-5 | 1st round | Rothmans Grand Prix |
| | v Kearney | 1-5 | 1st round | Dubai Classic |
| | v Miles | 6-2 | 1st round | Stormseal UK Open |
| | v Spencer | 3-6 | 2nd round | Stormseal UK Open |
| **1990** | v M. Smith | 5-2 | 1st round | Mercantile Credit Classic |
| | v Robidoux | 5-4 | 2nd round | Mercantile Credit Classic |
| | v Clark | 2-5 | 3rd round | Mercantile Credit Classic |
| | v John Rea | 5-1 | 1st round | Pearl Assurance British Open |
| | v David Taylor | 0-5 | 2nd round | Pearl Assurance British Open |
| | v Bear | 5-4 | 1st round | European Open |
| | v N. Gilbert | 3-5 | 2nd round | European Open |
| | v B. Bennett | 10-4 | Qualifying | Embassy World Championship |
| | v Scott | 10-3 | Qualifying | Embassy World Championship |
| | v Reardon | 10-8 | Qualifying | Embassy World Championship |
| | v N. Gilbert | 6-10 | Qualifying | Embassy World Championship |

## DUNCAN CAMPBELL (Scotland)

**Born** 24.9.66. **Turned professional** 1989. **World ranking** 109.

| | | | | |
|---|---|---|---|---|
| **1989** | v B. Harris | 5-2 | 1st round | Hong Kong Open |
| | v Dodd | 4-5 | 2nd round | Hong Kong Open |
| | v Lawlor | 5-4 | 1st round | 555 Asian Open |
| | v John Rea | 2-5 | 2nd round | 555 Asian Open |
| | v P. Gibson | 5-1 | 1st round | BCE International |
| | v J. McLaughlin | 0-5 | 2nd round | BCE International |
| | v Williamson | 5-0 | 1st round | Rothmans Grand Prix |
| | v J. Campbell | 3-5 | 2nd round | Rothmans Grand Prix |
| | v Foldvari | 5-2 | 1st round | Dubai Classic |
| | v Wright | 1-5 | 2nd round | Dubai Classic |
| | v B. Harris | 2-6 | 1st round | Stormseal UK Open |
| **1990** | v Dunning | 5-2 | 1st round | Mercantile Credit Classic |
| | v Edmonds | 3-5 | 2nd round | Mercantile Credit Classic |
| | v B. Harris | 2-5 | 1st round | Pearl Assurance British Open |
| | v Houlihan | 5-4 | 1st round | European Open |
| | v D. Gilbert | 5-2 | 2nd round | European Open |
| | v Virgo | 4-5 | 3rd round | European Open |
| | v Greaves | 10-3 | Qualifying | Embassy World Championship |
| | v Wright | 10-6 | Qualifying | Embassy World Championship |
| | v J. Campbell | 5-10 | Qualifying | Embassy World Championship |

## JOHN CAMPBELL (Australia)

**Born** 10.4.53. **Turned professional** 1982. **World ranking** 48 (42).

| | | | | |
|---|---|---|---|---|
| **1983** | v Watterson | 10-6 | Qualifying | Embassy World Championship |
| | v Donnelly | 10-2 | Qualifying | Embassy World Championship |
| | v Thorburn | 5-10 | 1st round | Embassy World Championship |
| | v E. McLaughlin | 2-5 | Qualifying | Jameson International |
| | v Mountjoy | 5-3 | 1st round | Professional Players Tournament |
| | v Miles | 5-2 | 2nd round | Professional Players Tournament |
| | v Martin | 5-0 | 3rd round | Professional Players Tournament |
| | v Knowles | 3-5 | Quarter-final | Professional Players Tournament |
| **1984** | v White | 1-5 | Qualifying | Lada Classic |
| | v Gauvreau | 7-10 | Qualifying | Embassy World Championship |
| | v G. Foulds | 5-3 | Qualifying | Jameson International |
| | v S. Davis | 1-5 | 1st round | Jameson International |
| | v W. Jones | 5-4 | 1st round | Rothmans Grand Prix |
| | v Thorburn | 1-5 | 2nd round | Rothmans Grand Prix |
| | v Donnelly | 9-6 | Qualifying | Coral UK Open |
| | v White | 7-9 | 1st round | Coral UK Open |
| **1985** | v Scott | 4-5 | Qualifying | Mercantile Credit Classic |
| | v O'Kane | 4-6 | 1st round | Dulux British Open |
| | v Morra | 10-9 | Qualifying | Embassy World Championship |
| | v Charlton | 3-10 | 1st round | Embassy World Championship |
| | v Charlton | 5-4 | Quarter-final | Winfield Australian Masters |
| | v Parrott | 6-4 | Semi-final | Winfield Australian Masters |
| | v Meo | 2-7 | Final | Winfield Australian Masters |
| | v Foldvari | 8-5 | Quarter-final | Australian Championship |
| | v King | 9-6 | Semi-final | Australian Championship |
| | **v Charlton** | **10-7** | **Final** | **Australian Championship** |
| | v Morra | 5-2 | 3rd round | Goya Matchroom Trophy |
| | v Mountjoy | 5-1 | 4th round | Goya Matchroom Trophy |
| | v Thorburn | 0-5 | 5th round | Goya Matchroom Trophy |
| | v Van Rensberg | 5-4 | 3rd round | Rothmans Grand Prix |
| | v Mountjoy | 5-2 | 4th round | Rothmans Grand Prix |
| | v Knowles | 2-5 | 5th round | Rothmans Grand Prix |
| | v Medati | 9-7 | 3rd round | Coral UK Open |
| | v David Taylor | 4-9 | 4th round | Coral UK Open |
| **1986** | v Donnelly | 5-2 | 3rd round | Mercantile Credit Classic |
| | v Mikkelsen | 5-2 | 4th round | Mercantile Credit Classic |
| | v N. Foulds | 1-5 | 5th round | Mercantile Credit Classic |
| | v West | 5-4 | 3rd round | Dulux British Open |
| | v Medati | 5-4 | 4th round | Dulux British Open |
| | v S. Davis | 0-5 | 5th round | Dulux British Open |
| | v Van Rensberg | 10-6 | Qualifying | Embassy World Championship |
| | v Reardon | 10-8 | 1st round | Embassy World Championship |
| | v Thorne | 9-13 | 2nd round | Embassy World Championship |
| | v Wilkinson | 6-1 | Quarter-final | Australian Championship |
| | v Foldvari | 8-3 | Semi-final | Australian Championship |
| | v King | 3-10 | Final | Australian Championship |
| | v Duggan | 3-5 | 3rd round | BCE International |
| | v G. Foulds | 5-0 | 3rd round | Rothmans Grand Prix |
| | v Griffiths | 1-5 | 4th round | Rothmans Grand Prix |
| | v W. Jones | 3-9 | 3rd round | Tennents UK Open |
| **1987** | v Browne | 5-2 | 3rd round | Mercantile Credit Classic |
| | v Spencer | 5-3 | 4th round | Mercantile Credit Classic |
| | v Griffiths | 3-5 | 5th round | Mercantile Credit Classic |
| | v James | 1-5 | 3rd round | Dulux British Open |
| | v Chappel | 10-6 | Qualifying | Embassy World Championship |
| | v S. Francisco | 3-10 | 1st round | Embassy World Championship |
| | v Wilkinson | 6-4 | Quarter-final | Australian Championship |
| | v Charlton | 6-8 | Semi-final | Australian Championship |
| | v James | 4-5 | 3rd round | Fidelity International |

| | | | | |
|---|---|---|---|---|
| | v Bales | 3-5 | 3rd round | Rothmans Grand Prix |
| | v Chambers | 9-7 | 3rd round | Tennents UK Open |
| | v M. Smith | 9-8 | 4th round | Tennents UK Open |
| | v Thorburn | 4-9 | 5th round | Tennents UK Open |
| **1988** | v Murphy | 3-5 | 3rd round | Mercantile Credit Classic |
| | v W. Jones | 5-3 | 3rd round | MIM Britannia British Open |
| | v O'Boye | 1-5 | 4th round | MIM Britannia British Open |
| | v F. Davis | 10-3 | Qualifying | Embassy World Championship |
| | v White | 3-10 | 1st round | Embassy World Championship |
| | v Anderson | 5-0 | Quarter-final | Australian Championship |
| | v Charlton | 8-6 | Semi-final | Australian Championship |
| | **v Foldvari** | **9-7** | **Final** | **Australian Championship** |
| | v Stevens | *wo* | 3rd round | Fidelity International |
| | v Dennis Taylor | 4-5 | 4th round | Fidelity International |
| | v W. Jones | 2-5 | 3rd round | Rothmans Grand Prix |
| | v Oliver | 3-5 | 2nd round | BCE Canadian Masters |
| | v Foldvari | 9-7 | 2nd round | Tennents UK Open |
| | v White | 5-9 | 3rd round | Tennents UK Open |
| **1989** | v S. Campbell | 2-5 | 2nd round | Mercantile Credit Classic |
| | v Watchorn | 5-1 | 2nd round | European Open |
| | v P. Francisco | 5-0 | 3rd round | European Open |
| | v M. Bennett | 5-3 | 4th round | European Open |
| | v Parrott | 0-5 | 5th round | European Open |
| | v M. Gibson | 5-2 | 2nd round | Anglian British Open |
| | v P. Francisco | 2-5 | 3rd round | Anglian British Open |
| | v D. Morgan | 4-10 | Qualifying | Embassy World Championship |
| | v Houlihan | 3-5 | 2nd round | Hong Kong Open |
| | v Oliver | 3-5 | 2nd round | 555 Asian Open |
| | v Fitzmaurice | 5-3 | 2nd round | BCE International |
| | v S. Francisco | 4-5 | 3rd round | BCE International |
| | v D. Campbell | 5-3 | 2nd round | Rothmans Grand Prix |
| | v Dennis Taylor | 3-5 | 3rd round | Rothmans Grand Prix |
| | v Meakin | 5-0 | 2nd round | Dubai Classic |
| | v Newbury | 5-1 | 3rd round | Dubai Classic |
| | v J. McLaughlin | 1-5 | 4th round | Dubai Classic |
| | v Marshall | 4-6 | 2nd round | Stormseal UK Open |
| **1990** | v Owers | 5-3 | 2nd round | Mercantile Credit Classic |
| | v Knowles | 5-2 | 3rd round | Mercantile Credit Classic |
| | v Gary Wilkinson | 4-5 | 4th round | Mercantile Credit Classic |
| | v Terry | 1-5 | 2nd round | Pearl Assurance British Open |
| | v Gollan | 5-3 | 2nd round | European Open |
| | v C. Wilson | 5-0 | 3rd round | European Open |
| | v Robidoux | 5-4 | 4th round | European Open |
| | v Bond | 4-5 | 5th round | European Open |
| | v D. Campbell | 10-5 | Qualifying | Embassy World Championship |
| | v Price | 6-10 | Qualifying | Embassy World Championship |

## STEVE CAMPBELL (England)

**Born** 7.3.66. **Turned professional** 1988. **World ranking** 92 (98).

| | | | | |
|---|---|---|---|---|
| **1988** | v F. Davis | 4-5 | 1st round | Fidelity International |
| | v Black | 5-1 | 1st round | Rothmans Grand Prix |
| | v Stevens | 3-5 | 2nd round | Rothmans Grand Prix |
| | v Kearney | 5-2 | 1st round | BCE Canadian Masters |
| | v Bales | 5-2 | 2nd round | BCE Canadian Masters |
| | v Hendry | 2-5 | 3rd round | BCE Canadian Masters |
| | v Dunning | 9-5 | 1st round | Tennents UK Open |
| | v Clark | 3-9 | 2nd round | Tennents UK Open |
| **1989** | v Oliver | 5-4 | 1st round | Mercantile Credit Classic |
| | v J. Campbell | 5-2 | 2nd round | Mercantile Credit Classic |

| | | | | |
|---|---|---|---|---|
| | v C. Wilson | 3-5 | 3rd round | Mercantile Credit Classic |
| | v Morra | 3-5 | 1st round | European Open |
| | v Dunning | 5-3 | 1st round | English Championship |
| | v Fowler | 1-5 | 2nd round | English Championship |
| | v Medati | 5-3 | 1st round | Anglian British Open |
| | v Reardon | 4-5 | 2nd round | Anglian British Open |
| | v M. Smith | 9-10 | Qualifying | Embassy World Championship |
| | v Watterson | 5-0 | 1st round | Hong Kong Open |
| | v Bales | 2-5 | 2nd round | Hong Kong Open |
| | v G. Foulds | 5-4 | 1st round | 555 Asian Open |
| | v Robidoux | 5-2 | 2nd round | 555 Asian Open |
| | v W. Jones | 3-5 | 3rd round | 555 Asian Open |
| | v John Rea | 5-4 | 1st round | BCE International |
| | v Bales | 3-5 | 2nd round | BCE International |
| | v Foldvari | 5-4 | 1st round | Rothmans Grand Prix |
| | v Bales | 5-2 | 2nd round | Rothmans Grand Prix |
| | v White | 0-5 | 3rd round | Rothmans Grand Prix |
| | v Brumby | 4-5 | 1st round | Dubai Classic |
| | v Foldvari | 6-5 | 1st round | Stormseal UK Open |
| | v D. Morgan | 6-5 | 2nd round | Stormseal UK Open |
| | v P. Francisco | 5-9 | 3rd round | Stormseal UK Open |
| **1990** | v Williamson | 2-5 | 1st round | Mercantile Credit Classic |
| | v Price | 5-3 | 1st round | Pearl Assurance British Open |
| | v Spencer | 3-5 | 2nd round | Pearl Assurance British Open |
| | v Scott | 5-2 | 1st round | European Open |
| | v Johnston-Allen | 0-5 | 2nd round | European Open |
| | v Glen Wilkinson | 10-2 | Qualifying | Embassy World Championship |
| | v Longworth | 10-6 | Qualifying | Embassy World Championship |
| | v Dodd | 10-7 | Qualifying | Embassy World Championship |
| | v N. Foulds | 7-10 | Qualifying | Embassy World Championship |

## JIM CHAMBERS (England)

**Born** 7.2.57. **Turned professional** 1987. **World ranking** 59 (60).

| | | | | |
|---|---|---|---|---|
| **1987** | v Grace | 4-5 | 2nd round | Fidelity International |
| | v Fitzmaurice | 5-2 | 1st round | Rothmans Grand Prix |
| | v O'Boye | 5-3 | 2nd round | Rothmans Grand Prix |
| | v Mountjoy | 5-2 | 3rd round | Rothmans Grand Prix |
| | v Hendry | 1-5 | 4th round | Rothmans Grand Prix |
| | v Roscoe | 9-4 | 1st round | Tennents UK Open |
| | v Wildman | 9-5 | 2nd round | Tennents UK Open |
| | v J. Campbell | 7-9 | 3rd round | Tennents UK Open |
| **1988** | v Rowswell | 2-5 | 1st round | Mercantile Credit Classic |
| | v P. Gibson | 6-0 | 1st round | English Championship |
| | v Scott | 6-2 | 2nd round | English Championship |
| | v Longworth | 4-6 | 3rd round | English Championship |
| | v Roe | 3-5 | 1st round | MIM Britannia British Open |
| | v Watterson | 10-3 | Qualifying | Embassy World Championship |
| | v Wright | 2-10 | Qualifying | Embassy World Championship |
| | v Graham | 5-2 | 1st round | Fidelity International |
| | v Gary Wilkinson | 5-4 | 2nd round | Fidelity International |
| | v Thorne | 2-5 | 3rd round | Fidelity International |
| | v Meakin | 5-0 | 1st round | Rothmans Grand Prix |
| | v Owers | 5-3 | 2nd round | Rothmans Grand Prix |
| | v West | 3-5 | 3rd round | Rothmans Grand Prix |
| | v Fagan | 5-2 | 1st round | BCE Canadian Masters |
| | v Murphy | 3-5 | 2nd round | BCE Canadian Masters |
| | v Owers | 4-9 | 2nd round | Tennents UK Open |
| **1989** | v Mienie | 5-2 | 1st round | Mercantile Credit Classic |
| | v Reardon | 4-5 | 2nd round | Mercantile Credit Classic |
| | v Mikkelsen | 5-3 | 1st round | European Open |

| | | | | |
|---|---|---|---|---|
| | v Bales | 5-1 | 2nd round | European Open |
| | v S. Davis | *wo* | 3rd round | European Open |
| | v Charlton | 2-5 | 4th round | European Open |
| | v Bradley | 2-5 | 1st round | English Championship |
| | v Marshall | 2-5 | 1st round | Anglian British Open |
| | v Anderson | 10-7 | Qualifying | Embassy World Championship |
| | v Stevens | 8-10 | Qualifying | Embassy World Championship |
| | v D. Hughes | 5-2 | 2nd round | Hong Kong Open |
| | v Reynolds | 5-4 | 3rd round | Hong Kong Open |
| | v N. Foulds | 0-5 | 4th round | Hong Kong Open |
| | v F. Davis | 5-1 | 2nd round | 555 Asian Open |
| | v West | 3-5 | 3rd round | 555 Asian Open |
| | v Dyson | 3-5 | 2nd round | BCE International |
| | v G. Foulds | 5-2 | 2nd round | Rothmans Grand Prix |
| | v West | 5-4 | 3rd round | Rothmans Grand Prix |
| | v White | 1-5 | 4th round | Rothmans Grand Prix |
| | v Everton | 5-1 | 2nd round | Dubai Classic |
| | v O'Boye | 5-4 | 3rd round | Dubai Classic |
| | v James | 4-5 | 4th round | Dubai Classic |
| | v Gauvreau | 6-2 | 2nd round | Stormseal UK Open |
| | v Johnson | 7-9 | 3rd round | Stormseal UK Open |
| **1990** | v Miles | 5-3 | 2nd round | Mercantile Credit Classic |
| | v James | 4-5 | 3rd round | Mercantile Credit Classic |
| | v Wattana | 3-5 | 2nd round | Pearl Assurance British Open |
| | v Watterson | 5-0 | 2nd round | European Open |
| | v Mountjoy | 4-5 | 3rd round | European Open |
| | v Bear | 10-3 | Qualifying | Embassy World Championship |
| | v Miles | 10-5 | Qualifying | Embassy World Championship |
| | v W. Jones | 6-10 | Qualifying | Embassy World Championship |

## ROBERT CHAPERON (Canada)

**Born** 18.5.58. **Turned professional** 1983. **World ranking** 26 (29).

| | | | | |
|---|---|---|---|---|
| **1983** | v Watson | 9-5 | 1st round | Canadian Championship |
| | v Jonik | 4-9 | 2nd round | Canadian Championship |
| **1984** | v Fowler | 0-5 | Qualifying | Jameson International |
| | v Kearney | 5-1 | Qualifying | Rothmans Grand Prix |
| | v Gibson | 5-4 | Qualifying | Rothmans Grand Prix |
| | v Martin | 4-5 | Qualifying | Rothmans Grand Prix |
| | v T. Jones | 1-9 | Qualifying | Coral UK Open |
| **1985** | v G. Foulds | 3-5 | Qualifying | Mercantile Credit Clasic |
| | v Fagan | 6-5 | Qualifying | Dulux British Open |
| | v Werbeniuk | 6-1 | 1st round | Dulux British Open |
| | v W. Jones | 5-2 | 2nd round | Dulux British Open |
| | v S. Francisco | 2-5 | 3rd round | Dulux British Open |
| | v Bales | 10-7 | Qualifying | Embassy World Championship |
| | v Heywood | 10-1 | Qualifying | Embassy World Championship |
| | v Morgan | 10-3 | Qualifying | Embassy World Championship |
| | v F. Davis | 9-10 | Qualifying | Embassy World Championship |
| | v Thornley | 5-1 | 1st round | Canadian Championship |
| | v Stevens | 6-4 | Quarter-final | Canadian Championship |
| | v Jonik | 6-3 | Semi-final | Canadian Championship |
| | v Thorburn | 4-6 | Final | Canadian Championship |
| | v Chalmers | 5-2 | 2nd round | Goya Matchroom Trophy |
| | v S. Francisco | 5-3 | 3rd round | Goya Matchroom Trophy |
| | v Macleod | 4-5 | 4th round | Goya Matchroom Trophy |
| | v O'Boye | 3-5 | 2nd round | Rothmans Grand Prix |
| | v J. McLaughlin | 5-9 | 2nd round | Coral UK Open |
| **1986** | v Burke | 5-2 | 2nd round | Mercantile Credit Classic |
| | S. Davis | 1-5 | 3rd round | Mercantile Credit Classic |
| | v V. Harris | 5-0 | 2nd round | Dulux British Open |

| | | | | |
|---|---|---|---|---|
| | v Wilson | 3-5 | 3rd round | Dulux British Open |
| | v Jonik | 10-8 | Qualifying | Embassy World Championship |
| | v Gauvreau | 8-10 | Qualifying | Embassy World Championship |
| | v Bear | 6-3 | 1st round | Canadian Championship |
| | v Jonik | 3-6 | 2nd round | Canadian Championship |
| | v N. Gilbert | 5-3 | 2nd round | BCE International |
| | v Martin | 5-4 | 3rd round | BCE International |
| | v Drago | 5-1 | 4th round | BCE International |
| | v E. Hughes | 0-5 | 5th round | BCE International |
| | v Chalmers | 5-2 | 2nd round | Rothmans Grand Prix |
| | v Reardon | 5-3 | 3rd round | Rothmans Grand Prix |
| | v Hendry | 2-5 | 4th round | Rothmans Grand Prix |
| | v Dodd | 9-4 | 2nd round | Tennents UK Open |
| | v David Taylor | 8-9 | 3rd round | Tennents UK Open |
| **1987** | v Roe | 5-4 | 2nd round | Mercantile Credit Classic |
| | v Stevens | 3-5 | 3rd round | Mercantile Credit Classic |
| | v Fisher | 5-2 | 2nd round | Dulux British Open |
| | v Stevens | 4-5 | 3rd round | Dulux British Open |
| | v Fitzmaurice | 10-2 | Qualifying | Embassy World Championship |
| | v Spencer | 4-10 | Qualifying | Embassy World Championship |
| | v Morra | 5-6 | 1st round | Canadian Championship |
| | v V. Harris | 5-4 | 2nd round | Fidelity International |
| | v West | 5-4 | 3rd round | Fidelity International |
| | v Parrott | 1-5 | 4th round | Fidelity International |
| | v Rowswell | 5-4 | 2nd round | Rothmans Grand Prix |
| | v Reynolds | 5-4 | 3rd round | Rothmans Grand Prix |
| | v Houlihan | 5-0 | 4th round | Rothmans Grand Prix |
| | v Fisher | 5-2 | 5th round | Rothmans Grand Prix |
| | v Parrott | 2-5 | Quarter-final | Rothmans Grand Prix |
| | v Jack Rea | 9-6 | 2nd round | Tennents UK Open |
| | v David Taylor | 6-9 | 3rd round | Tennents UK Open |
| **1988** | v Medati | 5-3 | 2nd round | Mercantile Credit Classic |
| | v N. Foulds | 1-5 | 3rd round | Mercantile Credit Classic |
| | v Rigitano | 5-2 | 2nd round | MIM Britannia British Open |
| | v Stevens | *wo* | 3rd round | MIM Britannia British Open |
| | v T. Jones | 4-5 | 4th round | MIM Britannia British Open |
| | v Marshall | 10-3 | Qualifying | Embassy World Championship |
| | v Murphy | 10-5 | Qualifying | Embassy World Championship |
| | v David Taylor | 10-6 | Qualifying | Embassy World Championship |
| | v Hallett | 2-10 | 1st round | Embassy World Championship |
| | v Robidoux | 3-6 | 1st round | BCE Canadian Championship |
| | v Fisher | 5-3 | 3rd round | Fidelity International |
| | v S. Francisco | 5-2 | 4th round | Fidelity International |
| | v Meo | 4-5 | 5th round | Fidelity International |
| | v Martin | 5-0 | 3rd round | Rothmans Grand Prix |
| | v Dennis Taylor | 4-5 | 4th round | Rothmans Grand Prix |
| | v Reardon | 4-5 | 3rd round | BCE Canadian Masters |
| | v Gary Wilkinson | 0-9 | 3rd round | Tennents UK Open |
| **1989** | v J. McLaughlin | 5-3 | 3rd round | Mercantile Credit Classic |
| | v Virgo | 1-5 | 4th round | Mercantile Credit Classic |
| | v Edwards | 3-5 | 3rd round | European Open |
| | v Marshall | 2-5 | 3rd round | Anglian British Open |
| | v Clark | 10-4 | Qualifying | Embassy World Championship |
| | v Griffiths | 6-10 | 1st round | Embassy World Championship |
| | v Macleod | 5-3 | 3rd round | Hong Kong Open |
| | v Clark | 2-5 | 4th round | Hong Kong Open |
| | v King | 2-5 | 3rd round | 555 Asian Open |
| | v Williamson | 5-4 | 3rd round | BCE International |
| | v White | 3-5 | 4th round | BCE International |
| | v Bond | 4-5 | 3rd round | Rothmans Grand Prix |
| | v Rowswell | 4-5 | 3rd round | Dubai Classic |
| | v Price | 9-6 | 3rd round | Stormseal UK Open |
| | v Parrott | 8-9 | 4th round | Stormseal UK Open |

| | | | | |
|---|---|---|---|---|
| **1990** | v Rowswell | 5-1 | 3rd round | Mercantile Credit Classic |
| | v James | 2-5 | 4th round | Mercantile Credit Classic |
| | v Donnelly | 5-0 | 3rd round | Pearl Assurance British Open |
| | v Hallett | 5-3 | 4th round | Pearl Assurance British Open |
| | v Robidoux | 5-4 | 5th round | Pearl Assurance British Open |
| | v N. Foulds | 5-3 | Quarter-final | Pearl Assurance British Open |
| | v Marshall | 9-5 | Semi-final | Pearl Assurance British Open |
| | **v Higgins** | **10-8** | **Final** | **Pearl Assurance British Open** |
| | v Grace | 5-2 | 3rd round | European Open |
| | v S. Davis | 0-5 | 4th round | European Open |
| | v D. Morgan | 0-10 | Qualifying | Embassy World Championship |

## TONY CHAPPEL (Wales)

**Born** 28.5.60. **Turned professional** 1984. **World ranking** 44 (41).

| | | | | |
|---|---|---|---|---|
| **1984** | v Mikkelsen | 4-5 | Qualifying | Jameson International |
| | v Scott | 5-1 | Qualifying | Rothmans Grand Prix |
| | v Stevens | 3-5 | 1st round | Rothmans Grand Prix |
| | v Houlihan | 9-3 | Qualifying | Coral UK Open |
| | v Black | 9-3 | Qualifying | Coral UK Open |
| | v Reynolds | 9-6 | Qualifying | Coral UK Open |
| | v Stevens | 7-9 | 1st round | Coral UK Open |
| | v Giannaros | 2-5 | Qualifying | Mercantile Credit Classic |
| | v Williamson | 6-5 | Qualifying | Dulux British Open |
| | v S. Davis | 5-6 | 1st round | Dulux British Open |
| | v Hines | 8-10 | Qualifying | Embassy World Championship |
| | v M. Owen | 6-0 | 1st round | BCE Welsh Championship |
| | v Griffiths | 0-6 | Quarter-final | BCE Welsh Championship |
| **1985** | v Meadowcroft | 5-2 | 2nd round | Goya Matchroom Trophy |
| | v Stevens | 5-3 | 3rd round | Goya Matchroom Trophy |
| | v Wilson | 0-5 | 4th round | Goya Matchroom Trophy |
| | v Dodd | 5-2 | 2nd round | Rothmans Grand Prix |
| | v Mountjoy | 1-5 | 3rd round | Rothmans Grand Prix |
| | v O'Kane | 9-5 | 1st round | Coral UK Open |
| | v White | 5-9 | 2nd round | Coral UK Open |
| **1986** | v Murphy | 4-5 | 2nd round | Mercantile Credit Classic |
| | v Griffiths | 4-6 | Quarter-final | Zetters Welsh Championship |
| | v Fowler | 4-5 | 2nd round | Dulux British Open |
| | v Wych | 6-10 | Qualifying | Embassy World Championship |
| | v Roscoe | 5-3 | 2nd round | BCE International |
| | v E. Hughes | 4-5 | 3rd round | BCE International |
| | v Kearney | 5-1 | 2nd round | Rothmans Grand Prix |
| | v Meo | 1-5 | 3rd round | Rothmans Grand Prix |
| | v Wilkinson | 9-2 | 2nd round | Tennents UK Open |
| | v S. Davis | 7-9 | 3rd round | Tennents UK Open |
| **1987** | v Wright | 4-5 | 2nd round | Mercantile Credit Classic |
| | v Reardon | 6-4 | Quarter-final | Matchroom Welsh Championship |
| | v Mountjoy | 2-9 | Semi-final | Matchroom Welsh Championship |
| | v Kearney | 5-3 | 2nd round | Dulux British Open |
| | v White | 1-5 | 3rd round | Dulux British Open |
| | v Morra | 10-8 | Qualifying | Embassy World Championship |
| | v Duggan | 10-3 | Qualifying | Embassy World Championship |
| | v J. Campbell | 6-10 | Qualifying | Embassy World Championship |
| | v M. Gibson | 5-2 | 2nd round | Fidelity International |
| | v Parrott | 1-5 | 3rd round | Fidelity International |
| | v Jonik | 5-4 | 2nd round | Rothmans Grand Prix |
| | v Spencer | 5-1 | 3rd round | Rothmans Grand Prix |
| | v Griffiths | 3-5 | 4th round | Rothmans Grand Prix |
| | v D. Gilbert | 9-2 | 2nd round | Tennents UK Open |
| | v Reynolds | 9-5 | 3rd round | Tennents UK Open |
| | v Longworth | 9-6 | 4th round | Tennents UK Open |

| | | | | |
|---|---|---|---|---|
| | v Johnson | 4-9 | 5th round | Tennents UK Open |
| **1988** | v D. Hughes | 5-3 | 2nd round | Mercantile Credit Classic |
| | v Johnson | 2-5 | 3rd round | Mercantile Credit Classic |
| | v Roscoe | 6-4 | 1st round | Welsh Championship |
| | v Griffiths | 4-6 | Quarter-final | Welsh Championship |
| | v Ellis | 5-0 | 2nd round | MIM Britannia British Open |
| | v Hendry | 1-5 | 3rd round | MIM Britannia British Open |
| | v N. Gilbert | 10-8 | Qualifying | Embassy World Championship |
| | v Miles | 10-7 | Qualifying | Embassy World Championship |
| | v Drago | 7-10 | Qualifying | Embassy World Championship |
| | v Watchorn | 5-4 | 2nd round | Fidelity International |
| | v Dennis Taylor | 1-5 | 3rd round | Fidelity International |
| | v T. Wilson | 5-4 | 2nd round | Rothmans Grand Prix |
| | v C. Wilson | 2-5 | 3rd round | Rothmans Grand Prix |
| | v Darrington | 5-1 | 2nd round | BCE Canadian Masters |
| | v Thorburn | 1-5 | 3rd round | BCE Canadian Masters |
| | v J. Smith | 9-6 | 2nd round | Tennents UK Open |
| | v Reynolds | 4-9 | 3rd round | Tennents UK Open |
| **1989** | v Johnston-Allen | 5-2 | 2nd round | Mercantile Credit Classic |
| | v S. Davis | 5-3 | 3rd round | Mercantile Credit Classic |
| | v A. Harris | 5-1 | 4th round | Mercantile Credit Classic |
| | v Browne | 1-5 | 5th round | Mercantile Credit Classic |
| | v Darrington | 5-0 | 2nd round | European Open |
| | v O'Kane | 5-0 | 3rd round | European Open |
| | v Griffiths | 2-5 | 4th round | European Open |
| | v D. Morgan | 5-6 | 1st round | Senator Welsh Championship |
| | v Lawlor | 5-2 | 2nd round | Anglian British Open |
| | v James | 5-3 | 3rd round | Anglian British Open |
| | v Wilson | 3-5 | 4th round | Anglian British Open |
| | v Edwards | 7-10 | Qualifying | Embassy World Championship |
| | v B. Morgan | 3-5 | 2nd round | Hong Kong Open |
| | v Sinclair | 5-0 | 2nd round | 555 Asian Open |
| | v Hendry | 1-5 | 3rd round | 555 Asian Open |
| | v Wattana | 3-5 | 2nd round | BCE International |
| | v Bond | 2-5 | 2nd round | Rothmans Grand Prix |
| | v Wildman | 5-1 | 2nd round | Dubai Classic |
| | v Williams | 5-2 | 3rd round | Dubai Classic |
| | v Virgo | 4-5 | 4th round | Dubai Classic |
| | v S. Murphy | 6-1 | 2nd round | Stormseal UK Open |
| | v S. Davis | 3-9 | 3rd round | Stormseal UK Open |
| **1990** | v Houlihan | 5-0 | 2nd round | Mercantile Credit Classic |
| | v S. Davis | 4-5 | 3rd round | Mercantile Credit Classic |
| | v Wilson | 6-4 | Quarter-final | Senator Welsh Championship |
| | v D. Morgan | 8-9 | Semi-final | Senator Welsh Championship |
| | v Bond | 5-4 | 2nd round | Pearl Assurance British Open |
| | v Reynolds | 2-5 | 3rd round | Pearl Assurance British Open |
| | v Jack Rea | 5-1 | 2nd round | European Open |
| | v Knowles | 5-3 | 3rd round | European Open |
| | v David Taylor | 5-2 | 4th round | European Open |
| | v Hendry | 2-5 | 5th round | European Open |
| | v Morra | 10-8 | Qualifying | Embassy World Championship |
| | v Pinches | 10-3 | Qualifying | Embassy World Championship |
| | v Clark | 10-9 | Qualifying | Embassy World Championship |
| | v Knowles | 4-10 | 1st round | Embassy World Championship |

## EDDIE CHARLTON A.M. (Australia)

**Born** 31.10.29. **Turned professional** 1960. **World ranking** 32 (22).

| | | | | |
|---|---|---|---|---|
| **1970** | v Simpson | 22-27 | Semi-final | World Championship |
| **1972** | v David Taylor | 31-25 | Quarter-final | World Championship |
| | v Spencer | 32-37 | Semi-final | World Championship |

| | | | | |
|---|---|---|---|---|
| **1973** | v Mans | 16-8 | 2nd round | World Championship |
| | v Miles | 16-6 | Quarter-final | World Championship |
| | v Higgins | 23-9 | Semi-final | World Championship |
| | v Reardon | 32-38 | Final | World Championship |
| **1974** | v Dunning | 13-15 | 2nd round | World Championship |
| **1975** | v F. Davis | 5-3 | Quarter-final | Benson & Hedges Masters |
| | v Spencer | 2-5 | Semi-final | Benson & Hedges Masters |
| | v Werbeniuk | 15-11 | 2nd round | World Championship |
| | v Thorburn | 19-12 | Quarter-final | World Championship |
| | v Dennis Taylor | 19-12 | Semi-final | World Championship |
| | v Reardon | 30-31 | Final | World Championship |
| **1976** | v Williams | 4-1 | 2nd round | Benson & Hedges Masters |
| | v Reardon | 4-5 | Semi-final | Benson & Hedges Masters |
| | v Pulman | 15-9 | 1st round | Embassy World Championship |
| | v F. Davis | 15-13 | Quarter-final | Embassy World Championship |
| | v Higgins | 18-20 | Semi-final | Embassy World Championship |
| **1977** | v David Taylor | 13-5 | 1st round | Embassy World Championship |
| | v Thorburn | 12-13 | Quarter-final | Embassy World Championship |
| **1978** | v Thorne | 13-12 | 1st round | Embassy World Championship |
| | v Thorburn | 13-12 | Quarter-final | Embassy World Championship |
| | v Reardon | 14-18 | Semi-final | Embassy World Championship |
| **1979** | v Higgins | 2-5 | Quarter-final | Benson & Hedges Masters |
| | v Mountjoy | 13-6 | 1st round | Embassy World Championship |
| | v F. Davis | 13-4 | Quarter-final | Embassy World Championship |
| | v Griffiths | 17-19 | Semi-final | Embassy World Championship |
| **1980** | v Spencer | 2-5 | Quarter-final | Benson & Hedges Masters |
| | v Virgo | 13-12 | 2nd round | Embassy World Championship |
| | v Stevens | 7-13 | Quarter-final | Embassy World Championship |
| **1981** | v Mountjoy | 0-5 | 1st round | Benson & Hedges Masters |
| | v Mountjoy | 7-13 | 2nd round | Embassy World Championship |
| | v Martin | 2-5 | 3rd round | Jameson International |
| **1982** | v White | 5-4 | 1st round | Benson & Hedges Masters |
| | v Higgins | 1-5 | Quarter-final | Benson & Hedges Masters |
| | v Wilson | 10-5 | 1st round | Embassy World Championship |
| | v Werbeniuk | 13-5 | 2nd round | Embassy World Championship |
| | v Knowles | 13-11 | Quarter-final | Embassy World Championship |
| | v Reardon | 11-16 | Semi-final | Embassy World Championship |
| | v Virgo | 4-5 | 1st round | Jameson International |
| | v D. Hughes | 5-2 | 1st round | Professional Players Tournament |
| | v Williams | 5-2 | 2nd round | Professional Players Tournament |
| | v Meo | 5-3 | 3rd round | Professional Players Tournament |
| | v Reynolds | 5-2 | Quarter-final | Professional Players Tournament |
| | v Reardon | 7-10 | Semi-final | Professional Players Tournament |
| **1983** | v Virgo | 5-2 | 1st round | Lada Classic |
| | v S. Davis | 4-5 | Quarter-final | Lada Classic |
| | v Meo | 5-3 | 1st round | Benson & Hedges Masters |
| | v Werbeniuk | 5-3 | Quarter-final | Benson & Hedges Masters |
| | v Thorburn | 5-6 | Semi-final | Benson & Hedges Masters |
| | v David Taylor | 5-4 | 1st round | Benson & Hedges Irish Masters |
| | v S. Davis | 1-5 | Quarter-final | Benson & Hedges Irish Masters |
| | v Dodd | 10-7 | 1st round | Embassy World Championship |
| | v Spencer | 13-11 | 2nd round | Embassy World Championship |
| | v S. Davis | 5-13 | Quarter-final | Embassy World Championship |
| | v Johnson | 5-2 | 1st round | Jameson International |
| | v Morra | 5-3 | 2nd round | Jameson International |
| | v Thorne | 5-0 | Quarter-final | Jameson International |
| | v S. Davis | 2-9 | Semi-final | Jameson International |
| | v E. McLaughlin | 5-0 | 1st round | Professional Players Tournament |
| | v Fisher | 5-4 | 2nd round | Professional Players Tournament |
| | v Johnson | 0-5 | 3rd round | Professional Players Tournament |
| **1984** | v Wilson | 5-0 | Qualifying | Lada Classic |
| | v White | 5-3 | 1st round | Lada Classic |
| | v Wildman | 4-5 | Quarter-final | Lada Classic |
| | v White | 2-5 | 1st round | Benson & Hedges Masters |

| | | | | |
|---|---|---|---|---|
| | v Higgins | 2-5 | 1st round | Benson & Hedges Irish Masters |
| | v Stevens | 3-5 | 1st round | Tolly Cobbold Classic |
| | v Andrewartha | 10-4 | 1st round | Embassy World Championship |
| | v White | 7-13 | 2nd round | Embassy World Championship |
| | v David Taylor | 5-4 | Quarter-final | Winfield Australian Masters |
| | v Knowles | 0-6 | Semi-final | Winfield Australian Masters |
| | v Johnson | 1-5 | 1st round | Jameson International |
| | v Everton | 5-1 | 1st round | Rothmans Grand Prix |
| | v Parrott | 5-1 | 2nd round | Rothmans Grand Prix |
| | v Mountjoy | 4-5 | 3rd round | Rothmans Grand Prix |
| | v S. Francisco | 9-4 | 1st round | Coral UK Open |
| | v Thorne | 7-9 | 2nd round | Coral UK Open |
| **1985** | v Macleod | 1-5 | 1st round | Mercantile Credit Classic |
| | v Spencer | 3-5 | 1st round | Benson & Hedges Masters |
| | v B. Harris | 3-6 | 1st round | Dulux British Open |
| | v Dennis Taylor | 5-4 | 1st round | Benson & Hedges Irish Masters |
| | v Knowles | 3-5 | Quarter-final | Benson & Hedges Irish Masters |
| | v J. Campbell | 10-3 | 1st round | Embassy World Championship |
| | v Dennis Taylor | 6-13 | 2nd round | Embassy World Championship |
| | v J. Campbell | 4-5 | Quarter-final | Winfield Australian Masters |
| | v Wilkinson | 8-2 | Quarter-final | Australian Championship |
| | v Morgan | 9-3 | Semi-final | Australian Championship |
| | v J. Campbell | 7-10 | Final | Australian Championship |
| | v Gibson | 4-5 | 3rd round | Goya Matchroom Trophy |
| | v G. Foulds | 5-1 | 3rd round | Rothmans Grand Prix |
| | v Drago | 3-5 | 4th round | Rothmans Grand Prix |
| | v P. Francisco | 5-9 | 3rd round | Coral UK Open |
| **1986** | v P. Francisco | 1-5 | 3rd round | Mercantile Credit Classic |
| | v Stevens | 5-4 | 1st round | Benson & Hedges Masters |
| | v Knowles | 4-5 | Quarter-final | Benson & Hedges Masters |
| | v Gilbert | 5-2 | 3rd round | Dulux British Open |
| | v Browne | 5-1 | 4th round | Dulux British Open |
| | v Virgo | 4-5 | 5th round | Dulux British Open |
| | v Wilson | 10-6 | 1st round | Embassy World Championship |
| | v Stevens | 12-13 | 2nd round | Embassy World Championship |
| | v Anderson | 6-2 | Quarter-final | Australian Championship |
| | v King | 6-8 | Semi-final | Australian Championship |
| | v Black | 5-0 | 3rd round | BCE International |
| | v Knowles | 1-5 | 4th round | BCE International |
| | v Drago | 4-5 | 3rd round | Rothmans Grand Prix |
| | v V. Harris | 9-2 | 3rd round | Tennents UK Open |
| | v S. Davis | 6-9 | 4th round | Tennents UK Open |
| **1987** | v Fisher | 5-0 | 3rd round | Mercantile Credit Classic |
| | v Williams | 5-4 | 4th round | Mercantile Credit Classic |
| | v Parrott | 4-5 | 5th round | Mercantile Credit Classic |
| | v Medati | 5-4 | 3rd round | Dulux British Open |
| | v Dennis Taylor | 1-5 | 4th round | Dulux British Open |
| | v King | 4-10 | Qualifying | Embassy World Championship |
| | v Anderson | 6-2 | Quarter-final | Australian Championship |
| | v J. Campbell | 8-6 | Semi-final | Australian Championship |
| | v King | 7-10 | Final | Australian Championship |
| | v Reardon | 5-4 | 3rd round | Fidelity International |
| | v Griffiths | 5-2 | 4th round | Fidelity International |
| | v N. Gilbert | 5-0 | 5th round | Fidelity International |
| | v Hallett | 4-5 | Quarter-final | Fidelity International |
| | v Van Rensberg | 5-3 | 3rd round | Rothmans Grand Prix |
| | v Edmonds | 5-3 | 4th round | Rothmans Grand Prix |
| | v Knowles | 0-5 | 5th round | Rothmans Grand Prix |
| | v O'Kane | 8-9 | 3rd round | Tennents UK Open |
| **1988** | v Roscoe | 3-5 | 3rd round | Mercantile Credit Classic |
| | v James | 2-5 | 3rd round | MIM Britannia British Open |
| | v B. Harris | 10-4 | Qualifying | Embassy World Championship |
| | v S. Francisco | 10-7 | 1st round | Embassy World Championship |

| | | | | |
|---|---|---|---|---|
| | v Knowles | 7-13 | 2nd round | Embassy World Championship |
| | v Jenkins | 5-0 | Quarter-final | Australian Championship |
| | v J. Campbell | 6-8 | Semi-final | Australian Championship |
| | v Robidoux | 2-5 | 3rd round | Fidelity International |
| | v Houlihan | 5-3 | 3rd round | Rothmans Grand Prix |
| | v N. Gilbert | 0-5 | 4th round | Rothmans Grand Prix |
| | v Wych | 5-4 | 3rd round | BCE Canadian Masters |
| | v Graham | 2-5 | 4th round | BCE Canadian Masters |
| | v Stevens | 7-9 | 3rd round | Tennents UK Open |
| **1989** | v Reardon | 1-5 | 3rd round | Mercantile Credit Classic |
| | v Duggan | 5-2 | 3rd round | European Open |
| | v Chambers | 5-2 | 4th round | European Open |
| | v Virgo | 5-4 | 5th round | European Open |
| | v Parrott | 1-5 | Quarter-final | European Open |
| | v D. Morgan | 3-5 | 3rd round | Anglian British Open |
| | v Dodd | 10-6 | Qualifying | Embassy World Championship |
| | v Thorburn | 10-9 | 1st round | Embassy World Championship |
| | v Meo | 8-13 | 2nd round | Embassy World Championship |
| | v D. Gilbert | 5-2 | 3rd round | Hong Kong Open |
| | v White | 2-5 | 4th round | Hong Kong Open |
| | v Gary Wilkinson | 3-5 | 3rd round | 555 Asian Open |
| | v Brumby | 5-4 | 3rd round | BCE International |
| | v Marshall | 2-5 | 4th round | BCE International |
| | v King | 0-5 | 3rd round | Rothmans Grand Prix |
| | v Lawlor | 5-3 | 3rd round | Dubai Classic |
| | v Roe | 2-5 | 4th round | Dubai Classic |
| | v Gollan | 2-9 | 3rd round | Stormseal UK Open |
| **1990** | v B. Harris | 5-2 | 3rd round | Mercantile Credit Classic |
| | v King | 2-5 | 4th round | Mercantile Credit Classic |
| | v Robidoux | 3-5 | 3rd round | Pearl Assurance British Open |
| | v Ellis | 5-3 | 3rd round | European Open |
| | v Price | 5-4 | 4th round | European Open |
| | v Mountjoy | 2-5 | 5th round | European Open |
| | v Price | 10-5 | Qualifying | Embassy World Championship |
| | v S. Davis | 1-10 | 1st round | Embassy World Championship |

**MARTIN CLARK** (England)

**Born** 27.10.68. **Turned professional** 1987. **World ranking** 12 (17).

| | | | | |
|---|---|---|---|---|
| **1987** | v Bear | 5-2 | 1st round | Fidelity International |
| | v Duggan | 5-2 | 2nd round | Fidelity International |
| | v Drago | 5-2 | 3rd round | Fidelity International |
| | v Dennis Taylor | 5-0 | 4th round | Fidelity International |
| | v O'Boye | 2-5 | 5th round | Fidelity International |
| | v Williamson | 5-1 | 1st round | Rothmans Grand Prix |
| | v Grace | 5-1 | 2nd round | Rothmans Grand Prix |
| | v N. Foulds | 5-4 | 3rd round | Rothmans Grand Prix |
| | v Fisher | 4-5 | 4th round | Rothmans Grand Prix |
| | v Foldvari | 8-9 | 1st round | Tennents UK Open |
| **1988** | v Wych | 5-2 | 2nd round | Mercantile Credit Classic |
| | v Hallett | 5-4 | 3rd round | Mercantile Credit Classic |
| | v Bennett | 5-2 | 4th round | Mercantile Credit Classic |
| | v Newbury | 2-5 | 5th round | Mercantile Credit Classic |
| | v G. Foulds | 6-0 | 2nd round | English Championship |
| | v White | 5-6 | 3rd round | English Championship |
| | v Fisher | 5-1 | 1st round | MIM Britannia British Open |
| | v Grace | 5-0 | 2nd round | MIM Britannia British Open |
| | v White | 2-5 | 3rd round | MIM Britannia British Open |
| | v Parrott | 1-5 | Final | Kent Cup |
| | v Darrington | 10-5 | Qualifying | Embassy World Championship |
| | v Scott | 10-4 | Qualifying | Embassy World Championship |

*Martin Clark*

| | | | | |
|---|---|---|---|---|
| | v King | 9-10 | Qualifying | Embassy World Championship |
| | v Kearney | 5-3 | 2nd round | Fidelity International |
| | v White | 2-5 | 3rd round | Fidelity International |
| | v Whitthread | 5-1 | 2nd round | Rothmans Grand Prix |
| | v E. Hughes | 3-5 | 3rd round | Rothmans Grand Prix |
| | v T. Wilson | 5-3 | 2nd round | BCE Canadian Masters |
| | v Higgins | 3-5 | 3rd round | BCE Canadian Masters |
| | v S. Campbell | 9-3 | 2nd round | Tennents UK Open |
| | v Hallett | 9-6 | 3rd round | Tennents UK Open |
| | v Fowler | 6-9 | 4th round | Tennents UK Open |
| **1989** | v Morgan | 5-1 | 2nd round | Mercantile Credit Classic |
| | v Spencer | 5-2 | 3rd round | Mercantile Credit Classic |
| | v N. Foulds | 5-4 | 4th round | Mercantile Credit Classic |
| | v Johnson | 5-3 | 5th round | Mercantile Credit Classic |
| | v Thorne | 4-5 | Quarter-final | Mercantile Credit Classic |
| | v Rowing | 5-0 | 2nd round | European Open |
| | v N. Foulds | 5-3 | 3rd round | European Open |
| | v E. Hughes | 5-1 | 4th round | European Open |
| | v Johnson | 5-4 | 5th round | European Open |
| | v Griffiths | 1-5 | Quarter-final | European Open |
| | v Oliver | 5-2 | 2nd round | English Championship |
| | v Thorne | 1-5 | 3rd round | English Championship |
| | v Darrington | 5-2 | 2nd round | Anglian British Open |
| | v David Taylor | 5-2 | 3rd round | Anglian British Open |
| | v Virgo | 5-1 | 4th round | Anglian British Open |
| | v N. Foulds | 5-4 | 5th round | Anglian British Open |
| | v Hallett | 3-5 | Quarter-final | Anglian British Open |
| | v Morra | 10-6 | Qualifying | Embassy World Championship |
| | v Martin | 10-2 | Qualifying | Embassy World Championship |
| | v Chaperon | 4-10 | Qualifying | Embassy World Championship |
| | v Foldvari | 5-2 | 3rd round | Hong Kong Open |
| | v Chaperon | 5-2 | 4th round | Hong Kong Open |
| | v Dennis Taylor | 3-5 | 5th round | Hong Kong Open |
| | v Price | 5-2 | 3rd round | 555 Asian Open |
| | v King | 5-3 | 4th round | 555 Asian Open |
| | v West | 5-0 | 5th round | 555 Asian Open |
| | v Gary Wilkinson | 0-5 | Quarter-final | 555 Asian Open |
| | v King | 5-4 | 3rd round | BCE International |
| | v Dennis Taylor | 4-5 | 4th round | BCE International |
| | v Roscoe | 5-3 | 3rd round | Rothmans Grand Prix |
| | v Knowles | 2-5 | 4th round | Rothmans Grand Prix |
| | v Gauvreau | 5-1 | 3rd round | Dubai Classic |
| | v Rowswell | 5-4 | 4th round | Dubai Classic |
| | v Fowler | 2-5 | 5th round | Dubai Classic |
| | v Rowswell | 9-1 | 3rd round | Stormseal UK Open |
| | v Johnson | 6-9 | 4th round | Stormseal UK Open |
| **1990** | v Cairns | 5-2 | 3rd round | Mercantile Credit Classic |
| | v N. Gilbert | 5-2 | 4th round | Mercantile Credit Classic |
| | v O'Kane | 1-5 | 5th round | Mercantile Credit Classic |
| | v S. Murphy | 5-2 | 3rd round | Pearl Assurance British Open |
| | v Browne | 5-2 | 4th round | Pearl Assurance British Open |
| | v Dennis Taylor | 5-3 | 5th round | Pearl Assurance British Open |
| | v Higgins | 3-5 | Quarter-final | Pearl Assurance British Open |
| | v Spencer | 5-1 | 3rd round | European Open |
| | v Dyson | 2-5 | 4th round | European Open |
| | v Chappel | 9-10 | Qualifying | Embassy World Championship |

## GRAHAM CRIPSEY (England)

**Born** 8.12.54. **Turned professional** 1982. **World ranking** 88 (51).

| | | | | |
|---|---|---|---|---|
| **1982** | v French | 1-5 | Qualifying | Jameson International |

| | | | | |
|---|---|---|---|---|
| | v B. Harris | 6-9 | Qualifying | Coral UK Championship |
| **1983** | v D. Hughes | 10-2 | Qualifying | Embassy World Championship |
| | v Meadowcroft | 6-10 | Qualifying | Embassy World Championship |
| | v Ganim | 4-5 | Qualifying | Professional Players Tournament |
| | v Darrington | 3-9 | Qualifying | Coral UK Championship |
| **1984** | v Parkin | 10-4 | Qualifying | Embassy World Championship |
| | v Gauvreau | 1-10 | Qualifying | Embassy World Championship |
| | v Thornley | 5-3 | Qualifying | Jameson Internaitonal |
| | v Dunning | 3-5 | Qualifying | Jameson International |
| | v Morra | 3-5 | Qualifying | Rothmans Grand Prix |
| | v Foldvari | 9-7 | Qualifying | Coral UK Open |
| | v Fitzmaurice | 8-9 | Qualifying | Coral UK Open |
| **1985** | v Medati | 4-5 | Qualifying | Mercantile Credit Classic |
| | v Bennett | 9-0 | Qualifying | Tolly Cobbold English Championship |
| | v David Taylor | 5-9 | 1st round | Tolly Cobbold English Championship |
| | v O'Kane | 4-6 | Qualifying | Dulux British Open |
| | v Longworth | 8-10 | Qualifying | Embassy World Championship |
| | v Bennett | 5-3 | 1st round | Goya Matchroom Trophy |
| | v Medati | 5-2 | 2nd round | Goya Matchroom Trophy |
| | v Dennis Taylor | 1-5 | 3rd round | Goya Matchroom Trophy |
| | v Hargreaves | 1-5 | 1st round | Rothmans Grand Prix |
| | v Greaves | 9-4 | 1st round | Coral UK Open |
| | v Dunning | *wo* | 2nd round | Coral UK Open |
| | v Wilson | 9-7 | 3rd round | Coral UK Open |
| | v Dennis Taylor | 2-9 | 4th round | Coral UK Open |
| **1986** | v Drago | 5-4 | 1st round | Mercantile Credit Classic |
| | v Newbury | 5-4 | 2nd round | Mercantile Credit Classic |
| | v Spencer | 5-1 | 3rd round | Mercantile Credit Classic |
| | v Higgins | 2-5 | 4th round | Mercantile Credit Classic |
| | v Meadowcroft | 9-1 | 2nd round | Tolly Cobbold English Championship |
| | v Wildman | 5-9 | 3rd round | Tolly Cobbold English Championship |
| | v Darrington | 5-4 | 1st round | Dulux British Open |
| | v Williamson | 4-5 | 2nd round | Dulux British Open |
| | v Drago | 4-10 | Qualifying | Embassy World Championship |
| | v Houlihan | 1-5 | 2nd round | BCE International |
| | v P. Gibson | 5-3 | 2nd round | Rothmans Grand Prix |
| | v Parrott | 4-5 | 3rd round | Rothmans Grand Prix |
| | v Bales | 9-6 | 2nd round | Tennents UK Open |
| | v N. Foulds | 7-9 | 3rd round | Tennents UK Open |
| **1987** | v Mienie | 5-0 | 2nd round | Mercantile Credit Classic |
| | v Thorburn | 0-5 | 3rd round | Mercantile Credit Classic |
| | v Dunning | 6-1 | 2nd round | Tolly Ales English Championship |
| | v White | 4-6 | 3rd round | Tolly Ales English Championship |
| | v Watchorn | 5-4 | 2nd round | Dulux British Open |
| | v Werbeniuk | 5-2 | 3rd round | Dulux British Open |
| | v Thorburn | 2-5 | 4th round | Dulux British Open |
| | v Meadowcroft | 10-9 | Qualifying | Embassy World Championship |
| | v M. Gibson | 10-4 | Qualifying | Embassy World Championship |
| | v David Taylor | 7-10 | Qualifying | Embassy World Championship |
| | v Anderson | 5-4 | 2nd round | Fidelity International |
| | v Werbeniuk | 1-5 | 3rd round | Fidelity International |
| | v M. Gibson | 5-2 | 2nd round | Rothmans Grand Prix |
| | v West | 5-3 | 3rd round | Rothmans Grand Prix |
| | v P. Gibson | 5-4 | 4th round | Rothmans Grand Prix |
| | v P. Francisco | 1-5 | 5th round | Rothmans Grand Prix |
| | v P. Gibson | 9-6 | 2nd round | Tennents UK Open |
| | v Thorburn | 6-9 | 3rd round | Tennents UK Open |
| **1988** | v M. Gibson | 5-4 | 2nd round | Mercantile Credit Classic |
| | v P. Francisco | 2-5 | 3rd round | Mercantile Credit Classic |
| | v Greaves | 4-6 | 2nd round | English Championship |
| | v Donnelly | 5-4 | 2nd round | MIM Britannia British Open |
| | v E. Hughes | 5-3 | 3rd round | MIM Britannia British Open |
| | v Hallett | 2-5 | 4th round | MIM Britannia British Open |

| | | | | |
|---|---|---|---|---|
| | v Meadowcroft | 10-3 | Qualifying | Embassy World Championship |
| | v Houlihan | 10-4 | Qualifying | Embassy World Championship |
| | v Longworth | 2-10 | Qualifying | Embassy World Championship |
| | v Johnson | 3-5 | 3rd round | Fidelity International |
| | v M. Smith | 0-5 | 2nd round | Rothmans Grand Prix |
| | v Medati | 0-5 | 2nd round | BCE Canadian Masters |
| | v John Rea | 2-9 | 2nd round | Tennents UK Open |
| **1989** | v Kearney | 5-2 | 2nd round | Mercantile Credit Classic |
| | v Longworth | 5-3 | 3rd round | Mercantile Credit Classic |
| | v Thorburn | 1-5 | 4th round | Mercantile Credit Classic |
| | v Roscoe | 5-4 | 2nd round | European Open |
| | v Johnson | 2-5 | 3rd round | European Open |
| | v Whitthread | 5-2 | 2nd round | English Championship |
| | v James | 5-3 | 3rd round | English Championship |
| | v N. Foulds | 1-5 | 4th round | English Championship |
| | v Bradley | 5-4 | 2nd round | Anglian British Open |
| | v S. Davis | 1-5 | 3rd round | Anglian British Open |
| | v Graham | 2-10 | Qualifying | Embassy World Championship |
| | v Gollan | 1-5 | 2nd round | Hong Kong Open |
| | v Gauvreau | 5-4 | 2nd round | 555 Asian Open |
| | v P. Francisco | 0-5 | 3rd round | 555 Asian Open |
| | v Williamson | 3-5 | 2nd round | BCE International |
| | v M. Smith | 5-4 | 2nd round | Rothmans Grand Prix |
| | v Hendry | 2-5 | 3rd round | Rothmans Grand Prix |
| | v Van Rensberg | 3-5 | 2nd round | Dubai Classic |
| | v B. Morgan | 2-6 | 2nd round | Stormseal UK Open |
| **1990** | v Terry | 3-5 | 2nd round | Mercantile Credit Classic |
| | v Miles | 2-5 | 2nd round | Pearl Assurance British Open |
| | v S. Murphy | 2-5 | 2nd round | European Open |
| | v T. Wilson | 6-10 | Qualifying | Embassy World Championship |

## MIKE DARRINGTON (England)

**Born** 13.9.31. **Turned professional** 1982. **World ranking** 120 (102).

| | | | | |
|---|---|---|---|---|
| **1983** | v Williams | 0-10 | Qualifying | Embassy World Championship |
| | v Williamson | 5-3 | Qualifying | Jameson International |
| | v S. Francisco | 2-5 | Qualifying | Jameson International |
| | v Duggan | 4-5 | Qualifying | Professional Players Tournament |
| | v Cripsey | 9-3 | Qualifying | Coral UK Championship |
| | v Hallett | 1-9 | Qualifying | Coral UK Championship |
| **1984** | v Caggianello | 7-10 | Qualifying | Embassy World Championship |
| | v Bradley | 3-5 | Qualifying | Jameson International |
| | v Burke | 3-5 | Qualifying | Rothmans Grand Prix |
| | v Longworth | 5-9 | Qualifying | Coral UK Open |
| **1985** | v Hargreaves | 2-5 | Qualifying | Mercantile Credit Classic |
| | v Virgo | 0-9 | 1st round | Tolly Cobbold English Championship |
| | v Scott | 3-6 | Qualifying | Dulux British Open |
| | v T. Jones | 2-10 | Qualifying | Embassy World Championship |
| | v Gilbert | 5-2 | 1st round | Goya Matchroom Trophy |
| | v Sinclair | 0-5 | 2nd round | Goya Matchroom Trophy |
| | v Greaves | 5-2 | 1st round | Rothmans Grand Prix |
| | v Foldvari | 5-3 | 2nd round | Rothmans Grand Prix |
| | v N. Foulds | 0-5 | 3rd round | Rothmans Grand Prix |
| | v Foldvari | 9-6 | 2nd round | Coral UK Open |
| | v Martin | 3-9 | 3rd round | Coral UK Open |
| **1986** | v O'Boye | 0-5 | 1st round | Mercantile Credit Classic |
| | v Fowler | 3-9 | 2nd round | Tolly Cobbold English Championship |
| | v Cripsey | 4-5 | 1st round | Dulux British Open |
| | v Meadowcroft | 10-6 | Qualifying | Embassy World Championship |
| | v Edmonds | 5-10 | Qualifying | Embassy World Championship |
| | v Jack Rea | 4-5 | 1st round | BCE International |

| | | | | |
|---|---|---|---|---|
| | v Watchorn | 2-5 | 1st round | Rothmans Grand Prix |
| | v Whitthread | 9-8 | 1st round | Tennents UK Open |
| | v Fowler | 6-9 | 2nd round | Tennents UK Open |
| **1987** | v Roe | 0-5 | 1st round | Mercantile Credit Classic |
| | v V. Harris | 3-6 | 2nd round | Tolly Ales English Championship |
| | v James | 3-5 | 1st round | Dulux British Open |
| | v Demarco | 10-6 | Qualifying | Embassy World Championship |
| | v Hendry | 7-10 | 2nd round | Embassy World Championship |
| | v Kelly | 4-5 | 1st round | Fidelity International |
| | v Chalmers | 5-2 | 1st round | Rothmans Grand Prix |
| | v Kearney | 0-5 | 2nd round | Rothmans Grand Prix |
| | v Watchorn | 2-9 | 1st round | Tennents UK Open |
| **1988** | v Meakin | 4-5 | 1st round | Mercantile Credit Classic |
| | v Meakin | 3-6 | 1st round | English Championship |
| | v Burke | 5-4 | 1st round | MIM Britannia British Open |
| | v Dodd | 5-4 | 2nd round | MIM Britannia British Open |
| | v P. Francisco | 1-5 | 3rd round | MIM Britannia British Open |
| | v Clark | 5-10 | Qualifying | Embassy World Championship |
| | v Williamson | 1-5 | 1st round | Fidelity International |
| | v John Rea | 4-5 | 1st round | Rothmans Grand Prix |
| | v V. Harris | 5-0 | 1st round | BCE Canadian Masters |
| | v Chappel | 1-5 | 2nd round | BCE Canadian Masters |
| | v Roscoe | 7-9 | 1st round | Tennents UK Open |
| **1989** | v Morra | 5-2 | 1st round | Mercantile Credit Classic |
| | v Houlihan | 5-4 | 2nd round | Mercantile Credit Classic |
| | v David Taylor | 2-5 | 3rd round | Mercantile Credit Classic |
| | v Dunning | 5-4 | 1st round | European Open |
| | v Chappel | 0-5 | 2nd round | European Open |
| | v Graham | 3-5 | 1st round | English Championship |
| | v Scott | 5-4 | 1st round | Anglian British Open |
| | v Clark | 2-5 | 2nd round | Anglian British Open |
| | v M. Gibson | 0-10 | Qualifying | Embassy World Championship |
| | v Williamson | 5-4 | 1st round | Hong Kong Open |
| | v Macleod | 0-5 | 2nd round | Hong Kong Open |
| | v P. Gibson | 4-5 | 1st round | 555 Asian Open |
| | v V. Harris | 5-2 | 1st round | BCE International |
| | v O'Boye | 3-5 | 2nd round | BCE International |
| | v Rowswell | 2-5 | 1st round | Rothmans Grand Prix |
| | v B. Morgan | 2-5 | 1st round | Dubai Classic |
| | v Rowswell | 2-6 | 1st round | Stormseal UK Open |
| **1990** | v Sinclair | 3-5 | 1st round | Mercantile Credit Classic |
| | v M. Smith | 4-5 | 1st round | Pearl Assurance British Open |
| | v Miles | 2-5 | 1st round | European Open |
| | v Owers | 1-10 | Qualifying | Embassy World Championship |

## FRED DAVIS O.B.E. (England)

**Born** 14.8.13. **Turned professional** 1930. **World ranking** 128 (89).

| | | | | |
|---|---|---|---|---|
| **1969** | v Reardon | 25-24 | Quarter-final | World Championship |
| | v G. Owen | 28-45 | Semi-final | World Championship |
| **1970** | v Reardon | 26-31 | Quarter-final | World Championship |
| **1972** | v Spencer | 21-31 | Quarter-final | World Championship |
| **1973** | v Greaves | 16-1 | 2nd round | World Championship |
| | v Higgins | 14-16 | Quarter-final | World Championship |
| **1974** | v Werbeniuk | 15-5 | 2nd round | World Championship |
| | v Higgins | 15-14 | Quarter-final | World Championship |
| | v Reardon | 3-15 | Semi-final | World Championship |
| **1975** | v Charlton | 3-5 | Quarter-final | Benson & Hedges Masters |
| | v Dennis Taylor | 14-15 | 2nd round | World Championship |
| **1976** | v Thorburn | 4-2 | 1st round | Benson & Hedges Masters |
| | v Spencer | 0-4 | 2nd round | Benson & Hedges Masters |

| | | | | |
|---|---|---|---|---|
| | v Werbeniuk | 15-12 | 1st round | Embassy World Championship |
| | v Charlton | 13-15 | Quarter-final | Embassy World Championship |
| **1977** | v Mountjoy | 2-4 | Quarter-final | Benson & Hedges Masters |
| | v Pulman | 12-13 | 1st round | Embassy World Championship |
| | v Fagan | 0-5 | 2nd round | Super Crystalate UK Championship |
| **1978** | v Miles | 3-4 | 1st round | Benson & Hedges Masters |
| | v Virgo | 9-8 | Qualifying | Embassy World Championship |
| | v Dennis Taylor | 13-9 | 1st round | Embassy World Championship |
| | v Fagan | 13-10 | Quarter-final | Embassy World Championship |
| | v Mans | 16-18 | Semi-final | Embassy World Championship |
| | v Dunning | 9-2 | 1st round | Coral UK Championship |
| | v Higgins | 4-9 | Quarter-final | Coral UK Championship |
| **1979** | v Mountjoy | 2-5 | 1st round | Benson & Hedges Masters |
| | v Stevens | 13-8 | 1st round | Embassy World Championship |
| | v Charlton | 4-13 | Quarter-final | Embassy World Championship |
| | v Edmonds | 6-9 | 3rd round | Coral UK Championship |
| **1980** | v David Taylor | 5-13 | 2nd round | Embassy World Championship |
| | v Wildman | 9-6 | 2nd round | Coral UK Championship |
| | v Higgins | 6-9 | Quarter-final | Coral UK Championship |
| **1981** | v Stevens | 5-4 | 1st round | Benson & Hedges Masters |
| | v Griffiths | 2-5 | Quarter-final | Benson & Hedges Masters |
| | v Edmonds | 6-9 | 1st round | John Courage English |
| | v David Taylor | 3-13 | 2nd round | Embassy World Championship |
| | v Williams | 0-5 | 2nd round | Jameson International |
| | v Knowles | 6-9 | 2nd round | Coral UK Championship |
| **1982** | v Reynolds | 7-10 | 1st round | Embassy World Championship |
| | v Fisher | 3-5 | Qualifying | Jameson International |
| | v Sinclair | 2-5 | 1st round | Professional Players Tournament |
| | v Hallett | 7-9 | 1st round | Coral UK Open |
| **1983** | vWilliams | 1-10 | Qualifying | Embassy World Championship |
| | v Kelly | 5-1 | Qualifying | Jameson International |
| | v Morgan | 3-5 | Qualifying | Jameson International |
| | v Fisher | 4-5 | 1st round | Professional Players Tournament |
| | v Watterson | 6-9 | Qualifying | Coral UK Championship |
| | v Donnelly | 10-5 | Qualifying | Embassy World Championship |
| | v Werbeniuk | 4-10 | 1st round | Embassy World Championship |
| **1984** | v Dunning | 5-4 | Qualifying | Jameson International |
| | v Virgo | 3-5 | Qualifying | Jameson International |
| | v V. Harris | 1-5 | Qualifying | Rothmans Grand Prix |
| | v Fowler | 4-9 | Qualifying | Coral UK Open |
| **1985** | v E. McLaughlin | 1-5 | Qualifying | Mercantile Credit Classic |
| | v G. Foulds | 2-9 | Qualifying | Tolly Cobbold English Championship |
| | v Longworth | 1-6 | Qualifying | Dulux British Open |
| | v Chaperon | 10-9 | Qualifying | Embassy World Championship |
| | v Williams | 6-10 | Qualifying | Embassy World Championship |
| | v Duggan | 1-5 | 2nd round | Goya Matchroom Trophy |
| | v Simngam | 2-5 | 2nd round | Rothmans Grand Prix |
| | v John Rea | 9-8 | 2nd round | Coral UK Open |
| | v Werbeniuk | 9-7 | 3rd round | Coral UK Open |
| | v Higgins | 2-9 | 4th round | Coral UK Open |
| **1986** | v Kelly | 5-3 | 2nd round | Mercantile Credit Classic |
| | v Stevens | 5-2 | 3rd round | Mercantile Credit Classic |
| | v E. Hughes | 3-5 | 4th round | Mercantile Credit Classic |
| | v D. Hughes | 9-6 | 2nd round | Tolly Cobbold English Championship |
| | v Martin | 8-9 | 3rd round | Tolly Cobbold English Championship |
| | v Kelly | 5-4 | 2nd round | Dulux British Open |
| | v Macleod | 4-5 | 3rd round | Dulux British Open |
| | v Chalmers | 10-6 | Qualifying | Embassy World Championship |
| | v P. Francisco | 1-10 | Qualifying | Embassy World Championship |
| | v Bales | 4-5 | 2nd round | BCE International |
| | v Bales | 5-4 | 2nd round | Rothmans Grand Prix |
| | v Higgins | 0-5 | 3rd round | Rothmans Grand Prix |
| | v Rowswell | 4-9 | 2nd round | Tennents UK Open |

| | | | | |
|---|---|---|---|---|
| **1987** | v Fisher | 2-5 | 2nd round | Mercantile Credit Classic |
| | v James | 2-6 | 2nd round | Tolly Ales English Championship |
| | v Owers | 3-5 | 2nd round | Dulux British Open |
| | v Owers | 5-10 | Qualifying | Embassy World Championship |
| | v Roe | 3-5 | 2nd round | Fidelity International |
| | v Fisher | 0-5 | 2nd round | Rothmans Grand Prix |
| | v Ellis | 9-6 | 2nd round | Tennents UK Open |
| | v Virgo | 4-9 | 3rd round | Tennents UK Open |
| **1988** | v Meakin | 5-4 | 2nd round | Mercantile Credit Classic |
| | v Mountjoy | 0-5 | 3rd round | Mercantile Credit Classic |
| | v N. Gilbert | 6-5 | 2nd round | English Championship |
| | v Meo | 3-6 | 3rd round | English Championship |
| | v D. Hughes | 5-2 | 2nd round | MIM Britannia British Open |
| | v Spencer | 0-5 | 3rd round | MIM Britannia British Open |
| | v Fitzmaurice | 10-8 | Qualifying | Embassy World Championship |
| | v Bear | 10-4 | Qualifying | Embassy World Championship |
| | v J. Campbell | 3-10 | Qualifying | Embassy World Championship |
| | v S. Campbell | 5-4 | 1st round | Fidelity International |
| | v Murphy | 1-5 | 2nd round | Fidelity International |
| | v Kelly | 3-5 | 1st round | Rothmans Grand Prix |
| | v Morgan | 2-5 | 1st round | BCE Canadian Masters |
| | v Sheehan | 7-9 | 1st round | Tennents UK Open |
| **1989** | v Everton | 5-0 | 1st round | European Open |
| | v M. Bennett | 2-5 | 2nd round | European Open |
| | v Lawlor | 2-5 | 1st round | English Championship |
| | v T. Wilson | 1-5 | 1st round | Anglian British Open |
| | v B. Bennett | 10-4 | Qualifying | Embassy World Championship |
| | v Duggan | 3-10 | Qualifying | Embassy World Championship |
| | v Dyson | 1-5 | 1st round | Hong Kong Open |
| | v Watterson | 5-2 | 1st round | 555 Asian Open |
| | v Chambers | 1-5 | 2nd round | 555 Asian Open |
| | v Van Rensberg | 5-4 | 1st round | BCE International |
| | v Duggan | 1-5 | 2nd round | BCE International |
| | v Kelly | 4-5 | 1st round | Rothmans Grand Prix |
| | v Wattana | 1-5 | 1st round | Dubai Classic |
| | v Rowing | 5-6 | 1st round | Stormseal UK Open |
| **1990** | v B. Morgan | 0-5 | 1st round | Mercantile Credit Classic |
| | v Rowing | 2-5 | 1st round | Pearl Assurance British Open |
| | v S. Murphy | 0-5 | 1st round | European Open |
| | v Brumby | 6-10 | Qualifying | Embassy World Championship |

## STEVE DAVIS M.B.E. (England)

**Born** 22.8.57. **Turned professional** 1978. **World ranking** 2 (1).

| | | | | |
|---|---|---|---|---|
| **1979** | v Anderson | 9-1 | Prelim | Embassy World Championship |
| | v Fagan | 9-2 | Qualifying | Embassy World Championship |
| | v Dennis Taylor | 11-13 | 1st round | Embassy World Championship |
| | v Dunning | 9-3 | 2nd round | Coral UK Championship |
| | v Mountjoy | 9-5 | 3rd round | Coral UK Championship |
| | v Virgo | 7-9 | Quarter-final | Coral UK Championship |
| **1980** | v Morgan | 9-0 | Qualifying | Embassy World Championship |
| | v Fagan | 10-6 | 1st round | Embassy World Championship |
| | v Griffiths | 13-10 | 2nd round | Embassy World Championship |
| | v Higgins | 9-13 | Quarter-final | Embassy World Championship |
| | v Hallett | 9-1 | 1st round | Coral UK Championship |
| | v Werbeniuk | 9-3 | 2nd round | Coral UK Championship |
| | v Meo | 9-5 | Quarter-final | Coral UK Championship |
| | v Griffiths | 9-0 | Semi-final | Coral UK Championship |
| | **v Higgins** | **16-6** | **Final** | **Coral UK Championship** |
| **1981** | v Mans | 3-5 | 1st round | Benson & Hedges Masters |
| | v Dennis Taylor | 5-2 | Semi-final | Yamaha International Masters |

*Steve Davis*

| | | | | |
|---|---|---|---|---|
| | **v David Taylor** | **9-6** | **Final** | **Yamaha International Masters** |
| | v Meadowcroft | 9-2 | 1st round | John Courage English |
| | v Spencer | 9-7 | 2nd round | John Courage English |
| | v Edmonds | 9-0 | Semi-final | John Courage English |
| | **v Meo** | **9-3** | **Final** | **John Courage English** |
| | v White | 10-8 | 1st round | Embassy World Championship |
| | v Higgins | 13-8 | 2nd round | Embassy World Championship |
| | v Griffiths | 13-9 | Quarter-final | Embassy World Championship |
| | v Thorburn | 16-10 | Semi-final | Embassy World Championship |
| | **v Mountjoy** | **18-12** | **Final** | **Embassy World Championship** |
| | v Mountjoy | 5-0 | Quarter-final | Langs Scottish Masters |
| | v White | 5-6 | Semi-final | Langs Scottish Masters |
| | v Mans | 5-3 | 3rd round | Jameson International |
| | v David Taylor | 5-1 | Quarter-final | Jameson International |
| | v Higgins | 9-8 | Semi-final | Jameson International |
| | **v Dennis Taylor** | **9-0** | **Final** | **Jameson International** |
| | v Higgins | 5-2 | 1st round | Northern Ireland Classic |
| | v Griffiths | 9-6 | Semi-final | Northern Ireland Classic |
| | v White | 9-11 | Final | Northern Ireland Classic |
| | v Thorne | 9-2 | 3rd round | Coral UK Championship |
| | v Werbeniuk | 9-5 | Quarter-final | Coral UK Championship |
| | v White | 9-0 | Semi-final | Coral UK Championship |
| | **v Griffiths** | **16-3** | **Final** | **Coral UK Championship** |
| **1982** | v Spencer | 5-2 | 1st round | Lada Classic |
| | v Reardon | 5-4 | Semi-final | Lada Classic |
| | v Griffiths | 8-9 | Final | Lada Classic |
| | v Mountjoy | 5-2 | Quarter-final | Benson & Hedges Masters |
| | v Meo | 6-4 | Semi-final | Benson & Hedges Masters |
| | **v Griffiths** | **9-5** | **Final** | **Benson & Hedges Masters** |
| | **v Griffiths** | **9-7** | **Final** | **Yamaha International Masters** |
| | v Miles | 5-2 | Semi-final | Tolly Cobbold Classic |
| | **v Dennis Taylor** | **8-3** | **Final** | **Tolly Cobbold Classic** |
| | v Mountjoy | 5-2 | Quarter-final | Benson & Hedges Irish Masters |
| | v Higgins | 6-2 | Semi-final | Benson & Hedges Irish Masters |
| | v Griffiths | 5-9 | Final | Benson & Hedges Irish Masters |
| | v Knowles | 1-10 | 1st round | Embassy World Championship |
| | v Knowles | 5-4 | 1st round | Langs Scottish Masters |
| | v Dennis Taylor | 6-1 | Semi-final | Langs Scottish Masters |
| | **v Higgins** | **9-4** | **Final** | **Langs Scottish Masters** |
| | v Roscoe | 5-0 | 1st round | Jameson International |
| | v Reynolds | 5-0 | 2nd round | Jameson International |
| | v David Taylor | 3-5 | Quarter-final | Jameson International |
| | v Williams | 9-6 | 1st round | Coral UK Open |
| | v Fagan | 9-3 | 2nd round | Coral UK Open |
| | v Griffiths | 6-9 | Quarter-final | Coral UK Open |
| **1983** | v Dennis Taylor | 5-2 | 1st round | Lada Classic |
| | v Charlton | 5-4 | Quarter-final | Lada Classic |
| | v Spencer | 5-4 | Semi-final | Lada Classic |
| | **v Werbeniuk** | **9-5** | **Final** | **Lada Classic** |
| | v Wildman | 5-2 | 1st round | Benson & Hedges Masters |
| | v Mountjoy | 4-5 | Quarter-final | Benson & Hedges Masters |
| | v Dennis Taylor | 5-1 | Semi-final | Tolly Cobbold Classic |
| | **v Griffiths** | **7-5** | **Final** | **Tolly Cobbold Classic** |
| | v Charlton | 5-1 | Quarter-final | Benson & Hedges Irish Masters |
| | v Griffiths | 6-2 | Semi-final | Benson & Hedges Irish Masters |
| | **v Reardon** | **9-2** | **Final** | **Benson & Hedges Irish Masters** |
| | v Williams | 10-4 | 1st round | Embassy World Championship |
| | v Dennis Taylor | 13-11 | 2nd round | Embassy World Championship |
| | v Charlton | 13-5 | Quarter-final | Embassy World Championship |
| | v Higgins | 16-5 | Semi-final | Embassy World Championship |
| | **v Thorburn** | **18-6** | **Final** | **Embassy World Championship** |
| | v Macleod | 5-1 | 1st round | Langs Scottish Masters |
| | v Higgins | 6-2 | Semi-final | Langs Scottish Masters |

| | | | | |
|---|---|---|---|---|
| | **v Knowles** | **9-6** | **Final** | **Langs Scottish Masters** |
| | v E. Hughes | 5-1 | 1st round | Jameson International |
| | v Watterson | 5-0 | 2nd round | Jameson International |
| | v S. Francisco | 5-1 | Quarter-final | Jameson International |
| | v Charlton | 9-2 | Semi-final | Jameson International |
| | **v Thorburn** | **9-4** | **Final** | **Jameson International** |
| | v Donnelly | 5-1 | 1st round | Professional Players Tournament |
| | v Hallett | 2-5 | 2nd round | Professional Players Tournament |
| | v G. Foulds | 9-1 | 1st round | Coral UK Championship |
| | v Thorne | 9-3 | 2nd round | Coral UK Championship |
| | v Meo | 9-4 | Quarter-final | Coral UK Championship |
| | v White | 9-4 | Semi-final | Coral UK Championship |
| | v Higgins | 15-16 | Final | Coral UK Championship |
| **1984** | v Spencer | 5-2 | 1st round | Lada Classic |
| | v Griffiths | 5-4 | Quarter-final | Lada Classic |
| | v Parrott | 5-4 | Semi-final | Lada Classic |
| | **v Meo** | **9-8** | **Final** | **Lada Classic** |
| | v Meo | 5-0 | 1st round | Benson & Hedges Masters |
| | v Stevens | 3-5 | Quarter-final | Benson & Hedges Masters |
| | v Meo | 5-4 | Quarter-final | Benson & Hedges Irish Masters |
| | v Higgins | 6-4 | Semi-final | Benson & Hedges Irish Masters |
| | **v Griffiths** | **9-1** | **Final** | **Benson & Hedges Irish Masters** |
| | v Thorne | 5-2 | 1st round | Tolly Cobbold Classic |
| | v Stevens | 5-4 | Semi-final | Tolly Cobbold Classic |
| | **v Knowles** | **8-2** | **Final** | **Tolly Cobbold Classic** |
| | v King | 10-3 | 1st round | Embassy World Championship |
| | v Spencer | 13-5 | 2nd round | Embassy World Championship |
| | v Griffiths | 13-10 | Quarter-final | Embassy World Championship |
| | v Dennis Taylor | 16-9 | Semi-final | Embassy World Championship |
| | **v White** | **18-16** | **Final** | **Embassy World Championship** |
| | v Thorburn | 5-2 | 1st round | Langs Supreme Scottish Masters |
| | v Higgins | 6-4 | Semi-final | Langs Supreme Scottish Masters |
| | **v White** | **9-4** | **Final** | **Langs Supreme Scottish Masters** |
| | v J. Campbell | 5-1 | 1st round | Jameson International |
| | v David Taylor | 5-1 | 2nd round | Jameson International |
| | v Higgins | 5-1 | Quarter-final | Jameson International |
| | v E. Hughes | 9-3 | Semi-final | Jameson International |
| | **v Knowles** | **9-2** | **Final** | **Jameson International** |
| | v Morra | 5-2 | 1st round | Rothmans Grand Prix |
| | v Miles | 5-0 | 2nd round | Rothmans Grand Prix |
| | v David Taylor | 5-1 | 3rd round | Rothmans Grand Prix |
| | v Reynolds | 5-0 | Quarter-final | Rothmans Grand Prix |
| | v Thorburn | 7-9 | Semi-final | Rothmans Grand Prix |
| | v Murphy | 9-1 | 1st round | Coral UK Open |
| | v Meo | 9-7 | 2nd round | Coral UK Open |
| | v White | 9-4 | Quarter-final | Coral UK Open |
| | v Stevens | 9-2 | Semi-final | Coral UK Open |
| | **v Higgins** | **16-8** | **Final** | **Coral UK Open** |
| **1985** | v S. Francisco | 5-0 | 1st round | Mercantile Credit Classic |
| | v Higgins | 5-2 | 2nd round | Mercantile Credit Classic |
| | v Reardon | 5-1 | Quarter-final | Mercantile Credit Classic |
| | v Thorne | 8-9 | Semi-final | Mercantile Credit Classic |
| | v Higgins | 4-5 | 1st round | Benson & Hedges Masters |
| | v Fowler | 9-3 | 1st round | Tolly Cobbold English Championship |
| | v Williams | 9-2 | 2nd round | Tolly Cobbold English Championship |
| | v Virgo | 9-2 | Quarter-final | Tolly Cobbold English Championship |
| | v Meo | 9-8 | Semi-final | Tolly Cobbold English Championship |
| | **v Knowles** | **9-2** | **Final** | **Tolly Cobbold English Championship** |
| | v Chappel | 6-5 | 1st round | Dulux British Open |
| | v Virgo | 5-2 | 2nd round | Dulux British Open |
| | v Bradley | 5-2 | 3rd round | Dulux British Open |
| | v O'Kane | 5-1 | Quarter-final | Dulux British Open |
| | v Stevens | 7-9 | Semi-final | Dulux British Open |

| | | | | |
|---|---|---|---|---|
| | v E. Hughes | 5-4 | Quarter-final | Benson & Hedges Irish Masters |
| | v Higgins | 2-6 | Semi-final | Benson & Hedges Irish Masters |
| | v N. Foulds | 10-8 | 1st round | Embassy World Championship |
| | v David Taylor | 13-4 | 2nd round | Embassy World Championship |
| | v Griffiths | 13-6 | Quarter-final | Embassy World Championship |
| | v Reardon | 16-5 | Semi-final | Embassy World Championship |
| | v Dennis Taylor | 17-18 | Final | Embassy World Championship |
| | v Bales | 5-2 | 3rd round | Goya Matchroom Trophy |
| | v Virgo | 5-1 | 4th round | Goya Matchroom Trophy |
| | v Macleod | 5-1 | 5th round | Goya Matchroom Trophy |
| | v White | 3-5 | Quarter-final | Goya Matchroom Trophy |
| | v Agrawal | 5-0 | 3rd round | Rothmans Grand Prix |
| | v Fowler | 5-1 | 4th round | Rothmans Grand Prix |
| | v Higgins | 5-0 | 5th round | Rothmans Grand Prix |
| | v S. Francisco | 5-2 | Quarter-final | Rothmans Grand Prix |
| | v Thorburn | 9-5 | Semi-final | Rothmans Grand Prix |
| | **v Dennis Taylor** | **10-9** | **Final** | **Rothmans Grand Prix** |
| | v Griffiths | 5-4 | 1st round | BCE Canadian Masters |
| | v Thorburn | 8-1 | Semi-final | BCE Canadian Masters |
| | v Dennis Taylor | 5-9 | Final | BCE Canadian Masters |
| | v Sheehan | 9-1 | 3rd round | Coral UK Open |
| | v Drago | 9-2 | 4th round | Coral UK Open |
| | v Meo | 9-5 | 5th round | Coral UK Open |
| | v West | 9-1 | Quarter-final | Coral UK Open |
| | v White | 9-5 | Semi-final | Coral UK Open |
| | **v Thorne** | **16-14** | **Final** | **Coral UK Open** |
| | v Reardon | 5-2 | 1st round | Kit Kat |
| | v Higgins | 6-1 | Semi-final | Kit Kat |
| | v Dennis Taylor | 5-9 | Final | Kit Kat |
| **1986** | v Chaperon | 5-1 | 3rd round | Mercantile Credit Classic |
| | v Van Rensberg | 5-1 | 4th round | Mercantile Credit Classic |
| | v P. Francisco | 5-0 | 5th round | Mercantile Credit Classic |
| | v White | 2-5 | Quarter-final | Mercantile Credit Classic |
| | v Griffiths | 2-5 | 1st round | BCE Belgian Classic |
| | v David Taylor | 5-4 | 1st round | Benson & Hedges Masters |
| | v Thorne | 5-4 | Quarter-final | Benson & Hedges Masters |
| | v White | 3-6 | Semi-final | Benson & Hedges Masters |
| | v Bradley | 9-3 | 3rd round | Tolly Cobbold English Championship |
| | v Martin | 9-4 | 4th round | Tolly Cobbold English Championship |
| | v Virgo | 9-2 | Quarter-final | Tolly Cobbold English Championship |
| | v Meo | 7-9 | Semi-final | Tolly Cobbold English Championship |
| | v Black | 5-2 | 3rd round | Dulux British Open |
| | v Martin | 5-1 | 4th round | Dulux British Open |
| | v J. Campbell | 5-0 | 5th round | Dulux British Open |
| | v Wych | 5-2 | Quarter-final | Dulux British Open |
| | v Higgins | 9-3 | Semi-final | Dulux British Open |
| | **v Thorne** | **12-7** | **Final** | **Dulux British Open** |
| | v Edmonds | 10-4 | 1st round | Embassy World Championship |
| | v Mountjoy | 13-5 | 2nd round | Embassy World Championship |
| | v White | 13-5 | Quarter-final | Embassy World Championship |
| | v Thorburn | 16-12 | Semi-final | Embassy World Championship |
| | v Johnson | 12-18 | Final | Embassy World Championship |
| | v Thorne | 2-5 | Semi-final | Camus Hong Kong Masters |
| | v Griffiths | 6-2 | Semi-final | Matchroom Trophy |
| | v Thorne | 9-10 | Final | Matchroom Trophy |
| | v John Rea | 5-1 | 3rd round | BCE International |
| | v King | 5-4 | 4th round | BCE International |
| | v Williams | 5-4 | 5th round | BCE International |
| | v E. Hughes | 4-5 | Quarter-final | BCE International |
| | v M. Gibson | 5-1 | 3rd round | Rothmans Grand Prix |
| | v Drago | 5-1 | 4th round | Rothmans Grand Prix |
| | v Griffiths | 5-2 | 5th round | Rothmans Grand Prix |
| | v Williams | 1-5 | Quarter-final | Rothmans Grand Prix |

| | | | | |
|---|---|---|---|---|
| | v White | 5-2 | 1st round | BCE Canadian Masters |
| | v Higgins | 8-2 | Semi-final | BCE Canadian Masters |
| | **v Thorne** | **9-3** | **Final** | **BCE Canadian Masters** |
| | v Chappel | 9-7 | 3rd round | Tennents UK Open |
| | v Charlton | 9-6 | 4th round | Tennents UK Open |
| | v Reynolds | 9-5 | 5th round | Tennents UK Open |
| | v Drago | 9-8 | Quarter-final | Tennents UK Open |
| | v Higgins | 9-3 | Semi-final | Tennents UK Open |
| | **v N. Foulds** | **16-7** | **Final** | **Tennents UK Open** |
| **1987** | v Jenkins | 5-0 | 3rd round | Mercantile Credit Classic |
| | v Virgo | 5-2 | 4th round | Mercantile Credit Classic |
| | v Meo | 5-2 | 5th round | Mercantile Credit Classic |
| | v Parrott | 5-4 | Quarter-final | Mercantile Credit Classic |
| | v Hendry | 9-3 | Semi-final | Mercantile Credit Classic |
| | **v White** | **13-12** | **Final** | **Mercantile Credit Classic** |
| | v Mountjoy | 2-5 | 1st round | Benson & Hedges Masters |
| | v Gauvreau | 5-0 | 3rd round | Dulux British Open |
| | v Virgo | 4-5 | 4th round | Dulux British Open |
| | v Meo | 5-2 | Quarter-final | Benson & Hedges Irish Masters |
| | v Griffiths | 6-2 | Semi-final | Benson & Hedges Irish Masters |
| | **v Thorne** | **9-1** | **Final** | **Benson & Hedges Irish Masters** |
| | v King | 10-7 | 1st round | Embassy World Championship |
| | v Reardon | 13-4 | 2nd round | Embassy World Championship |
| | v Griffiths | 13-5 | Quarter-final | Embassy World Championship |
| | v White | 16-11 | Semi-final | Embassy World Championship |
| | **v Johnson** | **18-14** | **Final** | **Embassy World Championship** |
| | v Dennis Taylor | 5-4 | Semi-final | Riley Hong Kong Masters (WS) |
| | **v Hendry** | **9-3** | **Final** | **Riley Hong Kong Masters (WS)** |
| | v O'Kane | 5-2 | 3rd round | Fidelity International |
| | v Meo | 5-3 | 4th round | Fidelity International |
| | v Parrott | 5-2 | 5th round | Fidelity International |
| | v Virgo | 5-2 | Quarter-final | Fidelity International |
| | v Hallett | 9-3 | Semi-final | Fidelity International |
| | **v Thorburn** | **12-5** | **Final** | **Fidelity International** |
| | v Miles | 5-1 | 3rd round | Rothmans Grand Prix |
| | v Wych | 5-1 | 4th round | Rothmans Grand Prix |
| | v Hendry | 2-5 | 5th round | Rothmans Grand Prix |
| | v Dennis Taylor | 1-5 | 1st round | Labatts Canadian Masters (WS) |
| | v Meo | 6-5 | 1st round | Matchroom Trophy |
| | v Dennis Taylor | 3-6 | Semi-final | Matchroom Trophy |
| | v King | 9-2 | 3rd round | Tennents UK Open |
| | v P. Francisco | 9-6 | 4th round | Tennents UK Open |
| | v Higgins | 9-2 | 5th round | Tennents UK Open |
| | v Parrott | 9-5 | Quarter-final | Tennents UK Open |
| | v Thorne | 9-2 | Semi-final | Tennents UK Open |
| | **v White** | **16-14** | **Final** | **Tennents UK Open** |
| **1988** | v Dodd | 5-0 | 3rd round | Mercantile Credit Classic |
| | v Donnelly | 5-0 | 4th round | Mercantile Credit Classic |
| | v Higgins | 5-0 | 5th round | Mercantile Credit Classic |
| | v Hendry | 5-3 | Quarter-final | Mercantile Credit Classic |
| | v Newbury | 9-2 | Semi-final | Mercantile Credit Classic |
| | **v Parrott** | **13-11** | **Final** | **Mercantile Credit Classic** |
| | v Reynolds | 5-2 | 1st round | Benson and Hedges Masters |
| | v Griffiths | 5-0 | Quarter-final | Benson and Hedges Masters |
| | v Johnson | 6-3 | Semi-final | Benson and Hedges Masters |
| | **v Hallett** | **9-0** | **Final** | **Benson and Hedges Masters** |
| | v Reardon | 0-5 | 3rd round | MIM Britannia British Open |
| | v Johnson | 5-0 | Quarter-final | Benson and Hedges Irish Masters |
| | v Higgins | 6-2 | Semi-final | Benson and Hedges Irish Masters |
| | **v N. Foulds** | **9-4** | **Final** | **Benson and Hedges Irish Masters** |
| | v Virgo | 10-8 | 1st round | Embassy World Championship |
| | v Hallett | 13-1 | 2nd round | Embassy World Championship |
| | v Drago | 13-4 | Quarter-final | Embassy World Championship |

| | | | | |
|---|---|---|---|---|
| | v Thorburn | 16-8 | Semi-final | Embassy World Championship |
| | **v Griffiths** | **18-11** | **Final** | **Embassy World Championship** |
| | v W. Jones | 5-1 | 3rd round | Fidelity International |
| | v Robidoux | 5-4 | 4th round | Fidelity International |
| | v David Taylor | 5-1 | 5th round | Fidelity International |
| | v Dennis Taylor | 5-2 | Quarter-final | Fidelity International |
| | v James | 9-1 | Semi-final | Fidelity International |
| | **v White** | **12-6** | **Final** | **Fidelity International** |
| | v Newbury | 5-1 | 4th round | Rothmans Grand Prix |
| | v C. Wilson | 5-1 | 5th round | Rothmans Grand Prix |
| | v Griffiths | 5-3 | Quarter-final | Rothmans Grand Prix |
| | v Dennis Taylor | 9-1 | Semi-final | Rothmans Grand Prix |
| | **v Higgins** | **10-6** | **Final** | **Rothmans Grand Prix** |
| | v M. Smith | 5-0 | 3rd round | BCE Canadian Masters |
| | v Scott | 5-1 | 4th round | BCE Canadian Masters |
| | v James | 5-0 | 5th round | BCE Canadian Masters |
| | v Griffiths | 5-3 | Quarter-final | BCE Canadian Masters |
| | v Hendry | 9-5 | Semi-final | BCE Canadian Masters |
| | v White | 4-9 | Final | BCE Canadian Masters |
| | v Thorne | 6-2 | 1st round | LEP Matchroom Championship |
| | v White | 6-4 | Semi-final | LEP Matchroom Championship |
| | **v Dennis Taylor** | **10-7** | **Final** | **LEP Matchroom Championship** |
| | v Thorne | 5-2 | Semi-final | Dubai Duty Free Masters |
| | v N. Foulds | 4-5 | Final | Dubai Duty Free Masters |
| | v King | 9-7 | 3rd round | Tennents UK Open |
| | v Gary Wilkinson | 9-3 | 4th round | Tennents UK Open |
| | v Fowler | 9-6 | 5th round | Tennents UK Open |
| | v Parrott | 9-4 | Quarter-final | Tennents UK Open |
| | v Hendry | 3-9 | Semi-final | Tennents UK Open |
| | v Hallett | 9-2 | Quarter-final | Everest World Matchplay |
| | v White | 9-5 | Semi-final | Everest World Matchplay |
| | **v Parrott** | **9-5** | **Final** | **Everest World Matchplay** |
| | **v White** | **5-4** | **Final** | **Norwich Union European Grand Prix** |
| **1989** | v Chappel | 3-5 | 3rd round | Mercantile Credit Classic |
| | v C. Wilson | 5-2 | 1st round | Benson and Hedges Masters |
| | v Knowles | 5-0 | Quarter-final | Benson and Hedges Masters |
| | v Hendry | 3-6 | Semi-final | Benson and Hedges Masters |
| | v Cripsey | 5-1 | 3rd round | Anglian British Open |
| | v Higgins | 5-0 | 4th round | Anglian British Open |
| | v Thorne | 5-0 | 5th round | Anglian British Open |
| | v Parrott | 1-5 | Quarter-final | Anglian British Open |
| | v Hallett | 5-4 | Quarter-final | Benson and Hedges Irish Masters |
| | v Hendry | 4-6 | Semi-final | Benson and Hedges Irish Masters |
| | v Newbury | 10-5 | 1st round | Embassy World Championship |
| | v Duggan | 13-3 | 2nd round | Embassy World Championship |
| | v Hallett | 13-3 | Quarter-final | Embassy World Championship |
| | v Hendry | 16-9 | Semi-final | Embassy World Championship |
| | **v Parrott** | **18-3** | **Final** | **Embassy World Championship** |
| | v John Rea | 6-2 | Quarter-final | Regal Scottish Masters |
| | v Griffiths | 2-6 | Semi-final | Regal Scottish Masters |
| | v Kearney | 5-1 | 3rd round | BCE International |
| | v W. Jones | 5-2 | 4th round | BCE International |
| | v N. Foulds | 5-3 | 5th round | BCE International |
| | v B. Morgan | 5-2 | Quarter-final | BCE International |
| | v Robidoux | 6-3 | Semi-final | BCE International |
| | **v Hendry** | **9-4** | **Final** | **BCE International** |
| | v Duggan | 5-1 | 3rd round | Rothmans Grand Prix |
| | v N. Foulds | 5-4 | 4th round | Rothmans Grand Prix |
| | v J. Smith | 5-1 | 5th round | Rothmans Grand Prix |
| | v Knowles | 5-2 | Quarter-final | Rothmans Grand Prix |
| | v Fowler | 9-2 | Semi-final | Rothmans Grand Prix |
| | **v Reynolds** | **10-0** | **Final** | **Rothmans Grand Prix** |
| | v Chappel | 9-3 | 3rd round | Stormseal UK Open |

| | | | | |
|---|---|---|---|---|
| | v C. Wilson | 9-3 | 4th round | Stormseal UK Open |
| | v Thorne | 9-4 | 5th round | Stormseal UK Open |
| | v Hallett | 9-5 | Quarter-final | Stormseal UK Open |
| | v Wilkinson | 9-8 | Semi-final | Stormseal UK Open |
| | v Hendry | 12-16 | Final | Stormseal UK Open |
| | v Reynolds | 7-9 | Quarter-final | Everest World Matchplay |
| **1990** | v Chappel | 5-4 | 3rd round | Mercantile Credit Classic |
| | v Williams | 5-0 | 4th round | Mercantile Credit Classic |
| | v Drago | 5-3 | 5th round | Mercantile Credit Classic |
| | v B. Morgan | 5-1 | Quarter-final | Mercantile Credit Classic |
| | v James | 4-6 | Semi-final | Mercantile Credit Classic |
| | v Wattana | 5-2 | 1st round | Benson and Hedges Masters |
| | v Mountjoy | 5-0 | Quarter-final | Benson and Hedges Masters |
| | v Parrott | 2-6 | Semi-final | Benson and Hedges Masters |
| | v Stevens | 5-2 | 3rd round | Pearl Assurance British Open |
| | v D. Morgan | 5-4 | 4th round | Pearl Assurance British Open |
| | v Newbury | 2-5 | 5th round | Pearl Assurance British Open |
| | v Bales | 5-2 | 3rd round | European Open |
| | v Chaperon | 5-0 | 4th round | European Open |
| | v Edwards | 5-4 | 5th round | European Open |
| | v Mountjoy | 5-0 | Quarter-final | European Open |
| | v Hendry | 3-6 | Semi-final | European Open |
| | v Thorne | 5-3 | Quarter-final | Benson and Hedges Irish Masters |
| | v Griffiths | 6-3 | Semi-final | Benson and Hedges Irish Masters |
| | **v Dennis Taylor** | **9-4** | **Final** | **Benson and Hedges Irish Masters** |
| | v Charlton | 10-1 | 1st round | Embassy World Championship |
| | v James | 13-7 | 2nd round | Embassy World Championship |
| | v N. Foulds | 13-8 | Quarter-final | Embassy World Championship |
| | v White | 14-16 | Semi-final | Embassy World Championship |

## **LES DODD** (England)

**Born** 11.2.54. **Turned professional** 1982. **World ranking** 46 (65).

| | | | | |
|---|---|---|---|---|
| **1982** | v Macleod | 5-1 | Qualifying | Jameson International |
| | v Fitzmaurice | 5-3 | Qualifying | Jameson International |
| | v Mans | 3-5 | 1st round | Jameson International |
| | v Williamson | 9-1 | Qualifying | Coral UK Championship |
| | v French | 9-7 | Qualifying | Coral UK Championship |
| | v David Taylor | 7-9 | 1st round | Coral UK Championship |
| **1983** | v Williamson | 10-9 | Qualifying | Embassy World Championship |
| | v Charlton | 7-10 | 1st round | Embassy World Championship |
| | v Gibson | 1-5 | Qualifying | Jameson International |
| | v Griffiths | 3-5 | 1st round | Professional Players Tournament |
| | v G. Foulds | 7-9 | Qualifying | Coral UK Championship |
| **1984** | v Giannaros | 10-1 | Qualifying | Embassy World Championship |
| | v N. Foulds | 4-10 | Qualifying | Embassy World Championship |
| | v Foldvari | 5-3 | Qualifying | Jameson International |
| | v Wilson | 5-1 | Qualifying | Jameson International |
| | v Reardon | 4-5 | 1st round | Jameson International |
| | v Medati | 4-5 | Qualifying | Rothmans Grand Prix |
| | v Newbury | 9-6 | Qualifying | Coral UK Open |
| | v Wilson | 8-9 | Qualifying | Coral UK Open |
| **1985** | v T. Jones | 1-5 | Qualifying | Mercantile Credit Classic |
| | v Bales | 9-5 | Qualifying | Tolly Cobbold English Championship |
| | v Thorne | 1-9 | 1st round | Tolly Cobbold English Championship |
| | v V. Harris | 1-6 | Qualifying | Dulux British Open |
| | v O'Kane | 7-10 | Qualifying | Embassy World Championship |
| | v Simngam | 5-4 | 2nd round | Goya Matchroom Trophy |
| | v N. Foulds | 3-5 | 3rd round | Goya Matchroom Trophy |
| | v Chappel | 2-5 | 2nd round | Rothmans Grand Prix |
| | v Thorburn | 4-9 | 3rd round | Coral UK Open |

| | | | | |
|---|---|---|---|---|
| **1986** | v Rigitano | 3-5 | 2nd round | Mercantile Credit Classic |
| | v Oliver | 5-9 | 2nd round | Tolly Cobbold English Championship |
| | v Jonik | 5-4 | 2nd round | Dulux British Open |
| | v Thorne | 2-5 | 3rd round | Dulux British Open |
| | v Fitzmaurice | 10-6 | Qualifying | Embassy World Championship |
| | v Watterson | 10-1 | Qualifying | Embassy World Championship |
| | v Mans | 7-10 | Qualifying | Embassy World Championship |
| | v Reynolds | 2-5 | 3rd round | BCE International |
| | v Scott | 5-2 | 2nd round | Rothmans Grand Prix |
| | v Stevens | 5-4 | 3rd round | Rothmans Grand Prix |
| | v Hallett | 2-5 | 4th round | Rothmans Grand Prix |
| | v Chaperon | 4-9 | 2nd round | Tennents UK Open |
| **1987** | v Medati | 5-4 | 2nd round | Mercantile Credit Classic |
| | v Mountjoy | 5-4 | 3rd round | Mercantile Credit Classic |
| | v Wilson | 4-5 | 4th round | Mercantile Credit Classic |
| | v Smith | 6-3 | 2nd round | Tolly Ales English Championship |
| | v Knowles | 6-2 | 3rd round | Tolly Ales English Championship |
| | v West | 6-3 | 4th round | Tolly Ales English Championship |
| | v Hallett | 6-5 | Quarter-final | Tolly Ales English Championship |
| | v Johnson | 9-5 | Semi-final | Tolly Ales English Championship |
| | v Meo | 5-9 | Final | Tolly Ales English Championship |
| | v Fowler | 1-5 | 2nd round | Dulux British Open |
| | v Newbury | 7-10 | Qualifying | Embassy World Championship |
| | v Morra | 3-5 | 2nd round | Fidelity International |
| | v Kelly | 5-2 | 2nd round | Rothmans Grand Prix |
| | v Parrott | 1-5 | 3rd round | Rothmans Grand Prix |
| | v Medati | 9-6 | 2nd round | Tennents UK Open |
| | v Dennis Taylor | 8-9 | 3rd round | Tennents UK Open |
| **1988** | v Roe | 2-5 | 2nd round | Mercantile Credit Classic |
| | v S. Davis | 0-5 | 3rd round | Mercantile Credit Classic |
| | v Heaton | 6-0 | 2nd round | English Championship |
| | v Virgo | 3-6 | 3rd round | English Championship |
| | v Darrington | 4-5 | 2nd round | MIM Britannia British Open |
| | v Medati | 10-6 | Qualifying | Embassy World Championship |
| | v Fowler | 8-10 | Qualifying | Embassy World Championship |
| | v Roscoe | 5-1 | 2nd round | Fidelity International |
| | v Parrott | 5-4 | 3rd round | Fidelity International |
| | v West | 3-5 | 4th round | Fidelity International |
| | v M. Gibson | 5-1 | 2nd round | Rothmans Grand Prix |
| | v Reynolds | 3-5 | 3rd round | Rothmans Grand Prix |
| | v Marshall | 5-3 | 2nd round | BCE Canadian Masters |
| | v David Taylor | 3-5 | 3rd round | BCE Canadian Masters |
| | v Glen Wilkinson | 9-6 | 2nd round | Tennents UK Open |
| | v Higgins | 7-9 | 3rd round | Tennents UK Open |
| **1989** | v Sinclair | 5-3 | 2nd round | Mercantile Credit Classic |
| | v Virgo | 2-5 | 3rd round | Mercantile Credit Classic |
| | v Higgins | 2-5 | 3rd round | European Open |
| | v Edwards | 1-5 | 2nd round | English Championship |
| | v Rempe | 5-0 | 2nd round | Anglian British Open |
| | v Reynolds | 2-5 | 3rd round | Anglian British Open |
| | v Grech | 10-9 | Qualifying | Embassy World Championship |
| | v Glen Wilkinson | 10-4 | Qualifying | Embassy World Championship |
| | v Charlton | 6-10 | Qualifying | Embassy World Championship |
| | v D. Campbell | 5-4 | 2nd round | Hong Kong Open |
| | v Johnson | 5-0 | 3rd round | Hong Kong Open |
| | v B. Morgan | 5-2 | 4th round | Hong Kong Open |
| | v Hendry | 3-5 | 5th round | Hong Kong Open |
| | v Price | 1-5 | 2nd round | 555 Asian Open |
| | v A. Harris | 5-2 | 2nd round | BCE International |
| | v Hallett | 4-5 | 3rd round | BCE International |
| | v Kearney | 5-1 | 2nd round | Rothmans Grand Prix |
| | v Williams | 5-3 | 3rd round | Rothmans Grand Prix |
| | v Gibson | 4-5 | 4th round | Rothmans Grand Prix |

| | | | | |
|---|---|---|---|---|
| | v Williamson | 5-0 | 2nd round | Dubai Classic |
| | v Gary Wilkinson | 3-5 | 3rd round | Dubai Classic |
| | v Wattana | 2-6 | 1st round | Stormseal UK Open |
| **1990** | v Dyson | 3-5 | 1st round | Mercantile Credit Classic |
| | v King | 5-2 | 2nd round | Pearl Assurance British Open |
| | v C. Wilson | 5-3 | 3rd round | Pearl Assurance British Open |
| | v Rowing | 5-2 | 4th round | Pearl Assurance British Open |
| | v Knowles | 5-4 | 5th round | Pearl Assurance British Open |
| | v James | 2-5 | Quarter-final | Pearl Assurance British Open |
| | v Grace | 3-5 | 2nd round | European Open |
| | v Watterson | 10-3 | Qualifying | Embassy World Championship |
| | v King | 10-8 | Qualifying | Embassy World Championship |
| | v S. Campbell | 7-10 | Qualifying | Embassy World Championship |

## JIM DONNELLY (Scotland)

**Born** 13.6.46. **Turned professional** 1981. **World ranking** 114 (84).

| | | | | |
|---|---|---|---|---|
| **1981** | v Johnson | 4-5 | Qualifying | Jameson International |
| | v Sinclair | 5-0 | Quarter-final | Scottish Championship |
| | v Gibson | 4-6 | Semi-final | Scottish Championship |
| | v Medati | 7-9 | Qualifying | Coral UK Championship |
| **1982** | v Gibson | 9-8 | Qualifying | Embassy World Championship |
| | v Sinclair | 9-8 | Qualifying | Embassy World Championship |
| | v Reardon | 5-10 | 1st round | Embassy World Championship |
| | v Macleod | 5-6 | 1st round | Scottish Championship |
| | v Williamson | 3-5 | Qualifying | Jameson International |
| | v Watterson | 4-5 | 1st round | Professional Players Tournament |
| | v Ross | 9-5 | Qualifying | Coral UK Championship |
| | v Knowles | 6-9 | 1st round | Coral UK Championship |
| **1983** | v Sheehan | 10-6 | Qualifying | Embassy World Championship |
| | v Campbell | 2-10 | Qualifying | Embassy World Championship |
| | v Demarco | 6-4 | 1st round | Scottish Championship |
| | v Sinclair | 5-6 | Semi-final | Scottish Championship |
| | v Bennett | 5-1 | Qualifying | Jameson International |
| | v Wilson | 5-1 | Qualifying | Jameson International |
| | v David Taylor | 5-3 | 1st round | Jameson International |
| | v S. Francisco | 1-5 | 2nd round | Jameson International |
| | v S. Davis | 1-5 | 1st round | Professional Players Tournament |
| | v Murphy | 4-9 | Qualifying | Coral UK Championship |
| **1984** | v Watchorn | 10-7 | Qualifying | Embassy World Championship |
| | v Anderson | 10-6 | Qualifying | Embassy World Championship |
| | v F. Davis | 5-10 | Qualifying | Embassy World Championship |
| | v G. Foulds | 3-5 | Qualifying | Jameson International |
| | v Hargreaves | 5-4 | Qualifying | Rothmans Grand Prix |
| | v Wilson | 2-5 | 1st round | Rothmans Grand Prix |
| | v Gibson | 9-6 | Qualifying | Coral UK Open |
| | v Campbell | 6-9 | Qualifying | Coral UK Open |
| **1985** | v Watchorn | 5-1 | Qualifying | Mercantile Credit Classic |
| | v Williams | 3-5 | Qualifying | Mercantile Credit Classic |
| | v John Rea | 2-6 | 1st round | Scottish Championship |
| | v W. Jones | 1-6 | Qualifying | Dulux British Open |
| | v Fowler | 0-10 | Qualifying | Embassy World Championship |
| | v Jim Bear | 2-5 | 2nd round | Goya Matchroom Trophy |
| | v Kelly | 4-5 | 2nd round | Rothmans Grand Prix |
| | v Drago | 8-9 | 1st round | Coral UK Open |
| **1986** | v Chalmers | 5-0 | 2nd round | Mercantile Credit Classic |
| | v Campbell | 2-5 | 3rd round | Mercantile Credit Classic |
| | v Wilkinson | 5-4 | 2nd round | Dulux British Open |
| | v Meo | 3-5 | 3rd round | Dulux British Open |
| | v John Rea | 1-6 | Quarter-final | Canada Dry Scottish Championship |
| | v Smith | 10-6 | Qualifying | Embassy World Championship |

| | | | | |
|---|---|---|---|---|
| | v West | 5-10 | Qualifying | Embassy World Championship |
| | v Murphy | 2-5 | 2nd round | BCE International |
| | v N. Gilbert | 5-1 | 1st round | Rothmans Grand Prix |
| | v King | 2-5 | 2nd round | Rothmans Grand Prix |
| | v N. Gilbert | 8-9 | 1st round | Tennents UK Open |
| **1987** | v Watchorn | 0-5 | 1st round | Mercantile Credit Classic |
| | v Macleod | 6-2 | 1st round | Scottish Championship |
| | v Sinclair | 6-4 | Semi-final | Scottish Championship |
| | v Hendry | 7-10 | Final | Scottish Championship |
| | v T. Jones | 2-5 | 2nd round | Dulux British Open |
| | v W. Jones | 3-10 | Qualifying | Embassy World Championship |
| | v M. Smith | 3-5 | 1st round | Fidelity International |
| | v D. Hughes | 5-1 | 1st round | Rothmans Grand Prix |
| | v W. Jones | 3-5 | 2nd round | Rothmans Grand Prix |
| | v Anderson | 9-4 | 1st round | Tennents UK Open |
| | v O'Boye | 2-9 | 2nd round | Tennents UK Open |
| **1988** | v N. Gilbert | 5-2 | 1st round | Mercantile Credit Classic |
| | v Duggan | 5-4 | 2nd round | Mercantile Credit Classic |
| | v Macleod | 5-4 | 3rd round | Mercantile Credit Classic |
| | v S. Davis | 0-5 | 4th round | Mercantile Credit Classic |
| | v Macleod | 5-6 | Quarter-final | Scottish Championship |
| | v Greaves | 5-4 | 1st round | MIM Britannia British Open |
| | v Cripsey | 4-5 | 2nd round | MIM Britannia British Open |
| | v J. Smith | 4-10 | Qualifying | Embassy World Championship |
| | v J. Smith | 5-2 | 1st round | Fidelity International |
| | v Reardon | 1-5 | 2nd round | Fidelity International |
| | v Watterson | 0-5 | 1st round | Rothmans Grand Prix |
| | v Terry | 1-5 | 1st round | BCE Canadian Masters |
| | v Whitthread | 8-9 | 1st round | Tennents UK Open |
| **1989** | v Ellis | 0-5 | 1st round | Mercantile Credit Classic |
| | v Johnston-Allen | 3-5 | 1st round | European Open |
| | v Demarco | 5-1 | 1st round | Scottish Championship |
| | v John Rea | 1-5 | Semi-final | Scottish Championship |
| | v Whitthread | 4-5 | 1st round | Anglian British Open |
| | v Whitthread | 7-10 | Qualifying | Embassy World Championship |
| | v Meakin | 4-5 | 1st round | Hong Kong Open |
| | v Rowing | 5-4 | 1st round | 555 Asian Open |
| | v Spencer | 3-5 | 2nd round | 555 Asian Open |
| | v J. Smith | 4-5 | 1st round | BCE International |
| | v Watchorn | 2-5 | 1st round | Rothmans Grand Prix |
| | v Rigitano | 1-5 | 1st round | Dubai Classic |
| | v Fitzmaurice | 6-2 | 1st round | Stormseal UK Open |
| | v Duggan | 1-6 | 2nd round | Stormseal UK Open |
| **1990** | v J. Smith | 2-5 | 1st round | Mercantile Credit Classic |
| | v D. Hughes | 5-2 | 1st round | Pearl Assurance British Open |
| | v D. Gilbert | 5-4 | 2nd round | Pearl Assurance British Open |
| | v Chaperon | 0-5 | 3rd round | Pearl Assurance British Open |
| | v Watterson | 3-5 | 1st round | European Open |
| | v Rigitano | 6-10 | Qualifying | Embassy World Championship |

## TONY DRAGO (Malta)

**Born** 22.9.65. **Turned professional** 1985. **World ranking** 31 (32).

| | | | | |
|---|---|---|---|---|
| **1985** | v Bales | 2-5 | 1st round | Goya Matchroom Trophy |
| | v Watchorn | 5-2 | 1st round | Rothmans Grand Prix |
| | v King | 5-4 | 2nd round | Rothmans Grand Prix |
| | v Macleod | 5-3 | 3rd round | Rothmans Grand Prix |
| | v Charlton | 5-3 | 4th round | Rothmans Grand Prix |
| | v Wilson | 2-5 | 5th round | Rothmans Grand Prix |
| | v Gilbert | 9-5 | 1st round | Coral UK Open |
| | v Donnelly | 9-8 | 2nd round | Coral UK Open |

| | | | | |
|---|---|---|---|---|
| | v Wildman | 9-5 | 3rd round | Coral UK Open |
| | v S. Davis | 2-9 | 4th round | Coral UK Open |
| **1986** | v Cripsey | 4-5 | 1st round | Mercantile Credit Classic |
| | v Gauvreau | 5-3 | 2nd round | Dulux British Open |
| | v Williams | 1-5 | 3rd round | Dulux British Open |
| | v Cripsey | 10-4 | Qualifying | Embassy World Championship |
| | v P. Francisco | 4-10 | Qualifying | Embassy World Championship |
| | v Morra | 5-3 | 2nd round | BCE International |
| | v Thorne | 5-2 | 3rd round | BCE International |
| | v Chaperon | 1-5 | 4th round | BCE International |
| | v Watchorn | 5-3 | 2nd round | Rothmans Grand Prix |
| | v Charlton | 5-4 | 3rd round | Rothmans Grand Prix |
| | v S. Davis | 1-5 | 4th round | Rothmans Grand Prix |
| | v Morra | 9-6 | 2nd round | Tennents UK Open |
| | v Williams | 9-7 | 3rd round | Tennents UK Open |
| | v Virgo | 9-6 | 4th round | Tennents UK Open |
| | v Thorne | 9-5 | 5th round | Tennents UK Open |
| | v S. Davis | 8-9 | Quarter-final | Tennents UK Open |
| **1987** | v Jonik | 2-5 | 2nd round | Mercantile Credit Classic |
| | v Oliver | 5-1 | 2nd round | Dulux British Open |
| | v Johnson | 0-5 | 3rd round | Dulux British Open |
| | v Sinclair | 9-10 | Qualifying | Embassy World Championship |
| | v Clark | 2-5 | 3rd round | Fidelity International |
| | v Meadowcroft | 5-1 | 3rd round | Rothmans Grand Prix |
| | v Thorne | 2-5 | 4th round | Rothmans Grand Prix |
| | v Murphy | 7-9 | 3rd round | Tennents UK Open |
| **1988** | v Scott | 5-3 | 3rd round | Mercantile Credit Classic |
| | v Dennis Taylor | 0-5 | 4th round | Mercantile Credit Classic |
| | v Roe | 3-5 | 3rd round | MIM Britannia British Open |
| | v Chappel | 10-7 | Qualifying | Embassy World Championship |
| | v Higgins | 10-2 | 1st round | Embassy World Championship |
| | v Dennis Taylor | 13-5 | 2nd round | Embassy World Championship |
| | v S. Davis | 4-13 | Quarter-final | Embassy World Championship |
| | v Fowler | 5-3 | 3rd round | Fidelity International |
| | v Thorne | 2-5 | 4th round | Fidelity International |
| | v Foldvari | 5-3 | 3rd round | Rothmans Grand Prix |
| | v C. Wilson | 4-5 | 4th round | Rothmans Grand Prix |
| | v Fowler | 1-5 | 3rd round | BCE Canadian Masters |
| | v Duggan | 7-9 | 3rd round | Tennents UK Open |
| **1989** | v Marshall | 5-1 | 3rd round | Mercantile Credit Classic |
| | v Griffiths | 0-5 | 4th round | Mercantile Credit Classic |
| | v M. Bennett | 1-5 | 3rd round | European Open |
| | v Bear | 5-2 | 3rd round | Anglian British Open |
| | v Johnson | 3-5 | 4th round | Anglian British Open |
| | v Gary Wilkinson | 9-10 | Qualifying | Embassy World Championship |
| | v Gauvreau | 0-5 | 3rd round | Hong Kong Open |
| | v O'Boye | 5-3 | 3rd round | 555 Asian Open |
| | v Johnson | 5-2 | 4th round | 555 Asian Open |
| | v Griffiths | 3-5 | 5th round | 555 Asian Open |
| | v Macleod | 5-4 | 3rd round | BCE International |
| | v Parrott | 2-5 | 4th round | BCE International |
| | v Gary Wilkinson | 1-5 | 3rd round | Rothmans Grand Prix |
| | v Marshall | 5-0 | 3rd round | Dubai Classic |
| | v C. Wilson | 5-0 | 4th round | Dubai Classic |
| | v Hendry | 3-5 | 5th round | Dubai Classic |
| | v Johnston-Allen | 9-7 | 3rd round | Stormseal UK Open |
| | v Knowles | 7-9 | 4th round | Stormseal UK Open |
| **1990** | v Dyson | 5-3 | 3rd round | Mercantile Credit Classic |
| | v Dennis Taylor | 5-4 | 4th round | Mercantile Credit Classic |
| | v S. Davis | 3-5 | 5th round | Mercantile Credit Classic |
| | v Longworth | 5-0 | 3rd round | Pearl Assurance British Open |
| | v N. Foulds | 0-5 | 4th round | Pearl Assurance British Open |
| | v Bond | 2-5 | 3rd round | European Open |

| | | | | |
|---|---|---|---|---|
| | v Graham | 10-7 | Qualifying | Embassy World Championship |
| | v Thorne | 4-10 | 1st round | Embassy World Championship |

## STEVE DUGGAN (England)

**Born** 10.4.58. **Turned professional** 1983. **World ranking** 42 (43).

| | | | | |
|---|---|---|---|---|
| **1983** | v Darrington | 5-4 | Qualifying | Professional Players Tournament |
| | v Dunning | 5-2 | 1st round | Professional Players Tournament |
| | v Reardon | 2-5 | 2nd round | Professional Players Tournament |
| | v G. Foulds | 8-9 | Qualifying | Coral UK Championship |
| **1984** | v Browne | 9-10 | Qualifying | Embassy World Championship |
| | v T. Jones | 5-2 | Qualifying | Jameson International |
| | v Sinclair | 0-5 | Qualifying | Jameson International |
| | v Browne | 5-2 | Qualifying | Rothmans Grand Prix |
| | v S. Francisco | 3-5 | 1st round | Rothmans Grand Prix |
| | v O'Kane | 6-9 | Qualifying | Coral UK Open |
| **1985** | v W. Jones | 5-0 | Qualifying | Mercantile Credit Classic |
| | v King | 4-5 | Qualifying | Mercantile Credit Classic |
| | v B. Harris | 9-8 | Qualifying | Tolly Cobbold English Championship |
| | v Hallett | 4-9 | 1st round | Tolly Cobbold English Championship |
| | v Foldvari | 4-6 | Qualifying | Dulux British Open |
| | v T. Jones | 8-10 | Qualifying | Embassy World Championship |
| | v F. Davis | 5-1 | 2nd round | Goya Matchroom Trophy |
| | v Reardon | 5-3 | 3rd round | Goya Matchroom Trophy |
| | v Black | 5-1 | 4th round | Goya Matchroom Trophy |
| | v Thorne | 5-4 | 5th round | Goya Matchroom Trophy |
| | v Thorburn | 2-5 | Quarter-final | Goya Matchroom Trophy |
| | v Gauvreau | 5-4 | 2nd round | Rothmans Grand Prix |
| | v Wildman | 4-5 | 3rd round | Rothmans Grand Prix |
| | v Wych | 5-9 | 2nd round | Coral UK Open |
| **1986** | v King | 2-5 | 2nd round | Mercantile Credit Classic |
| | v Longworth | 4-9 | 2nd round | Tolly Cobbold English Championship |
| | v Murphy | 5-1 | 2nd round | Dulux British Open |
| | v Hallett | 3-5 | 3rd round | Dulux British Open |
| | v Fisher | 10-3 | Qualifying | Embassy World Championship |
| | v Wych | 5-10 | Qualifying | Embassy World Championship |
| | v Bear | 5-4 | 2nd round | BCE International |
| | v Campbell | 5-3 | 3rd round | BCE International |
| | v Williams | 4-5 | 4th round | BCE International |
| | v Whitthread | 5-1 | 2nd round | Rothmans Grand Prix |
| | v Thorne | 0-5 | 3rd round | Rothmans Grand Prix |
| | v O'Boye | 4-9 | 2nd round | Tennents UK Open |
| **1987** | v Watchorn | 5-1 | 2nd round | Mercantile Credit Classic |
| | v N. Foulds | 5-3 | 3rd round | Mercantile Credit Classic |
| | v Werbeniuk | 5-0 | 4th round | Mercantile Credit Classic |
| | v White | 2-5 | 5th round | Mercantile Credit Classic |
| | v Fisher | 6-0 | 2nd round | Tolly Ales English Championship |
| | v Meo | 3-6 | 3rd round | Tolly Ales English Championship |
| | v P. Gibson | 5-3 | 2nd round | Dulux British Open |
| | v Longworth | 5-2 | 3rd round | Dulux British Open |
| | v Thorne | 2-5 | 4th round | Dulux British Open |
| | v Roscoe | 10-7 | Qualifying | Embassy World Championship |
| | v Chappel | 3-10 | Qualifying | Embassy World Championship |
| | v Clark | 2-5 | 2nd round | Fidelity International |
| | v P. Gibson | 4-5 | 2nd round | Rothmans Grand Prix |
| | v Williamson | 9-7 | 2nd round | Tennents UK Open |
| | v Higgins | 4-9 | 3rd round | Tennents UK Open |
| **1988** | v Donnelly | 4-5 | 2nd round | Mercantile Credit Classic |
| | v Williamson | 6-2 | 2nd round | English Championship |
| | v Hallett | 3-6 | 3rd round | English Championship |
| | v M. Gibson | 2-5 | 2nd round | MIM Britannia British Open |

| | | | | |
|---|---|---|---|---|
| | v A. Harris | 10-4 | Qualifying | Embassy World Championship |
| | v P. Gibson | 10-9 | Qualifying | Embassy World Championship |
| | v Virgo | 5-10 | Qualifying | Embassy World Championship |
| | v Oliver | 5-3 | 2nd round | Fidelity International |
| | v C. Wilson | 5-2 | 3rd round | Fidelity International |
| | v Williams | 4-5 | 4th round | Fidelity International |
| | v Edwards | 5-4 | 2nd round | Rothmans Grand Prix |
| | v David Taylor | 5-1 | 3rd round | Rothmans Grand Prix |
| | v N. Foulds | 4-5 | 4th round | Rothmans Grand Prix |
| | v Wildman | 5-1 | 2nd round | BCE Canadian Masters |
| | v West | 5-3 | 3rd round | BCE Canadian Masters |
| | v King | 4-5 | 4th round | BCE Canadian Masters |
| | v Morra | 9-8 | 2nd round | Tennents UK Open |
| | v Drago | 9-7 | 3rd round | Tennents UK Open |
| | v Griffiths | 2-9 | 4th round | Tennents UK Open |
| **1989** | v Dunning | 5-2 | 2nd round | Mercantile Credit Classic |
| | v Reynolds | 1-5 | 3rd round | Mercantile Credit Classic |
| | v D. Morgan | 5-4 | 2nd round | European Open |
| | v Charlton | 2-5 | 3rd round | European Open |
| | v Graham | 2-5 | 2nd round | English Championship |
| | v Graham | 2-5 | 2nd round | Anglian British Open |
| | v F. Davis | 10-3 | Qualifying | Embassy World Championship |
| | v Rowing | 10-6 | Qualifying | Embassy World Championship |
| | v C. Wilson | 10-1 | 1st round | Embassy World Championship |
| | v S. Davis | 3-13 | 2nd round | Embassy World Championship |
| | v Rowswell | 5-3 | 2nd round | Hong Kong Open |
| | v C. Wilson | 4-5 | 3rd round | Hong Kong Open |
| | v Fitzmaurice | 5-1 | 2nd round | 555 Asian Open |
| | v Newbury | 5-3 | 3rd round | 555 Asian Open |
| | v James | 5-3 | 4th round | 555 Asian Open |
| | v T. Jones | 3-5 | 5th round | 555 Asian Open |
| | v F. Davis | 5-1 | 2nd round | BCE International |
| | v Newbury | 2-5 | 3rd round | BCE International |
| | v Meadowcroft | 5-1 | 2nd round | Rothmans Grand Prix |
| | v S. Davis | 1-5 | 3rd round | Rothmans Grand Prix |
| | v B. Harris | 3-5 | 2nd round | Dubai Classic |
| | v Donnelly | 6-1 | 2nd round | Stormseal UK Open |
| | v Higgins | 7-9 | 3rd round | Stormseal UK Open |
| **1990** | v Meadowcroft | 5-3 | 2nd round | Mercantile Credit Classic |
| | v Mountjoy | 5-4 | 3rd round | Mercantile Credit Classic |
| | v P. Francisco | 2-5 | 4th round | Mercantile Credit Classic |
| | v Williamson | 5-3 | 2nd round | Pearl Assurance British Open |
| | v Parrott | 5-1 | 3rd round | Pearl Assurance British Open |
| | v Robidoux | 4-5 | 4th round | Pearl Assurance British Open |
| | v Sinclair | 3-5 | 2nd round | European Open |
| | v Price | 9-10 | Qualifying | Embassy World Championship |

## JOHN DUNNING (England)

**Born** 18.4.27. **Turned professional** 1970. **World ranking** 117 (95).

| | | | | |
|---|---|---|---|---|
| **1972** | v Houlihan | 11-10 | Qualifying | World Championship |
| | v Miles | 11-5 | Qualifying | World Championship |
| | v Pulman | 7-19 | 1st round | World Championship |
| **1973** | v David Taylor | 4-9 | 1st round | World Championship |
| **1974** | v David Taylor | 8-6 | 1st round | World Championship |
| | v Charlton | 15-13 | 2nd round | World Championship |
| | v Miles | 13-15 | Quarter-final | World Championship |
| **1975** | v G. Owen | 8-15 | 2nd round | World Championship |
| **1976** | v Reardon | 7-15 | 1st round | Embassy World Championship |
| **1977** | v Virgo | 6-11 | Qualifying | Embassy World Championship |
| | v Parkin | 5-4 | 1st round | Super Crystalate UK Championship |

| | | | | |
|---|---|---|---|---|
| | v Higgins | 0-5 | Quarter-final | Super Crystalate UK Championship |
| **1978** | v Fagan | 5-9 | Qualifying | Embassy World Championship |
| | v Greaves | 9-3 | Qualifying | Coral UK Championship |
| | v F. Davis | 2-9 | 1st round | Coral UK Championship |
| **1979** | v Jack Rea | 9-5 | Prelim | Embassy World Championship |
| | v David Taylor | 8-9 | Qualifying | Embassy World Championship |
| | v Greaves | 9-8 | 1st round | Coral UK Championship |
| | v S. Davis | 3-9 | 2nd round | Coral UK Championship |
| **1980** | v Johnson | 6-9 | Qualifying | Coral UK Championship |
| **1981** | v Greaves | 9-4 | Qualifying | John Courage English |
| | v David Taylor | 9-8 | 1st round | John Courage English |
| | v Thorne | 0-9 | 2nd round | John Courage English |
| | v Bennett | 9-6 | Qualifying | Embassy World Championship |
| | v Fagan | 9-7 | Qualifying | Embassy World Championship |
| | v Stevens | 4-10 | 1st round | Embassy World Championship |
| | v Gibson | 5-3 | Qualifying | Jameson International |
| | v Martin | 2-5 | 1st round | Jameson International |
| **1982** | v Macleod | 9-4 | Qualifying | Embassy World Championship |
| | v Spencer | 4-10 | 1st round | Embassy World Championship |
| | v Roscoe | 2-5 | Qualifying | Jameson International |
| | v Wildman | 4-5 | 1st round | Professional Players Tournament |
| **1983** | v B. Harris | 3-5 | Qualifying | Jameson International |
| | v Duggan | 2-5 | 1st round | Professional Players Tournament |
| | v Andrewartha | 9-2 | Qualifying | Coral UK Championship |
| | v Spencer | 7-9 | 1st round | Coral UK Championship |
| **1984** | v Oliver | 3-10 | Qualifying | Embassy World Championship |
| | v Cripsey | 5-3 | Qualifying | Jameson International |
| | v F. Davis | 4-5 | Qualifying | Jameson International |
| | v D. Hughes | 5-0 | Qualifying | Rothmans Grand Prix |
| | v Mans | 5-4 | 1st round | Rothmans Grand Prix |
| | v Knowles | 1-5 | 2nd round | Rothmans Grand Prix |
| | v John Rea | 3-9 | Qualifying | Coral UK Open |
| **1985** | v W. Jones | 6-10 | Qualifying | Embassy World Championship |
| | v Everton | 5-2 | 2nd round | Goya Matchroom Trophy |
| | v Meo | 0-5 | 3rd round | Goya Matchroom Trophy |
| | v Agrawal | 0-5 | 2nd round | Rothmans Grand Prix |
| **1986** | v West | 3-10 | Qualifying | Embassy World Championship |
| | v Demarco | 5-4 | 1st round | BCE International |
| | v Newbury | 4-5 | 2nd round | BCE International |
| | v P. Gibson | 1-5 | 1st round | Rothmans Grand Prix |
| | v Kearney | 9-6 | 1st round | Tennents UK Open |
| | v M. Gibson | 2-9 | 2nd round | Tennents UK Open |
| **1987** | v B. Bennett | 5-2 | 1st round | Mercantile Credit Classic |
| | v Browne | 1-5 | 2nd round | Mercantile Credit Classic |
| | v Cripsey | 1-6 | 2nd round | Tolly Ales English Championship |
| | v Watchorn | 2-5 | 1st round | Dulux British Open |
| | v Caggianello | 10-7 | Qualifying | Embassy World Championship |
| | v Scott | 7-10 | Qualifying | Embassy World Championship |
| | v Sheehan | 5-1 | 1st round | Fidelity International |
| | v W. Jones | 1-5 | 2nd round | Fidelity International |
| | v Foldvari | 0-5 | 1st round | Rothmans Grand Prix |
| | v Fagan | 9-4 | 1st round | Tennents UK Open |
| | v Bales | 9-8 | 2nd round | Tennents UK Open |
| | v White | 0-9 | 3rd round | Tennents UK Open |
| **1988** | v Jonik | 2-5 | 1st round | Mercantile Credit Classic |
| | v Williamson | 5-6 | 1st round | English Championship |
| | v Jonik | 5-3 | 1st round | MIM Britannia British Open |
| | v Scott | 5-3 | 2nd round | MIM Britannia British Open |
| | v West | 0-5 | 3rd round | MIM Britannia British Open |
| | v Rigitano | 7-10 | Qualifying | Embassy World Championship |
| | v Kelly | 5-0 | 1st round | Fidelity International |
| | v N. Gilbert | 0-5 | 2nd round | Fidelity International |
| | v Heaton | 5-1 | 1st round | Rothmans Grand Prix |

| | | | | |
|---|---|---|---|---|
| | v Edmonds | 3-5 | 2nd round | Rothmans Grand Prix |
| | v Sheehan | 5-3 | 1st round | BCE Canadian Masters |
| | v Werbeniuk | 3-5* | 2nd round | BCE Canadian Masters |
| | v Parrott | 2-5 | 3rd round | BCE Canadian Masters |
| **1989** | v Price | 5-3 | 1st round | Mercantile Credit Classic |
| | v Duggan | 2-5 | 2nd round | Mercantile Credit Classic |
| | v Darrington | 4-5 | 1st round | European Open |
| | v S. Campbell | 3-5 | 1st round | English Championship |
| | v Fitzmaurice | 1-5 | 1st round | Anglian British Open |
| | v Rowing | 9-10 | Qualifying | Embassy World Championship |
| | v S. Murphy | 5-3 | 1st round | Hong Kong Open |
| | v Wych | 1-5 | 2nd round | Hong Kong Open |
| | v Gollan | 1-5 | 1st round | 555 Asian Open |
| | v Rowing | 0-5 | 1st round | BCE International |
| | v Fitzmaurice | 5-3 | 1st round | Rothmans Grand Prix |
| | v D. Gilbert | 1-5 | 2nd round | Rothmans Grand Prix |
| | v Fagan | 5-2 | 1st round | Dubai Classic |
| | v T. Jones | 2-5 | 2nd round | Dubai Classic |
| | v Gollan | 4-6 | 1st round | Stormseal UK Open |
| **1990** | v D. Campbell | 2-5 | 1st round | Mercantile Credit Classic |
| | v M. Gibson | 5-4 | 1st round | Pearl Assurance British Open |
| | v Macleod | 1-5 | 2nd round | Pearl Assurance British Open |
| | v Bond | 0-5 | 1st round | European Open |
| | v Wattana | 2-10 | Qualifying | Embassy World Championship |

* Dunning deemed lucky loser after Werbeniuk suspended for contravening drug regulations.

## NICK DYSON (England)

**Born** 19.12.69. **Turned professional** 1989. **World ranking** 65.

| | | | | |
|---|---|---|---|---|
| **1989** | v F. Davis | 5-1 | 1st round | Hong Kong Open |
| | v T. Jones | 1-5 | 2nd round | Hong Kong Open |
| | v Owers | 5-1 | 1st round | 555 Asian Open |
| | v T. Jones | 3-5 | 2nd round | 555 Asian Open |
| | v Glen Wilkinson | 5-1 | 1st round | BCE International |
| | v Chambers | 5-3 | 2nd round | BCE International |
| | v Dennis Taylor | 1-5 | 3rd round | BCE International |
| | v Medati | 4-5 | 1st round | Rothmans Grand Prix |
| | v Bradley | 4-5 | 1st round | Dubai Classic |
| | v John Rea | 6-4 | 1st round | Stormseal UK Open |
| | v Stevens | 4-6 | 2nd round | Stormseal UK Open |
| **1990** | v Dodd | 5-3 | 1st round | Mercantile Credit Classic |
| | v Graham | 5-3 | 2nd round | Mercantile Credit Classic |
| | v Drago | 3-5 | 3rd round | Mercantile Credit Classic |
| | v Miles | 3-5 | 1st round | Pearl Assurance British Open |
| | v Williamson | 5-3 | 1st round | European Open |
| | v Longworth | 5-3 | 2nd round | European Open |
| | v Dennis Taylor | 5-3 | 3rd round | European Open |
| | v Clark | 5-2 | 4th round | European Open |
| | v Roscoe | 2-5 | 5th round | European Open |
| | v Black | 10-5 | Qualifying | Embassy World Championship |
| | v Bradley | 10-6 | Qualifying | Embassy World Championship |
| | v Macleod | 9-10 | Qualifying | Embassy World Championship |

## RAY EDMONDS (England)

**Born** 28.5.36. **Turned professional** 1978. **World ranking** 73 (49).

| | | | | |
|---|---|---|---|---|
| **1978** | v Virgo | 4-9 | Qualifying | Coral UK Championship |
| **1979** | v Meadowcroft | 9-3 | 2nd round | Coral UK Championship |
| | v F. Davis | 9-6 | 3rd round | Coral UK Championship |

| | | | | |
|---|---|---|---|---|
| | v Werbeniuk | 8-9 | Quarter-final | Coral UK Championship |
| **1980** | v Hood | 9-6 | Qualifying | Embassy World Championship |
| | v David Taylor | 3-10 | 1st round | Embassy World Championship |
| | v Hallett | 8-9 | Qualifying | Coral UK Championship |
| **1981** | v Hallett | 9-3 | Qualifying | John Courage English |
| | v F. Davis | 9-6 | 1st round | John Courage English |
| | v Johnson | 9-5 | 2nd round | John Courage English |
| | v S. Davis | 0-9 | Semi-final | John Courage English |
| | v Wildman | 9-3 | Qualifying | Embassy World Championship |
| | v Williams | 9-7 | Qualifying | Embassy World Championship |
| | v Spencer | 9-10 | 1st round | Embassy World Championship |
| | v E. Hughes | 5-4 | 1st round | Jameson International |
| | v Spencer | 3-5 | 2nd round | Jameson International |
| | v Thorne | 4-9 | 2nd round | Coral UK Championship |
| **1982** | v Reynolds | 6-9 | Qualifying | Embassy World Championship |
| | v D. Hughes | 5-0 | Qualifying | Jameson International |
| | v Miles | 5-1 | Qualifying | Jameson International |
| | v Spencer | 2-5 | 1st round | Jameson International |
| | v Dennis Taylor | 4-5 | 1st round | Professional Players Tournament |
| | v Fisher | 8-9 | Qualifying | Coral UK Championship |
| **1983** | v Jonik | 10-4 | Qualifying | Embassy World Championship |
| | v Reynolds | 6-10 | Qualifying | Embassy World Championship |
| | v Jack Rea | 5-1 | Qualifying | Jameson International |
| | v E. McLaughlin | 5-1 | Qualifying | Jameson International |
| | v Knowles | 1-5 | 1st round | Jameson International |
| | v Stevens | 1-5 | 1st round | Professional Players Tournament |
| | v Medati | 7-9 | Qualifying | Coral UK Championship |
| **1984** | v Greaves | 10-0 | Qualifying | Embassy World Championship |
| | v Van Rensberg | 9-10 | Qualifying | Embassy World Championship |
| | v Foldvari | 1-5 | Qualifying | Jameson International |
| | v Rigitano | 3-5 | Qualifying | Rothmans Grand Prix |
| | v John Rea | 6-9 | Qualifying | Coral UK Open |
| **1985** | v Hargreaves | 5-2 | Qualifying | Mercantile Credit Classic |
| | v Watterson | 5-2 | Qualifying | Mercantile Credit Classic |
| | v Johnson | 4-5 | Qualifying | Mercantile Credit Classic |
| | v Longworth | 4-9 | Qualifying | Tolly Cobbold English Championship |
| | v Mienie | 6-1 | Qualifying | Dulux British Open |
| | v Miles | 1-6 | 1st round | Dulux British Open |
| | v Foldvari | 10-3 | Qualifying | Embassy World Championship |
| | v Wildman | 10-7 | Qualifying | Embassy World Championship |
| | v Stevens | 8-10 | 1st round | Embassy World Championship |
| | v Bales | 0-5 | 2nd round | Goya Matchroom Trophy |
| | v Kearney | 5-2 | 2nd round | Rothmans Grand Prix |
| | v O'Kane | 5-2 | 3rd round | Rothmans Grand Prix |
| | v Knowles | 3-5 | 4th round | Rothmans Grand Prix |
| | v Van Rensberg | 9-5 | 2nd round | Coral UK Open |
| | v Higgins | 8-9 | 3rd round | Coral UK Open |
| **1986** | v Smith | 2-5 | 2nd round | Mecantile Credit Classic |
| | v Smith | 9-8 | 2nd round | Tolly Cobbold English Championship |
| | v David Taylor | 9-6 | 3rd round | Tolly Cobbold English Championship |
| | v N. Foulds | 4-9 | 4th round | Tolly Cobbold English Championship |
| | v Hargreaves | 3-5 | 2nd round | Dulux British Open |
| | v Kelly | 10-0 | Qualifying | Embassy World Championship |
| | v Darrington | 10-5 | Qualifying | Embassy World Championship |
| | v Wildman | 10-9 | Qualifying | Embassy World Championship |
| | v S. Davis | 4-10 | 1st round | Embassy World Championship |
| | v James | 5-2 | 2nd round | BCE International |
| | v David Taylor | 4-5 | 3rd round | BCE International |
| | v O'Boye | 2-5 | 2nd round | Rothmans Grand Prix |
| | v Bear | 9-6 | 2nd round | Tennents UK Open |
| | v White | 4-9 | 3rd round | Tennents UK Open |
| **1987** | v Williamson | 2-5 | 2nd round | Mercantile Credit Classic |
| | v Bennett | 6-1 | 2nd round | Tolly Ales English Championship |

| | | | | |
|---|---|---|---|---|
| | v Reynolds | 3-6 | 3rd round | Tolly Ales English Championship |
| | v G. Foulds | 3-5 | 2nd round | Dulux British Open |
| | v James | 10-1 | Qualifying | Embassy World Championship |
| | v Sinclair | 10-6 | Qualifying | Embassy World Championship |
| | v Macleod | 7-10 | Qualifying | Embassy World Championship |
| | v Sinclair | 4-5 | 2nd round | Fidelity International |
| | v Sinclair | 5-2 | 2nd round | Rothmans Grand Prix |
| | v Williams | 5-3 | 3rd round | Rothmans Grand Prix |
| | v Charlton | 3-5 | 4th round | Rothmans Grand Prix |
| | v D. Hughes | 9-4 | 2nd round | Tennents UK Open |
| | v Macleod | 9-4 | 3rd round | Tennents UK Open |
| | v Griffiths | 5-9 | 4th round | Tennents UK Open |
| **1988** | v Foldvari | 5-4 | 2nd round | Mercantile Credit Classic |
| | v Longworth | 3-5 | 3rd round | Mercantile Credit Classic |
| | v Gary Wilkinson | 3-6 | 2nd round | English Championship |
| | v Roe | 1-5 | 2nd round | MIM Britannia British Open |
| | v Morra | 8-10 | Qualifying | Embassy World Championship |
| | v Bear | 5-1 | 2nd round | Fidelity International |
| | v Hendry | 1-5 | 3rd round | Fidelity International |
| | v Dunning | 5-2 | 2nd round | Rothmans Grand Prix |
| | v Longworth | 5-3 | 3rd round | Rothmans Grand Prix |
| | v Parrott | 5-3 | 4th round | Rothmans Grand Prix |
| | v Williams | 3-5 | 5th round | Rothmans Grand Prix |
| | v Scott | 2-5 | 2nd round | BCE Canadian Masters |
| | v Wildman | 9-4 | 2nd round | Tennents UK Open |
| | v C. Wilson | 1-9 | 3rd round | Tennents UK Open |
| **1989** | v Marshall | 2-5 | 2nd round | Mercantile Credit Classic |
| | v Grace | 5-1 | 2nd round | European Open |
| | v Thorburn | 2-5 | 3rd round | European Open |
| | v Price | 4-5 | 2nd round | English Championship |
| | v Johnston-Allen | 4-5 | 2nd round | Anglian British Open |
| | v Black | 10-3 | Qualifying | Embassy World Championship |
| | v John Rea | 7-10 | Qualifying | Embassy World Championship |
| | v P. Gibson | 5-2 | 2nd round | Hong Kong Open |
| | v Newbury | 4-5 | 3rd round | Hong Kong Open |
| | v Terry | 2-5 | 2nd round | 555 Asian Open |
| | v Houlihan | 2-5 | 2nd round | BCE International |
| | v Brumby | 5-2 | 2nd round | Rothmans Grand Prix |
| | v Knowles | 4-5 | 3rd round | Rothmans Grand Prix |
| | v B. Morgan | 0-5 | 2nd round | Dubai Classic |
| | v Rowing | 4-6 | 2nd round | Stormseal UK Open |
| **1990** | v D. Campbell | 5-3 | 2nd round | Mercantile Credit Classic |
| | v W. Jones | 1-5 | 3rd round | Mercantile Credit Classic |
| | v Sinclair | 3-5 | 2nd round | Pearl Assurance British Open |
| | v Wright | 4-5 | 2nd round | European Open |
| | v B. Harris | 10-4 | Qualifying | Embassy World Championship |
| | v Robidoux | 6-10 | Qualifying | Embassy World Championship |

## CRAIG EDWARDS (England)

**Born** 23.12.68. **Turned professional** 1988. **World ranking** 62 (69).

| | | | | |
|---|---|---|---|---|
| **1988** | v John Rea | 2-5 | 1st round | Fidelity International |
| | v Duggan | 4-5 | 2nd round | Rothmans Grand Prix |
| | v Medati | 3-5 | 1st round | BCE Canadian Masters |
| | v Sinclair | 9-8 | 1st round | Tennents UK Open |
| | v Stevens | 4-9 | 2nd round | Tennents UK Open |
| **1989** | v Lawlor | 5-1 | 1st round | Mercantile Credit Classic |
| | v Stevens | 4-5 | 2nd round | Mercantile Credit Classic |
| | v M. Smith | 4-5 | 1st round | European Open |
| | v Werbeniuk | *wo* | 2nd round | European Open |
| | v Chaperon | 5-3 | 3rd round | European Open |

| | | | | |
|---|---|---|---|---|
| | v Virgo | 3-5 | 4th round | European Open |
| | v Watterson | 5-0 | 1st round | English Championship |
| | v Dodd | 5-1 | 2nd round | English Championship |
| | v Spencer | 5-1 | 3rd round | English Championship |
| | v Johnson | 0-5 | 4th round | English Championship |
| | v Black | 5-3 | 1st round | Anglian British Open |
| | v O'Boye | 5-4 | 2nd round | Anglian British Open |
| | v Hendry | 0-5 | 3rd round | Anglian British Open |
| | v Giannaros | 10-4 | Qualifying | Embassy World Championship |
| | v Bear | 10-7 | Qualifying | Embassy World Championship |
| | v Chappel | 10-7 | Qualifying | Embassy World Championship |
| | v N. Gilbert | 8-10 | Qualifying | Embassy World Championship |
| | v Rigitano | 3-5 | 1st round | Hong Kong Open |
| | v Bond | 5-4 | 1st round | 555 Asian Open |
| | v Fisher | 5-3 | 2nd round | 555 Asian Open |
| | v Hallett | 0-5 | 3rd round | 555 Asian Open |
| | v Wattana | 2-5 | 1st round | BCE International |
| | v S. Murphy | 4-5 | 1st round | Rothmans Grand Prix |
| | v Miles | 4-5 | 2nd round | Dubai Classic |
| | v M. Gibson | 0-6 | 1st round | Stormseal UK Open |
| **1990** | v Meakin | 5-4 | 1st round | Mercantile Credit Classic |
| | v Longworth | 5-4 | 2nd round | Mercantile Credit Classic |
| | v Parrott | 2-5 | 3rd round | Mercantile Credit Classic |
| | v Wattana | 2-5 | 1st round | Pearl Assurance British Open |
| | v B. Morgan | 5-2 | 1st round | European Open |
| | v T. Jones | 5-0 | 2nd round | European Open |
| | v Meo | 5-4 | 3rd round | European Open |
| | v O'Kane | 5-2 | 4th round | European Open |
| | v S. Davis | 4-5 | 5th round | European Open |
| | v Sheehan | 10-8 | Qualifying | Embassy World Championship |
| | v Robidoux | 3-10 | Qualifying | Embassy World Championship |

## FRANÇOIS ELLIS (South Africa)

**Born** 11.9.59. **Turned professional** 1983. **World ranking** 106 (105).

| | | | | |
|---|---|---|---|---|
| **1986** | v Mans | 7-6 | 2nd round | South African Championship |
| | v Van Rensberg | 8-2 | Semi-final | South African Championship |
| | v S. Francisco | 1-9 | Final | South African Championship |
| | v Morra | 3-5 | 1st round | BCE International |
| | v Wildman | 1-5 | 2nd round | Rothmans Grand Prix |
| | v D. Hughes | 6-9 | 1st round | Tennents UK Open |
| **1987** | v Morra | 1-5 | 1st round | Mercantile Credit Classic |
| | v Smith | 5-2 | 1st round | Dulux British Open |
| | v Medati | 0-5 | 2nd round | Dulux British Open |
| | v Roe | 4-5 | 1st round | Fidelity International |
| | v Sinclair | 4-5 | 1st round | Rothmans Grand Prix |
| | v Sheehan | 9-8 | 1st round | Tennents UK Open |
| | v F. Davis | 6-9 | 2nd round | Tennents UK Open |
| **1988** | v V. Harris | 1-5 | 1st round | Mercantile Credit Classic |
| | v Chappel | 0-5 | 2nd round | MIM Britannia British Open |
| | v G. Foulds | 2-5 | 1st round | Fidelity International |
| | v Lawlor | 5-4 | 1st round | Rothmans Grand Prix |
| | v Gauvreau | 5-2 | 2nd round | Rothmans Grand Prix |
| | v Dennis Taylor | 1-5 | 3rd round | Rothmans Grand Prix |
| | v Rowswell | 1-5 | 1st round | BCE Canadian Masters |
| | v Bear | 9-7 | 1st round | Tennents UK Open |
| | v Fowler | 3-9 | 2nd round | Tennents UK Open |
| **1989** | v Donnelly | 5-0 | 1st round | Mercantile Credit Classic |
| | v Roe | 0-5 | 2nd round | Mercantile Credit Classic |
| | v Kearney | 5-4 | 1st round | European Open |
| | v D. Gilbert | 2-5 | 2nd round | European Open |

| | | | | |
|---|---|---|---|---|
| | v Rowswell | 1-5 | 1st round | Anglian British Open |
| | v Wildman | 10-7 | Qualifying | Embassy World Championship |
| | v J. McLaughlin | 9-10 | Qualifying | Embassy World Championship |
| | v Price | 2-5 | 1st round | Hong Kong Open |
| | v Morra | 3-5 | 1st round | 555 Asian Open |
| | v Sinclair | 5-2 | 1st round | BCE International |
| | v T. Murphy | 4-5 | 2nd round | BCE International |
| | v A. Harris | 2-5 | 1st round | Rothmans Grand Prix |
| | v Grech | 1-5 | 1st round | Dubai Classic |
| | v Oliver | 5-6 | 1st round | Stormseal UK Open |
| **1990** | v P. Gibson | 3-5 | 1st round | Mercantile Credit Classic |
| | v A. Harris | 3-5 | 1st round | Pearl Assurance British Open |
| | v Terry | 5-3 | 1st round | European Open |
| | v King | 5-4 | 2nd round | European Open |
| | v Charlton | 3-5 | 3rd round | European Open |
| | v M. Smith | 6-10 | Qualifying | Embassy World Championship |

## MICK FISHER (England)

**Born** 12.7.44. **Turned professional** 1982. **World ranking** 99 (64).

| | | | | |
|---|---|---|---|---|
| **1982** | v Murphy | 5-1 | Qualifying | Jameson International |
| | v F. Davis | 5-3 | Qualifying | Jameson International |
| | v David Taylor | 1-5 | 1st round | Jameson International |
| | v Black | 9-3 | Qualifying | Coral UK Championship |
| | v Edmonds | 9-8 | Qualifying | Coral UK Championship |
| | v Reynolds | 6-9 | 1st round | Coral UK Championship |
| **1983** | v Fagan | 10-8 | Qualifying | Embassy World Championship |
| | v E. McLaughlin | 10-9 | Qualifying | Embassy World Championship |
| | v Stevens | 2-10 | 1st round | Embassy World Championship |
| | v E. Hughes | 4-5 | Qualifying | Jameson International |
| | v F. Davis | 5-4 | 1st round | Professional Players Tournament |
| | v Charlton | 4-5 | 2nd round | Professional Players Tournament |
| | v Parrott | 0-9 | Qualifying | Coral UK Championship |
| **1984** | v Thornley | 10-8 | Qualifying | Embassy World Championship |
| | v Gibson | 7-10 | Qualifying | Embassy World Championship |
| | v Bales | 3-5 | Qualifying | Jameson International |
| | v Newbury | 0-5 | Qualifying | Rothmans Grand Prix |
| | v Watchorn | 9-5 | Qualifying | Coral UK Open |
| | v Williams | 8-9 | Qualifying | Coral UK Open |
| **1985** | v Longworth | 1-5 | Qualifying | Mercantile Credit Classic |
| | v French | 9-8 | Qualifying | Tolly Cobbold English Championship |
| | v Meo | 3-9 | 1st round | Tolly Cobbold English Championship |
| | v John Rea | 0-6 | Qualifying | Dulux British Open |
| | v Rigitano | 2-10 | Qualifying | Embassy World Championship |
| | v Mikkelsen | 3-5 | 1st round | Goya Matchroom Trophy |
| | v Bales | 3-5 | 2nd round | Rothmans Grand Prix |
| | v Simngam | 4-9 | 2nd round | Coral UK Open |
| **1986** | v Jack Rea | 5-3 | 2nd round | Mercantile Credit Classic |
| | v Higgins | 0-5 | 3rd round | Mercantile Credit Classic |
| | v Chalmers | 2-9 | 2nd round | Tolly Cobbold English Championship |
| | v J. McLaughlin | 3-5 | 2nd round | Dulux British Open |
| | v Duggan | 3-10 | Qualifying | Embassy World Championship |
| | v Hines | 2-5 | 1st round | BCE International |
| | v Wright | 1-5 | 1st round | Rothmans Grand Prix |
| | v Greaves | 9-4 | 1st round | Tennents UK Open |
| | v V. Harris | 4-9 | 2nd round | Tennents UK Open |
| **1987** | v Demarco | 5-0 | 1st round | Mercantile Credit Classic |
| | v F. Davis | 5-2 | 2nd round | Mercantile Credit Classic |
| | v Charlton | 0-5 | 3rd round | Mercantile Credit Classic |
| | v Whitthread | 6-3 | 1st round | Tolly Ales English Championship |
| | v Duggan | 0-6 | 2nd round | Tolly Ales English Championship |

| | | | | |
|---|---|---|---|---|
| | v Chaperon | 2-5 | 2nd round | Dulux British Open |
| | v Owers | 5-10 | Qualifying | Embassy World Championship |
| | v Newbury | 0-5 | 2nd round | Fidelity International |
| | v Watchorn | 5-4 | 1st round | Rothmans Grand Prix |
| | v F. Davis | 5-0 | 2nd round | Rothmans Grand Prix |
| | v E. Hughes | 5-4 | 3rd round | Rothmans Grand Prix |
| | v Clark | 5-4 | 4th round | Rothmans Grand Prix |
| | v Chaperon | 2-5 | 5th round | Rothmans Grand Prix |
| | v Wych | 6-9 | 2nd round | Tennents UK Open |
| **1988** | v Owers | 0-5 | 2nd round | Mercantile Credit Classic |
| | v Wright | 2-6 | 2nd round | English Championship |
| | v Clark | 1-5 | 1st round | MIM Britannia British Open |
| | v A. Harris | 4-10 | Qualifying | Embassy World Championship |
| | v Glen Wilkinson | 5-4 | 2nd round | Fidelity International |
| | v Chaperon | 3-5 | 3rd round | Fidelity International |
| | v J. Smith | 5-3 | 2nd round | Rothmans Grand Prix |
| | v Mountjoy | 1-5 | 3rd round | Rothmans Grand Prix |
| | v Robidoux | 0-5 | 2nd round | BCE Canadian Masters |
| | v Medati | 3-9 | 2nd round | Tennents UK Open |
| **1989** | v Sheehan | 3-5 | 2nd round | Mercantile Credit Classic |
| | v Robidoux | 1-5 | 2nd round | European Open |
| | v Miles | 4-5 | 2nd round | English Championship |
| | v Foldvari | 0-5 | 2nd round | Anglian British Open |
| | v Robidoux | 2-10 | Qualifying | Embassy World Championship |
| | v Wright | 0-5 | 2nd round | Hong Kong Open |
| | v Edwards | 3-5 | 2nd round | 555 Asian Open |
| | v Rowing | 5-4 | 2nd round | BCE International |
| | v Parrott | 2-5 | 3rd round | BCE International |
| | v P. Gibson | 3-5 | 2nd round | Rothmans Grand Prix |
| | v Kearney | 5-3 | 2nd round | Dubai Classic |
| | v P. Francisco | 0-5 | 3rd round | Dubai Classic |
| | v Rowswell | 5-6 | 2nd round | Stormseal UK Open |
| **1990** | v Watchorn | 3-5 | 2nd round | Mercantile Credit Classic |
| | v B. Harris | 1-5 | 2nd round | Pearl Assurance British Open |
| | v Bond | 2-5 | 2nd round | European Open |
| | v Watchorn | 7-10 | Qualifying | Embassy World Championship |

## **JACK FITZMAURICE** (England)

**Born** 25.4.28. **Turned professional** 1981. **World ranking** 116 (106).

| | | | | |
|---|---|---|---|---|
| **1981** | v Bennett | 5-1 | Qualifying | Jameson International |
| | v E. Hughes | 3-5 | Qualifying | Jameson International |
| | v Gibson | 6-9 | Qualifying | Coral UK Championship |
| **1982** | v Morra | 9-7 | Qualifying | Embassy World Championship |
| | v Stevens | 4-10 | 1st round | Embassy World Championship |
| | v Black | 5-3 | Qualifying | Jameson International |
| | v Dodd | 3-5 | Qualifying | Jameson International |
| | v Sheehan | 5-1 | 1st round | Professional Players Tournament |
| | v Reynolds | 0-5 | 2nd round | Professional Players Tournament |
| | v Kelly | 0-8 *retd* | Qualifying | Coral UK Championship |
| **1983** | v E. Hughes | 7-10 | Qualifying | Embassy World Championship |
| | v Morgan | 4-5 | Qualifying | Jameson International |
| | v Martin | 0-5 | 1st round | Professional Players Tournament |
| | v B. Harris | 3-9 | Qualifying | Coral UK Championship |
| **1984** | v Murphy | 8-10 | Qualifying | Embassy World Championship |
| | v O'Kane | 4-5 | Qualifying | Jameson International |
| | v John Rea | 2-5 | Qualifying | Rothmans Grand Prix |
| | v Cripsey | 9-8 | Qualifying | Coral UK Open |
| | v Parrott | 6-9 | Qualifying | Coral UK Open |
| **1985** | v G. Foulds | 1-5 | Qualifying | Mercantile Credit Classic |

| | | | | |
|---|---|---|---|---|
| | v Greaves | 9-3 | Qualifying | Tolly Cobbold English Championship |
| | v Reynolds | 2-9 | 1st round | Tolly Cobbold English Championship |
| | v Watterson | 1-6 | Qualifying | Dulux British Open |
| | v T. Jones | 4-10 | Qualifying | Embassy World Championship |
| | v Watterson | 5-2 | 2nd round | Goya Matchroom Trophy |
| | v Macleod | 1-5 | 3rd round | Goya Matchroom Trophy |
| | v Sinclair | 5-3 | 2nd round | Rothmans Grand Prix |
| | v White | 0-5 | 3rd round | Rothmans Grand Prix |
| | v W. Jones | 3-9 | 2nd round | Coral UK Open |
| **1986** | v Fagan | 5-3 | 2nd round | Mercantile Credit Classic |
| | v Dennis Taylor | 1-5 | 3rd round | Mercantile Credit Classic |
| | v Miles | 5-9 | 2nd round | Tolly Cobbold English Championship |
| | v Fagan | 4-5 | 2nd round | Dulux British Open |
| | v Dodd | 6-10 | Qualifying | Embassy World Championship |
| | v Burke | 4-5 | 1st round | BCE International |
| | v Mienie | 2-5 | 1st round | Rothmans Grand Prix |
| | v Hines | 9-4 | 1st round | Tennents UK Open |
| | v T. Jones | 0-9 | 2nd round | Tennents UK Open |
| **1987** | v Wilkinson | 2-5 | 1st round | Mercantile Credit Classic |
| | v Scott | 6-2 | 2nd round | Tolly Ales English Championship |
| | v David Taylor | 1-6 | 3rd round | Tolly Ales English Championship |
| | v Wilkinson | 0-5 | 1st round | Dulux British Open |
| | v Everton | 10-2 | Qualifying | Embassy World Championship |
| | v Chaperon | 2-10 | Qualifying | Embassy World Championship |
| | v Chalmers | 4-5 | 1st round | Fidelity International |
| | v Chambers | 2-5 | 1st round | Rothmans Grand Prix |
| | v Lawlor | 0-9 | 1st round | Tennents UK Open |
| **1988** | v M. Smith | 2-5 | 1st round | Mercantile Credit Classic |
| | v Marshall | 1-6 | 1st round | English Championship |
| | v T. Jones | 3-5 | 2nd round | MIM Britannia British Open |
| | v Parkin | 10-6 | Qualifying | Embassy World Championship |
| | v F. Davis | 8-10 | Qualifying | Embassy World Championship |
| | v Mikkelsen | 2-5 | 1st round | Fidelity International |
| | v Oliver | 3-5 | 1st round | Rothmans Grand Prix |
| | v Van Rensberg | 5-3 | 1st round | BCE Canadian Masters |
| | v J. McLaughlin | 5-2 | 2nd round | BCE Canadian Masters |
| | v Thorne | 0-5 | 3rd round | BCE Canadian Masters |
| | v Lawlor | 1-9 | 1st round | Tennents UK Open |
| **1989** | v Meadowcroft | 5-2 | 1st round | Mercantile Credit Classic |
| | v N. Gilbert | 3-5 | 2nd round | Mercantile Credit Classic |
| | v Lawlor | 0-5 | 1st round | European Open |
| | v B. Harris | 5-4 | 1st round | English Championship |
| | v Houlihan | 4-5 | 2nd round | English Championship |
| | v Dunning | 5-1 | 1st round | Anglian British Open |
| | v Bales | 1-5 | 2nd round | Anglian British Open |
| | v Roscoe | 10-9 | Qualifying | Embassy World Championship |
| | v Reardon | 5-10 | Qualifying | Embassy World Championship |
| | v John Rea | 4-5 | 2nd round | Hong Kong Open |
| | v Foldvari | 5-2 | 1st round | 555 Asian Open |
| | v Duggan | 1-5 | 2nd round | 555 Asian Open |
| | v Rowswell | 5-4 | 1st round | BCE International |
| | v J. Campbell | 3-5 | 2nd round | BCE International |
| | v Dunning | 3-5 | 1st round | Rothmans Grand Prix |
| | v Oliver | 5-4 | 1st round | Dubai Classic |
| | v Terry | 3-5 | 2nd round | Dubai Classic |
| | v Donnelly | 2-6 | 1st round | Stormseal UK Open |
| **1990** | v Bradley | 4-5 | 1st round | Mercantile Credit Classic |
| | v Morra | 5-2 | 1st round | Pearl Assurance British Open |
| | v Gary Wilkinson | 3-5 | 2nd round | Pearl Assurance British Open |
| | v B. Harris | 3-5 | 1st round | European Open |
| | v Bear | 5-10 | Qualifying | Embassy World Championship |

**ROBBY FOLDVARI** (Australia)

**Born** 2.6.60. **Turned professional** 1984. **World ranking** 100 (77).

| | | | | |
|---|---|---|---|---|
| **1984** | v Rigitano | 5-2 | Qualifying | Jameson International |
| | v Edmonds | 5-1 | Qualifying | Jameson International |
| | v Dodd | 3-5 | Qualifying | Jameson International |
| | v Gauvreau | 2-5 | Qualifying | Rothmans Grand Prix |
| | v Greaves | 9-5 | Qualifying | Coral UK Open |
| | v Cripsey | 7-9 | Qualifying | Coral UK Open |
| **1985** | v Houlihan | 5-1 | Qualifying | Mercantile Credit Classic |
| | v Jack Rea | 5-4 | Qualifying | Mercantile Credit Classic |
| | v Martin | 5-2 | Qualifying | Mercantile Credit Classic |
| | v Thorne | 2-5 | 1st round | Mercantile Credit Classic |
| | v Duggan | 6-4 | Qualifying | Dulux British Open |
| | v Meo | 0-6 | 1st round | Dulux British Open |
| | v Oliver | 10-3 | Qualifying | Embassy World Championship |
| | v Edmonds | 3-10 | Qualifying | Embassy World Championship |
| | v Robinson | 7-2 | 2nd round | Australian Championship |
| | v Campbell | 5-8 | Quarter-final | Australian Championship |
| | v V. Harris | 5-4 | 2nd round | Goya Matchroom Trophy |
| | v Spencer | 4-5 | 3rd round | Goya Matchroom Trophy |
| | v Darrington | 3-5 | 2nd round | Rothmans Grand Prix |
| | v Darrington | 6-9 | 2nd round | Coral UK Open |
| **1986** | v Houlihan | 4-5 | 2nd round | Mercantile Credit Classic |
| | v Kearney | 5-2 | 2nd round | Dulux British Open |
| | v Werbeniuk | 4-5 | 3rd round | Dulux British Open |
| | v Rigitano | 10-6 | Qualifying | Embassy World Championship |
| | v Miles | 10-7 | Qualifying | Embassy World Championship |
| | v Parrott | 6-10 | Qualifying | Embassy World Championship |
| | v Jenkins | 6-3 | 2nd round | Australian Championship |
| | v Morgan | 6-2 | Quarter-final | Australian Championship |
| | v Campbell | 3-8 | Semi-final | Australian Championship |
| | v B. Harris | 5-0 | 2nd round | BCE International |
| | v Dennis Taylor | 1-5 | 3rd round | BCE International |
| | v W. Jones | 3-5 | 2nd round | Rothmans Grand Prix |
| | v Spencer | 6-9 | 2nd round | Tennents UK Open |
| **1987** | v Mikkelsen | 1-5 | 2nd round | Mercantile Credit Classic |
| | v Mikkelsen | 5-3 | 2nd round | Dulux British Open |
| | v Williams | 4-5 | 3rd round | Dulux British Open |
| | v Wildman | 5-10 | Qualifying | Embassy World Championship |
| | v King | 1-8 | Semi-final | Australian Championship |
| | v Meakin | 3-5 | 1st round | Fidelity International |
| | v Kearney | 5-1 | 2nd round | Fidelity International |
| | v Williams | 5-0 | 3rd round | Fidelity International |
| | v D. Gilbert | 4-5 | 4th round | Fidelity International |
| | v Dunning | 5-0 | 1st round | Rothmans Grand Prix |
| | v King | 5-4 | 2nd round | Rothmans Grand Prix |
| | v Werbeniuk | 1-5 | 3rd round | Rothmans Grand Prix |
| | v Clark | 9-8 | 1st round | Tennents UK Open |
| | v Newbury | 5-9 | 2nd round | Tennents UK Open |
| **1988** | v Greaves | 5-3 | 1st round | Mercantile Credit Classic |
| | v Edmonds | 4-5 | 2nd round | Mercantile Credit Classic |
| | v Heaton | 5-1 | 1st round | MIM Britannia British Open |
| | v G. Foulds | 5-3 | 2nd round | MIM Britannia British Open |
| | v Parrott | 1-5 | 3rd round | MIM Britannia British Open |
| | v Rempe | 10-4 | Qualifying | Embassy World Championship |
| | v T. Jones | 10-9 | Qualifying | Embassy World Championship |
| | v Wildman | 10-1 | Qualifying | Embassy World Championship |
| | v P. Francisco | 5-10 | Qualifying | Embassy World Championship |
| | v Potaszyk | 5-3 | Quarter-final | Australian Championship |
| | v King | 8-4 | Semi-final | Australian Championship |
| | v J. Campbell | 7-9 | Final | Australian Championship |

| | | | | |
|---|---|---|---|---|
| | v A. Harris | 5-1 | 1st round | Fidelity International |
| | v T. Jones | 4-5 | 2nd round | Fidelity International |
| | v Price | 5-1 | 1st round | Rothmans Grand Prix |
| | v Wright | 5-4 | 2nd round | Rothmans Grand Prix |
| | v Drago | 3-5 | 3rd round | Rothmans Grand Prix |
| | v Burke | 5-2 | 1st round | BCE Canadian Masters |
| | v Wych | 2-5 | 2nd round | BCE Canadian Masters |
| | v Burke | 9-0 | 1st round | Tennents UK Open |
| | v J. Campbell | 7-9 | 2nd round | Tennents UK Open |
| **1989** | v T. Wilson | 5-4 | 1st round | Mercantile Credit Classic |
| | v Martin | 2-5 | 2nd round | Mercantile Credit Classic |
| | v Rowing | 4-5 | 1st round | European Open |
| | v Sheehan | 5-1 | 1st round | Anglian British Open |
| | v Fisher | 5-0 | 2nd round | Anglian British Open |
| | v Higgins | 1-5 | 3rd round | Anglian British Open |
| | v J. Smith | 4-10 | Qualifying | Embassy World Championship |
| | v G. Foulds | 5-1 | 1st round | Hong Kong Open |
| | v O'Boye | 5-0 | 2nd round | Hong Kong Open |
| | v Clark | 4-5 | 3rd round | Hong Kong Open |
| | v Fitzmaurice | 2-5 | 1st round | 555 Asian Open |
| | v Cairns | 4-5 | 1st round | BCE International |
| | v S. Campbell | 4-5 | 1st round | Rothmans Grand Prix |
| | v D. Campbell | 2-5 | 1st round | Dubai Classic |
| | v S. Campbell | 5-6 | 1st round | Stormseal UK Open |
| **1990** | v Wych | 2-5 | 2nd round | Mercantile Credit Classic |
| | v S. Murphy | 3-5 | 1st round | Pearl Assurance British Open |
| | v D. Hughes | 7-1 | 1st round | European Open |
| | v Macleod | 5-4 | 2nd round | European Open |
| | v Hendry | 1-5 | 3rd round | European Open |
| | v Rowing | 9-10 | Qualifying | Embassy World Championship |

## GEOFF FOULDS (England)

**Born** 20.11.39. **Turned professional** 1981. **World ranking** 129 (118).

| | | | | |
|---|---|---|---|---|
| **1981** | v French | 2-5 | Qualifying | Jameson International |
| | v Kelly | 9-7 | Qualifying | Coral UK Championship |
| | v Knowles | 1-9 | Qualifying | Coral UK Championship |
| **1982** | v Wildman | 8-9 | Qualifying | Embassy World Championship |
| | v Kelly | 4-5 | Qualifying | Jameson International |
| | v Spencer | 1-5 | 1st round | Professional Players Tournament |
| | v Gibson | 9-3 | Qualifying | Coral UK Championship |
| | v Williams | 7-9 | Qualifying | Coral UK Championship |
| **1983** | v Gibson | 10-6 | Qualifying | Embassy World Championship |
| | v Meo | 4-10 | Qualifying | Embassy World Championship |
| | v Burke | 5-2 | Qualifying | Jameson International |
| | v E. Hughes | 1-5 | Qualifying | Jameson International |
| | v Burke | 4-5 | Qualifying | Professional Players Tournament |
| | v Duggan | 9-8 | Qualifying | Coral UK Championship |
| | v Dodd | 9-7 | Qualifying | Coral UK Championship |
| | v S. Davis | 1-9 | 1st round | Coral UK Championship |
| **1984** | v Morra | 2-10 | Qualifying | Embassy World Championship |
| | v P. Francisco | 5-4 | Qualifying | Jameson International |
| | v Williamson | 5-4 | Qualifying | Jameson International |
| | v Donnelly | 5-3 | Qualifying | Jameson International |
| | v Campbell | 3-5 | Qualifying | Jameson International |
| | v Murphy | 1-5 | Qualifying | Rothmans Grand Prix |
| | v D. Hughes | 9-7 | Qualifying | Coral UK Open |
| | v Browne | 5-9 | Qualifying | Coral UK Open |
| **1985** | v Chaperon | 5-3 | Qualifying | Mercantile Credit Classic |
| | v Jonik | 5-2 | Qualifying | Mercantile Credit Classic |
| | v Fitzmaurice | 5-1 | Qualifying | Mercantile Credit Classic |

| | | | | |
|---|---|---|---|---|
| | v Hallett | 4-5 | Qualifying | Mercantile Credit Classic |
| | v F. Davis | 9-2 | Qualifying | Tolly Cobbold English Championship |
| | v Parrott | 4-9 | 1st round | Tolly Cobbold English Championship |
| | v T. Jones | 0-6 | Qualifying | Dulux British Open |
| | v Parkin | 10-6 | Qualifying | Embassy World Championship |
| | v Everton | 10-2 | Qualifying | Embassy World Championship |
| | v Roscoe | 10-7 | Qualifying | Embassy World Championship |
| | v Johnson | 6-10 | Qualifying | Embassy World Championship |
| | v Roscoe | 3-5 | 2nd round | Goya Matchroom Trophy |
| | v Black | 5-3 | 2nd round | Rothmans Grand Prix |
| | v Charlton | 1-5 | 3rd round | Rothmans Grand Prix |
| | v Sinclair | 4-9 | 2nd round | Coral UK Open |
| **1986** | v Black | 5-2 | 2nd round | Mercantile Credit Classic |
| | v Werbeniuk | 3-5 | 3rd round | Mercantile Credit Classic |
| | v Watterson | 9-1 | 2nd round | Tolly Cobbold English Championship |
| | v N. Foulds | 4-9 | 3rd round | Tolly Cobbold English Championship |
| | v P. Francisco | 2-5 | 2nd round | Dulux British Open |
| | v Roscoe | 3-10 | Qualifying | Embassy World Championship |
| | v V. Harris | 5-4 | 2nd round | BCE International |
| | v Werbeniuk | 5-2 | 3rd round | BCE International |
| | v N. Foulds | 0-5 | 4th round | BCE International |
| | v Wilkinson | 5-3 | 1st round | Rothmans Grand Prix |
| | v Mikkelsen | 5-1 | 2nd round | Rothmans Grand Prix |
| | v Campbell | 0-5 | 3rd round | Rothmans Grand Prix |
| | v Roe | 1-7 *retd* | 1st round | Tennents UK Open |
| **1987** | v Chalmers | 5-4 | 1st round | Mercantile Credit Classic |
| | v O'Kane | 5-4 | 2nd round | Mercantile Credit Classic |
| | v Martin | 4-5 | 3rd round | Mercantile Credit Classic |
| | v B. Harris | 1-6 | 2nd round | Tolly Ales English Championship |
| | v Edmonds | 5-3 | 2nd round | Dulux British Open |
| | v Wilson | 3-5 | 3rd round | Dulux British Open |
| | v Watchorn | 10-6 | Qualifying | Embassy World Championship |
| | v Fowler | 6-10 | Qualifying | Embassy World Championship |
| | v Jack Rea | 1-5 | 2nd round | Fidelity International |
| | v James | 0-5 | 2nd round | Rothmans Grand Prix |
| | v N. Gilbert | 4-9 | 2nd round | Tennents UK Open |
| **1988** | v Whitthread | 3-5 | 2nd round | Mercantile Credit Classic |
| | v Clark | 0-6 | 2nd round | English Championship |
| | v Foldvari | 3-5 | 2nd round | MIM Britannia British Open |
| | v Bear | 2-10 | Qualifying | Embassy World Championship |
| | v Ellis | 5-2 | 1st round | Fidelity International |
| | v Miles | 3-5 | 2nd round | Fidelity International |
| | v J. Smith | 3-5 | 1st round | Rothmans Grand Prix |
| | v J. Smith | 1-5 | 1st round | BCE Canadian Masters |
| | v Rowing | 4-9 | 1st round | Tennents UK Open |
| **1989** | v Everton | 5-0 | 1st round | Mercantile Credit Classic |
| | v Wright | 4-5 | 2nd round | Mercantile Credit Classic |
| | v Jack Rea | 5-4 | 1st round | European Open |
| | v Wych | 0-5 | 2nd round | European Open |
| | v Oliver | 1-5 | 1st round | English Championship |
| | v J. Smith | 3-5 | 1st round | Anglian British Open |
| | v Fagan | 6-10 | Qualifying | Embassy World Championship |
| | v Foldvari | 1-5 | 1st round | Hong Kong Open |
| | v S. Campbell | 4-5 | 1st round | 555 Asian Open |
| | v Bradley | 1-5 | 1st round | BCE International |
| | v Owers | 5-1 | 1st round | Rothmans Grand Prix |
| | v Chambers | 2-5 | 2nd round | Rothmans Grand Prix |
| | v Rowing | 5-4 | 1st round | Dubai Classic |
| | v Macleod | 1-5 | 2nd round | Dubai Classic |
| | v Wright | 1-6 | 1st round | Stormseal UK Open |
| **1990** | v Wright | 4-5 | 1st round | Mercantile Credit Classic |
| | v Williamson | 0-5 | 1st round | Pearl Assurance British Open |

| | | | | |
|---|---|---|---|---|
| | v Owers | 1-5 | 1st round | European Open |
| | v Jenkins | 5-10 | Qualifying | Embassy World Championship |

## NEAL FOULDS (England)

**Born** 13.7.63. **Turned professional** 1983. **World ranking** 13 (20).

| | | | | |
|---|---|---|---|---|
| **1983** | v French | 2-5 | Qualifying | Professional Players Tournament |
| | v Roscoe | 9-2 | Qualifying | Coral UK Championship |
| | v Meadowcroft | 9-2 | Qualifying | Coral UK Championship |
| | v David Taylor | 4-9 | 1st round | Coral UK Championship |
| **1984** | v French | 10-5 | Qualifying | Embassy World Championship |
| | v Dodd | 10-4 | Qualifying | Embassy World Championship |
| | v Meadowcroft | 10-2 | Qualifying | Embassy World Championship |
| | v Higgins | 10-9 | 1st round | Embassy World Championship |
| | v Mountjoy | 6-13 | 2nd round | Embassy World Championship |
| | v Bennett | 5-0 | Qualifying | Jameson International |
| | v Griffiths | 3-5 | 1st round | Jameson International |
| | v Demarco | 5-2 | 1st round | Rothmans Grand Prix |
| | v T. Jones | 5-0 | 2nd round | Rothmans Grand Prix |
| | v Thorne | 5-1 | 3rd round | Rothmans Grand Prix |
| | v Knowles | 5-2 | Quarter-final | Rothmans Grand Prix |
| | v Dennis Taylor | 3-9 | Semi-final | Rothmans Grand Prix |
| | v Fowler | 6-9 | Qualifying | Coral UK Open |
| **1985** | v Longworth | 3-5 | Qualifying | Mercantile Credit Classic |
| | v D. Hughes | 9-3 | 1st round | Tolly Cobbold English Championship |
| | v White | 7-9 | 2nd round | Tolly Cobbold English Championship |
| | v Hargreaves | 6-1 | 1st round | Dulux British Open |
| | v Higgins | 1-5 | 2nd round | Dulux British Open |
| | v Rigitano | 10-8 | Qualifying | Embassy World Championship |
| | v S. Davis | 8-10 | 1st round | Embassy World Championship |
| | v Dodd | 5-3 | 3rd round | Goya Matchroom Trophy |
| | v Knowles | 5-3 | 4th round | Goya Matchroom Trophy |
| | v David Taylor | 5-4 | 5th round | Goya Matchroom Trophy |
| | v Johnson | 5-2 | Quarter-final | Goya Matchroom Trophy |
| | v White | 5-9 | Semi-final | Goya Matchroom Trophy |
| | v Darrington | 5-0 | 3rd round | Rothmans Grand Prix |
| | v Higgins | 3-5 | 4th round | Rothmans Grand Prix |
| | v Fagan | 9-5 | 3rd round | Coral UK Open |
| | v Johnson | 9-8 | 4th round | Coral UK Open |
| | v Dennis Taylor | 5-9 | 5th round | Coral UK Open |
| **1986** | v Bradley | 5-3 | 3rd round | Mercantile Credit Classic |
| | v Hendry | 5-4 | 4th round | Mercantile Credit Classic |
| | v Campbell | 5-1 | 5th round | Mercantile Credit Classic |
| | v Mountjoy | 3-5 | Quarter-final | Mercantile Credit Classic |
| | v G. Foulds | 9-4 | 3rd round | Tolly Cobbold English Championship |
| | v Edmonds | 9-4 | 4th round | Tolly Cobbold English Championship |
| | v White | 9-4 | Quarter-final | Tolly Cobbold English Championship |
| | v Hallett | 9-8 | Semi-final | Tolly Cobbold English Championship |
| | v Meo | 7-9 | Final | Tolly Cobbold English Championship |
| | v Hargreaves | 5-4 | 3rd round | Dulux British Open |
| | v Griffiths | 3-5 | 4th round | Dulux British Open |
| | v P. Francisco | 10-9 | Qualifying | Embassy World Championship |
| | v Knowles | 9-10 | 1st round | Embassy World Championship |
| | v Thorne | 3-6 | 1st round | Matchroom Trophy |
| | v Miles | 5-2 | 3rd round | BCE International |
| | v G. Foulds | 5-0 | 4th round | BCE International |
| | v Owers | 5-1 | 5th round | BCE International |
| | v Reynolds | 5-2 | Quarter-final | BCE International |
| | v E. Hughes | 9-8 | Semi-final | BCE International |
| | **v Thorburn** | **12-9** | **Final** | **BCE International** |
| | v Miles | 5-1 | 3rd round | Rothmans Grand Prix |

*Neal Foulds*

| | | | | |
|---|---|---|---|---|
| | v Wilson | 5-0 | 4th round | Rothmans Grand Prix |
| | v Thorne | 5-3 | 5th round | Rothmans Grand Prix |
| | v Meo | 5-3 | Quarter-final | Rothmans Grand Prix |
| | v Williams | 8-9 | Semi-final | Rothmans Grand Prix |
| | v Cripsey | 9-7 | 3rd round | Tennents UK Open |
| | v Wych | 9-3 | 4th round | Tennents UK Open |
| | v White | 9-7 | 5th round | Tennents UK Open |
| | v Thorburn | 9-2 | Quarter-final | Tennents UK Open |
| | v Parrott | 9-2 | Semi-final | Tennents UK Open |
| | v S. Davis | 7-16 | Final | Tennents UK Open |
| **1987** | v Duggan | 3-5 | 3rd round | Mercantile Credit Classic |
| | v Dennis Taylor | 2-5 | 1st round | Benson & Hedges Masters |
| | v Owers | 3-6 | 3rd round | Tolly Ales English Championship |
| | v Roe | 5-1 | 3rd round | Dulux British Open |
| | v King | 5-4 | 4th round | Dulux British Open |
| | v Thorne | 5-2 | 5th round | Dulux British Open |
| | v Virgo | 5-3 | Quarter-final | Dulux British Open |
| | v Knowles | 9-2 | Semi-final | Dulux British Open |
| | v White | 9-13 | Final | Dulux British Open |
| | v Virgo | 10-4 | 1st round | Embassy World Championship |
| | v Dennis Taylor | 13-10 | 2nd round | Embassy World Championship |
| | v Hallett | 13-9 | Quarter-final | Embassy World Championship |
| | v Johnson | 9-16 | Semi-final | Embassy World Championship |
| | v Johnson | 4-5 | 1st round | Carling Champions |
| | v Griffiths | 4-5 | 1st round | Langs Scottish Masters |
| | v P. Gibson | 5-2 | 3rd round | Fidelity International |
| | v Hendry | 2-5 | 4th round | Fidelity International |
| | v Clark | 4-5 | 3rd round | Rothmans Grand Prix |
| | v Griffiths | 5-4 | 1st round | Labatts Canadian Masters (WS) |
| | v White | 7-8 | Semi-final | Labatts Canadian Masters (WS) |
| | v Griffiths | 6-2 | 1st round | Matchroom Trophy |
| | v Thorne | 5-6 | Semi-final | Matchroom Trophy |
| | v Fowler | 5-9 | 3rd round | Tennents UK Open |
| **1988** | v Chaperon | 5-1 | 3rd round | Mercantile Credit Classic |
| | v Virgo | 3-5 | 4th round | Mercantile Credit Classic |
| | v Parrott | 4-5 | 1st round | Benson & Hedges Masters |
| | v Gary Wilkinson | 6-3 | 3rd round | English Championship |
| | v Fowler | 6-1 | 4th round | English Championship |
| | v Thorne | 6-2 | Quarter-final | English Championship |
| | v West | 9-6 | Semi-final | English Championship |
| | v Reynolds | 5-9 | Final | English Championship |
| | v Fowler | 5-3 | 3rd round | MIM Britannia British Open |
| | v P. Francisco | 5-3 | 4th round | MIM Britannia British Open |
| | v Parrott | 0-5 | 5th round | MIM Britannia British Open |
| | v Knowles | 5-3 | Quarter-final | Benson & Hedges Irish Masters |
| | v Griffiths | 6-4 | Semi-final | Benson & Hedges Irish Masters |
| | v S. Davis | 4-9 | Final | Benson & Hedges Irish Masters |
| | v W. Jones | 10-7 | 1st round | Embassy World Championship |
| | v Mountjoy | 13-1 | 2nd round | Embassy World Championship |
| | v Griffiths | 9-13 | Quarter-final | Embassy World Championship |
| | v Thorne | 5-4 | Semi-final | LEP Hong Kong Masters |
| | v White | 3-6 | Final | LEP Hong Kong Masters |
| | v Murphy | 5-3 | 3rd round | Fidelity International |
| | v Reynolds | 3-5 | 4th round | Fidelity International |
| | v Meo | 5-4 | Semi-final | Dubai Duty Free Masters |
| | **v S. Davis** | **5-4** | **Final** | **Dubai Duty Free Masters** |
| | v Griffiths | 6-4 | 1st round | LEP Matchroom Championship |
| | v Dennis Taylor | 3-6 | Semi-final | LEP Matchroom Championship |
| | v Terry | 5-4 | 3rd round | Rothmans Grand Prix |
| | v Duggan | 5-4 | 4th round | Rothmans Grand Prix |
| | v Higgins | 3-5 | 5th round | Rothmans Grand Prix |
| | v King | 3-5 | 3rd round | BCE Canadian Masters |
| | v Rowing | 9-4 | 3rd round | Tennents UK Open |

| | | | | |
|---|---|---|---|---|
| | v Mountjoy | 4-9 | 4th round | Tennents UK Open |
| **1989** | v Martin | 5-1 | 3rd round | Mercantile Credit Classic |
| | v Clark | 4-5 | 4th round | Mercantile Credit Classic |
| | v P. Francisco | 5-2 | 1st round | Benson and Hedges Masters |
| | v Thorburn | 5-2 | Quarter-final | Benson and Hedges Masters |
| | v Parrott | 5-6 | Semi-final | Benson and Hedges Masters |
| | v Clark | 3-5 | 3rd round | European Open |
| | v Medati | 5-3 | 3rd round | English Championship |
| | v Cripsey | 5-1 | 4th round | English Championship |
| | v Thorne | 3-5 | Quarter-final | English Championship |
| | v Reardon | 5-1 | 3rd round | Anglian British Open |
| | v Robidoux | 5-1 | 4th round | Anglian British Open |
| | v Clark | 4-5 | 5th round | Anglian British Open |
| | v Higgins | 2-5 | Quarter-final | Benson and Hedges Irish Masters |
| | v W. Jones | 9-10 | 1st round | Embassy World Championship |
| | v Bond | 5-2 | 3rd round | Hong Kong Open |
| | v Chambers | 5-0 | 4th round | Hong Kong Open |
| | v Thorne | 5-1 | 5th round | Hong Kong Open |
| | v White | 2-5 | Quarter-final | Hong Kong Open |
| | v Wych | 5-2 | 3rd round | 555 Asian Open |
| | v Knowles | 3-5 | 4th round | 555 Asian Open |
| | v O'Boye | 5-0 | 3rd round | BCE International |
| | v M. Bennett | 5-2 | 4th round | BCE International |
| | v S. Davis | 3-5 | 5th round | BCE International |
| | v N. Gilbert | 5-1 | 3rd round | Rothmans Grand Prix |
| | v S. Davis | 4-5 | 4th round | Rothmans Grand Prix |
| | v Meakin | 9-1 | 3rd round | Stormseal UK Open |
| | v White | 5-9 | 4th round | Stormseal UK Open |
| **1990** | v D. Morgan | 4-5 | 3rd round | Mercantile Credit Classic |
| | v Graham | 5-2 | 3rd round | Pearl Assurance British Open |
| | v Drago | 5-0 | 4th round | Pearl Assurance British Open |
| | v P. Francisco | 5-3 | 5th round | Pearl Assurance British Open |
| | v Chaperon | 3-5 | Quarter-final | Pearl Assurance British Open |
| | v Johnston-Allen | 5-3 | 3rd round | European Open |
| | v Thorne | 5-3 | 4th round | European Open |
| | v M. Bennett | 5-2 | 5th round | European Open |
| | v Hendry | 3-5 | Quarter-final | European Open |
| | v S. Campbell | 10-7 | Qualifying | Embassy World Championship |
| | v Dennis Taylor | 10-8 | 1st round | Embassy World Championship |
| | v Thorne | 13-11 | 2nd round | Embassy World Championship |
| | v S. Davis | 8-13 | Quarter-final | Embassy World Championship |

## DANNY FOWLER (England)

**Born** 30.7.56. **Turned professional** 1984. **World ranking** 30 (36).

| | | | | |
|---|---|---|---|---|
| **1984** | v Chaperon | 5-0 | Qualifying | Jameson International |
| | v Andrewartha | 5-0 | Qualifying | Jameson International |
| | v Martin | 5-0 | Qualifying | Jameson International |
| | v Dennis Taylor | 0-5 | 1st round | Jameson International |
| | v Reynolds | 2-5 | 1st round | Rothmans Grand Prix |
| | v Demarco | 9-3 | Qualifying | Coral UK Open |
| | v Oliver | 9-3 | Qualifying | Coral UK Open |
| | v F. Davis | 9-4 | Qualifying | Coral UK Open |
| | v N. Foulds | 9-6 | Qualifying | Coral UK Open |
| | v Reardon | 2-9 | 1st round | Coral UK Open |
| **1985** | v Rigitano | 5-0 | Qualifying | Mercantile Credit Classic |
| | v Murphy | 5-0 | Qualifying | Mercantile Credit Classic |
| | v Meadowcroft | 5-2 | Qualifying | Mercantile Credit Classic |
| | v Wilson | 4-5 | Qualifying | Mercantile Credit Classic |
| | v Oliver | 9-7 | Qualifying | Tolly Cobbold English Championship |
| | v S. Davis | 3-9 | 1st round | Tolly Cobbold English Championship |

| Year | Opponent | Score | Round | Event |
|---|---|---|---|---|
| | v Everton | 6-1 | Qualifying | Dulux British Open |
| | v Williams | 6-4 | 1st round | Dulux British Open |
| | v Bradley | 4-5 | 2nd round | Dulux British Open |
| | v Hargreaves | 10-0 | Qualifying | Embassy World Championship |
| | v Donnelly | 10-0 | Qualifying | Embassy World Championship |
| | v Parrott | 2-10 | Qualifying | Embassy World Championship |
| | v Agrawal | 5-2 | 2nd round | Goya Matchroom Trophy |
| | v Thorne | 1-5 | 3rd round | Goya Matchroom Trophy |
| | v Jonik | 5-4 | 2nd round | Rothmans Grand Prix |
| | v Werbeniuk | 5-1 | 3rd round | Rothmans Grand Prix |
| | v S. Davis | 1-5 | 4th round | Rothmans Grand Prix |
| | v Wilkinson | 9-6 | 2nd round | Coral UK Open |
| | v Mans | 9-2 | 3rd round | Coral UK Open |
| | v Meo | 2-9 | 4th round | Coral UK Open |
| **1986** | v Bales | 5-4 | 2nd round | Mercantile Credit Classic |
| | v White | 1-5 | 3rd round | Mercantile Credit Classic |
| | v Darrington | 9-3 | 2nd round | Tolly Cobbold English Championship |
| | v Johnson | 7-9 | 3rd round | Tolly Cobbold English Championship |
| | v Chappel | 5-4 | 2nd round | Dulux British Open |
| | v Virgo | 1-5 | 3rd round | Dulux British Open |
| | v Oliver | 10-8 | Qualifying | Embassy World Championship |
| | v Scott | 10-7 | Qualifying | Embassy World Championship |
| | v Macleod | 10-6 | Qualifying | Embassy World Championship |
| | v Griffiths | 2-10 | 1st round | Embassy World Championship |
| | v J. McLaughlin | 2-5 | 2nd round | BCE International |
| | v Bear | 2-5 | 2nd round | Rothmans Grand Prix |
| | v Darrington | 9-6 | 2nd round | Tennents UK Open |
| | v Thorburn | 7-9 | 3rd round | Tennents UK Open |
| **1987** | v Wilkinson | 5-1 | 2nd round | Mercantile Credit Classic |
| | v Knowles | 5-4 | 3rd round | Mercantile Credit Classic |
| | v Hallett | 5-4 | 4th round | Mercantile Credit Classic |
| | v Hendry | 4-5 | 5th round | Mercantile Credit Classic |
| | v Bradley | 6-3 | 3rd round | Tolly Ales English Championship |
| | v Meo | 0-6 | 4th round | Tolly Ales English Championship |
| | v Dodd | 5-1 | 2nd round | Dulux British Open |
| | v Knowles | 4-5 | 3rd round | Dulux British Open |
| | v G. Foulds | 10-6 | Qualifying | Embassy World Championship |
| | v B. Harris | 10-6 | Qualifying | Embassy World Championship |
| | v Parrott | 3-10 | Qualifying | Embassy World Championship |
| | v Watchorn | 5-1 | 2nd round | Fidelity International |
| | v Knowles | 4-5 | 3rd round | Fidelity International |
| | v D. Gilbert | 5-1 | 2nd round | Rothmans Grand Prix |
| | v S. Francisco | 1-5 | 3rd round | Rothmans Grand Prix |
| | v Kearney | 9-7 | 2nd round | Tennents UK Open |
| | v N. Foulds | 9-5 | 3rd round | Tennents UK Open |
| | v Miles | 9-4 | 4th round | Tennents UK Open |
| | v Hallett | 4-9 | 5th round | Tennents UK Open |
| **1988** | v Rigitano | 2-5 | 2nd round | Mercantile Credit Classic |
| | v Medati | 6-1 | 2nd round | English Championship |
| | v Spencer | 6-3 | 3rd round | English Championship |
| | v Foulds | 1-6 | 4th round | English Championship |
| | v Kearney | 5-1 | 2nd round | MIM Britannia British Open |
| | v N. Foulds | 3-5 | 3rd round | MIM Britannia British Open |
| | v Black | 10-1 | Qualifying | Embassy World Championship |
| | v Dodd | 10-8 | Qualifying | Embassy World Championship |
| | v Macleod | 10-3 | Qualifying | Embassy World Championship |
| | v Knowles | 8-10 | 1st round | Embassy World Championship |
| | v Grace | 5-3 | 2nd round | Fidelity International |
| | v Drago | 3-5 | 3rd round | Fidelity International |
| | v Kelly | 5-4 | 2nd round | Rothmans Grand Prix |
| | v White | 0-5 | 3rd round | Rothmans Grand Prix |
| | v Rowswell | 5-4 | 2nd round | BCE Canadian Masters |
| | v Drago | 5-1 | 3rd round | BCE Canadian Masters |

| | | | | |
|---|---|---|---|---|
| | v Hendry | 2-5 | 4th round | BCE Canadian Masters |
| | v Ellis | 9-3 | 2nd round | Tennents UK Open |
| | v Longworth | 9-8 | 3rd round | Tennents UK Open |
| | v Clark | 9-6 | 4th round | Tennents UK Open |
| | v S. Davis | 6-9 | 5th round | Tennents UK Open |
| **1989** | v Dennis Taylor | 3-5 | 3rd round | Mercantile Credit Classic |
| | v A. Harris | 5-1 | 2nd round | European Open |
| | v Knowles | 5-2 | 3rd round | European Open |
| | v T. Wilson | 5-2 | 4th round | European Open |
| | v Wych | 4-5 | 5th round | European Open |
| | v S. Campbell | 5-1 | 2nd round | English Championship |
| | v Meo | 5-3 | 3rd round | English Championship |
| | v Parrott | 4-5 | 4th round | English Championship |
| | v Van Rensberg | 5-1 | 2nd round | Anglian British Open |
| | v Virgo | 2-5 | 3rd round | Anglian British Open |
| | v Whitthread | 10-6 | Qualifying | Embassy World Championship |
| | v O'Boye | 6-10 | Qualifying | Embassy World Championship |
| | v V. Harris | 5-0 | 2nd round | Hong Kong Open |
| | v Hallett | 2-5 | 3rd round | Hong Kong Open |
| | v Rowswell | 5-3 | 2nd round | 555 Asian Open |
| | v Johnson | 4-5 | 3rd round | 555 Asian Open |
| | v B. Morgan | 4-5 | 2nd round | BCE International |
| | v Rigitano | 5-4 | 2nd round | Rothmans Grand Prix |
| | v Roe | 5-4 | 3rd round | Rothmans Grand Prix |
| | v Hallett | 5-3 | 4th round | Rothmans Grand Prix |
| | v Robidoux | 5-4 | 5th round | Rothmans Grand Prix |
| | v Johnson | 5-4 | Quarter-final | Rothmans Grand Prix |
| | v S. Davis | 2-9 | Semi-final | Rothmans Grand Prix |
| | v Browne | 5-4 | 3rd round | Dubai Classic |
| | v T. Jones | 5-4 | 4th round | Dubai Classic |
| | v Clark | 5-2 | 5th round | Dubai Classic |
| | v J. McLaughlin | 5-1 | Quarter-final | Dubai Classic |
| | v Hendry | 4-5 | Semi-final | Dubai Classic |
| | v T. Wilson | 6-3 | 2nd round | Stormseal UK Open |
| | v W. Jones | 7-9 | 3rd round | Stormseal UK Open |
| **1990** | v Marshall | 5-2 | 2nd round | Mercantile Credit Classic |
| | v O'Kane | 4-5 | 3rd round | Mercantile Credit Classic |
| | v Gary Wilkinson | 5-1 | 2nd round | Pearl Assurance British Open |
| | v Dennis Taylor | 1-5 | 3rd round | Pearl Assurance British Open |
| | v B. Harris | 5-3 | 2nd round | European Open |
| | v West | 5-2 | 3rd round | European Open |
| | v Johnson | 1-5 | 4th round | European Open |
| | v Rigitano | 10-6 | Qualifying | Embassy World Championship |
| | v D. Gilbert | 10-3 | Qualifying | Embassy World Championship |
| | v West | 10-9 | Qualifying | Embassy World Championship |
| | v White | 4-10 | 1st round | Embassy World Championship |

## **PETER FRANCISCO** (South Africa)

**Born** 14.2.62. **Turned professional** 1984. **World ranking** 25 (25).

| | | | | |
|---|---|---|---|---|
| **1984** | v G. Foulds | 4-5 | Qualifying | Jameson International |
| | v Black | 5-4 | Qualifying | Rothmans Grand Prix |
| | v Spencer | 5-2 | 1st round | Rothmans Grand Prix |
| | v Reynolds | 4-5 | 2nd round | Rothmans Grand Prix |
| | v Sheehan | 9-5 | Qualifying | Coral UK Open |
| | v Williamson | 9-2 | Qualifying | Coral UK Open |
| | v Sinclair | 8-9 | Qualifying | Coral UK Open |
| **1985** | v Longworth | 4-5 | Qualifying | Mercantile Credit Classic |
| | v Kelly | 6-3 | Qualifying | Dulux British Open |
| | v Virgo | 2-6 | 1st round | Dulux British Open |
| | v Demarco | 10-4 | Qualifying | Embassy World Championship |

| | | | | |
|---|---|---|---|---|
| | v Murphy | 10-4 | Qualifying | Embassy World Championship |
| | v Meadowcroft | 10-5 | Qualifying | Embassy World Championship |
| | v Macleod | 7-10 | Qualifying | Embassy World Championship |
| | v Gibson | 4-5 | 2nd round | Goya Matchroom Trophy |
| | v Everton | 5-0 | 2nd round | Rothmans Grand Prix |
| | v Virgo | 5-4 | 3rd round | Rothmans Grand Prix |
| | v W. Jones | 5-3 | 4th round | Rothmans Grand Prix |
| | v Griffiths | 2-5 | 5th round | Rothmans Grand Prix |
| | v Charlton | 9-5 | 3rd round | Coral UK Open |
| | v Williams | 7-9 | 4th round | Coral UK Open |
| **1986** | v Jonik | 5-2 | 2nd round | Mercantile Credit Classic |
| | v Charlton | 5-1 | 3rd round | Mercantile Credit Classic |
| | v Martin | 5-2 | 4th round | Mercantile Credit Classic |
| | v S. Davis | 0-5 | 5th round | Mercantile Credit Classic |
| | v G. Foulds | 5-2 | 2nd round | Dulux British Open |
| | v White | 5-4 | 3rd round | Dulux British Open |
| | v Longworth | 5-2 | 4th round | Dulux British Open |
| | v Higgins | 2-5 | 5th round | Dulux British Open |
| | v Drago | 10-4 | Qualifying | Embassy World Championship |
| | v F. Davis | 10-1 | Qualifying | Embassy World Championship |
| | v N. Foulds | 9-10 | Qualifying | Embassy World Championship |
| | v Grace | 7-1 | 2nd round | South African Championship |
| | v S. Francisco | 3-8 | Semi-final | South African Championship |
| | v Wildman | 5-2 | 3rd round | BCE International |
| | v Higgins | 5-4 | 4th round | BCE International |
| | v Gauvreau | 5-2 | 5th round | BCE International |
| | v S. Francisco | 5-3 | Quarter-final | BCE International |
| | v Thorburn | 7-9 | Semi-final | BCE International |
| | v Medati | 5-1 | 3rd round | Rothmans Grand Prix |
| | v Knowles | 3-5 | 4th round | Rothmans Grand Prix |
| | v Watterson | 9-4 | 3rd round | Tennents UK Open |
| | v White | 5-9 | 4th round | Tennents UK Open |
| **1987** | v Gauvreau | 5-3 | 3rd round | Mercantile Credit Classic |
| | v Johnson | 5-3 | 4th round | Mercantile Credit Classic |
| | v S. Francisco | 1-5 | 5th round | Mercantile Credit Classic |
| | v Sinclair | 5-3 | 3rd round | Dulux British Open |
| | v Mountjoy | 3-5 | 4th round | Dulux British Open |
| | v O'Kane | 5-10 | Qualifying | Embassy World Championship |
| | v Newbury | 2-5 | 3rd round | Fidelity International |
| | v John Rea | 5-3 | 3rd round | Rothmans Grand Prix |
| | v Johnson | 5-2 | 4th round | Rothmans Grand Prix |
| | v Cripsey | 5-1 | 5th round | Rothmans Grand Prix |
| | v Thorne | 5-3 | Quarter-final | Rothmans Grand Prix |
| | v Dennis Taylor | 4-9 | Semi-final | Rothmans Grand Prix |
| | v Lawlor | 9-4 | 3rd round | Tennents UK Open |
| | v S. Davis | 6-9 | 4th round | Tennents UK Open |
| **1988** | v Cripsey | 5-2 | 3rd round | Mercantile Credit Classic |
| | v Owers | 5-0 | 4th round | Mercantile Credit Classic |
| | v Dennis Taylor | 3-5 | 5th round | Mercantile Credit Classic |
| | v Darrington | 5-1 | 3rd round | MIM Britannia British Open |
| | v N. Foulds | 3-5 | 4th round | MIM Britannia British Open |
| | v Foldvari | 10-5 | Qualifying | Embassy World Championship |
| | v Thorne | 6-10 | 1st round | Embassy World Championship |
| | v John Rea | 0-5 | 3rd round | Fidelity International |
| | v J. McLaughlin | 2-5 | 3rd round | Rothmans Grand Prix |
| | v Graham | 3-5 | 3rd round | BCE Canadian Masters |
| | v John Rea | 9-2 | 3rd round | Tennents UK Open |
| | v Roe | 7-9 | 4th round | Tennents UK Open |
| | v Griffiths | 7-9 | 1st round | Everest World Matchplay |
| **1989** | v Terry | 4-5 | 3rd round | Mercantile Credit Classic |
| | v N. Foulds | 2-5 | 1st round | Benson and Hedges Masters |
| | v J. Campbell | 0-5 | 3rd round | European Open |
| | v J. Campbell | 5-2 | 3rd round | Anglian British Open |

| | | | | |
|---|---|---|---|---|
| | v Roe | 5-3 | 4th round | Anglian British Open |
| | v West | 5-1 | 5th round | Anglian British Open |
| | v Meo | 3-5 | Quarter-final | Anglian British Open |
| | v Reynolds | 7-10 | 1st round | Embassy World Championship |
| | v Robidoux | 3-5 | 3rd round | Hong Kong Open |
| | v Cripsey | 5-1 | 3rd round | 555 Asian Open |
| | v Roscoe | 5-4 | 4th round | 555 Asian Open |
| | v Gary Wilkinson | 4-5 | 5th round | 555 Asian Open |
| | v Wattana | 0-5 | 3rd round | BCE International |
| | v J. Smith | 3-5 | 3rd round | Rothmans Grand Prix |
| | v Fisher | 5-0 | 3rd round | Dubai Classic |
| | v Medati | 5-1 | 4th round | Dubai Classic |
| | v Bond | 5-4 | 5th round | Dubai Classic |
| | v Parrott | 1-5 | Quarter-final | Dubai Classic |
| | v S. Campbell | 9-5 | 3rd round | Stormseal UK Open |
| | v Thorburn | 9-5 | 4th round | Stormseal UK Open |
| | v M. Bennett | 3-9 | 5th round | Stormseal UK Open |
| **1990** | v Macleod | 5-2 | 3rd round | Mercantile Credit Classic |
| | v Duggan | 5-2 | 4th round | Mercantile Credit Classic |
| | v Newbury | 3-5 | 5th round | Mercantile Credit Classic |
| | v David Taylor | 5-4 | 3rd round | Pearl Assurance British Open |
| | v Griffiths | 5-1 | 4th round | Pearl Assurance British Open |
| | v N. Foulds | 3-5 | 5th round | Pearl Assurance British Open |
| | v Roscoe | 3-5 | 3rd round | European Open |
| | v Johnston-Allen | 10-7 | Qualifying | Embassy World Championship |
| | v Reynolds | 7-10 | 1st round | Embassy World Championship |

## **SILVINO FRANCISCO** (South Africa)

**Born** 3.5.46. **Turned professional** 1978. **World ranking** 27 (23).

| | | | | |
|---|---|---|---|---|
| **1982** | v Ross | 9-0 | Qualifying | Embassy World Championship |
| | v Morgan | 9-1 | Qualifying | Embassy World Championship |
| | v Dennis Taylor | 10-7 | 1st round | Embassy World Championship |
| | v Reynolds | 13-8 | 2nd round | Embassy World Championship |
| | v Reardon | 8-13 | Quarter-final | Embassy World Championship |
| **1983** | v Kelly | 10-5 | Qualifying | Embassy World Championship |
| | v Dennis Taylor | 9-10 | 1st round | Embassy World Championship |
| | v Darrington | 5-2 | Qualifying | Jameson International |
| | v Donnelly | 5-1 | 2nd round | Jameson International |
| | v S. Davis | 1-5 | Quarter-final | Jameson International |
| | v Morra | 5-3 | 1st round | Professional Players Tournament |
| | v Scott | 5-1 | 2nd round | Professional Players Tournament |
| | v Knowles | 0-5 | 3rd round | Professional Players Tournament |
| **1984** | v Thorburn | 5-1 | Qualifying | Lada Classic |
| | v Wildman | 1-5 | 1st round | Lada Classic |
| | v Van Rensberg | 10-3 | Qualifying | Embassy World Championship |
| | v Meo | 10-5 | 1st round | Embassy World Championship |
| | v Reardon | 8-13 | 2nd round | Embassy World Championship |
| | v Kelly | 5-3 | Qualifying | Jameson International |
| | v Spencer | 5-2 | 1st round | Jameson International |
| | v Virgo | 5-2 | 2nd round | Jameson International |
| | v Knowles | 6-9 | Semi-final | Jameson International |
| | v Duggan | 5-3 | 1st round | Rothmans Grand Prix |
| | v White | 5-1 | 2nd round | Rothmans Grand Prix |
| | v Reynolds | 1-5 | 3rd round | Rothmans Grand Prix |
| | v Sinclair | 9-4 | Qualifying | Coral UK Open |
| | v Charlton | 4-9 | 1st round | Coral UK Open |
| **1985** | v T. Jones | 5-1 | Qualifying | Mercantile Credit Classic |
| | v S. Davis | 0-5 | 1st round | Mercantile Credit Classic |
| | v Kearney | 6-4 | 1st round | Dulux British Open |
| | v White | 5-4 | 2nd round | Dulux British Open |

| Year | Opponent | Score | Round | Event |
|---|---|---|---|---|
| | v Chaperon | 5-2 | 3rd round | Dulux British Open |
| | v Meo | 5-4 | Quarter-final | Dulux British Open |
| | v Higgins | 9-6 | Semi-final | Dulux British Open |
| | **v Stevens** | **12-9** | **Final** | **Dulux British Open** |
| | v Medati | 10-7 | Qualifying | Embassy World Championship |
| | v Dennis Taylor | 2-10 | 1st round | Embassy World Championship |
| | v Parrott | 3-4 | 1st round | Winfield Australian Masters |
| | v Knowles | 5-4 | 1st round | Langs Scottish Masters |
| | v Thorburn | 0-6 | Semi-final | Langs Scottish Masters |
| | v Chaperon | 3-5 | 3rd round | Goya Matchroom Trophy |
| | v Kelly | 5-2 | 3rd round | Rothmans Grand Prix |
| | v Martin | 5-3 | 4th round | Rothmans Grand Prix |
| | v White | 5-4 | 5th round | Rothmans Grand Prix |
| | v S. Davis | 2-5 | Quarter-final | Rothmans Grand Prix |
| | v Wych | 9-8 | 3rd round | Coral UK Open |
| | v Martin | 9-6 | 4th round | Coral UK Open |
| | v Griffiths | 5-9 | 5th round | Coral UK Open |
| **1986** | v Hendry | 4-5 | 3rd round | Mercantile Credit Classic |
| | v Knowles | 1-5 | 1st round | Benson & Hedges Masters |
| | v T. Jones | 5-2 | 3rd round | Dulux British Open |
| | v Macleod | 1-5 | 4th round | Dulux British Open |
| | v Williams | 10-4 | 1st round | Embassy World Championship |
| | v Knowles | 10-13 | 2nd round | Embassy World Championship |
| | v P. Francisco | 8-3 | Semi-final | South African Championship |
| | **v Ellis** | **9-1** | **Final** | **South African Championship** |
| | v Newbury | 5-4 | 3rd round | BCE International |
| | v Virgo | 5-0 | 4th round | BCE International |
| | v Dennis Taylor | 5-0 | 5th round | BCE International |
| | v P. Francisco | 3-5 | Quarter-final | BCE International |
| | v Spencer | 5-4 | 3rd round | Rothmans Grand Prix |
| | v W. Jones | 5-4 | 4th round | Rothmans Grand Prix |
| | v Newbury | 5-2 | 5th round | Rothmans Grand Prix |
| | v Knowles | 5-2 | Quarter-final | Rothmans Grand Prix |
| | v White | 6-9 | Semi-final | Rothmans Grand Prix |
| **1987** | v Van Rensberg | 5-4 | 3rd round | Mercantile Credit Classic |
| | v B. Harris | 5-3 | 4th round | Mercantile Credit Classic |
| | v P. Francisco | 5-1 | 5th round | Mercantile Credit Classic |
| | v Hendry | 0-5 | Quarter-final | Mercantile Credit Classic |
| | v Knowles | 5-2 | 1st round | Benson & Hedges Masters |
| | v Dennis Taylor | 3-5 | Quarter-final | Benson & Hedges Masters |
| | v Rowswell | 5-0 | 3rd round | Dulux British Open |
| | v Wilson | 4-5 | 4th round | Dulux British Open |
| | v J. Campbell | 10-3 | 1st round | Embassy World Championship |
| | v Hallett | 9-13 | 2nd round | Embassy World Championship |
| | v King | 5-2 | 3rd round | Fidelity International |
| | v Werbeniuk | 5-3 | 4th round | Fidelity International |
| | v E. Hughes | 4-5 | 5th round | Fidelity International |
| | v Fowler | 5-1 | 3rd round | Rothmans Grand Prix |
| | v Gary Wilkinson | 3-5 | 4th round | Rothmans Grand Prix |
| | v Reardon | 9-3 | 3rd round | Tennents UK Open |
| | v Wilson | 9-1 | 4th round | Tennents UK Open |
| | v Griffiths | 3-9 | 5th round | Tennents UK Open |
| **1988** | v Rowswell | 5-3 | 3rd round | Mercantile Credit Classic |
| | v Longworth | 5-2 | 4th round | Mercantile Credit Classic |
| | v Hendry | 3-5 | 5th round | Mercantile Credit Classic |
| | v Griffiths | 3-5 | 1st round | Benson & Hedges Masters |
| | v Bear | 5-0 | 3rd round | MIM Britannia British Open |
| | v Gary Wilkinson | 3-5 | 4th round | MIM Britannia British Open |
| | v Charlton | 7-10 | 1st round | Embassy World Championship |
| | v Owers | 5-1 | 3rd round | Fidelity International |
| | v Chaperon | 2-5 | 4th round | Fidelity International |
| | v N. Gilbert | 4-5 | 3rd round | Rothmans Grand Prix |
| | v Macleod | 4-5 | 3rd round | BCE Canadian Masters |

| | | | | |
|---|---|---|---|---|
| | v Medati | 9-8 | 3rd round | Tennents UK Open |
| | v West | 4-9 | 4th round | Tennents UK Open |
| **1989** | v Werbeniuk | *wo* | 3rd round | Mercantile Credit Classic |
| | v Meo | 5-1 | 4th round | Mercantile Credit Classic |
| | v Parrott | 1-5 | 5th round | Mercantile Credit Classic |
| | v Griffiths | 1-5 | 1st round | Benson and Hedges Masters |
| | v Wych | 1-5 | 3rd round | European Open |
| | v Macleod | 4-5 | 3rd round | Anglian British Open |
| | v O'Boye | 10-6 | 1st round | Embassy World Championship |
| | v Griffiths | 9-13 | 2nd round | Embassy World Championship |
| | v Pinches | 4-5 | 3rd round | Hong Kong Open |
| | v Spencer | 5-1 | 3rd round | 555 Asian Open |
| | v Graham | 5-4 | 4th round | 555 Asian Open |
| | v Knowles | 5-2 | 5th round | 555 Asian Open |
| | v Wattana | 2-5 | Quarter-final | 555 Asian Open |
| | v J. Campbell | 5-4 | 3rd round | BCE International |
| | v Bond | 3-5 | 4th round | BCE International |
| | v Wattana | 2-5 | 3rd round | Rothmans Grand Prix |
| | v Medati | 4-5 | 3rd round | Dubai Classic |
| | v Longworth | 9-7 | 3rd round | Stormseal UK Open |
| | v Robidoux | 3-9 | 4th round | Stormseal UK Open |
| **1990** | v Roscoe | 5-1 | 3rd round | Mercantile Credit Classic |
| | v Brumby | 5-0 | 4th round | Mercantile Credit Classic |
| | v Rowing | 5-1 | 5th round | Mercantile Credit Classic |
| | v O'Kane | 5-4 | Quarter-final | Mercantile Credit Classic |
| | v King | 5-6 | Semi-final | Mercantile Credit Classic |
| | v T. Wilson | 4-5 | 3rd round | Pearl Assurance British Open |
| | v Oliver | 5-2 | 3rd round | European Open |
| | v M. Bennett | 3-5 | 4th round | European Open |
| | v Gary Wilkinson | 7-10 | Qualifying | Embassy World Championship |

## MARCEL GAUVREAU (Canada)

**Born** 9.1.55. **Turned professional** 1983. **World ranking** 72 (68).

| | | | | |
|---|---|---|---|---|
| **1983** | v Rigitano | 6-9 | 1st round | Canadian Championship |
| | v Miles | 3-5 | 1st round | Professional Players Tournament |
| **1984** | v J. Campbell | 10-7 | Qualifying | Embassy World Championship |
| | v Cripsey | 10-1 | Qualifying | Embassy World Championship |
| | v Macleod | 10-6 | Qualifying | Embassy World Championship |
| | v David Taylor | 5-10 | 1st round | Embassy World Championship |
| | v Jonik | 5-1 | Qualifying | Jameson International |
| | v Parrott | 5-4 | Qualifying | Jameson International |
| | v Stevens | 5-1 | 1st round | Jameson International |
| | v Thorne | 3-5 | 2nd round | Jameson International |
| | v Foldvari | 5-2 | Qualifying | Rothmans Grand Prix |
| | v Parrott | 3-5 | 1st round | Rothmans Grand Prix |
| | v Bales | 9-8 | Qualifying | Coral UK Open |
| | v Mans | 9-6 | Qualifying | Coral UK Open |
| | v Knowles | 5-9 | 1st round | Coral UK Open |
| **1985** | v Giannaros | 5-3 | Qualifying | Mercantile Credit Classic |
| | v Sinclair | 5-1 | Qualifying | Mercantile Credit Classic |
| | v Higgins | 3-5 | 1st round | Mercantile Credit Classic |
| | v Greaves | 6-3 | Qualifying | Dulux British Open |
| | v Stevens | 3-6 | 1st round | Dulux British Open |
| | v Van Rensberg | 10-9 | Qualifying | Embassy World Championship |
| | v Reynolds | 1-10 | Qualifying | Embassy World Championship |
| | v D. Hughes | 4-5 | 2nd round | Goya Matchroom Trophy |
| | v Duggan | 4-5 | 2nd round | Rothmans Grand Prix |
| | v O'Boye | 5-9 | 2nd round | Coral UK Open |
| **1986** | v Simngam | 5-1 | 2nd round | Mercantile Credit Classic |
| | v David Taylor | 5-3 | 3rd round | Mercantile Credit Classic |

| | | | | |
|---|---|---|---|---|
| | v Browne | 5-3 | 4th round | Mercantile Credit Classic |
| | v White | 2-5 | 5th round | Mercantile Credit Classic |
| | v Drago | 3-5 | 2nd round | Dulux British Open |
| | v Jim Bear | 10-5 | Qualifying | Embassy World Championship |
| | v Chaperon | 10-8 | Qualifying | Embassy World Championship |
| | v Williams | 3-10 | Qualifying | Embassy World Championship |
| | v Jenkins | 5-1 | 2nd round | BCE International |
| | v Macleod | 5-4 | 3rd round | BCE International |
| | v Reardon | 5-2 | 4th round | BCE International |
| | v P. Francisco | 2-5 | 5th round | BCE International |
| | v J. McLaughlin | 3-5 | 2nd round | Rothmans Grand Prix |
| | v J. McLaughlin | 8-9 | 2nd round | Tennents UK Open |
| **1987** | v Rigitano | 5-0 | 2nd round | Mercantile Credit Classic |
| | v P. Francisco | 3-5 | 3rd round | Mercantile Credit Classic |
| | v Bales | 5-0 | 2nd round | Dulux British Open |
| | v S. Davis | 0-5 | 3rd round | Dulux British Open |
| | v Bear | 10-3 | Qualifying | Embassy World Championship |
| | v Medati | 3-10 | Qualifying | Embassy World Championship |
| | v Caggianello | 3-6 | 1st round | Canadian Championship |
| | v Williamson | 1-5 | 2nd round | Fidelity International |
| | v M. Smith | 5-3 | 2nd round | Rothmans Grand Prix |
| | v Virgo | 1-5 | 3rd round | Rothmans Grand Prix |
| | v A. Harris | 9-3 | 2nd round | Tennents UK Open |
| | v West | 6-9 | 3rd round | Tennents UK Open |
| **1988** | v Morra | 4-5 | 2nd round | Mercantile Credit Classic |
| | v Medati | 1-5 | 2nd round | MIM Britannia British Open |
| | v P. Gibson | 9-10 | Qualifying | Embassy World Championship |
| | v Meakin | 3-5 | 2nd round | Fidelity International |
| | v Ellis | 2-5 | 2nd round | Rothmans Grand Prix |
| | v Williamson | 5-1 | 2nd round | BCE Canadian Masters |
| | v Meo | 5-0 | 3rd round | BCE Canadian Masters |
| | v Hallett | 3-5 | 4th round | BCE Canadian Masters |
| | v Rowswell | 7-9 | 2nd round | Tennents UK Open |
| **1989** | v Miles | 3-5 | 2nd round | Mercantile Credit Classic |
| | v T. Wilson | 3-5 | 2nd round | European Open |
| | v Kelly | 5-0 | 2nd round | Anglian British Open |
| | v Mountjoy | 0-5 | 3rd round | Anglian British Open |
| | v Rowswell | 7-10 | Qualifying | Embassy World Championship |
| | v Stevens | 5-3 | 2nd round | Hong Kong Open |
| | v Drago | 5-0 | 3rd round | Hong Kong Open |
| | v Virgo | 2-5 | 4th round | Hong Kong Open |
| | v Cripsey | 4-5 | 2nd round | 555 Asian Open |
| | v Kearney | 3-5 | 1st round | BCE International |
| | v Jack Rea | 5-2 | 1st round | Rothmans Grand Prix |
| | v J. McLaughlin | 3-5 | 2nd round | Rothmans Grand Prix |
| | v Bradley | 5-4 | 2nd round | Dubai Classic |
| | v Clark | 1-5 | 3rd round | Dubai Classic |
| | v Meadowcroft | 6-1 | 1st round | Stormseal UK Open |
| | v Chambers | 2-6 | 2nd round | Stormseal UK Open |
| **1990** | v Sheehan | 5-0 | 1st round | Mercantile Credit Classic |
| | v Gary Wilkinson | 1-5 | 2nd round | Mercantile Credit Classic |
| | v Pinches | 5-4 | 1st round | Pearl Assurance British Open |
| | v Bales | 1-5 | 2nd round | Pearl Assurance British Open |
| | v Meakin | 5-3 | 1st round | European Open |
| | v Martin | 4-5 | 2nd round | European Open |
| | v Jack Rea | 10-9 | Qualifying | Embassy World Championship |
| | v Gary Wilkinson | 5-10 | Qualifying | Embassy World Championship |

## **MATT GIBSON** (Scotland)

**Born** 7.5.53. **Turned professional** 1981. **World ranking** 110 (112).

| | | | | |
|---|---|---|---|---|
| **1981** | v Hood | 5-3 | Qualifying | Jameson International |
| | v Parkin | 5-3 | Qualifying | Jameson International |
| | v Dunning | 3-5 | Qualifying | Jameson International |
| | v Demarco | 5-3 | Quarter-final | Scottish Championship |
| | v Donnelly | 6-4 | Semi-final | Scottish Championship |
| | v Black | 7-11 | Final | Scottish Championship |
| | v Fitzmaurice | 9-6 | Qualifying | Coral UK Championship |
| | v Everton | 7-9 | Qualifying | Coral UK Championship |
| **1982** | v Donnelly | 8-9 | Qualifying | Embassy World Championship |
| | v E. McLaughlin | 6-3 | Quarter-final | Scottish Championship |
| | v Sinclair | 2-6 | Semi-final | Scottish Championship |
| | v Wildman | 1-5 | Qualifying | Jameson International |
| | v Martin | 2-5 | 1st round | Professional Players Tournament |
| | v G. Foulds | 3-9 | Qualifying | Coral UK Championship |
| **1983** | v G. Foulds | 6-10 | Qualifying | Embassy World Championship |
| | v Macleod | 5-6 | 1st round | Scottish Championship |
| | v Dodd | 5-1 | Qualifying | Jameson International |
| | v Scott | 3-5 | Qualifying | Jameson International |
| | v Morgan | 4-5 | Qualifying | Professional Players Tournament |
| | v Johnson | 6-9 | Qualifying | Coral UK Championship |
| **1984** | v Rigitano | 10-7 | Qualifying | Embassy World Championship |
| | v Fisher | 10-7 | Qualifying | Embassy World Championship |
| | v Johnson | 3-10 | Qualifying | Embassy World Championship |
| | v Medati | 5-3 | Qualifying | Jameson International |
| | v W. Jones | 2-5 | Qualifying | Jameson International |
| | v Chaperon | 4-5 | Qualifying | Rothmans Grand Prix |
| | v Hargreaves | 9-8 | Qualifying | Coral UK Open |
| | v Donnelly | 6-9 | Qualifying | Coral UK Open |
| **1985** | v T. Jones | 0-5 | Qualifying | Mercantile Credit Classic |
| | v Black | 6-2 | 1st round | Scottish Championship |
| | v Macleod | 4-6 | Semi-final | Scottish Championship |
| | v Demarco | 6-1 | Qualifying | Dulux British Open |
| | v Wildman | 1-6 | 1st round | Dulux British Open |
| | v Hines | 10-7 | Qualifying | Embassy World Championship |
| | v Fagan | 8-10 | Qualifying | Embassy World Championship |
| | v P. Francisco | 5-4 | 2nd round | Goya Matchroom Trophy |
| | v Charlton | 5-4 | 3rd round | Goya Matchroom Trophy |
| | v Reynolds | 0-5 | 4th round | Goya Matchroom Trophy |
| | v Bradley | 5-4 | 2nd round | Rothmans Grand Prix |
| | v Knowles | 1-5 | 3rd round | Rothmans Grand Prix |
| | v Longworth | 2-9 | 2nd round | Coral UK Open |
| **1986** | v Virgo | 3-5 | 3rd round | Mercantile Credit Classic |
| | v Black | 0-5 | 2nd round | Dulux British Open |
| | v Sinclair | 6-4 | Quarter-final | Canada Dry Scottish Championship |
| | v John Rea | 6-0 | Semi-final | Canada Dry Scottish Championship |
| | v Hendry | 5-10 | Final | Canada Dry Scottish Championship |
| | v Jenkins | 10-4 | Qualifying | Embassy World Championship |
| | v Morra | 10-9 | Qualifying | Embassy World Championship |
| | v Medati | 6-10 | Qualifying | Embassy World Championship |
| | v Hines | 5-1 | 2nd round | BCE International |
| | v Mountjoy | 3-5 | 3rd round | BCE International |
| | v Mienie | 5-4 | 2nd round | Rothmans Grand Prix |
| | v S. Davis | 1-5 | 3rd round | Rothmans Grand Prix |
| | v Dunning | 9-2 | 2nd round | Tennents UK Open |
| | v Reardon | 6-9 | 3rd round | Tennents UK Open |
| **1987** | v J. McLaughlin | 3-5 | 2nd round | Mercantile Credit Classic |
| | v Sinclair | 2-6 | 1st round | Scottish Championship |
| | v J. McLaughlin | 1-5 | 2nd round | Dulux British Open |
| | v Kelly | 10-9 | Qualifying | Embassy World Championship |
| | v Cripsey | 4-10 | Qualifying | Embassy World Championship |
| | v Chappel | 2-5 | 2nd round | Fidelity International |
| | v Cripsey | 2-5 | 2nd round | Rothmans Grand Prix |
| | v Murphy | 0-9 | 2nd round | Tennents UK Open |

| | | | | |
|---|---|---|---|---|
| 1988 | v Cripsey | 4-5 | 2nd round | Mercantile Credit Classic |
| | v Black | 6-2 | Quarter-final | Scottish Championship |
| | v Hendry | 1-6 | Semi-final | Scottish Championship |
| | v Duggan | 5-2 | 2nd round | MIM Britannia British Open |
| | v Knowles | 4-5 | 3rd round | MIM Britannia British Open |
| | v Watchorn | 7-10 | Qualifying | Embassy World Championship |
| | v T. Wilson | 1-5 | 1st round | Fidelity International |
| | v Burke | 5-4 | 1st round | Rothmans Grand Prix |
| | v Dodd | 1-5 | 2nd round | Rothmans Grand Prix |
| | v D. Hughes | 5-1 | 1st round | BCE Canadian Masters |
| | v King | 3-5 | 2nd round | BCE Canadian Masters |
| | v A. Harris | 9-8 | 1st round | Tennents UK Open |
| | v Roe | 3-9 | 2nd round | Tennents UK Open |
| 1989 | v Jack Rea | 3-5 | 1st round | Mercantile Credit Classic |
| | v T. Wilson | 3-5 | 1st round | European Open |
| | v Sinclair | 5-4 | 1st round | Scottish Championship |
| | v Macleod | 1-5 | Semi-final | Scottish Championship |
| | v Rowing | 5-0 | 1st round | Anglian British Open |
| | v J. Campbell | 2-5 | 2nd round | Anglian British Open |
| | v Darrington | 1-0 | Qualifying | Embassy World Championship |
| | v Martin | 7-10 | Qualifying | Embassy World Championship |
| | v Marshall | 5-1 | 1st round | Hong Kong Open |
| | v Browne | 5-3 | 2nd round | Hong Kong Open |
| | v Parrott | 3-5 | 3rd round | Hong Kong Open |
| | v Sinclair | 2-5 | 1st round | 555 Asian Open |
| | v Wright | 4-5 | 1st round | BCE International |
| | v Price | 4-5 | 1st round | Rothmans Grand Prix |
| | v V. Harris | 5-3 | 1st round | Dubai Classic |
| | v Bales | 4-5 | 2nd round | Dubai Classic |
| | v Edwards | 6-0 | 1st round | Stormseal UK Open |
| | v Longworth | 4-6 | 2nd round | Stormseal UK Open |
| 1990 | v Miles | 3-5 | 1st round | Mercantile Credit Classic |
| | v Dunning | 4-5 | 1st round | Pearl Assurance British Open |
| | v Wright | 1-5 | 1st round | European Open |
| | v Lawlor | 6-10 | Qualifying | Embassy World Championship |

## **PAUL GIBSON** (England)

**Born** 9.6.63. **Turned professional** 1986. **World ranking** 67 (82).

| | | | | |
|---|---|---|---|---|
| 1986 | v Meadowcroft | 5-2 | 1st round | BCE International |
| | v Hendry | 2-5 | 2nd round | BCE International |
| | v Dunning | 5-1 | 1st round | Rothmans Grand Prix |
| | v Cripsey | 3-5 | 2nd round | Rothmans Grand Prix |
| | v Agrawal | 9-6 | 1st round | Tennents UK Open |
| | v Mans | *wo* | 2nd round | Tennents UK Open |
| | v Griffiths | 3-9 | 3rd round | Tennents UK Open |
| 1987 | v B. Harris | 3-5 | 2nd round | Mercantile Credit Classic |
| | v D. Hughes | 6-3 | 1st round | Tolly Ales English Championship |
| | v Medati | 2-6 | 2nd round | Tolly Ales English Championship |
| | v Agrawal | 5-0 | 1st round | Dulux British Open |
| | v Duggan | 3-5 | 2nd round | Dulux British Open |
| | v Morra | 6-10 | Qualifying | Embassy World Championship |
| | v Glen Wilkinson | 5-3 | 1st round | Fidelity International |
| | v T. Jones | 5-4 | 2nd round | Fidelity International |
| | v N. Foulds | 2-5 | 3rd round | Fidelity International |
| | v Fagan | 5-0 | 1st round | Rothmans Grand Prix |
| | v Duggan | 5-4 | 2nd round | Rothmans Grand Prix |
| | v Hallett | 5-4 | 3rd round | Rothmans Grand Prix |
| | v Cripsey | 4-5 | 4th round | Rothmans Grand Prix |
| | v Rigitano | 9-5 | 1st round | Tennents UK Open |
| | v Cripsey | 6-9 | 2nd round | Tennents UK Open |

| | | | | |
|---|---|---|---|---|
| **1988** | v Black | 5-2 | 1st round | Mercantile Credit Classic |
| | v J. McLaughlin | 4-5 | 2nd round | Mercantile Credit Classic |
| | v Chambers | 0-6 | 1st round | English Championship |
| | v Roscoe | 4-5 | 1st round | MIM Britannia British Open |
| | v Sheehan | 10-9 | Qualifying | Embassy World Championship |
| | v Gauvreau | 10-9 | Qualifying | Embassy World Championship |
| | v Duggan | 9-10 | Qualifying | Embassy World Championship |
| **1989** | v Marshall | 10-3 | Qualifying | Embassy World Championship |
| | v Owers | 8-10 | Qualifying | Embassy World Championship |
| | v Grace | 5-3 | 1st round | Hong Kong Open |
| | v Edmonds | 2-5 | 2nd round | Hong Kong Open |
| | v Darrington | 5-4 | 1st round | 555 Asian Open |
| | v Gary Wilkinson | 4-5 | 2nd round | 555 Asian Open |
| | v D. Campbell | 1-5 | 1st round | BCE International |
| | v Gollan | 5-4 | 1st round | Rothmans Grand Prix |
| | v Fisher | 5-3 | 2nd round | Rothmans Grand Prix |
| | v Griffiths | 5-2 | 3rd round | Rothmans Grand Prix |
| | v Dodd | 5-4 | 4th round | Rothmans Grand Prix |
| | v Wattana | 3-5 | 5th round | Rothmans Grand Prix |
| | v Meadowcroft | 5-4 | 1st round | Dubai Classic |
| | v Johnston-Allen | 5-0 | 2nd round | Dubai Classic |
| | v Parrott | 2-5 | 3rd round | Dubai Classic |
| | v Watchorn | 3-6 | 1st round | Stormseal UK Open |
| **1990** | v Ellis | 5-3 | 1st round | Mercantile Credit Classic |
| | v David Taylor | 1-5 | 2nd round | Mercantile Credit Classic |
| | v Gollan | 1-5 | 1st round | Pearl Assurance British Open |
| | v Kearney | 1-5 | 1st round | European Open |
| | v Gollan | 5-10 | Qualifying | Embassy World Championship |

## DAVE GILBERT (England)

**Born** 15.8.61. **Turned professional** 1985. **World ranking** 75 (63).

| | | | | |
|---|---|---|---|---|
| **1985** | v Darrington | 2-5 | 1st round | Goya Matchroom Trophy |
| | v Wilkinson | 5-4 | 1st round | Rothmans Grand Prix |
| | v Williamson | 5-4 | 2nd round | Rothmans Grand Prix |
| | v Johnson | 2-5 | 3rd round | Rothmans Grand Prix |
| | v Drago | 5-9 | 1st round | Coral UK Open |
| **1986** | v Watson | 5-4 | 1st round | Mercantile Credit Classic |
| | v T. Jones | 3-5 | 2nd round | Mercantile Credit Classic |
| | v West | 9-8 | 1st round | Tolly Cobbold English Championship |
| | v Bradley | 5-9 | 2nd round | Tolly Cobbold English Championship |
| | v Burke | 5-1 | 1st round | Dulux British Open |
| | v Morra | 5-4 | 2nd round | Dulux British Open |
| | v Charlton | 2-5 | 3rd round | Dulux British Open |
| | v Bales | 10-7 | Qualifying | Embassy World Championship |
| | v Bradley | 10-7 | Qualifying | Embassy World Championship |
| | v T. Jones | 10-7 | Qualifying | Embassy World Championship |
| | v Martin | 5-10 | Qualifying | Embassy World Championship |
| | v James | 2-5 | 1st round | BCE International |
| | v Rowswell | 5-1 | 1st round | Rothmans Grand Prix |
| | v Newbury | 1-5 | 2nd round | Rothmans Grand Prix |
| | v Owers | 8-9 | 1st round | Tennents UK Open |
| **1987** | v Spencer | 4-5 | 2nd round | Mercantile Credit Classic |
| | v Bradley | 3-6 | 2nd round | Tolly Ales English Championship |
| | v Murphy | 4-5 | 2nd round | Dulux British Open |
| | v O'Kane | 2-10 | Qualifying | Embassy World Championship |
| | v A. Harris | 5-4 | 1st round | Fidelity International |
| | v Houlihan | 5-3 | 2nd round | Fidelity International |
| | v Martin | 5-2 | 3rd round | Fidelity International |
| | v Wilson | 5-1 | 4th round | Fidelity International |
| | v Hendry | 0-5 | 5th round | Fidelity International |

| | | | | |
|---|---|---|---|---|
| | v Lawlor | 5-2 | 1st round | Rothmans Grand Prix |
| | v Fowler | 1-5 | 2nd round | Rothmans Grand Prix |
| | v Heaton | 9-5 | 1st round | Tennents UK Open |
| | v Chappel | 2-9 | 2nd round | Tennents UK Open |
| **1988** | v Jack Rea | 5-2 | 1st round | Mercantile Credit Classic |
| | v B. Harris | 5-4 | 2nd round | Mercantile Credit Classic |
| | v C. Wilson | 3-5 | 3rd round | Mercantile Credit Classic |
| | v Whitthread | 6-1 | 1st round | English Championship |
| | v Bales | 6-2 | 2nd round | English Championship |
| | v Reynolds | 3-6 | 3rd round | English Championship |
| | v Wright | 5-2 | 2nd round | MIM Britannia British Open |
| | v Macleod | 4-5 | 3rd round | MIM Britannia British Open |
| | v Heaton | 10-2 | Qualifying | Embassy World Championship (withdrew from 2nd qualifying round) |
| | v Johnston-Allen | 3-5 | 2nd round | Fidelity International |
| | v Mienie | 5-0 | 2nd round | Rothmans Grand Prix |
| | v O'Kane | 4-5 | 3rd round | Rothmans Grand Prix |
| | v Price | 4-5 | 2nd round | BCE Canadian Masters |
| | v Lawlor | 9-2 | 2nd round | Tennents UK Open |
| | v Thorne | 3-9 | 3rd round | Tennents UK Open |
| **1989** | v A. Harris | 4-5 | 2nd round | Mercantile Credit Classic |
| | v Ellis | 5-2 | 2nd round | European Open |
| | v Hallett | 3-5 | 3rd round | European Open |
| | v Bradley | 5-4 | 2nd round | English Championship |
| | v Johnson | 2-5 | 3rd round | English Championship |
| | v John Rea | 3-5 | 2nd round | Anglian British Open |
| | v Fagan | 10-4 | Qualifying | Embassy World Championship |
| | v Thornley | 10-4 | Qualifying | Embassy World Championship |
| | v Mountjoy | 7-10 | Qualifying | Embassy World Championship |
| | v Meadowcroft | 5-3 | 2nd round | Hong Kong Open |
| | v Charlton | 2-5 | 3rd round | Hong Kong Open |
| | v Williamson | 5-1 | 2nd round | 555 Asian Open |
| | v Dennis Taylor | 5-1 | 3rd round | 555 Asian Open |
| | v West | 3-5 | 4th round | 555 Asian Open |
| | v Wright | 1-5 | 2nd round | BCE International |
| | v Dunning | 5-1 | 2nd round | Rothmans Grand Prix |
| | v Higgins | 3-5 | 3rd round | Rothmans Grand Prix |
| | v Medati | 3-5 | 2nd round | Dubai Classic |
| | v B. Harris | 6-2 | 2nd round | Stormseal UK Open |
| | v Dennis Taylor | 2-9 | 3rd round | Stormseal UK Open |
| **1990** | v Rowing | 1-5 | 2nd round | Mercantile Credit Classic |
| | v Donnelly | 4-5 | 2nd round | Pearl Assurance British Open |
| | v D. Campbell | 2-5 | 2nd round | European Open |
| | v Grace | 10-9 | Qualifying | Embassy World Championship |
| | v Fowler | 3-10 | Qualifying | Embassy World Championship |

## NIGEL GILBERT (England)

**Born** 20.3.59. **Turned professional** 1986. **World ranking** 52 (46).

| | | | | |
|---|---|---|---|---|
| **1986** | v Agrawal | 5-0 | 1st round | BCE International |
| | v Chaperon | 3-5 | 2nd round | BCE International |
| | v Donnelly | 1-5 | 1st round | Rothmans Grand Prix |
| | v Donnelly | 8-9 | 1st round | Tennents UK Open |
| **1987** | v Smith | 5-0 | 1st round | Mercantile Credit Classic |
| | v Van Rensberg | 3-5 | 2nd round | Mercantile Credit Classic |
| | v B. Bennett | 5-6 | 1st round | Tolly Ales English Championship |
| | v Houlihan | 5-4 | 1st round | Dulux British Open |
| | v W. Jones | 5-3 | 2nd round | Dulux British Open |
| | v Reynolds | 2-5 | 3rd round | Dulux British Open |
| | v Sheehan | 10-6 | Qualifying | Embassy World Championship |
| | v O'Boye | 5-10 | Qualifying | Embassy World Championship |

| | | | | |
|---|---|---|---|---|
| | v Black | 5-3 | 1st round | Fidelity International |
| | v J. McLaughlin | 5-4 | 2nd round | Fidelity International |
| | v Macleod | 5-1 | 3rd round | Fidelity International |
| | v W. Jones | 5-4 | 4th round | Fidelity International |
| | v Charlton | 0-5 | 5th round | Fidelity International |
| | v Jonik | 3-5 | 1st round | Rothmans Grand Prix |
| | v Sinclair | 9-8 | 1st round | Tennents UK Open |
| | v G. Foulds | 9-4 | 2nd round | Tennents UK Open |
| | v E. Hughes | 7-9 | 3rd round | Tennents UK Open |
| **1988** | v Donnelly | 2-5 | 1st round | Mercantile Credit Classic |
| | v A. Harris | 6-3 | 1st round | English Championship |
| | v F. Davis | 5-6 | 2nd round | English Championship |
| | v Sheehan | 5-3 | 1st round | MIM Britannia British Open |
| | v Werbeniuk | 5-1 | 2nd round | MIM Britannia British Open |
| | v Williams | 2-5 | 3rd round | MIM Britannia British Open |
| | v John Rea | 10-5 | Qualifying | Embassy World Championship |
| | v Chappel | 8-10 | Qualifying | Embassy World Championship |
| | v Dunning | 5-0 | 2nd round | Fidelity International |
| | v Meo | 1-5 | 3rd round | Fidelity International |
| | v Oliver | 5-4 | 2nd round | Rothmans Grand Prix |
| | v S. Francisco | 5-4 | 3rd round | Rothmans Grand Prix |
| | v Charlton | 5-0 | 4th round | Rothmans Grand Prix |
| | v Knowles | 5-4 | 5th round | Rothmans Grand Prix |
| | v Robidoux | 4-5 | Quarter-final | Rothmans Grand Prix |
| | v Johnston-Allen | 5-4 | 2nd round | BCE Canadian Masters |
| | v Newbury | 3-5 | 3rd round | BCE Canadian Masters |
| | v Whitthread | 9-5 | 2nd round | Tennents UK Open |
| | v Spencer | 9-7 | 3rd round | Tennents UK Open |
| | v Parrott | 8-9 | 4th round | Tennents UK Open |
| **1989** | v Fitzmaurice | 5-3 | 2nd round | Mercantile Credit Classic |
| | v O'Kane | 2-5 | 3rd round | Mercantile Credit Classic |
| | v Morra | 1-5 | 2nd round | European Open |
| | v Marshall | 4-5 | 2nd round | English Championship |
| | v T. Wilson | 5-2 | 2nd round | Anglian British Open |
| | v Hallett | 3-5 | 3rd round | Anglian British Open |
| | v Terry | 10-5 | Qualifying | Embassy World Championship |
| | v Edwards | 10-8 | Qualifying | Embassy World Championship |
| | v Newbury | 7-10 | Qualifying | Embassy World Championship |
| | v Rigitano | 3-5 | 2nd round | Hong Kong Open |
| | v Gollan | 2-5 | 2nd round | 555 Asian Open |
| | v J. Smith | 2-5 | 2nd round | BCE International |
| | v A. Harris | 5-2 | 2nd round | Rothmans Grand Prix |
| | v N. Foulds | 1-5 | 3rd round | Rothmans Grand Prix |
| | v Morra | 4-5 | 2nd round | Dubai Classic |
| | v Meakin | 5-6 | 2nd round | Stormseal UK Open |
| **1990** | v Bradley | 5-1 | 2nd round | Mercantile Credit Classic |
| | v Johnson | 5-0 | 3rd round | Mercantile Credit Classic |
| | v Clark | 2-5 | 4th round | Mercantile Credit Classic |
| | v Marshall | 2-5 | 2nd round | Pearl Assurance British Open |
| | v Cairns | 5-3 | 2nd round | European Open |
| | v Johnson | 2-5 | 3rd round | European Open |
| | v Kearney | 10-6 | Qualifying | Embassy World Championship |
| | v Cairns | 10-6 | Qualifying | Embassy World Championship |
| | v Roe | 10-6 | Qualifying | Embassy World Championship |
| | v Griffiths | 4-10 | 1st round | Embassy World Championship |

## BRADY GOLLAN (Canada)

**Born** 28.3.65. **Turned professional** 1989. **World ranking** 55.

| | | | | |
|---|---|---|---|---|
| **1989** | v Sinclair | 5-3 | 1st round | Hong Kong Open |

| | | | | |
|---|---|---|---|---|
| | v Cripsey | 5-1 | 2nd round | Hong Kong Open |
| | v E. Hughes | 5-3 | 3rd round | Hong Kong Open |
| | v Dennis Taylor | 4-5 | 4th round | Hong Kong Open |
| | v Dunning | 5-1 | 1st round | 555 Asian Open |
| | v N. Gilbert | 5-2 | 2nd round | 555 Asian Open |
| | v C. Wilson | 5-4 | 3rd round | 555 Asian Open |
| | v Thorne | 1-5 | 4th round | 555 Asian Open |
| | v T. Wilson | 5-2 | 1st round | BCE International |
| | v Longworth | 5-0 | 2nd round | BCE International |
| | v Griffiths | 4-5 | 3rd round | BCE International |
| | v P. Gibson | 4-5 | 1st round | Rothmans Grand Prix |
| | v Marshall | 2-5 | 2nd round | Dubai Classic |
| | v Dunning | 6-4 | 1st round | Stormseal UK Open |
| | v Martin | 6-0 | 2nd round | Stormseal UK Open |
| | v Charlton | 9-2 | 3rd round | Stormseal UK Open |
| | v O'Boye | 9-5 | 4th round | Stormseal UK Open |
| | v Robidoux | 5-9 | 5th round | Stormseal UK Open |
| **1990** | v Owers | 2-5 | 1st round | Mercantile Credit Classic |
| | v P. Gibson | 5-1 | 1st round | Pearl Assurance British Open |
| | v T. Jones | 5-1 | 2nd round | Pearl Assurance British Open |
| | v Knowles | 2-5 | 3rd round | Pearl Assurance British Open |
| | v V. Harris | 5-2 | 1st round | European Open |
| | v J. Campbell | 3-5 | 2nd round | European Open |
| | v Everton | 10-2 | Qualifying | Embassy World Championship |
| | v P. Gibson | 10-5 | Qualifying | Embassy World Championship |
| | v Stevens | 10-6 | Qualifying | Embassy World Championship |
| | v B. Morgan | 10-6 | Qualifying | Embassy World Championship |
| | v E. Hughes | 10-7 | Qualifying | Embassy World Championship |
| | v Mountjoy | 8-10 | 1st round | Embassy World Championship |

## **ROBBIE GRACE** (South Africa)

**Born** 14.6.54. **Turned professional** 1985. **World ranking** 113 (113).

| | | | | |
|---|---|---|---|---|
| **1986** | v Parkin | 10-8 | Qualifying | Embassy World Championship |
| | v W. Jones | 3-10 | Qualifying | Embassy World Championship |
| | v P. Francisco | 1-7 | 2nd round | South African Championship |
| | v Houlihan | 5-1 | 1st round | Rothmans Grand Prix |
| | v Fagan | 3-5 | 2nd round | Rothmans Grand Prix |
| | v Houlihan | 9-6 | 1st round | Tennents UK Open |
| | v Medati | 9-5 | 2nd round | Tennents UK Open |
| | v Macleod | 9-6 | 3rd round | Tennents UK Open |
| | v Thorne | 1-9 | 4th round | Tennents UK Open |
| **1987** | v Rigitano | 4-5 | 1st round | Mercantile Credit Classic |
| | v Meadowcroft | 5-4 | 1st round | Dulux British Open |
| | v Fagan | 5-3 | 2nd round | Dulux British Open |
| | v West | 2-5 | 3rd round | Dulux British Open |
| | v Jenkins | 9-10 | Qualifying | Embassy World Championship |
| | v Chambers | 5-4 | 2nd round | Fidelity International |
| | v Thorburn | 1-5 | 3rd round | Fidelity International |
| | v Clark | 1-5 | 2nd round | Rothmans Grand Prix |
| | v Gary Wilkinson | 5-9 | 2nd round | Tennents UK Open |
| **1988** | v Van Rensberg | 3-5 | 2nd round | Mercantile Credit Classic |
| | v Clark | 0-5 | 2nd round | MIM Britannia British Open |
| | v Fowler | 3-5 | 2nd round | Fidelity International |
| | v Whitthread | 4-5 | 1st round | Rothmans Grand Prix |
| | v T. Wilson | 2-5 | 1st round | BCE Canadian Masters |
| | v Price | 3-9 | 1st round | Tennents UK Open |
| **1989** | v Graham | 4-5 | 1st round | Mercantile Credit Classic |
| | v Meakin | 5-4 | 1st round | European Open |
| | v Edmonds | 1-5 | 2nd round | European Open |
| | v Fagan | 5-2 | 1st round | Anglian British Open |

| | | | | |
|---|---|---|---|---|
| | v Wright | 1-5 | 2nd round | Anglian British Open |
| | v Watchorn | 6-10 | Qualifying | Embassy World Championship |
| | v P. Gibson | 3-5 | 1st round | Hong Kong Open |
| | v Rowswell | 0-5 | 1st round | 555 Asian Open |
| | v Lawlor | 5-4 | 1st round | BCE International |
| | v Johnston-Allen | 0-5 | 2nd round | BCE International |
| | v Marshall | 2-5 | 1st round | Rothmans Grand Prix |
| | v Medati | 3-5 | 1st round | Dubai Classic |
| | v Bradley | 6-4 | 1st round | Stormseal UK Open |
| | v T. Murphy | 0-6 | 2nd round | Stormseal UK Open |
| **1990** | v Houlihan | 2-5 | 1st round | Mercantile Credit Classic |
| | v Bradley | 1-5 | 1st round | Pearl Assurance British Open |
| | v T. Wilson | 5-3 | 1st round | European Open |
| | v Dodd | 5-3 | 2nd round | European Open |
| | v Chaperon | 2-5 | 3rd round | European Open |
| | v A. Harris | 10-8 | Qualifying | Embassy World Championship |
| | v D. Gilbert | 9-10 | Qualifying | Embassy World Championship |

## IAN GRAHAM (England)

**Born** 17.2.67. **Turned professional** 1988. **World ranking** 51 (59).

| | | | | |
|---|---|---|---|---|
| **1988** | v Chambers | 2-5 | 1st round | Fidelity International |
| | v Glen Wilkinson | 4-5 | 1st round | Rothmans Grand Prix |
| | v Sinclair | 5-3 | 1st round | BCE Canadian Masters |
| | v Wright | 5-2 | 2nd round | BCE Canadian Masters |
| | v P. Francisco | 5-3 | 3rd round | BCE Canadian Masters |
| | v Charlton | 5-2 | 4th round | BCE Canadian Masters |
| | v Thorburn | 4-5 | 5th round | BCE Canadian Masters |
| | v B. Harris | 4-9 | 1st round | Tennents UK Open |
| **1989** | v Grace | 5-4 | 1st round | Mercantile Credit Classic |
| | v Macleod | 4-5 | 2nd round | Mercantile Credit Classic |
| | v Scott | 5-1 | 1st round | European Open |
| | v Gary Wilkinson | 3-5 | 2nd round | European Open |
| | v Heaton | 5-1 | Prelim | English Championship |
| | v Darrington | 5-3 | 1st round | English Championship |
| | v Duggan | 5-2 | 2nd round | English Championship |
| | v Williams | 5-3 | 3rd round | English Championship |
| | v Gary Wilkinson | 1-5 | 4th round | English Championship |
| | v Williamson | 5-4 | 1st round | Anglian British Open |
| | v Duggan | 5-2 | 2nd round | Anglian British Open |
| | v West | 1-5 | 3rd round | Anglian British Open |
| | v Greaves | 10-0 | Qualifying | Embassy World Championship |
| | v B. Harris | *wo* | Qualifying | Embassy World Championship |
| | v Cripsey | 10-2 | Qualifying | Embassy World Championship |
| | v M. Smith | 10-6 | Qualifying | Embassy World Championship |
| | v Reynolds | 5-10 | Qualifying | Embassy World Championship |
| | v Wattana | 5-4 | 2nd round | Hong Kong Open |
| | v Williams | 5-1 | 3rd round | Hong Kong Open |
| | v James | 5-3 | 4th round | Hong Kong Open |
| | v T. Jones | 5-3 | 5th round | Hong Kong Open |
| | v O'Kane | 1-5 | Quarter-final | Hong Kong Open |
| | v Van Rensberg | 5-0 | 2nd round | 555 Asian Open |
| | v Parrott | *wo* | 3rd round | 555 Asian Open |
| | v S. Francisco | 4-5 | 4th round | 555 Asian Open |
| | v Pinches | 5-0 | 2nd round | BCE International |
| | v Hendry | 0-5 | 3rd round | BCE International |
| | v Morra | 0-5 | 2nd round | Rothmans Grand Prix |
| | v Sinclair | 4-5 | 2nd round | Dubai Classic |
| | v Houlihan | 6-0 | 2nd round | Stormseal UK Open |
| | v O'Kane | 7-9 | 3rd round | Stormseal UK Open |
| **1990** | v Dyson | 3-5 | 2nd round | Mercantile Credit Classic |

| | | | |
|---|---|---|---|
| v Kearney | 5-4 | 2nd round | Pearl Assurance British Open |
| v N. Foulds | 2-5 | 3rd round | Pearl Assurance British Open |
| v Bradley | 5-0 | 2nd round | European Open |
| v W. Jones | 1-5 | 3rd round | European Open |
| v Sinclair | 10-3 | Qualifying | Embassy World Championship |
| v Rowing | 10-8 | Qualifying | Embassy World Championship |
| v Drago | 7-10 | Qualifying | Embassy World Championship |

## TERRY GRIFFITHS (Wales)

**Born** 16.10.47. **Turned professional** 1978. **World ranking** 6 (5).

| | | | | |
|---|---|---|---|---|
| **1978** | v Williams | 8-9 | Qualifying | Coral UK Championship |
| **1979** | v Bennett | 9-2 | Prelim | Embassy World Championship |
| | v Meadowcroft | 9-6 | Qualifying | Embassy World Championship |
| | v Mans | 13-8 | 1st round | Embassy World Championship |
| | v Higgins | 13-12 | Quarter-final | Embassy World Championship |
| | v Charlton | 19-17 | Semi-final | Embassy World Championship |
| | **v Dennis Taylor** | **24-16** | **Final** | **Embassy World Championship** |
| | v Wilson | 9-4 | 3rd round | Coral UK Championship |
| | v Higgins | 9-7 | Quarter-final | Coral UK Championship |
| | v Werbeniuk | 9-3 | Semi-final | Coral UK Championship |
| | v Virgo | 13-14 | Final | Coral UK Championship |
| **1980** | v Thorburn | 5-3 | Quarter-final | Benson & Hedges Masters |
| | v Spencer | 5-0 | Semi-final | Benson & Hedges Masters |
| | **v Higgins** | **9-5** | **Final** | **Benson & Hedges Masters** |
| | v Mountjoy | 6-9 | 1st round | Woodpecker Welsh Championship |
| | **v Mountjoy** | **9-8** | **Final** | **Benson & Hedges Irish Masters** |
| | v S. Davis | 10-13 | 2nd round | Embassy World Championship |
| | v Fagan | 9-8 | 2nd round | Coral UK Championship |
| | v Dennis Taylor | 9-7 | Quarter-final | Coral UK Championship |
| | v S. Davis | 0-9 | Semi-final | Coral UK Championship |
| **1981** | v F. Davis | 5-2 | Quarter-final | Benson & Hedges Masters |
| | v Spencer | 6-5 | Semi-final | Benson & Hedges Masters |
| | v Higgins | 6-9 | Final | Benson & Hedges Masters |
| | v Reardon | 6-9 | Semi-final | Woodpecker Welsh Championship |
| | v Thorburn | 6-5 | Semi-final | Benson & Hedges Irish Masters |
| | **v Reardon** | **9-7** | **Final** | **Benson & Hedges Irish Masters** |
| | v Meo | 13-6 | 2nd round | Embassy World Championship |
| | v S. Davis | 9-13 | Quarter-final | Embassy World Championship |
| | v Spencer | 5-2 | 3rd round | Jameson International |
| | v Higgins | 2-5 | Quarter-final | Jameson International |
| | v Stevens | 5-0 | 1st round | Northern Ireland Classic |
| | v S. Davis | 6-9 | Semi-final | Northern Ireland Classic |
| | v Miles | 9-4 | 3rd round | Coral UK Championship |
| | v Knowles | 9-5 | Quarter-final | Coral UK Championship |
| | v Meo | 9-3 | Semi-final | Coral UK Championship |
| | v S. Davis | 3-16 | Final | Coral UK Championship |
| **1982** | v Thorburn | 5-1 | 1st round | Lada Classic |
| | v Higgins | 5-1 | Semi-final | Lada Classic |
| | **v S. Davis** | **9-8** | **Final** | **Lada Classic** |
| | v Reardon | 5-3 | Quarter-final | Benson & Hedges Masters |
| | v Higgins | 6-4 | Semi-final | Benson & Hedges Masters |
| | v S. Davis | 5-9 | Final | Benson & Hedges Masters |
| | v S. Davis | 7-9 | Final | Yamaha International Masters |
| | v Roscoe | 6-2 | 1st round | Woodpecker Welsh Championship |
| | v Wilson | 9-6 | Semi-final | Woodpecker Welsh Championship |
| | v Mountjoy | 8-9 | Final | Woodpecker Welsh Championship |
| | v Meo | 5-3 | Quarter-final | Benson & Hedges Irish Masters |
| | v Reardon | 6-3 | Semi-final | Benson & Hedges Irish Masters |
| | **v S. Davis** | **9-5** | **Final** | **Benson & Hedges Irish Masters** |
| | v Thorne | 6-10 | 1st round | Embassy World Championship |

*Terry Griffiths*

| | | | | |
|---|---|---|---|---|
| | v Reardon | 5-3 | 1st round | Langs Scottish Masters |
| | v Higgins | 5-6 | Semi-final | Langs Scottish Masters |
| | v Williams | 5-2 | 1st round | Jameson International |
| | v Higgins | 5-2 | 2nd round | Jameson International |
| | v Stevens | 3-5 | Quarter-final | Jameson International |
| | v Roscoe | 5-1 | 1st round | Professional Players Tournament |
| | v Watterson | 5-2 | 2nd round | Professional Players Tournament |
| | v Sinclair | 5-3 | 3rd round | Professional Players Tournament |
| | v White | 2-5 | Quarter-final | Professional Players Tournament |
| | v Johnson | 9-1 | 1st round | Coral UK Championship |
| | v Dennis Taylor | 9-7 | 2nd round | Coral UK Championship |
| | v S. Davis | 9-6 | Quarter-final | Coral UK Championship |
| | v Meo | 9-7 | Semi-final | Coral UK Championship |
| | **v Higgins** | **16-15** | **Final** | **Coral UK Championship** |
| **1983** | v Mountjoy | 1-5 | 1st round | Lada Classic |
| | v Stevens | 5-3 | 1st round | Benson & Hedges Masters |
| | v Thorburn | 3-5 | Quarter-final | Benson & Hedges Masters |
| | v Everton | 6-1 | Quarter-final | Woodpecker Welsh Championship |
| | v Reardon | 4-9 | Semi-final | Woodpecker Welsh Championship |
| | v Werbeniuk | 5-3 | Semi-final | Tolly Cobbold Classic |
| | v S. Davis | 5-7 | Final | Tolly Cobbold Classic |
| | v Mountjoy | 5-4 | Quarter-final | Benson & Hedges Irish Masters |
| | v S. Davis | 2-6 | Semi-final | Benson & Hedges Irish Masters |
| | v Wildman | 10-8 | 1st round | Embassy World Championship |
| | v Thorburn | 12-13 | 2nd round | Embassy World Championship |
| | v Thorburn | 1-5 | 1st round | Langs Scottish Masters |
| | v Miles | 5-2 | 1st round | Jameson International |
| | v Scott | 5-0 | 2nd round | Jameson International |
| | v Spencer | 5-4 | Quarter-final | Jameson International |
| | v Thorburn | 8-9 | Semi-final | Jameson International |
| | v Dodd | 5-3 | 1st round | Professional Players Tournament |
| | v Parrott | 5-1 | 2nd round | Professional Players Tournament |
| | v E. Hughes | 2-5 | 3rd round | Professional Players Tournament |
| | v Martin | 9-4 | 1st round | Coral UK Championship |
| | v Hallett | 9-5 | 2nd round | Coral UK Championship |
| | v Johnson | 9-2 | Quarter-final | Coral UK Championship |
| | v Higgins | 4-9 | Semi-final | Coral UK Championship |
| **1984** | v Reynolds | 5-2 | Qualifying | Lada Classic |
| | v Roscoe | 5-2 | 1st round | Lada Classic |
| | v S. Davis | 4-5 | Quarter-final | Lada Classic |
| | v Werbeniuk | 5-1 | 1st round | Benson & Hedges Masters |
| | v Spencer | 5-4 | Quarter-final | Benson & Hedges Masters |
| | v Knowles | 6-4 | Semi-final | Benson & Hedges Masters |
| | v White | 5-9 | Final | Benson & Hedges Masters |
| | v Andrewartha | 6-1 | 1st round | Strongbow Welsh Championship |
| | v Mountjoy | 5-9 | Semi-final | Strongbow Welsh Championship |
| | v Werbeniuk | 5-2 | 1st round | Benson & Hedges Irish Masters |
| | v Knowles | 5-0 | Quarter-final | Benson & Hedges Irish Masters |
| | v Dennis Taylor | 5-4 | Semi-final | Benson & Hedges Irish Masters |
| | v S. Davis | 1-9 | Final | Benson & Hedges Irish Masters |
| | v Mifsud | 10-2 | 1st round | Embassy World Championship |
| | v Werbeniuk | 10-5 | 2nd round | Embassy World Championship |
| | v S. Davis | 10-13 | Quarter-final | Embassy World Championship |
| | v Knowles | 3-5 | 1st round | Langs Scottish Masters |
| | v N. Foulds | 5-3 | 1st round | Jameson International |
| | v Higgins | 4-5 | 2nd round | Jameson International |
| | v T. Jones | 3-5 | 1st round | Rothmans Grand Prix |
| | v Wilson | 6-9 | 1st round | Coral UK Open |
| **1985** | v Fagan | 5-0 | 1st round | Mercantile Credit Classic |
| | v Williams | 5-3 | 2nd round | Mercantile Credit Classic |
| | v Thorburn | 4-5 | Quarter-final | Mercantile Credit Classic |
| | v Werbeniuk | 5-2 | 1st round | Benson & Hedges Masters |
| | v Higgins | 5-1 | Quarter-final | Benson & Hedges Masters |

| | | | | |
|---|---|---|---|---|
| | v Mountjoy | 2-6 | Semi-final | Benson & Hedges Masters |
| | v Chalmers | 6-0 | 1st round | Dulux British Open |
| | v Newbury | 3-5 | 2nd round | Dulux British Open |
| | v Higgins | 2-5 | 1st round | Benson & Hedges Irish Masters |
| | v Williams | 10-3 | 1st round | Embassy World Championship |
| | v Higgins | 13-7 | 2nd round | Embassy World Championship |
| | v S. Davis | 6-13 | Quarter-final | Embassy World Championship |
| | v Chappel | 6-0 | Quarter-final | BCE Welsh Championship |
| | v Reardon | 9-3 | Semi-final | BCE Welsh Championship |
| | **v Mountjoy** | **9-4** | **Final** | **BCE Welsh Championship** |
| | v Newbury | 5-2 | 3rd round | Goya Matchroom Trophy |
| | v Spencer | 5-1 | 4th round | Goya Matchroom Trophy |
| | v Parrott | 1-5 | 5th round | Goya Matchroom Trophy |
| | v J. McLaughlin | 5-4 | 3rd round | Rothmans Grand Prix |
| | v B. Harris | 5-3 | 4th round | Rothmans Grand Prix |
| | v P. Francisco | 5-2 | 5th round | Rothmans Grand Prix |
| | v Thorburn | 1-5 | Quarter-final | Rothmans Grand Prix |
| | v S. Davis | 4-5 | 1st round | BCE Canadian Masters |
| | v T. Jones | 9-5 | 3rd round | Coral UK Open |
| | v Reynolds | 9-7 | 4th round | Coral UK Open |
| | v S. Francisco | 9-5 | 5th round | Coral UK Open |
| | v Thorne | 7-9 | Quarter-final | Coral UK Open |
| | v Reardon | 5-2 | 1st round | Kit Kat |
| | v Dennis Taylor | 4-6 | Semi-final | Kit Kat |
| **1986** | v V. Harris | 3-5 | 3rd round | Mercantile Credit Classic |
| | v S. Davis | 5-2 | 1st round | BCE Belgian Classic |
| | v Knowles | 5-2 | Semi-final | BCE Belgian Classic |
| | **v Stevens** | **9-7** | **Final** | **BCE Belgian Classic** |
| | v Higgins | 5-4 | 1st round | Benson & Hedges Masters |
| | v Thorburn | 2-5 | Quarter-final | Benson & Hedges Masters |
| | v Chappel | 6-4 | Quarter-final | Zetters Welsh Championship |
| | v Wilson | 9-1 | Semi-final | Zetters Welsh Championship |
| | **v Mountjoy** | **9-3** | **Final** | **Zetters Welsh Championship** |
| | v Scott | 5-3 | 3rd round | Dulux British Open |
| | v N. Foulds | 5-3 | 4th round | Dulux British Open |
| | v Macleod | 5-2 | 5th round | Dulux British Open |
| | v Thorne | 4-5 | Quarter-final | Dulux British Open |
| | v Thorne | 2-5 | 1st round | Benson & Hedges Irish Masters |
| | v Fowler | 10-2 | 1st round | Embassy World Championship |
| | v Higgins | 13-12 | 2nd round | Embassy World Championship |
| | v Johnson | 12-13 | Quarter-final | Embassy World Championship |
| | v Dennis Taylor | 4-5 | Semi-final | Camus Hong Kong Masters |
| | v Meo | 6-3 | 1st round | Matchroom Trophy |
| | v S. Davis | 2-6 | Semi-final | Matchroom Trophy |
| | v Medati | 5-3 | 3rd round | BCE International |
| | v West | 5-1 | 4th round | BCE International |
| | v Thorburn | 4-5 | 5th round | BCE International |
| | v Morra | 5-3 | 3rd round | Rothmans Grand Prix |
| | v J. Campbell | 5-1 | 4th round | Rothmans Grand Prix |
| | v S. Davis | 2-5 | 5th round | Rothmans Grand Prix |
| | v P. Gibson | 9-3 | 3rd round | Tennents UK Open |
| | v O'Kane | 9-0 | 4th round | Tennents UK Open |
| | v Knowles | 6-9 | 5th round | Tennents UK Open |
| **1987** | v O'Boye | 5-1 | 3rd round | Mercantile Credit Classic |
| | v Martin | 5-4 | 4th round | Mercantile Credit Classic |
| | v J. Campbell | 5-3 | 5th round | Mercantile Credit Classic |
| | v White | 3-5 | Quarter-final | Mercantile Credit Classic |
| | v Higgins | 4-5 | 1st round | Benson & Hedges Masters |
| | v W. Jones | 6-2 | Quarter-final | Matchroom Welsh Championship |
| | v Newbury | 6-9 | Semi-final | Matchroom Welsh Championship |
| | v John Rea | 5-2 | 3rd round | Dulux British Open |
| | v T. Jones | 5-3 | 4th round | Dulux British Open |
| | v Dennis Taylor | 4-5 | 5th round | Dulux British Open |

| | | | | |
|---|---|---|---|---|
| | v Higgins | 5-1 | 1st round | Benson & Hedges Irish Masters |
| | v Johnson | 5-0 | Quarter-final | Benson & Hedges Irish Masters |
| | v S. Davis | 2-6 | Semi-final | Benson & Hedges Irish Masters |
| | v Wych | 10-4 | 1st round | Embassy World Championship |
| | v Higgins | 13-10 | 2nd round | Embassy World Championship |
| | v S. Davis | 5-13 | Quarter-final | Embassy World Championship |
| | v Dennis Taylor | 3-6 | Final | British Caledonian Tokyo Masters (WS) |
| | v N. Foulds | 5-4 | 1st round | Langs Scottish Masters |
| | v White | 6-2 | Semi-final | Langs Scottish Masters |
| | v Johnson | 7-9 | Final | Langs Scottish Masters |
| | v Wildman | 5-1 | 3rd round | Fidelity International |
| | v Charlton | 2-5 | 4th round | Fidelity International |
| | v Kearney | 5-0 | 3rd round | Rothmans Grand Prix |
| | v Chappel | 5-3 | 4th round | Rothmans Grand Prix |
| | v Parrott | 4-5 | 5th round | Rothmans Grand Prix |
| | v N. Foulds | 4-5 | 1st round | Labatts Canadian Masters (WS) |
| | v N. Foulds | 2-6 | 1st round | Matchroom Trophy |
| | v Gary Wilkinson | 9-5 | 3rd round | Tennents UK Open |
| | v Edmonds | 9-5 | 4th round | Tennents UK Open |
| | v S. Francisco | 9-3 | 5th round | Tennents UK Open |
| | v White | 7-9 | Quarter-final | Tennents UK Open |
| **1988** | v Van Rensberg | 5-2 | 3rd round | Mercantile Credit Classic |
| | v C. Wilson | 5-2 | 4th round | Mercantile Credit Classic |
| | v West | 5-2 | 5th round | Mercantile Credit Classic |
| | v Newbury | 4-5 | Quarter-final | Mercantile Credit Classic |
| | v S. Francisco | 5-3 | 1st round | Benson and Hedges Masters |
| | v S. Davis | 0-5 | Quarter-final | Benson and Hedges Masters |
| | v Chappel | 6-4 | Quarter-final | Welsh Championship |
| | v C. Wilson | 9-7 | Semi-final | Welsh Championship |
| | **v W. Jones** | **9-3** | **Final** | **Welsh Championship** |
| | v Morra | 5-1 | 3rd round | MIM Britannia British Open |
| | v Hendry | 1-5 | 4th round | MIM Britannia British Open |
| | v Williams | 5-1 | 1st round | Benson & Hedges Irish Masters |
| | v White | 5-2 | Quarter-final | Benson & Hedges Irish Masters |
| | v N. Foulds | 4-6 | Semi-final | Benson & Hedges Irish Masters |
| | v Longworth | 10-1 | 1st round | Embassy World Championship |
| | v Thorne | 13-9 | 2nd round | Embassy World Championship |
| | v N. Foulds | 13-9 | Quarter-final | Embassy World Championship |
| | v White | 16-11 | Semi-final | Embassy World Championship |
| | v S. Davis | 11-18 | Final | Embassy World Championship |
| | v Wych | 0-5 | 3rd round | Fidelity International |
| | v N. Foulds | 4-6 | 1st round | LEP Matchroom Championship |
| | v Watterson | 5-3 | 3rd round | Rothmans Grand Prix |
| | v West | 5-1 | 4th round | Rothmans Grand Prix |
| | v E. Hughes | 5-2 | 5th round | Rothmans Grand Prix |
| | v S. Davis | 3-5 | Quarter-final | Rothmans Grand Prix |
| | v Oliver | 5-4 | 3rd round | BCE Canadian Masters |
| | v Reardon | 5-2 | 4th round | BCE Canadian Masters |
| | v Mountjoy | 5-4 | 5th round | BCE Canadian Masters |
| | v S. Davis | 3-5 | Quarter-final | BCE Canadian Masters |
| | v Owers | 9-2 | 3rd round | Tennents UK Open |
| | v Duggan | 9-2 | 4th round | Tennents UK Open |
| | v Reynolds | 9-6 | 5th round | Tennents UK Open |
| | v West | 9-5 | Quarter-final | Tennents UK Open |
| | v Mountjoy | 4-9 | Semi-final | Tennents UK Open |
| | v P. Francisco | 9-7 | 1st round | Everest World Matchplay |
| | v White | 5-9 | Quarter-final | Everest World Matchplay |
| **1989** | v King | 5-2 | 3rd round | Mercantile Credit Classic |
| | v Drago | 5-0 | 4th round | Mercantile Credit Classic |
| | v Thorne | 1-5 | 5th round | Mercantile Credit Classic |
| | v S. Francisco | 5-1 | 1st round | Benson and Hedges Masters |
| | v Hendry | 3-5 | Quarter-final | Benson and Hedges Masters |
| | v J. McLaughlin | 5-3 | 3rd round | European Open |

| | | | | |
|---|---|---|---|---|
| | v Chappel | 5-2 | 4th round | European Open |
| | v Robidoux | 5-3 | 5th round | European Open |
| | v Clark | 5-1 | Quarter-final | European Open |
| | v White | 5-4 | Semi-final | European Open |
| | v Parrott | 8-9 | Final | European Open |
| | v D. Morgan | 6-5 | Quarter-final | Senator Welsh Championship |
| | v Newbury | 9-7 | Semi-final | Senator Welsh Championship |
| | v Mountjoy | 6-9 | Final | Senator Welsh Championship |
| | v Johnston-Allen | 1-5 | 3rd round | Anglian British Open |
| | v J. McLaughlin | 5-4 | 1st round | Benson and Hedges Irish Masters |
| | v Hendry | 2-5 | Quarter-final | Benson and Hedges Irish Masters |
| | v Chaperon | 10-6 | 1st round | Embassy World Championship |
| | v S. Francisco | 13-9 | 2nd round | Embassy World Championship |
| | v Hendry | 5-13 | Quarter-final | Embassy World Championship |
| | v Rigitano | 5-3 | 3rd round | Hong Kong Open |
| | v O'Kane | 4-5 | 4th round | Hong Kong Open |
| | v Cairns | 5-2 | 3rd round | 555 Asian Open |
| | v Roe | 5-3 | 4th round | 555 Asian Open |
| | v Drago | 5-3 | 5th round | 555 Asian Open |
| | v T. Jones | 5-3 | Quarter-final | 555 Asian Open |
| | v Wattana | 0-5 | Semi-final | 555 Asian Open |
| | v White | 6-3 | Quarter-final | Regal Scottish Masters |
| | v S. Davis | 6-2 | Semi-final | Regal Scottish Masters |
| | v Hendry | 1-10 | Final | Regal Scottish Masters |
| | v Gollan | 5-4 | 3rd round | BCE International |
| | v Newbury | 2-5 | 4th round | BCE International |
| | v P. Gibson | 2-5 | 3rd round | Rothmans Grand Prix |
| | v King | 9-4 | 3rd round | Stormseal UK Open |
| | v T. Jones | 9-8 | 4th round | Stormseal UK Open |
| | v Knowles | 9-7 | 5th round | Stormseal UK Open |
| | v Robidoux | 9-2 | Quarter-final | Stormseal UK Open |
| | v Hendry | 7-9 | Semi-final | Stormseal UK Open |
| | v Thorburn | 9-5 | 1st round | Everest World Matchplay |
| | v Hendry | 3-9 | Quarter-final | Everest World Matchplay |
| **1990** | v King | 1-5 | 3rd round | Mercantile Credit Classic |
| | v Knowles | 4-5 | 1st round | Benson and Hedges Masters |
| | v D. Morgan | 4-6 | Quarter-final | Senator Welsh Championship |
| | v Gary Wilkinson | 5-4 | 3rd round | Pearl Assurance British Open |
| | v P. Francisco | 1-5 | 4th round | Pearl Assurance British Open |
| | v M. Bennett | 2-5 | 3rd round | European Open |
| | v Mountjoy | 5-1 | 1st round | Benson and Hedges Irish Masters |
| | v Parrott | 5-3 | Quarter-final | Benson and Hedges Irish Masters |
| | v S. Davis | 3-6 | Semi-final | Benson and Hedges Irish Masters |
| | v N. Gilbert | 10-4 | 1st round | Embassy World Championship |
| | v Knowles | 13-6 | 2nd round | Embassy World Championship |
| | v White | 5-13 | Quarter-final | Embassy World Championship |

## MIKE HALLETT (England)

**Born** 6.7.59. **Turned professional** 1979. **World ranking** 7 (6).

| | | | | |
|---|---|---|---|---|
| **1979** | v Parkin | 9-1 | 1st round | Coral UK Championship |
| | v Fagan | 4-9 | 2nd round | Coral UK Championship |
| **1980** | v Stevens | 3-9 | Qualifying | Embassy World Championship |
| | v Bennett | 9-4 | Qualifying | Coral UK Championship |
| | v Edmonds | 9-8 | Qualifying | Coral UK Championship |
| | v S. Davis | 1-9 | 1st round | Coral UK Championship |
| **1981** | v Edmonds | 3-9 | Qualifying | John Courage English |
| | v Jonik | 9-1 | Qualifying | Embassy World Championship |
| | v Meo | 4-9 | Qualifying | Embassy World Championship |
| | v Demarco | 5-4 | Qualifying | Jameson International |
| | v Knowles | 2-5 | 1st round | Jameson International |

*Mike Hallett*

| | | | | |
|---|---|---|---|---|
| | v V. Harris | 9-4 | Qualifying | Coral UK Championship |
| | v D. Hughes | 9-6 | Qualifying | Coral UK Championship |
| | v Fagan | 9-5 | Qualifying | Coral UK Championship |
| | v Stevens | 4-9 | 2nd round | Coral UK Championship |
| **1982** | v Johnson | 9-8 | Qualifying | Embassy World Championship |
| | v Virgo | 4-10 | 1st round | Embassy World Championship |
| | v Jonik | 5-2 | Qualifying | Jameson International |
| | v Wildman | 2-5 | Qualifying | Jameson International |
| | v V. Harris | 5-3 | 1st round | Professional Players Tournament |
| | v Virgo | 2-5 | 2nd round | Professional Players Tournament |
| | v Demarco | 9-1 | Qualifying | Coral UK Championship |
| | v F. Davis | 9-7 | 1st round | Coral UK Championship |
| | v Reardon | 8-9 | 2nd round | Coral UK Championship |
| **1983** | v Andrewartha | 10-7 | Qualifying | Embassy World Championship |
| | v King | 10-6 | Qualifying | Embassy World Championship |
| | v Spencer | 7-10 | 1st round | Embassy World Championship |
| | v Roscoe | 5-2 | Qualifying | Jameson International |
| | v Morra | 3-5 | Qualifying | Jameson International |
| | v Kelly | 5-0 | 1st round | Professional Players Tournament |
| | v S. Davis | 5-2 | 2nd round | Professional Players Tournament |
| | v Meo | 3-5 | 3rd round | Professional Players Tournament |
| | v Darrington | 9-1 | Qualifying | Coral UK Championship |
| | v Miles | 9-4 | 1st round | Coral UK Championship |
| | v Griffiths | 5-9 | 2nd round | Coral UK Championship |
| **1984** | v Dennis Taylor | 5-4 | Qualifying | Lada Classic |
| | v Knowles | 3-5 | 1st round | Lada Classic |
| | v Burke | 10-5 | Qualifying | Embassy World Championship |
| | v Mountjoy | 4-10 | 1st round | Embassy World Championship |
| | v O'Kane | 4-5 | Qualifying | Jameson International |
| | v Sheehan | 5-1 | 1st round | Rothmans Grand Prix |
| | v Higgins | 5-3 | 2nd round | Rothmans Grand Prix |
| | v Stevens | 3-5 | 3rd round | Rothmans Grand Prix |
| | v Bradley | 9-8 | Qualifying | Coral UK Open |
| | v Mountjoy | 2-9 | 1st round | Coral UK Open |
| **1985** | v G. Foulds | 5-4 | Qualifying | Mercantile Credit Classic |
| | v Reardon | 3-5 | 1st round | Mercantile Credit Classic |
| | v Duggan | 9-4 | 1st round | Tolly Cobbold English Championship |
| | v Meo | 4-9 | 2nd round | Tolly Cobbold English Championship |
| | v Meo | 4-5 | 2nd round | Dulux British Open |
| | v Chalmers | 10-1 | Qualifying | Embassy World Championship |
| | v Thorburn | 8-10 | 1st round | Embassy World Championship |
| | v Bradley | 4-5 | 3rd round | Goya Matchroom Trophy |
| | v Mikkelsen | 5-3 | 3rd round | Rothmans Grand Prix |
| | v Johnson | 4-5 | 4th round | Rothmans Grand Prix |
| | v Meadowcroft | 9-1 | 3rd round | Coral UK Open |
| | v Stevens | 5-9 | 4th round | Coral UK Open |
| **1986** | v John Rea | 5-2 | 3rd round | Mercantile Credit Classic |
| | v Thorburn | 3-5 | 4th round | Mercantile Credit Classic |
| | v Chalmers | 9-1 | 3rd round | Tolly Cobbold English Championship |
| | v Knowles | 9-5 | 4th round | Tolly Cobbold English Championship |
| | v Johnson | 9-6 | Quarter-final | Tolly Cobbold English Championship |
| | v N. Foulds | 8-9 | Semi-final | Tolly Cobbold English Championship |
| | v Duggan | 5-3 | 3rd round | Dulux British Open |
| | v Higgins | 1-5 | 4th round | Dulux British Open |
| | v Wych | 10-7 | Qualifying | Embassy World Championship |
| | v Dennis Taylor | 10-6 | 1st round | Embassy World Championship |
| | v Johnson | 6-13 | 2nd round | Embassy World Championship |
| | v O'Kane | 1-5 | 3rd round | BCE International |
| | v V. Harris | 5-2 | 3rd round | Rothmans Grand Prix |
| | v Dodd | 5-2 | 4th round | Rothmans Grand Prix |
| | v White | 3-5 | 5th round | Rothmans Grand Prix |
| | v King | 9-5 | 3rd round | Tennents UK Open |
| | v Meo | 9-4 | 4th round | Tennents UK Open |

| | | | | |
|---|---|---|---|---|
| | v Higgins | 7-9 | 5th round | Tennents UK Open |
| **1987** | v Mikkelsen | 5-3 | 3rd round | Mercantile Credit Classic |
| | v Fowler | 4-5 | 4th round | Mercantile Credit Classic |
| | v Williamson | 2-6 | 3rd round | Tolly Ales English Championship |
| | v Owers | 6-2 | 4th round | Tolly Ales English Championship |
| | v Dodd | 5-6 | Quarter-final | Tolly Ales English Championship |
| | v Rigitano | 5-0 | 3rd round | Dulux British Open |
| | v White | 2-5 | 4th round | Dulux British Open |
| | v Newbury | 10-4 | Qualifying | Embassy World Championship |
| | v Knowles | 10-6 | 1st round | Embassy World Championship |
| | v S. Francisco | 13-9 | 2nd round | Embassy World Championship |
| | v N. Foulds | 9-13 | Quarter-final | Embassy World Championship |
| | v Roscoe | 5-3 | 3rd round | Fidelity International |
| | v Longworth | 5-1 | 4th round | Fidelity International |
| | v White | 5-4 | 5th round | Fidelity International |
| | v Charlton | 5-4 | Quarter-final | Fidelity International |
| | v S. Davis | 3-9 | Semi-final | Fidelity International |
| | v P. Gibson | 4-5 | 3rd round | Rothmans Grand Prix |
| | v T. Jones | 9-2 | 3rd round | Tennents UK Open |
| | v Meo | 9-5 | 4th round | Tennents UK Open |
| | v Fowler | 9-4 | 5th round | Tennents UK Open |
| | v Johnson | 7-9 | Quarter-final | Tennents UK Open |
| **1988** | v Clark | 4-5 | 3rd round | Mercantile Credit Classic |
| | v Dennis Taylor | 5-3 | 1st round | Benson & Hedges Masters |
| | v Higgins | 5-2 | Quarter-final | Benson & Hedges Masters |
| | v Parrott | 6-5 | Semi-final | Benson & Hedges Masters |
| | v S. Davis | 0-9 | Final | Benson & Hedges Masters |
| | v Duggan | 6-3 | 3rd round | English Championship |
| | v Williams | 6-3 | 4th round | English Championship |
| | v West | 5-6 | Quarter-final | English Championship |
| | v Williamson | 5-0 | 3rd round | MIM Britannia British Open |
| | v Cripsey | 5-2 | 4th round | MIM Britannia British Open |
| | v Macleod | 5-2 | 5th round | MIM Britannia British Open |
| | v O'Boye | 5-4 | Quarter-final | MIM Britannia British Open |
| | v Parrott | 9-8 | Semi-final | MIM Britannia British Open |
| | v Hendry | 2-13 | Final | MIM Britannia British Open |
| | v Chaperon | 10-2 | 1st round | Embassy World Championship |
| | v S. Davis | 1-13 | 2nd round | Embassy World Championship |
| | v O'Kane | 5-1 | 1st round | New Zealand Masters |
| | v Knowles | 5-3 | Semi-final | New Zealand Masters |
| | v Hendry | 1-6 | Final | New Zealand Masters |
| | v O'Boye | 5-3 | 3rd round | Fidelity International |
| | v Meo | 3-5 | 4th round | Fidelity International |
| | v Parrott | 5-3 | 1st round | Fosters Professional |
| | **v Hendry** | **8-5** | **Final** | **Fosters Professional** |
| | v T. Jones | 5-2 | 3rd round | Rothmans Grand Prix |
| | v James | 5-2 | 4th round | Rothmans Grand Prix |
| | v Dennis Taylor | 2-5 | 5th round | Rothmans Grand Prix |
| | v O'Boye | 5-0 | 3rd round | BCE Canadian Masters |
| | v Gauvreau | 5-3 | 4th round | BCE Canadian Masters |
| | v King | 5-2 | 5th round | BCE Canadian Masters |
| | v Parrott | 5-3 | Quarter-final | BCE Canadian Masters |
| | v White | 2-9 | Semi-final | BCE Canadian Masters |
| | v Clark | 6-9 | 3rd round | Tennents UK Open |
| | v Thorne | 9-8 | 1st round | Everest World Matchplay |
| | v S. Davis | 2-9 | Quarter-final | Everest World Matchplay |
| **1989** | v Browne | 2-5 | 3rd round | Mercantile Credit Classic |
| | v Knowles | 3-5 | 1st round | Benson and Hedges Masters |
| | v D. Gilbert | 5-3 | 3rd round | European Open |
| | v Browne | 5-4 | 4th round | European Open |
| | v Hendry | 5-3 | 5th round | European Open |
| | v Wych | 5-3 | Quarter-final | European Open |
| | v Parrott | 4-5 | Semi-final | European Open |

| | | | | |
|---|---|---|---|---|
| | v Houlihan | 5-2 | 3rd round | English Championship |
| | v Price | 5-4 | 4th round | English Championship |
| | v Longworth | 5-1 | Quarter-final | English Championship |
| | v Gary Wilkinson | 5-3 | Semi-final | English Championship |
| | **v Parrott** | **9-7** | **Final** | **English Championship** |
| | v N. Gilbert | 5-3 | 3rd round | Anglian British Open |
| | v Bales | 5-0 | 4th round | Anglian British Open |
| | v Thorburn | 5-4 | 5th round | Anglian British Open |
| | v Clark | 5-3 | Quarter-final | Anglian British Open |
| | v Meo | 8-9 | Semi-final | Anglian British Open |
| | v Knowles | 5-0 | 1st round | Benson and Hedges Irish Masters |
| | v S. Davis | 4-5 | Quarter-final | Benson and Hedges Irish Masters |
| | v Mountjoy | 10-7 | 1st round | Embassy World Championship |
| | v Roe | 13-12 | 2nd round | Embassy World Championship |
| | v S. Davis | 3-13 | Quarter-final | Embassy World Championship |
| | v Johnson | 5-6 | 1st round | Lion Brown New Zealand Masters |
| | v Fowler | 5-2 | 3rd round | Hong Kong Open |
| | v West | 5-4 | 4th round | Hong Kong Open |
| | v Virgo | 5-1 | 5th round | Hong Kong Open |
| | v Hendry | 5-4 | Quarter-final | Hong Kong Open |
| | v White | 5-2 | Semi-final | Hong Kong Open |
| | **v O'Kane** | **9-8** | **Final** | **Hong Kong Open** |
| | v Edwards | 5-0 | 3rd round | 555 Asian Open |
| | v Wattana | 3-5 | 4th round | 555 Asian Open |
| | v White | 1-6 | Quarter-final | Regal Scottish Masters |
| | v Dodd | 5-4 | 3rd round | BCE International |
| | v C. Wilson | 4-5 | 4th round | BCE International |
| | v Johnston-Allen | 5-1 | 3rd round | Rothmans Grand Prix |
| | v Fowler | 3-5 | 4th round | Rothmans Grand Prix |
| | v T. Jones | 4-5 | 3rd round | Dubai Classic |
| | v Wattana | 9-7 | 3rd round | Stormseal UK Open |
| | v O'Kane | 9-0 | 4th round | Stormseal UK Open |
| | v Dennis Taylor | 9-6 | 5th round | Stormseal UK Open |
| | v S. Davis | 5-9 | Quarter-final | Stormseal UK Open |
| | v Dennis Taylor | 6-9 | 1st round | Everest World Matchplay |
| **1990** | v S. Murphy | 5-1 | 3rd round | Mercantile Credit Classic |
| | v W. Jones | 3-5 | 4th round | Mercantile Credit Classic |
| | v Johnson | 3-5 | 1st round | Benson and Hedges Masters |
| | v Miles | 5-1 | 3rd round | Pearl Assurance British Open |
| | v Chaperon | 3-5 | 4th round | Pearl Assurance British Open |
| | v Robidoux | 1-5 | 3rd round | European Open |
| | v Thorne | 1-5 | 1st round | Benson and Hedges Irish Masters |
| | v Newbury | 10-9 | 1st round | Embassy World Championship |
| | v D. Morgan | 8-13 | 2nd round | Embassy World Championship |

## ANTHONY HARRIS (England)

**Born** 19.4.68. **Turned professional** 1987. **World ranking** 90 (74).

| | | | | |
|---|---|---|---|---|
| **1987** | v D. Gilbert | 4-5 | 1st round | Fidelity International |
| | v Meadowcroft | 3-5 | 1st round | Rothmans Grand Prix |
| | v Morra | 9-8 | 1st round | Tennents UK Open |
| | v Gauvreau | 3-9 | 2nd round | Tennents UK Open |
| **1988** | v Jenkins | 5-4 | 1st round | Mercantile Credit Classic |
| | v T. Jones | 2-5 | 2nd round | Mercantile Credit Classic |
| | v N. Gilbert | 3-5 | 1st round | English Championship |
| | v Bear | 2-5 | 1st round | MIM Britannia British Open |
| | v Mizerak | 10-3 | Preliminary | Embassy World Championship |
| | v Fisher | 10-4 | Qualifying | Embassy World Championship |
| | v Duggan | 4-10 | Qualifying | Embassy World Championship |
| | v Foldvari | 1-5 | 1st round | Fidelity International |
| | v Kearney | 5-2 | 1st round | Rothmans Grand Prix |

| | | | | |
|---|---|---|---|---|
| | v Werbeniuk | 1-5 | 2nd round | Rothmans Grand Prix |
| | v Morra | 5-3 | 1st round | BCE Canadian Masters |
| | v O'Boye | 3-5 | 2nd round | BCE Canadian Masters |
| | v M. Gibson | 8-9 | 1st round | Tennents UK Open |
| **1989** | v Bear | 5-3 | 1st round | Mercantile Credit Classic |
| | v D. Gilbert | 5-4 | 2nd round | Mercantile Credit Classic |
| | v West | 5-4 | 3rd round | Mercantile Credit Classic |
| | v Chappel | 1-5 | 4th round | Mercantile Credit Classic |
| | v Glen Wilkinson | 5-4 | 1st round | European Open |
| | v Fowler | 1-5 | 2nd round | European Open |
| | v T. Jones | 5-3 | 2nd round | English Championship |
| | v Reynolds | 1-5 | 3rd round | English Championship |
| | v Wildman | 5-4 | 1st round | Anglian British Open |
| | v Wych | 4-5 | 2nd round | Anglian British Open |
| | v Van Rensberg | 10-7 | Qualifying | Embassy World Championship |
| | v W. Jones | 4-10 | Qualifying | Embassy World Championship |
| | v Rowing | 4-5 | 1st round | Hong Kong Open |
| | v Van Rensberg | 3-5 | 1st round | 555 Asian Open |
| | v M. Gibson | 5-4 | 1st round | BCE International |
| | v Dodd | 3-5 | 2nd round | BCE International |
| | v Ellis | 5-2 | 1st round | Rothmans Grand Prix |
| | v N. Gilbert | 2-5 | 2nd round | Rothmans Grand Prix |
| | v Thornley | 5-1 | 1st round | Dubai Classic |
| | v King | 3-5 | 2nd round | Dubai Classic |
| | v Meakin | 2-6 | 1st round | Stormseal UK Open |
| **1990** | v Wattana | 3-5 | 1st round | Mercantile Credit Classic |
| | v Ellis | 5-3 | 1st round | Pearl Assurance British Open |
| | v D. Morgan | 3-5 | 2nd round | Pearl Assurance British Open |
| | v Jack Rea | 4-5 | 1st round | European Open |
| | v Grace | 8-10 | Qualifying | Embassy World Championship |

## BOB HARRIS (England)

**Born** 12.3.56. **Turned professional** 1982. **World ranking** 93 (93).

| | | | | |
|---|---|---|---|---|
| **1982** | v Scott | 4-5 | Qualifying | Jameson International |
| | v Cripsey | 9-6 | Qualifying | Coral UK Championship |
| | v Watterson | 9-3 | Qualifying | Coral UK Championship |
| | v Fagan | 6-9 | 1st round | Coral UK Championship |
| **1983** | v Wildman | 7-10 | Qualifying | Embassy World Championship |
| | v Dunning | 5-3 | Qualifying | Jameson International |
| | v Wildman | 2-5 | Qualifying | Jameson International |
| | v King | 3-5 | Qualifying | Professional Players Tournament |
| | v E. McLaughlin | 9-8 | Qualifying | Coral UK Championship |
| | v Fitzmaurice | 9-3 | Qualifying | Coral UK Championship |
| | v Reardon | 7-9 | 1st round | Coral UK Championship |
| **1984** | v Sheehan | 10-3 | Qualifying | Embassy World Championship |
| | v Burke | 4-10 | Qualifying | Embassy World Championship |
| | v Watchorn | 7-9 | Qualifying | Coral UK Open |
| **1985** | v Duggan | 8-9 | Qualifying | Tolly Cobbold English Championship |
| | v Meadowcroft | 6-1 | Qualifying | Dulux British Open |
| | v Charlton | 6-3 | 1st round | Dulux British Open |
| | v E. Hughes | 4-5 | 2nd round | Dulux British Open |
| | v Rigitano | 4-10 | Qualifying | Embassy World Championship |
| | v Browne | 5-3 | 2nd round | Goya Matchroom Trophy |
| | v O'Kane | 5-3 | 3rd round | Goya Matchroom Trophy |
| | v Dennis Taylor | 3-5 | 4th round | Goya Matchroom Trophy |
| | v Browne | 5-3 | 2nd round | Rothmans Grand Prix |
| | v Spencer | 5-2 | 3rd round | Rothmans Grand Prix |
| | v Griffiths | 3-5 | 4th round | Rothmans Grand Prix |
| | v Fagan | 2-9 | 2nd round | Coral UK Open |
| **1986** | v Morra | 5-3 | 2nd round | Mercantile Credit Classic |

| | | | | |
|---|---|---|---|---|
| | v Johnson | 4-5 | 3rd round | Mercantile Credit Classic |
| | v T. Jones | 5-9 | 2nd round | Tolly Cobbold English Championship |
| | v Sinclair | 5-3 | 2nd round | Dulux British Open |
| | v Martin | 1-5 | 3rd round | Dulux British Open |
| | v Black | 8-10 | Qualifying | Embassy World Championship |
| | v Foldvari | 0-5 | 2nd round | BCE International |
| | v Jack Rea | 5-0 | 2nd round | Rothmans Grand Prix |
| | v Mountjoy | 2-5 | 3rd round | Rothmans Grand Prix |
| | v Jack Rea | 9-5 | 2nd round | Tennents UK Open |
| | v Wych | 6-9 | 3rd round | Tennents UK Open |
| **1987** | v P. Gibson | 5-3 | 2nd round | Mercantile Credit Classic |
| | v Wych | 5-3 | 3rd round | Mercantile Credit Classic |
| | v S. Francisco | 3-5 | 4th round | Mercantile Credit Classic |
| | v G. Foulds | 6-1 | 2nd round | Tolly Ales English Championship |
| | v Thorne | 2-6 | 3rd round | Tolly Ales English Championship |
| | v Kelly | 5-2 | 2nd round | Dulux British Open |
| | v Thorne | 1-5 | 3rd round | Dulux British Open |
| | v D. Hughes | 10-2 | Qualifying | Embassy World Championship |
| | v Fowler | 6-10 | Qualifying | Embassy World Championship |
| | v James | 0-5 | 2nd round | Fidelity International |
| | v Bear | 3-5 | 2nd round | Rothmans Grand Prix |
| | v Bear | 4-9 | 2nd round | Tennents UK Open |
| **1988** | v D. Gilbert | 4-5 | 2nd round | Mercantile Credit Classic |
| | v M. Smith | 4-6 | 2nd round | English Championship |
| | v Lawlor | 2-5 | 2nd round | MIM Britannia British Open |
| | v Fagan | 10-1 | Qualifying | Embassy World Championship |
| | v Sinclair | 10-0 | Qualifying | Embassy World Championship |
| | v Charlton | 4-10 | Qualifying | Embassy World Championship |
| | v Watchorn | 2-5 | 1st round | Fidelity International |
| | v Jack Rea | 5-2 | 1st round | Rothmans Grand Prix |
| | v Roe | 2-5 | 2nd round | Rothmans Grand Prix |
| | v Johnston-Allen | 4-5 | 1st round | BCE Canadian Masters |
| | v Graham | 9-4 | 1st round | Tennents UK Open |
| | v Macleod | 9-8 | 2nd round | Tennents UK Open |
| | v Williams | 4-9 | 3rd round | Tennents UK Open |
| **1989** | v Robidoux | 1-5 | 1st round | Mercantile Credit Classic |
| | v Watchorn | 4-5 | 1st round | European Open |
| | v Fitzmaurice | 4-5 | 1st round | English Championship |
| | v Robidoux | 0-5 | 1st round | Anglian British Open |
| | v D. Campbell | 2-5 | 1st round | Hong Kong Open |
| | v B. Morgan | 5-3 | 1st round | 555 Asian Open |
| | v T. Murphy | 5-3 | 2nd round | 555 Asian Open |
| | v Virgo | 4-5 | 3rd round | 555 Asian Open |
| | v Watterson | 5-3 | 1st round | BCE International |
| | v Gary Wilkinson | 5-4 | 2nd round | BCE International |
| | v Knowles | 1-5 | 3rd round | BCE International |
| | v B. Morgan | 5-2 | 1st round | Rothmans Grand Prix |
| | v Longworth | 2-5 | 2nd round | Rothmans Grand Prix |
| | v Sheehan | 5-3 | 1st round | Dubai Classic |
| | v Duggan | 5-3 | 2nd round | Dubai Classic |
| | v Spencer | 3-5 | 3rd round | Dubai Classic |
| | v D. Campbell | 6-2 | 1st round | Stormseal UK Open |
| | v D. Gilbert | 2-6 | 2nd round | Stormseal UK Open |
| **1990** | v Wildman | 5-2 | 1st round | Mercantile Credit Classic |
| | v Browne | 5-3 | 2nd round | Mercantile Credit Classic |
| | v Charlton | 2-5 | 3rd round | Mercantile Credit Classic |
| | v D. Campbell | 5-2 | 1st round | Pearl Assurance British Open |
| | v Fisher | 5-1 | 2nd round | Pearl Assurance British Open |
| | v Higgins | 3-5 | 3rd round | Pearl Assurance British Open |
| | v Fitzmaurice | 5-3 | 1st round | European Open |
| | v Fowler | 3-5 | 2nd round | European Open |
| | v Jenkins | 10-4 | Qualifying | Embassy World Championship |
| | v Edmonds | 4-10 | Qualifying | Embassy World Championship |

## VIC HARRIS (England)

**Born** 16.8.45. **Turned professional** 1981. **World ranking** 111 (83).

| | | | | |
|---|---|---|---|---|
| **1981** | v Sheehan | 1-5 | Qualifying | Jameson International |
| | v Higgins | 3-5 | Quarter-final | Langs Scottish Masters |
| | v Hallett | 4-9 | Qualifying | Coral UK Championship |
| | v Johnson | 4-9 | Qualifying | Embassy World Championship |
| **1982** | v Hallett | 3-5 | 1st round | Professional Players Tournament |
| | v M. Owen | 9-4 | Qualifying | Coral UK Championship |
| | v Johnson | 8-9 | Qualifying | Coral UK Championship |
| | v Sheehan | 5-3 | Qualifying | Jameson International |
| | v Virgo | 2-5 | Qualifying | Jameson International |
| **1983** | v Meo | 0-10 | Qualifying | Embassy World Championship |
| | v Medati | 0-5 | Qualifying | Jameson International |
| | v Thorburn | 1-5 | 1st round | Professional Players Tournament |
| | v Houlihan | 9-6 | Qualifying | Coral UK Championship |
| | v Williams | 6-9 | Qualifying | Coral UK Championship |
| **1984** | v Van Rensberg | 7-10 | Qualifying | Embassy World Championship |
| | v Williamson | 0-5 | Qualifying | Jameson International |
| | v F. Davis | 5-1 | Qualifying | Rothmans Grand Prix |
| | v Knowles | 1-5 | 1st round | Rothmans Grand Prix |
| | v Bradley | 8-9 | Qualifying | Coral UK Open |
| **1985** | v Newbury | 3-5 | Qualifying | Mercantile Credit Classic |
| | v Scott | 7-9 | Qualifying | Tolly Cobbold English Championship |
| | v Dodd | 6-1 | Qualifying | Dulux British Open |
| | v Mountjoy | 6-5 | 1st round | Dulux British Open |
| | v O'Kane | 3-5 | 2nd round | Dulux British Open |
| | v O'Kane | 5-10 | Qualifying | Embassy World Championship |
| | v Foldvari | 4-5 | 2nd round | Goya Matchroom Trophy |
| | v Wych | 5-3 | 2nd round | Rothmans Grand Prix |
| | v Higgins | 1-5 | 3rd round | Rothmans Grand Prix |
| | v Black | 9-3 | 2nd round | Coral UK Open |
| | v Spencer | 5-9 | 3rd round | Coral UK Open |
| **1986** | v Roscoe | 5-1 | 2nd round | Mercantile Credit Classic |
| | v Griffiths | 5-3 | 3rd round | Mercantile Credit Classic |
| | v Williams | 1-5 | 4th round | Mercantile Credit Classic |
| | v Bales | 7-9 | 2nd round | Tolly Cobbold English Championship |
| | v Chaperon | 0-5 | 2nd round | Dulux British Open |
| | v T. Jones | 7-10 | Qualifying | Embassy World Championship |
| | v G. Foulds | 4-5 | 2nd round | BCE International |
| | v Kelly | 5-3 | 2nd round | Rothmans Grand Prix |
| | v Hallett | 2-5 | 3rd round | Rothmans Grand Prix |
| | v Fisher | 9-4 | 2nd round | Tennents UK Open |
| | v Charlton | 2-9 | 3rd round | Tennents UK Open |
| **1987** | v O'Boye | 1-5 | 2nd round | Mercantile Credit Classic |
| | v Darrington | 6-3 | 2nd round | Tolly Ales English Championship |
| | v West | 3-6 | 3rd round | Tolly Ales English Championship |
| | v Sheehan | 5-4 | 2nd round | Dulux British Open |
| | v E. Hughes | 1-5 | 3rd round | Dulux British Open |
| | v Rigitano | 6-10 | Qualifying | Embassy World Championship |
| | v Marshall | 5-1 | 1st round | Fidelity International |
| | v Chaperon | 4-5 | 2nd round | Fidelity International |
| | v Gary Wilkinson | 0-5 | 1st round | Rothmans Grand Prix |
| | v Greaves | 9-1 | 1st round | Tennents UK Open |
| | v M. Bennett | 9-7 | 2nd round | Tennents UK Open |
| | v Martin | 9-7 | 3rd round | Tennents UK Open |
| | v Roe | 5-9 | 4th round | Tennents UK Open |
| **1988** | v Ellis | 5-1 | 1st round | Mercantile Credit Classic |
| | v Murphy | 2-5 | 2nd round | Mercantile Credit Classic |
| | v J. Smith | 3-6 | 1st round | English Championship |
| | v Thornley | 4-5 | 1st round | MIM Britannia British Open |
| | v M. Smith | 6-10 | Qualifying | Embassy World Championship |

| | | | | |
|---|---|---|---|---|
| | v Burke | 5-2 | 1st round | Fidelity International |
| | v Wych | 3-5 | 2nd round | Fidelity International |
| | v Marshall | 5-3 | 1st round | Rothmans Grand Prix |
| | v J. McLaughlin | 4-5 | 2nd round | Rothmans Grand Prix |
| | v Darrington | 0-5 | 1st round | BCE Canadian Masters |
| | v Mikkelsen | 9-3 | 1st round | Tennents UK Open |
| | v M. Bennett | 7-9 | 2nd round | Tennents UK Open |
| **1989** | v D. Morgan | 3-5 | 1st round | Mercantile Credit Classic |
| | v Terry | 5-2 | 1st round | European Open |
| | v Roe | 1-5 | 2nd round | European Open |
| | v Rowswell | 3-5 | 1st round | English Championship |
| | v Johnston-Allen | 1-5 | 1st round | Anglian British Open |
| | v Watterson | 10-5 | Qualifying | Embassy World Championship |
| | v Gary Wilkinson | 6-10 | Qualifying | Embassy World Championship |
| | v Watchorn | 5-4 | 1st round | Hong Kong Open |
| | v Fowler | 0-5 | 2nd round | Hong Kong Open |
| | v Meakin | 3-5 | 1st round | 555 Asian Open |
| | v Darrington | 2-5 | 1st round | BCE International |
| | v D. Hughes | 5-4 | 1st round | Rothmans Grand Prix |
| | v David Taylor | 5-3 | 2nd round | Rothmans Grand Prix |
| | v Reynolds | 0-5 | 3rd round | Rothmans Grand Prix |
| | v M. Gibson | 3-5 | 1st round | Dubai Classic |
| | v B. Morgan | 3-6 | 1st round | Stormseal UK Open |
| **1990** | v Jack Rea | 5-2 | 1st round | Pearl Assurance British Open |
| | v M. Bennett | 0-5 | 2nd round | Pearl Assurance British Open |
| | v Gollan | 2-5 | 1st round | European Open |
| | v Watchorn | 6-10 | Qualifying | Embassy World Championship |

## STEPHEN HENDRY (Scotland)

**Born** 13.1.69. **Turned professional** 1985. **World ranking** 1 (3).

| | | | | |
|---|---|---|---|---|
| **1985** | v West | 5-4 | 1st round | Goya Matchroom Trophy |
| | v E. McLaughlin | 3-5 | 2nd round | Goya Matchroom Trophy |
| | v O'Boye | 4-5 | 1st round | Rothmans Grand Prix |
| | v Agrawal | 2-9 | Qualifying | Coral UK Open |
| **1986** | v Sheehan | 5-2 | 1st round | Mercantile Credit Classic |
| | v Miles | 5-1 | 2nd round | Mercantile Credit Classic |
| | v S. Francisco | 5-4 | 3rd round | Mercantile Credit Classic |
| | v N. Foulds | 4-5 | 4th round | Mercantile Credit Classic |
| | v D. Hughes | 5-1 | 1st round | Dulux British Open |
| | v Browne | 0-5 | 2nd round | Dulux British Open |
| | v Demarco | 6-1 | 1st round | Canada Dry Scottish Championship |
| | v Macleod | 6-5 | Quarter-final | Canada Dry Scottish Championship |
| | v Black | 6-2 | Semi-final | Canada Dry Scottish Championship |
| | **v Gibson** | **10-5** | **Final** | **Canada Dry Scottish Championship** |
| | v Demarco | 10-7 | Qualifying | Embassy World Championship |
| | v Browne | 10-9 | Qualifying | Embassy World Championship |
| | v W. Jones | 10-8 | Qualifying | Embassy World Championship |
| | v O'Kane | 10-9 | Qualifying | Embassy World Championship |
| | v Thorne | 8-10 | 1st round | Embassy World Championship |
| | v White | 1-5 | 1st round | Langs Scottish Masters |
| | v P. Gibson | 5-2 | 2nd round | BCE International |
| | v Parrott | 5-3 | 3rd round | BCE International |
| | v Dennis Taylor | 3-5 | 4th round | BCE International |
| | v Williamson | 5-1 | 2nd round | Rothmans Grand Prix |
| | v E. Hughes | 5-1 | 3rd round | Rothmans Grand Prix |
| | v Chaperon | 5-2 | 4th round | Rothmans Grand Prix |
| | v M. Bennett | 5-3 | 5th round | Rothmans Grand Prix |
| | v White | 4-5 | Quarter-final | Rothmans Grand Prix |
| | v Oliver | 9-1 | 2nd round | Tennents UK Open |

| | | | | |
|---|---|---|---|---|
| | v Higgins | 8-9 | 3rd round | Tennents UK Open |
| **1987** | v Jack Rea | 5-1 | 2nd round | Mercantile Credit Classic |
| | v Reardon | 5-3 | 3rd round | Mercantile Credit Classic |
| | v Wright | 5-1 | 4th round | Mercantile Credit Classic |
| | v Fowler | 5-4 | 5th round | Mercantile Credit Classic |
| | v S. Francisco | 5-0 | Quarter-final | Mercantile Credit Classic |
| | v S. Davis | 3-9 | Semi-final | Mercantile Credit Classic |
| | v Demarco | 6-2 | 1st round | Scottish Championship |
| | v John Rea | 6-0 | Semi-final | Scottish Championship |
| | **v Donnelly** | **10-7** | **Final** | **Scottish Championship** |
| | v Sinclair | 2-5 | 2nd round | Dulux British Open |
| | v Darrington | 10-7 | Qualifying | Embassy World Championship |
| | v Rempe | 10-4 | Qualifying | Embassy World Championship |
| | v Martin | 10-7 | Qualifying | Embassy World Championship |
| | v Thorne | 10-7 | 1st round | Embassy World Championship |
| | v Longworth | 13-7 | 2nd round | Embassy World Championship |
| | v Johnson | 12-13 | Quarter-final | Embassy World Championship |
| | v White | 5-2 | Semi-final | Riley Hong Kong Masters (WS) |
| | v S. Davis | 3-9 | Final | Riley Hong Kong Masters (WS) |
| | v Dennis Taylor | 3-5 | 1st round | Carling Champions |
| | v Johnson | 2-5 | 1st round | Langs Scottish Masters |
| | v Gary Wilkinson | 5-4 | 3rd round | Fidelity International |
| | v N. Foulds | 5-2 | 4th round | Fidelity International |
| | v D. Gilbert | 5-0 | 5th round | Fidelity International |
| | v O'Boye | 5-2 | Quarter-final | Fidelity International |
| | v Thorburn | 1-9 | Semi-final | Fidelity International |
| | v M. Bennett | 5-1 | 3rd round | Rothmans Grand Prix |
| | v Chambers | 5-1 | 4th round | Rothmans Grand Prix |
| | v S. Davis | 5-2 | 5th round | Rothmans Grand Prix |
| | v Knowles | 5-2 | Quarter-final | Rothmans Grand Prix |
| | v Parrott | 9-7 | Semi-final | Rothmans Grand Prix |
| | **v Dennis Taylor** | **10-7** | **Final** | **Rothmans Grand Prix** |
| | v Wych | 7-9 | 3rd round | Tennents UK Open |
| **1988** | v Werbeniuk | 5-2 | 3rd round | Mercantile Credit Classic |
| | v Johnson | 5-3 | 4th round | Mercantile Credit Classic |
| | v S. Francisco | 5-3 | 5th round | Mercantile Credit Classic |
| | v S. Davis | 3-5 | Quarter-final | Mercantile Credit Classic |
| | v Demarco | 6-0 | Quarter-final | Scottish Championship |
| | v M. Gibson | 6-1 | Semi-final | Scottish Championship |
| | **v Macleod** | **10-4** | **Final** | **Scottish Championship** |
| | v Chappel | 5-1 | 3rd round | MIM Britannia British Open |
| | v Griffiths | 5-1 | 4th round | MIM Britannia British Open |
| | v T. Jones | 5-3 | 5th round | MIM Britannia British Open |
| | v White | 5-4 | Quarter-final | MIM Britannia British Open |
| | v Thorburn | 9-5 | Semi-final | MIM Britannia British Open |
| | **v Hallett** | **13-2** | **Final** | **MIM Britannia British Open** |
| | v Wright | 10-4 | Qualifying | Embassy World Championship |
| | v Reynolds | 10-6 | 1st round | Embassy World Championship |
| | v White | 12-13 | 2nd round | Embassy World Championship |
| | v D. Morgan | 5-2 | 1st round | New Zealand Masters |
| | v Johnson | 5-2 | Semi-final | New Zealand Masters |
| | **v Hallett** | **6-1** | **Final** | **New Zealand Masters** |
| | v Edmonds | 5-1 | 3rd round | Fidelity International |
| | v Longworth | 5-3 | 4th round | Fidelity International |
| | v James | 2-5 | 5th round | Fidelity International |
| | v E. Hughes | 5-1 | 1st round | Fosters Professional |
| | v Hallett | 5-8 | Final | Fosters Professional |
| | v Williamson | 5-2 | 3rd round | Rothmans Grand Prix |
| | v Mountjoy | 1-5 | 4th round | Rothmans Grand Prix |
| | v S. Campbell | 5-2 | 3rd round | BCE Canadian Masters |
| | v Fowler | 5-2 | 4th round | BCE Canadian Masters |
| | v C. Wilson | 5-1 | 5th round | BCE Canadian Masters |
| | v Thorburn | 5-4 | Quarter-final | BCE Canadian Masters |

*Stephen Hendry*

| | | | | |
|---|---|---|---|---|
| | v S. Davis | 5-9 | Semi-final | BCE Canadian Masters |
| | v Murphy | 9-4 | 3rd round | Tennents UK Open |
| | v Roscoe | 9-3 | 4th round | Tennents UK Open |
| | v Thorne | 9-4 | 5th round | Tennents UK Open |
| | v Thorburn | 9-2 | Quarter-final | Tennents UK Open |
| | v S. Davis | 9-3 | Semi-final | Tennents UK Open |
| | v Mountjoy | 12-16 | Final | Tennents UK Open |
| | v Dennis Taylor | 9-7 | Quarter-final | Everest World Matchplay |
| | v Parrott | 6-9 | Semi-final | Everest World Matchplay |
| **1989** | v Murphy | 5-2 | 3rd round | Mercantile Credit Classic |
| | v Reardon | 5-4 | 4th round | Mercantile Credit Classic |
| | v Newbury | 5-1 | 5th round | Mercantile Credit Classic |
| | v Thorburn | 4-5 | Quarter-final | Mercantile Credit Classic |
| | v Thorne | 5-2 | 1st round | Benson and Hedges Masters |
| | v Griffiths | 5-3 | Quarter-final | Benson and Hedges Masters |
| | v S. Davis | 6-3 | Semi-final | Benson and Hedges Masters |
| | **v Parrott** | **9-6** | **Final** | **Benson and Hedges Masters** |
| | v O'Boye | 5-2 | 3rd round | European Open |
| | v Longworth | 5-0 | 4th round | European Open |
| | v Hallett | 3-5 | 5th round | European Open |
| | v Edwards | 5-0 | 3rd round | Anglian British Open |
| | v O'Kane | 5-2 | 4th round | Anglian British Open |
| | v Meo | 3-5 | 5th round | Anglian British Open |
| | v Griffiths | 5-2 | Quarter-final | Benson and Hedges Irish Masters |
| | v S. Davis | 6-4 | Semi-final | Benson and Hedges Irish Masters |
| | v Higgins | 8-9 | Final | Benson and Hedges Irish Masters |
| | v Gary Wilkinson | 10-9 | 1st round | Embassy World Championship |
| | v Thorne | 10-4 | 2nd round | Embassy World Championship |
| | v Griffiths | 13-5 | Quarter-final | Embassy World Championship |
| | v S. Davis | 9-16 | Semi-final | Embassy World Championship |
| | v O'Kane | 6-3 | 1st round | Lion Brown New Zealand Masters |
| | v Thorne | 5-6 | Semi-final | Lion Brown New Zealand Masters |
| | v Wright | 5-4 | 3rd round | Hong Kong Open |
| | v Robidoux | 5-4 | 4th round | Hong Kong Open |
| | v Dodd | 5-3 | 5th round | Hong Kong Open |
| | v Hallett | 4-5 | Quarter-final | Hong Kong Open |
| | v Chappel | 5-1 | 3rd round | 555 Asian Open |
| | v Higgins | 5-3 | 4th round | 555 Asian Open |
| | v W. Jones | 5-0 | 5th round | 555 Asian Open |
| | v Thorne | 5-2 | Quarter-final | 555 Asian Open |
| | v Gary Wilkinson | 5-4 | Semi-final | 555 Asian Open |
| | **v Wattana** | **9-6** | **Final** | **555 Asian Open** |
| | v Hallett | 6-1 | Quarter-final | Regal Scottish Masters |
| | v Parrott | 6-4 | Semi-final | Regal Scottish Masters |
| | **v Griffiths** | **10-1** | **Final** | **Regal Scottish Masters** |
| | v Graham | 5-0 | 3rd round | BCE International |
| | v Wattana | 5-3 | 4th round | BCE International |
| | v T. Jones | 5-4 | 5th round | BCE International |
| | v C. Wilson | 5-2 | Quarter-final | BCE International |
| | v Bond | 6-5 | Semi-final | BCE International |
| | v S. Davis | 4-9 | Final | BCE International |
| | v Cripsey | 5-2 | 3rd round | Rothmans Grand Prix |
| | v Bond | 5-1 | 4th round | Rothmans Grand Prix |
| | v Mountjoy | 3-5 | 5th round | Rothmans Grand Prix |
| | v Macleod | 5-3 | 3rd round | Dubai Classic |
| | v Wych | *wo* | 4th round | Dubai Classic |
| | v Drago | 5-3 | 5th round | Dubai Classic |
| | v Reynolds | 5-3 | Quarter-final | Dubai Classic |
| | v Fowler | 5-4 | Semi-final | Dubai Classic |
| | **v Mountjoy** | **9-2** | **Final** | **Dubai Classic** |
| | v Spencer | 9-1 | 3rd round | Stormseal UK Open |
| | v West | 9-1 | 4th round | Stormseal UK Open |
| | v Reynolds | 9-8 | 5th round | Stormseal UK Open |

| | | | | |
|---|---|---|---|---|
| | v M. Bennett | 9-2 | Quarter-final | Stormseal UK Open |
| | v Griffiths | 9-7 | Semi-final | Stormseal UK Open |
| | **v S. Davis** | **16-12** | **Final** | **Stormseal UK Open** |
| | v Griffiths | 9-3 | Quarter-final | Everest World Matchplay |
| | v Parrott | 8-9 | Semi-final | Everest World Matchplay |
| **1990** | v T. Jones | 5-3 | 3rd round | Mercantile Credit Classic |
| | v O'Kane | 2-5 | 4th round | Mercantile Credit Classic |
| | v James | 5-2 | 1st round | Benson and Hedges Irish Masters |
| | v Thorne | 5-1 | Quarter-final | Benson and Hedges Irish Masters |
| | v White | 5-4 | Semi-final | Benson and Hedges Irish Masters |
| | **v Parrott** | **9-4** | **Final** | **Benson and Hedges Masters** |
| | v D. Morgan | 4-5 | 3rd round | Pearl Assurance British Open |
| | v Foldvari | 5-1 | 3rd round | European Open |
| | v Newbury | 5-1 | 4th round | European Open |
| | v Chappel | 5-2 | 5th round | European Open |
| | v N. Foulds | 5-3 | Quarter-final | European Open |
| | v S. Davis | 6-3 | Semi-final | European Open |
| | v Parrott | 6-10 | Final | European Open |
| | v White | 2-5 | Quarter-final | Benson and Hedges Irish Masters |
| | v Robidoux | 10-7 | 1st round | Embassy World Championship |
| | v Meo | 13-7 | 2nd round | Embassy World Championship |
| | v D. Morgan | 13-6 | Quarter-final | Embassy World Championship |
| | v Parrott | 16-11 | Semi-final | Embassy World Championship |
| | **v White** | **18-12** | **Final** | **Embassy World Championship** |

## ALEX HIGGINS (Northern Ireland)

**Born** 18.3.49. **Turned professional** 1971. **World ranking** 14 (24).

| | | | | |
|---|---|---|---|---|
| **1972** | v Gross | 15-6 | Qualifying | World Championship |
| | v Parkin | 11-3 | Qualifying | World Championship |
| | v Jack Rea | 19-11 | 1st round | World Championship |
| | v Pulman | 31-23 | Quarter-final | World Championship |
| | v Williams | 31-30 | Semi-final | World Championship |
| | **v Spencer** | **37-32** | **Final** | **World Championship** |
| **1973** | v Houlihan | 16-3 | 2nd round | World Championship |
| | v Davis | 16-14 | Quarter-final | World Championship |
| | v Charlton | 9-23 | Semi-final | World Championship |
| | v Spencer | 2-8 | Semi-final | Norwich Union Open |
| **1974** | v Bennett | 15-4 | 2nd round | World Championship |
| | v F. Davis | 14-15 | Quarter-final | World Championship |
| | v Dennis Taylor | 5-1 | 1st round | Norwich Union Open |
| | v Werbeniuk | 5-4 | Quarter-final | Norwich Union Open |
| | v Reardon | 8-9 | Semi-final | Norwich Union Open |
| **1975** | v Werbeniuk | 5-0 | 1st round | Benson & Hedges Masters |
| | v Williams | 3-5 | Quarter-final | Benson & Hedges Masters |
| | v David Taylor | 15-2 | 2nd round | World Championship |
| | v Williams | 19-12 | Quarter-final | World Championship |
| | v Reardon | 14-19 | Semi-final | World Championship |
| **1976** | v Miles | 1-4 | 2nd round | Benson & Hedges Masters |
| | v Thorburn | 15-14 | 1st round | Embassy World Championship |
| | v Spencer | 15-14 | Quarter-final | Embassy World Championship |
| | v Charlton | 20-18 | Semi-final | Embassy World Championship |
| | v Reardon | 16-27 | Final | Embassy World Championship |
| **1977** | v Mans | 4-2 | Quarter-final | Benson & Hedges Masters |
| | v Mountjoy | 3-5 | Semi-final | Benson & Hedges Masters |
| | v Mountjoy | 12-13 | 1st round | Embassy World Championship |
| | v David Taylor | 5-4 | 2nd round | Super Crystalate UK Championship |
| | v Dunning | 5-0 | Quarter-final | Super Crystalate UK Championship |
| | v Mountjoy | 2-9 | Semi-final | Super Crystalate UK Championship |
| **1978** | v Dennis Taylor | 4-3 | Quarter-final | Benson & Hedges Masters |
| | v Reardon | 5-1 | Semi-final | Benson & Hedges Masters |

| | | | | |
|---|---|---|---|---|
| | **v Thorburn** | **7-5** | **Final** | **Benson & Hedges Masters** |
| | v Fagan | 12-13 | 1st round | Embassy World Championship |
| | v Meadowcroft | 9-6 | 1st round | Coral UK Championship |
| | v F. Davis | 9-4 | Quarter-final | Coral UK Championship |
| | v David Taylor | 5-9 | Semi-final | Coral UK Championship |
| **1979** | v Miles | 3-6 | Semi-final | Holsten Lager International |
| | v Charlton | 5-2 | Quarter-final | Benson & Hedges Masters |
| | v Mountjoy | 5-1 | Semi-final | Benson & Hedges Masters |
| | v Mans | 4-8 | Final | Benson & Hedges Masters |
| | v David Taylor | 13-5 | 1st round | Embassy World Championship |
| | v Griffiths | 12-13 | Quarter-final | Embassy World Championship |
| | v Houlihan | 9-3 | 3rd round | Coral UK Championship |
| | v Griffiths | 7-9 | Quarter-final | Coral UK Championship |
| **1980** | v F. Davis | 5-1 | 1st round | Benson & Hedges Masters |
| | v Mans | 5-1 | Quarter-final | Benson & Hedges Masters |
| | v Reardon | 5-2 | Semi-final | Benson & Hedges Masters |
| | v Griffiths | 5-9 | Final | Benson & Hedges Masters |
| | **v Reardon** | **5-1** | **Final** | **British Gold Cup** |
| | v Meo | 10-9 | 1st round | Embassy World Championship |
| | v Mans | 13-6 | 2nd round | Embassy World Championship |
| | v S. Davis | 13-9 | Quarter-final | Embassy World Championship |
| | v Stevens | 16-13 | Semi-final | Embassy World Championship |
| | v Thorburn | 16-18 | Final | Embassy World Championship |
| | v Thorne | 9-7 | 2nd round | Coral UK Championship |
| | v F. Davis | 9-6 | Quarter-final | Coral UK Championship |
| | v Reardon | 9-7 | Semi-final | Coral UK Championship |
| | v S. Davis | 6-16 | Final | Coral UK Championship |
| **1981** | v Mountjoy | 5-1 | Quarter-final | Benson & Hedges Masters |
| | v Thorburn | 6-5 | Semi-final | Benson & Hedges Masters |
| | **v Griffiths** | **9-6** | **Final** | **Benson & Hedges Masters** |
| | v Reardon | 5-6 | Semi-final | Benson & Hedges Irish Masters |
| | v S. Davis | 8-13 | 2nd round | Embassy World Championship |
| | v V. Harris | 5-3 | Quarter-final | Langs Scottish Masters |
| | v Thorburn | 2-6 | Semi-final | Langs Scottish Masters |
| | v Fagan | 5-3 | 2nd round | Jameson International |
| | v Mountjoy | 5-1 | 3rd round | Jameson International |
| | v Griffiths | 5-2 | Quarter-final | Jameson International |
| | v S. Davis | 8-9 | Semi-final | Jameson International |
| | v S. Davis | 2-5 | 1st round | Northern Ireland Classic |
| | v Martin | 9-7 | 2nd round | Coral UK Championship |
| | v David Taylor | 9-5 | 3rd round | Coral UK Championship |
| | v Meo | 4-9 | Quarter-final | Coral UK Championship |
| **1982** | v Dennis Taylor | 5-1 | 1st round | Lada Classic |
| | v Griffiths | 1-5 | Semi-final | Lada Classic |
| | v Charlton | 5-1 | Quarter-final | Benson & Hedges Masters |
| | v Griffiths | 4-6 | Semi-final | Benson & Hedges Masters |
| | v D. Hughes | 6-2 | Semi-final | Irish Championship |
| | v Dennis Taylor | 13-16 | Final | Irish Championship |
| | v Wych | 5-3 | 1st round | Benson & Hedges Irish Masters |
| | v Thorburn | 5-4 | Quarter-final | Benson & Hedges Irish Masters |
| | v S. Davis | 2-6 | Semi-final | Benson & Hedges Irish Masters |
| | v Meadowcroft | 10-5 | 1st round | Embassy World Championship |
| | v Mountjoy | 13-12 | 2nd round | Embassy World Championship |
| | v Thorne | 13-10 | Quarter-final | Embassy World Championship |
| | v White | 16-15 | Semi-final | Embassy World Championship |
| | **v Reardon** | **18-15** | **Final** | **Embassy World Championship** |
| | v Sinclair | 5-1 | 1st round | Langs Scottish Masters |
| | v Griffiths | 6-5 | Semi-final | Langs Scottish Masters |
| | v S. Davis | 4-9 | Final | Langs Scottish Masters |
| | v Kelly | 5-3 | 1st round | Jameson International |
| | v Griffiths | 2-5 | 2nd round | Jameson International |
| | v French | 5-3 | 1st round | Professional Players Tournament |
| | v Reardon | 2-5 | 2nd round | Professional Players Tournament |

| | | | | |
|---|---|---|---|---|
| | v Martin | 9-7 | 1st round | Coral UK Championship |
| | v Reynolds | 9-8 | 2nd round | Coral UK Championship |
| | v Spencer | 9-5 | Quarter-final | Coral UK Championship |
| | v Reardon | 9-6 | Semi-final | Coral UK Championship |
| | v Griffiths | 15-16 | Final | Coral UK Championship |
| **1983** | v Werbeniuk | 4-5 | 1st round | Lada Classic |
| | v Werbeniuk | 4-5 | 1st round | Benson & Hedges Masters |
| | v Jack Rea | 6-3 | Quarter-final | Irish Championship |
| | v E. Hughes | 6-2 | Semi-final | Irish Championship |
| | **v Dennis Taylor** | **16-11** | **Final** | **Irish Championship** |
| | v White | 5-2 | Quarter-final | Benson & Hedges Irish Masters |
| | v Reardon | 3-6 | Semi-final | Benson & Hedges Irish Masters |
| | v Reynolds | 10-4 | 1st round | Embassy World Championship |
| | v Thorne | 13-8 | 2nd round | Embassy World Championship |
| | v Werbeniuk | 13-11 | Quarter-final | Embassy World Championship |
| | v S. Davis | 5-16 | Semi-final | Embassy World Championship |
| | v White | 5-3 | 1st round | Langs Supreme Scottish Masters |
| | v S. Davis | 2-6 | Semi-final | Langs Supreme Scottish Masters |
| | v Martin | 2-5 | 1st round | Jameson International |
| | v Watterson | 2-5 | 1st round | Professional Players Tournament |
| | v Macleod | 9-6 | 1st round | Coral UK Championship |
| | v Medati | 9-1 | 2nd round | Coral UK Championship |
| | v Knowles | 9-5 | Quarter-final | Coral UK Championship |
| | v Griffiths | 9-4 | Semi-final | Coral UK Championship |
| | **v S. Davis** | **16-15** | **Final** | **Coral UK Championship** |
| **1984** | v Fagan | 5-3 | Qualifying | Lada Classic |
| | v Parrott | 2-5 | 1st round | Lada Classic |
| | v Mountjoy | 5-2 | 1st round | Benson & Hedges Masters |
| | v Knowles | 1-5 | Quarter-final | Benson & Hedges Masters |
| | v Charlton | 5-2 | 1st round | Benson & Hedges Irish Masters |
| | v Reardon | 5-2 | Quarter-final | Benson & Hedges Irish Masters |
| | v S. Davis | 4-6 | Semi-final | Benson & Hedges Irish Masters |
| | v N. Foulds | 9-10 | 1st round | Embassy World Championship |
| | v Stevens | 5-2 | 1st round | Langs Supreme Scottish Masters |
| | v S. Davis | 4-6 | Semi-final | Langs Supreme Scottish Masters |
| | v Knowles | 3-5 | 1st round | Carlsberg Challenge |
| | v Sinclair | 5-1 | 1st round | Jameson International |
| | v Griffiths | 5-4 | 2nd round | Jameson International |
| | v S. Davis | 1-5 | Quarter-final | Jameson International |
| | v Bales | 5-1 | 1st round | Rothmans Grand Prix |
| | v Hallett | 3-5 | 2nd round | Rothmans Grand Prix |
| | v T. Jones | 9-7 | 1st round | Coral UK Open |
| | v Williams | 9-7 | 2nd round | Coral UK Open |
| | v Thorne | 9-5 | Quarter-final | Coral UK Open |
| | v Thorburn | 9-7 | Semi-final | Coral UK Open |
| | v S. Davis | 8-16 | Final | Coral UK Open |
| **1985** | v Gauvreau | 5-3 | 1st round | Mercantile Credit Classic |
| | v S. Davis | 2-5 | 2nd round | Mercantile Credit Classic |
| | v S. Davis | 5-4 | 1st round | Benson & Hedges Masters |
| | v Griffiths | 1-5 | Quarter-final | Benson & Hedges Masters |
| | v Bales | 6-3 | 1st round | Dulux British Open |
| | v N. Foulds | 5-1 | 2nd round | Dulux British Open |
| | v Thorburn | 5-2 | 3rd round | Dulux British Open |
| | v E. Hughes | 5-2 | Quarter-final | Dulux British Open |
| | v S. Francisco | 6-9 | Semi-final | Dulux British Open |
| | v Griffiths | 5-2 | 1st round | Benson & Hedges Irish Masters |
| | v Stevens | 5-3 | Quarter-final | Benson & Hedges Irish Masters |
| | v S. Davis | 6-2 | Semi-final | Benson & Hedges Irish Masters |
| | v White | 5-9 | Final | Benson & Hedges Irish Masters |
| | v Burke | 6-0 | Quarter-final | Irish Championship |
| | v Fagan | 6-3 | Semi-final | Irish Championship |
| | v Dennis Taylor | 5-10 | Final | Irish Championship |
| | v Reynolds | 10-4 | 1st round | Embassy World Championship |

*Alex Higgins*

| | | | | |
|---|---|---|---|---|
| | v Griffiths | 7-13 | 2nd round | Embassy World Championship |
| | v Thorburn | 5-4 | Semi-final | Carlsberg Challenge |
| | v White | 3-8 | Final | Carlsberg Challenge |
| | v White | 0-5 | 1st round | Langs Scottish Masters |
| | v D. Hughes | 5-1 | 3rd round | Goya Matchroom Trophy |
| | v Murphy | 5-2 | 4th round | Goya Matchroom Trophy |
| | v Dennis Taylor | 1-5 | 5th round | Goya Matchroom Trophy |
| | v V. Harris | 5-1 | 3rd round | Rothmans Grand Prix |
| | v N. Foulds | 5-3 | 4th round | Rothmans Grand Prix |
| | v S. Davis | 0-5 | 5th round | Rothmans Grand Prix |
| | v Edmonds | 9-8 | 3rd round | Coral UK Open |
| | v F. Davis | 9-2 | 4th round | Coral UK Open |
| | v White | 6-9 | 5th round | Coral UK Open |
| | v Thorburn | 5-4 | 1st round | Kit Kat |
| | v S. Davis | 1-6 | Semi-final | Kit Kat |
| **1986** | v Fisher | 5-0 | 3rd round | Mercantile Credit Classic |
| | v Cripsey | 5-2 | 4th round | Mercantile Credit Classic |
| | v Dennis Taylor | 5-4 | 5th round | Mercantile Credit Classic |
| | v Williams | 2-5 | Quarter-final | Mercantile Credit Classic |
| | v Dennis Taylor | 5-1 | 1st round | BCE Belgian Classic |
| | v Stevens | 4-5 | Semi-final | BCE Belgian Classic |
| | v Griffiths | 4-5 | 1st round | Benson & Hedges Masters |
| | v Bradley | 5-3 | 3rd round | Dulux British Open |
| | v Hallett | 5-1 | 4th round | Dulux British Open |
| | v P. Francisco | 5-2 | 5th round | Dulux British Open |
| | v Werbeniuk | 5-1 | Quarter-final | Dulux British Open |
| | v S. Davis | 3-9 | Semi-final | Dulux British Open |
| | v Meo | 4-5 | 1st round | Benson & Hedges Irish Masters |
| | v Spencer | 10-7 | 1st round | Embassy World Championship |
| | v Griffiths | 12-13 | 2nd round | Embassy World Championship |
| | v J. McLaughlin | 6-2 | Quarter-final | Strongbow Irish Championship |
| | v E. Hughes | 6-2 | Semi-final | Strongbow Irish Championship |
| | v Dennis Taylor | 7-10 | Final | Strongbow Irish Championship |
| | v White | 1-5 | 1st round | Carlsberg Challenge |
| | v Johnson | 5-2 | 1st round | Langs Scottish Masters |
| | v Stevens | 6-2 | Semi-final | Langs Scottish Masters |
| | v Thorburn | 8-9 | Final | Langs Scottish Masters |
| | v Sinclair | 5-3 | 3rd round | BCE International |
| | v P. Francisco | 4-5 | 4th round | BCE International |
| | v F. Davis | 5-0 | 3rd round | Rothmans Grand Prix |
| | v Martin | 5-2 | 4th round | Rothmans Grand Prix |
| | v Williams | 1-5 | 5th round | Rothmans Grand Prix |
| | v Johnson | 5-3 | 1st round | BCE Canadian Masters |
| | v S. Davis | 2-8 | Semi-final | BCE Canadian Masters |
| | v Hendry | 9-8 | 3rd round | Tennents UK Open |
| | v Martin | 9-6 | 4th round | Tennents UK Open |
| | v Hallett | 9-7 | 5th round | Tennents UK Open |
| | v W. Jones | 9-5 | Quarter-final | Tennents UK Open |
| | v S. Davis | 3-9 | Semi-final | Tennents UK Open |
| **1987** | v Roscoe | 5-2 | 3rd round | Mercantile Credit Classic |
| | v Parrott | 2-5 | 4th round | Mercantile Credit Classic |
| | v Griffiths | 5-4 | 1st round | Benson & Hedges Masters |
| | v Johnson | 5-1 | Quarter-final | Benson & Hedges Masters |
| | v Meo | 6-2 | Semi-final | Benson & Hedges Masters |
| | v Dennis Taylor | 8-9 | Final | Benson & Hedges Masters |
| | v J. McLaughlin | 4-5 | 3rd round | Dulux British Open |
| | v Griffiths | 1-5 | 1st round | Benson & Hedges Irish Masters |
| | v Wright | 10-6 | 1st round | Embassy World Championship |
| | v Griffiths | 10-13 | 2nd round | Embassy World Championship |
| | v White | 3-5 | 1st round | Langs Scottish Masters |
| | v Duggan | 9-4 | 3rd round | Tennents UK Open |
| | v David Taylor | 9-6 | 4th round | Tennents UK Open |
| | v S. Davis | 2-9 | 5th round | Tennents UK Open |

| | | | | |
|---|---|---|---|---|
| **1988** | v T. Jones | 5-0 | 3rd round | Mercantile Credit Classic |
| | v S. Davis | 0-5 | 4th round | Mercantile Credit Classic |
| | v Knowles | 5-4 | 1st round | Benson & Hedges Masters |
| | v Hallett | 2-5 | 2nd round | Benson & Hedges Masters |
| | v O'Boye | 4-6 | Quarter-final | Irish Championship |
| | v T. Jones | 3-5 | 3rd round | MIM Britannia British Open |
| | v Dennis Taylor | 5-3 | 1st round | Benson & Hedges Irish Masters |
| | v Thorburn | 5-3 | Quarter-final | Benson & Hedges Irish Masters |
| | v Davis | 2-6 | Semi-final | Benson & Hedges Irish Masters |
| | v Drago | 2-10 | 1st round | Embassy World Championship |
| | v Macleod | 2-5 | 3rd round | Fidelity International |
| | v Roe | 5-4 | 3rd round | Rothmans Grand Prix |
| | v O'Kane | 5-0 | 4th round | Rothmans Grand Prix |
| | v N. Foulds | 5-3 | 5th round | Rothmans Grand Prix |
| | v Williams | 5-4 | Quarter-final | Rothmans Grand Prix |
| | v Robidoux | 9-7 | Semi-final | Rothmans Grand Prix |
| | v S. Davis | 6-10 | Final | Rothmans Grand Prix |
| | v Clark | 3-5 | 3rd round | BCE Canadian Masters |
| | v Dodd | 9-7 | 3rd round | Tennents UK Open |
| | v Knowles | 6-9 | 4th round | Tennents UK Open |
| **1989** | v Macleod | 5-2 | 3rd round | Mercantile Credit Classic |
| | v Johnson | 0-5 | 4th round | Mercantile Credit Classic |
| | v Dodd | 5-2 | 3rd round | European Open |
| | v Thorne | 1-5 | 4th round | European Open |
| | v Watchorn | 5-2 | Quarter-final | Irish Championship |
| | v E. Hughes | 6-2 | Semi-final | Irish Championship |
| | **v J. McLaughlin** | **9-7** | **Final** | **Irish Championship** |
| | v Foldvari | 5-1 | 3rd round | Anglian British Open |
| | v S. Davis | 0-5 | 4th round | Anglian British Open |
| | v Thorburn | 5-4 | 1st round | Benson and Hedges Irish Masters |
| | v N. Foulds | 5-2 | Quarter-final | Benson and Hedges Irish Masters |
| | v Parrott | 6-4 | Semi-final | Benson and Hedges Irish Masters |
| | **v Hendry** | **9-8** | **Final** | **Benson and Hedges Irish Masters** |
| | v D. Morgan | 8-10 | Qualifying | Embassy World Championship |
| | v Spencer | 5-2 | 3rd round | Hong Kong Open |
| | v Meo | 5-4 | 4th round | Hong Kong Open |
| | v O'Kane | 2-5 | 5th round | Hong Kong Open |
| | v Martin | 5-3 | 3rd round | 555 Asian Open |
| | v Hendry | 3-5 | 4th round | 555 Asian Open |
| | v Johnston-Allen | 1-5 | 3rd round | BCE International |
| | v D. Gilbert | 5-3 | 3rd round | Rothmans Grand Prix |
| | v Johnson | 2-5 | 4th round | Rothmans Grand Prix |
| | v Sinclair | 5-2 | 3rd round | Dubai Classic |
| | v O'Kane | 5-3 | 4th round | Dubai Classic |
| | v Grech | 5-4 | 5th round | Dubai Classic |
| | v Mountjoy | 2-5 | Quarter-final | Dubai Classic |
| | v Duggan | 9-7 | 3rd round | Stormseal UK Open |
| | v Thorne | 3-9 | 4th round | Stormseal UK Open |
| **1990** | v Johnston-Allen | 5-0 | 3rd round | Mercantile Credit Classic |
| | v Parrott | 4-5 | 4th round | Mercantile Credit Classic |
| | v James | 2-5 | Play-offs | Benson and Hedges Masters |
| | v B. Harris | 5-3 | 3rd round | Pearl Assurance British Open |
| | v M. Bennett | 5-2 | 4th round | Pearl Assurance British Open |
| | v Mountjoy | 5-3 | 5th round | Pearl Assurance British Open |
| | v Clark | 5-3 | Quarter-final | Pearl Assurance British Open |
| | v James | 9-3 | Semi-final | Pearl Assurance British Open |
| | v Chaperon | 8-10 | Final | Pearl Assurance British Open |
| | v Owers | 5-2 | 3rd round | European Open |
| | v James | 2-5 | 4th round | European Open |
| | v Dennis Taylor | 2-5 | Quarter-final | Benson and Hedges Irish Masters |
| | v Wattana | 10-6 | Qualifying | Embassy World Championship |
| | v James | 5-10 | 1st round | Embassy World Championship |

## PAT HOULIHAN (England)

**Born** 7.11.29. **Turned professional** 1969. **World ranking** 97 (81).

| | | | | |
|---|---|---|---|---|
| **1972** | v Dunning | 10-11 | Qualifying | World Championship |
| **1973** | v Jack Rea | 9-2 | 1st round | World Championship |
| | v Higgins | 3-16 | 2nd round | World Championship |
| **1977** | v Meadowcroft | 1-5 | 1st round | Super Crystalate UK |
| **1978** | v Ross | 9-1 | Prelim | Embassy World Championship |
| | v Meadowcroft | 9-6 | Qualifying | Embassy World Championship |
| | v Thorburn | 8-13 | 1st round | Embassy World Championship |
| | v Andrewartha | 3-9 | Qualifying | Coral UK Championship |
| **1979** | v Barrie | 9-5 | Prelim | Embassy World Championship |
| | v Mountjoy | 6-9 | Qualifying | Embassy World Championship |
| | v Jack Rea | 9-3 | 2nd round | Coral UK Championship |
| | v Higgins | 3-9 | 3rd round | Coral UK Championship |
| **1980** | v Meo | 1-9 | Qualifying | Embassy World Championship |
| | v Meo | 1-9 | 1st round | Coral UK Championship |
| **1981** | v Spencer | 1-9 | 1st round | John Courage English |
| | v French | 3-5 | Qualifying | Jameson International |
| | v Kennerley | 9-1 | Qualifying | Coral UK Championship |
| | v Black | 9-4 | Qualifying | Coral UK Championship |
| | v Meadowcroft | 9-4 | Qualifying | Coral UK Championship |
| | v Miles | 3-9 | 2nd round | Coral UK Championship |
| **1982** | v Anderson | 9-5 | Qualifying | Embassy World Championship |
| | v Martin | 3-9 | Qualifying | Embassy World Championship |
| | v E. McLaughlin | 2-5 | Qualifying | Jameson International |
| | v Knowles | 4-5 | 1st round | Professional Players Tournament |
| | v Mountjoy | 3-9 | 1st round | Coral UK Championship |
| **1983** | v Murphy | 9-10 | Qualifying | Embassy World Championship |
| | v Scott | 0-5 | Qualifying | Jameson International |
| | v Sheehan | 2-5 | Qualifying | Professional Players Tournament |
| | v V. Harris | 6-9 | Qualifying | Coral UK Championship |
| **1984** | v Williamson | 5-10 | Qualifying | Embassy World Championship |
| | v Hargreaves | 2-5 | Qualifying | Jameson International |
| | v Everton | 3-5 | Qualifying | Rothmans Grand Prix |
| | v Chappel | 3-9 | Qualifying | Coral UK Open |
| **1985** | v Foldvari | 1-5 | Qualifying | Mercantile Credit Classic |
| | v T. Jones | 1-9 | Qualifying | Tolly Cobbold English Championship |
| | v Bear | 2-5 | 1st round | Goya Matchroom Trophy |
| | v Robinson | 5-0 | 1st round | Rothmans Grand Prix |
| | v T. Jones | 4-5 | 2nd round | Rothmans Grand Prix |
| | v Watson | 9-4 | 1st round | Coral UK Open |
| | v Newbury | 3-9 | 2nd round | Coral UK Open |
| **1986** | v Bennett | 5-0 | 1st round | Mercantile Credit Classic |
| | v Foldvari | 5-4 | 2nd round | Mercantile Credit Classic |
| | v Reynolds | 1-5 | 3rd round | Mercantile Credit Classic |
| | v Hargreaves | 9-5 | 1st round | Tolly Cobbold English Championship |
| | v Dunning | *wo* | 2nd round | Tolly Cobbold English Championship |
| | v Spencer | 5-9 | 3rd round | Tolly Cobbold English Championship |
| | v Longworth | 3-5 | 2nd round | Dulux British Open |
| | v Sheehan | 7-10 | Qualifying | Embassy World Championship |
| | v Chalmers | 5-1 | 1st round | BCE International |
| | v Cripsey | 5-1 | 2nd round | BCE International |
| | v Meo | 5-4 | 3rd round | BCE International |
| | v E. Hughes | 1-5 | 4th round | BCE International |
| | v Grace | 1-5 | 1st round | Rothmans Grand Prix |
| **1987** | v Owers | 1-5 | 1st round | Mercantile Credit Classic |
| | v N. Gilbert | 4-5 | 1st round | Dulux British Open |
| | v Wright | 4-10 | Qualifying | Embassy World Championship |
| | v D. Gilbert | 3-5 | 2nd round | Fidelity International |
| | v Heaton | 5-0 | 2nd round | Rothmans Grand Prix |
| | v Reynolds | 5-4 | 3rd round | Rothmans Grand Prix |

| | | | | |
|---|---|---|---|---|
| | v Chaperon | 0-5 | 4th round | Rothmans Grand Prix |
| | v Miles | 3-9 | 2nd round | Tennents UK Open |
| **1988** | v James | 2-5 | 2nd round | Mercantile Credit Classic |
| | v Marshall | 4-6 | 2nd round | English Championship |
| | v Bear | 0-5 | 2nd round | MIM Britannia British Open |
| | v Cripsey | 4-10 | Qualifying | Embassy World Championship |
| | v Robidoux | 2-5 | 2nd round | Fidelity International |
| | v John Rea | 5-1 | 2nd round | Rothmans Grand Prix |
| | v Charlton | 3-5 | 3rd round | Rothmans Grand Prix |
| | v M. Smith | 2-5 | 2nd round | BCE Canadian Masters |
| | v Roscoe | 8-9 | 2nd round | Tennents UK Open |
| **1989** | v Darrington | 4-5 | 2nd round | Mercantile Credit Classic |
| | v Sinclair | 1-5 | 2nd round | European Open |
| | v Fitzmaurice | 5-4 | 2nd round | English Championship |
| | v Hallett | 2-5 | 3rd round | English Championship |
| | v Terry | 5-2 | 2nd round | Anglian British Open |
| | v John Rea | 5-10 | Qualifying | Embassy World Championship |
| | v Kearney | 5-1 | 1st round | Hong Kong Open |
| | v J. Campbell | 5-3 | 2nd round | Hong Kong Open |
| | v Meo | 0-5 | 3rd round | Hong Kong Open |
| | v Cairns | 0-5 | 1st round | 555 Asian Open |
| | v Jack Rea | 5-4 | 1st round | BCE International |
| | v Edmonds | 5-2 | 2nd round | BCE International |
| | v W. Jones | 2-5 | 3rd round | BCE International |
| | v Watterson | 5-4 | 1st round | Rothmans Grand Prix |
| | v T. Jones | 0-5 | 2nd round | Rothmans Grand Prix |
| | v Pinches | 5-1 | 1st round | Dubai Classic |
| | v D. Morgan | 2-5 | 2nd round | Dubai Classic |
| | v Wildman | 6-3 | 1st round | Stormseal UK Open |
| | v Graham | 0-6 | 2nd round | Stormseal UK Open |
| **1990** | v Grace | 5-2 | 1st round | Mercantile Credit Classic |
| | v Chappel | 0-5 | 2nd round | Mercantile Credit Classic |
| | v Kearney | 2-5 | 1st round | Pearl Assurance British Open |
| | v D. Campbell | 4-5 | 1st round | European Open |
| | v Mienie | 10-5 | Qualifying | Embassy World Championship |
| | v J. McLaughlin | 10-5 | Qualifying | Embassy World Championship |
| | v T. Wilson | 6-10 | Qualifying | Embassy World Championship |

## DENNIS HUGHES (England)

**Born** 30.1.37. **Turned professional** 1981. **World ranking** 122 (108).

| | | | | |
|---|---|---|---|---|
| **1981** | v Jack Rea | 5-4 | Qualifying | Jameson International |
| | v Demarco | 1-5 | Qualifying | Jameson International |
| | v Hallett | 6-9 | Qualifying | Coral UK Championship |
| **1982** | v Higgins | 2-6 | Semi-final | Irish Championship |
| | v Everton | 9-4 | Qualifying | Embassy World Championship |
| | v Meo | 4-9 | Qualifying | Embassy World Championship |
| | v Edmonds | 0-5 | Qualifying | Jameson International |
| | v Charlton | 2-5 | 1st round | Professional Players Tournament |
| | v Meadowcroft | 8-9 | Qualifying | Coral UK Championship |
| **1983** | v Parkin | 5-0 | Qualifying | Jameson International |
| | v Johnson | 1-5 | Qualifying | Jameson International |
| | v Medati | 1-5 | Qualifying | Professional Players Tournament |
| | v Medati | 2-9 | Qualifying | Coral UK Championship |
| **1984** | v Parrott | 3-10 | Qualifying | Embassy World Championship |
| | v Oliver | 4-5 | Qualifying | Jameson International |
| | v Dunning | 0-5 | Qualifying | Rothmans Grand Prix |
| | v G. Foulds | 7-9 | Qualifying | Coral UK Open |
| **1985** | v Watchorn | 0-5 | Prelim | Mercantile Credit Classic |
| | v Watterson | 9-5 | Qualifying | Tolly Cobbold English Championship |

| | | | | |
|---|---|---|---|---|
| | v N. Foulds | 3-9 | 1st round | Tolly Cobbold English Championship |
| | v Mikkelsen | 0-6 | Qualifying | Dulux British Open |
| | v French | 10-5 | Qualifying | Embassy World Championship |
| | v Newbury | 9-10 | Qualifying | Embassy World Championship |
| | v Kearney | 5-1 | 1st round | Goya Matchroom Trophy |
| | v Gauvreau | 5-4 | 2nd round | Goya Matchroom Trophy |
| | v Higgins | 1-5 | 3rd round | Goya Matchroom Trophy |
| | v Bennett | 5-4 | 1st round | Rothmans Grand Prix |
| | v Morra | 2-5 | 2nd round | Rothmans Grand Prix |
| | v Kearney | 9-8 | 1st round | Coral UK Open |
| | v King | 0-9 | 2nd round | Coral UK Open |
| **1986** | v Burke | 3-5 | 1st round | Mercantile Credit Classic |
| | v F. Davis | 6-9 | 2nd round | Tolly Cobbold English Championship |
| | v Hendry | 1-5 | 1st round | Dulux British Open |
| | v Agrawal | 6-10 | Qualifying | Embassy World Championship |
| | v Roe | 2-5 | 1st round | BCE International |
| | v Jack Rea | 2-5 | 1st round | Rothmans Grand Prix |
| | v Ellis | 9-6 | 1st round | Tennents UK Open |
| | v Murphy | 0-9 | 2nd round | Tennents UK Open |
| **1987** | v Wright | 2-5 | 1st round | Mercantile Credit Classic |
| | v P. Gibson | 3-6 | 1st round | Tolly Ales English Championship |
| | v Whitthread | 1-5 | 1st round | Dulux British Open |
| | v Parkin | 10-5 | Qualifying | Embassy World Championship |
| | v B. Harris | 2-10 | Qualifying | Embassy World Championship |
| | v Rowswell | 1-5 | 1st round | Fidelity International |
| | v Donnelly | 1-5 | 1st round | Rothmans Grand Prix |
| | v Edmonds | 4-9 | 2nd round | Tennents UK Open |
| **1988** | v Williamson | 5-3 | 1st round | Mercantile Credit Classic |
| | v Chappel | 3-5 | 2nd round | Mercantile Credit Classic |
| | v Fitzmaurice | 6-1 | 1st round | English Championship |
| | v Wildman | 6-0 | 2nd round | English Championship |
| | v Williams | 1-6 | 3rd round | English Championship |
| | v Fagan | 5-4 | 1st round | MIM Britannia British Open |
| | v F. Davis | 2-5 | 2nd round | MIM Britannia British Open |
| | v Miles | 3-10 | Qualifying | Embassy World Championship |
| | v Rigitano | 5-4 | 1st round | Fidelity International |
| | v Stevens | 2-5 | 2nd round | Fidelity International |
| | v Mikkelsen | 4-5 | 1st round | Rothmans Grand Prix |
| | v M. Gibson | 1-5 | 1st round | BCE Canadian Masters |
| | v Morra | 2-9 | 1st round | Tennents UK Open |
| **1989** | v O'Boye | 5-1 | 2nd round | Mercantile Credit Classic |
| | v Mountjoy | 0-5 | 3rd round | Mercantile Credit Classic |
| | v Williamson | 1-5 | 1st round | European Open |
| | v Whitthread | 1-5 | 1st round | English Championship |
| | v M. Smith | 1-5 | 1st round | Anglian British Open |
| | v John Rea | 3-10 | Qualifying | Embassy World Championship |
| | v Lawlor | 5-1 | 1st round | Hong Kong Open |
| | v Chambers | 2-5 | 2nd round | Hong Kong Open |
| | v Medati | 5-2 | 1st round | 555 Asian Open |
| | v King | 0-5 | 2nd round | 555 Asian Open |
| | v M. Smith | 0-5 | 1st round | BCE International |
| | v V. Harris | 4-5 | 1st round | Rothmans Grand Prix |
| | v Williamson | 1-5 | 1st round | Dubai Classic |
| | v Williamson | 0-6 | 1st round | Stormseal UK Open |
| **1990** | v Terry | 0-5 | 1st round | Mercantile Credit Classic |
| | v Donnelly | 2-5 | 1st round | Pearl Assurance British Open |
| | v Foldvari | 1-5 | 1st round | European Open |
| | v Miles | 5-10 | Qualifying | Embassy World Championship |

## **EUGENE HUGHES** (Republic of Ireland)

**Born** 4.11.55. **Turned professional** 1981. **World ranking** 35 (27).

| | | | | |
|---|---|---|---|---|
| **1981** | v M. Owen | 5-1 | Qualifying | Jameson International |
| | v Fitzmaurice | 5-3 | Qualifying | Jameson International |
| | v Sinclair | 5-2 | Qualifying | Jameson International |
| | v Edmonds | 4-5 | 1st round | Jameson International |
| **1982** | v Mountjoy | 4-5 | 1st round | Benson & Hedges Irish Masters |
| | v Jack Rea | 6-1 | Quarter-final | Irish Championship |
| | v Higgins | 2-6 | Semi-final | Irish Championship |
| | v Knowles | 7-9 | Qualifying | Embassy World Championship |
| | v Parkin | 5-2 | Qualifying | Jameson International |
| | v Martin | 5-4 | Qualifying | Jameson International |
| | v Reardon | 3-5 | 1st round | Jameson International |
| | v Stevens | 2-5 | 1st round | Professional Players Tournament |
| **1983** | v Burke | 6-2 | Quarter-final | Irish Championship |
| | v Higgins | 2-6 | Semi-final | Irish Championship |
| | v Fitzmaurice | 10-7 | Qualifying | Embassy World Championship |
| | v Sinclair | 10-8 | Qualifying | Embassy World Championship |
| | v Reardon | 7-10 | 1st round | Embassy World Championship |
| | v Fisher | 5-4 | Qualifying | Jameson International |
| | v G. Foulds | 5-1 | Qualifying | Jameson International |
| | v S. Davis | 1-5 | 1st round | Jameson International |
| | v Sinclair | 5-4 | 1st round | Professional Players Tournament |
| | v Werbeniuk | 5-0 | 2nd round | Professional Players Tournament |
| | v Griffiths | 5-2 | 3rd round | Professional Players Tournament |
| | v Thorne | 1-5 | Quarter-final | Professional Players Tournament |
| **1984** | v Knowles | 1-5 | Qualifying | Lada Classic |
| | v Dennis Taylor | 1-5 | 1st round | Benson & Hedges Irish Masters |
| | v Mifsud | 5-10 | Qualifying | Embassy World Championship |
| | v Roscoe | 5-1 | Qualifying | Jameson International |
| | v Mountjoy | 5-1 | 1st round | Jameson International |
| | v Reardon | 5-1 | 2nd round | Jameson International |
| | v Thorne | 5-2 | Quarter-final | Jameson International |
| | v S. Davis | 3-9 | Semi-final | Jameson International |
| | v John Rea | 4-5 | 1st round | Rothmans Grand Prix |
| | v Morra | 9-8 | Qualifying | Coral UK Open |
| | v Meo | 4-9 | 1st round | Coral UK Open |
| **1985** | v Newbury | 5-3 | Qualifying | Mercantile Credit Classic |
| | v Meo | 5-4 | 1st round | Mercantile Credit Classic |
| | v Reardon | 1-5 | 2nd round | Mercantile Credit Classic |
| | v Watchorn | 6-4 | 1st round | Dulux British Open |
| | v B. Harris | 5-4 | 2nd round | Dulux British Open |
| | v Macleod | 5-2 | 3rd round | Dulux British Open |
| | v Higgins | 2-5 | Quarter-final | Dulux British Open |
| | v Reardon | 5-0 | 1st round | Benson & Hedges Irish Masters |
| | v S. Davis | 4-5 | Quarter-final | Benson & Hedges Irish Masters |
| | v Kelly | 6-2 | Quarter-final | Irish Championship |
| | v Dennis Taylor | 5-6 | Semi-final | Irish Championship |
| | v Newbury | 10-6 | Qualifying | Embassy World Championship |
| | v Reardon | 9-10 | 1st round | Embassy World Championship |
| | v Murphy | 3-5 | 3rd round | Goya Matchroom Trophy |
| | v Simngam | 5-1 | 3rd round | Rothmans Grand Prix |
| | v Meo | 3-5 | 4th round | Rothmans Grand Prix |
| | v West | 3-9 | 3rd round | Coral UK Open |
| **1986** | v Wych | 5-2 | 3rd round | Mercantile Credit Classic |
| | v F. Davis | 5-3 | 4th round | Mercantile Credit Classic |
| | v Johnson | 1-5 | 5th round | Mercantile Credit Classic |
| | v Longworth | 4-5 | 3rd round | Dulux British Open |
| | v Reardon | 5-2 | 1st round | Benson & Hedges Irish Masters |
| | v Thorburn | 1-5 | Quarter-final | Benson & Hedges Irish Masters |
| | v Murphy | 10-7 | Qualifying | Embassy World Championship |
| | v David Taylor | 10-7 | 1st round | Embassy World Championship |
| | v Thorburn | 6-13 | 2nd round | Embassy World Championship |
| | v Sheehan | 5-0 | 1st round | Strongbow Irish Championship |
| | v Burke | 6-3 | Quarter-final | Strongbow Irish Championship |

| | | | | |
|---|---|---|---|---|
| | v Higgins | 2-6 | Semi-final | Strongbow Irish Championship |
| | v Chappel | 5-4 | 3rd round | BCE International |
| | v Houlihan | 5-1 | 4th round | BCE International |
| | v Chaperon | 5-0 | 5th round | BCE International |
| | v S. Davis | 5-4 | Quarter-final | BCE International |
| | v N. Foulds | 8-9 | Semi-final | BCE International |
| | v Hendry | 1-5 | 3rd round | Rothmans Grand Prix |
| | v Roscoe | 9-8 | 3rd round | Tennents UK Open |
| | v Reardon | 9-5 | 4th round | Tennents UK Open |
| | v W. Jones | 5-9 | 5th round | Tennents UK Open |
| **1987** | v Wright | 4-5 | 3rd round | Mercantile Credit Classic |
| | v V. Harris | 5-0 | 3rd round | Dulux British Open |
| | v Johnson | 3-5 | 4th round | Dulux British Open |
| | v Dennis Taylor | 4-5 | 1st round | Benson & Hedges Irish Masters |
| | v Medati | 10-2 | Qualifying | Embassy World Championship |
| | v Johnson | 9-10 | 1st round | Embassy World Championship |
| | v Watchorn | 5-2 | 1st round | Matchroom Irish Championship |
| | v Kearney | 6-1 | Quarter-final | Matchroom Irish Championship |
| | v O'Boye | 3-6 | Semi-final | Matchroom Irish Championship |
| | v Owers | 5-4 | 3rd round | Fidelity International |
| | v Wych | 5-4 | 4th round | Fidelity International |
| | v S. Francisco | 5-4 | 5th round | Fidelity International |
| | v Thorburn | 1-5 | Quarter-final | Fidelity International |
| | v Fisher | 4-5 | 3rd round | Rothmans Grand Prix |
| | v N. Gilbert | 9-7 | 3rd round | Tennents UK Open |
| | v White | 4-9 | 4th round | Tennents UK Open |
| **1988** | v Newbury | 1-5 | 3rd round | Mercantile Credit Classic |
| | v Watchorn | 2-5 | 1st round | Irish Championship |
| | v Cripsey | 3-5 | 3rd round | MIM Britannia British Open |
| | v Johnson | 4-5 | 1st round | Benson & Hedges Irish Masters |
| | v James | 6-10 | Qualifying | Embassy World Championship |
| | v Meakin | 5-0 | 3rd round | Fidelity International |
| | v White | 1-5 | 4th round | Fidelity International |
| | v Hendry | 1-5 | 1st round | Fosters Professional |
| | v Clark | 5-3 | 3rd round | Rothmans Grand Prix |
| | v Johnson | 5-2 | 4th round | Rothmans Grand Prix |
| | v Griffiths | 2-5 | 5th round | Rothmans Grand Prix |
| | v M. Bennett | 2-5 | 3rd round | BCE Canadian Masters |
| | v O'Boye | 8-9 | 3rd round | Tennents UK Open |
| **1989** | v Miles | 5-2 | 3rd round | Mercantile Credit Classic |
| | v W. Jones | 1-5 | 4th round | Mercantile Credit Classic |
| | v Morra | 5-1 | 3rd round | European Open |
| | v Clark | 1-5 | 4th round | European Open |
| | v Kearney | 5-1 | Quarter-final | Irish Championship |
| | v Higgins | 2-6 | Semi-final | Irish Championship |
| | v W. Jones | 5-2 | 3rd round | Anglian British Open |
| | v Johnston-Allen | 2-5 | 4th round | Anglian British Open |
| | v Rowswell | 10-9 | Qualifying | Embassy World Championship |
| | v Dennis Taylor | 3-10 | 1st round | Embassy World Championship |
| | v Gollan | 3-5 | 3rd round | Hong Kong Open |
| | v Terry | 5-1 | 3rd round | 555 Asian Open |
| | v Mountjoy | 4-5 | 4th round | 555 Asian Open |
| | v D. Morgan | 5-4 | 3rd round | BCE International |
| | v B. Morgan | 3-5 | 4th round | BCE International |
| | v M. Bennett | 5-2 | 3rd round | Rothmans Grand Prix |
| | v Robidoux | 1-5 | 4th round | Rothmans Grand Prix |
| | v Wattana | 0-5 | 3rd round | Dubai Classic |
| | v M. Bennett | 3-9 | 3rd round | Stormseal UK Open |
| **1990** | v B. Morgan | 1-5 | 3rd round | Mercantile Credit Classic |
| | v Johnston-Allen | 5-1 | 3rd round | Pearl Assurance British Open |
| | v Williams | 5-2 | 4th round | Pearl Assurance British Open |
| | v Marshall | 0-5 | 5th round | Pearl Assurance British Open |
| | v David Taylor | 4-5 | 3rd round | European Open |

| | | | | |
|---|---|---|---|---|
| | v Gollan | 7-10 | Qualifying | Embassy World Championship |

## STEVE JAMES (England)

**Born** 2.5.61. **Turned professional** 1986. **World ranking** 9 (16).

| | | | | |
|---|---|---|---|---|
| **1986** | v N. Gilbert | 5-2 | 1st round | BCE International |
| | v Edmonds | 2-5 | 2nd round | BCE International |
| | v Morra | 3-5 | 1st round | Rothmans Grand Prix |
| | v Rigitano | 9-5 | 1st round | Tennents UK Open |
| | v King | 8-9 | 2nd round | Tennents UK Open |
| **1987** | v Jonik | 4-5 | 1st round | Mercantile Credit Classic |
| | v Hargreaves | 6-5 | 1st round | Tolly Ales English Championship |
| | v F. Davis | 6-2 | 2nd round | Tolly Ales English Championship |
| | v Longworth | 6-2 | 3rd round | Tolly Ales English Championship |
| | v Johnson | 3-6 | 4th round | Tolly Ales English Championship |
| | v Darrington | 5-3 | 1st round | Dulux British Open |
| | v Miles | 5-2 | 2nd round | Dulux British Open |
| | v J. Campbell | 5-1 | 3rd round | Dulux British Open |
| | v Williams | 2-5 | 4th round | Dulux British Open |
| | v Watterson | 10-2 | Qualifying | Embassy World Championship |
| | v Edmonds | 1-10 | Qualifying | Embassy World Championship |
| | v B. Harris | 5-0 | 2nd round | Fidelity International |
| | v J. Campbell | 5-4 | 3rd round | Fidelity International |
| | v Roe | 3-5 | 4th round | Fidelity International |
| | v G. Foulds | 5-0 | 2nd round | Rothmans Grand Prix |
| | v Johnson | 4-5 | 3rd round | Rothmans Grand Prix |
| | v T. Jones | 6-9 | 2nd round | Tennents UK Open |
| **1988** | v Houlihan | 5-2 | 2nd round | Mercantile Credit Classic |
| | v White | 1-5 | 3rd round | Mercantile Credit Classic |
| | v Greaves | 5-6 | 1st round | English Championship |
| | v King | 5-2 | 2nd round | MIM Britannia British Open |
| | v Charlton | 5-2 | 3rd round | MIM Britannia British Open |
| | v White | 1-5 | 4th round | MIM Britannia British Open |
| | v O'Boye | 10-7 | Qualifying | Embassy World Championship |
| | v Browne | 10-1 | Qualifying | Embassy World Championship |
| | v E. Hughes | 10-6 | Qualifying | Embassy World Championship |
| | v Williams | 10-6 | 1st round | Embassy World Championship |
| | v Johnson | 13-9 | 2nd round | Embassy World Championship |
| | v Thorburn | 11-13 | Quarter-final | Embassy World Championship |
| | v Wright | 5-3 | 3rd round | Fidelity International |
| | v Macleod | 5-2 | 4th round | Fidelity International |
| | v Hendry | 5-2 | 5th round | Fidelity International |
| | v Meo | 5-1 | Quarter-final | Fidelity International |
| | v S. Davis | 1-9 | Semi-final | Fidelity International |
| | v M. Smith | 5-3 | 3rd round | Rothmans Grand Prix |
| | v Hallett | 2-5 | 4th round | Rothmans Grand Prix |
| | v Murphy | 5-3 | 3rd round | BCE Canadian Masters |
| | v Johnson | 5-4 | 4th round | BCE Canadian Masters |
| | v S. Davis | 0-5 | 5th round | BCE Canadian Masters |
| | v Kearney | 9-1 | 3rd round | Tennents UK Open |
| | v Thorburn | 6-9 | 4th round | Tennents UK Open |
| **1989** | v Gary Wilkinson | 5-1 | 3rd round | Mercantile Credit Classic |
| | v Browne | 4-5 | 4th round | Mercantile Credit Classic |
| | v Johnston-Allen | 1-5 | 3rd round | European Open |
| | v Cripsey | 3-5 | 3rd round | English Championship |
| | v Chappel | 3-5 | 3rd round | Anglian British Open |
| | v John Rea | 10-7 | Qualifying | Embassy World Championship |
| | v Parrott | 9-10 | 1st round | Embassy World Championship |
| | v Rowing | 5-1 | 3rd round | Hong Kong Open |
| | v Graham | 3-5 | 4th round | Hong Kong Open |
| | v M. Bennett | 5-3 | 3rd round | 555 Asian Open |

*Steve James*

| | | | | |
|---|---|---|---|---|
| | v Duggan | 3-5 | 4th round | 555 Asian Open |
| | v J. McLaughlin | 5-3 | 3rd round | BCE International |
| | v M. Smith | 5-3 | 4th round | BCE International |
| | v Bond | 0-5 | 5th round | BCE International |
| | v Robidoux | 2-5 | 3rd round | Rothmans Grand Prix |
| | v Wright | 5-2 | 3rd round | Dubai Classic |
| | v Chambers | 5-4 | 4th round | Dubai Classic |
| | v Parrott | 3-5 | 5th round | Dubai Classic |
| | v B. Morgan | 4-9 | 3rd round | Stormseal UK Open |
| **1990** | v Chambers | 5-4 | 3rd round | Mercantile Credit Classic |
| | v Chaperon | 5-2 | 4th round | Mercantile Credit Classic |
| | v Parrott | 5-3 | 5th round | Mercantile Credit Classic |
| | v W. Jones | 5-2 | Quarter-final | Mercantile Credit Classic |
| | v S. Davis | 6-4 | Semi-final | Mercantile Credit Classic |
| | **v King** | **10-6** | **Final** | **Mercantile Credit Classic** |
| | v Higgins | 5-2 | Play-offs | Benson and Hedges Masters |
| | v Hendry | 2-5 | 1st round | Benson and Hedges Masters |
| | v Oliver | 5-1 | 3rd round | Pearl Assurance British Open |
| | v T. Wilson | 5-0 | 4th round | Pearl Assurance British Open |
| | v White | 5-4 | 5th round | Pearl Assurance British Open |
| | v Dodd | 5-2 | Quarter-final | Pearl Assurance British Open |
| | v Higgins | 3-9 | Semi-final | Pearl Assurance British Open |
| | v Pinches | 5-2 | 3rd round | European Open |
| | v Higgins | 5-2 | 4th round | European Open |
| | v White | 5-4 | 5th round | European Open |
| | v Roscoe | 5-2 | Quarter-final | European Open |
| | v Parrott | 3-6 | Semi-final | European Open |
| | v Higgins | 10-5 | 1st round | Embassy World Championship |
| | v S. Davis | 7-13 | 2nd round | Embassy World Championship |

## JOE JOHNSON (England)

**Born** 29.7.52. **Turned professional** 1979. **World ranking** 18 (11).

| | | | | |
|---|---|---|---|---|
| **1979** | v Werbeniuk | 3-9 | 2nd round | Coral UK Championship |
| **1980** | v Dunning | 9-6 | Qualifying | Coral UK Championship |
| | v Fagan | 4-9 | 1st round | Coral UK Championship |
| **1981** | v Knowles | 9-2 | Qualifying | John Courage English |
| | v Johnson | *wo* | 1st round | John Courage English |
| | v Edmonds | 5-9 | 2nd round | John Courage English |
| | v Meo | 8-9 | Qualifying | Embassy World Championship |
| | v Donnelly | 5-4 | Qualifying | Jameson International |
| | v Macleod | 5-1 | Qualifying | Jameson International |
| | v Wych | 5-2 | 1st round | Jameson International |
| | v Miles | 3-5 | 2nd round | Jameson International |
| | v Murphy | 9-1 | Qualifying | Coral UK Championship |
| | v Watterson | 9-3 | Qualifying | Coral UK Championship |
| | v Wilson | 9-5 | Qualifying | Coral UK Championship |
| | v Spencer | 9-5 | 2nd round | Coral UK Championship |
| | v Reardon | 7-9 | 3rd round | Coral UK Championship |
| **1982** | v Harris | 9-4 | Qualifying | Embassy World Championship |
| | v Hallett | 8-9 | Qualifying | Embassy World Championship |
| | v Wilson | 4-5 | Qualifying | Jameson International |
| | v Miles | 5-1 | 1st round | Professional Players Tournament |
| | v Stevens | 5-1 | 2nd round | Professional Players Tournament |
| | v Wildman | 5-4 | 3rd round | Professional Players Tournament |
| | v Virgo | 1-5 | Quarter-final | Professional Players Tournament |
| | v V. Harris | 9-8 | Qualifying | Coral UK Championship |
| | v Griffiths | 1-9 | 1st round | Coral UK Championship |
| **1983** | v Thorburn | 2-5 | 1st round | Benson & Hedges Masters |
| | v Watchorn | 10-0 | Qualifying | Embassy World Championship |
| | v Wilson | 8-10 | Qualifying | Embassy World Championship |

| Year | Opponent | Score | Round | Tournament |
|---|---|---|---|---|
| | v D. Hughes | 5-1 | Qualifying | Jameson International |
| | v Charlton | 2-5 | 1st round | Jameson International |
| | v Burke | 5-3 | 1st round | Professional Players Tournament |
| | v White | 5-3 | 2nd round | Professional Players Tournament |
| | v Charlton | 5-0 | 3rd round | Professional Players Tournament |
| | v Thorburn | 5-1 | Quarter-final | Professional Players Tournament |
| | v Meo | 9-6 | Semi-final | Professional Players Tournament |
| | v Knowles | 8-9 | Final | Professional Players Tournament |
| | v Gibson | 9-6 | Qualifying | Coral UK Championship |
| | v Virgo | 9-6 | 1st round | Coral UK Championship |
| | v David Taylor | 9-3 | 2nd round | Coral UK Championship |
| | v Griffiths | 2-9 | Quarter-final | Coral UK Championship |
| **1984** | v Spencer | 4-5 | Qualifying | Lada Classic |
| | v Gibson | 10-3 | Qualifying | Embassy World Championship |
| | v Dennis Taylor | 1-10 | 1st round | Embassy World Championship |
| | v Morra | 5-0 | Qualifying | Jameson International |
| | v Charlton | 5-1 | 1st round | Jameson International |
| | v Dennis Taylor | 2-5 | 2nd round | Jameson International |
| | v Medati | 5-1 | 1st round | Rothmans Grand Prix |
| | v Williamson | 4-5 | 2nd round | Rothmans Grand Prix |
| | v John Rea | 9-6 | Qualifying | Coral UK Open |
| | v Spencer | 9-6 | 1st round | Coral UK Open |
| | v Stevens | 2-9 | 2nd round | Coral UK Open |
| **1985** | v Edmonds | 5-4 | Qualifying | Mercantile Credit Classic |
| | v Knowles | 5-1 | 1st round | Mercantile Credit Classic |
| | v Wilson | 5-0 | 2nd round | Mercantile Credit Classic |
| | v King | 5-3 | Quarter-final | Mercantile Credit Classic |
| | v Thorburn | 2-9 | Semi-final | Mercantile Credit Classic |
| | v Scott | 9-1 | 1st round | Tolly Cobbold English Championship |
| | v Virgo | 4-9 | 2nd round | Tolly Cobbold English Championship |
| | v W. Jones | 5-6 | 1st round | Dulux British Open |
| | v G. Foulds | 10-6 | Qualifying | Embassy World Championship |
| | v Werbeniuk | 8-10 | 1st round | Embassy World Championship |
| | v White | 4-5 | Quarter-final | Winfield Australian Masters |
| | v Bear | 5-1 | 3rd round | Goya Matchroom Trophy |
| | v Bradley | 5-2 | 4th round | Goya Matchroom Trophy |
| | v Wilson | 5-1 | 5th round | Goya Matchroom Trophy |
| | v N. Foulds | 2-5 | Quarter-final | Goya Matchroom Trophy |
| | v Gilbert | 5-2 | 3rd round | Rothmans Grand Prix |
| | v Hallett | 5-4 | 4th round | Rothmans Grand Prix |
| | v Thorburn | 1-5 | 5th round | Rothmans Grand Prix |
| | v Simngam | 9-4 | 3rd round | Coral UK Open |
| | v N. Foulds | 8-9 | 4th round | Coral UK Open |
| **1986** | v B. Harris | 5-4 | 3rd round | Mercantile Credit Classic |
| | v Mans | 5-2 | 4th round | Mercantile Credit Classic |
| | v E. Hughes | 5-1 | 5th round | Mercantile Credit Classic |
| | v Thorburn | 4-5 | Quarter-final | Mercantile Credit Classic |
| | v Thorburn | 3-5 | 1st round | Benson & Hedges Masters |
| | v Fowler | 9-7 | 3rd round | Tolly Cobbold English Championship |
| | v Spencer | 9-7 | 4th round | Tolly Cobbold English Championship |
| | v Hallett | 6-9 | Quarter-final | Tolly Cobbold English Championship |
| | v J. McLaughlin | 5-2 | 3rd round | Dulux British Open |
| | v Werbeniuk | 5-2 | 4th round | Dulux British Open |
| | v Martin | 10-3 | 1st round | Embassy World Championship |
| | v Hallett | 13-6 | 2nd round | Embassy World Championship |
| | v Griffiths | 13-12 | Quarter-final | Embassy World Championship |
| | v Knowles | 16-8 | Semi-final | Embassy World Championship |
| | **v S. Davis** | **18-12** | **Final** | **Embassy World Championship** |
| | v Dennis Taylor | 3-5 | 1st round | Carlsberg Challenge |
| | v Higgins | 2-5 | 1st round | Langs Scottish Masters |
| | v Murphy | 5-4 | 3rd round | BCE International |
| | v David Taylor | 3-5 | 4th round | BCE International |
| | v Browne | 2-5 | 3rd round | Rothmans Grand Prix |

*Joe Johnson*

| | | | | |
|---|---|---|---|---|
| | v Higgins | 3-5 | 1st round | BCE Canadian Masters |
| | v Parrott | 1-9 | 3rd round | Tennents UK Open |
| **1987** | v Sinclair | 5-0 | 3rd round | Mercantile Credit Classic |
| | v P. Francisco | 3-5 | 4th round | Mercantile Credit Classic |
| | v Reardon | 5-2 | 1st round | Benson & Hedges Masters |
| | v Higgins | 1-5 | Quarter-final | Benson & Hedges Masters |
| | v Miles | 6-3 | 3rd round | Tolly Ales English Championship |
| | v James | 6-2 | 4th round | Tolly Ales English Championship |
| | v Williams | 6-5 | Quarter-final | Tolly Ales English Championship |
| | v Dodd | 5-9 | Semi-final | Tolly Ales English Championship |
| | v Drago | 5-0 | 3rd round | Dulux British Open |
| | v E. Hughes | 5-3 | 4th round | Dulux British Open |
| | v Spencer | 3-5 | 5th round | Dulux British Open |
| | v Griffiths | 0-5 | Quarter-final | Benson & Hedges Irish Masters |
| | v E. Hughes | 10-9 | 1st round | Embassy World Championship |
| | v Macleod | 13-7 | 2nd round | Embassy World Championship |
| | v Hendry | 13-12 | Quarter-final | Embassy World Championship |
| | v N. Foulds | 16-9 | Semi-final | Embassy World Championship |
| | v S. Davis | 14-18 | Final | Embassy World Championship |
| | v N. Foulds | 5-4 | 1st round | Carling Champions |
| | v Dennis Taylor | 5-8 | Final | Carling Champions |
| | v Hendry | 5-2 | 1st round | Langs Scottish Masters |
| | v Thorburn | 6-3 | Semi-final | Langs Scottish Masters |
| | **v Griffiths** | **9-7** | **Final** | **Langs Scottish Masters** |
| | v Wych | 4-5 | 3rd round | Fidelity International |
| | v James | 5-4 | 3rd round | Rothmans Grand Prix |
| | v P. Francisco | 2-5 | 4th round | Rothmans Grand Prix |
| | v Thorburn | 3-5 | 1st round | Labatts Canadian Masters (WS) |
| | v Bear | 9-5 | 3rd round | Tennents UK Open |
| | v West | 9-6 | 4th round | Tennents UK Open |
| | v Chappel | 9-4 | 5th round | Tennents UK Open |
| | v Hallett | 9-7 | Quarter-final | Tennents UK Open |
| | v White | 4-9 | Semi-final | Tennents UK Open |
| **1988** | v Chappel | 5-2 | 3rd round | Mercantile Credit Classic |
| | v Hendry | 3-5 | 4th round | Mercantile Credit Classic |
| | v Thorne | 5-4 | 1st round | Benson & Hedges Masters |
| | v White | 5-3 | Quarter-final | Benson & Hedges Masters |
| | v S. Davis | 3-6 | Semi-final | Benson & Hedges Masters |
| | v J. Smith | 6-5 | 3rd round | English Championship |
| | v Martin | 6-4 | 4th round | English Championship |
| | v Knowles | 6-4 | Quarter-final | English Championship |
| | v Reynolds | 8-9 | Semi-final | English Championship |
| | v Lawlor | 5-1 | 3rd round | MIM Britannia British Open |
| | v Rowswell | 5-2 | 4th round | MIM Britannia British Open |
| | v O'Kane | 2-5 | 5th round | MIM Britannia British Open |
| | v E. Hughes | 5-4 | 1st round | Benson & Hedges Irish Masters |
| | v S. Davis | 0-5 | Quarter-final | Benson & Hedges Irish Masters |
| | v C. Wilson | 10-7 | 1st round | Embassy World Championship |
| | v James | 9-13 | 2nd round | Embassy World Championship |
| | v Reynolds | 5-4 | 1st round | New Zealand Masters |
| | v Hendry | 2-5 | 2nd round | New Zealand Masters |
| | v Knowles | 5-4 | Play-off for 3rd | New Zealand Masters |
| | v Cripsey | 5-3 | 3rd round | Fidelity International |
| | v Mountjoy | 5-4 | 4th round | Fidelity International |
| | v Newbury | 5-2 | 5th round | Fidelity International |
| | v Reynolds | 1-5 | Quarter-final | Fidelity International |
| | v Bradley | 5-2 | 3rd round | Rothmans Grand Prix |
| | v E. Hughes | 2-5 | 4th round | Rothmans Grand Prix |
| | v Robidoux | 5-1 | 3rd round | BCE Canadian Masters |
| | v James | 4-5 | 4th round | BCE Canadian Masters |
| | v M. Smith | 9-2 | 3rd round | Tennents UK Open |
| | v Williams | 9-7 | 4th round | Tennents UK Open |
| | v Mountjoy | 5-9 | 5th round | Tennents UK Open |

| | | | | |
|---|---|---|---|---|
| | v Thorburn | 9-4 | 1st round | Everest World Matchplay |
| | v Parrott | 7-9 | Quarter-final | Everest World Matchplay |
| **1989** | v Sheehan | 5-2 | 3rd round | Mercantile Credit Classic |
| | v Higgins | 5-0 | 4th round | Mercantile Credit Classic |
| | v Clark | 3-5 | 5th round | Mercantile Credit Classic |
| | v Thorburn | 2-5 | 1st round | Benson and Hedges Masters |
| | v Cripsey | 5-2 | 3rd round | European Open |
| | v Roe | 5-2 | 4th round | European Open |
| | v Clark | 4-5 | 5th round | European Open |
| | v D. Gilbert | 5-2 | 3rd round | English Championship |
| | v Edwards | 5-0 | 4th round | English Championship |
| | v Parrott | 4-5 | Quarter-final | English Championship |
| | v Whitthread | 5-2 | 3rd round | Anglian British Open |
| | v Drago | 5-3 | 4th round | Anglian British Open |
| | v Johnston-Allen | 5-2 | 5th round | Anglian British Open |
| | v Reynolds | 4-5 | Quarter-final | Anglian British Open |
| | v Meo | 5-10 | 1st round | Embassy World Championship |
| | v Hallett | 6-5 | 1st round | Lion Brown New Zealand Masters |
| | v Knowles | 6-3 | Semi-final | Lion Brown New Zealand Masters |
| | v Thorne | 4-7 | Final | Lion Brown New Zealand Masters |
| | v Dodd | 0-5 | 3rd round | Hong Kong Open |
| | v Fowler | 5-4 | 3rd round | 555 Asian Open |
| | v Drago | 2-5 | 4th round | 555 Asian Open |
| | v B. Morgan | 2-5 | 3rd round | BCE International |
| | v D. Morgan | 5-2 | 3rd round | Rothmans Grand Prix |
| | v Higgins | 5-2 | 4th round | Rothmans Grand Prix |
| | v White | 5-0 | 5th round | Rothmans Grand Prix |
| | v Fowler | 4-5 | Quarter-final | Rothmans Grand Prix |
| | v Bond | 3-5 | 3rd round | Dubai Classic |
| | v Chambers | 9-7 | 3rd round | Stormseal UK Open |
| | v Clark | 9-6 | 4th round | Stormseal UK Open |
| | v White | 6-9 | 5th round | Stormseal UK Open |
| **1990** | v N. Gilbert | 0-5 | 3rd round | Mercantile Credit Classic |
| | v Hallett | 5-4 | 1st round | Benson and Hedges Masters |
| | v Parrott | 3-5 | Quarter-final | Benson and Hedges Masters |
| | v Wych | *wo* | 3rd round | Pearl Assurance British Open |
| | v Marshall | 4-5 | 4th round | Pearl Assurance British Open |
| | v N. Gilbert | 5-2 | 3rd round | European Open |
| | v Fowler | 5-1 | 4th round | European Open |
| | v Parrott | 2-5 | 5th round | European Open |
| | v White | 4-5 | 1st round | Benson and Hedges Irish Masters |
| | v D. Morgan | 8-10 | 1st round | Embassy World Championship |

## MARK JOHNSTON-ALLEN (England)

**Born** 28.12.88. **Turned professional** 1988. **World ranking** 60 (52).

| | | | | |
|---|---|---|---|---|
| **1988** | v Scott | 5-2 | 1st round | Fidelity International |
| | v D. Gilbert | 5-3 | 2nd round | Fidelity International |
| | v O'Kane | 3-5 | 3rd round | Fidelity International |
| | v Roscoe | 5-1 | 1st round | Rothmans Grand Prix |
| | v Browne | 5-2 | 2nd round | Rothmans Grand Prix |
| | v Spencer | 3-5 | 3rd round | Rothmans Grand Prix |
| | v B. Harris | 5-4 | 1st round | BCE Canadian Masters |
| | v N. Gilbert | 4-5 | 2nd round | BCE Canadian Masters |
| | v Van Rensberg | 9-4 | 1st round | Tennents UK Open |
| | v W. Jones | 8-9 | 2nd round | Tennents UK Open |
| **1989** | v Scott | 5-0 | 1st round | Mercantile Credit Classic |
| | v Chappel | 2-5 | 2nd round | Mercantile Credit Classic |
| | v Donnelly | 5-3 | 1st round | European Open |
| | v Wright | 5-4 | 2nd round | European Open |
| | v James | 5-1 | 3rd round | European Open |

| | | | | |
|---|---|---|---|---|
| | v Wych | 4-5 | 4th round | European Open |
| | v B. Bennett | 5-2 | Prelim | English Championship |
| | v Price | 4-5 | 1st round | English Championship |
| | v V. Harris | 5-1 | 1st round | Anglian British Open |
| | v Edmonds | 5-4 | 2nd round | Anglian British Open |
| | v Griffiths | 5-1 | 3rd round | Anglian British Open |
| | v E. Hughes | 5-2 | 4th round | Anglian British Open |
| | v Johnson | 2-5 | 5th round | Anglian British Open |
| | v E. McLaughlin | 10-3 | Qualifying | Embassy World Championship |
| | v Rigitano | 10-3 | Qualifying | Embassy World Championship |
| | v Wych | 3-10 | Qualifying | Embassy World Championship |
| | v Price | 1-5 | 2nd round | Hong Kong Open |
| | v Meakin | 5-1 | 2nd round | 555 Asian Open |
| | v Reynolds | 2-5 | 3rd round | 555 Asian Open |
| | v Grace | 5-0 | 2nd round | BCE International |
| | v Higgins | 5-1 | 3rd round | BCE International |
| | v T. Jones | 2-5 | 4th round | BCE International |
| | v Kelly | 5-1 | 2nd round | Rothmans Grand Prix |
| | v Hallett | 1-5 | 3rd round | Rothmans Grand Prix |
| | v P. Gibson | 0-5 | 2nd round | Dubai Classic |
| | v Pinches | 6-1 | 2nd round | Stormseal UK Open |
| | v Drago | 7-9 | 3rd round | Stormseal UK Open |
| **1990** | v John Rea | 5-4 | 2nd round | Mercantile Credit Classic |
| | v Higgins | 0-5 | 3rd round | Mercantile Credit Classic |
| | v Owers | 5-4 | 2nd round | Pearl Assurance British Open |
| | v E. Hughes | 1-5 | 3rd round | Pearl Assurance British Open |
| | v S. Campbell | 5-0 | 2nd round | European Open |
| | v N. Foulds | 3-5 | 3rd round | European Open |
| | v Terry | 10-1 | Qualifying | Embassy World Championship |
| | v Browne | 10-2 | Qualifying | Embassy World Championship |
| | v P. Francisco | 7-10 | Qualifying | Embassy World Championship |

## TONY JONES (England)

**Born** 15.4.60. **Turned professional** 1983. **World ranking** 36 (62).

| | | | | |
|---|---|---|---|---|
| **1983** | v Oliver | 5-2 | Qualifying | Professional Players Tournament |
| | v Werbeniuk | 4-5 | 1st round | Professional Players Tournament |
| | v Sinclair | 9-3 | Qualifying | Coral UK Championship |
| | v Knowles | 5-9 | 1st round | Coral UK Championship |
| **1984** | v King | 9-10 | Qualifying | Embassy World Championship |
| | v French | 5-1 | Qualifying | Jameson International |
| | v Duggan | 2-5 | Qualifying | Jameson International |
| | v Sinclair | 5-4 | Qualifying | Rothmans Grand Prix |
| | v Griffiths | 5-3 | 1st round | Rothmans Grand Prix |
| | v N. Foulds | 0-5 | 2nd round | Rothmans Grand Prix |
| | v Chaperon | 9-1 | Qualifying | Coral UK Open |
| | v Fagan | 9-2 | Qualifying | Coral UK Open |
| | v Wildman | 9-2 | Qualifying | Coral UK Open |
| | v Higgins | 7-9 | 1st round | Coral UK Open |
| **1985** | v Greaves | 5-2 | Qualifying | Mercantile Credit Classic |
| | v Gibson | 5-0 | Qualifying | Mercantile Credit Classic |
| | v Dodd | 5-1 | Qualifying | Mercantile Credit Classic |
| | v S. Francisco | 1-5 | Qualifying | Mercantile Credit Classic |
| | v Houlihan | 9-1 | Qualifying | Tolly Cobbold English Championship |
| | v Williams | 6-9 | 1st round | Tolly Cobbold English Championship |
| | v G. Foulds | 6-0 | Qualifying | Dulux British Open |
| | v White | 5-6 | 1st round | Dulux British Open |
| | v Darrington | 10-2 | Qualifying | Embassy World Championship |
| | v Duggan | 10-8 | Qualifying | Embassy World Championship |
| | v Fitzmaurice | 10-4 | Qualifying | Embassy World Championship |
| | v Sinclair | 10-2 | Qualifying | Embassy World Championship |

| | | | | |
|---|---|---|---|---|
| | v Knowles | 8-10 | 1st round | Embassy World Championship |
| | v Kelly | 5-3 | 2nd round | Goya Matchroom Trophy |
| | v David Taylor | 4-5 | 3rd round | Goya Matchroom Trophy |
| | v Houlihan | 5-4 | 2nd round | Rothmans Grand Prix |
| | v Meo | 2-5 | 3rd round | Rothmans Grand Prix |
| | v Jonik | 9-4 | 2nd round | Coral UK Open |
| | v Griffiths | 5-9 | 3rd round | Coral UK Open |
| **1986** | v Gilbert | 5-3 | 2nd round | Mercantile Credit Classic |
| | v Thorne | 5-3 | 3rd round | Mercantile Credit Classic |
| | v Werbeniuk | 3-5 | 4th round | Mercantile Credit Classic |
| | v B. Harris | 9-5 | 2nd round | Tolly Cobbold English Championship |
| | v Virgo | 7-9 | 3rd round | Tolly Cobbold English Championship |
| | v O'Boye | 5-2 | 2nd round | Dulux British Open |
| | v S. Francisco | 2-5 | 3rd round | Dulux British Open |
| | v V. Harris | 10-7 | Qualifying | Embassy World Championship |
| | v Gilbert | 7-10 | Qualifying | Embassy World Championship |
| | v Burke | 4-5 | 2nd round | BCE International |
| | v Smith | 5-0 | 2nd round | Rothmans Grand Prix |
| | v White | 0-5 | 3rd round | Rothmans Grand Prix |
| | v Fitzmaurice | 9-0 | 2nd round | Tennents UK Open |
| | v West | 9-4 | 3rd round | Tennents UK Open |
| | v Knowles | 2-9 | 4th round | Tennents UK Open |
| **1987** | v Oliver | 5-0 | 2nd round | Mercantile Credit Classic |
| | v Parrott | 2-5 | 3rd round | Mercantile Credit Classic |
| | v Oliver | 6-1 | 2nd round | Tolly Ales English Championship |
| | v Williams | 4-6 | 3rd round | Tolly Ales English Championship |
| | v Donnelly | 5-2 | 2nd round | Dulux British Open |
| | v Macleod | 5-4 | 3rd round | Dulux British Open |
| | v Griffiths | 3-5 | 4th round | Dulux British Open |
| | v Chalmers | 10-1 | Qualifying | Embassy World Championship |
| | v Van Rensberg | 10-0 | Qualifying | Embassy World Championship |
| | v Virgo | 9-10 | Qualifying | Embassy World Championship |
| | v P. Gibson | 4-5 | 2nd round | Fidelity International |
| | v Roscoe | 5-1 | 2nd round | Rothmans Grand Prix |
| | v Thorburn | 2-5 | 3rd round | Rothmans Grand Prix |
| | v James | 9-6 | 2nd round | Tennents UK Open |
| | v Hallett | 2-9 | 3rd round | Tennents UK Open |
| **1988** | v A. Harris | 5-2 | 2nd round | Mercantile Credit Classic |
| | v Higgins | 0-5 | 3rd round | Mercantile Credit Classic |
| | v J. Smith | 0-5 | 2nd round | English Championship |
| | v Fitzmaurice | 5-3 | 2nd round | MIM Britannia British Open |
| | v Higgins | 5-3 | 3rd round | MIM Britannia British Open |
| | v Chaperon | 5-4 | 4th round | MIM Britannia British Open |
| | v Hendry | 3-5 | 5th round | MIM Britannia British Open |
| | v Foldvari | 9-10 | Qualifying | Embassy World Championship |
| | v Foldvari | 5-4 | 2nd round | Fidelity International |
| | v Reynolds | 4-5 | 3rd round | Fidelity International |
| | v Mikkelsen | 5-3 | 2nd round | Rothmans Grand Prix |
| | v Hallett | 2-5 | 3rd round | Rothmans Grand Prix |
| | v D. Morgan | 0-5 | 2nd round | BCE Canadian Masters |
| | v Scott | 9-5 | 2nd round | Tennents UK Open |
| | v West | 5-9 | 3rd round | Tennents UK Open |
| **1989** | v Bradley | 4-5 | 2nd round | Mercantile Credit Classic |
| | v Medati | 5-2 | 2nd round | European Open |
| | v C. Wilson | 3-5 | 3rd round | European Open |
| | v A. Harris | 3-5 | 2nd round | English Championship |
| | v Meadowcroft | 5-1 | 2nd round | Anglian British Open |
| | v O'Kane | 4-5 | 3rd round | Anglian British Open |
| | v J. Smith | 10-7 | Qualifying | Embassy World Championship |
| | v Stevens | 10-2 | Qualifying | Embassy World Championship |
| | v Meo | 7-10 | Qualifying | Embassy World Championship |
| | v Dyson | 5-1 | 2nd round | Hong Kong Open |
| | v Thorburn | 5-2 | 3rd round | Hong Kong Open |

| | | | | |
|---|---|---|---|---|
| | v Roe | 5-1 | 4th round | Hong Kong Open |
| | v Graham | 3-5 | 5th round | Hong Kong Open |
| | v Dyson | 5-3 | 2nd round | 555 Asian Open |
| | v Thorburn | 5-2 | 3rd round | 555 Asian Open |
| | v Oliver | 5-1 | 4th round | 555 Asian Open |
| | v Duggan | 5-3 | 5th round | 555 Asian Open |
| | v Griffiths | 3-5 | Quarter-final | 555 Asian Open |
| | v Oliver | 5-1 | 2nd round | BCE International |
| | v Virgo | 5-0 | 3rd round | BCE International |
| | v Johnston-Allen | 5-2 | 4th round | BCE International |
| | v Hendry | 4-5 | 5th round | BCE International |
| | v Houlihan | 5-0 | 2nd round | Rothmans Grand Prix |
| | v O'Kane | 5-2 | 3rd round | Rothmans Grand Prix |
| | v Thorburn | 5-4 | 4th round | Rothmans Grand Prix |
| | v Knowles | 4-5 | 5th round | Rothmans Grand Prix |
| | v Dunning | 5-2 | 2nd round | Dubai Classic |
| | v Hallett | 5-4 | 3rd round | Dubai Classic |
| | v Fowler | 4-5 | 4th round | Dubai Classic |
| | v Morra | 6-3 | 2nd round | Stormseal UK Open |
| | v Newbury | 9-7 | 3rd round | Stormseal UK Open |
| | v Griffiths | 8-9 | 4th round | Stormseal UK Open |
| **1990** | v Kearney | 5-1 | 2nd round | Mercantile Credit Classic |
| | v Hendry | 3-5 | 3rd round | Mercantile Credit Classic |
| | v Gollan | 1-5 | 2nd round | Pearl Assurance British Open |
| | v Edwards | 0-5 | 2nd round | European Open |
| | v Bond | 2-10 | Qualifying | Embassy World Championship |

## WAYNE JONES (Wales)

**Born** 24.12.59. **Turned professional** 1984. **World ranking** 23 (31).

| | | | | |
|---|---|---|---|---|
| **1984** | v Watchorn | 5-0 | Qualifying | Jameson International |
| | v Gibson | 5-2 | Qualifying | Jameson International |
| | v Scott | 5-0 | Qualifying | Jameson International |
| | v Wildman | 5-0 | Qualifying | Jameson International |
| | v David Taylor | 4-5 | 1st round | Jameson International |
| | v Watterson | 5-3 | Qualifying | Rothmans Grand Prix |
| | v J. Campbell | 4-5 | 1st round | Rothmans Grand Prix |
| | v O'Kane | 7-9 | Qualifying | Coral UK Open |
| **1985** | v O'Kane | 5-0 | Qualifying | Mercantile Credit Classic |
| | v Duggan | 0-5 | Qualifying | Mercantile Credit Classic |
| | v Donnelly | 6-1 | Qualifying | Dulux British Open |
| | v Johnson | 6-5 | 1st round | Dulux British Open |
| | v Chaperon | 2-5 | 2nd round | Dulux British Open |
| | v Jack Rea | 10-3 | Qualifying | Embassy World Championship |
| | v Dunning | 10-6 | Qualifying | Embassy World Championship |
| | v Watterson | 10-5 | Qualifying | Embassy World Championship |
| | v Miles | 10-8 | Qualifying | Embassy World Championship |
| | v White | 4-10 | 1st round | Embassy World Championship |
| | v Newbury | 2-6 | 1st round | BCE Welsh Championship |
| | v Smith | 5-3 | 2nd round | Goya Matchroom Trophy |
| | v Parrott | 3-5 | 3rd round | Goya Matchroom Trophy |
| | v John Rea | 5-0 | 2nd round | Rothmans Grand Prix |
| | v Thorne | 5-0 | 3rd round | Rothmans Grand Prix |
| | v P. Francisco | 3-5 | 4th round | Rothmans Grand Prix |
| | v Fitzmaurice | 9-3 | 2nd round | Coral UK Open |
| | v Virgo | 7-9 | 3rd round | Coral UK Open |
| **1986** | v Van Rensberg | 4-5 | 2nd round | Mercantile Credit Classic |
| | v Everton | 6-2 | 1st round | Zetters Welsh Championship |
| | v Reardon | 6-4 | Quarter-final | Zetters Welsh Championship |
| | v Mountjoy | 7-9 | Semi-final | Zetters Welsh Championship |
| | v Rigitano | 5-1 | 2nd round | Dulux British Open |

| | | | | |
|---|---|---|---|---|
| | v Mans | 2-5 | 3rd round | Dulux British Open |
| | v Grace | 10-3 | Qualifying | Embassy World Championship |
| | v Hendry | 8-10 | Qualifying | Embassy World Championship |
| | v Jack Rea | 5-1 | 2nd round | BCE International |
| | v Reardon | 4-5 | 3rd round | BCE International |
| | v Foldvari | 5-3 | 2nd round | Rothmans Grand Prix |
| | v David Taylor | 5-1 | 3rd round | Rothmans Grand Prix |
| | v S. Francisco | 4-5 | 4th round | Rothmans Grand Prix |
| | v Hargreaves | 9-0 | 2nd round | Tennents UK Open |
| | v J. Campbell | 9-3 | 3rd round | Tennents UK Open |
| | v Dennis Taylor | 9-2 | 4th round | Tennents UK Open |
| | v E. Hughes | 9-5 | 5th round | Tennents UK Open |
| | v Higgins | 5-9 | Quarter-final | Tennents UK Open |
| **1987** | v Everton | 5-0 | 2nd round | Mercantile Credit Classic |
| | v Dennis Taylor | 5-2 | 3rd round | Mercantile Credit Classic |
| | v Kearney | 5-1 | 4th round | Mercantile Credit Classic |
| | v Wilson | 3-5 | 5th round | Mercantile Credit Classic |
| | v M. Bennett | 6-3 | 1st round | Matchroom Welsh Championship |
| | v Griffiths | 2-6 | Quarter-final | Matchroom Welsh Championship |
| | v Gilbert | 3-5 | 2nd round | Dulux British Open |
| | v Donnelly | 10-3 | Qualifying | Embassy World Championship |
| | v M. Bennett | 3 10 | Qualifying | Embassy World Championship |
| | v Dunning | 5-1 | 2nd round | Fidelity International |
| | v Reynolds | 5-4 | 3rd round | Fidelity International |
| | v N. Gilbert | 4-5 | 4th round | Fidelity International |
| | v Donnelly | 5-3 | 2nd round | Rothmans Grand Prix |
| | v Stevens | 1-5 | 3rd round | Rothmans Grand Prix |
| | v Meakin | 9-1 | 2nd round | Tennents UK Open |
| | v Wilson | 6-9 | 3rd round | Tennents UK Open |
| **1988** | v Roscoe | 4-5 | 2nd round | Mercantile Credit Classic |
| | v Reardon | 6-5 | Quarter-final | Welsh Championship |
| | v Mountjoy | 9-5 | Semi-final | Welsh Championship |
| | v Griffiths | 3-9 | Final | Welsh Championship |
| | v John Rea | 5-3 | 2nd round | MIM Britannia British Open |
| | v J. Campbell | 3-5 | 3rd round | MIM Britannia British Open |
| | v Glen Wilkinson | 10-4 | Qualifying | Embassy World Championship |
| | v Morra | 10-8 | Qualifying | Embassy World Championship |
| | v Martin | 10-5 | Qualifying | Embassy World Championship |
| | v N. Foulds | 7-10 | 1st round | Embassy World Championship |
| | v M. Smith | 5-2 | 2nd round | Fidelity International |
| | v S. Davis | 1-5 | 3rd round | Fidelity International |
| | v Rigitano | 5-3 | 2nd round | Rothmans Grand Prix |
| | v J. Campbell | 5-2 | 3rd round | Rothmans Grand Prix |
| | v White | 1-5 | 4th round | Rothmans Grand Prix |
| | v Roscoe | 4-5 | 3rd round | BCE Canadian Masters |
| | v Johnston-Allen | 9-8 | 2nd round | Tennents UK Open |
| | v Mountjoy | 7-9 | 3rd round | Tennents UK Open |
| **1989** | v Rowswell | 5-3 | 2nd round | Mercantile Credit Classic |
| | v White | 5-3 | 3rd round | Mercantile Credit Classic |
| | v E. Hughes | 5-1 | 4th round | Mercantile Credit Classic |
| | v David Taylor | 5-3 | 5th round | Mercantile Credit Classic |
| | v Parrott | 5-4 | Quarter-final | Mercantile Credit Classic |
| | v Thorne | 9-4 | Semi-final | Mercantile Credit Classic |
| | v Mountjoy | 11-13 | Final | Mercantile Credit Classic |
| | v Newbury | 5-6 | Quarter-final | Senator Welsh Championship |
| | v Rowswell | 5-0 | 2nd round | Anglian British Open |
| | v E. Hughes | 2-5 | 3rd round | Anglian British Open |
| | v A. Harris | 10-4 | Qualifying | Embassy World Championship |
| | v Wych | 10-9 | Qualifying | Embassy World Championship |
| | v David Taylor | 10-7 | Qualifying | Embassy World Championship |
| | v N. Foulds | 10-9 | 1st round | Embassy World Championship |
| | v Reynolds | 3-13 | 2nd round | Embassy World Championship |
| | v King | 5-1 | 3rd round | Hong Kong Open |

| | | | | |
|---|---|---|---|---|
| | v Thorne | 1-5 | 4th round | Hong Kong Open |
| | v S. Campbell | 5-3 | 3rd round | 555 Asian Open |
| | v Reynolds | 5-3 | 4th round | 555 Asian Open |
| | v Hendry | 0-5 | 5th round | 555 Asian Open |
| | v Houlihan | 5-2 | 3rd round | BCE International |
| | v S. Davis | 2-5 | 4th round | BCE International |
| | v Morra | 4-5 | 3rd round | Rothmans Grand Prix |
| | v Scott | 5-3 | 3rd round | Dubai Classic |
| | v West | 2-5 | 4th round | Dubai Classic |
| | v Fowler | 9-7 | 3rd round | Stormseal UK Open |
| | v Reynolds | 8-9 | 4th round | Stormseal UK Open |
| **1990** | v Edmonds | 5-1 | 3rd round | Mercantile Credit Classic |
| | v Hallett | 5-3 | 4th round | Mercantile Credit Classic |
| | v Gary Wilkinson | 5-2 | 5th round | Mercantile Credit Classic |
| | v James | 2-5 | Quarter-final | Mercantile Credit Classic |
| | v Newbury | 6-3 | Quarter-final | Senator Welsh Championship |
| | v Mountjoy | 7-9 | Semi-final | Senator Welsh Championship |
| | v Rowing | 4-5 | 3rd round | Pearl Assurance British Open |
| | v Graham | 5-1 | 3rd round | European Open |
| | v Parrott | 0-5 | 4th round | European Open |
| | v Chambers | 10-6 | Qualifying | Embassy World Championship |
| | v Meo | 8-10 | 1st round | Embassy World Championship |

## TONY KEARNEY (Republic of Ireland)

**Born** 24.6.54. **Turned professional** 1984. **World ranking** 104 (101).

| | | | | |
|---|---|---|---|---|
| **1984** | v Burke | 4-5 | Qualifying | Jameson International |
| | v Chaperon | 1-5 | Qualifying | Rothmans Grand Prix |
| | v Murphy | 2-9 | Qualifying | Coral UK Open |
| **1985** | v French | 5-1 | Qualifying | Mercantile Credit Classic |
| | v Williamson | 3-5 | Qualifying | Mercantile Credit Classic |
| | v Watterson | 6-4 | Qualifying | Dulux British Open |
| | v S. Francisco | 4-6 | 1st round | Dulux British Open |
| | v Burke | 4-6 | Qualifying | Irish Championship |
| | v Anderson | 8-10 | Qualifying | Embassy World Championship |
| | v D. Hughes | 1-5 | 1st round | Goya Matchroom Trophy |
| | v Bear | 5-3 | 1st round | Rothmans Grand Prix |
| | v Edmonds | 2-5 | 2nd round | Rothmans Grand Prix |
| | v D. Hughes | 8-9 | 1st round | Coral UK Open |
| **1986** | v Jim Bear | 5-0 | 1st round | Mercantile Credit Classic |
| | v Medati | 2-5 | 2nd round | Mercantile Credit Classic |
| | v Smith | 5-2 | 1st round | Dulux British Open |
| | v Foldvari | 5-2 | 2nd round | Dulux British Open |
| | v Wilkinson | 10-5 | Qualifying | Embassy World Championship |
| | v Scott | 8-10 | Qualifying | Embassy World Championship |
| | v Fagan | 5-0 | 1st round | Strongbow Irish Championship |
| | v Murphy | 2-6 | Quarter-final | Strongbow Irish Championship |
| | v Medati | 3-5 | 2nd round | BCE International |
| | v Jenkins | 5-3 | 1st round | Rothmans Grand Prix |
| | v Chappel | 1-5 | 2nd round | Rothmans Grand Prix |
| | v Dunning | 6-9 | 1st round | Tennents UK Open |
| **1987** | v Agrawal | 5-0 | 1st round | Mercantile Credit Classic |
| | v Wildman | 5-3 | 2nd round | Mercantile Credit Classic |
| | v Macleod | 5-0 | 3rd round | Mercantile Credit Classic |
| | v W. Jones | 1-5 | 4th round | Mercantile Credit Classic |
| | v Chappel | 3-5 | 2nd round | Dulux British Open |
| | v Medati | 8-10 | Qualifying | Embassy World Championship |
| | v Murphy | 5-1 | 1st round | Matchroom Irish Championship |
| | v E. Hughes | 1-6 | Quarter-final | Matchroom Irish Championship |
| | v Foldvari | 1-5 | 2nd round | Fidelity International |
| | v Darrington | 5-0 | 2nd round | Rothmans Grand Prix |
| | v Griffiths | 0-5 | 3rd round | Rothmans Grand Prix |

| | | | | |
|---|---|---|---|---|
| | v Fowler | 7-9 | 2nd round | Tennents UK Open |
| **1988** | v Newbury | 1-5 | 2nd round | Mercantile Credit Classic |
| | v Fagan | 5-3 | 1st round | Irish Championship |
| | v Dennis Taylor | 3-6 | Quarter-final | Irish Championship |
| | v Fowler | 1-5 | 2nd round | MIM Britannia British Open |
| | v Kelly | 4-10 | Qualifying | Embassy World Championship |
| | v Watterson | 5-1 | 1st round | Fidelity International |
| | v Clark | 3-5 | 2nd round | Fidelity International |
| | v A. Harris | 2-5 | 1st round | Rothmans Grand Prix |
| | v S. Campbell | 2-5 | 1st round | BCE Canadian Masters |
| | v Watterson | 9-3 | 1st round | Tennents UK Open |
| | v Browne | 9-6 | 2nd round | Tennents UK Open |
| | v James | 1-9 | 3rd round | Tennents UK Open |
| **1989** | v Kelly | 5-3 | 1st round | Mercantile Credit Classic |
| | v Cripsey | 2-5 | 2nd round | Mercantile Credit Classic |
| | v Ellis | 4-5 | 1st round | European Open |
| | v Kelly | 5-2 | 1st round | Irish Championship |
| | v E. Hughes | 1-5 | Quarter-final | Irish Championship |
| | v Terry | 3-5 | 1st round | Anglian British Open |
| | v Meakin | 3-10 | Qualifying | Embassy World Championship |
| | v Houlihan | 1-5 | 1st round | Hong Kong Open |
| | v Oliver | 3-5 | 1st round | 555 Asian Open |
| | v Gauvreau | 5-3 | 1st round | BCE International |
| | v Stevens | 5-4 | 2nd round | BCE International |
| | v S. Davis | 1-5 | 3rd round | BCE International |
| | v T. Wilson | 5-2 | 1st round | Rothmans Grand Prix |
| | v Dodd | 1-5 | 2nd round | Rothmans Grand Prix |
| | v Cairns | 5-1 | 1st round | Dubai Classic |
| | v Fisher | 3-5 | 2nd round | Dubai Classic |
| | v Price | 1-6 | 1st round | Stormseal UK Open |
| **1990** | v T. Jones | 1-5 | 2nd round | Mercantile Credit Classic |
| | v Houlihan | 5-2 | 1st round | Pearl Assurance British Open |
| | v Graham | 4-5 | 2nd round | Pearl Assurance British Open |
| | v P. Gibson | 5-1 | 1st round | European Open |
| | v Bales | 3-5 | 2nd round | European Open |
| | v Medati | 10-7 | Qualifying | Embassy World Championship |
| | v N. Gilbert | 6-10 | Qualifying | Embassy World Championship |

## WARREN KING (Australia)

**Born** 1.4.55. **Turned professional** 1982. **World ranking** 40 (55).

| | | | | |
|---|---|---|---|---|
| **1983** | v Anderson | 10-6 | Qualifying | Embassy World Championship |
| | v Hallett | 6-10 | Qualifying | Embassy World Championship |
| | v Black | 5-3 | Qualifying | Jameson International |
| | v Miles | 3-5 | Qualifying | Jameson International |
| | v B. Harris | 5-3 | Qualifying | Professional Players Tournament |
| | v Meo | 2-5 | 1st round | Professional Players Tournament |
| **1984** | v Jones | 10-9 | Qualifying | Embassy World Championship |
| | v Watterson | 10-8 | Qualifying | Embassy World Championship |
| | v Martin | 10-8 | Qualifying | Embassy World Championship |
| | v S. Davis | 3-10 | 1st round | Embassy World Championship |
| | v Kelly | 4-5 | Qualifying | Jameson International |
| | v Greaves | 5-0 | Qualifying | Rothmans Grand Prix |
| | v Macleod | 4-5 | 1st round | Rothmans Grand Prix |
| | v Browne | 9-5 | Qualifying | Coral UK Open |
| | v Virgo | 9-4 | Qualifying | Coral UK Open |
| | v Dennis Taylor | 5-9 | 1st round | Coral UK Open |
| **1985** | v Duggan | 5-4 | Qualifying | Mercantile Credit Classic |
| | v Reynolds | 5-2 | Qualifying | Mercantile Credit Classic |
| | v Spencer | 5-2 | 1st round | Mercantile Credit Classic |
| | v White | 5-2 | 2nd round | Mercantile Credit Classic |
| | v Johnson | 3-5 | Quarter-final | Mercantile Credit Classic |

| | | | | |
|---|---|---|---|---|
| | v Medati | 6-4 | Qualifying | Dulux British Open |
| | v Reardon | 5-6 | 1st round | Dulux British Open |
| | v Medati | 9-10 | Qualifying | Embassy World Championship |
| | v Anderson | 8-2 | Quarter-final | Australian Championship |
| | v J. Campbell | 6-9 | Semi-final | Australian Championship |
| | v Caggianello | 5-0 | 2nd round | Goya Matchroom Trophy |
| | v Williams | 5-3 | 3rd round | Goya Matchroom Trophy |
| | v White | 2-5 | 4th round | Goya Matchroom Trophy |
| | v Drago | 4-5 | 2nd round | Rothmans Grand Prix |
| | v D. Hughes | 9-0 | 2nd round | Coral UK Open |
| | v Williams | 5-9 | 3rd round | Coral UK Open |
| **1986** | v Duggan | 5-2 | 2nd round | Mercantile Credit Classic |
| | v Mountjoy | 4-5 | 3rd round | Mercantile Credit Classic |
| | v John Rea | 1-5 | 2nd round | Dulux British Open |
| | v Sheehan | 10-4 | Qualifying | Embassy World Championship |
| | v Roscoe | 10-5 | Qualifying | Embassy World Championship |
| | v Reynolds | 7-10 | Qualifying | Embassy World Championship |
| | v Charlton | 8-6 | Semi-final | Australian Championship |
| | **v J. Campbell** | **10-3** | **Final** | **Australian Championship** |
| | v Rigitano | 5-0 | 2nd round | BCE International |
| | v Longworth | 5-0 | 3rd round | BCE International |
| | v S. Davis | 4-5 | 4th round | BCE International |
| | v Donnelly | 5-2 | 2nd round | Rothmans Grand Prix |
| | v Werbeniuk | 5-2 | 3rd round | Rothmans Grand Prix |
| | v Thorne | 2-5 | 4th round | Rothmans Grand Prix |
| | v James | 9-8 | 2nd round | Tennents UK Open |
| | v Hallett | 5-9 | 3rd round | Tennents UK Open |
| **1987** | v Burke | 5-0 | 2nd round | Mercantile Credit Classic |
| | v Reynolds | 4-5 | 3rd round | Mercantile Credit Classic |
| | v Williamson | 5-3 | 2nd round | Dulux British Open |
| | v Parrott | 5-1 | 3rd round | Dulux British Open |
| | v N. Foulds | 4-5 | 4th round | Dulux British Open |
| | v Roe | 10-4 | Qualifying | Embassy World Championship |
| | v Owers | 10-4 | Qualifying | Embassy World Championship |
| | v Charlton | 10-4 | Qualifying | Embassy World Championship |
| | v S. Davis | 7-10 | 1st round | Embassy World Championship |
| | v Jenkins | 6-4 | Quarter-final | Australian Championship |
| | v Foldvari | 8-1 | Semi-final | Australian Championship |
| | **v Charlton** | **10-7** | **Final** | **Australian Championship** |
| | v M. Smith | 5-3 | 2nd round | Fidelity International |
| | v S. Francisco | 2-5 | 3rd round | Fidelity International |
| | v Foldvari | 4-5 | 2nd round | Rothmans Grand Prix |
| | v Meadowcroft | 9-4 | 2nd round | Tennents UK Open |
| | v S. Davis | 2-9 | 3rd round | Tennents UK Open |
| **1988** | v Oliver | 3-5 | 2nd round | Mercantile Credit Classic |
| | v James | 2-5 | 2nd round | MIM Britannia British Open |
| | v Watchorn | 10-4 | Qualifying | Embassy World Championship |
| | v Clark | 10-9 | Qualifying | Embassy World Championship |
| | v Spencer | 10-7 | Qualifying | Embassy World Championship |
| | v Parrott | 4-10 | 1st round | Embassy World Championship |
| | v Frangie | 5-4 | Quarter-final | Australian Championship |
| | v Foldvari | 4-8 | Semi-final | Australian Championship |
| | v Knowles | 4-5 | 1st round | New Zealand Masters |
| | v Morra | 5-4 | 2nd round | Fidelity International |
| | v West | 4-5 | 3rd round | Fidelity International |
| | v Medati | 1-5 | 2nd round | Rothmans Grand Prix |
| | v M. Gibson | 5-3 | 2nd round | BCE Canadian Masters |
| | v N. Foulds | 5-3 | 3rd round | BCE Canadian Masters |
| | v Duggan | 5-4 | 4th round | BCE Canadian Masters |
| | v Hallett | 2-5 | 5th round | BCE Canadian Masters |
| | v Terry | 9-7 | 2nd round | Tennents UK Open |
| | v S. Davis | 7-9 | 3rd round | Tennents UK Open |
| **1989** | v Rowing | 5-4 | 2nd round | Mercantile Credit Classic |

| | | | | |
|---|---|---|---|---|
| | v Griffiths | 2-5 | 3rd round | Mercantile Credit Classic |
| | v Miles | 5-2 | 2nd round | European Open |
| | v Williams | 2-5 | 3rd round | European Open |
| | v Robidoux | 2-5 | 2nd round | Anglian British Open |
| | v Rowing | 7-10 | Qualifying | Embassy World Championship |
| | v Jenkins | 5-4 | 2nd round | Hong Kong Open |
| | v W. Jones | 1-5 | 3rd round | Hong Kong Open |
| | v D. Hughes | 5-0 | 2nd round | 555 Asian Open |
| | v Chaperon | 5-2 | 3rd round | 555 Asian Open |
| | v Clark | 3-5 | 4th round | 555 Asian Open |
| | v Kelly | 5-0 | 2nd round | BCE International |
| | v Clark | 4-5 | 3rd round | BCE International |
| | v Watchorn | 5-3 | 2nd round | Rothmans Grand Prix |
| | v Charlton | 5-0 | 3rd round | Rothmans Grand Prix |
| | v Reynolds | 3-5 | 4th round | Rothmans Grand Prix |
| | v A. Harris | 5-3 | 2nd round | Dubai Classic |
| | v David Taylor | 5-1 | 3rd round | Dubai Classic |
| | v Mountjoy | 2-5 | 4th round | Dubai Classic |
| | v Watchorn | 6-5 | 2nd round | Stormseal UK Open |
| | v Griffiths | 4-9 | 3rd round | Stormseal UK Open |
| **1990** | v Morra | 5-3 | 2nd round | Mercantile Credit Classic |
| | v Griffiths | 5-1 | 3rd round | Mercantile Credit Classic |
| | v Charlton | 5-2 | 4th round | Mercantile Credit Classic |
| | v Virgo | 5-1 | 5th round | Mercantile Credit Classic |
| | v Newbury | 5-3 | Quarter-final | Mercantile Credit Classic |
| | v S. Francisco | 6-5 | Semi-final | Mercantile Credit Classic |
| | v James | 6-10 | Final | Mercantile Credit Classic |
| | v Dodd | 2-5 | 2nd round | Pearl Assurance British Open |
| | v Ellis | 4-5 | 2nd round | European Open |
| | v Dodd | 8-10 | Qualifying | Embassy World Championship |

**TONY KNOWLES** (England)

**Born** 13.6.55. **Turned professional** 1980. **World ranking** 22 (12).

| | | | | |
|---|---|---|---|---|
| **1980** | v Andrewartha | 8-9 | Qualifying | Coral UK Championship |
| **1981** | v Johnson | 2-9 | Qualifying | John Courage English Professional |
| | v Ross | 7-0 | Qualifying | Embassy World Championship |
| | v Wych | 9-3 | Qualifying | Embassy World Championship |
| | v Miles | 8-10 | 1st round | Embassy World Championship |
| | v Hallet | 5-2 | 1st round | Jameson International |
| | v Virgo | 2-5 | 2nd round | Jameson International |
| | v G. Foulds | 9-1 | Qualifying | Coral UK Championship |
| | v F. Davis | 9-6 | 2nd round | Coral UK Championship |
| | v Mountjoy | 9-6 | 3rd round | Coral UK Championship |
| | v Griffiths | 5-9 | Quarter-final | Coral UK Championship |
| **1982** | v Dennis Taylor | 2-5 | Semi-final | Tolly Cobbold Classic |
| | v E. Hughes | 9-7 | Qualifying | Embassy World Championship |
| | v S. Davis | 10-1 | 1st round | Embassy World Championship |
| | v Miles | 13-7 | 2nd round | Embassy World Championship |
| | v Charlton | 11-13 | Quarter-final | Embassy World Championship |
| | v S. Davis | 4-5 | 1st round | Langs Scottish Masters |
| | v Sinclair | 5-2 | 1st round | Jameson International |
| | v Reardon | 5-2 | 2nd round | Jameson International |
| | v Wilson | 5-4 | Quarter-final | Jameson International |
| | v Stevens | 9-8 | Semi-final | Jameson International |
| | **v David Taylor** | **9-6** | **Final** | **Jameson International** |
| | v Houlihan | 5-4 | 1st round | Professional Players Tournament |
| | v Wilson | 4-5 | 2nd round | Professional Players Tournament |
| | v Donnelly | 9-6 | 1st round | Coral UK Championship |
| | v Spencer | 6-9 | 2nd round | Coral UK Championship |
| **1983** | v Stevens | 0-5 | 1st round | Lada Classic |

| | | | | |
|---|---|---|---|---|
| | v Mountjoy | 1-5 | 1st round | Benson & Hedges Irish Masters |
| | v Miles | 10-3 | 1st round | Embassy World Championship |
| | v Reardon | 13-12 | 2nd round | Embassy World Championship |
| | v Meo | 13-9 | Quarter-final | Embassy World Championship |
| | v Thorburn | 15-16 | Semi-final | Embassy World Championship |
| | v Werbeniuk | 0-5 | Semi-final | Winfield Masters |
| | v Meo | 5-4 | 1st round | Langs Scottish Masters |
| | v Thorburn | 6-2 | Semi-final | Langs Scottish Masters |
| | v S. Davis | 6-9 | Final | Langs Scottish Masters |
| | v Edmonds | 5-1 | 1st round | Jameson International |
| | v Spencer | 4-5 | 2nd round | Jameson International |
| | v Medati | 5-1 | 1st round | Professional Players Tournament |
| | v Williams | 5-4 | 2nd round | Professional Players Tournament |
| | v S. Francisco | 5-0 | 3rd round | Professional Players Tournament |
| | v J. Campbell | 5-3 | Quarter-final | Professional Players Tournament |
| | v Thorne | 9-7 | Semi-final | Professional Players Tournament |
| | **v Johnson** | **9-8** | **Final** | **Professional Players Tournament** |
| | v T. Jones | 9-5 | 1st round | Coral UK Championship |
| | v Mountjoy | 9-5 | 2nd round | Coral UK Championship |
| | v Higgins | 5-9 | Quarter-final | Coral UK Championship |
| **1984** | v E. Hughes | 5-1 | Qualifying | Lada Classic |
| | v Hallett | 5-3 | 1st round | Lada Classic |
| | v Parrott | 1-5 | Quarter-final | Lada Classic |
| | v Dennis Taylor | 5-2 | 1st round | Benson & Hedges Masters |
| | v Higgins | 5-1 | Quarter-final | Benson & Hedges Masters |
| | v Griffiths | 4-6 | Semi-final | Benson & Hedges Masters |
| | v Griffiths | 0-5 | Quarter-final | Benson & Hedges Irish Masters |
| | v White | 5-1 | 1st round | Tolly Cobbold Classic |
| | v Thorburn | 5-3 | Semi-final | Tolly Cobbold Classic |
| | v S. Davis | 2-8 | Final | Tolly Cobbold Classic |
| | v Parrott | 7-10 | 1st round | Embassy World Championship |
| | v White | 5-3 | Quarter-final | Winfield Australian Masters |
| | v Charlton | 6-0 | Semi-final | Winfield Australian Masters |
| | **v Virgo** | **7-3** | **Final** | **Winfield Australian Masters** |
| | v Griffiths | 5-3 | 1st round | Langs Scottish Masters |
| | v White | 5-6 | Semi-final | Langs Scottish Masters |
| | v Higgins | 5-3 | 1st round | Carlsberg Challenge |
| | v White | 7-9 | Final | Carlsberg Challenge |
| | v Reynolds | 5-1 | 1st round | Jameson International |
| | v Newbury | 5-4 | 2nd round | Jameson International |
| | v White | 5-4 | Quarter-final | Jameson International |
| | v S. Francisco | 9-6 | Semi-final | Jameson International |
| | v S. Davis | 2-9 | Final | Jameson International |
| | v V. Harris | 5-1 | 1st round | Rothmans Grand Prix |
| | v Dunning | 5-1 | 2nd round | Rothmans Grand Prix |
| | v Williamson | 5-2 | 3rd round | Rothmans Grand Prix |
| | v N. Foulds | 2-5 | Quarter-final | Rothmans Grand Prix |
| | v Gauvreau | 9-5 | 1st round | Coral UK Open |
| | v Dennis Taylor | 9-2 | 2nd round | Coral UK Open |
| | v Stevens | 7-9 | Quarter-final | Coral UK Open |
| **1985** | v Johnson | 1-5 | 1st round | Mercantile Credit Classic |
| | v Mountjoy | 3-5 | 1st round | Benson & Hedges Masters |
| | v Bradley | 9-8 | 1st round | Tolly Cobbold English Championship |
| | v Martin | 9-3 | 2nd round | Tolly Cobbold English Championship |
| | v David Taylor | 9-2 | Quarter-final | Tolly Cobbold English Championship |
| | v Longworth | 9-6 | Semi-final | Tolly Cobbold English Championship |
| | v S. Davis | 2-9 | Final | Tolly Cobbold English Championship |
| | v French | 6-2 | 1st round | Dulux British Open |
| | v Longworth | 5-2 | 2nd round | Dulux British Open |
| | v Meo | 2-5 | 3rd round | Dulux British Open |
| | v Charlton | 5-3 | Quarter-final | Benson & Hedges Irish Masters |
| | v White | 4-6 | Semi-final | Benson & Hedges Irish Masters |
| | v T. Jones | 10-8 | 1st round | Embassy World Championship |

| | | | | |
|---|---|---|---|---|
| | v Mountjoy | 13-6 | 2nd round | Embassy World Championship |
| | v White | 13-10 | Quarter-final | Embassy World Championship |
| | v Dennis Taylor | 5-16 | Semi-final | Embassy World Championship |
| | v S. Francisco | 4-5 | 1st round | Langs Scottish Masters |
| | v E. McLaughlin | 5-1 | 3rd round | Goya Matchroom Trophy |
| | v N. Foulds | 4-5 | 4th round | Goya Matchroom Trophy |
| | v Gibson | 5-1 | 3rd round | Rothmans Grand Prix |
| | v Edmonds | 5-3 | 4th round | Rothmans Grand Prix |
| | v J. Campbell | 5-2 | 5th round | Rothmans Grand Prix |
| | v Stevens | 5-4 | Quarter-final | Rothmans Grand Prix |
| | v Dennis Taylor | 6-9 | Semi-final | Rothmans Grand Prix |
| | v Reardon | 5-2 | 1st round | BCE Canadian Masters |
| | v O'Boye | 9-5 | 3rd round | Coral UK Open |
| | v Spencer | 9-7 | 4th round | Coral UK Open |
| | v David Taylor | 9-7 | 5th round | Coral UK Open |
| | v White | 4-9 | Quarter-final | Coral UK Open |
| **1986** | v Rigitano | 5-4 | 3rd round | Mercantile Credit Classic |
| | v Macleod | 5-4 | 4th round | Mercantile Credit Classic |
| | v Williams | 2-5 | 5th round | Mercantile Credit Classic |
| | v White | 5-3 | 1st round | BCE Belgian Classic |
| | v Griffiths | 2-5 | Semi-final | BCE Belgian Classic |
| | v S. Francisco | 5-1 | 1st round | Benson & Hedges Masters |
| | v Charlton | 5-4 | Quarter-final | Benson & Hedges Masters |
| | v Thorburn | 4-6 | Semi-final | Benson & Hedges Masters |
| | v Bales | 9-4 | 3rd round | Tolly Cobbold English Championship |
| | v Hallett | 5-9 | 4th round | Tolly Cobbold English Championship |
| | v Williamson | 5-1 | 3rd round | Dulux British Open |
| | v Wych | 4-5 | 4th round | Dulux British Open |
| | v Fagan | 4-5 | Quarter-final | Benson & Hedges Irish Masters |
| | v N. Foulds | 10-9 | 1st round | Embassy World Championship |
| | v S. Francisco | 13-10 | 2nd round | Embassy World Championship |
| | v Stevens | 13-9 | Quarter-final | Embassy World Championship |
| | v Johnson | 8-16 | Semi-final | Embassy World Championship |
| | v Stevens | 3-5 | 1st round | Langs Scottish Masters |
| | v Spencer | 5-0 | 3rd round | BCE International |
| | v Charlton | 5-1 | 4th round | BCE International |
| | v Wilson | 4-5 | 5th round | BCE International |
| | v Roe | 5-3 | 3rd round | Rothmans Grand Prix |
| | v P. Francisco | 5-3 | 4th round | Rothmans Grand Prix |
| | v Mountjoy | 5-1 | 5th round | Rothmans Grand Prix |
| | v S. Francisco | 2-5 | Quarter-final | Rothmans Grand Prix |
| | v Thorburn | 5-1 | 1st round | BCE Canadian Masters |
| | v Thorne | 7-8 | Semi-final | BCE Canadian Masters |
| | v John Rea | 9-4 | 3rd round | Tennents UK Open |
| | v T. Jones | 9-2 | 4th round | Tennents UK Open |
| | v Griffiths | 9-6 | 5th round | Tennents UK Open |
| | v Parrott | 4-9 | Quarter-final | Tennents UK Open |
| **1987** | v Fowler | 4-5 | 3rd round | Mercantile Credit Classic |
| | v S. Francisco | 2-5 | 1st round | Benson & Hedges Masters |
| | v Dodd | 2-6 | 3rd round | Tolly Ales English Championship |
| | v Fowler | 5-4 | 3rd round | Dulux British Open |
| | v Reynolds | 5-0 | 4th round | Dulux British Open |
| | v Murphy | 5-3 | 5th round | Dulux British Open |
| | v Dennis Taylor | 5-4 | Quarter-final | Dulux British Open |
| | v N. Foulds | 2-9 | Semi-final | Dulux British Open |
| | v Meo | 2-5 | 1st round | Benson & Hedges Irish Masters |
| | v Hallett | 6-10 | 1st round | Embassy World Championship |
| | v Fowler | 5-4 | 3rd round | Fidelity International |
| | v David Taylor | 5-2 | 4th round | Fidelity International |
| | v Virgo | 2-5 | 5th round | Fidelity International |
| | v J. McLaughlin | 5-0 | 3rd round | Rothmans Grand Prix |
| | v Roe | 5-2 | 4th round | Rothmans Grand Prix |
| | v Charlton | 5-0 | 5th round | Rothmans Grand Prix |

| | | | | |
|---|---|---|---|---|
| | v Hendry | 2-5 | Quarter-final | Rothmans Grand Prix |
| | v White | 1-5 | 1st round | Labatts Canadian Masters (WS) |
| | v John Rea | 9-6 | 3rd round | Tennents UK Open |
| | v Stevens | 9-8 | 4th round | Tennents UK Open |
| | v Parrott | 4-9 | 5th round | Tennents UK Open |
| **1988** | v Wright | 5-1 | 3rd round | Mercantile Credit Classic |
| | v Roscoe | 5-0 | 4th round | Mercantile Credit Classic |
| | v Murphy | 5-3 | 5th round | Mercantile Credit Classic |
| | v Dennis Taylor | 5-1 | Quarter-final | Mercantile Credit Classic |
| | v Parrott | 4-9 | Semi-final | Mercantile Credit Classic |
| | v Higgins | 4-5 | 1st round | Benson & Hedges Masters |
| | v Wright | 6-2 | 3rd round | English Championship |
| | v Owers | 6-4 | 4th round | English Championship |
| | v Johnson | 4-6 | Quarter-final | English Championship |
| | v M. Gibson | 5-4 | 3rd round | MIM Britannia British Open |
| | v Macleod | 4-5 | 4th round | MIM Britannia British Open |
| | v Thorne | 5-3 | 1st round | Benson & Hedges Irish Masters |
| | v N. Foulds | 3-5 | Quarter-final | Benson & Hedges Irish Masters |
| | v Fowler | 10-8 | 1st round | Embassy World Championship |
| | v Charlton | 13-7 | 2nd round | Embassy World Championship |
| | v White | 6-13 | Quarter-final | Embassy World Championship |
| | v King | 5-4 | 1st round | New Zealand Masters |
| | v Hallett | 3-5 | Semi-final | New Zealand Masters |
| | v Miles | 5-4 | 3rd round | Fidelity International |
| | v Newbury | 4-5 | 4th round | Fidelity International |
| | v O'Boye | 5-4 | 3rd round | Rothmans Grand Prix |
| | v Reynolds | 5-3 | 4th round | Rothmans Grand Prix |
| | v N. Gilbert | 4-5 | 5th round | Rothmans Grand Prix |
| | v Roscoe | 2-5 | 3rd round | BCE Canadian Masters |
| | v Wych | 9-4 | 3rd round | Tennents UK Open |
| | v Higgins | 9-6 | 4th round | Tennents UK Open |
| | v Virgo | 3-9 | 5th round | Tennents UK Open |
| | v Dennis Taylor | 7-9 | 1st round | Everest World Matchplay |
| **1989** | v Roscoe | 5-4 | 3rd round | Mercantile Credit Classic |
| | v Reynolds | 5-4 | 4th round | Mercantile Credit Classic |
| | v Mountjoy | 4-5 | 5th round | Mercantile Credit Classic |
| | v Hallett | 5-3 | 1st round | Benson and Hedges Masters |
| | v S. Davis | 0-5 | Quarter-final | Benson and Hedges Masters |
| | v Fowler | 2-5 | 3rd round | European Open |
| | v Williamson | 5-2 | 3rd round | English Championship |
| | v Longworth | 4-5 | 4th round | English Championship |
| | v Wych | 5-2 | 3rd round | Anglian British Open |
| | v West | 0-5 | 4th round | Anglian British Open |
| | v Hallett | 0-5 | 1st round | Benson and Hedges Irish Masters |
| | v Roe | 6-10 | 1st round | Embassy World Championship |
| | v Parrott | 6-3 | 1st round | Lion Brown New Zealand Masters |
| | v Johnson | 3-6 | Semi-final | Lion Brown New Zealand Masters |
| | v Gary Wilkinson | 2-5 | 3rd round | Hong Kong Open |
| | v Miles | 5-3 | 3rd round | 555 Asian Open |
| | v N. Foulds | 5-3 | 4th round | 555 Asian Open |
| | v S. Francisco | 2-5 | 5th round | 555 Asian Open |
| | v B. Harris | 5-1 | 3rd round | BCE International |
| | v Cairns | 5-2 | 4th round | BCE International |
| | v Parrott | 2-5 | 5th round | BCE International |
| | v Edmonds | 5-4 | 3rd round | Rothmans Grand Prix |
| | v Clark | 5-2 | 4th round | Rothmans Grand Prix |
| | v T. Jones | 5-4 | 5th round | Rothmans Grand Prix |
| | v S. Davis | 2-5 | Quarter-final | Rothmans Grand Prix |
| | v Grech | 3-5 | 3rd round | Dubai Classic |
| | v Marshall | 9-2 | 3rd round | Stormseal UK Open |
| | v Drago | 9-7 | 4th round | Stormseal UK Open |
| | v Griffiths | 7-9 | 5th round | Stormseal UK Open |
| **1990** | v J. Campbell | 2-5 | 3rd round | Mercantile Credit Classic |

| | | | | |
|---|---|---|---|---|
| | v Griffiths | 5-4 | 1st round | Benson and Hedges Masters |
| | v White | 3-5 | Quarter-final | Benson and Hedges Masters |
| | v Gollan | 5-3 | 3rd round | Pearl Assurance British Open |
| | v Wattana | 5-3 | 4th round | Pearl Assurance British Open |
| | v Dodd | 4-5 | 5th round | Pearl Assurance British Open |
| | v Chappel | 3-5 | 3rd round | European Open |
| | v Chappel | 10-4 | 1st round | Embassy World Championship |
| | v Griffiths | 6-13 | 2nd round | Embassy World Championship |

## ERIC LAWLOR (England)

**Born** 1.7.37. **Turned professional** 1987. **World ranking** 105 (96).

| | | | | |
|---|---|---|---|---|
| **1987** | v Roscoe | 4-5 | 1st round | Fidelity International |
| | v D. Gilbert | 2-5 | 1st round | Rothmans Grand Prix |
| | v Fitzmaurice | 9-0 | 1st round | Tennents UK Open |
| | v Wright | 9-7 | 2nd round | Tennents UK Open |
| | v P. Francisco | 4-9 | 3rd round | Tennents UK Open |
| **1988** | v Sinclair | 3-5 | 1st round | Mercantile Credit Classic |
| | v Roe | 6-5 | 1st round | English Championship |
| | v Bradley | 6-5 | 2nd round | English Championship |
| | v Parrott | 3-6 | 3rd round | English Championship |
| | v Sinclair | 5-3 | 1st round | MIM Britannia British Open |
| | v B. Harris | 5-2 | 2nd round | MIM Britannia British Open |
| | v Johnson | 1-5 | 3rd round | MIM Britannia British Open |
| | v Newbury | 3-10 | Qualifying | Embassy World Championship |
| | v Jack Rea | 5-2 | 1st round | Fidelity International |
| | v J. McLaughlin | 3-5 | 2nd round | Fidelity International |
| | v Ellis | 4-5 | 1st round | Rothmans Grand Prix |
| | v Mikkelsen | 5-2 | 1st round | BCE Canadian Masters |
| | v Owers | 2-5 | 2nd round | BCE Canadian Masters |
| | v Fitzmaurice | 9-1 | 1st round | Tennents UK Open |
| | v D. Gilbert | 2-9 | 2nd round | Tennents UK Open |
| **1989** | v Edwards | 1-5 | 1st round | Mercantile Credit Classic |
| | v Fitzmaurice | 5-0 | 1st round | European Open |
| | v Owers | 5-4 | 2nd round | European Open |
| | v Parrott | *scr* | 3rd round | European Open |
| | v F. Davis | 5-2 | 1st round | English Championship |
| | v Roe | 1-5 | 2nd round | English Championship |
| | v Watterson | 5-9 | 1st round | Anglian British Open |
| | v Chappel | 2-5 | 2nd round | Anglian British Open |
| | v D. Morgan | 2-10 | Qualifying | Embassy World Championship |
| | v D. Hughes | 1-5 | 1st round | Hong Kong Open |
| | v D. Campbell | 4-5 | 1st round | 555 Asian Open |
| | v Grace | 4-5 | 1st round | BCE International |
| | v Thornley | 5-4 | 1st round | Rothmans Grand Prix |
| | v D. Morgan | 3-5 | 2nd round | Rothmans Grand Prix |
| | v Jack Rea | 5-3 | 1st round | Dubai Classic |
| | v T. Wilson | 5-2 | 2nd round | Dubai Classic |
| | v Charlton | 3-5 | 3rd round | Dubai Classic |
| | v Brumby | 6-5 | 1st round | Stormseal UK Open |
| | v J. McLaughlin | 3-6 | 2nd round | Stormseal UK Open |
| **1990** | v Brumby | 4-5 | 1st round | Mercantile Credit Classic |
| | v Meadowcroft | 2-5 | 1st round | Pearl Assurance British Open |
| | v Sheehan | 5-3 | 1st round | European Open |
| | v David Taylor | 2-5 | 2nd round | European Open |
| | v M. Gibson | 10-6 | Qualifying | Embassy World Championship |
| | v M. Bennett | 3-10 | Qualifying | Embassy World Championship |

## STEVE LONGWORTH (England)

**Born** 27.7.48. **Turned professional** 1984. **World ranking** 58 (34).

| | | | | |
|---|---|---|---|---|
| **1984** | v Newbury | 4-5 | Qualifying | Jameson International |
| | v E. McLaughlin | 2-5 | Qualifying | Rothmans Grand Prix |
| | v Darrington | 9-5 | Qualifying | Coral UK Open |
| | v Burke | 9-4 | Qualifying | Coral UK Open |
| | v Morra | 1-9 | Qualifying | Coral UK Open |
| **1985** | v P. Francisco | 5-4 | Qualifying | Mercantile Credit Classic |
| | v Oliver | 5-1 | Qualifying | Mercantile Credit Classic |
| | v Fisher | 5-1 | Qualifying | Mercantile Credit Classic |
| | v N. Foulds | 5-3 | Qualifying | Mercantile Credit Classic |
| | v David Taylor | 5-4 | 1st round | Mercantile Credit Classic |
| | v Thorburn | 3-5 | 2nd round | Mercantile Credit Classic |
| | v Edmonds | 9-4 | Qualifying | Tolly Cobbold English Championship |
| | v Wildman | 9-3 | 1st round | Tolly Cobbold English Championship |
| | v Medati | 9-7 | 2nd round | Tolly Cobbold English Championship |
| | v White | 9-5 | Quarter-final | Tolly Cobbold English Championship |
| | v Knowles | 6-9 | Semi-final | Tolly Cobbold English Championship |
| | v F. Davis | 6-1 | Qualifying | Dulux British Open |
| | v Wilson | 6-3 | 1st round | Dulux British Open |
| | v Knowles | 2-5 | 2nd round | Dulux British Open |
| | v Giannaros | 10-1 | Qualifying | Embassy World Championship |
| | v Cripsey | 10-8 | Qualifying | Embassy World Championship |
| | v Van Rensberg | 7-10 | Qualifying | Embassy World Championship |
| | v Wilkinson | 5-0 | 2nd round | Goya Matchroom Trophy |
| | v Thorburn | 3-5 | 3rd round | Goya Matchroom Trophy |
| | v Hargreaves | 5-2 | 2nd round | Rothmans Grand Prix |
| | v Parrott | 5-2 | 3rd round | Rothmans Grand Prix |
| | v David Taylor | 5-1 | 4th round | Rothmans Grand Prix |
| | v Stevens | 3-5 | 5th round | Rothmans Grand Prix |
| | v Gibson | 9-2 | 2nd round | Coral UK Open |
| | v Meo | 5-9 | 3rd round | Coral UK Open |
| **1986** | v O'Boye | 1-5 | 2nd round | Mercantile Credit Classic |
| | v Duggan | 9-4 | 2nd round | Tolly Cobbold English Championship |
| | v Reynolds | 5-9 | 3rd round | Tolly Cobbold English Championship |
| | v Houlihan | 5-3 | 2nd round | Dulux British Open |
| | v E. Hughes | 5-4 | 3rd round | Dulux British Open |
| | v P. Francisco | 2-5 | 4th round | Dulux British Open |
| | v Watchorn | 10-7 | Qualifying | Embassy World Championship |
| | v John Rea | 10-4 | Qualifying | Embassy World Championship |
| | v Virgo | 8-10 | Qualifying | Embassy World Championship |
| | v King | 0-5 | 3rd round | BCE International |
| | v Wildman | 2-5 | 3rd round | Rothmans Grand Prix |
| | v Rowswell | 9-3 | 3rd round | Tennents UK Open |
| | v Mountjoy | 9-1 | 4th round | Tennents UK Open |
| | v Parrott | 6-9 | 5th round | Tennents UK Open |
| **1987** | v Murphy | 5-3 | 3rd round | Mercantile Credit Classic |
| | v Meo | 0-5 | 4th round | Mercantile Credit Classic |
| | v James | 2-6 | 3rd round | Tolly Ales English Championship |
| | v Duggan | 2-5 | 3rd round | Dulux British Open |
| | v Murphy | 10-2 | Qualifying | Embassy World Championship |
| | v Stevens | 10-4 | 1st round | Embassy World Championship |
| | v Hendry | 7-13 | 2nd round | Embassy World Championship |
| | v Williamson | 5-4 | 3rd round | Fidelity International |
| | v White | 1-5 | 4th round | Fidelity International |
| | v Gary Wilkinson | 4-5 | 3rd round | Rothmans Grand Prix |
| | v Werbeniuk | 9-5 | 3rd round | Tennents UK Open |
| | v Chappel | 6-9 | 4th round | Tennents UK Open |
| **1988** | v Edmonds | 5-3 | 3rd round | Mercantile Credit Classic |
| | v S. Francisco | 2-5 | 4th round | Mercantile Credit Classic |
| | v Chambers | 6-4 | 3rd round | English Championship |
| | v Meo | 4-6 | 4th round | English Championship |
| | v Rowswell | 4-5 | 3rd round | MIM Britannia British Open |
| | v Cripsey | 10-2 | Qualifying | Embassy World Championship |
| | v Griffiths | 1-10 | 1st round | Embassy World Championship |

| | | | | |
|---|---|---|---|---|
| | v Price | 5-4 | 3rd round | Fidelity International |
| | v Hendry | 3-5 | 4th round | Fidelity International |
| | v Edmonds | 3-5 | 3rd round | Rothmans Grand Prix |
| | v Browne | 5-4 | 3rd round | BCE Canadian Masters |
| | v Macleod | 5-3 | 4th round | BCE Canadian Masters |
| | v White | 3-5 | 5th round | BCE Canadian Masters |
| | v Fowler | 8-9 | 3rd round | Tennents UK Open |
| **1989** | v Cripsey | 3-5 | 3rd round | Mercantile Credit Classic |
| | v Hendry | 0-5 | 4th round | European Open |
| | v Marshall | 5-3 | 3rd round | English Championship |
| | v Knowles | 5-4 | 4th round | English Championship |
| | v Hallett | 1-5 | Quarter-final | English Championship |
| | v Owers | 5-1 | 3rd round | Anglian British Open |
| | v Parrott | 1-5 | 4th round | Anglian British Open |
| | v Browne | 0-10 | Qualifying | Embassy World Championship |
| | v Rowing | 3-5 | 2nd round | Hong Kong Open |
| | v Cairns | 1-5 | 2nd round | 555 Asian Open |
| | v Gollan | 0-5 | 2nd round | BCE International |
| | v B. Harris | 5-2 | 2nd round | Rothmans Grand Prix |
| | v Virgo | 4-5 | 3rd round | Rothmans Grand Prix |
| | v J. McLaughlin | 1-5 | 3rd round | Dubai Classic |
| | v M. Gibson | 6-4 | 2nd round | Stormseal UK Open |
| | v S. Francisco | 7-9 | 3rd round | Stormseal UK Open |
| **1990** | v Edwards | 4-5 | 2nd round | Mercantile Credit Classic |
| | v B. Morgan | 5-3 | 2nd round | Pearl Assurance British Open |
| | v Drago | 0-5 | 3rd round | Pearl Assurance British Open |
| | v Dyson | 3-5 | 2nd round | European Open |
| | v S. Campbell | 6-10 | Qualifying | Embassy World Championship |

## JACK McLAUGHLIN (Northern Ireland)

**Born** 29.1.59. **Turned professional** 1984. **World ranking** 50 (58).

| | | | | |
|---|---|---|---|---|
| **1984** | v Greaves | 5-3 | Qualifying | Jameson International |
| | v Jonik | 2-5 | Qualifying | Jameson International |
| | v Meadowcroft | 5-1 | Qualifying | Rothmans Grand Prix |
| | v Wildman | 3-5 | 1st round | Rothmans Grand Prix |
| | v French | 9-3 | Qualifying | Coral UK Open |
| | v Roscoe | 9-8 | Qualifying | Coral UK Open |
| | v Miles | 9-8 | Qualifying | Coral UK Open |
| | v Thorburn | 4-9 | 1st round | Coral UK Open |
| **1985** | v Demarco | 5-1 | Qualifying | Mercantile Credit Classic |
| | v Black | 5-0 | Qualifying | Mercantile Credit Classic |
| | v Scott | 4-5 | Qualifying | Mercantile Credit Classic |
| | v Jonik | 2-6 | Qualifying | Dulux British Open |
| | v Sheehan | 6-3 | Qualifying | Irish Championship |
| | v Williamson | 3-5 | 2nd round | Goya Matchroom Trophy |
| | v Medati | 5-2 | 2nd round | Rothmans Grand Prix |
| | v Griffiths | 4-5 | 3rd round | Rothmans Grand Prix |
| | v Chaperon | 9-5 | Qualifying | Coral UK Open |
| | v Reynolds | 7-9 | 1st round | Coral UK Open |
| **1986** | v E. McLaughlin | 5-2 | 2nd round | Mercantile Credit Classic |
| | v Thorburn | 1-5 | 3rd round | Mercantile Credit Classic |
| | v Fisher | 5-3 | 2nd round | Dulux British Open |
| | v Johnson | 2-5 | 3rd round | Dulux British Open |
| | v Murphy | 7-10 | Qualifying | Embassy World Championship |
| | v Watchorn | 5-0 | 1st round | Strongbow Irish Championship |
| | v Higgins | 2-6 | Quarter-final | Strongbow Irish Championship |
| | v B. Bennett | 5-0 | 1st round | BCE International |
| | v Fowler | 5-2 | 2nd round | BCE International |
| | v Wilson | 2-5 | 3rd round | BCE International |
| | v Owers | 5-2 | 1st round | Rothmans Grand Prix |

| | | | | |
|---|---|---|---|---|
| | v Gauvreau | 5-3 | 2nd round | Rothmans Grand Prix |
| | v West | 5-1 | 3rd round | Rothmans Grand Prix |
| | v White | 2-5 | 4th round | Rothmans Grand Prix |
| | v Gauvreau | 9-8 | 2nd round | Tennents UK Open |
| | v Mountjoy | 6-9 | 3rd round | Tennents UK Open |
| **1987** | v M. Gibson | 5-3 | 2nd round | Mercantile Credit Classic |
| | v Werbeniuk | 1-5 | 3rd round | Mercantile Credit Classic |
| | v Gibson | 5-1 | 2nd round | Dulux British Open |
| | v Higgins | 5-4 | 3rd round | Dulux British Open |
| | v David Taylor | 2-5 | 4th round | Dulux British Open |
| | v Van Rensberg | 6-10 | Qualifying | Embassy World Championship |
| | v Sheehan | 4-5 | 1st round | Matchroom Irish Championship |
| | v N. Gilbert | 4-5 | 2nd round | Fidelity International |
| | v Oliver | 5-2 | 2nd round | Rothmans Grand Prix |
| | v Knowles | 0-5 | 3rd round | Rothmans Grand Prix |
| | v John Rea | 5-9 | 2nd round | Tennents UK Open |
| **1988** | v P. Gibson | 5-4 | 2nd round | Mercantile Credit Classic |
| | v Martin | 2-5 | 3rd round | Mercantile Credit Classic |
| | v Burke | 5-3 | 1st round | Irish Championship |
| | v Watchorn | 6-5 | Quarter-final | Irish Championship |
| | v O'Boye | 6-4 | Semi-final | Irish Championship |
| | **v Dennis Taylor** | **9-4** | **Final** | **Irish Championship** |
| | v Rowswell | 2-5 | 2nd round | MIM Britannia British Open |
| | v M. Smith | 3-10 | Qualifying | Embassy World Championship |
| | v Lawlor | 5-3 | 2nd round | Fidelity International |
| | v Virgo | 0-5 | 3rd round | Fidelity International |
| | v V. Harris | 5-4 | 2nd round | Rothmans Grand Prix |
| | v P. Francisco | 5-2 | 3rd round | Rothmans Grand Prix |
| | v Spencer | 5-3 | 4th round | Rothmans Grand Prix |
| | v White | 2-5 | 5th round | Rothmans Grand Prix |
| | v Fitzmaurice | 2-5 | 2nd round | BCE Canadian Masters |
| | v Bradley | 9-3 | 2nd round | Tennents UK Open |
| | v Dennis Taylor | 5-9 | 3rd round | Tennents UK Open |
| **1989** | v Watterson | 5-3 | 2nd round | Mercantile Credit Classic |
| | v Chaperon | 3-5 | 3rd round | Mercantile Credit Classic |
| | v Price | 5-3 | 2nd round | European Open |
| | v Griffiths | 3-5 | 3rd round | European Open |
| | v Jack Rea | 5-0 | Quarter-final | Irish Championship |
| | v Browne | 6-3 | Semi-final | Irish Championship |
| | v Higgins | 7-9 | Final | Irish Championship |
| | v Griffiths | 4-5 | 1st round | Benson and Hedges Irish Masters |
| | v Ellis | 10-0 | Qualifying | Embassy World Championship |
| | v Robidoux | 2-10 | Qualifying | Embassy World Championship |
| | v Wildman | 5-1 | 2nd round | Hong Kong Open |
| | v White | 2-5 | 3rd round | Hong Kong Open |
| | v J. Smith | 5-4 | 2nd round | 555 Asian Open |
| | v Mountjoy | 3-5 | 3rd round | 555 Asian Open |
| | v D. Campbell | 5-0 | 2nd round | BCE International |
| | v James | 3-5 | 3rd round | BCE International |
| | v Gauvreau | 5-3 | 2nd round | Rothmans Grand Prix |
| | v Thorne | 2-5 | 3rd round | Rothmans Grand Prix |
| | v Glen Wilkinson | 5-3 | 2nd round | Dubai Classic |
| | v Longworth | 5-1 | 3rd round | Dubai Classic |
| | v J. Campbell | 5-1 | 4th round | Dubai Classic |
| | v Virgo | 5-4 | 5th round | Dubai Classic |
| | v Fowler | 1-5 | Quarter-final | Dubai Classic |
| | v Lawlor | 6-3 | 2nd round | Stormseal UK Open |
| | v Parrott | 2-9 | 3rd round | Stormseal UK Open |
| **1990** | v J. Smith | 5-1 | 2nd round | Mercantile Credit Classic |
| | v Roe | 5-2 | 3rd round | Mercantile Credit Classic |
| | v Virgo | 2-5 | 4th round | Mercantile Credit Classic |
| | v T. Wilson | 3-5 | 2nd round | Pearl Assurance British Open |
| | v Morra | 5-0 | 2nd round | European Open |

| | | | | |
|---|---|---|---|---|
| | v Newbury | 2-5 | 3rd round | European Open |
| | v Houlihan | 5-10 | Qualifying | Embassy World Championship |

## MURDO MACLEOD (Scotland)

**Born** 14.1.47. **Turned professional** 1981. **World ranking** 57 (45).

| | | | | |
|---|---|---|---|---|
| **1981** | v Kelly | 5-1 | Qualifying | Jameson International |
| | v Johnson | 1-5 | Qualifying | Jameson International |
| | v Black | 4-5 | Quarter-final | Scottish Championship |
| | v Roscoe | 7-9 | Qualifying | Coral UK Championship |
| **1982** | v E. McLaughlin | 9-8 | Qualifying | Embassy World Championship |
| | v Dunning | 4-9 | Qualifying | Embassy World Championship |
| | v Donnelly | 6-5 | 1st round | Scottish Championship |
| | v Black | 0-6 | Quarter-final | Scottish Championship |
| | v Dodd | 1-5 | Qualifying | Jameson International |
| | v Thorne | 5-2 | 2nd round | Professional Players Tournament |
| | v Reardon | 2-5 | 3rd round | Professional Players Tournament |
| | v Martin | 6-9 | Qualifying | Coral UK Championship |
| **1983** | v M. Owen | 10-5 | Qualifying | Embassy World Championship |
| | v Martin | 7-10 | Qualifying | Embassy World Championship |
| | v Gibson | 6-5 | 1st round | Scottish Championship |
| | v Black | 6-2 | Semi-final | Scottish Championship |
| | **v Sinclair** | **11-9** | **Final** | **Scottish Championship** |
| | v S. Davis | 1-5 | 1st round | Langs Supreme Scottish Masters |
| | v Medati | 5-3 | Qualifying | Jameson International |
| | v Reardon | 2-5 | 1st round | Jameson International |
| | v Murphy | 0-5 | 1st round | Professional Players Tournament |
| | v Bennett | 9-0 | Qualifying | Coral UK Championship |
| | v Higgins | 6-9 | 1st round | Coral UK Championship |
| **1984** | v David Taylor | 5-4 | Qualifying | Lada Classic |
| | v Stevens | 1-5 | 1st round | Lada Classic |
| | v Gauvreau | 6-10 | Qualifying | Embassy World Championship |
| | v White | 0-5 | 1st round | Langs Supreme Scottish Masters |
| | v Black | 5-3 | Qualifying | Jameson International |
| | v Meo | 1-5 | 1st round | Jameson International |
| | v King | 5-4 | 1st round | Rothmans Grand Prix |
| | v Thorne | 3-5 | 2nd round | Rothmans Grand Prix |
| | v Scott | 9-5 | Qualifying | Coral UK Open |
| | v David Taylor | 6-9 | 1st round | Coral UK Open |
| **1985** | v E. McLaughlin | 5-4 | Qualifying | Mercantile Credit Classic |
| | v Charlton | 5-1 | 1st round | Mercantile Credit Classic |
| | v Virgo | 0-5 | 2nd round | Mercantile Credit Classic |
| | v E. McLaughlin | 6-4 | 1st round | Scottish Championship |
| | v M. Gibson | 6-4 | Semi-final | Scottish Championship |
| | **v Sinclair** | **10-2** | **Final** | **Scottish Championship** |
| | v Murphy | 6-5 | 1st round | Dulux British Open |
| | v Thorne | 5-0 | 2nd round | Dulux British Open |
| | v E. Hughes | 2-5 | 3rd round | Dulux British Open |
| | v P. Francisco | 10-7 | Qualifying | Embassy World Championship |
| | v Mountjoy | 5-10 | 1st round | Embassy World Championship |
| | v Thorburn | 1-5 | 1st round | Langs Scottish Masters |
| | v Fitzmaurice | 5-1 | 3rd round | Goya Matchroom Trophy |
| | v Chaperon | 5-4 | 4th round | Goya Matchroom Trophy |
| | v S. Davis | 1-5 | 5th round | Goya Matchroom Trophy |
| | v Drago | 3-5 | 3rd round | Rothmans Grand Prix |
| | v Murphy | 9-7 | 3rd round | Coral UK Open |
| | v Reardon | 9-5 | 4th round | Coral UK Open |
| | v West | 4-9 | 5th round | Coral UK Open |
| **1986** | v Sinclair | 5-3 | 3rd round | Mercantile Credit Classic |
| | v Knowles | 4-5 | 4th round | Mercantile Credit Classic |
| | v F. Davis | 5-4 | 3rd round | Dulux British Open |

| | | | | |
|---|---|---|---|---|
| | v S. Francisco | 5-1 | 4th round | Dulux British Open |
| | v Griffiths | 2-5 | 5th round | Dulux British Open |
| | v Hendry | 5-6 | Quarter-final | Canada Dry Scottish Championship |
| | v Fowler | 6-10 | Qualifying | Embassy World Championship |
| | v Gauvreau | 4-5 | 3rd round | BCE International |
| | v M. Bennett | 1-5 | 3rd round | Rothmans Grand Prix |
| | v Grace | 6-9 | 3rd round | Tennents UK Open |
| **1987** | v Kearney | 0-5 | 3rd round | Mercantile Credit Classic |
| | v Donnelly | 2-6 | 1st round | Scottish Championship |
| | v T. Jones | 4-5 | 3rd round | Dulux British Open |
| | v Edmonds | 10-7 | Qualifying | Embassy World Championship |
| | v Williams | 10-5 | 1st round | Embassy World Championship |
| | v Johnson | 7-13 | 2nd round | Embassy World Championship |
| | v N. Gilbert | 1-5 | 3rd round | Fidelity International |
| | v Wych | 4-5 | 3rd round | Rothmans Grand Prix |
| | v Edmonds | 4-9 | 3rd round | Tennents UK Open |
| **1988** | v Donnelly | 4-5 | 3rd round | Mercantile Credit Classic |
| | v Donnelly | 6-5 | Quarter-final | Scottish Championship |
| | v John Rea | 6-5 | Semi-final | Scottish Championship |
| | v Hendry | 4-10 | Final | Scottish Championship |
| | v D. Gilbert | 5-4 | 3rd round | MIM Britannia British Open |
| | v Knowles | 5-4 | 4th round | MIM Britannia British Open |
| | v Hallett | 2-5 | 5th round | MIM Britannia British Open |
| | v Fowler | 3-10 | Qualifying | Embassy World Championship |
| | v Sheehan | 5-0 | 2nd round | Fidelity International |
| | v Higgins | 5-2 | 3rd round | Fidelity International |
| | v James | 2-5 | 4th round | Fidelity International |
| | v Glen Wilkinson | 5-2 | 2nd round | Rothmans Grand Prix |
| | v Newbury | 3-5 | 3rd round | Rothmans Grand Prix |
| | v Watchorn | 5-1 | 2nd round | BCE Canadian Masters |
| | v S. Francisco | 5-4 | 3rd round | BCE Canadian Masters |
| | v Longworth | 3-5 | 4th round | BCE Canadian Masters |
| | v B. Harris | 8-9 | 2nd round | Tennents UK Open |
| **1989** | v Graham | 5-4 | 2nd round | Mercantile Credit Classic |
| | v Higgins | 2-5 | 3rd round | Mercantile Credit Classic |
| | v Black | 5-1 | 2nd round | European Open |
| | v West | 5-4 | 3rd round | European Open |
| | v Thorburn | 1-5 | 4th round | European Open |
| | v E. McLaughlin | 5-0 | 1st round | Scottish Championship |
| | v M. Gibson | 5-1 | Semi-final | Scottish Championship |
| | v John Rea | 7-9 | Final | Scottish Championship |
| | v M. Smith | 5-4 | 2nd round | Anglian British Open |
| | v S. Francisco | 5-4 | 3rd round | Anglian British Open |
| | v Mountjoy | 0-5 | 4th round | Anglian British Open |
| | v Meadowcroft | 10-9 | Qualifying | Embassy World Championship |
| | v Browne | 6-10 | Qualifying | Embassy World Championship |
| | v Darrington | 5-0 | 2nd round | Hong Kong Open |
| | v Chaperon | 3-5 | 3rd round | Hong Kong Open |
| | v Wattana | 2-5 | 2nd round | 555 Asian Open |
| | v Thorburn | 2-6 | 1st round | Regal Scottish Masters |
| | v Meakin | 5-4 | 2nd round | BCE International |
| | v Drago | 4-5 | 3rd round | BCE International |
| | v Wattana | 1-5 | 2nd round | Rothmans Grand Prix |
| | v G. Foulds | 5-1 | 2nd round | Dubai Classic |
| | v Hendry | 3-5 | 3rd round | Dubai Classic |
| | v Bond | 3-6 | 2nd round | Stormseal UK Open |
| **1990** | v Pinches | 5-4 | 2nd round | Mercantile Credit Classic |
| | v P. Francisco | 2-5 | 3rd round | Mercantile Credit Classic |
| | v Dunning | 5-1 | 2nd round | Pearl Assurance British Open |
| | v West | 5-0 | 3rd round | Pearl Assurance British Open |
| | v Dennis Taylor | 2-5 | 4th round | Pearl Assurance British Open |
| | v Foldvari | 4-5 | 2nd round | European Open |
| | v Dyson | 10-9 | Qualifying | Embassy World Championship |

| | | | | |
|---|---|---|---|---|
| | v M. Bennett | 1-10 | Qualifying | Embassy World Championship |

## ROBERT MARSHALL (England)

**Born** 25.8.64. **Turned professional** 1987. **World ranking** 47 (70).

| | | | | |
|---|---|---|---|---|
| **1987** | v V. Harris | 1-5 | 1st round | Fidelity International |
| | v Sheehan | 5-1 | 1st round | Rothmans Grand Prix |
| | v Wych | 2-5 | 2nd round | Rothmans Grand Prix |
| | v Roe | 3-9 | 1st round | Tennents UK Open |
| **1988** | v Morra | 0-5 | 1st round | Mercantile Credit Classic |
| | v Oliver | 6-3 | 1st round | English Championship |
| | v Houlihan | 6-4 | 2nd round | English Championship |
| | v Thorne | 3-6 | 3rd round | English Championship |
| | v Rigitano | 2-5 | 1st round | MIM Britannia British Open |
| | v Chaperon | 3-10 | Qualifying | Embassy World Championship |
| | v Rowswell | 5-4 | 1st round | Fidelity International |
| | v M. Bennett | 1-5 | 2nd round | Fidelity International |
| | v V. Harris | 3-5 | 1st round | Rothmans Grand Prix |
| | v Black | 5-1 | 1st round | BCE Canadian Masters |
| | v Dodd | 3-5 | 2nd round | BCE Canadian Masters |
| | v M. Smith | 6-9 | 1st round | Tennents UK Open |
| **1989** | v Black | 5-0 | 1st round | Mercantile Credit Classic |
| | v Edmonds | 5-2 | 2nd round | Mercantile Credit Classic |
| | v Drago | 1-5 | 3rd round | Mercantile Credit Classic |
| | v Van Rensberg | 5-1 | 1st round | European Open |
| | v Murphy | 4-5 | 2nd round | European Open |
| | v Terry | 5-3 | 1st round | English Championship |
| | v N. Gilbert | 5-4 | 2nd round | English Championship |
| | v Longworth | 3-5 | 3rd round | English Championship |
| | v Chambers | 5-2 | 1st round | Anglian British Open |
| | v Stevens | 5-4 | 2nd round | Anglian British Open |
| | v Chaperon | 5-2 | 3rd round | Anglian British Open |
| | v Thorne | 1-5 | 4th round | Anglian British Open |
| | v Hines | 10-1 | Qualifying | Embassy World Championship |
| | v P. Gibson | 3-10 | Qualifying | Embassy World Championship |
| | v M. Gibson | 1-5 | 1st round | Hong Kong Open |
| | v Brumby | 5-4 | 1st round | 555 Asian Open |
| | v Stevens | 5-3 | 2nd round | 555 Asian Open |
| | v O'Kane | 1-5 | 3rd round | 555 Asian Open |
| | v Watchorn | 5-3 | 1st round | BCE International |
| | v Roscoe | 5-4 | 2nd round | BCE International |
| | v Reynolds | 5-3 | 3rd round | BCE International |
| | v Charlton | 5-2 | 4th round | BCE International |
| | v C. Wilson | 3-5 | 5th round | BCE International |
| | v Grace | 5-2 | 1st round | Rothmans Grand Prix |
| | v Roscoe | 4-5 | 2nd round | Rothmans Grand Prix |
| | v Gollan | 5-2 | 2nd round | Dubai Classic |
| | v Drago | 0-5 | 3rd round | Dubai Classic |
| | v Van Rensberg | 6-5 | 1st round | Stormseal UK Open |
| | v J. Campbell | 6-4 | 2nd round | Stormseal UK Open |
| | v Knowles | 2-9 | 3rd round | Stormseal UK Open |
| **1990** | v Jack Rea | 5-2 | 1st round | Mercantile Credit Classic |
| | v Fowler | 2-5 | 2nd round | Mercantile Credit Classic |
| | v Meakin | 5-2 | 1st round | Pearl Assurance British Open |
| | v N. Gilbert | 5-2 | 2nd round | Pearl Assurance British Open |
| | v Roe | 5-3 | 3rd round | Pearl Assurance British Open |
| | v Johnson | 5-4 | 4th round | Pearl Assurance British Open |
| | v E. Hughes | 5-0 | 5th round | Pearl Assurance British Open |
| | v Newbury | 5-4 | Quarter-final | Pearl Assurance British Open |
| | v Chaperon | 5-9 | Semi-final | Pearl Assurance British Open |
| | v Pinches | 4-5 | 1st round | European Open |

| | | | | |
|---|---|---|---|---|
| | v Thornley | 10-0 | Qualifying | Embassy World Championship |
| | v Martin | 10-6 | Qualifying | Embassy World Championship |
| | v Gary Wilkinson | 7-10 | Qualifying | Embassy World Championship |

## **DAVE MARTIN** (England)

**Born** 9.5.48. **Turned professional** 1981. **World ranking** 91 (56).

| | | | | |
|---|---|---|---|---|
| **1981** | v Anderson | 9-3 | Qualifying | Embassy World Championship |
| | v Pulman | 9-2 | Qualifying | Embassy World Championship |
| | v Werbeniuk | 4-10 | 1st round | Embassy World Championship |
| | v Dunning | 5-2 | 1st round | Jameson International |
| | v Werbeniuk | 5-2 | 2nd round | Jameson International |
| | v Charlton | 5-2 | 3rd round | Jameson International |
| | v Miles | 5-1 | Quarter-final | Jameson International |
| | v Dennis Taylor | 1-9 | Semi-final | Jameson International |
| | v Sinclair | 9-7 | Qualifying | Coral UK Championship |
| | v Higgins | 7-9 | 2nd round | Coral UK Championship |
| **1982** | v Houlihan | 9-3 | Qualifying | Embassy World Championship |
| | v Miles | 5-10 | Qualifying | Embassy World Championship |
| | v E. Hughes | 4-5 | Qualifying | Jameson International |
| | v Gibson | 5-2 | 1st round | Professional Players Tournament |
| | v Spencer | 3-5 | 2nd round | Professional Players Tournament |
| | v Macleod | 9-6 | Qualifying | Coral UK Championship |
| | v Higgins | 7-9 | 1st round | Coral UK Championship |
| **1983** | v Parkin | 10-1 | Qualifying | Embassy World Championship |
| | v Macleod | 10-7 | Qualifying | Embassy World Championship |
| | v Werbeniuk | 4-10 | Qualifying | Embassy World Championship |
| | v Greaves | 5-1 | Qualifying | Jameson International |
| | v Fagan | 5-0 | Qualifying | Jameson International |
| | v Higgins | 5-2 | 1st round | Jameson International |
| | v Mountjoy | 0-5 | 2nd round | Jameson International |
| | v Fitzmaurice | 5-0 | 1st round | Professional Players Tournament |
| | v Watterson | 5-4 | 2nd round | Professional Players Tournament |
| | v J. Campbell | 0-5 | 3rd round | Professional Players Tournament |
| | v French | 9-3 | Qualifying | Coral UK Championship |
| | v Griffiths | 4-9 | Qualifying | Coral UK Championship |
| **1984** | v King | 8-10 | Qualifying | Embassy World Championship |
| | v Fowler | 0-5 | Qualifying | Jameson International |
| | v Chaperon | 5-4 | 1st round | Rothmans Grand Prix |
| | v Meo | 4-5 | 2nd round | Rothmans Grand Prix |
| | v Murphy | 8-9 | Qualifying | Coral UK Open |
| **1985** | v Foldvari | 2-5 | Qualifying | Mercantile Credit Classic |
| | v Miles | 9-7 | 1st round | Tolly Cobbold English Championship |
| | v Knowles | 3-9 | 2nd round | Tolly Cobbold English Championship |
| | v Bennett | 6-0 | 1st round | Dulux British Open |
| | v Reardon | 5-4 | 2nd round | Dulux British Open |
| | v O'Kane | 4-5 | 3rd round | Dulux British Open |
| | v O'Kane | 8-10 | Qualifying | Embassy World Championship |
| | v Sinclair | 5-1 | 3rd round | Goya Matchroom Trophy |
| | v Thorburn | 3-5 | 4th round | Goya Matchroom Trophy |
| | v Morra | 5-2 | 3rd round | Rothmans Grand Prix |
| | v S. Francisco | 3-5 | 4th round | Rothmans Grand Prix |
| | v Darrington | 9-3 | 3rd round | Coral UK Open |
| | v S. Francisco | 6-9 | 4th round | Coral UK Open |
| **1986** | v Murphy | 5-3 | 3rd round | Mercantile Credit Classic |
| | v P. Francisco | 2-5 | 4th round | Mercantile Credit Classic |
| | v F. Davis | 9-8 | 3rd round | Tolly Cobbold English Championship |
| | v S. Davis | 4-9 | 4th round | Tolly Cobbold English Championship |
| | v B. Harris | 5-1 | 3rd round | Dulux British Open |
| | v S. Davis | 1-5 | 4th round | Dulux British Open |
| | v Gilbert | 10-5 | Qualifying | Embassy World Championship |

| | | | | |
|---|---|---|---|---|
| | v Johnson | 3-10 | 1st round | Embassy World Championship |
| | v Chaperon | 4-5 | 3rd round | BCE International |
| | v Higgins | 2-5 | 4th round | Rothmans Grand Prix |
| | v Williamson | 9-5 | 3rd round | Tennents UK Open |
| | v Higgins | 6-9 | 4th round | Tennents UK Open |
| **1987** | v G. Foulds | 5-4 | 3rd round | Mercantile Credit Classic |
| | v Griffiths | 4-5 | 4th round | Mercantile Credit Classic |
| | v Spencer | 6-5 | 3rd round | Tolly Ales English Championship |
| | v Thorne | 3-6 | 4th round | Tolly Ales English Championship |
| | v Scott | 5-3 | 3rd round | Dulux British Open |
| | v Spencer | 2-5 | 4th round | Dulux British Open |
| | v Hendry | 7-10 | Qualifying | Embassy World Championship |
| | v D. Gilbert | 2-5 | 3rd round | Fidelity International |
| | v Roe | 4-5 | 3rd round | Rothmans Grand Prix |
| | v V. Harris | 7-9 | 3rd round | Tennents UK Open |
| **1988** | v J. McLaughlin | 5-2 | 3rd round | Mercantile Credit Classic |
| | v Mountjoy | 5-4 | 4th round | Mercantile Credit Classic |
| | v White | 5-2 | 5th round | Mercantile Credit Classic |
| | v Knowles | 1-5 | Quarter-final | Mercantile Credit Classic |
| | v M. Smith | 6-5 | 3rd round | English Championship |
| | v Johnson | 4-6 | 4th round | English Championship |
| | v Browne | 4-5 | 3rd round | MIM Britannia British Open |
| | v W. Jones | 5-10 | Qualifying | Embassy World Championship |
| | v Mikkelsen | 5-4 | 2nd round | Fidelity International |
| | v Mountjoy | 1-5 | 3rd round | Fidelity International |
| | v Wildman | 5-1 | 2nd round | Rothmans Grand Prix |
| | v Chaperon | 0-5 | 3rd round | Rothmans Grand Prix |
| | v Watterson | 5-1 | 2nd round | BCE Canadian Masters |
| | v Reynolds | 0-5 | 3rd round | BCE Canadian Masters |
| | v Miles | 9-7 | 2nd round | Tennents UK Open |
| | v Parrott | 6-9 | 3rd round | Tennents UK Open |
| **1989** | v Foldvari | 5-2 | 2nd round | Mercantile Credit Classic |
| | v N. Foulds | 1-5 | 3rd round | Mercantile Credit Classic |
| | v Oliver | 4-5 | 2nd round | European Open |
| | v Rowswell | 2-5 | 3rd round | English Championship |
| | v Bear | 2-5 | 2nd round | Anglian British Open |
| | v M. Gibson | 10-7 | Qualifying | Embassy World Championship |
| | v Clark | 2-10 | Qualifying | Embassy World Championship |
| | v Kelly | 5-2 | 2nd round | Hong Kong Open |
| | v O'Kane | 1-5 | 3rd round | Hong Kong Open |
| | v Wildman | 5-2 | 2nd round | 555 Asian Open |
| | v Higgins | 3-5 | 3rd round | 555 Asian Open |
| | v M. Smith | 3-5 | 2nd round | BCE International |
| | v Oliver | 3-5 | 2nd round | Rothmans Grand Prix |
| | v Price | 5-3 | 2nd round | Dubai Classic |
| | v Reynolds | 2-5 | 3rd round | Dubai Classic |
| | v Gollan | 0-6 | 2nd round | Stormseal UK Open |
| **1990** | v Wright | 1-5 | 2nd round | Mercantile Credit Classic |
| | v Wright | 2-5 | 2nd round | Pearl Assurance British Open |
| | v Gauvreau | 5-4 | 2nd round | European Open |
| | v Roe | 1-5 | 3rd round | European Open |
| | v Marshall | 6-10 | Qualifying | Embassy World Championship |

## JIM MEADOWCROFT (England)

**Born** 15.12.46. **Turned professional** 1971. **World ranking** 127 (115).

| | | | | |
|---|---|---|---|---|
| **1973** | v Reardon | 10-16 | 2nd round | World Championship |
| **1974** | v Kennerley | 8-5 | 1st round | World Championship |
| | v Reardon | 3-15 | 2nd round | World Championship |
| **1975** | v Werbeniuk | 9-15 | Qualifying | World Championship |

| | | | | |
|---|---|---|---|---|
| **1976** | v Wheelwright | 8-1 | Qualifying | Embassy World Championship |
| | v Gross | 8-4 | Qualifying | Embassy World Championship |
| | v Thorne | 8-5 | Qualifying | Embassy World Championship |
| | v Williams | 15-7 | 1st round | Embassy World Championship |
| | v Mans | 8-15 | Quarter-final | Embassy World Championship |
| **1977** | v Fagan | 9-11 | Qualifying | Embassy World Championship |
| | v Houlihan | 5-1 | 1st round | Super Crystalate UK Championship |
| | v Reardon | 5-4 | 2nd round | Super Crystalate UK Championship |
| | v Fagan | 4-5 | Quarter-final | Super Crystalate UK Championship |
| **1978** | v Houlihan | 6-9 | Qualifying | Embassy World Championship |
| | v Jack Rea | 9-5 | Qualifying | Coral UK Championship |
| | v Higgins | 6-9 | 1st round | Coral UK Championship |
| **1979** | v Van Rensberg | 9-7 | Prelim | Embassy World Championship |
| | v Griffiths | 6-9 | Qualifying | Embassy World Championship |
| | v Edmonds | 3-9 | 2nd round | Coral UK Championship |
| **1980** | v Sinclair | 9-1 | Qualifying | Embassy World Championship |
| | v Virgo | 2-10 | 1st round | Embassy World Championship |
| | v Greaves | 9-1 | Qualifying | Coral UK Championship |
| | v Thorne | 1-9 | 1st round | Coral UK Championship |
| **1981** | v Barrie | 9-3 | Qualifying | John Courage English |
| | v S. Davis | 2-9 | 1st round | John Courage English |
| | v White | 8-9 | Qualifying | Embassy World Championship |
| | v Roscoe | 5-4 | Qualifying | Jameson International |
| | v Wilson | 5-4 | 1st round | Jameson International |
| | v Stevens | 1-5 | 2nd round | Jameson International |
| | v Houlihan | 4-9 | Qualifying | Coral UK Championship |
| **1982** | v Watterson | 9-7 | Qualifying | Embassy World Championship |
| | v Higgins | 5-10 | 1st round | Embassy World Championship |
| | v Ross | 5-0 | Qualifying | Jameson International |
| | v White | 1-5 | 1st round | Jameson International |
| | v Bennett | 5-4 | 1st round | Professional Players Tournament |
| | v Sinclair | 3-5 | 2nd round | Professional Players Tournament |
| | v D. Hughes | 9-8 | Qualifying | Coral UK Championship |
| | v Dennis Taylor | 7-9 | 1st round | Coral UK Championship |
| **1983** | v Bennett | 10-3 | Qualifying | Embassy World Championship |
| | v Cripsey | 10-6 | Qualifying | Embassy World Championship |
| | v David Taylor | 2-10 | 1st round | Embassy World Championship |
| | v Roscoe | 5-4 | 1st round | Professional Players Tournament |
| | v Thorburn | 1-5 | 2nd round | Professional Players Tournament |
| | v N. Foulds | 2-9 | Qualifying | Coral UK Championship |
| **1984** | v Meo | 1-5 | Qualifying | Lada Classic |
| | v N. Foulds | 2-10 | Qualifying | Embassy World Championship |
| | v Chalmers | 5-1 | Qualifying | Jameson International |
| | v Williams | 4-5 | Qualifying | Jameson International |
| | v J. McLaughlin | 1-5 | Qualifying | Rothmans Grand Prix |
| | v Bradley | 7-9 | Qualifying | Coral UK Open |
| **1985** | v Fowler | 2-5 | Qualifying | Mercantile Credit Classic |
| | v Chalmers | 3-9 | Qualifying | Tolly Cobbold English Championship |
| | v B. Harris | 1-6 | Qualifying | Dulux British Open |
| | v P. Francisco | 5-10 | Qualifying | Embassy World Championship |
| | v Chappel | 2-5 | 2nd round | Goya Matchroom Trophy |
| | v West | 2-5 | 2nd round | Rothmans Grand Prix |
| | v Hargreaves | 9-8 | 2nd round | Coral UK Open |
| | v Hallett | 1-9 | 3rd round | Coral UK Open |
| **1986** | v West | 0-5 | 2nd round | Mercantile Credit Classic |
| | v Cripsey | 1-9 | 2nd round | Tolly Cobbold English Championship |
| | v Jenkins | 2-5 | 2nd round | Dulux British Open |
| | v Darrington | 6-10 | Qualifying | Embassy World Championship |
| | v P. Gibson | 2-5 | 1st round | BCE International |
| | v Greaves | 5-2 | 1st round | Rothmans Grand Prix |
| | v Mans | *wo* | 2nd round | Rothmans Grand Prix |
| | v Martin | *scr* | 3rd round | Rothmans Grand Prix |
| | v Demarco | 9-2 | 1st round | Tennents UK Open |

| | | | | |
|---|---|---|---|---|
| | v Bradley | 2-9 | 2nd round | Tennents UK Open |
| 1987 | v Newbury | 1-5 | 2nd round | Mercantile Credit Classic |
| | v Grace | 4-5 | 1st round | Dulux British Open |
| | v Mienie | 10-3 | Qualifying | Embassy World Championship |
| | v Cripsey | 9-10 | Qualifying | Embassy World Championship |
| | v Greaves | 5-1 | 1st round | Fidelity International |
| | v Owers | 3-5 | 2nd round | Fidelity International |
| | v A. Harris | 5-3 | 1st round | Rothmans Grand Prix |
| | v Browne | 3-5 | 2nd round | Rothmans Grand Prix |
| | v King | 4-9 | 2nd round | Tennents UK Open |
| 1988 | v Everton | 3-5 | 1st round | Mercantile Credit Classic |
| | v Heaton | 0-6 | 1st round | English Championship |
| | v Kelly | 5-1 | 1st round | MIM Britannia British Open |
| | v Murphy | 4-5 | 2nd round | MIM Britannia British Open |
| | v B. Bennett | 10-5 | Qualifying | Embassy World Championship |
| | v Cripsey | 3-10 | Qualifying | Embassy World Championship |
| | v Whitthread | 4-5 | 1st round | Fidelity International |
| | v Price | 0-5 | 1st round | BCE Canadian Masters |
| | v J. Smith | 7-9 | 1st round | Tennents UK Open |
| 1989 | v Fitzmaurice | 2-5 | 1st round | Mercantile Credit Classic |
| | v Robidoux | 0-5 | 1st round | European Open |
| | v Jenkins | 5-4 | 1st round | Anglian British Open |
| | v T. Jones | 1-5 | 2nd round | Anglian British Open |
| | v Mienie | 10-7 | Qualifying | Embassy World Championship |
| | v Macleod | 9-10 | Qualifying | Embassy World Championship |
| | v Bradley | 5-2 | 1st round | Hong Kong Open |
| | v D. Gilbert | 3-5 | 2nd round | Hong Kong Open |
| | v Price | 2-5 | 1st round | 555 Asian Open |
| | v Terry | 1-5 | 1st round | BCE International |
| | v Glen Wilkinson | 5-4 | 1st round | Rothmans Grand Prix |
| | v Duggan | 1-5 | 2nd round | Rothmans Grand Prix |
| | v P. Gibson | 4-5 | 1st round | Dubai Classic |
| | v Gauvreau | 1-6 | 1st round | Stormseal UK Open |
| 1990 | v Oliver | 5-3 | 1st round | Mercantile Credit Classic |
| | v Duggan | 3-5 | 2nd round | Mercantile Credit Classic |
| | v Lawlor | 5-2 | 1st round | Pearl Assurance British Open |
| | v Stevens | 4-5 | 2nd round | Pearl Assurance British Open |
| | v Mienie | 1-10 | Qualifying | Embassy World Championship |

## STEVE MEAKIN (England)

**Born** 19.7.61. **Turned professional** 1987. **World ranking** 101 (107).

| | | | | |
|---|---|---|---|---|
| 1987 | v Foldvari | 3-5 | 1st round | Fidelity International |
| | v Morra | 5-2 | 1st round | Rothmans Grand Prix |
| | v Newbury | 1-5 | 2nd round | Rothmans Grand Prix |
| | v Glen Wilkinson | 9-0 | 1st round | Tennents UK Open |
| | v W. Jones | 1-9 | 2nd round | Tennents UK Open |
| 1988 | v Darrington | 5-4 | 1st round | Mercantile Credit Classic |
| | v F. Davis | 4-5 | 2nd round | Mercantile Credit Classic |
| | v Darrington | 6-3 | 1st round | English Championship |
| | v Owers | 2-6 | 2nd round | English Championship |
| | v Williamson | 1-5 | 1st round | MIM Britannia British Open |
| | v Morra | 5-10 | Qualifying | Embassy World Championship |
| | v Van Rensberg | 5-4 | 1st round | Fidelity International |
| | v Gauvreau | 5-3 | 2nd round | Fidelity International |
| | v E. Hughes | 0-5 | 3rd round | Fidelity International |
| | v Chambers | 0-5 | 1st round | Rothmans Grand Prix |
| | v John Ree | 6-9 | 1st round | Tennents UK Open |
| 1989 | v Sinclair | 1-5 | 1st round | Mercantile Credit Classic |
| | v Grace | 4-5 | 1st round | European Open |

| | | | | |
|---|---|---|---|---|
| | v Roscoe | 1-5 | 1st round | Anglian British Open |
| | v Kearney | 10-3 | Qualifying | Embassy World Championship |
| | v Browne | 9-10 | Qualifying | Embassy World Championship |
| | v Donnelly | 5-4 | 1st round | Hong Kong Open |
| | v Roscoe | 1-5 | 2nd round | Hong Kong Open |
| | v V. Harris | 5-3 | 1st round | 555 Asian Open |
| | v Johnston-Allen | 1-5 | 2nd round | 555 Asian Open |
| | v Wildman | 5-3 | 1st round | BCE International |
| | v Macleod | 4-5 | 2nd round | BCE International |
| | v Wildman | 5-2 | 1st round | Rothmans Grand Prix |
| | v Stevens | 5-4 | 2nd round | Rothmans Grand Prix |
| | v Thorburn | 3-5 | 3rd round | Rothmans Grand Prix |
| | v J. Smith | 5-4 | 1st round | Dubai Classic |
| | v J. Campbell | 0-5 | 2nd round | Dubai Classic |
| | v A. Harris | 6-2 | 1st round | Stormseal UK Open |
| | v N. Gilbert | 6-5 | 2nd round | Stormseal UK Open |
| | v N. Foulds | 1-9 | 3rd round | Stormseal UK Open |
| **1990** | v Edwards | 4-5 | 1st round | Mercantile Credit Classic |
| | v Marshall | 2-5 | 1st round | Pearl Assurance British Open |
| | v Gauvreau | 3-5 | 1st round | European Open |
| | v T. Wilson | 8-10 | Qualifying | Embassy World Championship |

## PAUL MEDATI (England)

**Born** 14.11.44. **Turned professional** 1981. **World ranking** 79 (80).

| | | | | |
|---|---|---|---|---|
| **1981** | v Watterson | 3-5 | Qualifying | Jameson International |
| | v E. McLaughlin | 9-5 | Qualifying | Coral UK Championship |
| | v Donnelly | 9-7 | Qualifying | Coral UK Championship |
| | v Thorne | 6-9 | Qualifying | Coral UK Championship |
| **1982** | v Phillips | 9-3 | Qualifying | Embassy World Championship |
| | v Wilson | 5-9 | Qualifying | Embassy World Championship |
| | v Williams | 3-5 | Qualifying | Jameson International |
| | v Thorburn | 1-5 | 1st round | Professional Players Tournament |
| | v Bennett | 9-1 | Qualifying | Coral UK Championship |
| | v White | 7-9 | 1st round | Coral UK Championship |
| **1983** | v John Bear | 10-7 | Qualifying | Embassy World Championship |
| | v Black | 4-10 | Qualifying | Embassy World Championship |
| | v V. Harris | 5-0 | Qualifying | Jameson International |
| | v Macleod | 3-5 | Qualifying | Jameson International |
| | v D. Hughes | 5-1 | Qualifying | Professional Players Tournament |
| | v Knowles | 1-5 | 1st round | Professional Players Tournament |
| | v D. Hughes | 9-2 | Qualifying | Coral UK Championship |
| | v Edmonds | 9-7 | Qualifying | Coral UK Championship |
| | v Reynolds | 9-3 | 1st round | Coral UK Championship |
| | v Higgins | 1-9 | 2nd round | Coral UK Championship |
| **1984** | v Mikkelsen | 8-10 | Qualifying | Embassy World Championship |
| | v Gibson | 3-5 | Qualifying | Jameson International |
| | v Dodd | 5-4 | Qualifying | Rothmans Grand Prix |
| | v Johnson | 1-5 | 1st round | Rothmans Grand Prix |
| | v Hargreaves | 6-9 | Qualifying | Coral UK Open |
| **1985** | v Cripsey | 5-4 | Qualifying | Mercantile Credit Classic |
| | v Roscoe | 5-4 | Qualifying | Mercantile Credit Classic |
| | v Parrott | 5-3 | Qualifying | Mercantile Credit Classic |
| | v Stevens | 4-5 | 1st round | Mercantile Credit Classic |
| | v Hargreaves | 9-8 | Qualifying | Tolly Cobbold English Championship |
| | v Spencer | 9-4 | 1st round | Tolly Cobbold English Championship |
| | v Longworth | 7-9 | 2nd round | Tolly Cobbold English Championship |
| | v King | 4-6 | Qualifying | Dulux British Open |
| | v Bennett | 10-4 | Qualifying | Embassy World Championship |
| | v Williamson | 10-8 | Qualifying | Embassy World Championship |
| | v King | 10-9 | Qualifying | Embassy World Championship |

| | | | | |
|---|---|---|---|---|
| | v S. Francisco | 7-10 | Qualifying | Embassy World Championship |
| | v Cripsey | 2-5 | 2nd round | Goya Matchroom Trophy |
| | v J. McLaughlin | 2-5 | 2nd round | Rothmans Grand Prix |
| | v Kelly | 9-1 | 2nd round | Coral UK Open |
| | v J. Campbell | 7-9 | 3rd round | Coral UK Open |
| **1986** | v Kearney | 5-2 | 2nd round | Mercantile Credit Classic |
| | v O'Kane | 0-5 | 3rd round | Mercantile Credit Classic |
| | v Greaves | 9-4 | 2nd round | Tolly Cobbold English Championship |
| | v Thorne | 2-9 | 3rd round | Tolly Cobbold English Championship |
| | v Everton | 5-1 | 2nd round | Dulux British Open |
| | v David Taylor | 5-1 | 3rd round | Dulux British Open |
| | v J. Campbell | 4-5 | 4th round | Dulux British Open |
| | v Simngam | 10-9 | Qualifying | Embassy World Championship |
| | v Gibson | 10-6 | Qualifying | Embassy World Championship |
| | v Wilson | 6-10 | Qualifying | Embassy World Championship |
| | v Kearney | 5-3 | 2nd round | BCE International |
| | v Griffiths | 3-5 | 3rd round | BCE International |
| | v Rigitano | 5-1 | 2nd round | Rothmans Grand Prix |
| | v P. Francisco | 1-5 | 3rd round | Rothmans Grand Prix |
| | v Grace | 5-9 | 2nd round | Tennents UK Open |
| **1987** | v Dodd | 4-5 | 2nd round | Mercantile Credit Classic |
| | v N. Gibson | 6-2 | 2nd round | Tolly Ales English Championship |
| | v Virgo | 1-6 | 3rd round | Tolly Ales English Championship |
| | v Ellis | 5-0 | 2nd round | Dulux British Open |
| | v Charlton | 4-5 | 3rd round | Dulux British Open |
| | v Kearney | 10-8 | Qualifying | Embassy World Championship |
| | v Gauvreau | 10-3 | Qualifying | Embassy World Championship |
| | v E. Hughes | 2-10 | Qualifying | Embassy World Championship |
| | v Murphy | 3-5 | 2nd round | Fidelity International |
| | v M. Bennett | 4-5 | 2nd round | Rothmans Grand Prix |
| | v Dodd | 6-9 | 2nd round | Tennents UK Open |
| **1988** | v Chaperon | 3-5 | 2nd round | Mercantile Credit Classic |
| | v B. Bennett | 6-0 | 1st round | English Championship |
| | v Fowler | 1-6 | 2nd round | English Championship |
| | v Gauvreau | 5-1 | 2nd round | MIM Britannia British Open |
| | v David Taylor | 5-4 | 3rd round | MIM Britannia British Open |
| | v Thorburn | 2-5 | 4th round | MIM Britannia British Open |
| | v Gary Wilkinson | 10-9 | Qualifying | Embassy World Championship |
| | v Dodd | 6-10 | Qualifying | Embassy World Championship |
| | v Price | 4-5 | 1st round | Fidelity International |
| | v Watchorn | 5-2 | 1st round | Rothmans Grand Prix |
| | v King | 5-1 | 2nd round | Rothmans Grand Prix |
| | v Williams | 2-5 | 3rd round | Rothmans Grand Prix |
| | v Edwards | 5-3 | 1st round | BCE Canadian Masters |
| | v Cripsey | 5-0 | 2nd round | BCE Canadian Masters |
| | v Virgo | 1-5 | 3rd round | BCE Canadian Masters |
| | v Fisher | 9-3 | 2nd round | Tennents UK Open |
| | v S. Francisco | 8-9 | 3rd round | Tennents UK Open |
| **1989** | v Gary Wilkinson | 1-5 | 2nd round | Mercantile Credit Classic |
| | v Sheehan | 5-1 | 1st round | European Open |
| | v T. Jones | 2-5 | 2nd round | European Open |
| | v Wildman | 5-4 | 1st round | English Championship |
| | v Bales | 5-3 | 2nd round | English Championship |
| | v N. Foulds | 3-5 | 3rd round | English Championship |
| | v S. Campbell | 3-5 | 1st round | Anglian British Open |
| | v Terry | 8-10 | Qualifying | Embassy World Championship |
| | v Jenkins | 2-5 | 1st round | Hong Kong Open |
| | v D. Hughes | 2-5 | 1st round | 555 Asian Open |
| | v Whitthread | 3-5 | 1st round | BCE International |
| | v Dyson | 5-4 | 1st round | Rothmans Grand Prix |
| | v M. Bennett | 2-5 | 2nd round | Rothmans Grand Prix |
| | v Grace | 5-3 | 1st round | Dubai Classic |
| | v D. Gilbert | 5-3 | 2nd round | Dubai Classic |

| | | | | |
|---|---|---|---|---|
| | v S. Francisco | 5-4 | 3rd round | Dubai Classic |
| | v P. Francisco | 1-5 | 4th round | Dubai Classic |
| | v Thornley | 6-3 | 1st round | Stormseal UK Open |
| | v Roscoe | 6-5 | 2nd round | Stormseal UK Open |
| | v Thorne | 3-9 | 3rd round | Stormseal UK Open |
| **1990** | v Watchorn | 2-5 | 1st round | Mercantile Credit Classic |
| | v Sheehan | 5-2 | 1st round | Pearl Assurance British Open |
| | v Robidoux | 1-5 | 2nd round | Pearl Assurance British Open |
| | v Wattana | 1-5 | 1st round | European Open |
| | v Kearney | 7-10 | Qualifying | Embassy World Championship |

## TONY MEO (England)

**Born** 4.10.59. **Turned professional** 1979. **World ranking** 16 (14).

| | | | | |
|---|---|---|---|---|
| **1979** | v David Taylor | 9-7 | 2nd round | Coral UK Championship |
| | v Virgo | 6-9 | 3rd round | Coral UK Championship |
| **1980** | v Van Rensberg | 9-1 | Qualifying | Embassy World Championship |
| | v Houlihan | 9-1 | Qualifying | Embassy World Championship |
| | v Higgins | 9-10 | 1st round | Embassy World Championship |
| | v Hood | 9-5 | Qualifying | Coral UK Championship |
| | v Houlihan | 9-1 | 1st round | Coral UK Championship |
| | v Virgo | 9-1 | 2nd round | Coral UK Championship |
| | v S. Davis | 5-9 | Quarter-final | Coral UK Championship |
| **1981** | v Virgo | 9-6 | Qualifying | John Courage English |
| | v Miles | 9-7 | 2nd round | John Courage English |
| | v Thorne | 9-8 | Semi-final | John Courage English |
| | v S. Davis | 3-9 | Final | John Courage English |
| | v Johnson | 9-8 | Qualifying | Embassy World Championship |
| | v Hallett | 9-4 | Qualifying | Embassy World Championship |
| | v Virgo | 10-6 | 1st round | Embassy World Championship |
| | v Griffiths | 6-13 | 2nd round | Embassy World Championship |
| | v E. McLaughlin | 5-2 | 1st round | Jameson International |
| | v Mans | 3-5 | 2nd round | Jameson International |
| | v Williams | 9-8 | 2nd round | Coral UK Championship |
| | v Thorburn | 9-6 | 3rd round | Coral UK Championship |
| | v Higgins | 9-4 | Quarter-final | Coral UK Championship |
| | v Griffiths | 3-9 | Semi-final | Coral UK Championship |
| **1982** | v David Taylor | 5-2 | 1st round | Benson & Hedges Masters |
| | v Thorburn | 5-0 | Quarter-final | Benson & Hedges Masters |
| | v S. Davis | 4-6 | Semi-final | Benson & Hedges Masters |
| | v Spencer | 5-3 | 1st round | Benson & Hedges Irish Masters |
| | v Griffiths | 3-5 | Quarter-final | Benson & Hedges Irish Masters |
| | v D. Hughes | 9-4 | Qualifying | Embassy World Championship |
| | v Mans | 8-10 | 1st round | Embassy World Championship |
| | v Sinclair | 3-5 | Qualifying | Jameson International |
| | v M. Owen | 5-4 | 1st round | Professional Players Tournament |
| | v Jonik | 5-0 | 2nd round | Professional Players Tournament |
| | v Charlton | 3-5 | 3rd round | Professional Players Tournament |
| | v Scott | 9-5 | Qualifying | Coral UK Championship |
| | v Miles | 9-4 | 1st round | Coral UK Championship |
| | v David Taylor | 9-6 | 2nd round | Coral UK Championship |
| | v Virgo | 9-6 | Quarter-final | Coral UK Championship |
| | v Griffiths | 7-9 | Semi-final | Coral UK Championship |
| **1983** | v Charlton | 3-5 | 1st round | Benson & Hedges Masters |
| | v Burke | 5-0 | 1st round | Benson & Hedges Irish Masters |
| | v Reardon | 4-5 | Quarter-final | Benson & Hedges Irish Masters |
| | v V. Harris | 10-0 | Qualifying | Embassy World Championship |
| | v G. Foulds | 10-4 | Qualifying | Embassy World Championship |
| | v White | 10-8 | 1st round | Embassy World Championship |
| | v Mountjoy | 13-11 | 2nd round | Embassy World Championship |
| | v Knowles | 9-13 | Quarter-final | Embassy World Championship |

*Tony Meo*

| | | | | |
|---|---|---|---|---|
| | v Knowles | 4-5 | 1st round | Langs Supreme Scottish Masters |
| | v Watterson | 3-5 | 1st round | Jameson International |
| | v King | 5-2 | 1st round | Professional Players Tournament |
| | v Reynolds | 5-0 | 2nd round | Professional Players Tournament |
| | v Hallett | 5-3 | 3rd round | Professional Players Tournament |
| | v Stevens | 5-3 | Quarter-final | Professional Players Tournament |
| | v Johnson | 6-9 | Semi-final | Professional Players Tournament |
| | v Parrott | 9-7 | 1st round | Coral UK Championship |
| | v Spencer | 9-5 | 2nd round | Coral UK Championship |
| | v Davis | 4-9 | Quarter-final | Coral UK Championship |
| **1984** | v Meadowcroft | 5-1 | Qualifying | Lada Classic |
| | v Williams | 5-3 | 1st round | Lada Classic |
| | v Stevens | 5-2 | Quarter-final | Lada Classic |
| | v Wildman | 5-3 | Semi-final | Lada Classic |
| | v S. Davis | 8-9 | Final | Lada Classic |
| | v S. Davis | 0-5 | 1st round | Benson & Hedges Masters |
| | v White | 5-4 | 1st round | Benson & Hedges Irish Masters |
| | v S. Davis | 4-5 | Quarter-final | Benson & Hedges Irish Masters |
| | v Thorburn | 4-5 | 1st round | Tolly Cobbold Classic |
| | v S. Francisco | 5-10 | 1st round | Embassy World Championship |
| | v Stevens | 5-1 | Quarter-final | Winfield Australian Masters |
| | v Virgo | 2-6 | Semi-final | Winfield Australian Masters |
| | v Macleod | 5-1 | 1st round | Jameson International |
| | v White | 1-5 | 2nd round | Jameson International |
| | v Burke | 5-1 | 1st round | Rothmans Grand Prix |
| | v Martin | 5-4 | 2nd round | Rothmans Grand Prix |
| | v Thorburn | 4-5 | 3rd round | Rothmans Grand Prix |
| | v E. Hughes | 9-4 | 1st round | Coral UK Open |
| | v S. Davis | 7-9 | 2nd round | Coral UK Open |
| **1985** | v E. Hughes | 4-5 | 1st round | Mercantile Credit Classic |
| | v Fisher | 9-3 | 1st round | Tolly Cobbold English Championship |
| | v Hallett | 9-4 | 2nd round | Tolly Cobbold English Championship |
| | v Reynolds | 9-4 | Quarter-final | Tolly Cobbold English Championship |
| | v S. Davis | 8-9 | Semi-final | Tolly Cobbold English Championship |
| | v Foldvari | 6-0 | 1st round | Dulux British Open |
| | v Hallett | 5-4 | 2nd round | Dulux British Open |
| | v Knowles | 5-2 | 3rd round | Dulux British Open |
| | v S. Francisco | 4-5 | Quarter-final | Dulux British Open |
| | v White | 1-5 | 1st round | Benson & Hedges Irish Masters |
| | v Virgo | 10-6 | 1st round | Embassy World Championship |
| | v White | 11-13 | 2nd round | Embassy World Championship |
| | v Virgo | 5-3 | Quarter-final | Winfield Australian Masters |
| | v White | 6-3 | Semi-final | Winfield Australian Masters |
| | **v J. Campbell** | **7-2** | **Final** | **Winfield Australian Masters** |
| | v Dunning | 5-0 | 3rd round | Goya Matchroom Trophy |
| | v Parrott | 4-5 | 4th round | Goya Matchroom Trophy |
| | v T. Jones | 5-2 | 3rd round | Rothmans Grand Prix |
| | v E. Hughes | 5-3 | 4th round | Rothmans Grand Prix |
| | v Dennis Taylor | 3-5 | 5th round | Rothmans Grand Prix |
| | v Longworth | 9-5 | 3rd round | Coral UK Open |
| | v Fowler | 9-2 | 4th round | Coral UK Open |
| | v S. Davis | 5-9 | 5th round | Coral UK Open |
| **1986** | v O'Boye | 5-3 | 3rd round | Mercantile Credit Classic |
| | v West | 5-1 | 4th round | Mercantile Credit Classic |
| | v Thorburn | 1-5 | 5th round | Mercantile Credit Classic |
| | v White | 4-5 | 1st round | Benson & Hedges Masters |
| | v Scott | 9-1 | 3rd round | Tolly Cobbold English Championship |
| | v Wildman | 9-3 | 4th round | Tolly Cobbold English Championship |
| | v Reynolds | 9-4 | Quarter-final | Tolly Cobbold English Championship |
| | v S. Davis | 9-7 | Semi-final | Tolly Cobbold English Championship |
| | **v N. Foulds** | **9-7** | **Final** | **Tolly Cobbold English Championship** |
| | v Donnelly | 5-3 | 3rd round | Dulux British Open |
| | v Newbury | 5-0 | 4th round | Dulux British Open |

| | | | | |
|---|---|---|---|---|
| | v Thorburn | 5-3 | 5th round | Dulux British Open |
| | v Virgo | 3-5 | Quarter-final | Dulux British Open |
| | v Higgins | 5-4 | 1st round | Benson & Hedges Irish Masters |
| | v White | 2-5 | Quarter-final | Benson & Hedges Irish Masters |
| | v Parrott | 6-10 | 1st round | Embassy World Championship |
| | v Griffiths | 3-6 | 1st round | Matchroom Trophy |
| | v Houlihan | 5-1 | 3rd round | BCE International |
| | v Chappel | 5-1 | 3rd round | Rothmans Grand Prix |
| | v Parrott | 5-3 | 4th round | Rothmans Grand Prix |
| | v Dennis Taylor | 5-2 | 5th round | Rothmans Grand Prix |
| | v N. Foulds | 3-5 | Quarter-final | Rothmans Grand Prix |
| | v O'Boye | 9-3 | 3rd round | Tennents UK Open |
| | v Hallett | 4-9 | 4th round | Tennents UK Open |
| **1987** | v John Rea | 5-4 | 3rd round | Mercantile Credit Classic |
| | v Longworth | 5-0 | 4th round | Mercantile Credit Classic |
| | v S. Davis | 2-5 | 5th round | Mercantile Credit Classic |
| | v White | 5-4 | 1st round | Benson & Hedges Masters |
| | v Mountjoy | 5-4 | Quarter-final | Benson & Hedges Masters |
| | v Higgins | 2-6 | Semi-final | Benson & Hedges Masters |
| | v Duggan | 6-3 | 3rd round | Tolly Ales English Championship |
| | v Fowler | 6-0 | 4th round | Tolly Ales English Championship |
| | v Parrott | 6-3 | Quarter-final | Tolly Ales English Championship |
| | v Thorne | 9-3 | Semi-final | Tolly Ales English Championship |
| | **v Dodd** | **9-5** | **Final** | **Tolly Ales English Championship** |
| | v Spencer | 1-5 | 3rd round | Dulux British Open |
| | v Knowles | 5-2 | 1st round | Benson & Hedges Irish Masters |
| | v S. Davis | 2-5 | Quarter-final | Benson & Hedges Irish Masters |
| | v Parrott | 8-10 | 1st round | Embassy World Championship |
| | v Wright | 5-2 | 3rd round | Fidelity International |
| | v S. Davis | 3-5 | 4th round | Fidelity International |
| | v Newbury | 0-5 | 3rd round | Rothmans Grand Prix |
| | v S. Davis | 5-6 | 1st round | Matchroom Trophy |
| | v Watchorn | 9-1 | 3rd round | Tennents UK Open |
| | v Hallett | 5-9 | 4th round | Tennents UK Open |
| **1988** | v Morra | 5-1 | 3rd round | Mercantile Credit Classic |
| | v Higgins | 3-5 | 4th round | Mercantile Credit Classic |
| | v F. Davis | 6-3 | 3rd round | English Championship |
| | v Longworth | 6-4 | 4th round | English Championship |
| | v Reynolds | 4-6 | Quarter-final | English Championship |
| | v Gary Wilkinson | 2-5 | 3rd round | MIM Britannia British Open |
| | v Werbeniuk | 4-10 | Qualifying | Embassy World Championship |
| | v N. Gilbert | 5-1 | 3rd round | Fidelity International |
| | v Hallett | 5-3 | 4th round | Fidelity International |
| | v Chaperon | 5-4 | 5th round | Fidelity International |
| | v James | 1-5 | Quarter-final | Fidelity International |
| | v N. Foulds | 4-5 | Semi-final | Dubai Duty Free Masters |
| | v Stevens | 5-3 | 3rd round | Rothmans Grand Prix |
| | v Robidoux | 0-5 | 4th round | Rothmans Grand Prix |
| | v Gauvreau | 0-5 | 3rd round | BCE Canadian Masters |
| | v Roe | 6-9 | 3rd round | Tennents UK Open |
| **1989** | v Stevens | 5-3 | 3rd round | Mercantile Credit Classic |
| | v S. Francisco | 1-5 | 4th round | Mercantile Credit Classic |
| | v Roe | 1-5 | 3rd round | European Open |
| | v Fowler | 3-5 | 3rd round | English Championship |
| | v M. Bennett | 5-1 | 3rd round | Anglian British Open |
| | v Roscoe | 5-3 | 4th round | Anglian British Open |
| | v Hendry | 5-3 | 5th round | Anglian British Open |
| | v P. Francisco | 5-3 | Quarter-final | Anglian British Open |
| | v Hallett | 9-8 | Semi-final | Anglian British Open |
| | **v Reynolds** | **13-6** | **Final** | **Anglian British Open** |
| | v T. Jones | 10-5 | Qualifying | Embassy World Championship |
| | v Johnson | 10-5 | 1st round | Embassy World Championship |
| | v Charlton | 13-8 | 2nd round | Embassy World Championship |

| | | | | |
|---|---|---|---|---|
| | v Reynolds | 13-9 | Quarter-final | Embassy World Championship |
| | v Parrott | 7-16 | Semi-final | Embassy World Championship |
| | v Houlihan | 5-0 | 3rd round | Hong Kong Open |
| | v Higgins | 4-5 | 4th round | Hong Kong Open |
| | v John Rea | 5-2 | 3rd round | 555 Asian Open |
| | v Gary Wilkinson | 2-5 | 4th round | 555 Asian Open |
| | v M. Bennett | 2-5 | 3rd round | BCE International |
| | v Sinclair | 5-2 | 3rd round | Rothmans Grand Prix |
| | v J. Smith | 3-5 | 4th round | Rothmans Grand Prix |
| | v Robidoux | 5-9 | 3rd round | Stormseal UK Open |
| | v Reynolds | 7-9 | 1st round | Everest World Matchplay |
| **1990** | v T. Murphy | 5-2 | 3rd round | Mercantile Credit Classic |
| | v Newbury | 4-5 | 4th round | Mercantile Credit Classic |
| | v Parrott | 3-5 | 1st round | Benson and Hedges Masters |
| | v Bales | 5-2 | 3rd round | Pearl Assurance British Open |
| | v White | 0-5 | 4th round | Pearl Assurance British Open |
| | v Edwards | 4-5 | 3rd round | European Open |
| | v W. Jones | 10-8 | 1st round | Embassy World Championship |
| | v Hendry | 7-13 | 2nd round | Embassy World Championship |

## **GRAHAM MILES** (England)

**Born** 11.5.41. **Turned professional** 1969. **World ranking** 95 (78).

| | | | | |
|---|---|---|---|---|
| **1972** | v Bennett | 15-6 | Qualifying | World Championship |
| | v Dunning | 5-11 | Qualifying | World Championship |
| **1973** | v Thompson | 9-5 | 1st round | World Championship |
| | v Pulman | 16-10 | 2nd round | World Championship |
| | v Charlton | 6-16 | Quarter-final | World Championship |
| **1974** | v Morgan | 15-7 | 2nd round | World Championship |
| | v Dunning | 15-13 | Quarter-final | World Championship |
| | v Williams | 15-7 | Semi-final | World Championship |
| | v Reardon | 12-22 | Final | World Championship |
| **1975** | v Reardon | 3-5 | Quarter-final | Benson & Hedges Masters |
| | v Thorburn | 2-15 | 2nd round | World Championship |
| **1976** | v Spencer | 5-4 | Semi-final | Benson & Hedges Masters |
| | v Reardon | 3-7 | Final | Benson & Hedges Masters |
| | v Mans | 10-15 | 1st round | Embassy World Championship |
| **1977** | v Reardon | 2-5 | Semi-final | Benson & Hedges Masters |
| | v Thorne | 13-4 | 1st round | Embassy World Championship |
| | v Pulman | 10-13 | Quarter-final | Embassy World Championship |
| | v Ross | 5-1 | 2nd round | Super Crystalate UK Championship |
| | v Virgo | 2-5 | Quarter-final | Super Crystalate UK Championship |
| **1978** | v David Taylor | 13-10 | 1st round | Embassy World Championship |
| | v Mans | 7-13 | Quarter-final | Embassy World Championship |
| | v Williams | 9-8 | 1st round | Coral UK Championship |
| | v Thorne | 9-1 | Quarter-final | Coral UK Championship |
| | v Mountjoy | 1-9 | Semi-final | Coral UK Championship |
| **1979** | v Higgins | 6-3 | Semi-final | Holsten Lager International |
| | v Spencer | 7-11 | Final | Holsten Lager International |
| | v Williams | 9-5 | Qualifying | Embassy World Championship |
| | v Reardon | 8-13 | 1st round | Embassy World Championship |
| | v Fagan | 5-9 | 3rd round | Coral UK Championship |
| **1980** | v Stevens | 3-10 | 1st round | Embassy World Championship |
| | v Sinclair | 5-9 | 1st round | Coral UK Championship |
| **1981** | v Hood | 9-1 | 1st round | John Courage English |
| | v Meo | 7-9 | 2nd round | John Courage English |
| | v Knowles | 10-8 | 1st round | Embassy World Championship |
| | v Thorburn | 2-13 | 2nd round | Embassy World Championship |
| | v Johnson | 5-3 | 2nd round | Jameson International |
| | v Thorburn | 5-0 | 3rd round | Jameson International |
| | v Martin | 1-5 | Quarter-final | Jameson International |

| | | | | |
|---|---|---|---|---|
| | v Houlihan | 9-5 | 2nd round | Coral UK Championship |
| | v Griffiths | 4-9 | 3rd round | Coral UK Championship |
| **1982** | v S. Davis | 2-5 | Semi-final | Tolly Cobbold Classic |
| | v Martin | 10-5 | 1st round | Embassy World Championship |
| | v Knowles | 7-13 | 2nd round | Embassy World Championship |
| | v Edmonds | 1-5 | Qualifying | Jameson International |
| | v Johnson | 1-5 | 1st round | Professional Players Tournament |
| | v Meo | 4-9 | 1st round | Coral UK Championship |
| **1983** | v Morgan | 10-6 | Qualifying | Embassy World Championship |
| | v Knowles | 3-10 | 1st round | Embassy World Championship |
| | v King | 5-3 | Qualifying | Jameson International |
| | v Griffiths | 2-5 | 1st round | Jameson International |
| | v Gauvreau | 5-3 | 1st round | Professional Players Tournament |
| | v J. Campbell | 2-5 | 2nd round | Professional Players Tournament |
| | v Hallett | 4-9 | 1st round | Coral UK Championship |
| **1984** | v Williamson | 10-6 | Qualifying | Embassy World Championship |
| | v Spencer | 3-10 | 1st round | Embassy World Championship |
| | v Newbury | 1-5 | Qualifying | Jameson International |
| | v Murphy | 5-3 | 1st round | Rothmans Grand Prix |
| | v S. Davis | 0-5 | 2nd round | Rothmans Grand Prix |
| | v J. McLaughlin | 8-9 | Qualifying | Coral UK Open |
| **1985** | v Browne | 3-5 | Qualifying | Mercantile Credit Classic |
| | v Martin | 7-9 | 1st round | Tolly Cobbold English Championship |
| | v Edmonds | 6-1 | 1st round | Dulux British Open |
| | v Spencer | 2-5 | 2nd round | Dulux British Open |
| | v Stevens | 2-5 | 3rd round | Dulux British Open |
| | v W. Jones | 8-10 | Qualifying | Embassy World Championship |
| | v O'Boye | 5-2 | 2nd round | Goya Matchroom Trophy |
| | v Virgo | 2-5 | 3rd round | Goya Matchroom Trophy |
| | v Rigitano | 5-4 | 2nd round | Rothmans Grand Prix |
| | v Reynolds | 5-3 | 3rd round | Rothmans Grand Prix |
| | v Stevens | 2-5 | 4th round | Rothmans Grand Prix |
| | v Oliver | 9-4 | 2nd round | Coral UK Open |
| | v Reardon | 4-9 | 3rd round | Coral UK Open |
| **1986** | v Hendry | 1-5 | 2nd round | Mercantile Credit Classic |
| | v Fitzmaurice | 9-5 | 2nd round | Tolly Cobbold English Championship |
| | v Williams | 6-9 | 3rd round | Tolly Cobbold English Championship |
| | v Agrawal | 5-4 | 2nd round | Dulux British Open |
| | v Stevens | 3-5 | 3rd round | Dulux British Open |
| | v Everton | 10-3 | Qualifying | Embassy World Championship |
| | v Foldvari | 7-10 | Qualifying | Embassy World Championship |
| | v Roe | 5-1 | 2nd round | BCE International |
| | v N. Foulds | 2-5 | 3rd round | BCE International |
| | v Jonik | 5-1 | 2nd round | Rothmans Grand Prix |
| | v N. Foulds | 1-5 | 3rd round | Rothmans Grand Prix |
| | v Sheehan | 9-8 | 2nd round | Tennents UK Open |
| | v Virgo | 7-9 | 3rd round | Tennents UK Open |
| **1987** | v Sinclair | 1-5 | 2nd round | Mercantile Credit Classic |
| | v Johnson | 3-6 | 3rd round | Tolly Ales English Championship |
| | v Greaves | 10-7 | Qualifying | Embassy World Championship |
| | v Murphy | 7-10 | Qualifying | Embassy World Championship |
| | v Wildman | 3-5 | 2nd round | Fidelity International |
| | v Scott | 5-2 | 2nd round | Rothmans Grand Prix |
| | v Davis | 1-5 | 3rd round | Rothmans Grand Prix |
| | v Houlihan | 9-3 | 2nd round | Tennents UK Open |
| | v Spencer | 9-5 | 3rd round | Tennents UK Open |
| | v Fowler | 4-9 | 4th round | Tennents UK Open |
| **1988** | v M. Bennett | 1-5 | 2nd round | Mercantile Credit Classic |
| | v M. Smith | 1-6 | 1st round | English Championship |
| | v Owers | 5-3 | 2nd round | MIM Britannia British Open |
| | v Dennis Taylor | 1-5 | 3rd round | MIM Britannia British Open |
| | v D. Hughes | 10-3 | Qualifying | Embassy World Championship |
| | v Bales | 10-7 | Qualifying | Embassy World Championship |

| | | | | |
|---|---|---|---|---|
| | v Chappel | 7-10 | Qualifying | Embassy World Championship |
| | v G. Foulds | 5-3 | 2nd round | Fidelity International |
| | v Knowles | 4-5 | 3rd round | Fidelity International |
| | v Terry | 1-5 | 2nd round | Rothmans Grand Prix |
| | v Watchorn | 2-5 | 1st round | BCE Canadian Masters |
| | v Watchorn | 9-6 | 1st round | Tennents UK Open |
| | v Martin | 7-9 | 2nd round | Tennents UK Open |
| **1989** | v Mikkelsen | 5-3 | 1st round | Mercantile Credit Classic |
| | v Gauvreau | 5-3 | 2nd round | Mercantile Credit Classic |
| | v E. Hughes | 2-5 | 3rd round | Mercantile Credit Classic |
| | v Jenkins | 5-3 | 1st round | European Open |
| | v King | 2-5 | 2nd round | European Open |
| | v M. Smith | 5-4 | 1st round | English Championship |
| | v M. Fisher | 5-4 | 2nd round | English Championship |
| | v Parrott | 3-5 | 3rd round | English Championship |
| | v Chalmers | 5-4 | 1st round | Anglian British Open |
| | v Gary Wilkinson | 2-5 | 2nd round | Anglian British Open |
| | v Robidoux | 8-10 | Qualifying | Embassy World Championship |
| | v Brumby | 3-5 | 1st round | Hong Kong Open |
| | v Watchorn | 5-3 | 1st round | 555 Asian Open |
| | v Bales | 5-4 | 2nd round | 555 Asian Open |
| | v Knowles | 3-5 | 3rd round | 555 Asian Open |
| | v B. Morgan | 0-5 | 1st round | BCE International |
| | v Rigitano | 3-5 | 1st round | Rothmans Grand Prix |
| | v Watchorn | 5-3 | 1st round | Dubai Classic |
| | v Edwards | 5-4 | 2nd round | Dubai Classic |
| | v Mountjoy | 2-5 | 3rd round | Dubai Classic |
| | v Cairns | 2-6 | 1st round | Stormseal UK Open |
| **1990** | v M. Gibson | 5-3 | 1st round | Mercantile Credit Classic |
| | v Chambers | 3-5 | 2nd round | Mercantile Credit Classic |
| | v Dyson | 5-3 | 1st round | Pearl Assurance British Open |
| | v Cripsey | 5-2 | 2nd round | Pearl Assurance British Open |
| | v Hallett | 1-5 | 3rd round | Pearl Assurance British Open |
| | v Darrington | 5-2 | 1st round | European Open |
| | v O'Boye | 1-5 | 2nd round | European Open |
| | v D. Hughes | 10-5 | Qualifying | Embassy World Championship |
| | v Bales | 10-7 | Qualifying | Embassy World Championship |
| | v Chambers | 5-10 | Qualifying | Embassy World Championship |

## BRIAN MORGAN (England)

**Born** 16.7.68. **Turned professional** 1989. **World ranking** 43.

| | | | | |
|---|---|---|---|---|
| **1989** | v Scott | 5-1 | 1st round | Hong Kong Open |
| | v Chappel | 5-3 | 2nd round | Hong Kong Open |
| | v David Taylor | 5-4 | 3rd round | Hong Kong Open |
| | v Dodd | 2-5 | 4th round | Hong Kong Open |
| | v B. Harris | 3-5 | 1st round | 555 Asian Open |
| | v Miles | 5-0 | 1st round | BCE International |
| | v Fowler | 5-4 | 2nd round | BCE International |
| | v Johnson | 5-2 | 3rd round | BCE International |
| | v E. Hughes | 5-3 | 4th round | BCE International |
| | v Dennis Taylor | 5-4 | 5th round | BCE International |
| | v S. Davis | 2-5 | Quarter-final | BCE International |
| | v B. Harris | 2-5 | 1st round | Rothmans Grand Prix |
| | v Darrington | 2-5 | 1st round | Dubai Classic |
| | v V. Harris | 6-3 | 1st round | Stormseal UK Open |
| | v Cripsey | 6-2 | 2nd round | Stormseal UK Open |
| | v James | 9-4 | 3rd round | Stormseal UK Open |
| | v Gary Wilkinson | 6-9 | 4th round | Stormseal UK Open |
| **1990** | v F. Davis | 5-0 | 1st round | Mercantile Credit Classic |
| | v Bales | 5-3 | 2nd round | Mercantile Credit Classic |

| | | | | |
|---|---|---|---|---|
| | v E. Hughes | 5-1 | 3rd round | Mercantile Credit Classic |
| | v David Taylor | 5-4 | 4th round | Mercantile Credit Classic |
| | v D. Morgan | 5-1 | 5th round | Mercantile Credit Classic |
| | v S. Davis | 1-5 | Quarter-final | Mercantile Credit Classic |
| | v Scott | 5-1 | 1st round | Pearl Assurance British Open |
| | v Longworth | 3-5 | 2nd round | Pearl Assurance British Open |
| | v Edwards | 2-5 | 1st round | European Open |
| | v Heaton | 10-1 | Qualifying | Embassy World Championship |
| | v Williamson | 10-4 | Qualifying | Embassy World Championship |
| | v O'Boye | 10-2 | Qualifying | Embassy World Championship |
| | v Gollan | 6-10 | Qualifying | Embassy World Championship |

## DARREN MORGAN (Wales)

**Born** 3.5.66. **Turned professional** 1988. **World ranking** 41 (53).

| | | | | |
|---|---|---|---|---|
| **1988** | v Hendry | 2-5 | 1st round | New Zealand Masters |
| | v M. Smith | 3-5 | 1st round | Fidelity International |
| | v Rowswell | 5-0 | 1st round | Rothmans Grand Prix |
| | v Gary Wilkinson | 1-5 | 2nd round | Rothmans Grand Prix |
| | v F. Davis | 5-2 | 1st round | BCE Canadian Masters |
| | v T. Jones | 5-0 | 2nd round | BCE Canadian Masters |
| | v O'Kane | 5-3 | 3rd round | BCE Canadian Masters |
| | v Parrott | 3-5 | 4th round | BCE Canadian Masters |
| | v Reardon | 5-9 | 2nd round | Tennents UK Open |
| **1989** | v V. Harris | 5-3 | 1st round | Mercantile Credit Classic |
| | v Clark | 1-5 | 2nd round | Mercantile Credit Classic |
| | v Wildman | 5-1 | 1st round | European Open |
| | v Duggan | 4-5 | 2nd round | European Open |
| | v Chappel | 6-5 | 1st round | Senator Welsh Championship |
| | v Griffiths | 5-6 | Quarter-final | Senator Welsh Championship |
| | v Glen Wilkinson | 5-0 | 1st round | Anglian British Open |
| | v J. McLaughlin | 5-0 | 2nd round | Anglian British Open |
| | v Charlton | 5-3 | 3rd round | Anglian British Open |
| | v Thorburn | 4-5 | 4th round | Anglian British Open |
| | v Frangie | 10-5 | Qualifying | Embassy World Championship |
| | v Lawlor | 10-2 | Qualifying | Embassy World Championship |
| | v J. Campbell | 10-4 | Qualifying | Embassy World Championship |
| | v Owers | 10-8 | Qualifying | Embassy World Championship |
| | v Higgins | 10-8 | Qualifying | Embassy World Championship |
| | v Virgo | 4-10 | 1st round | Embassy World Championship |
| | v Bond | 2-5 | 2nd round | Hong Kong Open |
| | v T. Wilson | 5-2 | 2nd round | 555 Asian Open |
| | v Roe | 2-5 | 3rd round | 555 Asian Open |
| | v Whitthread | 5-0 | 2nd round | BCE International |
| | v E. Hughes | 4-5 | 3rd round | BCE International |
| | v Lawlor | 5-3 | 2nd round | Rothmans Grand Prix |
| | v Johnson | 2-5 | 3rd round | Rothmans Grand Prix |
| | v Houlihan | 5-2 | 2nd round | Dubai Classic |
| | v West | 1-5 | 3rd round | Dubai Classic |
| | v S. Campbell | 5-6 | 2nd round | Stormseal UK Open |
| **1990** | v Wattana | 5-1 | 2nd round | Mercantile Credit Classic |
| | v N. Foulds | 5-4 | 3rd round | Mercantile Credit Classic |
| | v Thorburn | 5-4 | 4th round | Mercantile Credit Classic |
| | v B. Morgan | 1-5 | 5th round | Mercantile Credit Classic |
| | v Roscoe | 6-4 | 1st round | Senator Welsh Championship |
| | v Griffiths | 6-4 | Quarter-final | Senator Welsh Championship |
| | v Chappel | 9-8 | Semi-final | Senator Welsh Championship |
| | **v Mountjoy** | **9-7** | **Final** | **Senator Welsh Championship** |
| | v A. Harris | 5-3 | 2nd round | Pearl Assurance British Open |
| | v Hendry | 5-4 | 3rd round | Pearl Assurance British Open |
| | v S. Davis | 4-5 | 4th round | Pearl Assurance British Open |

| | | | |
|---|---|---|---|
| v Rowswell | 5-2 | 2nd round | European Open |
| v Reynolds | 3-5 | 3rd round | European Open |
| v M. Smith | 10-6 | Qualifying | Embassy World Championship |
| v John Rea | 10-7 | Qualifying | Embassy World Championship |
| v Chaperon | 10-9 | Qualifying | Embassy World Championship |
| v Johnson | 10-8 | 1st round | Embassy World Championship |
| v Hallett | 13-8 | 2nd round | Embassy World Championship |
| v Hendry | 6-13 | Quarter-final | Embassy World Championship |

## MARIO MORRA (Canada)

**Born** 8.9.53. **Turned professional** 1979. **World ranking** 82 (86).

| | | | | |
|---|---|---|---|---|
| **1981** | v Thorne | 5-9 | Qualifying | Embassy World Championship |
| | v Wildman | 3-5 | Qualifying | Jameson International |
| **1982** | v Murphy | 9-5 | Qualifying | Embassy World Championship |
| | v Fitzmaurice | 7-9 | Qualifying | Embassy World Championship |
| | v Demarco | 5-2 | Qualifying | Jameson International |
| | v Reynolds | 1-5 | Qualifying | Jameson International |
| | v Wilson | 2-5 | 1st round | Professional Players Tournament |
| **1983** | v Black | 9-10 | Qualifying | Embassy World Championship |
| | v Jim Bear | 8-9 | 2nd round | Canadian Championship |
| | v Watchorn | 5-3 | Qualifying | Jameson International |
| | v Hallett | 5-3 | Qualifying | Jameson International |
| | v White | 5-3 | 1st round | Jameson International |
| | v Charlton | 3-5 | 2nd round | Jameson International |
| | v Hargreaves | 5-0 | Qualifying | Professional Players Tournament |
| | v S. Francisco | 3-5 | 1st round | Professional Players Tournament |
| | v Burke | 5-2 | Qualifying | Lada Classic |
| | v Everton | 5-0 | Qualifying | Lada Classic |
| | v S. Francisco | 1-5 | Qualifying | Lada Classic |
| **1984** | v G. Foulds | 10-2 | Qualifying | Embassy World Championship |
| | v Murphy | 10-5 | Qualifying | Embassy World Championship |
| | v Reynolds | 10-7 | Qualifying | Embassy World Championship |
| | v Thorburn | 3-10 | 1st round | Embassy World Championship |
| | v Bradley | 5-3 | Qualifying | Jameson International |
| | v Johnson | 0-5 | Qualifying | Jameson International |
| | v Cripsey | 5-3 | Qualifying | Rothmans Grand Prix |
| | v S. Davis | 2-5 | 1st round | Rothmans Grand Prix |
| | v Longworth | 9-1 | Qualifying | Coral UK Open |
| | v E. Hughes | 8-9 | Qualifying | Coral UK Open |
| **1985** | v Newbury | 2-5 | Qualifying | Mercantile Credit Classic |
| | v Bradley | 2-6 | Qualifying | Dulux British Open |
| | v Browne | 10-6 | Qualifying | Embassy World Championship |
| | v J. Campbell | 9-10 | Qualifying | Embassy World Championship |
| | v John Bear | 4-5 | 1st round | Canadian Championship |
| | v Oliver | 5-1 | 2nd round | Goya Matchroom Trophy |
| | v J. Campbell | 2-5 | 3rd round | Goya Matchroom Trophy |
| | v D. Hughes | 5-2 | 2nd round | Rothmans Grand Prix |
| | v Martin | 2-5 | 3rd round | Rothmans Grand Prix |
| | v Agrawal | 9-8 | 2nd round | Coral UK Open |
| | v Mountjoy | 2-9 | 3rd round | Coral UK Open |
| **1986** | v B. Harris | 3-5 | 2nd round | Mercantile Credit Classic |
| | v Gilbert | 4-5 | 2nd round | Dulux British Open |
| | v Gibson | 9-10 | Qualifying | Embassy World Championship |
| | v Thornley | 4-6 | 1st round | Canadian Championship |
| | v Ellis | 5-3 | 1st round | BCE International |
| | v Drago | 3-5 | 2nd round | BCE International |
| | v James | 5-3 | 1st round | Rothmans Grand Prix |
| | v Black | 5-4 | 2nd round | Rothmans Grand Prix |
| | v Griffiths | 3-5 | 3rd round | Rothmans Grand Prix |
| | v B. Bennett | 9-3 | 1st round | Tennents UK Open |

| | | | | |
|---|---|---|---|---|
| | v Drago | 6-9 | 2nd round | Tennents UK Open |
| **1987** | v Ellis | 5-1 | 1st round | Mercantile Credit Classic |
| | v Mans | 5-0 | 2nd round | Mercantile Credit Classic |
| | v Williams | 2-5 | 3rd round | Mercantile Credit Classic |
| | v M. Bennett | 5-4 | 1st round | Dulux British Open |
| | v Van Rensberg | 5-1 | 2nd round | Dulux British Open |
| | v Virgo | 3-5 | 3rd round | Dulux British Open |
| | v P. Gibson | 10-6 | Qualifying | Embassy World Championship |
| | v Chappel | 8-10 | Qualifying | Embassy World Championship |
| | v Chaperon | 6-5 | 1st round | Canadian Championship |
| | v Jonik | 6-2 | Quarter-final | Canadian Championship |
| | v Thorburn | 4-7 | Semi-final | Canadian Championship |
| | v Hargreaves | 5-4 | 1st round | Fidelity International |
| | v Dodd | 5-3 | 2nd round | Fidelity International |
| | v David Taylor | 3-5 | 3rd round | Fidelity International |
| | v Meakin | 2-5 | 1st round | Rothmans Grand Prix |
| | v A. Harris | 8-9 | 1st round | Tennents UK Open |
| **1988** | v Marshall | 5-0 | 1st round | Mercantile Credit Classic |
| | v Gauvreau | 5-4 | 2nd round | Mercantile Credit Classic |
| | v Meo | 1-5 | 3rd round | Mercantile Credit Classic |
| | v Watchorn | 5-1 | 1st round | MIM Britannia British Open |
| | v M. Bennett | 5-2 | 2nd round | MIM Britannia British Open |
| | v Griffiths | 1-5 | 3rd round | MIM Britannia British Open |
| | v Meakin | 10-5 | Qualifying | Embassy World Championship |
| | v Edmonds | 10-8 | Qualifying | Embassy World Championship |
| | v W. Jones | 8-10 | Qualifying | Embassy World Championship |
| | v Watson | 6-2 | 1st round | BCE Canadian Championship |
| | v Wych | 4-6 | Quarter-final | BCE Canadian Championship |
| | v Everton | 5-2 | 1st round | Fidelity International |
| | v King | 4-5 | 2nd round | Fidelity International |
| | v Reardon | 5-4 | 2nd round | Rothmans Grand Prix |
| | v Parrott | 3-5 | 3rd round | Rothmans Grand Prix |
| | v A. Harris | 3-5 | 1st round | BCE Canadian Masters |
| | v D. Hughes | 9-2 | 1st round | Tennents UK Open |
| | v Duggan | 8-9 | 2nd round | Tennents UK Open |
| **1989** | v Darrington | 2-5 | 1st round | Mercantile Credit Classic |
| | v S. Campbell | 5-3 | 1st round | European Open |
| | v N. Gilbert | 5-1 | 2nd round | European Open |
| | v E. Hughes | 1-5 | 3rd round | European Open |
| | v Rempe | 1-5 | 1st round | Anglian British Open |
| | v Mikkelsen | 10-4 | Qualifying | Embassy World Championship |
| | v Clark | 6-10 | Qualifying | Embassy World Championship |
| | v Kelly | 2-5 | 1st round | Hong Kong Open |
| | v Ellis | 5-3 | 1st round | 555 Asian Open |
| | v M. Bennett | 1-5 | 2nd round | 555 Asian Open |
| | v Kelly | 3-5 | 1st round | BCE International |
| | v Cairns | 5-4 | 1st round | Rothmans Grand Prix |
| | v Graham | 5-0 | 2nd round | Rothmans Grand Prix |
| | v W. Jones | 5-4 | 3rd round | Rothmans Grand Prix |
| | v Mountjoy | 0-5 | 4th round | Rothmans Grand Prix |
| | v Mikkelsen | 5-2 | 1st round | Dubai Classic |
| | v N. Gilbert | 5-4 | 2nd round | Dubai Classic |
| | v Robidoux | 1-5 | 3rd round | Dubai Classic |
| | v Rigitano | 6-4 | 1st round | Stormseal UK Open |
| | v T. Jones | 3-6 | 2nd round | Stormseal UK Open |
| **1990** | v Thornley | 5-3 | 1st round | Mercantile Credit Classic |
| | v King | 3-5 | 2nd round | Mercantile Credit Classic |
| | v Fitzmaurice | 2-5 | 1st round | Pearl Assurance British Open |
| | v J. Smith | 5-4 | 1st round | European Open |
| | v J. McLaughlin | 0-5 | 2nd round | European Open |
| | v Van Rensberg | *wo* | Qualifying | Embassy World Championship |
| | v Chappel | 8-10 | Qualifying | Embassy World Championship |

## DOUG MOUNTJOY (Wales)

**Born** 8.6.42. **Turned professional** 1976. **World ranking** 5 (10).

| | | | | |
|---|---|---|---|---|
| **1977** | v Higgins | 5-3 | Semi-final | Benson & Hedges Masters |
| | **v Reardon** | **7-6** | **Final** | **Benson & Hedges Masters** |
| | v Jack Rea | 11-9 | Qualifying | Embassy World Championship |
| | v Higgins | 13-12 | 1st round | Embassy World Championship |
| | v Dennis Taylor | 11-13 | Quarter-final | Embassy World Championship |
| | v Andrewartha | 5-2 | 1st round | Super Crystalate UK Championship |
| | v Spencer | 5-3 | 2nd round | Super Crystalate UK Championship |
| | v Thorne | 5-4 | Quarter-final | Super Crystalate UK Championship |
| | v Higgins | 9-2 | Semi-final | Super Crystalate UK Championship |
| | v Fagan | 9-12 | Final | Super Crystalate UK Championship |
| **1978** | v Spencer | 3-5 | Final | Benson & Hedges Irish Masters |
| | v Andrewartha | 9-3 | Qualifying | Embassy World Championship |
| | v Reardon | 9-13 | 1st round | Embassy World Championship |
| | v Barrie | 9-5 | Qualifying | Coral UK Championship |
| | v Dennis Taylor | 9-4 | 1st round | Coral UK Championship |
| | v Andrewartha | 9-4 | Quarter-final | Coral UK Championship |
| | v Miles | 9-1 | Semi-final | Coral UK Championship |
| | **v David Taylor** | **15-9** | **Final** | **Coral UK Championship** |
| **1979** | v F. Davis | 5-2 | 1st round | Benson & Hedges Masters |
| | v Spencer | 5-0 | Quarter-final | Benson & Hedges Masters |
| | v Higgins | 1-5 | Semi-final | Benson & Hedges Masters |
| | **v Reardon** | **6-5** | **Final** | **Benson & Hedges Irish Masters** |
| | v Mienie | 9-1 | Prelim | Embassy World Championship |
| | v Houlihan | 9-6 | Qualifying | Embassy World Championship |
| | v Charlton | 6-13 | 1st round | Embassy World Championship |
| | v S. Davis | 5-9 | 3rd round | Coral UK Championship |
| | v Griffiths | 9-6 | 1st round | Woodpecker Welsh Championship |
| | **v Reardon** | **9-6** | **Final** | **Woodpecker Welsh Championship** |
| **1980** | v Griffiths | 8-9 | Final | Benson & Hedges Irish Masters |
| | v Wilson | 10-6 | 1st round | Embassy World Championship |
| | v Thorburn | 10-13 | 2nd round | Embassy World Championship |
| | v Williams | 8-9 | 1st round | Coral UK Championship |
| **1981** | v Charlton | 5-0 | 1st round | Benson & Hedges Masters |
| | v Higgins | 1-5 | Quarter-final | Benson & Hedges Masters |
| | v Wilson | 6-9 | Semi-final | Woodpecker Welsh Championship |
| | v Thorne | 10-6 | 1st round | Embassy World Championship |
| | v Charlton | 13-7 | 2nd round | Embassy World Championship |
| | v Dennis Taylor | 13-8 | Quarter-final | Embassy World Championship |
| | v Reardon | 16-10 | Semi-final | Embassy World Championship |
| | v S. Davis | 12-18 | Final | Embassy World Championship |
| | v S. Davis | 0-5 | Quarter-final | Langs Supreme Scottish Masters |
| | v Higgins | 1-5 | 3rd round | Jameson International |
| | v Dennis Taylor | 5-4 | 1st round | Northern Ireland Classic |
| | v White | 8-9 | Semi-final | Northern Ireland Classic |
| | v Knowles | 6-9 | 3rd round | Coral UK Championship |
| **1982** | v Spencer | 5-4 | 1st round | Benson & Hedges Masters |
| | v S. Davis | 2-5 | Quarter-final | Benson & Hedges Masters |
| | v Andrewartha | 6-3 | 1st round | Welsh Championship |
| | v Reardon | 9-7 | Semi-final | Welsh Championship |
| | **v Griffiths** | **9-8** | **Final** | **Welsh Championship** |
| | v E. Hughes | 5-4 | 1st round | Benson & Hedges Irish Masters |
| | v S. Davis | 2-5 | Quarter-final | Benson & Hedges Irish Masters |
| | v Williams | 10-3 | 1st round | Embassy World Championship |
| | v Higgins | 12-13 | 2nd round | Embassy World Championship |
| | v Wilson | 4-5 | 1st round | Jameson International |
| | v Jonik | 3-5 | 1st round | Professional Players Tournament |
| | v Houlihan | 9-3 | 1st round | Coral UK Championship |
| | v Virgo | 5-9 | 2nd round | Coral UK Championship |

| | | | | |
|---|---|---|---|---|
| **1983** | v Griffiths | 5-1 | 1st round | Lada Classic |
| | v Werbeniuk | 2-5 | Quarter-final | Lada Classic |
| | v Virgo | 5-1 | 1st round | Benson & Hedges Masters |
| | v S. Davis | 5-4 | Quarter-final | Benson & Hedges Masters |
| | v Reardon | 3-6 | Semi-final | Benson & Hedges Masters |
| | v M. Owen | 6-0 | Quarter-final | Woodpecker Welsh Championship |
| | v Wilson | 9-3 | Semi-final | Woodpecker Welsh Championship |
| | v Reardon | 1-9 | Final | Woodpecker Welsh Championship |
| | v Knowles | 5-1 | 1st round | Benson & Hedges Irish Masters |
| | v Griffiths | 4-5 | Quarter-final | Benson & Hedges Irish Masters |
| | v Wilson | 10-2 | 1st round | Embassy World Championship |
| | v Meo | 11-13 | 2nd round | Embassy World Championship |
| | v Wildman | 5-4 | 1st round | Jameson International |
| | v Martin | 5-0 | 2nd round | Jameson International |
| | v Thorburn | 2-5 | Quarter-final | Jameson International |
| | v J. Campbell | 3-5 | 1st round | Professional Players Tournament |
| | v Watterson | 9-2 | 1st round | Coral UK Championship |
| | v Knowles | 5-9 | 2nd round | Coral UK Championship |
| **1984** | v Parrott | 4-5 | Qualifying | Lada Classic |
| | v Higgins | 2-5 | 1st round | Benson & Hedges Masters |
| | v Everton | 6-1 | 1st round | Strongbow Welsh Championship |
| | v Griffiths | 9 5 | Semi-final | Strongbow Welsh Championship |
| | **v Wilson** | **9-3** | **Final** | **Strongbow Welsh Championship** |
| | v Hallett | 10-4 | 1st round | Embassy World Championship |
| | v N. Foulds | 13-6 | 2nd round | Embassy World Championship |
| | v Dennis Taylor | 8-13 | Quarter-final | Embassy World Championship |
| | v E. Hughes | 1-5 | 1st round | Jameson International |
| | v E. McLaughlin | 5-4 | 1st round | Rothmans Grand Prix |
| | v Wildman | 5-0 | 2nd round | Rothmans Grand Prix |
| | v Charlton | 5-4 | 3rd round | Rothmans Grand Prix |
| | v Thorburn | 3-5 | Quarter-final | Rothmans Grand Prix |
| | v Hallett | 9-2 | 1st round | Coral UK Open |
| | v White | 2-9 | 2nd round | Coral UK Open |
| **1985** | v Wilson | 4-5 | 1st round | Mercantile Credit Classic |
| | v Knowles | 5-3 | 1st round | Benson & Hedges Masters |
| | v Meo | 5-4 | Quarter-final | Benson & Hedges Masters |
| | v Griffiths | 6-2 | Semi-final | Benson & Hedges Masters |
| | v Thorburn | 6-9 | Final | Benson & Hedges Masters |
| | v V. Harris | 5-6 | 1st round | Dulux British Open |
| | v Macleod | 10-5 | 1st round | Embassy World Championship |
| | v Knowles | 6-13 | 2nd round | Embassy World Championship |
| | v Newbury | 6-5 | Quarter-final | BCE Welsh Championship |
| | v Wilson | 9-2 | Semi-final | BCE Welsh Championship |
| | v Griffiths | 4-9 | Final | BCE Welsh Championship |
| | v Wych | 5-1 | 3rd round | Goya Matchroom Trophy |
| | v J. Campbell | 1-5 | 4th round | Goya Matchroom Trophy |
| | v Chappel | 5-1 | 3rd round | Rothmans Grand Prix |
| | v J. Campbell | 2-5 | 4th round | Rothmans Grand Prix |
| | v Morra | 9-2 | 3rd round | Coral UK Open |
| | v West | 4-9 | 4th round | Coral UK Open |
| **1986** | v King | 5-4 | 3rd round | Mercantile Credit Classic |
| | v O'Kane | 5-3 | 4th round | Mercantile Credit Classic |
| | v Werbeniuk | 5-3 | 5th round | Mercantile Credit Classic |
| | v N. Foulds | 5-3 | Quarter-final | Mercantile Credit Classic |
| | v Thorburn | 6-9 | Semi-final | Mercantile Credit Classic |
| | v Dennis Taylor | 2-5 | 1st round | Benson & Hedges Masters |
| | v Roscoe | 6-4 | Quarter-final | Zetters Welsh Championship |
| | v W. Jones | 9-7 | Semi-final | Zetters Welsh Championship |
| | v Griffiths | 3-9 | Final | Zetters Welsh Championship |
| | v Fagan | 1-5 | 3rd round | Dulux British Open |
| | v Mans | 10-3 | 1st round | Embassy World Championship |
| | v S. Davis | 5-13 | 2nd round | Embassy World Championship |
| | v M. Gibson | 5-3 | 3rd round | BCE International |

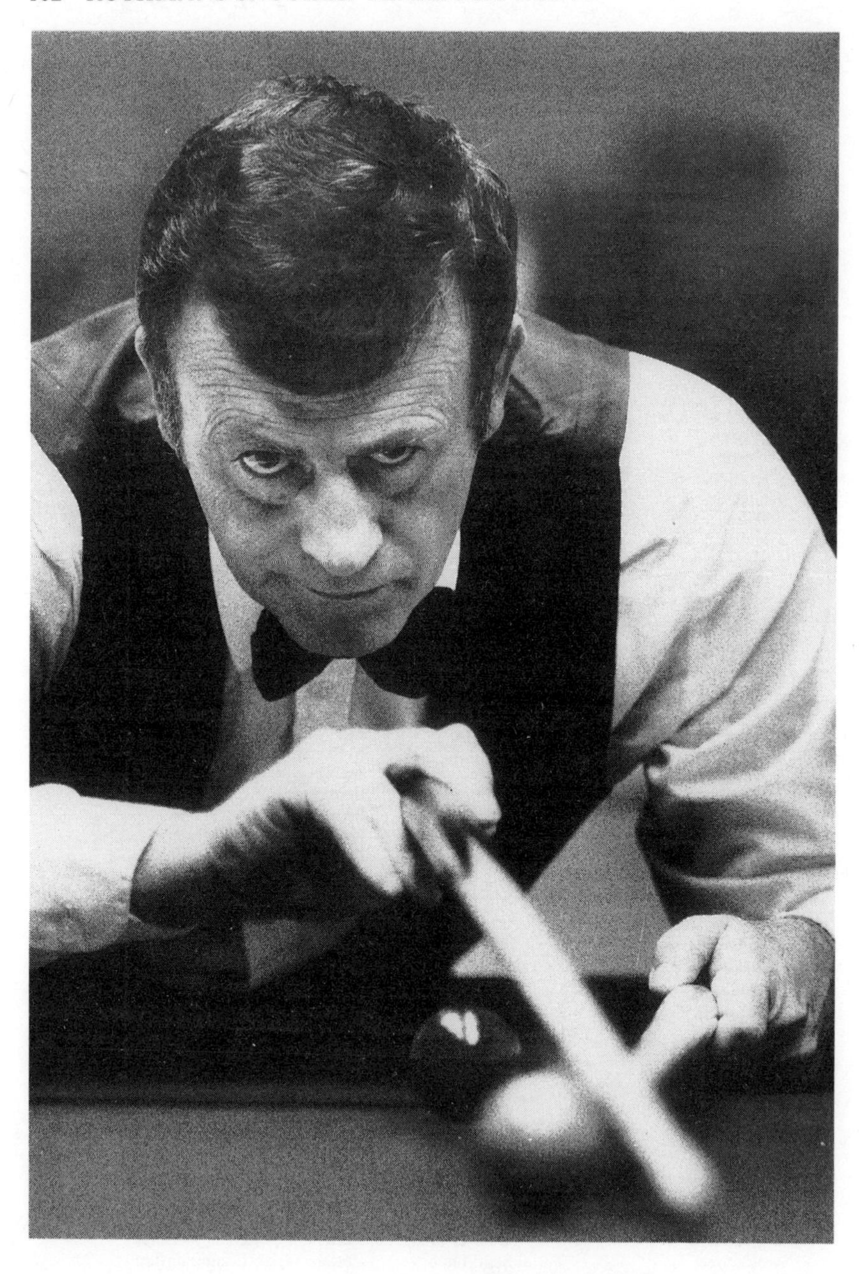

*Doug Mountjoy*

| | | | | |
|---|---|---|---|---|
| | v Reynolds | 2-5 | 4th round | BCE International |
| | v B. Harris | 5-2 | 3rd round | Rothmans Grand Prix |
| | v Wych | 5-1 | 4th round | Rothmans Grand Prix |
| | v Knowles | 1-5 | 5th round | Rothmans Grand Prix |
| | v J. McLaughlin | 9-6 | 3rd round | Tennents UK Open |
| | v Longworth | 1-9 | 4th round | Tennents UK Open |
| **1987** | v Dodd | 4-5 | 3rd round | Mercantile Credit Classic |
| | v S. Davis | 2-5 | 1st round | Benson & Hedges Masters |
| | v Meo | 4-5 | Quarter-final | Benson & Hedges Masters |
| | v Roscoe | 6-2 | Quarter-final | Matchroom Welsh Championship |
| | v Chappel | 9-2 | Semi-final | Matchroom Welsh Championship |
| | **v Newbury** | **9-7** | **Final** | **Matchroom Welsh Championship** |
| | v Owers | 5-3 | 3rd round | Dulux British Open |
| | v P. Francisco | 5-3 | 4th round | Dulux British Open |
| | v Thorburn | 4-5 | 5th round | Dulux British Open |
| | v David Taylor | 10-5 | 1st round | Embassy World Championship |
| | v O'Kane | 5-13 | 2nd round | Embassy World Championship |
| | v Roe | 4-5 | 3rd round | Fidelity International |
| | v Chambers | 2-5 | 3rd round | Rothmans Grand Prix |
| | v M. Smith | 7-9 | 3rd round | Tennents UK Open |
| **1988** | v F. Davis | 5-0 | 3rd round | Mercantile Credit Classic |
| | v Martin | 4-5 | 4th round | Mercantile Credit Classic |
| | v White | 0-5 | 1st round | Benson & Hedges Masters |
| | v M. Bennett | 6-3 | Quarter-final | Welsh Championship |
| | v W. Jones | 5-9 | Semi-final | Welsh Championship |
| | v O'Kane | 3-5 | 3rd round | MIM Britannia British Open |
| | v West | 10-6 | 1st round | Embassy World Championship |
| | v N. Foulds | 1-13 | 2nd round | Embassy World Championship |
| | v Martin | 5-1 | 3rd round | Fidelity International |
| | v Johnson | 4-5 | 4th round | Fidelity International |
| | v Fisher | 5-1 | 3rd round | Rothmans Grand Prix |
| | v Hendry | 5-1 | 4th round | Rothmans Grand Prix |
| | v Robidoux | 4-5 | 5th round | Rothmans Grand Prix |
| | v Price | 5-2 | 3rd round | BCE Canadian Masters |
| | v Thorne | 5-4 | 4th round | BCE Canadian Masters |
| | v Griffiths | 4-5 | 5th round | BCE Canadian Masters |
| | v W. Jones | 9-7 | 3rd round | Tennents UK Open |
| | v N. Foulds | 9-4 | 4th round | Tennents UK Open |
| | v Johnson | 9-5 | 5th round | Tennents UK Open |
| | v Virgo | 9-8 | Quarter-final | Tennents UK Open |
| | v Griffiths | 9-4 | Semi-final | Tennents UK Open |
| | **v Hendry** | **16-12** | **Final** | **Tennents UK Open** |
| **1989** | v D. Hughes | 5-0 | 3rd round | Mercantile Credit Classic |
| | v Terry | 5-4 | 4th round | Mercantile Credit Classic |
| | v Knowles | 5-4 | 5th round | Mercantile Credit Classic |
| | v Browne | 5-3 | Quarter-final | Mercantile Credit Classic |
| | v Thorburn | 9-5 | Semi-final | Mercantile Credit Classic |
| | **v W. Jones** | **13-11** | **Final** | **Mercantile Credit Classic** |
| | v Murphy | 5-1 | 3rd round | European Open |
| | v Dennis Taylor | 5-3 | 4th round | European Open |
| | v Thorburn | 0-5 | 5th round | European Open |
| | v Reardon | 6-3 | Quarter-final | Senator Welsh Championship |
| | v M. Bennett | 9-5 | Semi-final | Senator Welsh Championship |
| | **v Griffiths** | **9-6** | **Final** | **Senator Welsh Championship** |
| | v Gauvreau | 5-0 | 3rd round | Anglian British Open |
| | v Macleod | 5-0 | 4th round | Anglian British Open |
| | v Parrott | 2-5 | 5th round | Anglian British Open |
| | v D. Gilbert | 10-7 | Qualifying | Embassy World Championship |
| | v Hallett | 7-10 | 1st round | Embassy World Championship |
| | v Bales | 5-0 | 3rd round | Hong Kong Open |
| | v C. Wilson | *wo* | 4th round | Hong Kong Open |
| | v White | 3-5 | 5th round | Hong Kong Open |
| | v J. McLaughlin | 5-3 | 3rd round | 555 Asian Open |

| | | | | |
|---|---|---|---|---|
| | v E. Hughes | 5-4 | 4th round | 555 Asian Open |
| | v Wattana | 2-5 | 5th round | 555 Asian Open |
| | v Robidoux | 4-5 | 3rd round | BCE International |
| | v Wych | *wo* | 3rd round | Rothmans Grand Prix |
| | v Morra | 5-0 | 4th round | Rothmans Grand Prix |
| | v Hendry | 5-3 | 5th round | Rothmans Grand Prix |
| | v Wattana | 2-5 | Quarter-final | Rothmans Grand Prix |
| | v Miles | 5-2 | 3rd round | Dubai Classic |
| | v King | 5-2 | 4th round | Dubai Classic |
| | v Roe | 5-4 | 5th round | Dubai Classic |
| | v Higgins | 5-2 | Quarter-final | Dubai Classic |
| | v Parrott | 5-4 | Semi-final | Dubai Classic |
| | v Hendry | 2-9 | Final | Dubai Classic |
| | v O'Boye | 8-9 | 3rd round | Stormseal UK Open |
| | v Thorne | 9-2 | 1st round | Everest World Matchplay |
| | v White | 5-9 | Quarter-final | Everest World Matchplay |
| **1990** | v Duggan | 4-5 | 3rd round | Mercantile Credit Classic |
| | v Thorburn | 5-4 | 1st round | Benson and Hedges Masters |
| | v S. Davis | 0-5 | Quarter-final | Benson and Hedges Masters |
| | v Reardon | 6-3 | Quarter-final | Senator Welsh Championship |
| | v W. Jones | 9-7 | Semi-final | Senator Welsh Championship |
| | v D. Morgan | 7-9 | Final | Senator Welsh Championship |
| | v Terry | 5-3 | 3rd round | Pearl Assurance British Open |
| | v Reynolds | 5-2 | 4th round | Pearl Assurance British Open |
| | v Higgins | 3-5 | 5th round | Pearl Assurance British Open |
| | v Chambers | 5-4 | 3rd round | European Open |
| | v Williams | 5-0 | 4th round | European Open |
| | v Charlton | 5-2 | 5th round | European Open |
| | v S. Davis | 0-5 | Quarter-final | European Open |
| | v Griffiths | 1-5 | 1st round | Benson and Hedges Irish Masters |
| | v Gollan | 10-8 | 1st round | Embassy World Championship |
| | v Thorburn | 12-13 | 2nd round | Embassy World Championship |

## STEPHEN MURPHY (Republic of Ireland)

**Born** 23.9.69. **Turned professional** 1989. **World ranking** 98.

| | | | | |
|---|---|---|---|---|
| **1989** | v Dunning | 3-5 | 1st round | Hong Kong Open |
| | v Gauvreau | 4-5 | 1st round | 555 Asian Open |
| | v Price | 5-4 | 1st round | BCE International |
| | v Wych | 4-5 | 2nd round | BCE International |
| | v Edwards | 5-4 | 1st round | Rothmans Grand Prix |
| | v Browne | 5-3 | 2nd round | Rothmans Grand Prix |
| | v Parrott | 1-5 | 3rd round | Rothmans Grand Prix |
| | v M. Smith | 1-5 | 1st round | Dubai Classic |
| | v Glen Wilkinson | 6-1 | 1st round | Stormseal UK Open |
| | v Chappel | 1-6 | 2nd round | Stormseal UK Open |
| **1990** | v T. Wilson | 5-1 | 1st round | Mercantile Credit Classic |
| | v O'Boye | 5-0 | 2nd round | Mercantile Credit Classic |
| | v Hallett | 1-5 | 3rd round | Mercantile Credit Classic |
| | v Foldvari | 5-3 | 1st round | Pearl Assurance British Open |
| | v O'Boye | 5-3 | 2nd round | Pearl Assurance British Open |
| | v Clark | 2-5 | 3rd round | Pearl Assurance British Open |
| | v F. Davis | 5-0 | 1st round | European Open |
| | v Cripsey | 5-2 | 2nd round | European Open |
| | v White | 0-5 | 3rd round | European Open |
| | v Mikkelsen | 10-7 | Qualifying | Embassy World Championship |
| | v Terry | 4-10 | Qualifying | Embassy World Championship |

## TOMMY MURPHY (Northern Ireland)

**Born** 8.1.62. **Turned professional** 1981. **World ranking** 76 (57).

| | | | | |
|---|---|---|---|---|
| **1981** | v Johnson | 1-9 | Qualifying | Coral UK Championship |
| **1982** | v Fagan | 6-2 | Quarter-final | Irish Championship |
| | v Dennis Taylor | 0-6 | Semi-final | Irish Championship |
| | v Morra | 5-9 | Qualifying | Embassy World Championship |
| | v Fisher | 1-5 | Qualifying | Jameson International |
| | v Reardon | 0-5 | 1st round | Professional Players Tournament |
| | v Everton | 9-4 | Qualifying | Coral UK Championship |
| | v Sinclair | 5-9 | Qualifying | Coral UK Championship |
| **1983** | v Fagan | 4-6 | Quarter-final | Irish Championship |
| | v Houlihan | 10-9 | Qualifying | Embassy World Championship |
| | v Virgo | 8-10 | Qualifying | Embassy World Championship |
| | v Sheehan | 5-2 | Qualifying | Jameson International |
| | v Thorne | 2-5 | Qualifying | Jameson International |
| | v Macleod | 5-0 | 1st round | Professional Players Tournament |
| | v Stevens | 1-5 | 2nd round | Professional Players Tournament |
| | v Demarco | 9-4 | Qualifying | Coral UK Championship |
| | v Donnelly | 9-4 | Qualifying | Coral UK Championship |
| | v Dennis Taylor | 6-9 | 1st round | Coral UK Championship |
| **1984** | v Fitzmaurice | 10-8 | Qualifying | Embassy World Championship |
| | v Morra | 5-10 | Qualifying | Embassy World Championship |
| | v Bales | 4-5 | Qualifying | Jameson International |
| | v G. Foulds | 5-1 | Qualifying | Rothmans Grand Prix |
| | v Miles | 3-5 | 1st round | Rothmans Grand Prix |
| | v Kearney | 9-2 | Qualifying | Coral UK Open |
| | v Watterson | 9-4 | Qualifying | Coral UK Open |
| | v Martin | 9-8 | Qualifying | Coral UK Open |
| | v S. Davis | 1-9 | 1st round | Coral UK Open |
| **1985** | v Fowler | 0-5 | Qualifying | Mercantile Credit Classic |
| | v Sheehan | 6-3 | Qualifying | Dulux British Open |
| | v Macleod | 5-6 | 1st round | Dulux British Open |
| | v Browne | 6-3 | Qualifying | Irish Championship |
| | v Fagan | 2-6 | Quarter-final | Irish Championship |
| | v P. Francisco | 4-10 | Qualifying | Embassy World Championship |
| | v Jack Rea | 5-1 | 2nd round | Goya Matchroom Trophy |
| | v E. Hughes | 5-3 | 3rd round | Goya Matchroom Trophy |
| | v Higgins | 2-5 | 4th round | Goya Matchroom Trophy |
| | v Mikkelsen | 4-5 | 2nd round | Rothmans Grand Prix |
| | v Everton | 9-4 | 2nd round | Coral UK Open |
| | v Macleod | 7-9 | 3rd round | Coral UK Open |
| **1986** | v Chappel | 5-4 | 2nd round | Mercantile Credit Classic |
| | v Martin | 3-5 | 3rd round | Mercantile Credit Classic |
| | v Duggan | 1-5 | 2nd round | Dulux British Open |
| | v J. McLaughlin | 10-7 | Qualifying | Embassy World Championship |
| | v Thornley | 10-3 | Qualifying | Embassy World Championship |
| | v E. Hughes | 7-10 | Qualifying | Embassy World Championship |
| | v O'Boye | 5-0 | 1st round | Strongbow Irish Championship |
| | v Kearney | 6-2 | Quarter-final | Strongbow Irish Championship |
| | v Dennis Taylor | 3-6 | Semi-final | Strongbow Irish Championship |
| | v Donnelly | 5-2 | 2nd round | BCE International |
| | v Johnson | 4-5 | 3rd round | BCE International |
| | v Anderson | 4-5 | 2nd round | Rothmans Grand Prix |
| | v D. Hughes | 9-0 | 2nd round | Tennents UK Open |
| | v Thorne | 4-9 | 3rd round | Tennents UK Open |
| **1987** | v Bales | 5-2 | 2nd round | Mercantile Credit Classic |
| | v Longworth | 3-5 | 3rd round | Mercantile Credit Classic |
| | v D. Gilbert | 5-4 | 2nd round | Dulux British Open |
| | v Wych | 5-1 | 3rd round | Dulux British Open |
| | v Reardon | 5-4 | 4th round | Dulux British Open |

| | | | | |
|---|---|---|---|---|
| | v Knowles | 3-5 | 5th round | Dulux British Open |
| | v Jenkins | 10-4 | Qualifying | Embassy World Championship |
| | v Miles | 10-7 | Qualifying | Embassy World Championship |
| | v Longworth | 2-10 | Qualifying | Embassy World Championship |
| | v Kearney | 1-5 | 1st round | Matchroom Irish Championship |
| | v Medati | 5-3 | 2nd round | Fidelity International |
| | v Virgo | 1-5 | 3rd round | Fidelity International |
| | v Van Rensberg | 4-5 | 2nd round | Rothmans Grand Prix |
| | v M. Gibson | 9-0 | 2nd round | Tennents UK Open |
| | v Drago | 9-7 | 3rd round | Tennents UK Open |
| | v Thorne | 4-9 | 4th round | Tennents UK Open |
| **1988** | v V. Harris | 5-2 | 2nd round | Mercantile Credit Classic |
| | v J. Campbell | 5-3 | 3rd round | Mercantile Credit Classic |
| | v Reynolds | 5-4 | 4th round | Mercantile Credit Classic |
| | v Knowles | 3-5 | 5th round | Mercantile Credit Classic |
| | v Kelly | 5-1 | 1st round | Irish Championship |
| | v Browne | 5-6 | Quarter-final | Irish Championship |
| | v Meadowcroft | 5-4 | 2nd round | MIM Britannia British Open |
| | v Virgo | 1-5 | 3rd round | MIM Britannia British Open |
| | v Roscoe | 10-8 | Qualifying | Embassy World Championship |
| | v Chaperon | 5-10 | Qualifying | Embassy World Championship |
| | v F. Davis | 5-1 | 2nd round | Fidelity International |
| | v N. Foulds | 3-5 | 3rd round | Fidelity International |
| | v Bradley | 3-5 | 2nd round | Rothmans Grand Prix |
| | v Chambers | 5-3 | 2nd round | BCE Canadian Masters |
| | v James | 3-5 | 3rd round | BCE Canadian Masters |
| | v Price | 9-6 | 2nd round | Tennents UK Open |
| | v Hendry | 4-9 | 3rd round | Tennents UK Open |
| **1989** | v Jack Rea | 5-0 | 2nd round | Mercantile Credit Classic |
| | v Hendry | 2-5 | 3rd round | Mercantile Credit Classic |
| | v Marshall | 5-4 | 2nd round | European Open |
| | v Mountjoy | 1-5 | 3rd round | European Open |
| | v Browne | 3-5 | Quarter-final | Irish Championship |
| | v Whitthread | 2-5 | 2nd round | Anglian British Open |
| | v Oliver | 10-8 | Qualifying | Embassy World Championship |
| | v Roe | 7-10 | Qualifying | Embassy World Championship |
| | v Brumby | 0-5 | 2nd round | Hong Kong Open |
| | v B. Harris | 3-5 | 2nd round | 555 Asian Open |
| | v Ellis | 5-4 | 2nd round | BCE International |
| | v Thorne | 2-5 | 3rd round | BCE International |
| | v Rowswell | 1-5 | 2nd round | Rothmans Grand Prix |
| | v Bond | 0-5 | 2nd round | Dubai Classic |
| | v Grace | 6-0 | 2nd round | Stormseal UK Open |
| | v Williams | 6-9 | 3rd round | Stormseal UK Open |
| **1990** | v Williamson | 5-1 | 2nd round | Mercantile Credit Classic |
| | v Meo | 2-5 | 3rd round | Mercantile Credit Classic |
| | v Bear | 5-2 | 2nd round | Pearl Assurance British Open |
| | v Thorburn | 5-3 | 3rd round | Pearl Assurance British Open |
| | v Newbury | 2-5 | 4th round | Pearl Assurance British Open |
| | v Owers | 2-5 | 2nd round | European Open |
| | v John Rea | 7-10 | Qualifying | Embassy World Championship |

## STEVE NEWBURY (Wales)

**Born** 21.4.56. **Turned professional** 1984. **World ranking** 21 (19).

| | | | | |
|---|---|---|---|---|
| **1984** | v Longworth | 5-4 | Qualifying | Jameson International |
| | v Burke | 5-0 | Qualifying | Jameson International |
| | v Fagan | 5-0 | Qualifying | Jameson International |
| | v Miles | 5-1 | Qualifying | Jameson International |
| | v Werbeniuk | 5-2 | 1st round | Jameson International |

| | | | | |
|---|---|---|---|---|
| | v Knowles | 4-5 | 2nd round | Jameson International |
| | v Fisher | 5-0 | Qualifying | Rothmans Grand Prix |
| | v Thorne | 2-5 | 1st round | Rothmans Grand Prix |
| | v Rigitano | 9-6 | Qualifying | Coral UK Open |
| | v Jonik | 9-3 | Qualifying | Coral UK Open |
| | v Dodd | 6-9 | Qualifying | Coral UK Open |
| **1985** | v V. Harris | 5-3 | Qualifying | Mercantile Credit Classic |
| | v Burke | 5-1 | Qualifying | Mercantile Credit Classic |
| | v Morra | 5-2 | Qualifying | Mercantile Credit Classic |
| | v E. Hughes | 3-5 | Qualifying | Mercantile Credit Classic |
| | v Browne | 6-0 | Qualifying | Dulux British Open |
| | v Sinclair | 6-3 | 1st round | Dulux British Open |
| | v Griffiths | 5-3 | 2nd round | Dulux British Open |
| | v Dennis Taylor | 3-5 | 3rd round | Dulux British Open |
| | v D. Hughes | 10-9 | Qualifying | Embassy World Championship |
| | v Burke | 10-3 | Qualifying | Embassy World Championship |
| | v Scott | 10-2 | Qualifying | Embassy World Championship |
| | v E. Hughes | 6-10 | Qualifying | Embassy World Championship |
| | v W. Jones | 6-2 | 1st round | BCE Welsh Championship |
| | v Mountjoy | 5-6 | Quarter-final | BCE Welsh Championship |
| | v Jonik | 5-4 | 2nd round | Goya Matchroom Trophy |
| | v Griffiths | 2-5 | 3rd round | Goya Matchroom Trophy |
| | v Burke | 5-3 | 2nd round | Rothmans Grand Prix |
| | v David Taylor | 2-5 | 3rd round | Rothmans Grand Prix |
| | v Houlihan | 9-3 | 2nd round | Coral UK Open |
| | v Stevens | 7-9 | 3rd round | Coral UK Open |
| **1986** | v Cripsey | 4-5 | 2nd round | Mercantile Credit Classic |
| | v Wilson | 4-6 | Quarter-final | Zetters Welsh Championship |
| | v Oliver | 5-2 | 2nd round | Dulux British Open |
| | v O'Kane | 5-3 | 3rd round | Dulux British Open |
| | v Meo | 0-5 | 4th round | Dulux British Open |
| | v Agrawal | 10-5 | Qualifying | Embassy World Championship |
| | v Black | 10-2 | Qualifying | Embassy World Championship |
| | v Spencer | 7-10 | Qualifying | Embassy World Championship |
| | v Dunning | 5-4 | 2nd round | BCE International |
| | v S. Francisco | 4-5 | 3rd round | BCE International |
| | v D. Gilbert | 5-1 | 2nd round | Rothmans Grand Prix |
| | v Reynolds | 5-0 | 3rd round | Rothmans Grand Prix |
| | v O'Boye | 5-2 | 4th round | Rothmans Grand Prix |
| | v S. Francisco | 2-5 | 5th round | Rothmans Grand Prix |
| | v Owers | 8-9 | 2nd round | Tennents UK Open |
| **1987** | v Meadowcroft | 5-1 | 2nd round | Mercantile Credit Classic |
| | v White | 4-5 | 3rd round | Mercantile Credit Classic |
| | v Wilson | 6-2 | Quarter-final | Matchroom Welsh Championship |
| | v Griffiths | 9-6 | Semi-final | Matchroom Welsh Championship |
| | v Mountjoy | 7-9 | Final | Matchroom Welsh Championship |
| | v Roscoe | 3-5 | 2nd round | Dulux British Open |
| | v Dodd | 10-7 | Qualifying | Embassy World Championship |
| | v Rigitano | 10-4 | Qualifying | Embassy World Championship |
| | v Hallett | 4-10 | Qualifying | Embassy World Championship |
| | v Fisher | 5-0 | 2nd round | Fidelity International |
| | v P. Francisco | 5-2 | 3rd round | Fidelity International |
| | v Thorburn | 3-5 | 4th round | Fidelity International |
| | v Meakin | 5-1 | 2nd round | Rothmans Grand Prix |
| | v Meo | 5-0 | 3rd round | Rothmans Grand Prix |
| | v Thorburn | 5-0 | 4th round | Rothmans Grand Prix |
| | v Gary Wilkinson | 5-3 | 5th round | Rothmans Grand Prix |
| | v Dennis Taylor | 2-5 | Quarter-final | Rothmans Grand Prix |
| | v Foldvari | 9-5 | 2nd round | Tennents UK Open |
| | v Parrott | 5-9 | 3rd round | Tennents UK Open |
| **1988** | v Kearney | 5-1 | 2nd round | Mercantile Credit Classic |
| | v E. Hughes | 5-1 | 3rd round | Mercantile Credit Classic |
| | v Thorburn | 5-3 | 4th round | Mercantile Credit Classic |

| | | | | |
|---|---|---|---|---|
| | v Clark | 5-2 | 5th round | Mercantile Credit Classic |
| | v Griffiths | 5-4 | Quarter-final | Mercantile Credit Classic |
| | v S. Davis | 2-9 | Semi-final | Mercantile Credit Classic |
| | v C. Wilson | 3-6 | Quarter-final | Welsh Championship |
| | v Oliver | 5-3 | 2nd round | MIM Britannia British Open |
| | v Thorburn | 2-5 | 3rd round | MIM Britannia British Open |
| | v Lawlor | 10-3 | Qualifying | Embassy World Championship |
| | v M. Smith | 10-9 | Qualifying | Embassy World Championship |
| | v West | 8-10 | Qualifying | Embassy World Championship |
| | v M. Bennett | 5-0 | 3rd round | Fidelity International |
| | v Knowles | 5-4 | 4th round | Fidelity International |
| | v Johnson | 2-5 | 5th round | Fidelity International |
| | v Macleod | 5-3 | 3rd round | Rothmans Grand Prix |
| | v S. Davis | 1-5 | 4th round | Rothmans Grand Prix |
| | v N. Gilbert | 5-3 | 3rd round | BCE Canadian Masters |
| | v Virgo | 2-5 | 4th round | BCE Canadian Masters |
| | v Roscoe | 7-9 | 3rd round | Tennents UK Open |
| **1989** | v Bradley | 5-3 | 3rd round | Mercantile Credit Classic |
| | v Dennis Taylor | 5-4 | 4th round | Mercantile Credit Classic |
| | v Hendry | 1-5 | 5th round | Mercantile Credit Classic |
| | v Robidoux | 0-5 | 3rd round | European Open |
| | v W. Jones | 6-5 | Quarter-final | Senator Welsh Championship |
| | v Griffiths | 7-9 | Semi-final | Senator Welsh Championship |
| | v Bales | 3-5 | 3rd round | Anglian British Open |
| | v N. Gilbert | 10-7 | Qualifying | Embassy World Championship |
| | v S. Davis | 5-10 | 1st round | Embassy World Championship |
| | v Edmonds | 5-4 | 3rd round | Hong Kong Open |
| | v Parrott | 5-2 | 4th round | Hong Kong Open |
| | v Gary Wilkinson | 1-5 | 5th round | Hong Kong Open |
| | v Duggan | 3-5 | 3rd round | 555 Asian Open |
| | v Duggan | 5-2 | 3rd round | BCE International |
| | v Griffiths | 5-2 | 4th round | BCE International |
| | v Robidoux | 2-5 | 5th round | BCE International |
| | v Oliver | 5-4 | 3rd round | Rothmans Grand Prix |
| | v Virgo | 5-0 | 4th round | Rothmans Grand Prix |
| | v Dennis Taylor | 1-5 | 5th round | Rothmans Grand Prix |
| | v S. Campbell | 1-5 | 3rd round | Dubai Classic |
| | v T. Jones | 7-9 | 3rd round | Stormseal UK Open |
| **1990** | v Watchorn | 5-2 | 3rd round | Mercantile Credit Classic |
| | v Meo | 5-4 | 4th round | Mercantile Credit Classic |
| | v P. Francisco | 5-3 | 5th round | Mercantile Credit Classic |
| | v King | 3-5 | Quarter-final | Mercantile Credit Classic |
| | v W. Jones | 3-6 | Quarter-final | Senator Welsh Championship |
| | v Wright | 5-3 | 3rd round | Pearl Assurance British Open |
| | v T. Murphy | 5-2 | 4th round | Pearl Assurance British Open |
| | v S. Davis | 5-2 | 5th round | Pearl Assurance British Open |
| | v Marshall | 4-5 | Quarter-final | Pearl Assurance British Open |
| | v J. McLaughlin | 5-2 | 3rd round | European Open |
| | v Hendry | 1-5 | 4th round | European Open |
| | v Bond | 10-6 | Qualifying | Embassy World Championship |
| | v Hallett | 9-10 | 1st round | Embassy World Championship |

## JOE O'BOYE (Republic of Ireland)

**Born** 6.3.60. **Turned professional** 1985. **World ranking** 63 (40).

| | | | | |
|---|---|---|---|---|
| **1985** | v Parkin | 5-3 | 1st round | Goya Matchroom Trophy |
| | v Miles | 2-5 | 2nd round | Goya Matchroom Trophy |
| | v Hendry | 5-4 | 1st round | Rothmans Grand Prix |
| | v Chaperon | 5-3 | 2nd round | Rothmans Grand Prix |
| | v Mans | 5-3 | 3rd round | Rothmans Grand Prix |

| | | | | |
|---|---|---|---|---|
| | v White | 4-5 | 4th round | Rothmans Grand Prix |
| | v Bennett | 9-3 | 1st round | Coral UK Open |
| | v Gauvreau | 9-5 | 2nd round | Coral UK Open |
| | v Knowles | 5-9 | 3rd round | Coral UK Open |
| **1986** | v Wilkinson | 5-1 | 1st round | Mercantile Credit Classic |
| | v Longworth | 5-1 | 2nd round | Mercantile Credit Classic |
| | v Meo | 3-5 | 3rd round | Mercantile Credit Classic |
| | v Jim Bear | 5-1 | 1st round | Dulux British Open |
| | v T. Jones | 2-5 | 2nd round | Dulux British Open |
| | v Oliver | 8-10 | Qualifying | Embassy World Championship |
| | v Murphy | 0-5 | 1st round | Strongbow Irish Championship |
| | v Mikkelsen | 5-4 | 2nd round | BCE International |
| | v Williams | 0-5 | 3rd round | BCE International |
| | v Edmonds | 5-2 | 2nd round | Rothmans Grand Prix |
| | v Thorburn | 5-4 | 3rd round | Rothmans Grand Prix |
| | v Newbury | 2-5 | 4th round | Rothmans Grand Prix |
| | v Duggan | 9-4 | 2nd round | Tennents UK Open |
| | v Meo | 3-9 | 3rd round | Tennents UK Open |
| **1987** | v V. Harris | 5-1 | 2nd round | Mercantile Credit Classic |
| | v Griffiths | 1-5 | 3rd round | Mercantile Credit Classic |
| | v Bradley | 5-1 | 2nd round | Dulux British Open |
| | v Reardon | 5-4 | 3rd round | Dulux British Open |
| | v N. Gilbert | 10-5 | Qualifying | Embassy World Championship |
| | v Bradley | 7-10 | Qualifying | Embassy World Championship |
| | v Kelly | 5-0 | 1st round | Matchroom Irish Championship |
| | v Higgins | *wo* | Quarter-final | Matchroom Irish Championship |
| | v E. Hughes | 6-3 | Semi-final | Matchroom Irish Championship |
| | v Dennis Taylor | 2-9 | Final | Matchroom Irish Championship |
| | v Fagan | 5-1 | 2nd round | Fidelity International |
| | v Stevens | 5-1 | 3rd round | Fidelity International |
| | v Foldvari | 5-4 | 4th round | Fidelity International |
| | v Clark | 5-2 | 5th round | Fidelity International |
| | v Hendry | 2-5 | Quarter-final | Fidelity International |
| | v Chambers | 3-5 | 2nd round | Rothmans Grand Prix |
| | v Donnelly | 9-2 | 2nd round | Tennents UK Open |
| | v Stevens | 8-9 | 3rd round | Tennents UK Open |
| **1988** | v Sheehan | 5-3 | 2nd round | Mercantile Credit Classic |
| | v Reynolds | 3-5 | 3rd round | Mercantile Credit Classic |
| | v Sheehan | 5-0 | 1st round | Irish Championship |
| | v Higgins | 6-4 | Quarter-final | Irish Championship |
| | v J. McLaughlin | 4-6 | Semi-final | Irish Championship |
| | v Jenkins | 5-1 | 2nd round | MIM Britannia British Open |
| | v Reynolds | 5-2 | 3rd round | MIM Britannia British Open |
| | v J. Campbell | 5-1 | 4th round | MIM Britannia British Open |
| | v Roe | 5-1 | 5th round | MIM Britannia British Open |
| | v Hallett | 4-5 | Quarter-final | MIM Britannia British Open |
| | v James | 7-10 | Qualifying | Embassy World Championship |
| | v Whitthread | 5-1 | 2nd round | Fidelity International |
| | v Hallett | 3-5 | 3rd round | Fidelity International |
| | v Jenkins | 5-1 | 2nd round | Rothmans Grand Prix |
| | v Knowles | 4-5 | 3rd round | Rothmans Grand Prix |
| | v A. Harris | 5-3 | 2nd round | BCE Canadian Masters |
| | v Hallett | 0-5 | 3rd round | BCE Canadian Masters |
| | v Williamson | 9-4 | 2nd round | Tennents UK Open |
| | v E. Hughes | 9-8 | 3rd round | Tennents UK Open |
| | v Dennis Taylor | 4-9 | 4th round | Tennents UK Open |
| **1989** | v D. Hughes | 1-5 | 2nd round | Mercantile Credit Classic |
| | v Bradley | 5-3 | 2nd round | European Open |
| | v Hendry | 2-5 | 3rd round | European Open |
| | v Edwards | 4-5 | 2nd round | Anglian British Open |
| | v T. Wilson | 10-8 | Qualifying | Embassy World Championship |
| | v Fowler | 10-6 | Qualifying | Embassy World Championship |
| | v West | 10-7 | Qualifying | Embassy World Championship |

| | | | | |
|---|---|---|---|---|
| | v S. Francisco | 6-10 | 1st round | Embassy World Championship |
| | v Foldvari | 0-5 | 2nd round | Hong Kong Open |
| | v Bradley | 5-3 | 2nd round | 555 Asian Open |
| | v Drago | 3-5 | 3rd round | 555 Asian Open |
| | v Darrington | 5-3 | 2nd round | BCE International |
| | v N. Foulds | 0-5 | 3rd round | BCE International |
| | v J. Smith | 4-5 | 2nd round | Rothmans Grand Prix |
| | v Chambers | 4-5 | 3rd round | Dubai Classic |
| | v Williamson | 6-4 | 2nd round | Stormseal UK Open |
| | v Mountjoy | 9-8 | 3rd round | Stormseal UK Open |
| | v Gollan | 5-9 | 4th round | Stormseal UK Open |
| **1990** | v S. Murphy | 0-5 | 2nd round | Mercantile Credit Classic |
| | v S. Murphy | 3-5 | 2nd round | Pearl Assurance British Open |
| | v Miles | 5-1 | 2nd round | European Open |
| | v Williams | 2-5 | 3rd round | European Open |
| | v B. Morgan | 2-10 | Qualifying | Embassy World Championship |

## DENE O'KANE (New Zealand)

**Born** 24.2.63. **Turned professional** 1984. **World ranking** 24 (28).

| | | | | |
|---|---|---|---|---|
| **1984** | v Parkin | 5-2 | Qualifying | Jameson International |
| | v E. McLaughlin | 5-1 | Qualifying | Jameson International |
| | v Fitzmaurice | 5-4 | Qualifying | Jameson International |
| | v Hallett | 5-4 | Qualifying | Jameson International |
| | v Thorne | 3-5 | 1st round | Jameson International |
| | v Kelly | 5-4 | Qualifying | Rothmans Grand Prix |
| | v David Taylor | 1-5 | 1st round | Rothmans Grand Prix |
| | v W. Jones | 9-7 | Qualifying | Coral UK Open |
| | v Duggan | 9-6 | Qualifying | Coral UK Open |
| | v Scott | 7-9 | Qualifying | Coral UK Open |
| **1985** | v W. Jones | 0-5 | Qualifying | Mercantile Credit Classic |
| | v Cripsey | 6-4 | Qualifying | Dulux British Open |
| | v J. Campbell | 6-4 | 1st round | Dulux British Open |
| | v V. Harris | 5-3 | 2nd round | Dulux British Open |
| | v Martin | 5-4 | 3rd round | Dulux British Open |
| | v S. Davis | 1-5 | Quarter-final | Dulux British Open |
| | v J. McLaughlin | *wo* | Qualifying | Embassy World Championship |
| | v V. Harris | 10-5 | Qualifying | Embassy World Championship |
| | v Jonik | 10-5 | Qualifying | Embassy World Championship |
| | v Dodd | 10-7 | Qualifying | Embassy World Championship |
| | v Martin | 10-8 | Qualifying | Embassy World Championship |
| | v David Taylor | 4-10 | 1st round | Embassy World Championship |
| | v B. Harris | 3-5 | 3rd round | Goya Matchroom Trophy |
| | v Edmonds | 2-5 | 3rd round | Rothmans Grand Prix |
| | v Chappel | 5-9 | 3rd round | Coral UK Open |
| **1986** | v Medati | 5-0 | 3rd round | Mercantile Credit Classic |
| | v Mountjoy | 3-5 | 4th round | Mercantile Credit Classic |
| | v Newbury | 3-5 | 3rd round | Dulux British Open |
| | v Hendry | 9-10 | Qualifying | Embassy World Championship |
| | v Oliver | 5-2 | 2nd round | BCE International |
| | v Hallett | 5-1 | 3rd round | BCE International |
| | v Owers | 0-5 | 4th round | BCE International |
| | v M. Bennett | 2-5 | 2nd round | Rothmans Grand Prix |
| | v Jenkins | 9-5 | 2nd round | Tennents UK Open |
| | v Werbeniuk | 9-5 | 3rd round | Tennents UK Open |
| | v Griffiths | 0-9 | 4th round | Tennents UK Open |
| **1987** | v G. Foulds | 4-5 | 2nd round | Mercantile Credit Classic |
| | v Rowswell | 4-5 | 2nd round | Dulux British Open |
| | v D. Gilbert | 10-2 | Qualifying | Embassy World Championship |
| | v Black | 10-2 | Qualifying | Embassy World Championship |
| | v P. Francisco | 10-5 | Qualifying | Embassy World Championship |

| | | | | |
|---|---|---|---|---|
| | v Thorburn | 10-5 | 1st round | Embassy World Championship |
| | v Mountjoy | 13-5 | 2nd round | Embassy World Championship |
| | v White | 6-13 | Quarter-final | Embassy World Championship |
| | v Van Rensberg | 5-3 | 2nd round | Fidelity International |
| | v S. Davis | 2-5 | 3rd round | Fidelity International |
| | v Gary Wilkinson | 2-5 | 2nd round | Rothmans Grand Prix |
| | v Rowswell | 9-2 | 2nd round | Tennents UK Open |
| | v Charlton | 9-8 | 3rd round | Tennents UK Open |
| | v Dennis Taylor | 9-7 | 4th round | Tennents UK Open |
| | v Thorne | 7-9 | 5th round | Tennents UK Open |
| **1988** | v Rowswell | 4-5 | 2nd round | Mercantile Credit Classic |
| | v Whitthread | 5-2 | 2nd round | MIM Britannia British Open |
| | v Mountjoy | 5-3 | 3rd round | MIM Britannia British Open |
| | v Browne | 5-2 | 4th round | MIM Britannia British Open |
| | v Johnson | 5-2 | 5th round | MIM Britannia British Open |
| | v Parrott | 2-5 | Quarter-final | MIM Britannia British Open |
| | v Sinclair | 9-10 | Qualifying | Embassy World Championship |
| | v Hallett | 1-5 | 1st round | New Zealand Masters |
| | v Johnston-Allen | 5-3 | 3rd round | Fidelity International |
| | v Wych | 4-5 | 4th round | Fidelity International |
| | v D. Gilbert | 5-4 | 3rd round | Rothmans Grand Prix |
| | v Higgins | 0-5 | 4th round | Rothmans Grand Prix |
| | v D. Morgan | 3-5 | 3rd round | BCE Canadian Masters |
| | v Reardon | 9-8 | 3rd round | Tennents UK Open |
| | v Virgo | 8-9 | 4th round | Tennents UK Open |
| **1989** | v N. Gilbert | 5-2 | 3rd round | Mercantile Credit Classic |
| | v Thorne | 3-5 | 4th round | Mercantile Credit Classic |
| | v Chappel | 0-5 | 3rd round | European Open |
| | v T. Jones | 5-4 | 3rd round | Anglian British Open |
| | v Hendry | 2-5 | 4th round | Anglian British Open |
| | v Robidoux | 10-5 | Qualifying | Embassy World Championship |
| | v White | 7-10 | 1st round | Embassy World Championship |
| | v Hendry | 3-6 | 1st round | Lion Brown New Zealand Masters |
| | v Martin | 5-1 | 3rd round | Hong Kong Open |
| | v Griffiths | 5-4 | 4th round | Hong Kong Open |
| | v Higgins | 5-2 | 5th round | Hong Kong Open |
| | v Graham | 5-1 | Quarter-final | Hong Kong Open |
| | v Gary Wilkinson | 5-3 | Semi-final | Hong Kong Open |
| | v Hallett | 8-9 | Final | Hong Kong Open |
| | v Marshall | 5-1 | 3rd round | 555 Asian Open |
| | v Virgo | 3-5 | 4th round | 555 Asian Open |
| | v Cairns | 2-5 | 3rd round | BCE International |
| | v T. Jones | 2-5 | 3rd round | BCE International |
| | v M. Bennett | 5-2 | 3rd round | Dubai Classic |
| | v Higgins | 3-5 | 4th round | Dubai Classic |
| | v Graham | 9-7 | 3rd round | Stormseal UK Open |
| | v Hallett | 0-9 | 4th round | Stormseal UK Open |
| **1990** | v Fowler | 5-4 | 3rd round | Mercantile Credit Classic |
| | v Hendry | 5-2 | 4th round | Mercantile Credit Classic |
| | v Clark | 5-1 | 5th round | Mercantile Credit Classic |
| | v S. Francisco | 4-5 | Quarter-final | Mercantile Credit Classic |
| | v Wattana | 1-5 | 3rd round | Pearl Assurance British Open |
| | v Miles | 5-1 | 2nd round | European Open |
| | v Williams | 2-5 | 3rd round | European Open |
| | v Robidoux | 2-10 | Qualifying | Embassy World Championship |

## **BILL OLIVER** (England)

**Born** 3.12.48. **Turned professional** 1983. **World ranking** 78 (85).

| | | | | |
|---|---|---|---|---|
| **1983** | v T. Jones | 2-5 | Qualifying | Professional Players Tournament |
| | v Andrewartha | 1-9 | Qualifying | Coral UK Championship |

| | | | | |
|---|---|---|---|---|
| **1984** | v Dunning | 10-3 | Qualifying | Embassy World Championship |
| | v Caggianello | 10-7 | Qualifying | Embassy World Championship |
| | v Williams | 8-10 | Qualifying | Embassy World Championship |
| | v D. Hughes | 5-4 | Qualifying | Jameson International |
| | v Chalmers | 4-5 | Qualifying | Jameson International |
| | v Bennett | 5-3 | Qualifying | Rothmans Grand Prix |
| | v White | 1-5 | 1st round | Rothmans Grand Prix |
| | v Fowler | 3-9 | Qualifying | Coral UK Open |
| **1985** | v Longworth | 1-5 | Qualifying | Mercantile Credit Classic |
| | v Fowler | 7-9 | Qualifying | Tolly Cobbold English Championship |
| | v Thorne | 3-6 | 1st round | Dulux British Open |
| | v Foldvari | 3-10 | Qualifying | Embassy World Championship |
| | v Morra | 1-5 | 2nd round | Goya Matchroom Trophy |
| | v Fagan | 5-4 | 2nd round | Rothmans Grand Prix |
| | v Thorburn | 0-5 | 3rd round | Rothmans Grand Prix |
| | v Miles | 4-9 | 2nd round | Coral UK Open |
| **1986** | v Bradley | 3-5 | 2nd round | Mercantile Credit Classic |
| | v Dodd | 9-5 | 2nd round | Tolly Cobbold English Championship |
| | v Parrott | 0-9 | 3rd round | Tolly Cobbold English Championship |
| | v Newbury | 2-5 | 2nd round | Dulux British Open |
| | v O'Boye | 10-8 | Qualifying | Embassy World Championship |
| | v Fowler | 8-10 | Qualifying | Embassy World Championship |
| | v Mienie | 5-4 | 1st round | BCE International |
| | v O'Kane | 2-5 | 2nd round | BCE International |
| | v Anderson | 4-5 | 1st round | Rothmans Grand Prix |
| | v Chalmers | 9-6 | 1st round | Tennents UK Open |
| | v Hendry | 1-9 | 2nd round | Tennents UK Open |
| **1987** | v Greaves | 5-4 | 1st round | Mercantile Credit Classic |
| | v T. Jones | 0-5 | 2nd round | Mercantile Credit Classic |
| | v T. Jones | 1-6 | 2nd round | Tolly Ales English Championship |
| | v Jack Rea | 5-1 | 1st round | Dulux British Open |
| | v Drago | 1-5 | 2nd round | Dulux British Open |
| | v Watchorn | 3-5 | 1st round | Fidelity International |
| | v J. McLaughlin | 2-5 | 2nd round | Rothmans Grand Prix |
| | v Burke | 9-1 | 1st round | Tennents UK Open |
| | v Scott | 9-4 | 2nd round | Tennents UK Open |
| | v Thorne | 3-9 | 3rd round | Tennents UK Open |
| **1988** | v Burke | 5-2 | 1st round | Mercantile Credit Classic |
| | v King | 5-3 | 2nd round | Mercantile Credit Classic |
| | v West | 3-5 | 3rd round | Mercantile Credit Classic |
| | v Marshall | 3-6 | 1st round | English Championship |
| | v M. Smith | 5-0 | 1st round | MIM Britannia British Open |
| | v Newbury | 3-5 | 2nd round | MIM Britannia British Open |
| | v Chalmers | 10-9 | Qualifying | Embassy World Championship |
| | v Reardon | 10-6 | Qualifying | Embassy World Championship |
| | v Robidoux | 10-2 | Qualifying | Embassy World Championship |
| | v C. Wilson | 6-10 | Qualifying | Embassy World Championship |
| | v Fagan | 5-0 | 1st round | Fidelity International |
| | v Duggan | 3-5 | 2nd round | Fidelity International |
| | v Fitzmaurice | 5-3 | 1st round | Rothmans Grand Prix |
| | v N. Gilbert | 4-5 | 2nd round | Rothmans Grand Prix |
| | v Rempe | 5-3 | 1st round | BCE Canadian Masters |
| | v J. Campbell | 5-3 | 2nd round | BCE Canadian Masters |
| | v Griffiths | 4-5 | 3rd round | BCE Canadian Masters |
| | v Kelly | 9-2 | 1st round | Tennents UK Open |
| | v Wych | 6-9 | 2nd round | Tennents UK Open |
| **1989** | v S. Campbell | 4-5 | 1st round | Mercantile Credit Classic |
| | v Chalmers | 5-4 | 1st round | European Open |
| | v Martin | 5-4 | 2nd round | European Open |
| | v Thorne | 0-5 | 3rd round | European Open |
| | v G. Foulds | 5-1 | 1st round | English Championship |
| | v Clark | 2-5 | 2nd round | English Championship |
| | v Kelly | 4-5 | 1st round | Anglian British Open |

| | | | | |
|---|---|---|---|---|
| | v Rempe | 10-5 | Qualifying | Embassy World Championship |
| | v Murphy | 8-10 | Qualifying | Embassy World Championship |
| | v J. Smith | 3-5 | 1st round | Hong Kong Open |
| | v Kearney | 5-3 | 1st round | 555 Asian Open |
| | v J. Campbell | 5-3 | 2nd round | 555 Asian Open |
| | v Williams | 5-4 | 3rd round | 555 Asian Open |
| | v T. Jones | 1-5 | 4th round | 555 Asian Open |
| | v Rigitano | 5-1 | 1st round | BCE International |
| | v T. Jones | 1-5 | 2nd round | BCE International |
| | v Van Rensberg | 5-3 | 1st round | Rothmans Grand Prix |
| | v Martin | 5-3 | 2nd round | Rothmans Grand Prix |
| | v Newbury | 4-5 | 3rd round | Rothmans Grand Prix |
| | v Fitzmaurice | 4-5 | 1st round | Dubai Classic |
| | v Ellis | 6-5 | 1st round | Stormseal UK Open |
| | v Browne | 2-6 | 2nd round | Stormseal UK Open |
| **1990** | v Meadowcroft | 3-5 | 1st round | Mercantile Credit Classic |
| | v Watterson | 5-0 | 1st round | Pearl Assurance British Open |
| | v Roscoe | 5-4 | 2nd round | Pearl Assurance British Open |
| | v James | 1-5 | 3rd round | Pearl Assurance British Open |
| | v Rowing | 5-4 | 1st round | European Open |
| | v Wych | *wo* | 2nd round | European Open |
| | v S. Francisco | 2-5 | 3rd round | European Open |
| | v Pinches | 8-10 | Qualifying | Embassy World Championship |

## KEN OWERS (England)

**Born** 30.3.53. **Turned professional** 1986. **World ranking** 96 (75).

| | | | | |
|---|---|---|---|---|
| **1986** | v Scott | 5-1 | 2nd round | BCE International |
| | v White | 5-2 | 3rd round | BCE International |
| | v O'Kane | 5-0 | 4th round | BCE International |
| | v N. Foulds | 1-5 | 5th round | BCE International |
| | v J. McLaughlin | 2-5 | 1st round | Rothmans Grand Prix |
| | v D. Gilbert | 9-8 | 1st round | Tennents UK Open |
| | v Newbury | 9-8 | 2nd round | Tennents UK Open |
| | v S. Francisco | 3-9 | 3rd round | Tennents UK Open |
| **1987** | v Houlihan | 5-1 | 1st round | Mercantile Credit Classic |
| | v John Rea | 2-5 | 2nd round | Mercantile Credit Classic |
| | v Bales | 6-5 | 2nd round | Tolly Ales English Championship |
| | v N. Foulds | 6-3 | 3rd round | Tolly Ales English Championship |
| | v Hallett | 2-6 | 4th round | Tolly Ales English Championship |
| | v Jonik | 5-4 | 1st round | Dulux British Open |
| | v F. Davis | 5-3 | 2nd round | Dulux British Open |
| | v Mountjoy | 1-5 | 3rd round | Dulux British Open |
| | v Fisher | 10-5 | Qualifying | Embassy World Championship |
| | v F. Davis | 10-5 | Qualifying | Embassy World Championship |
| | v King | 4-10 | Qualifying | Embassy World Championship |
| | v Meadowcroft | 5-3 | 2nd round | Fidelity International |
| | v E. Hughes | 4-5 | 3rd round | Fidelity International |
| | v Glen Wilkinson | 4-5 | 2nd round | Rothmans Grand Prix |
| | v Roe | 7-9 | 2nd round | Tennents UK Open |
| **1988** | v Fisher | 5-0 | 2nd round | Mercantile Credit Classic |
| | v Williams | 5-3 | 3rd round | Mercantile Credit Classic |
| | v P. Francisco | 0-5 | 4th round | Mercantile Credit Classic |
| | v Meakin | 6-2 | 2nd round | English Championship |
| | v David Taylor | 6-3 | 3rd round | English Championship |
| | v Knowles | 4-6 | 4th round | English Championship |
| | v Miles | 3-5 | 2nd round | MIM Britannia British Open |
| | v Roe | 10-7 | Qualifying | Embassy World Championship |
| | v Wright | 8-10 | Qualifying | Embassy World Championship |
| | v Jenkins | 5-1 | 2nd round | Fidelity International |
| | v S. Francisco | 1-5 | 3rd round | Fidelity International |
| | v Chambers | 3-5 | 2nd round | Rothmans Grand Prix |

| | | | | |
|---|---|---|---|---|
| | v Lawlor | 5-2 | 2nd round | BCE Canadian Masters |
| | v Dennis Taylor | 1-5 | 3rd round | BCE Canadian Masters |
| | v Chambers | 9-4 | 2nd round | Tennents UK Open |
| | v Griffiths | 2-9 | 3rd round | Tennents UK Open |
| **1989** | v Roscoe | 3-5 | 2nd round | Mercantile Credit Classic |
| | v Lawlor | 4-5 | 2nd round | European Open |
| | v Williamson | 4-5 | 2nd round | English Championship |
| | v Burke | 5-2 | 2nd round | Anglian British Open |
| | v Longworth | 1-5 | 3rd round | Anglian British Open |
| | v P. Gibson | 10-8 | Qualifying | Embassy World Championship |
| | v D. Morgan | 8-10 | Qualifying | Embassy World Championship |
| | v Wattana | 2-5 | 1st round | Hong Kong Open |
| | v Dyson | 1-5 | 1st round | 555 Asian Open |
| | v Brumby | 4-5 | 1st round | BCE International |
| | v G. Foulds | 1-5 | 1st round | Rothmans Grand Prix |
| | v Bond | 1-5 | 1st round | Dubai Classic |
| | v J. Smith | 5-6 | 1st round | Stormseal UK Open |
| **1990** | v Gollan | 5-2 | 1st round | Mercantile Credit Classic |
| | v J. Campbell | 3-5 | 2nd round | Mercantile Credit Classic |
| | v Rigitano | 5-3 | 1st round | Pearl Assurance British Open |
| | v Johnston-Allen | 4-5 | 2nd round | Pearl Assurance British Open |
| | v G. Foulds | 5-1 | 1st round | European Open |
| | v T. Murphy | 5-3 | 2nd round | European Open |
| | v Higgins | 2-5 | 3rd round | European Open |
| | v Darrington | 10-1 | Qualifying | Embassy World Championship |
| | v Spencer | 8-10 | Qualifying | Embassy World Championship |

## JOHN PARROTT (England)

**Born** 11.5.64. **Turned professional** 1983. **World ranking** 3 (2).

| | | | | |
|---|---|---|---|---|
| **1983** | v Watchorn | 5-0 | Qualifying | Professional Players Tournament |
| | v Fagan | 5-2 | 1st round | Professional Players Tournament |
| | v Griffiths | 1-5 | 2nd round | Professional Players Tournament |
| | v Scott | 9-7 | Qualifying | Coral UK Championship |
| | v Fisher | 9-0 | Qualifying | Coral UK Championship |
| | v Meo | 7-9 | 1st round | Coral UK Championship |
| **1984** | v Mountjoy | 5-4 | Qualifying | Lada Classic |
| | v Higgins | 5-2 | 1st round | Lada Classic |
| | v Knowles | 5-1 | Quarter-final | Lada Classic |
| | v S. Davis | 4-5 | Semi-final | Lada Classic |
| | v D. Hughes | 10-3 | Qualifying | Embassy World Championship |
| | v Everton | 10-2 | Qualifying | Embassy World Championship |
| | v Mans | 10-0 | Qualifying | Embassy World Championship |
| | v Knowles | 10-7 | 1st round | Embassy World Championship |
| | v Dennis Taylor | 11-13 | 2nd round | Embassy World Championship |
| | v Gauvreau | 4-5 | Qualifying | Jameson International |
| | v Gauvreau | 5-3 | 1st round | Rothmans Grand Prix |
| | v Charlton | 1-5 | 2nd round | Rothmans Grand Prix |
| | v Fitzmaurice | 9-6 | Qualifying | Coral UK Open |
| | v Thorne | 7-9 | 1st round | Coral UK Open |
| **1985** | v Medati | 3-5 | Qualifying | Mercantile Credit Classic |
| | v G. Foulds | 9-4 | 1st round | Tolly Cobbold English Championship |
| | v David Taylor | 6-9 | 2nd round | Tolly Cobbold English Championship |
| | v John Rea | 6-4 | 1st round | Dulux British Open |
| | v Dennis Taylor | 2-5 | 2nd round | Dulux British Open |
| | v Fowler | 10-2 | Qualifying | Embassy World Championship |
| | v Spencer | 10-3 | 1st round | Embassy World Championship |
| | v Stevens | 13-6 | 2nd round | Embassy World Championship |
| | v Reardon | 12-13 | Quarter-final | Embassy World Championship |
| | v Thorne | 5-0 | Quarter-final | Winfield Australian Masters |
| | v J. Campbell | 4-6 | Semi-final | Winfield Australian Masters |
| | v White | 3-5 | Semi-final | Carlsberg Trophy |

| | | | | |
|---|---|---|---|---|
| | v W. Jones | 5-3 | 3rd round | Goya Matchroom Trophy |
| | v Meo | 5-4 | 4th round | Goya Matchroom Trophy |
| | v Griffiths | 5-1 | 5th round | Goya Matchroom Trophy |
| | v Dennis Taylor | 1-5 | Quarter-final | Goya Matchroom Trophy |
| | v Longworth | 2-5 | 3rd round | Rothmans Grand Prix |
| | v Dennis Taylor | 1-5 | 1st round | BCE Canadian Masters |
| | v Sinclair | 9-2 | 3rd round | Coral UK Open |
| | v Thorburn | 6-9 | 4th round | Coral UK Open |
| **1986** | v Van Rensberg | 3-5 | 3rd round | Mercantile Credit Classic |
| | v Oliver | 9-0 | 3rd round | Tolly Cobbold English Championship |
| | v Virgo | 6-9 | 4th round | Tolly Cobbold English Championship |
| | v Roscoe | 5-2 | 3rd round | Dulux British Open |
| | v Fagan | 5-0 | 4th round | Dulux British Open |
| | v Wych | 4-5 | 5th round | Dulux British Open |
| | v Foldvari | 10-6 | Qualifying | Embassy World Championship |
| | v Meo | 10-4 | 1st round | Embassy World Championship |
| | v White | 8-13 | 2nd round | Embassy World Championship |
| | v Thorburn | 1-5 | 1st round | Langs Scottish Masters |
| | v Hendry | 3-5 | 3rd round | BCE International |
| | v Cripsey | 5-4 | 3rd round | Rothmans Grand Prix |
| | v Meo | 3-5 | 4th round | Rothmans Grand Prix |
| | v Bradley | 9-4 | 3rd round | Tennents UK Open |
| | v Johnson | 9-1 | 4th round | Tennents UK Open |
| | v Longworth | 9-6 | 5th round | Tennents UK Open |
| | v Knowles | 9-4 | Quarter-final | Tennents UK Open |
| | v N. Foulds | 3-9 | Semi-final | Tennents UK Open |
| **1987** | v T. Jones | 5-2 | 3rd round | Mercantile Credit Classic |
| | v Higgins | 5-2 | 4th round | Mercantile Credit Classic |
| | v Charlton | 5-4 | 5th round | Mercantile Credit Classic |
| | v S. Davis | 4-5 | Quarter-final | Mercantile Credit Classic |
| | v Wildman | 6-1 | 3rd round | Tolly Ales English Championship |
| | v Virgo | 6-2 | 4th round | Tolly Ales English Championship |
| | v Meo | 3-6 | Quarter-final | Tolly Ales English Championship |
| | v King | 1-5 | 3rd round | Dulux British Open |
| | v Fowler | 10-3 | Qualifying | Embassy World Championship |
| | v Meo | 10-8 | 1st round | Embassy World Championship |
| | v White | 11-13 | 2nd round | Embassy World Championship |
| | v Chappel | 5-1 | 3rd round | Fidelity International |
| | v Chaperon | 5-1 | 4th round | Fidelity International |
| | v S. Davis | 2-5 | 5th round | Fidelity International |
| | v Dodd | 5-1 | 3rd round | Rothmans Grand Prix |
| | v Stevens | 5-0 | 4th round | Rothmans Grand Prix |
| | v Griffiths | 5-4 | 5th round | Rothmans Grand Prix |
| | v Chaperon | 5-2 | Quarter-final | Rothmans Grand Prix |
| | v Hendry | 7-9 | Semi-final | Rothmans Grand Prix |
| | v Newbury | 9-5 | 3rd round | Tennents UK Open |
| | v Wych | 9-6 | 4th round | Tennents UK Open |
| | v Knowles | 9-4 | 5th round | Tennents UK Open |
| | v S. Davis | 5-9 | Quarter-final | Tennents UK Open |
| **1988** | v Wildman | 5-2 | 3rd round | Mercantile Credit Classic |
| | v David Taylor | 5-0 | 4th round | Mercantile Credit Classic |
| | v Virgo | 5-0 | 5th round | Mercantile Credit Classic |
| | v Dennis Taylor | 5-1 | Quarter-final | Mercantile Credit Classic |
| | v Knowles | 9-4 | Semi-final | Mercantile Credit Classic |
| | v S. Davis | 11-13 | Final | Mercantile Credit Classic |
| | v Foulds | 5-4 | 1st round | Benson & Hedges Masters |
| | v Thorburn | 5-4 | Quarter-final | Benson & Hedges Masters |
| | v Hallett | 5-6 | Semi-final | Benson & Hedges Masters |
| | v Lawlor | 6-3 | 3rd round | English Championship |
| | v Reynolds | 2-6 | 4th round | English Championship |
| | v Foldvari | 5-1 | 3rd round | MIM Britannia British Open |
| | v Virgo | 5-1 | 4th round | MIM Britannia British Open |
| | v N. Foulds | 5-0 | 5th round | MIM Britannia British Open |

*John Parrott*

| | | | | |
|---|---|---|---|---|
| | v O'Kane | 5-2 | Quarter-final | MIM Britannia British Open |
| | v Hallett | 8-9 | Semi-final | MIM Britannia British Open |
| | v Clark | 5-1 | Semi-final | Kent Cup |
| | v King | 10-4 | 1st round | Embassy World Championship |
| | v Thorburn | 10-13 | 2nd round | Embassy World Championship |
| | v Dodd | 4-5 | 3rd round | Fidelity International |
| | v Hallett | 3-5 | 1st round | Fosters Professional |
| | v Morra | 5-3 | 3rd round | Rothmans Grand Prix |
| | v Edmonds | 3-5 | 4th round | Rothmans Grand Prix |
| | v Dunning | 5-2 | 3rd round | BCE Canadian Masters |
| | v D. Morgan | 5-3 | 4th round | BCE Canadian Masters |
| | v Virgo | 5-4 | 5th round | BCE Canadian Masters |
| | v Hallett | 3-5 | Quarter-final | BCE Canadian Masters |
| | v Martin | 9-6 | 3rd round | Tennents UK Open |
| | v N. Gilbert | 9-8 | 4th round | Tennents UK Open |
| | v Dennis Taylor | 9-4 | 5th round | Tennents UK Open |
| | v S. Davis | 4-9 | Quarter-final | Tennents UK Open |
| | v Johnson | 9-7 | Quarter-final | Everest World Matchplay |
| | v Hendry | 9-6 | Semi-final | Everest World Matchplay |
| | v S. Davis | 5-9 | Final | Everest World Matchplay |
| **1989** | v Roe | 5-2 | 3rd round | Mercantile Credit Classic |
| | v Wright | 5-2 | 4th round | Mercantile Credit Classic |
| | v S. Francisco | 5-1 | 5th round | Mercantile Credit Classic |
| | v W. Jones | 4-5 | Quarter-final | Mercantile Credit Classic |
| | v Dennis Taylor | 5-1 | 1st round | Benson and Hedges Masters |
| | v White | 5-4 | Quarter-final | Benson and Hedges Masters |
| | v N. Foulds | 6-5 | Semi-final | Benson and Hedges Masters |
| | v Hendry | 6-9 | Final | Benson and Hedges Masters |
| | v Gary Wilkinson | 5-2 | 4th round | European Open |
| | v J. Campbell | 5-0 | 5th round | European Open |
| | v Charlton | 5-1 | Quarter-final | European Open |
| | v Hallett | 5-4 | Semi-final | European Open |
| | **v Griffiths** | **9-8** | **Final** | **European Open** |
| | v Miles | 5-3 | 3rd round | English Championship |
| | v Fowler | 5-4 | 4th round | English Championship |
| | v Johnson | 5-4 | Quarter-final | English Championship |
| | v N. Foulds | 5-4 | Semi-final | English Championship |
| | v Hallett | 7-9 | Final | English Championship |
| | v Wright | 5-1 | 3rd round | Anglian British Open |
| | v Longworth | 5-1 | 4th round | Anglian British Open |
| | v Mountjoy | 5-2 | 5th round | Anglian British Open |
| | v S. Davis | 5-1 | Quarter-final | Anglian British Open |
| | v Reynolds | 8-9 | Semi-final | Anglian British Open |
| | v Dennis Taylor | 5-1 | 1st round | Benson and Hedges Irish Masters |
| | v White | 5-1 | Quarter-final | Benson and Hedges Irish Masters |
| | v Higgins | 4-6 | Semi-final | Benson and Hedges Irish Masters |
| | v James | 10-9 | 1st round | Embassy World Championship |
| | v Dennis Taylor | 13-10 | 2nd round | Embassy World Championship |
| | v White | 13-7 | Quarter-final | Embassy World Championship |
| | v Meo | 16-7 | Semi-final | Embassy World Championship |
| | v S. Davis | 3-18 | Final | Embassy World Championship |
| | v Knowles | 3-6 | 1st round | Lion Brown New Zealand Masters |
| | v M. Gibson | 5-3 | 3rd round | Hong Kong Open |
| | v Newbury | 2-5 | 4th round | Hong Kong Open |
| | v Thorburn | 6-5 | Quarter-final | Regal Scottish Masters |
| | v Hendry | 4-6 | Semi-final | Regal Scottish Masters |
| | v Fisher | 5-2 | 3rd round | BCE International |
| | v Drago | 5-3 | 4th round | BCE International |
| | v Knowles | 5-2 | 5th round | BCE International |
| | v Bond | 2-5 | Quarter-final | BCE International |
| | v S. Murphy | 5-1 | 3rd round | Rothmans Grand Prix |
| | v Gary Wilkinson | 5-1 | 4th round | Rothmans Grand Prix |
| | v Reynolds | 2-5 | 5th round | Rothmans Grand Prix |

| | | | | |
|---|---|---|---|---|
| | v P. Gibson | 5-2 | 3rd round | Dubai Classic |
| | v Wattana | 5-3 | 4th round | Dubai Classic |
| | v James | 5-3 | 5th round | Dubai Classic |
| | v P. Francisco | 5-1 | Quarter-final | Dubai Classic |
| | v Mountjoy | 4-5 | Semi-final | Dubai Classic |
| | v J. McLaughlin | 9-2 | 3rd round | Stormseal UK Open |
| | v Chaperon | 9-8 | 4th round | Stormseal UK Open |
| | v Gary Wilkinson | 6-9 | 5th round | Stormseal UK Open |
| | v Dennis Taylor | 9-6 | Quarter-final | Everest World Matchplay |
| | v Hendry | 9-8 | Semi-final | Everest World Matchplay |
| | v White | 9-18 | Final | Everest World Matchplay |
| **1990** | v Edwards | 5-2 | 3rd round | Mercantile Credit Classic |
| | v Higgins | 5-4 | 4th round | Mercantile Credit Classic |
| | v James | 3-5 | 5th round | Mercantile Credit Classic |
| | v Meo | 5-3 | 1st round | Benson and Hedges Masters |
| | v Johnson | 5-3 | Quarter-final | Benson and Hedges Masters |
| | v S. Davis | 6-2 | Semi-final | Benson and Hedges Masters |
| | v Hendry | 4-9 | Final | Benson and Hedges Masters |
| | v Duggan | 1-5 | 3rd round | Pearl Assurance British Open |
| | v Wright | 5-1 | 3rd round | European Open |
| | v W. Jones | 5-0 | 4th round | European Open |
| | v Johnson | 5-2 | 5th round | European Open |
| | v Bond | 5-3 | Quarter-final | European Open |
| | v James | 6-3 | Semi-final | European Open |
| | **v Hendry** | **10-6** | **Final** | **European Open** |
| | v Griffiths | 3-5 | Quarter-final | Benson and Hedges Irish Masters |
| | v M. Bennett | 10-9 | 1st round | Embassy World Championship |
| | v Reynolds | 13-11 | 2nd round | Embassy World Championship |
| | v Thorburn | 13-6 | Quarter-final | Embassy World Championship |
| | v Hendry | 11-16 | Semi-final | Embassy World Championship |

## BARRY PINCHES (England)

**Born** 13.7.70. **Turned professional** 1989. **World ranking** 83.

| | | | | |
|---|---|---|---|---|
| **1989** | v Terry | 5-1 | 1st round | Hong Kong Open |
| | v M. Bennett | 5-2 | 2nd round | Hong Kong Open |
| | v S. Francisco | 5-4 | 3rd round | Hong Kong Open |
| | v Gary Wilkinson | 4-5 | 4th round | Hong Kong Open |
| | v Glen Wilkinson | 5-4 | 1st round | 555 Asian Open |
| | v Roscoe | 2-5 | 2nd round | 555 Asian Open |
| | v Scott | 5-4 | 1st round | BCE International |
| | v Graham | 0-5 | 2nd round | BCE International |
| | v M. Smith | 2-5 | 1st round | Rothmans Grand Prix |
| | v Houlihan | 1-5 | 1st round | Dubai Classic |
| | v M. Smith | 6-4 | 1st round | Stormseal UK Open |
| | v Johnston-Allen | 1-6 | 2nd round | Stormseal UK Open |
| **1990** | v Scott | 5-0 | 1st round | Mercantile Credit Classic |
| | v Macleod | 4-5 | 2nd round | Mercantile Credit Classic |
| | v Gauvreau | 4-5 | 1st round | Pearl Assurance British Open |
| | v Marshall | 5-4 | 1st round | European Open |
| | v Stevens | 5-4 | 2nd round | European Open |
| | v James | 2-5 | 3rd round | European Open |
| | v Parkin | 10-0 | Qualifying | Embassy World Championship |
| | v Oliver | 10-8 | Qualifying | Embassy World Championship |
| | v Roscoe | 10-6 | Qualifying | Embassy World Championship |
| | v Chappel | 3-10 | Qualifying | Embassy World Championship |

## MICK PRICE (England)

**Born** 2.6.66. **Turned professional** 1988. **World ranking** 77 (90).

| | | | | |
|---|---|---|---|---|
| **1988** | v Medati | 5-4 | 1st round | Fidelity International |
| | v Werbeniuk | 5-2 | 2nd round | Fidelity International |
| | v Longworth | 4-5 | 3rd round | Fidelity International |
| | v Foldvari | 1-5 | 1st round | Rothmans Grand Prix |
| | v Meadowcroft | 5-0 | 1st round | BCE Canadian Masters |
| | v D. Gilbert | 5-4 | 2nd round | BCE Canadian Masters |
| | v Mountjoy | 2-5 | 3rd round | BCE Canadian Masters |
| | v Grace | 9-3 | 1st round | Tennents UK Open |
| | v Murphy | 6-9 | 2nd round | Tennents UK Open |
| **1989** | v Dunning | 3-5 | 1st round | Mercantile Credit Classic |
| | v John Rea | 5-4 | 1st round | European Open |
| | v J. McLaughlin | 3-5 | 2nd round | European Open |
| | v Johnston-Allen | 5-4 | 1st round | English Championship |
| | v Edmonds | 5-4 | 2nd round | English Championship |
| | v David Taylor | 5-1 | 3rd round | English Championship |
| | v Hallett | 4-5 | 4th round | English Championship |
| | v Rigitano | 5-0 | 1st round | Anglian British Open |
| | v Roe | 2-5 | 2nd round | Anglian British Open |
| | v Sinclair | 10-9 | Qualifying | Embassy World Championship |
| | v M. Bennett | 10-9 | Qualifying | Embassy World Championship |
| | v Rowswell | 6-10 | Qualifying | Embassy World Championship |
| | v Ellis | 5-2 | 1st round | Hong Kong Open |
| | v Johnston-Allen | 5-1 | 2nd round | Hong Kong Open |
| | v Roe | 4-5 | 3rd round | Hong Kong Open |
| | v Meadowcroft | 5-2 | 1st round | 555 Asian Open |
| | v Dodd | 5-1 | 2nd round | 555 Asian Open |
| | v Clark | 2-5 | 3rd round | 555 Asian Open |
| | v S. Murphy | 4-5 | 1st round | BCE International |
| | v M. Gibson | 5-4 | 1st round | Rothmans Grand Prix |
| | v Wych | 3-5 | 2nd round | Rothmans Grand Prix |
| | v Burke | 5-0 | 1st round | Dubai Classic |
| | v Martin | 3-5 | 2nd round | Dubai Classic |
| | v Kearney | 6-1 | 1st round | Stormseal UK Open |
| | v Bales | 6-2 | 2nd round | Stormseal UK Open |
| | v Chaperon | 6-9 | 3rd round | Stormseal UK Open |
| **1990** | v Rigitano | 2-5 | 1st round | Mercantile Credit Classic |
| | v S. Campbell | 3-5 | 1st round | Pearl Assurance British Open |
| | v Brumby | 5-1 | 1st round | European Open |
| | v Gary Wilkinson | 5-4 | 2nd round | European Open |
| | v Thorburn | 5-0 | 3rd round | European Open |
| | v Charlton | 4-5 | 4th round | European Open |
| | v Whitthread | 10-6 | Qualifying | Embassy World Championship |
| | v Duggan | 10-9 | Qualifying | Embassy World Championship |
| | v J. Campbell | 10-6 | Qualifying | Embassy World Championship |
| | v Charlton | 5-10 | Qualifying | Embassy World Championship |

## JACK REA (Northern Ireland)

**Born** 6.4.21. **Turned professional** 1948. **World ranking** 131 (117).

| | | | | |
|---|---|---|---|---|
| **1969** | v G. Owen | 17-25 | Quarter-final | World Championship |
| **1970** | v Spencer | 15-31 | Quarter-final | World Championship |
| **1972** | v Higgins | 11-19 | 1st round | World Championship |
| **1973** | v Houlihan | 2-9 | 1st round | World Championship |
| **1976** | v Anderson | 8-5 | Qualifying | Embassy World Championship |
| **1977** | v John Rea | 9-11 | Qualifying | Embassy World Championship |
| | v Fagan | 1-5 | 1st round | Super Crystalate UK Championship |
| **1978** | v Meadowcroft | 5-9 | Qualifying | Coral UK Championship |
| **1979** | v Dunning | 5-9 | Prelim | Embassy World Championship |
| | v Bennett | 9-8 | 1st round | Coral UK Championship |
| | v Houlihan | 3-9 | 2nd round | Coral UK Championship |
| **1980** | v Thorne | 1-9 | Qualifying | Embassy World Championship |

| | | | | |
|---|---|---|---|---|
| **1981** | v D. Hughes | 4-5 | Qualifying | Jameson International |
| **1982** | v E. Hughes | 1-6 | Quarter-final | Irish Championship |
| | v Bennett | 8-5 | Qualifying | Embassy World Championship |
| | v Werbeniuk | 2-5 | 2nd round | Professional Players Tournament |
| | v Roscoe | 6-9 | Qualifying | Coral UK Championship |
| **1983** | v Higgins | 3-6 | Quarter-final | Irish Championship |
| | v David Taylor | 7-8 | Qualifying | Embassy World Championship |
| | v Edmonds | 1-5 | Qualifying | Jameson International |
| | v French | 5-9 | Qualifying | Coral UK Championship |
| **1984** | v Bradley | 2-5 | Qualifying | Jameson International |
| **1985** | v Foldvari | 4-5 | Qualifying | Mercantile Credit Classic |
| | v Dennis Taylor | 0-6 | Quarter-final | Irish Championship |
| | v Murphy | 1-5 | 2nd round | Goya Matchroom Trophy |
| **1986** | v Fisher | 3-5 | 2nd round | Mercantile Credit Classic |
| | v Bradley | 1-5 | 2nd round | Dulux British Open |
| | v Kelly | 0-5 | 1st round | Strongbow Irish Championship |
| | v Darrington | 5-4 | 1st round | BCE International |
| | v W. Jones | 1-5 | 2nd round | BCE International |
| | v D. Hughes | 5-2 | 1st round | Rothmans Grand Prix |
| | v B. Harris | 0-5 | 2nd round | Rothmans Grand Prix |
| | v B. Harris | 5-9 | 2nd round | Tennents UK Open |
| **1987** | v Kelly | 5-3 | 1st round | Mercantile Credit Classic |
| | v Hendry | 1-5 | 2nd round | Mercantile Credit Classic |
| | v Oliver | 1-5 | 1st round | Dulux British Open |
| | v Bear | 5-10 | Qualifying | Embassy World Championship |
| | v Browne | 3-5 | 1st round | Matchroom Irish Championship |
| | v Burke | 5-1 | 1st round | Fidelity International |
| | v G. Foulds | 5-4 | 2nd round | Fidelity International |
| | v Spencer | 0-5 | 3rd round | Fidelity International |
| | v Rigitano | 4-5 | 1st round | Rothmans Grand Prix |
| | v Watterson | 9-6 | 1st round | Tennents UK Open |
| | v Chaperon | 6-9 | 2nd round | Tennents UK Open |
| **1988** | v D. Gilbert | 2-5 | 1st round | Mercantile Credit Classic |
| | v Browne | 0-5 | 1st round | Irish Championship |
| | v Rowswell | 1-5 | 1st round | MIM Britannia British Open |
| | v Mikkelsen | 3-10 | Qualifying | Embassy World Championship |
| | v Lawlor | 2-5 | 1st round | Fidelity International |
| | v B. Harris | 2-5 | 1st round | Rothmans Grand Prix |
| | v M. Smith | 1-5 | 1st round | BCE Canadian Masters |
| | v Glen Wilkinson | 0-9 | 1st round | Tennents UK Open |
| **1989** | v M. Gibson | 5-3 | 1st round | Mercantile Credit Classic |
| | v Murphy | 0-5 | 2nd round | Mercantile Credit Classic |
| | v G. Foulds | 4-5 | 1st round | European Open |
| | v J. McLaughlin | 0-5 | Quarter-final | Irish Championship |
| | v Bear | 4-5 | 1st round | Anglian British Open |
| | v Gauvreau | 1-5 | 1st round | Hong Kong Open |
| | v Bradley | 2-5 | 1st round | 555 Asian Open |
| | v Houlihan | 4-5 | 1st round | BCE International |
| | v Gauvreau | 2-5 | 1st round | Rothmans Grand Prix |
| | v Lawlor | 3-5 | 1st round | Dubai Classic |
| | v Bear | 0-6 | 1st round | Stormseal UK Open |
| **1990** | v Marshall | 2-5 | 1st round | Mercantile Credit Classic |
| | v V. Harris | 2-5 | 1st round | Pearl Assurance British Open |
| | v A. Harris | 5-4 | 1st round | European Open |
| | v Chappel | 1-5 | 2nd round | European Open |
| | v Gauvreau | 9-10 | Qualifying | Embassy World Championship |

## JOHN REA (Scotland)

**Born** 5.12.51. **Turned professional** 1984. **World ranking** 86 (66).

| | | | | |
|---|---|---|---|---|
| **1984** | v Browne | 2-5 | Qualifying | Jameson International |
| | v Fitzmaurice | 5-2 | Qualifying | Rothmans Grand Prix |
| | v E. Hughes | 5-4 | 1st round | Rothmans Grand Prix |
| | v David Taylor | 1-5 | 2nd round | Rothmans Grand Prix |
| | v Bennett | 9-5 | Qualifying | Coral UK Open |
| | v Dunning | 9-3 | Qualifying | Coral UK Open |
| | v Edmonds | 9-6 | Qualifying | Coral UK Open |
| | v Johnson | 6-9 | Qualifying | Coral UK Open |
| **1985** | v Sheehan | 2-5 | Qualifying | Mercantile Credit Classic |
| | v Donnelly | 6-2 | 1st round | Scottish Championship |
| | v Sinclair | 2-6 | Semi-final | Scottish Championship |
| | v Fisher | 6-0 | Qualifying | Dulux British Open |
| | v Parrott | 4-6 | 1st round | Dulux British Open |
| | v W. Jones | 3-10 | Qualifying | Embassy World Championship |
| | v Bradley | 1-5 | 2nd round | Goya Matchroom Trophy |
| | v W. Jones | 0-5 | 2nd round | Rothmans Grand Prix |
| | v F. Davis | 8-9 | 2nd round | Coral UK Open |
| **1986** | v Williamson | 5-4 | 2nd round | Mercantile Credit Classic |
| | v Hallett | 2-5 | 3rd round | Mercantile Credit Classic |
| | v King | 5-1 | 2nd round | Dulux British Open |
| | v Reardon | 5-3 | 3rd round | Dulux British Open |
| | v Virgo | 0-5 | 4th round | Dulux British Open |
| | v Donnelly | 6-1 | Quarter-final | Canada Dry Scottish Championship |
| | v Gibson | 0-6 | Semi-final | Canada Dry Scottish Championship |
| | v E. McLaughlin | 10-6 | Qualifying | Embassy World Championship |
| | v Longworth | 4-10 | Qualifying | Embassy World Championship |
| | v Anderson | 5-1 | 2nd round | BCE International |
| | v S. Davis | 1-5 | 3rd round | BCE International |
| | v Sinclair | 5-4 | 2nd round | Rothmans Grand Prix |
| | v Wych | 2-5 | 3rd round | Rothmans Grand Prix |
| | v N. Gilbert | 9-8 | 2nd round | Tennents UK Open |
| | v Knowles | 4-9 | 3rd round | Tennents UK Open |
| **1987** | v Owers | 5-2 | 2nd round | Mercantile Credit Classic |
| | v Meo | 4-5 | 3rd round | Mercantile Credit Classic |
| | v Black | 6-1 | 1st round | Scottish Championship |
| | v Hendry | 0-6 | Semi-final | Scottish Championship |
| | v Hargreaves | 5-3 | 2nd round | Dulux British Open |
| | v Griffiths | 2-5 | 3rd round | Dulux British Open |
| | v Rempe | 9-10 | Qualifying | Embassy World Championship |
| | v Bales | 5-2 | 2nd round | Fidelity International |
| | v Thorne | 3-5 | 3rd round | Fidelity International |
| | v Bradley | 5-1 | 2nd round | Rothmans Grand Prix |
| | v P. Francisco | 3-5 | 3rd round | Rothmans Grand Prix |
| | v J. McLaughlin | 9-5 | 2nd round | Rothmans Grand Prix |
| | v Knowles | 6-9 | 3rd round | Tennents UK Open |
| **1988** | v Bales | 5-0 | 2nd round | Mercantile Credit Classic |
| | v Spencer | 3-5 | 3rd round | Mercantile Credit Classic |
| | v Sinclair | 6-5 | Quarter-final | Scottish Championship |
| | v W. Jones | 3-5 | 2nd round | MIM Britannia British Open |
| | v N. Gilbert | 5-10 | Qualifying | Embassy World Championship |
| | v Edwards | 5-2 | 1st round | Fidelity International |
| | v Bales | 5-2 | 2nd round | Fidelity International |
| | v P. Francisco | 5-0 | 3rd round | Fidelity International |
| | v David Taylor | 4-5 | 4th round | Fidelity International |
| | v Darrington | 5-4 | 1st round | Rothmans Grand Prix |
| | v Houlihan | 1-5 | 2nd round | Rothmans Grand Prix |
| | v Rowing | 5-2 | 1st round | BCE Canadian Masters |
| | v M. Bennett | 4-5 | 2nd round | BCE Canadian Masters |
| | v Meakin | 9-6 | 1st round | Tennents UK Open |
| | v Cripsey | 9-2 | 2nd round | Tennents UK Open |
| | v P. Fransisco | 2-9 | 3rd round | Tennents UK Open |
| **1989** | v Terry | 3-5 | 1st round | Mercantile Credit Classic |
| | v Price | 4-5 | 1st round | European Open |

| | | | | |
|---|---|---|---|---|
| | v Black | 5-3 | 1st round | Scottish Championship |
| | v Donnelly | 5-1 | Semi-final | Scottish Championship |
| | **v Macleod** | **9-7** | **Final** | **Scottish Championship** |
| | v Watchorn | 5-3 | 1st round | Anglian British Open |
| | v D. Gilbert | 3-5 | 2nd round | Anglian British Open |
| | v D. Hughes | 10-3 | Qualifying | Embassy World Championship |
| | v Houlihan | 10-5 | Qualifying | Embassy World Championship |
| | v Edmonds | 10-7 | Qualifying | Embassy World Championship |
| | v James | 7-10 | Qualifying | Embassy World Championship |
| | v Fitzmaurice | 5-4 | 2nd round | Hong Kong Open |
| | v West | 4-5 | 3rd round | Hong Kong Open |
| | v D. Campbell | 5-2 | 2nd round | 555 Asian Open |
| | v Meo | 2-5 | 3rd round | 555 Asian Open |
| | v Dennis Taylor | 6-5 | 1st round | Regal Scottish Masters |
| | v S. Davis | 2-6 | Quarter-final | Regal Scottish Masters |
| | v S. Campbell | 4-5 | 1st round | BCE International |
| | v Wattana | 3-5 | 1st round | Rothmans Grand Prix |
| | v Rowswell | 4-5 | 2nd round | Dubai Classic |
| | v Dyson | 4-6 | 1st round | Stormseal UK Open |
| **1990** | v Van Rensberg | 5-1 | 1st round | Mercantile Credit Classic |
| | v Johnston-Allen | 4-5 | 2nd round | Mercantile Credit Classic |
| | v Cairns | 1-5 | 1st round | Pearl Assurance British Open |
| | v Rigitano | 5-4 | 1st round | European Open |
| | v Spencer | 1-5 | 2nd round | European Open |
| | v J. Smith | 10-4 | Qualifying | Embassy World Championship |
| | v T. Murphy | 10-7 | Qualifying | Embassy World Championship |
| | v D. Morgan | 7-10 | Qualifying | Embassy World Championship |

## RAY REARDON M.B.E. (Wales)

**Born** 8.10.32. **Turned professional** 1967. **World ranking** 74 (54).

| | | | | |
|---|---|---|---|---|
| **1969** | v F. Davis | 24-25 | Quarter-final | World Championship |
| **1970** | v F. Davis | 31-26 | Quarter-final | World Championship (Apr) |
| | v Spencer | 37-33 | Semi-final | World Championship (Apr) |
| | **v Pulman** | **39-34** | **Final** | **World Championship (Apr)** |
| | v Spencer | 15-34 | Semi-final | World Championship (Nov) |
| **1972** | v Williams | 23-25 | Quarter-final | World Championship |
| **1973** | v Meadowcroft | 16-10 | 2nd round | World Championship |
| | v G. Owen | 16-6 | Quarter-final | World Championship |
| | v Spencer | 23-22 | Semi-final | World Championship |
| | **v Charlton** | **38-32** | **Final** | **World Championship** |
| **1974** | v Meadowcroft | 15-3 | 2nd round | World Championship |
| | v M. Owen | 15-11 | Quarter-final | World Championship |
| | v F. Davis | 15-3 | Semi-final | World Championship |
| | **v Miles** | **22-12** | **Final** | **World Championship** |
| **1975** | v Miles | 5-3 | Quarter-final | Benson & Hedges Masters |
| | v Williams | 5-4 | Semi-final | Benson & Hedges Masters |
| | v Spencer | 8-9 | Final | Benson & Hedges Masters |
| | v Simpson | 15-11 | 2nd round | World Championship |
| | v Spencer | 19-17 | Quarter-final | World Championship |
| | v Higgins | 19-14 | Semi-final | World Championship |
| | **v Charlton** | **31-30** | **Final** | **World Championship** |
| **1976** | v Charlton | 5-4 | Semi-final | Benson & Hedges Masters |
| | **v Miles** | **7-3** | **Final** | **Benson & Hedges Masters** |
| | v Dunning | 15-7 | 1st round | Embassy World Championship |
| | v Dennis Taylor | 15-2 | Quarter-final | Embassy World Championship |
| | v Mans | 20-10 | Semi-final | Embassy World Championship |
| | **v Higgins** | **27-16** | **Final** | **Embassy World Championship** |
| **1977** | v Miles | 5-2 | Semi-final | Benson & Hedges Masters |
| | v Mountjoy | 6-7 | Final | Benson & Hedges Masters |
| | v Fagan | 13-7 | 1st round | Embassy World Championship |

| | | | | |
|---|---|---|---|---|
| | v Spencer | 6-13 | Quarter-final | Embassy World Championship |
| | v Meadowcroft | 4-5 | 2nd round | Super Crystalate UK Championship |
| **1978** | v Higgins | 1-5 | Semi-final | Benson & Hedges Masters |
| | v Mountjoy | 13-9 | 1st round | Embassy World Championship |
| | v Werbeniuk | 13-6 | Quarter-final | Embassy World Championship |
| | v Charlton | 18-14 | Semi-final | Embassy World Championship |
| | **v Mans** | **25-18** | **Final** | **Embassy World Championship** |
| | v Thorne | 6-9 | 1st round | Coral UK Championship |
| **1979** | v David Taylor | 5-2 | Quarter-final | Benson & Hedges Masters |
| | v Mans | 3-5 | Semi-final | Benson & Hedges Masters |
| | v Mountjoy | 5-6 | Final | Benson & Hedges Masters |
| | v Miles | 13-8 | 1st round | Embassy World Championship |
| | v Dennis Taylor | 8-13 | Quarter-final | Embassy World Championship |
| **1980** | v Dennis Taylor | 5-3 | Quarter-final | Benson & Hedges Masters |
| | v Higgins | 2-5 | Semi-final | Benson & Hedges Masters |
| | v Higgins | 1-5 | Final | British Gold Cup |
| | v Wilson | 9-3 | 1st round | Woodpecker Welsh Championship |
| | v Mountjoy | 6-9 | Final | Woodpecker Welsh Championship |
| | v Werbeniuk | 13-6 | 2nd round | Embassy World Championship |
| | v David Taylor | 11-13 | Quarter-final | Embassy World Championship |
| | v Andrewartha | 9-3 | 2nd round | Coral UK Championship |
| | v Williams | 9-4 | Quarter-final | Coral UK Championship |
| | v Higgins | 7-9 | Semi-final | Coral UK Championship |
| **1981** | v Spencer | 1-5 | Quarter-final | Benson & Hedges Masters |
| | v Griffiths | 9-6 | Semi-final | Woodpecker Welsh Championship |
| | **v Wilson** | **9-6** | **Final** | **Woodpecker Welsh Championship** |
| | v Higgins | 6-5 | Semi-final | Benson & Hedges Irish Masters |
| | v Griffiths | 7-9 | Final | Benson & Hedges Irish Masters |
| | v Spencer | 13-11 | 2nd round | Embassy World Championship |
| | v Werbeniuk | 13-10 | Quarter-final | Embassy World Championship |
| | v Mountjoy | 10-16 | Semi-final | Embassy World Championship |
| | v White | 4-5 | Quarter-final | Langs Supreme Scottish Masters |
| | v Virgo | 3-5 | 3rd round | Jameson International |
| | v Johnson | 9-7 | 3rd round | Coral UK Championship |
| | v White | 8-9 | Quarter-final | Coral UK Championship |
| **1982** | v David Taylor | 5-1 | 1st round | Lada Classic |
| | v S. Davis | 4-5 | Semi-final | Lada Classic |
| | v Dennis Taylor | 5-3 | 1st round | Benson & Hedges Masters |
| | v Griffiths | 3-5 | Quarter-final | Benson & Hedges Masters |
| | v Everton | 6-1 | 1st round | Welsh Championship |
| | v Mountjoy | 7-9 | Semi-final | Welsh Championship |
| | v Dennis Taylor | 5-4 | Quarter-final | Benson & Hedges Irish Masters |
| | v Griffiths | 3-6 | Semi-final | Benson & Hedges Irish Masters |
| | v Donnelly | 10-5 | 1st round | Embassy World Championship |
| | v Virgo | 13-8 | 2nd round | Embassy World Championship |
| | v S. Francisco | 13-8 | Quarter-final | Embassy World Championship |
| | v Charlton | 16-11 | Semi-final | Embassy World Championship |
| | v Higgins | 15-18 | Final | Embassy World Championship |
| | v Griffiths | 3-5 | 1st round | Langs Supreme Scottish Masters |
| | v E. Hughes | 5-3 | 1st round | Jameson International |
| | v Knowles | 2-5 | 2nd round | Jameson International |
| | v Murphy | 5-0 | 1st round | Professional Players Tournament |
| | v Higgins | 5-2 | 2nd round | Professional Players Tournament |
| | v Macleod | 5-2 | 3rd round | Professional Players Tournament |
| | v Werbeniuk | 5-3 | Quarter-final | Professional Players Tournament |
| | v Charlton | 10-7 | Semi-final | Professional Players Tournament |
| | **v White** | **10-5** | **Final** | **Professional Players Tournament** |
| | v Wildman | 9-5 | 1st round | Coral UK Championship |
| | v Hallett | 9-8 | 2nd round | Coral UK Championship |
| | v White | 9-8 | Quarter-final | Coral UK Championship |
| | v Higgins | 6-9 | Semi-final | Coral UK Championship |
| **1983** | v Spencer | 3-5 | 1st round | Lada Classic |
| | v Reynolds | 5-1 | 1st round | Benson & Hedges Masters |

| | | | | |
|---|---|---|---|---|
| | v White | 5-2 | Quarter-final | Benson & Hedges Masters |
| | v Mountjoy | 6-3 | Semi-final | Benson & Hedges Masters |
| | v Thorburn | 7-9 | Final | Benson & Hedges Masters |
| | **v White** | **9-6** | **Final** | **Yamaha International Masters** |
| | v Andrewartha | 6-2 | Quarter-final | Woodpecker Welsh Championship |
| | v Griffiths | 9-4 | Semi-final | Woodpecker Welsh Championship |
| | **v Mountjoy** | **9-1** | **Final** | **Woodpecker Welsh Championship** |
| | v Meo | 5-4 | Quarter-final | Benson & Hedges Irish Masters |
| | v Higgins | 6-3 | Semi-final | Benson & Hedges Irish Masters |
| | v S. Davis | 2-9 | Final | Benson & Hedges Irish Masters |
| | v E. Hughes | 10-7 | 1st round | Embassy World Championship |
| | v Knowles | 12-13 | 2nd round | Embassy World Championship |
| | v Macleod | 5-2 | 1st round | Jameson International |
| | v Thorne | 0-5 | 2nd round | Jameson International |
| | v Ganim | 5-4 | 1st round | Professional Players Tournament |
| | v Duggan | 5-2 | 2nd round | Professional Players Tournament |
| | v Thorne | 3-5 | 3rd round | Professional Players Tournament |
| | v B. Harris | 9-7 | 1st round | Coral UK Championship |
| | v Wilson | 9-4 | 2nd round | Coral UK Championship |
| | v White | 4-9 | Quarter-final | Coral UK Championship |
| **1984** | v Williams | 4-5 | Qualifying | Lada Classic |
| | v Virgo | 5-3 | 1st round | Benson & Hedges Masters |
| | v White | 3-5 | Quarter-final | Benson & Hedges Masters |
| | v M. Owen | 6-1 | 1st round | Strongbow Welsh Championship |
| | v Wilson | 4-9 | Semi-final | Strongbow Welsh Championship |
| | v Higgins | 2-5 | Quarter-final | Benson & Hedges Irish Masters |
| | v Wych | 10-7 | 1st round | Embassy World Championship |
| | v S. Francisco | 13-8 | 2nd round | Embassy World Championship |
| | v Stevens | 2-13 | Quarter-final | Embassy World Championship |
| | v Dodd | 5-4 | 1st round | Jameson International |
| | v E. Hughes | 1-5 | 2nd round | Jameson International |
| | v Roscoe | 5-1 | 1st round | Rothmans Grand Prix |
| | v Wilson | 5-4 | 2nd round | Rothmans Grand Prix |
| | v Dennis Taylor | 3-5 | 3rd round | Rothmans Grand Prix |
| | v Fowler | 9-2 | 1st round | Coral UK Open |
| | v David Taylor | 9-4 | 2nd round | Coral UK Open |
| | v Thorburn | 8-9 | Quarter-final | Coral UK Open |
| **1985** | v Hallett | 5-3 | 1st round | Mercantile Credit Classic |
| | v E. Hughes | 5-1 | 2nd round | Mercantile Credit Classic |
| | v S. Davis | 1-5 | Quarter-final | Mercantile Credit Classic |
| | v David Taylor | 5-1 | 1st round | Benson & Hedges Masters |
| | v Thorburn | 0-5 | Quarter-final | Benson & Hedges Masters |
| | v King | 6-5 | 1st round | Dulux British Open |
| | v Martin | 4-5 | 2nd round | Dulux British Open |
| | v E. Hughes | 0-5 | 1st round | Benson & Hedges Irish Masters |
| | v E. Hughes | 10-9 | 1st round | Embassy World Championship |
| | v Fagan | 13-9 | 2nd round | Embassy World Championship |
| | v Parrott | 13-12 | Quarter-final | Embassy World Championship |
| | v S. Davis | 5-16 | Semi-final | Embassy World Championship |
| | v Everton | 6-2 | Quarter-final | BCE Welsh Championship |
| | v Griffiths | 3-9 | Semi-final | BCE Welsh Championship |
| | v Duggan | 3-5 | 3rd round | Goya Matchroom Trophy |
| | v Scott | 4-5 | 3rd round | Rothmans Grand Prix |
| | v Knowles | 5-2 | 1st round | BCE Canadian Masters |
| | v Dennis Taylor | 3-8 | Semi-final | BCE Canadian Masters |
| | v Miles | 9-4 | 3rd round | Coral UK Open |
| | v Macleod | 5-9 | 4th round | Coral UK Open |
| | v Griffiths | 2-5 | 1st round | Kit Kat |
| **1986** | v Mikkelsen | 3-5 | 3rd round | Mercantile Credit Classic |
| | v Stevens | 1-5 | 1st round | BCE Belgian Classic |
| | v Thorne | 4-5 | 1st round | Benson & Hedges Masters |
| | v W. Jones | 4-6 | Quarter-final | Zetters Welsh Championship |
| | v John Rea | 3-5 | 3rd round | Dulux British Open |

| | | | | |
|---|---|---|---|---|
| | v E. Hughes | 2-5 | 1st round | Benson & Hedges Irish Masters |
| | v J. Campbell | 8-10 | 1st round | Embassy World Championship |
| | v W. Jones | 5-4 | 3rd round | BCE International |
| | v Gauvreau | 2-5 | 4th round | BCE International |
| | v Chaperon | 3-5 | 3rd round | Rothmans Grand Prix |
| | v M. Gibson | 9-6 | 3rd round | Tennents UK Open |
| | v E. Hughes | 5-9 | 4th round | Tennents UK Open |
| **1987** | v Hendry | 3-5 | 3rd round | Mercantile Credit Classic |
| | v Johnson | 2-5 | 1st round | Benson & Hedges Masters |
| | v Chappel | 4-6 | Quarter-final | Matchroom Welsh Championship |
| | v O'Boye | 5-4 | 3rd round | Dulux British Open |
| | v Murphy | 4-5 | 4th round | Dulux British Open |
| | v West | 10-5 | 1st round | Embassy World Championship |
| | v S. Davis | 4-13 | 2nd round | Embassy World Championship |
| | v Rowswell | 5-4 | 2nd round | Fidelity International |
| | v Charlton | 4-5 | 3rd round | Fidelity International |
| | v Burke | 5-2 | 2nd round | Rothmans Grand Prix |
| | v Dennis Taylor | 1-5 | 3rd round | Rothmans Grand Prix |
| | v Van Rensberg | 9-7 | 2nd round | Tennents UK Open |
| | v S. Francisco | 3-9 | 3rd round | Tennents UK Open |
| **1988** | v Gary Wilkinson | 5-3 | 2nd round | Mercantile Credit Classic |
| | v Thorburn | 3-5 | 3rd round | Mercantile Credit Classic |
| | v W. Jones | 5-6 | Quarter-final | Welsh Championship |
| | v Van Rensberg | 5-3 | 2nd round | MIM Britannia British Open |
| | v S. Davis | 5-0 | 3rd round | MIM Britannia British Open |
| | v Roe | 2-5 | 4th round | MIM Britannia British Open |
| | v Oliver | 6-10 | Qualifying | Embassy World Championship |
| | v Donnelly | 5-1 | 2nd round | Fidelity International |
| | v Spencer | 4-5 | 3rd round | Fidelity International |
| | v Morra | 4-5 | 2nd round | Rothmans Grand Prix |
| | v J. Smith | 5-2 | 2nd round | BCE Canadian Masters |
| | v Chaperon | 4-5 | 3rd round | BCE Canadian Masters |
| | v D. Morgan | 9-5 | 2nd round | Tennents UK Open |
| | v O'Kane | 8-9 | 3rd round | Tennents UK Open |
| **1989** | v Chambers | 5-4 | 2nd round | Mercantile Credit Classic |
| | v Charlton | 5-1 | 3rd round | Mercantile Credit Classic |
| | v Hendry | 4-5 | 4th round | Mercantile Credit Classic |
| | v Williamson | 5-3 | 2nd round | European Open |
| | v Virgo | 3-5 | 3rd round | European Open |
| | v Mountjoy | 3-6 | Quarter-final | Senator Welsh Championship |
| | v S. Campbell | 5-4 | 2nd round | Anglian British Open |
| | v N. Foulds | 1-5 | 3rd round | Anglian British Open |
| | v Fitzmaurice | 10-5 | Qualifying | Embassy World Championship |
| | v Gary Wilkinson | 5-10 | Qualifying | Embassy World Championship |
| | v Terry | 4-6 | 2nd round | Stormseal UK Open |
| **1990** | v Sinclair | 4-5 | 2nd round | Mercantile Credit Classic |
| | v M. Bennett | 6-2 | 1st round | Senator Welsh Championship |
| | v Mountjoy | 3-6 | Quarter-final | Senator Welsh Championship |
| | v Rowing | 4-5 | 2nd round | Pearl Assurance British Open |
| | v Cairns | 8-10 | Qualifying | Embassy World Championship |

## DEAN REYNOLDS (England)

**Born** 11.1.63. **Turned professional** 1981. **World ranking** 8 (15).

| | | | | |
|---|---|---|---|---|
| **1982** | v Sheehan | 9-5 | Qualifying | Embassy World Championship |
| | v Edmonds | 9-6 | Qualifying | Embassy World Championship |
| | v F. Davis | 10-7 | 1st round | Embassy World Championship |
| | v S. Francisco | 8-13 | 2nd round | Embassy World Championship |
| | v Morra | 5-1 | Qualifying | Jameson International |
| | v Thorne | 5-3 | 1st round | Jameson International |

| | | | | |
|---|---|---|---|---|
| | v S. Davis | 0-5 | 2nd round | Jameson International |
| | v Fitzmaurice | 5-0 | 2nd round | Professional Players Tournament |
| | v Wilson | 5-1 | 3rd round | Professional Players Tournament |
| | v Charlton | 2-5 | Quarter-final | Professional Players Tournament |
| | v Fisher | 9-6 | 1st round | Coral UK Championship |
| | v Higgins | 8-9 | 2nd round | Coral UK Championship |
| **1983** | v Reardon | 1-5 | 1st round | Benson & Hedges Masters |
| | v Edmonds | 10-6 | Qualifying | Embassy World Championship |
| | v Higgins | 4-10 | 1st round | Embassy World Championship |
| | v Williams | 5-3 | Qualifying | Jameson International |
| | v Dennis Taylor | 3-5 | 1st round | Jameson International |
| | v Greaves | 5-1 | 1st round | Professional Players Tournament |
| | v Meo | 0-5 | 2nd round | Professional Players Tournament |
| | v Medati | 3-9 | 1st round | Coral UK Championship |
| **1984** | v Griffiths | 2-5 | Qualifying | Lada Classic |
| | v Morra | 7-10 | Qualifying | Embassy World Championship |
| | v Bales | 5-4 | Qualifying | Jameson International |
| | v Knowles | 1-5 | 1st round | Jameson International |
| | v Fowler | 5-2 | 1st round | Rothmans Grand Prix |
| | v P. Francisco | 5-4 | 2nd round | Rothmans Grand Prix |
| | v S. Francisco | 5-1 | 3rd round | Rothmans Grand Prix |
| | v S. Davis | 0-5 | Quarter-final | Rothmans Grand Prix |
| | v Chappel | 6-9 | Qualifying | Coral UK Open |
| **1985** | v King | 2-5 | Qualifying | Mercantile Credit Classic |
| | v Fitzmaurice | 9-2 | 1st round | Tolly Cobbold English Championship |
| | v Thorne | 9-6 | 2nd round | Tolly Cobbold English Championship |
| | v Meo | 4-9 | Quarter-final | Tolly Cobbold English Championship |
| | v Giannaros | 6-3 | 1st round | Dulux British Open |
| | v Thorburn | 3-5 | 2nd round | Dulux British Open |
| | v Gauvreau | 10-1 | Qualifying | Embassy World Championship |
| | v Higgins | 4-10 | 1st round | Embassy World Championship |
| | v Mikkelsen | 5-0 | 3rd round | Goya Matchroom Trophy |
| | v Gibson | 5-0 | 4th round | Goya Matchroom Trophy |
| | v White | 1-5 | 5th round | Goya Matchroom Trophy |
| | v Miles | 3-5 | 3rd round | Rothmans Grand Prix |
| | v J. McLaughlin | 9-7 | 3rd round | Coral UK Open |
| | v Griffiths | 7-9 | 4th round | Coral UK Open |
| **1986** | v Houlihan | 5-1 | 3rd round | Mercantile Credit Classic |
| | v Dennis Taylor | 4-5 | 4th round | Mercantile Credit Classic |
| | v Longworth | 9-5 | 3rd round | Tolly Cobbold English Championship |
| | v Thorne | 9-8 | 4th round | Tolly Cobbold English Championship |
| | v Meo | 4-9 | Quarter-final | Tolly Cobbold English Championship |
| | v Wych | 3-5 | 3rd round | Dulux British Open |
| | v Stevens | 6-10 | 1st round | Embassy World Championship |
| | v Dodd | 5-2 | 3rd round | BCE International |
| | v Mountjoy | 5-2 | 4th round | BCE International |
| | v David Taylor | 5-1 | 5th round | BCE International |
| | v N. Foulds | 2-5 | Quarter-final | BCE International |
| | v Newbury | 0-5 | 3rd round | Rothmans Grand Prix |
| | v Mikkelsen | 9-6 | 3rd round | Tennents UK Open |
| | v S. Francisco | 9-8 | 4th round | Tennents UK Open |
| | v S. Davis | 5-9 | 5th round | Tennents UK Open |
| **1987** | v King | 5-4 | 3rd round | Mercantile Credit Classic |
| | v Thorburn | 5-4 | 4th round | Mercantile Credit Classic |
| | v West | 5-3 | 5th round | Mercantile Credit Classic |
| | v Wilson | 5-1 | Quarter-final | Mercantile Credit Classic |
| | v White | 8-9 | Semi-final | Mercantile Credit Classic |
| | v Edmonds | 6-3 | 3rd round | Tolly Ales English Championship |
| | v White | 6-5 | 4th round | Tolly Ales English Championship |
| | v Thorne | 4-6 | Quarter-final | Tolly Ales English Championship |
| | v N. Gilbert | 5-3 | 3rd round | Dulux British Open |
| | v Knowles | 0-5 | 4th round | Dulux British Open |
| | v Oliver | 10-7 | Qualifying | Embassy World Championship |

*Dean Reynolds*

| | | | | |
|---|---|---|---|---|
| | v White | 8-10 | 1st round | Embassy World Championship |
| | v W. Jones | 4-5 | 3rd round | Fidelity International |
| | v Houlihan | 4-5 | 3rd round | Rothmans Grand Prix |
| | v Chappel | 5-9 | 3rd round | Tennents UK Open |
| **1988** | v O'Boye | 5-3 | 3rd round | Mercantile Credit Classic |
| | v Murphy | 4-5 | 4th round | Mercantile Credit Classic |
| | v S. Davis | 2-5 | 1st round | Benson & Hedges Masters |
| | v D. Gilbert | 6-3 | 3rd round | English Championship |
| | v Parrott | 6-2 | 4th round | English Championship |
| | v Meo | 6-4 | Quarter-final | English Championship |
| | v Johnson | 9-8 | Semi-final | English Championship |
| | **v N. Foulds** | **9-5** | **Final** | **English Championship** |
| | v O'Boye | 2-5 | 3rd round | MIM Britannia British Open |
| | v Hendry | 6-10 | 1st round | Embassy World Championship |
| | v Johnson | 4-5 | 1st round | New Zealand Masters |
| | v T. Jones | 5-4 | 3rd round | Fidelity International |
| | v N. Foulds | 5-3 | 4th round | Fidelity International |
| | v Spencer | 5-2 | 5th round | Fidelity International |
| | v Johnson | 5-1 | Quarter-final | Fidelity International |
| | v White | 5-9 | Semi-final | Fidelity International |
| | v Dodd | 5-3 | 3rd round | Rothmans Grand Prix |
| | v Knowles | 3-5 | 4th round | Rothmans Grand Prix |
| | v Martin | 5-0 | 3rd round | BCE Canadian Masters |
| | v C. Wilson | 4-5 | 4th round | BCE Canadian Masters |
| | v Chappel | 9-4 | 3rd round | Tennents UK Open |
| | v C. Wilson | 9-3 | 4th round | Tennents UK Open |
| | v Griffiths | 6-9 | 5th round | Tennents UK Open |
| **1989** | v Duggan | 5-1 | 3rd round | Mercantile Credit Classic |
| | v Knowles | 4-5 | 4th round | Mercantile Credit Classic |
| | v A. Harris | 5-1 | 3rd round | English Championship |
| | v Rowswell | 4-5 | 4th round | English Championship |
| | v Dodd | 5-2 | 3rd round | Anglian British Open |
| | v White | *wo* | 4th round | Anglian British Open |
| | v C. Wilson | 5-0 | 5th round | Anglian British Open |
| | v Johnson | 5-4 | Quarter-final | Anglian British Open |
| | v Parrott | 9-8 | Semi-final | Anglian British Open |
| | v Meo | 6-13 | Final | Anglian British Open |
| | v Graham | 10-5 | Qualifying | Embassy World Championship |
| | v P. Francisco | 10-7 | 1st round | Embassy World Championship |
| | v W. Jones | 13-3 | 2nd round | Embassy World Championship |
| | v Meo | 9-13 | Quarter-final | Embassy World Championship |
| | v Chambers | 4-5 | 3rd round | Hong Kong Open |
| | v Johnston-Allen | 5-2 | 3rd round | 555 Asian Open |
| | v W. Jones | 2-5 | 4th round | 555 Asian Open |
| | v Marshall | 3-5 | 3rd round | BCE International |
| | v V. Harris | 5-0 | 3rd round | Rothmans Grand Prix |
| | v King | 5-3 | 4th round | Rothmans Grand Prix |
| | v Parrott | 5-2 | 5th round | Rothmans Grand Prix |
| | v Dennis Taylor | 5-3 | Quarter-final | Rothmans Grand Prix |
| | v Wattana | 9-8 | Semi-final | Rothmans Grand Prix |
| | v S. Davis | 0-10 | Final | Rothmans Grand Prix |
| | v Martin | 5-2 | 3rd round | Dubai Classic |
| | v Spencer | 5-4 | 4th round | Dubai Classic |
| | v West | 5-2 | 5th round | Dubai Classic |
| | v Hendry | 3-5 | Quarter-final | Dubai Classic |
| | v Terry | 9-6 | 3rd round | Stormseal UK Open |
| | v W. Jones | 9-8 | 4th round | Stormseal UK Open |
| | v Hendry | 8-9 | 5th round | Stormseal UK Open |
| | v Meo | 9-7 | 1st round | Everest World Matchplay |
| | v S. Davis | 9-7 | Quarter-final | Everest World Matchplay |
| | v White | 8-9 | Semi-final | Everest World Matchplay |
| **1990** | v Rowing | 4-5 | 4th round | Mercantile Credit Classic |
| | v Wattana | 4-5 | Play-offs | Benson and Hedges Masters |

| | | | | |
|---|---|---|---|---|
| | v Chappel | 5-2 | 3rd round | Pearl Assurance British Open |
| | v Mountjoy | 2-5 | 4th round | Pearl Assurance British Open |
| | v D. Morgan | 5-3 | 3rd round | European Open |
| | v Bond | 4-5 | 4th round | European Open |
| | v P. Francisco | 10-7 | 1st round | Embassy World Championship |
| | v Parrott | 11-13 | 2nd round | Embassy World Championship |

## GINO RIGITANO (Canada)

**Born** 14.8.57. **Turned professional** 1983. **World ranking** 112 (116).

| | | | | |
|---|---|---|---|---|
| **1983** | v Gauvreau | 9-6 | 1st round | Canadian Championship |
| | v Mikkelsen | 4-9 | 2nd round | Canadian Championship |
| **1984** | v Gibson | 7-10 | Qualifying | Embassy World Championship |
| | v Foldvari | 2-5 | Qualifying | Jameson International |
| | v Edmonds | 5-3 | Qualifying | Rothmans Grand Prix |
| | v Thorburn | 4-5 | 1st round | Rothmans Grand Prix |
| | v Newbury | 6-9 | Qualifying | Coral UK Open |
| **1985** | v Fowler | 0-5 | Qualifying | Mercantile Credit Classic |
| | v Thorburn | 3-6 | 1st round | Dulux British Open |
| | v Sheehan | 10-9 | Qualifying | Embassy World Championship |
| | v B. Harris | 10-4 | Qualifying | Embassy World Championship |
| | v Kelly | 10-6 | Qualifying | Embassy World Championship |
| | v Fisher | 10-2 | Qualifying | Embassy World Championship |
| | v N. Foulds | 8-10 | Qualifying | Embassy World Championship |
| | v Black | 4-5 | 2nd round | Goya Matchroom Trophy |
| | v Miles | 4-5 | 2nd round | Rothmans Grand Prix |
| **1986** | v Dodd | 5-3 | 2nd round | Mercantile Credit Classic |
| | v Knowles | 4-5 | 3rd round | Mercantile Credit Classic |
| | v W. Jones | 1-5 | 2nd round | Dulux British Open |
| | v Foldvari | 6-10 | Qualifying | Embassy World Championship |
| | v Jonik | 1-6 | 1st round | Canadian Championship |
| | v Greaves | 5-3 | 1st round | BCE International |
| | v King | 0-5 | 2nd round | BCE International |
| | v Everton | 5-1 | 1st round | Rothmans Grand Prix |
| | v Medati | 1-5 | 2nd round | Rothmans Grand Prix |
| | v James | 5-9 | 1st round | Tennents UK Open |
| **1987** | v Grace | 5-4 | 1st round | Mercantile Credit Classic |
| | v Gauvreau | 0-5 | 2nd round | Mercantile Credit Classic |
| | v Demarco | 5-1 | 1st round | Dulux British Open |
| | v Browne | 5-4 | 2nd round | Dulux British Open |
| | v Hallett | 0-5 | 3rd round | Dulux British Open |
| | v Morgan | 4-0 *retd* | Qualifying | Embassy World Championship |
| | v V. Harris | 10-6 | Qualifying | Embassy World Championship |
| | v Newbury | 4-10 | Qualifying | Embassy World Championship |
| | v Wych | 4-6 | 1st round | Canadian Championship |
| | v Gary Wilkinson | 1-5 | 1st round | Fidelity International |
| | v Jack Rea | 5-4 | 1st round | Rothmans Grand Prix |
| | v Wright | 0-5 | 2nd round | Rothmans Grand Prix |
| | v P. Gibson | 5-9 | 1st round | Tennents UK Open |
| **1988** | v Fowler | 5-2 | 2nd round | Mercantile Credit Classic |
| | v Virgo | 2-5 | 3rd round | Mercantile Credit Classic |
| | v Marshall | 5-2 | 1st round | MIM Britannia British Open |
| | v Chaperon | 2-5 | 2nd round | MIM Britannia British Open |
| | v Dunning | 10-7 | Qualifying | Embassy World Championship |
| | v M. Bennett | 4-10 | Qualifying | Embassy World Championship |
| | v D. Hughes | 4-5 | 1st round | Fidelity International |
| | v W. Jones | 3-5 | 2nd round | Rothmans Grand Prix |
| | v Watterson | 3-5 | 1st round | BCE Canadian Masters |
| | v Terry | 5-9 | 1st round | Tennents UK Open |

| | | | | |
|---|---|---|---|---|
| **1989** | v Watterson | 4-5 | 1st round | Mercantile Credit Classic |
| | v Burke | 5-2 | 1st round | European Open |
| | v W. Jones | 4-5 | 2nd round | European Open |
| | v Price | 0-5 | 1st round | Anglian British Open |
| | v Johnston-Allen | 3-10 | Qualifying | Embassy World Championship |
| | v Edwards | 5-3 | 1st round | Hong Kong Open |
| | v N. Gilbert | 5-3 | 2nd round | Hong Kong Open |
| | v Griffiths | 3-5 | 3rd round | Hong Kong Open |
| | v T. Wilson | 3-5 | 1st round | 555 Asian Open |
| | v Oliver | 1-5 | 1st round | BCE International |
| | v Miles | 5-3 | 1st round | Rothmans Grand Prix |
| | v Fowler | 4-5 | 2nd round | Rothmans Grand Prix |
| | v Donnelly | 5-1 | 1st round | Dubai Classic |
| | v M. Bennett | 2-5 | 2nd round | Dubai Classic |
| | v Morra | 4-6 | 1st round | Stormseal UK Open |
| **1990** | v Price | 5-2 | 1st round | Mercantile Credit Classic |
| | v M. Bennett | 2-5 | 2nd round | Mercantile Credit Classic |
| | v Owers | 3-5 | 1st round | Pearl Assurance British Open |
| | v E. McLaughlin | *wo* | Qualifying | Embassy World Championship |
| | v Donnelly | 10-6 | Qualifying | Embassy World Championship |
| | v Fowler | 6-10 | Qualifying | Embassy World Championship |

## ALAIN ROBIDOUX (Canada)

**Born** 25.7.60. **Turned professional** 1986 (earned full status 1988). **World ranking** 17 (35).

| | | | | |
|---|---|---|---|---|
| **1988** | v Chaperon | 6-3 | 1st round | BCE Canadian Championship |
| | v Caggianello | 6-5 | Quarter-final | BCE Canadian Championship |
| | v Mikkelsen | 7-3 | Semi-final | BCE Canadian Championship |
| | **v Wych** | **8-4** | **Final** | **BCE Canadian Championship** |
| | v Black | 5-1 | 1st round | Fidelity International |
| | v Houlihan | 5-2 | 2nd round | Fidelity International |
| | v Charlton | 5-2 | 3rd round | Fidelity International |
| | v S. Davis | 4-5 | 4th round | Fidelity International |
| | v Van Rensberg | 5-2 | 1st round | Rothmans Grand Prix |
| | v Bales | 5-1 | 2nd round | Rothmans Grand Prix |
| | v Virgo | 5-1 | 3rd round | Rothmans Grand Prix |
| | v Meo | 5-0 | 4th round | Rothmans Grand Prix |
| | v Mountjoy | 5-4 | 5th round | Rothmans Grand Prix |
| | v N. Gilbert | 5-4 | Quarter-final | Rothmans Grand Prix |
| | v Higgins | 7-9 | Semi-final | Rothmans Grand Prix |
| | v Glen Wilkinson | 5-3 | 1st round | BCE Canadian Masters |
| | v Fisher | 5-0 | 2nd round | BCE Canadian Masters |
| | v Johnson | 1-5 | 3rd round | BCE Canadian Masters |
| | v Black | 9-2 | 1st round | Tennents UK Open |
| | v Bales | 9-4 | 2nd round | Tennents UK Open |
| | v Thorburn | 4-9 | 3rd round | Tennents UK Open |
| **1989** | v B. Harris | 5-1 | 1st round | Mercantile Credit Classic |
| | v Werbeniuk | 4-5 | 2nd round | Mercantile Credit Classic |
| | v Meadowcroft | 5-0 | 1st round | European Open |
| | v Fisher | 5-1 | 2nd round | European Open |
| | v Newbury | 5-0 | 3rd round | European Open |
| | v C. Wilson | 5-0 | 4th round | European Open |
| | v Griffiths | 3-5 | 5th round | European Open |
| | v B. Harris | 5-0 | 1st round | Anglian British Open |
| | v King | 5-2 | 2nd round | Anglian British Open |
| | v Spencer | 5-1 | 3rd round | Anglian British Open |
| | v N. Foulds | 1-5 | 4th round | Anglian British Open |
| | v Miles | 10-8 | Qualifying | Embassy World Championship |
| | v Fisher | 10-2 | Qualifying | Embassy World Championship |
| | v J. McLaughlin | 10-2 | Qualifying | Embassy World Championship |

*Alain Robidoux*

| | | | | |
|---|---|---|---|---|
| | v O'Kane | 5-10 | Qualifying | Embassy World Championship |
| | v Van Rensberg | 5-1 | 2nd round | Hong Kong Open |
| | v P. Francisco | 5-3 | 3rd round | Hong Kong Open |
| | v Hendry | 4-5 | 4th round | Hong Kong Open |
| | v S. Campbell | 2-5 | 2nd round | 555 Asian Open |
| | v Bradley | 5-2 | 2nd round | BCE International |
| | v Mountjoy | 5-4 | 3rd round | BCE International |
| | v Bales | 5-1 | 4th round | BCE International |
| | v Newbury | 5-2 | 5th round | BCE International |
| | v White | 5-4 | Quarter-final | BCE International |
| | v S. Davis | 3-6 | Semi-final | BCE International |
| | v Rowing | 5-4 | 2nd round | Rothmans Grand Prix |
| | v James | 5-2 | 3rd round | Rothmans Grand Prix |
| | v E. Hughes | 5-1 | 4th round | Rothmans Grand Prix |
| | v Fowler | 4-5 | 5th round | Rothmans Grand Prix |
| | v Morra | 5-1 | 3rd round | Dubai Classic |
| | v Bond | 4-5 | 4th round | Dubai Classic |
| | v J. Smith | 6-0 | 2nd round | Stormseal UK Open |
| | v Meo | 9-5 | 3rd round | Stormseal UK Open |
| | v S. Francisco | 9-3 | 4th round | Stormseal UK Open |
| | v Gollan | 9-5 | 5th round | Stormseal UK Open |
| | v Griffiths | 2-9 | Quarter-final | Stormseal UK Open |
| **1990** | v Cairns | 4-5 | 2nd round | Mercantile Credit Classic |
| | v Medati | 5-1 | 2nd round | Pearl Assurance British Open |
| | v Charlton | 5-3 | 3rd round | Pearl Assurance British Open |
| | v Duggan | 5-4 | 4th round | Pearl Assurance British Open |
| | v Chaperon | 4-5 | 5th round | Pearl Assurance British Open |
| | v Wattana | 5-2 | 2nd round | European Open |
| | v Hallett | 5-1 | 3rd round | European Open |
| | v J. Campbell | 4-5 | 4th round | European Open |
| | v Edwards | 10-3 | Qualifying | Embassy World Championship |
| | v Edmonds | 10-6 | Qualifying | Embassy World Championship |
| | v O'Kane | 10-2 | Qualifying | Embassy World Championship |
| | v Hendry | 7-10 | 1st round | Embassy World Championship |

## **DAVID ROE** (England)

**Born** 11.9.65. **Turned professional** 1986. **World ranking** 37 (26).

| | | | | |
|---|---|---|---|---|
| **1986** | v D. Hughes | 5-2 | 1st round | BCE International |
| | v Miles | 1-5 | 2nd round | BCE International |
| | v Hargreaves | 5-1 | 1st round | Rothmans Grand Prix |
| | v Van Rensberg | 5-3 | 2nd round | Rothmans Grand Prix |
| | v Knowles | 3-5 | 3rd round | Rothmans Grand Prix |
| | v G. Foulds | 7-1 | 1st round | Tennents UK Open |
| | v Van Rensberg | 9-6 | 2nd round | Tennents UK Open |
| | v Dennis Taylor | 6-9 | 3rd round | Tennents UK Open |
| **1987** | v Darrington | 5-0 | 1st round | Mercantile Credit Classic |
| | v Chaperon | 4-5 | 2nd round | Mercantile Credit Classic |
| | v Greaves | 6-1 | 1st round | Tolly Ales English Championship |
| | v Williamson | 4-6 | 2nd round | Tolly Ales English Championship |
| | v Watterson | 5-3 | 1st round | Dulux British Open |
| | v Black | 5-0 | 2nd round | Dulux British Open |
| | v N. Foulds | 1-5 | 3rd round | Dulux British Open |
| | v King | 4-10 | Qualifying | Embassy World Championship |
| | v Ellis | 5-4 | 1st round | Fidelity International |
| | v F. Davis | 5-3 | 2nd round | Fidelity International |
| | v Mountjoy | 5-4 | 3rd round | Fidelity International |
| | v James | 3-5 | 4th round | Fidelity International |
| | v Whitthread | 5-1 | 1st round | Rothmans Grand Prix |
| | v Wildman | 5-3 | 2nd round | Rothmans Grand Prix |
| | v Martin | 5-4 | 3rd round | Rothmans Grand Prix |

| | | | | |
|---|---|---|---|---|
| | v Knowles | 2-5 | 4th round | Rothmans Grand Prix |
| | v Marshall | 9-3 | 1st round | Tennents UK Open |
| | v Owers | 9-7 | 2nd round | Tennents UK Open |
| | v Williams | 9-7 | 3rd round | Tennents UK Open |
| | v V. Harris | 9-5 | 4th round | Tennents UK Open |
| | v White | 5-9 | 5th round | Tennents UK Open |
| **1988** | v Kelly | 5-1 | 1st round | Mercantile Credit Classic |
| | v Dodd | 2-5 | 2nd round | Mercantile Credit Classic |
| | v Lawlor | 5-6 | 1st round | English Championship |
| | v Chambers | 5-3 | 1st round | MIM Britannia British Open |
| | v Edmonds | 5-1 | 2nd round | MIM Britannia British Open |
| | v Drago | 5-3 | 3rd round | MIM Britannia British Open |
| | v Reardon | 5-2 | 4th round | MIM Britannia British Open |
| | v O'Boye | 1-5 | 5th round | MIM Britannia British Open |
| | v Demarco | 10-2 | Qualifying | Embassy World Championship |
| | v Owers | 7-10 | Qualifying | Embassy World Championship |
| | v Sinclair | 5-1 | 2nd round | Fidelity International |
| | v Williams | 3-5 | 3rd round | Fidelity International |
| | v B. Harris | 5-2 | 2nd round | Rothmans Grand Prix |
| | v Higgins | 4-5 | 3rd round | Rothmans Grand Prix |
| | v Whitthread | 5-2 | 2nd round | BCE Canadian Masters |
| | v White | 3-5 | 3rd round | BCE Canadian Masters |
| | v M. Gibson | 9-3 | 2nd round | Tennents UK Open |
| | v Meo | 9-6 | 3rd round | Tennents UK Open |
| | v P. Francisco | 9-7 | 4th round | Tennents UK Open |
| | v Thorburn | 8-9 | 5th round | Tennents UK Open |
| **1989** | v Ellis | 5-0 | 2nd round | Mercantile Credit Classic |
| | v Parrott | 2-5 | 3rd round | Mercantile Credit Classic |
| | v V. Harris | 5-1 | 2nd round | European Open |
| | v Meo | 5-1 | 3rd round | European Open |
| | v Johnson | 2-5 | 4th round | European Open |
| | v Lawlor | 5-1 | 2nd round | English Championship |
| | v West | 5-4 | 3rd round | English Championship |
| | v Thorne | 1-5 | 4th round | English Championship |
| | v Price | 5-2 | 2nd round | Anglian British Open |
| | v Williams | 5-2 | 3rd round | Anglian British Open |
| | v P. Francisco | 3-5 | 4th round | Anglian British Open |
| | v Watchorn | 10-5 | Qualifying | Embassy World Championship |
| | v Murphy | 10-7 | Qualifying | Embassy World Championship |
| | v Williams | 10-3 | Qualifying | Embassy World Championship |
| | v Knowles | 10-6 | 1st round | Embassy World Championship |
| | v Hallett | 12-13 | 2nd round | Embassy World Championship |
| | v Price | 5-4 | 3rd round | Hong Kong Open |
| | v T. Jones | 1-5 | 4th round | Hong Kong Open |
| | v D. Morgan | 5-2 | 3rd round | 555 Asian Open |
| | v Griffiths | 3-5 | 4th round | 555 Asian Open |
| | v Bales | 4-5 | 3rd round | BCE International |
| | v Fowler | 4-5 | 3rd round | Rothmans Grand Prix |
| | v Bales | 5-3 | 3rd round | Dubai Classic |
| | v Charlton | 5-3 | 4th round | Dubai Classic |
| | v Mountjoy | 4-5 | 5th round | Dubai Classic |
| | v Gary Wilkinson | 2-9 | 3rd round | Stormseal UK Open |
| **1990** | v J. McLaughlin | 2-5 | 3rd round | Mercantile Credit Classic |
| | v Marshall | 3-5 | 3rd round | Pearl Assurance British Open |
| | v Martin | 5-1 | 3rd round | European Open |
| | v White | 1-5 | 4th round | European Open |
| | v N. Gilbert | 6-10 | Qualifying | Embassy World Championship |

## COLIN ROSCOE (Wales)

**Born** 30.6.45. **Turned professional** 1981. **World ranking** 49 (48).

| | | | | |
|---|---|---|---|---|
| **1981** | v Macleod | 9-7 | Qualifying | Coral UK Championship |
| | v Williams | 4-9 | Qualifying | Coral UK Championship |
| | v Andrewartha | 5-2 | Qualifying | Jameson International |
| | v Sheehan | 5-1 | Qualifying | Jameson International |
| | v Meadowcroft | 4-5 | Qualifying | Jameson International |
| **1982** | v Griffiths | 2-6 | 1st round | Welsh Championship |
| | v Mikkelsen | 9-6 | Qualifying | Embassy World Championship |
| | v Thorne | 1-9 | Qualifying | Embassy World Championship |
| | v Dunning | 5-2 | Qualifying | Jameson International |
| | v French | 5-2 | Qualifying | Jameson International |
| | v S. Davis | 0-5 | 1st round | Jameson International |
| | v Griffiths | 1-5 | 1st round | Professional Players Tournament |
| | v Jack Rea | 9-6 | Qualifying | Coral UK Championship |
| | v Wildman | 4-9 | Qualifying | Coral UK Championship |
| **1983** | v C. Wilson | 4-6 | Quarter-final | Woodpecker Welsh Championship |
| | v Sinclair | 2-10 | Qualifying | Jameson International |
| | v Hallett | 2-5 | Qualifying | Jameson International |
| | v Meadowcroft | 4-5 | 1st round | Professional Players Tournament |
| | v N. Foulds | 2-9 | Qualifying | Coral UK Championship |
| **1984** | v Ganim | 5-3 | Qualifying | Lada Classic |
| | v Miles | 5-2 | Qualifying | Lada Classic |
| | v Werbeniuk | 5-4 | 1st round | Lada Classic |
| | v Griffiths | 2-5 | 2nd round | Lada Classic |
| | v C. Wilson | 2-6 | 1st round | Strongbow Welsh Championship |
| | v Demarco | 10-7 | Qualifying | Embassy World Championship |
| | v Browne | 4-10 | Qualifying | Embassy World Championship |
| | v Mikkelsen | 5-1 | Qualifying | Jameson International |
| | v French | 5-0 | Qualifying | Rothmans Grand Prix |
| | v Reardon | 1-5 | 1st round | Rothmans Grand Prix |
| | v J. McLaughlin | 8-9 | Qualifying | Coral UK Open |
| **1985** | v Medati | 4-5 | Qualifying | Mercantile Credit Classic |
| | v Giannaros | 1-6 | Qualifying | Dulux British Open |
| | v G. Foulds | 7-10 | Qualifying | Embassy World Championship |
| | v C. Wilson | 3-6 | Quarter-final | BCE Welsh Championship |
| | v G. Foulds | 5-3 | 2nd round | Goya Matchroom Trophy |
| | v C. Wilson | 1-5 | 3rd round | Goya Matchroom Trophy |
| | v Watson | 2-5 | 2nd round | Rothmans Grand Prix |
| | v West | 5-9 | 2nd round | Coral UK Open |
| **1986** | v V. Harris | 1-5 | 2nd round | Mercantile Credit Classic |
| | v Mountjoy | 4-6 | Quarter-final | Zetters Welsh Championship |
| | v Mikkelsen | 5-4 | 2nd round | Dulux British Open |
| | v Parrott | 2-5 | 3rd round | Dulux British Open |
| | v G. Foulds | 10-3 | Qualifying | Embassy World Championship |
| | v King | 5-10 | Qualifying | Embassy World Championship |
| | v Parkin | 5-1 | 1st round | BCE International |
| | v Chappel | 3-5 | 2nd round | BCE International |
| | v Burke | 3-5 | 1st round | Rothmans Grand Prix |
| | v Parkin | 9-1 | 1st round | Tennents UK Open |
| | v Wildman | 9-6 | 2nd round | Tennents UK Open |
| | v E. Hughes | 8-9 | 3rd round | Tennents UK Open |
| **1987** | v Whitthread | 5-1 | 1st round | Mercantile Credit Classic |
| | v Fagan | *wo* | 2nd round | Mercantile Credit Classic |
| | v Higgins | 2-5 | 3rd round | Mercantile Credit Classic |
| | v Everton | 6-2 | 1st round | Matchroom Welsh Championship |
| | v Mountjoy | 2-6 | Quarter-final | Matchroom Welsh Championship |
| | v Mienie | 5-2 | 1st round | Dulux British Open |
| | v Newbury | 5-3 | 2nd round | Dulux British Open |
| | v Dennis Taylor | 1-5 | 3rd round | Dulux British Open |
| | v Whitthread | 10-2 | Qualifying | Embassy World Championship |
| | v Duggan | 7-10 | Qualifying | Embassy World Championship |
| | v Lawlor | 5-4 | 1st round | Fidelity International |
| | v Browne | 5-2 | 2nd round | Fidelity International |
| | v Hallett | 3-5 | 3rd round | Fidelity International |

| | | | | |
|---|---|---|---|---|
| | v T. Jones | 1-5 | 1st round | Rothmans Grand Prix |
| | v Chambers | 4-9 | 1st round | Tennents UK Open |
| **1988** | v Watchorn | 5-2 | 1st round | Mercantile Credit Classic |
| | v W. Jones | 5-4 | 2nd round | Mercantile Credit Classic |
| | v Charlton | 5-3 | 3rd round | Mercantile Credit Classic |
| | v Knowles | 0-5 | 4th round | Mercantile Credit Classic |
| | v Chappel | 4-6 | 1st round | Welsh Championship |
| | v P. Gibson | 5-4 | 1st round | MIM Britannia British Open |
| | v Wildman | 5-0 | 2nd round | MIM Britannia British Open |
| | v C. Wilson | 2-5 | 3rd round | MIM Britannia British Open |
| | v E. McLaughlin | 10-1 | Qualifying | Embassy World Championship |
| | v Murphy | 8-10 | Qualifying | Embassy World Championship |
| | v Terry | 5-2 | 1st round | Fidelity International |
| | v Dodd | 1-5 | 2nd round | Fidelity International |
| | v Johnston-Allen | 1-5 | 1st round | Rothmans Grand Prix |
| | v W. Jones | 5-4 | 2nd round | BCE Canadian Masters |
| | v Knowles | 5-2 | 3rd round | BCE Canadian Masters |
| | v David Taylor | 1-5 | 4th round | BCE Canadian Masters |
| | v Darrington | 9-7 | 1st round | Tennents UK Open |
| | v Houlihan | 9-8 | 2nd round | Tennents UK Open |
| | v Newbury | 9-7 | 3rd round | Tennents UK Open |
| | v Hendry | 3-9 | 4th round | Tennents UK Open |
| **1989** | v Whitthread | 5-3 | 1st round | Mercantile Credit Classic |
| | v Owers | 5-3 | 2nd round | Mercantile Credit Classic |
| | v Knowles | 4-5 | 3rd round | Mercantile Credit Classic |
| | v Watterson | 5-4 | 1st round | European Open |
| | v Cripsey | 4-5 | 2nd round | European Open |
| | v M. Bennett | 3-6 | 1st round | Senator Welsh Championship |
| | v Meakin | 5-1 | 1st round | Anglian British Open |
| | v Werbeniuk | *wo* | 2nd round | Anglian British Open |
| | v Dennis Taylor | 5-4 | 3rd round | Anglian British Open |
| | v Meo | 3-5 | 4th round | Anglian British Open |
| | v Fitzmaurice | 9-10 | Qualifying | Embassy World Championship |
| | v Meakin | 5-1 | 2nd round | Hong Kong Open |
| | v Dennis Taylor | 3-5 | 3rd round | Hong Kong Open |
| | v Pinches | 5-2 | 2nd round | 555 Asian Open |
| | v White | 5-3 | 3rd round | 555 Asian Open |
| | v P. Francisco | 4-5 | 4th round | 555 Asian Open |
| | v Marshall | 4-5 | 2nd round | BCE International |
| | v Marshall | 5-4 | 2nd round | Rothmans Grand Prix |
| | v Clark | 3-5 | 3rd round | Rothmans Grand Prix |
| | v Grech | 1-5 | 2nd round | Dubai Classic |
| | v Medati | 5-6 | 2nd round | Stormseal UK Open |
| **1990** | v Bond | 5-4 | 2nd round | Mercantile Credit Classic |
| | v S. Francisco | 1-5 | 3rd round | Mercantile Credit Classic |
| | v D. Morgan | 4-6 | 1st round | Senator Welsh Championship |
| | v Oliver | 4-5 | 2nd round | Pearl Assurance British Open |
| | v Wildman | 5-3 | 2nd round | European Open |
| | v P. Francisco | 5-3 | 3rd round | European Open |
| | v Virgo | 5-2 | 4th round | European Open |
| | v Dyson | 5-2 | 5th round | European Open |
| | v James | 2-5 | Quarter-final | European Open |
| | v Pinches | 6-10 | Qualifying | Embassy World Championship |

## MARK ROWING (England)

**Born** 24.3.66. **Turned professional** 1988. **World ranking** 61 (99).

| | | | | |
|---|---|---|---|---|
| **1988** | v Sinclair | 0-5 | 1st round | Fidelity International |
| | v Bradley | 3-5 | 1st round | Rothmans Grand Prix |
| | v John Rea | 2-5 | 1st round | BCE Canadian Masters |
| | v G. Foulds | 9-4 | 1st round | Tennents UK Open |

| | | | | |
|---|---|---|---|---|
| | v Wright | 9-7 | 2nd round | Tennents UK Open |
| | v N. Foulds | 4-9 | 3rd round | Tennents UK Open |
| **1989** | v M. Smith | 5-3 | 1st round | Mercantile Credit Classic |
| | v King | 4-5 | 2nd round | Mercantile Credit Classic |
| | v Foldvari | 5-4 | 1st round | European Open |
| | v Clark | 0-5 | 2nd round | European Open |
| | v Terry | 1-5 | Prelim | English Championship |
| | v M. Gibson | 0-5 | 1st round | Anglian British Open |
| | v Mizerak | 10-1 | Qualifying | Embassy World Championship |
| | v Dunning | 10-9 | Qualifying | Embassy World Championship |
| | v King | 10-7 | Qualifying | Embassy World Championship |
| | v Duggan | 6-10 | Qualifying | Embassy World Championship |
| | v A. Harris | 5-4 | 1st round | Hong Kong Open |
| | v Longworth | 5-3 | 2nd round | Hong Kong Open |
| | v James | 1-5 | 3rd round | Hong Kong Open |
| | v Donnelly | 4-5 | 1st round | 555 Asian Open |
| | v Dunning | 5-0 | 1st round | BCE International |
| | v Fisher | 4-5 | 2nd round | BCE International |
| | v Bradley | 5-4 | 1st round | Rothmans Grand Prix |
| | v Robidoux | 4-5 | 2nd round | Rothmans Grand Prix |
| | v G. Foulds | 4-5 | 1st round | Dubai Classic |
| | v F. Davis | 6-5 | 1st round | Stormseal UK Open |
| | v Edmonds | 6-4 | 2nd round | Stormseal UK Open |
| | v Thorburn | 2-9 | 3rd round | Stormseal UK Open |
| **1990** | v Bear | 5-3 | 1st round | Mercantile Credit Classic |
| | v D. Gilbert | 5-1 | 2nd round | Mercantile Credit Classic |
| | v West | 5-0 | 3rd round | Mercantile Credit Classic |
| | v Reynolds | 5-4 | 4th round | Mercantile Credit Classic |
| | v S. Francisco | 1-5 | 5th round | Mercantile Credit Classic |
| | v F. Davis | 5-2 | 1st round | Pearl Assurance British Open |
| | v Reardon | 5-4 | 2nd round | Pearl Assurance British Open |
| | v W. Jones | 5-4 | 3rd round | Pearl Assurance British Open |
| | v Dodd | 2-5 | 4th round | Pearl Assurance British Open |
| | v Oliver | 4-5 | 1st round | European Open |
| | v Foldvari | 10-9 | Qualifying | Embassy World Championship |
| | v Wych | *wo* | Qualifying | Embassy World Championship |
| | v Fowler | 8-10 | Qualifying | Embassy World Championship |

## BRIAN ROWSWELL (England)

**Born** 18.3.67. **Turned professional** 1986. **World ranking** 64 (79).

| | | | | |
|---|---|---|---|---|
| **1986** | v Sheehan | 5-4 | 1st round | BCE International |
| | v Wildman | 2-5 | 2nd round | BCE International |
| | v D. Gilbert | 1-5 | 1st round | Rothmans Grand Prix |
| | v F. Davis | 9-4 | 2nd round | Tennents UK Open |
| | v Longworth | 3-9 | 3rd round | Tennents UK Open |
| **1987** | v Watterson | 5-1 | 1st round | Mercantile Credit Classic |
| | v Bradley | 4-5 | 2nd round | Mercantile Credit Classic |
| | v Smith | 5-6 | 1st round | Tolly Ales English Championship |
| | v Jenkins | 5-1 | 1st round | Dulux British Open |
| | v O'Kane | 5-4 | 2nd round | Dulux British Open |
| | v S. Francisco | 0-5 | 3rd round | Dulux British Open |
| | v Bradley | 6-10 | Qualifying | Embassy World Championship |
| | v D. Hughes | 5-1 | 1st round | Fidelity International |
| | v Reardon | 4-5 | 2nd round | Fidelity International |
| | v J. Smith | 5-3 | 1st round | Rothmans Grand Prix |
| | v Chaperon | 4-5 | 2nd round | Rothmans Grand Prix |
| | v Everton | 9-4 | 1st round | Tennents UK Open |
| | v O'Kane | 2-9 | 2nd round | Tennents UK Open |
| **1988** | v Chambers | 5-2 | 1st round | Mercantile Credit Classic |
| | v O'Kane | 5-4 | 2nd round | Mercantile Credit Classic |

| | | | | |
|---|---|---|---|---|
| | v S. Francisco | 3-5 | 3rd round | Mercantile Credit Classic |
| | v Gary Wilkinson | 1-6 | 1st round | English Championship |
| | v Jack Rea | 5-1 | 1st round | MIM Britannia British Open |
| | v J. McLaughlin | 5-2 | 2nd round | MIM Britannia British Open |
| | v Longworth | 5-4 | 3rd round | MIM Britannia British Open |
| | v Johnson | 2-5 | 4th round | MIM Britannia British Open |
| | v Thornley | 10-7 | Qualifying | Embassy World Championship |
| | v Werbeniuk | 6-10 | Qualifying | Embassy World Championship |
| | v Marshall | 4-5 | 1st round | Fidelity International |
| | v D. Morgan | 0-5 | 1st round | Rothmans Grand Prix |
| | v Ellis | 5-1 | 1st round | BCE Canadian Masters |
| | v Fowler | 4-5 | 2nd round | BCE Canadian Masters |
| | v Jenkins | 9-4 | 1st round | Tennents UK Open |
| | v Gauvreau | 9-2 | 2nd round | Tennents UK Open |
| | v Virgo | 3-9 | 3rd round | Tennents UK Open |
| **1989** | v Burke | 5-2 | 1st round | Mercantile Credit Classic |
| | v W. Jones | 3-5 | 2nd round | Mercantile Credit Classic |
| | v J. Smith | 2-5 | 1st round | European Open |
| | v V. Harris | 5-3 | 1st round | English Championship |
| | v Wright | 5-2 | 2nd round | English Championship |
| | v Martin | 5-2 | 3rd round | English Championship |
| | v Reynolds | 5-4 | 4th round | English Championship |
| | v Gary Wilkinson | 1-5 | 5th round | English Championship |
| | v Ellis | 5-1 | 1st round | Anglian British Open |
| | v W. Jones | 0-5 | 2nd round | Anglian British Open |
| | v Burke | 10-0 | Qualifying | Embassy World Championship |
| | v Gauvreau | 10-7 | Qualifying | Embassy World Championship |
| | v Price | 10-6 | Qualifying | Embassy World Championship |
| | v E. Hughes | 9-10 | Qualifying | Embassy World Championship |
| | v Cairns | 5-3 | 1st round | Hong Kong Open |
| | v Duggan | 3-5 | 2nd round | Hong Kong Open |
| | v Grace | 5-0 | 1st round | 555 Asian Open |
| | v Fowler | 3-5 | 2nd round | 555 Asian Open |
| | v Fitzmaurice | 4-5 | 1st round | BCE International |
| | v Darrington | 5-2 | 1st round | Rothmans Grand Prix |
| | v T. Murphy | 5-1 | 2nd round | Rothmans Grand Prix |
| | v C. Wilson | 5-4 | 3rd round | Rothmans Grand Prix |
| | v Dennis Taylor | 2-5 | 4th round | Rothmans Grand Prix |
| | v Kelly | 5-0 | 1st round | Dubai Classic |
| | v John Rea | 5-4 | 2nd round | Dubai Classic |
| | v Chaperon | 5-4 | 3rd round | Dubai Classic |
| | v Clark | 4-5 | 4th round | Dubai Classic |
| | v Darrington | 6-2 | 1st round | Stormseal UK Open |
| | v Fisher | 6-5 | 2nd round | Stormseal UK Open |
| | v Clark | 1-9 | 3rd round | Stormseal UK Open |
| **1990** | v Watterson | 5-4 | 1st round | Mercantile Credit Classic |
| | v Stevens | 5-3 | 2nd round | Mercantile Credit Classic |
| | v Chaperon | 1-5 | 3rd round | Mercantile Credit Classic |
| | v Bond | 3-5 | 1st round | Pearl Assurance British Open |
| | v Watchorn | 5-3 | 1st round | European Open |
| | v D. Morgan | 2-5 | 2nd round | European Open |
| | v Bond | 1-10 | Qualifying | Embassy World Championship |

## GEORGE SCOTT (England)

**Born** 16.9.29. **Turned professional** 1981. **World ranking** 89 (73).

| | | | | |
|---|---|---|---|---|
| **1982** | v B. Harris | 5-4 | Qualifying | Jameson International |
| | v Thorburn | 1-5 | 1st round | Jameson International |
| | v Meo | 5-9 | Qualifying | Coral UK Championship |
| **1983** | v Houlihan | 5-0 | Qualifying | Jameson International |
| | v Gibson | 5-3 | Qualifying | Jameson International |

| | | | | |
|---|---|---|---|---|
| | v Werbeniuk | 5-3 | 1st round | Jameson International |
| | v Griffiths | 0-5 | 2nd round | Jameson International |
| | v Dennis Taylor | 5-4 | 1st round | Professional Players Tournament |
| | v S. Francisco | 1-5 | 2nd round | Professional Players Tournament |
| | v Parrott | 7-9 | Qualifying | Coral UK Championship |
| **1984** | v Heywood | 10-7 | Qualifying | Embassy World Championship |
| | v Wych | 6-10 | Qualifying | Embassy World Championship |
| | v W. Jones | 0-5 | Qualifying | Jameson International |
| | v Chappel | 1-5 | Qualifying | Rothmans Grand Prix |
| | v O'Kane | 9-7 | Qualifying | Coral UK Open |
| | v Macleod | 5-9 | Qualifying | Coral UK Open |
| **1985** | v J. McLaughlin | 5-4 | Qualifying | Mercantile Credit Classic |
| | v J. Campbell | 5-4 | Qualifying | Mercantile Credit Classic |
| | v Thorburn | 1-5 | 1st round | Mercantile Credit Classic |
| | v V. Harris | 9-7 | Qualifying | Tolly Cobbold English Championship |
| | v Johnson | 1-9 | 1st round | Tolly Cobbold English Championship |
| | v Darrington | 6-3 | Qualifying | Dulux British Open |
| | v Dennis Taylor | 2-6 | 1st round | Dulux British Open |
| | v Newbury | 2-10 | Qualifying | Embassy World Championship |
| | v Van Rensberg | 5-4 | 2nd round | Goya Matchroom Trophy |
| | v Wildman | 5-1 | 3rd round | Goya Matchroom Trophy |
| | v Thorne | 1-5 | 4th round | Goya Matchroom Trophy |
| | v Chalmers | 5-2 | 2nd round | Rothmans Grand Prix |
| | v Reardon | 5-4 | 3rd round | Rothmans Grand Prix |
| | v C. Wilson | 3-5 | 4th round | Rothmans Grand Prix |
| | v Sheehan | 6-9 | 2nd round | Coral UK Open |
| **1986** | v Mikkelsen | 1-5 | 2nd round | Mercantile Credit Classic |
| | v Bennett | 9-1 | 2nd round | Tolly Cobbold English Championship |
| | v Meo | 1-9 | 3rd round | Tolly Cobbold English Championship |
| | v Chalmers | 5-1 | 2nd round | Dulux British Open |
| | v Griffiths | 3-5 | 3rd round | Dulux British Open |
| | v Kearney | 10-8 | Qualifying | Embassy World Championship |
| | v Fowler | 7-10 | Qualifying | Embassy World Championship |
| | v Owers | 1-5 | 2nd round | BCE International |
| | v Dodd | 2-5 | 2nd round | Rothmans Grand Prix |
| | v Watchorn | 9-7 | 2nd round | Tennents UK Open |
| | v Stevens | 2-9 | 3rd round | Tennents UK Open |
| **1987** | v Jenkins | 4-5 | 2nd round | Mercantile Credit Classic |
| | v Fitzmaurice | 2-6 | 2nd round | Tolly Ales English Championship |
| | v Burke | 5-2 | 2nd round | Dulux British Open |
| | v Martin | 3-5 | 3rd round | Dulux British Open |
| | v Dunning | 10-7 | Qualifying | Embassy World Championship |
| | v Oliver | 5-10 | Qualifying | Embassy World Championship |
| | v Gary Wilkinson | 2-5 | 2nd round | Fidelity International |
| | v Miles | 2-5 | 2nd round | Rothmans Grand Prix |
| | v Oliver | 4-9 | 2nd round | Tennents UK Open |
| **1988** | v Bear | 5-3 | 2nd round | Mercantile Credit Classic |
| | v Drago | 3-5 | 3rd round | Mercantile Credit Classic |
| | v Chambers | 3-6 | 2nd round | English Championship |
| | v Dunning | 3-5 | 2nd round | MIM Britannia British Open |
| | v Clark | 4-10 | Qualifying | Embassy World Championship |
| | v Johnston-Allen | 2-5 | 1st round | Fidelity International |
| | v T. Wilson | 3-5 | 1st round | Rothmans Grand Prix |
| | v Everton | 5-0 | 1st round | BCE Canadian Masters |
| | v Edmonds | 5-2 | 2nd round | BCE Canadian Masters |
| | v Williams | 5-2 | 3rd round | BCE Canadian Masters |
| | v S. Davis | 1-5 | 4th round | BCE Canadian Masters |
| | v Fagan | 9-2 | 1st round | Tennents UK Open |
| | v T. Jones | 5-9 | 2nd round | Tennents UK Open |
| **1989** | v Johnston-Allen | 0-5 | 1st round | Mercantile Credit Classic |
| | v Graham | 1-5 | 1st round | European Open |
| | v Darrington | 4-5 | 2nd round | Anglian British Open |
| | v T. Wilson | 4-10 | Qualifying | Embassy World Championship |

| | | | | |
|---|---|---|---|---|
| | v B. Morgan | 1-5 | 1st round | Hong Kong Open |
| | v J. Smith | 0-5 | 1st round | 555 Asian Open |
| | v Pinches | 4-5 | 1st round | BCE International |
| | v Bond | 0-5 | 1st round | Rothmans Grand Prix |
| | v Brumby | 5-4 | 2nd round | Dubai Classic |
| | v W. Jones | 3-5 | 3rd round | Dubai Classic |
| | v Sheehan | 1-6 | 1st round | Stormseal UK Open |
| **1990** | v Pinches | 0-5 | 1st round | Mercantile Credit Classic |
| | v B. Morgan | 1-5 | 1st round | Pearl Assurance British Open |
| | v S. Campbell | 2-5 | 1st round | European Open |
| | v Cairns | 3-10 | Qualifying | Embassy World Championship |

**DESSIE SHEEHAN** (Republic of Ireland)

**Born** 3.9.49. **Turned professional** 1981. **World ranking** 121 (109).

| | | | | |
|---|---|---|---|---|
| **1981** | v V. Harris | 5-1 | Qualifying | Jameson International |
| | v Roscoe | 1-5 | Qualifying | Jameson International |
| **1982** | v E. Hughes | 1-6 | 1st round | Irish Championship |
| | v V. Harris | 3-5 | Qualifying | Jameson International |
| | v Dennis Taylor | 3-5 | 1st round | Benson & Hedges Irish Masters |
| | v Reynolds | 5-9 | Qualifying | Embassy World Championship |
| | v Fitzmaurice | 1-5 | 1st round | Professional Players Tournament |
| **1983** | v Donnelly | 6-10 | Qualifying | Embassy World Championship |
| | v Murphy | 2-5 | Qualifying | Jameson International |
| | v Houlihan | 5-2 | Qualifying | Professional Players Tournament |
| | v Williams | 1-5 | 1st round | Professional Players Tournament |
| **1984** | v B. Harris | 3-10 | Qualifying | Embassy World Championship |
| | v Bales | 2-5 | Qualifying | Jameson International |
| | v Mikkelsen | 5-3 | Qualifying | Rothmans Grand Prix |
| | v Hallett | 1-5 | 1st round | Rothmans Grand Prix |
| | v P. Francisco | 5-9 | Qualifying | Coral UK Open |
| **1985** | v John Rea | 5-2 | Qualifying | Mercantile Credit Classic |
| | v E. McLaughlin | 2-5 | Qualifying | Mercantile Credit Classic |
| | v Murphy | 3-6 | Qualifying | Dulux British Open |
| | v J. McLaughlin | 3-6 | Qualifying | Irish Championship |
| | v Rigitano | 9-10 | Qualifying | Embassy World Championship |
| | v Smith | 2-5 | 1st round | Goya Matchroom Trophy |
| | v Watson | 1-5 | 1st round | Rothmans Grand Prix |
| | v Watchorn | 9-7 | 1st round | Coral UK Open |
| | v Scott | 9-6 | 2nd round | Coral UK Open |
| | v S. Davis | 1-9 | 3rd round | Coral UK Open |
| **1986** | v Hendry | 2-5 | 1st round | Mercantile Credit Classic |
| | v Simngam | 5-2 | 1st round | Dulux British Open |
| | v Watterson | *wo* | 2nd round | Dulux British Open |
| | v Thorburn | 0-5 | 3rd round | Dulux British Open |
| | v Houlihan | 10-7 | Qualifying | Embassy World Championship |
| | v King | 4-10 | Qualifying | Embassy World Championship |
| | v E. Hughes | 0-5 | 1st round | Strongbow Irish Championship |
| | v Rowswell | 4-5 | 1st round | BCE International |
| | v Demarco | 5-1 | 1st round | Rothmans Grand Prix |
| | v Browne | 4-5 | 2nd round | Rothmans Grand Prix |
| | v M. Bennett | 9-8 | 1st round | Tennents UK Open |
| | v Miles | 8-9 | 2nd round | Tennents UK Open |
| **1987** | v M. Bennett | 3-5 | 1st round | Mercantile Credit Classic |
| | v Wright | 5-2 | 1st round | Dulux British Open |
| | v V. Harris | 4-5 | 2nd round | Dulux British Open |
| | v N. Gilbert | 6-10 | Qualifying | Embassy World Championship |
| | v J. McLaughlin | 5-4 | 1st round | Matchroom Irish Championship |
| | v Dennis Taylor | 3-6 | Quarter-final | Matchroom Irish Championship |
| | v Dunning | 1-5 | 1st round | Fidelity International |
| | v Marshall | 1-5 | 1st round | Rothmans Grand Prix |

| | | | | |
|---|---|---|---|---|
| | v Ellis | 8-9 | 1st round | Tennents UK Open |
| **1988** | v Heaton | 5-2 | 1st round | Mercantile Credit Classic |
| | v O'Boye | 3-5 | 2nd round | Mercantile Credit Classic |
| | v O'Boye | 0-5 | 1st round | Irish Championship |
| | v N. Gilbert | 3-5 | 1st round | MIM Britannia British Open |
| | v P. Gibson | 9-10 | Qualifying | Embassy World Championship |
| | v Bradley | 5-4 | 1st round | Fidelity International |
| | v Macleod | 0-5 | 2nd round | Fidelity International |
| | v M. Smith | 4-5 | 1st round | Rothmans Grand Prix |
| | v Dunning | 3-5 | 1st round | BCE Canadian Masters |
| | v F. Davis | 9-7 | 1st round | Tennents UK Open |
| | v Gary Wilkinson | 5-9 | 2nd round | Tennents UK Open |
| **1989** | v Fisher | 5-3 | 2nd round | Mercantile Credit Classic |
| | v Johnson | 2-5 | 3rd round | Mercantile Credit Classic |
| | v Medati | 1-5 | 1st round | European Open |
| | v Browne | 2-5 | 1st round | Irish Championship |
| | v Foldvari | 1-5 | 1st round | Anglian British Open |
| | v Black | 8-10 | Qualifying | Embassy World Championship |
| | v M. Smith | 5-2 | 1st round | Hong Kong Open |
| | v Spencer | 4-5 | 2nd round | Hong Kong Open |
| | v Wildman | 3-5 | 1st round | 555 Asian Open |
| | v Williamson | 1-5 | 1st round | BCE International |
| | v Terry | 4-5 | 1st round | Rothmans Grand Prix |
| | v B. Harris | 3-5 | 1st round | Dubai Classic |
| | v Scott | 6-1 | 1st round | Stormseal UK Open |
| | v Gary Wilkinson | 2-6 | 2nd round | Stormseal UK Open |
| **1990** | v Gauvreau | 0-5 | 1st round | Mercantile Credit Classic |
| | v Medati | 2-5 | 1st round | Pearl Assurance British Open |
| | v Lawlor | 3-5 | 1st round | European Open |
| | v Edwards | 8-10 | Qualifying | Embassy World Championship |

## EDDIE SINCLAIR (Scotland)

**Born** 5.5.37. **Turned professional** 1979. **World ranking** 94 (94).

| | | | | |
|---|---|---|---|---|
| **1980** | v Meadowcroft | 1-9 | Qualifying | Embassy World Championship |
| | v Kennerley | 9-1 | Qualifying | Coral UK Championship |
| | v Miles | 9-5 | 1st round | Coral UK Championship |
| | v Dennis Taylor | 6-9 | 2nd round | Coral UK Championship |
| **1981** | v Donnelly | 0-5 | Quarter-final | Scottish Championship |
| | v Morgan | 9-8 | Qualifying | Embassy World Championship |
| | v Wilson | 4-9 | Qualifying | Embassy World Championship |
| | v E. Hughes | 2-5 | Qualifying | Jameson International |
| | v Wildman | 9-8 | Qualifying | Coral UK Championship |
| | v Hood | 9-0 | Qualifying | Coral UK Championship |
| | v Martin | 7-9 | Qualifying | Coral UK Championship |
| **1982** | v Kelly | 9-8 | Qualifying | Embassy World Championship |
| | v Donnelly | 8-9 | Qualifying | Embassy World Championship |
| | v Phillips | 6-3 | Quarter-final | Scottish Championship |
| | v Gibson | 6-2 | Semi-final | Scottish Championship |
| | **v Black** | **11-7** | **Final** | **Scottish Championship** |
| | v Higgins | 1-5 | 1st round | Langs Supreme Scottish Masters |
| | v Anderson | 5-2 | Qualifying | Jameson International |
| | v Meo | 5-3 | Qualifying | Jameson International |
| | v Knowles | 2-5 | 1st round | Jameson International |
| | v F. Davis | 5-2 | 1st round | Professional Players Tournament |
| | v Meadowcroft | 5-3 | 2nd round | Professional Players Tournament |
| | v Griffiths | 3-5 | 3rd round | Professional Players Tournament |
| | v Murphy | 9-5 | Qualifying | Coral UK Championship |
| | v Spencer | 8-9 | 1st round | Coral UK Championship |
| **1983** | v Roscoe | 10-2 | Qualifying | Embassy World Championship |
| | v E. Hughes | 8-10 | Qualifying | Embassy World Championship |

| | | | | |
|---|---|---|---|---|
| | v Donnelly | 6-5 | Semi-final | Scottish Championship |
| | v Macleod | 9-11 | Final | Scottish Championship |
| | v Andrewartha | 5-4 | Qualifying | Jameson International |
| | v Thorburn | 0-5 | 1st round | Jameson International |
| | v E. Hughes | 4-5 | 1st round | Professional Players Tournament |
| | v T. Jones | 3-9 | Qualifying | Coral UK Championship |
| **1984** | v S. Davis | 2-5 | Qualifying | Lada Classic |
| | v Browne | 10-1 | Qualifying | Embassy World Championship |
| | v Stevens | 1-10 | 1st round | Embassy World Championship |
| | v Duggan | 5-0 | Qualifying | Jameson International |
| | v Mans | 5-2 | Qualifying | Jameson International |
| | v Higgins | 1-5 | 1st round | Jameson International |
| | v T. Jones | 4-5 | Qualifying | Rothmans Grand Prix |
| | v P. Francisco | 9-8 | Qualifying | Coral UK Open |
| | v S. Francisco | 4-9 | Qualifying | Coral UK Open |
| | v Demarco | 6-3 | 1st round | Scottish Championship |
| | v John Rea | 6-2 | Semi-final | Scottish Championship |
| | v Macleod | 2-10 | Final | Scottish Championship |
| **1985** | v Newbury | 3-6 | 1st round | Dulux British Open |
| | v T. Jones | 2-10 | Qualifying | Embassy World Championship |
| | v Darrington | 5-0 | 2nd round | Goya Matchroom Trophy |
| | v Martin | 1-5 | 3rd round | Goya Matchroom Trophy |
| | v Fitzmaurice | 3-5 | 2nd round | Rothmans Grand Prix |
| | v G. Foulds | 9-4 | 2nd round | Coral UK Open |
| | v Parrott | 2-9 | 3rd round | Coral UK Open |
| **1986** | v Greaves | 5-1 | 2nd round | Mercantile Credit Classic |
| | v Macleod | 2-5 | 3rd round | Mercantile Credit Classic |
| | v B. Harris | 3-5 | 2nd round | Dulux British Open |
| | v Gibson | 4-6 | Quarter-final | Canada Dry Scottish Championship |
| | v Morgan | 10-8 | Qualifying | Embassy World Championship |
| | v Van Rensberg | 2-10 | Qualifying | Embassy World Championship |
| | v Fagan | 5-0 | 2nd round | BCE International |
| | v Higgins | 3-5 | 3rd round | BCE International |
| | v John Rea | 4-5 | 2nd round | Rothmans Grand Prix |
| | v Mikkelsen | 8-9 | 2nd round | Tennents UK Open |
| **1987** | v Miles | 5-1 | 2nd round | Mercantile Credit Classic |
| | v Johnson | 0-5 | 3rd round | Mercantile Credit Classic |
| | v M. Gibson | 6-2 | 1st round | Scottish Championship |
| | v Donnelly | 4-6 | Semi-final | Scottish Championship |
| | v Hendry | 5-2 | 2nd round | Dulux British Open |
| | v P. Francisco | 3-5 | 3rd round | Dulux British Open |
| | v Drago | 10-9 | Qualifying | Embassy World Championship |
| | v Edmonds | 6-10 | Qualifying | Embassy World Championship |
| | v Heaton | 5-3 | 1st round | Fidelity International |
| | v Edmonds | 5-4 | 2nd round | Fidelity International |
| | v Wilson | 1-5 | 3rd round | Fidelity International |
| | v Ellis | 5-4 | 1st round | Rothmans Grand Prix |
| | v Edmonds | 2-5 | 2nd round | Rothmans Grand Prix |
| | v N. Gilbert | 8-9 | 1st round | Tennents UK Open |
| **1988** | v Lawlor | 5-3 | 1st round | Mercantile Credit Classic |
| | v Wright | 3-5 | 2nd round | Mercantile Credit Classic |
| | v John Rea | 5-6 | Quarter-final | Scottish Championship |
| | v Lawlor | 3-5 | 1st round | MIM Britannia British Open |
| | v Burke | 10-2 | Qualifying | Embassy World Championship |
| | v O'Kane | 10-9 | Qualifying | Embassy World Championship |
| | v B. Harris | 0-10 | Qualifying | Embassy World Championship |
| | v Rowing | 5-0 | 1st round | Fidelity International |
| | v Roe | 1-5 | 2nd round | Fidelity International |
| | v Terry | 3-5 | 1st round | Rothmans Grand Prix |
| | v Graham | 3-5 | 1st round | BCE Canadian Masters |
| | v Edwards | 8-9 | 1st round | Tennents UK Open |
| **1989** | v Meakin | 5-1 | 1st round | Mercantile Credit Classic |
| | v Dodd | 3-5 | 2nd round | Mercantile Credit Classic |

| | | | | |
|---|---|---|---|---|
| | v Whitthread | 5-4 | 1st round | European Open |
| | v Houlihan | 5-1 | 2nd round | European Open |
| | v White | 3-5 | 3rd round | European Open |
| | v M. Gibson | 4-5 | 1st round | Scottish Championship |
| | v Mikkelsen | 5-3 | 1st round | Anglian British Open |
| | v Browne | 3-5 | 2nd round | Anglian British Open |
| | v Price | 9-10 | Qualifying | Embassy World Championship |
| | v Gollan | 3-5 | 1st round | Hong Kong Open |
| | v M. Gibson | 5-2 | 1st round | 555 Asian Open |
| | v Chappel | 0-5 | 2nd round | 555 Asian Open |
| | v Ellis | 2-5 | 1st round | BCE International |
| | v Whitthread | *wo* | 1st round | Rothmans Grand Prix |
| | v Spencer | 5-0 | 2nd round | Rothmans Grand Prix |
| | v Meo | 2-5 | 3rd round | Rothmans Grand Prix |
| | v Heaton | 5-1 | 1st round | Dubai Classic |
| | v Graham | 5-4 | 2nd round | Dubai Classic |
| | v Higgins | 2-5 | 3rd round | Dubai Classic |
| | v Bond | 5-6 | 1st round | Stormseal UK Open |
| **1990** | v Darrington | 5-3 | 1st round | Mercantile Credit Classic |
| | v Reardon | 5-4 | 2nd round | Mercantile Credit Classic |
| | v Williams | 1-5 | 3rd round | Mercantile Credit Classic |
| | v Wildman | 5-4 | 1st round | Pearl Assurance British Open |
| | v Edmonds | 5-3 | 2nd round | Pearl Assurance British Open |
| | v Williams | 3-5 | 3rd round | Pearl Assurance British Open |
| | v Thornley | 5-2 | 1st round | European Open |
| | v Duggan | 5-3 | 2nd round | European Open |
| | v O'Kane | 4-5 | 3rd round | European Open |
| | v Graham | 3-10 | Qualifying | Embassy World Championship |

## **JASON SMITH** (England)

**Born** 6.1.64. **Turned professional** 1987. **World ranking** 66 (104).

| | | | | |
|---|---|---|---|---|
| **1987** | v Bradley | 1-5 | 2nd round | Fidelity International |
| | v Rowswell | 3-5 | 1st round | Rothmans Grand Prix |
| | v Black | 8-9 | 1st round | Tennents UK Open |
| **1988** | v Bear | 3-5 | 1st round | Mercantile Credit Classic |
| | v V. Harris | 6-3 | 1st round | English Championship |
| | v T. Jones | 6-5 | 2nd round | English Championship |
| | v Johnson | 5-6 | 3rd round | English Championship |
| | v Jenkins | 3-5 | 1st round | MIM Britannia British Open |
| | v Donnelly | 10-4 | Qualifying | Embassy World Championship |
| | v Wych | 3-10 | Qualifying | Embassy World Championship |
| | v Donnelly | 2-5 | 1st round | Fidelity International |
| | v G. Foulds | 5-3 | 1st round | Rothmans Grand Prix |
| | v Fisher | 3-5 | 2nd round | Rothmans Grand Prix |
| | v G. Foulds | 5-1 | 1st round | BCE Canadian Masters |
| | v Reardon | 2-5 | 2nd round | BCE Canadian Masters |
| | v Meadowcroft | 9-7 | 1st round | Tennents UK Open |
| | v Chappel | 6-9 | 2nd round | Tennents UK Open |
| **1989** | v Van Rensberg | 5-4 | 1st round | Mercantile Credit Classic |
| | v Bales | 5-1 | 2nd round | Mercantile Credit Classic |
| | v Thorne | 1-5 | 3rd round | Mercantile Credit Classic |
| | v Rowswell | 5-2 | 1st round | European Open |
| | v Browne | 4-5 | 2nd round | European Open |
| | v Gary Wilkinson | 3-5 | 2nd round | English Championship |
| | v G. Foulds | 5-3 | 1st round | Anglian British Open |
| | v M. Bennett | 4-5 | 2nd round | Anglian British Open |
| | v Foldvari | 10-4 | Qualifying | Embassy World Championship |
| | v T. Jones | 7-10 | Qualifying | Embassy World Championship |
| | v Oliver | 5-3 | 1st round | Hong Kong Open |
| | v Gary Wilkinson | 1-5 | 2nd round | Hong Kong Open |

| | | | | |
|---|---|---|---|---|
| | v Scott | 5-0 | 1st round | 555 Asian Open |
| | v J. McLaughlin | 4-5 | 2nd round | 555 Asian Open |
| | v Donnelly | 5-4 | 1st round | BCE International |
| | v N. Gilbert | 5-2 | 2nd round | BCE International |
| | v White | 3-5 | 3rd round | BCE International |
| | v Wright | 5-2 | 1st round | Rothmans Grand Prix |
| | v O'Boye | 5-4 | 2nd round | Rothmans Grand Prix |
| | v P. Francisco | 5-3 | 3rd round | Rothmans Grand Prix |
| | v Meo | 5-3 | 4th round | Rothmans Grand Prix |
| | v S. Davis | 1-5 | 5th round | Rothmans Grand Prix |
| | v Meakin | 4-5 | 1st round | Dubai Classic |
| | v Owers | 6-5 | 1st round | Stormseal UK Open |
| | v Robidoux | 0-6 | 2nd round | Stormseal UK Open |
| **1990** | v Donnelly | 5-2 | 1st round | Mercantile Credit Classic |
| | v J. McLaughlin | 1-5 | 2nd round | Mercantile Credit Classic |
| | v Bear | 4-5 | 1st round | Pearl Assurance British Open |
| | v John Rea | 4-10 | Qualifying | Embassy World Championship |

## MARTIN SMITH (England)

**Born** 12.6.61. **Turned professional** 1985. **World ranking** 80 (76).

| | | | | |
|---|---|---|---|---|
| **1985** | v Sheehan | 5-2 | 1st round | Goya Matchroom Trophy |
| | v W. Jones | 3-5 | 2nd round | Goya Matchroom Trophy |
| | v Bales | 1-5 | 1st round | Rothmans Grand Prix |
| | v Wilkinson | 4-9 | 1st round | Coral UK Open |
| **1986** | v Mienie | 5-1 | 1st round | Mercantile Credit Classic |
| | v Edmonds | 5-2 | 2nd round | Mercantile Credit Classic |
| | v Mans | 4-5 | 3rd round | Mercantile Credit Classic |
| | v Edmonds | 8-9 | 2nd round | Tolly Cobbold English Championship |
| | v Kearney | 2-5 | 1st round | Dulux British Open |
| | v Greaves | 10-4 | Qualifying | Embassy World Championship |
| | v Donnelly | 6-10 | Qualifying | Embassy World Championship |
| | v M. Bennett | 4-5 | 1st round | BCE International |
| | v Hines | 5-2 | 1st round | Rothmans Grand Prix |
| | v T. Jones | 0-5 | 2nd round | Rothmans Grand Prix |
| | v Wright | 7-9 | 1st round | Tennents UK Open |
| **1987** | v N. Gilbert | 2-5 | 1st round | Mercantile Credit Classic |
| | v Rowswell | 6-5 | 1st round | Tolly Ales English Championship |
| | v Dodd | 3-6 | 2nd round | Tolly Ales English Championship |
| | v Ellis | 2-5 | 1st round | Dulux British Open |
| | v Rempe | 9-10 | Qualifying | Embassy World Championship |
| | v Donnelly | 5-3 | 1st round | Fidelity International |
| | v King | 3-5 | 2nd round | Fidelity International |
| | v Black | 5-0 | 1st round | Rothmans Grand Prix |
| | v Gauvreau | 3-5 | 2nd round | Rothmans Grand Prix |
| | v Jonik | 9-5 | 1st round | Tennents UK Open |
| | v Browne | 9-4 | 2nd round | Tennents UK Open |
| | v Mountjoy | 9-7 | 3rd round | Tennents UK Open |
| | v J. Campbell | 8-9 | 4th round | Tennents UK Open |
| **1988** | v Fitzmaurice | 5-2 | 1st round | Mercantile Credit Classic |
| | v Browne | 5-1 | 2nd round | Mercantile Credit Classic |
| | v David Taylor | 3-5 | 3rd round | Mercantile Credit Classic |
| | v Miles | 6-1 | 1st round | English Championship |
| | v B. Harris | 6-4 | 2nd round | English Championship |
| | v Martin | 5-6 | 3rd round | English Championship |
| | v Oliver | 0-5 | 1st round | MIM Britannia British Open |
| | v V. Harris | 10-6 | Qualifying | Embassy World Championship |
| | v J. McLaughlin | 10-3 | Qualifying | Embassy World Championship |
| | v Newbury | 9-10 | Qualifying | Embassy World Championship |
| | v D. Morgan | 5-3 | 1st round | Fidelity International |
| | v W. Jones | 2-5 | 2nd round | Fidelity International |

| | | | | |
|---|---|---|---|---|
| | v Sheehan | 5-4 | 1st round | Rothmans Grand Prix |
| | v Cripsey | 5-0 | 2nd round | Rothmans Grand Prix |
| | v James | 3-5 | 3rd round | Rothmans Grand Prix |
| | v Marshall | 9-6 | 1st round | Tennents UK Open |
| | v Werbeniuk | 9-5 | 2nd round | Tennents UK Open |
| | v Johnson | 2-9 | 3rd round | Tennents UK Open |
| **1989** | v Rowing | 3-5 | 1st round | Mercantile Credit Classic |
| | v Edwards | 4-5 | 1st round | European Open |
| | v Miles | 4-5 | 1st round | English Championship |
| | v D. Hughes | 5-1 | 1st round | Anglian British Open |
| | v Macleod | 4-5 | 2nd round | Anglian British Open |
| | v S. Campbell | 10-9 | Qualifying | Embassy World Championship |
| | v Wright | 10-7 | Qualifying | Embassy World Championship |
| | v Graham | 6-10 | Qualifying | Embassy World Championship |
| | v Sheehan | 4-5 | 1st round | Hong Kong Open |
| | v Thornley | 5-2 | 1st round | 555 Asian Open |
| | v Wych | 3-5 | 2nd round | 555 Asian Open |
| | v D. Hughes | 5-0 | 1st round | BCE International |
| | v Martin | 5-3 | 2nd round | BCE International |
| | v Williams | 5-4 | 3rd round | BCE International |
| | v James | 3-5 | 4th round | BCE International |
| | v Pinches | 5-2 | 1st round | Rothmans Grand Prix |
| | v Cripsey | 4-5 | 2nd round | Rothmans Grand Prix |
| | v S. Murphy | 5-1 | 1st round | Dubai Classic |
| | v Browne | 1-5 | 2nd round | Dubai Classic |
| | v Pinches | 4-6 | 1st round | Stormseal UK Open |
| **1990** | v Cairns | 2-5 | 1st round | Mercantile Credit Classic |
| | v Darrington | 5-4 | 1st round | Pearl Assurance British Open |
| | v Wych | 2-5 | 2nd round | Pearl Assurance British Open |
| | v Whitthread | 5-1 | 1st round | European Open |
| | v Bennett | 3-5 | 2nd round | European Open |
| | v Ellis | 10-6 | Qualifying | Embassy World Championship |
| | v D. Morgan | 6-10 | Qualifying | Embassy World Championship |

## JOHN SPENCER (England)

**Born** 18.9.35. **Turned professional** 1967. **World ranking** 56 (38).

| | | | | |
|---|---|---|---|---|
| **1969** | v Pulman | 30-19 | Quarter-final | World Championship |
| | v Williams | 55-18 | Semi-final | World Championship |
| | **v G. Owen** | **46-27** | **Final** | **World Championship** |
| **1970** | v Jack Rea | 31-15 | Quarter-final | World Championship (Apr) |
| | v Reardon | 33-37 | Semi-final | World Championship (Apr) |
| | v Reardon | 34-15 | Semi-final | World Championship (Nov) |
| | **v Simpson** | **42-31** | **Final** | **World Championship (Nov)** |
| **1972** | v F. Davis | 31-21 | Quarter-final | World Championship |
| | v Charlton | 37-32 | Semi-final | World Championship |
| | v Higgins | 32-37 | Final | World Championship |
| **1973** | v David Taylor | 16-5 | 2nd round | World Championship |
| | v Williams | 16-7 | Quarter-final | World Championship |
| | v Reardon | 22-23 | Semi-final | World Championship |
| **1974** | v Mans | 13-15 | 2nd round | World Championship |
| **1975** | v Pulman | 5-3 | Quarter-final | Benson & Hedges Masters |
| | v Charlton | 5-2 | Semi-final | Benson & Hedges Masters |
| | **v Reardon** | **9-8** | **Final** | **Benson & Hedges Masters** |
| | v Pulman | 15-10 | 2nd round | World Championship |
| | v Reardon | 17-19 | Quarter-final | World Championship |
| **1976** | v Miles | 4-5 | Semi-final | Benson & Hedges Masters |
| | v David Taylor | 15-5 | 1st round | Embassy World Championship |
| | v Higgins | 14-15 | Quarter-final | Embassy World Championship |
| **1977** | v Virgo | 13-9 | 1st round | Embassy World Championship |
| | v Reardon | 13-6 | Quarter-final | Embassy World Championship |

| | | | | |
|---|---|---|---|---|
| | v Pulman | 18-16 | Semi-final | Embassy World Championship |
| | **v Thorburn** | **25-21** | **Final** | **Embassy World Championship** |
| | v Mountjoy | 3-5 | 2nd round | Super Crystalate UK Championship |
| **1978** | v Thorburn | 3-5 | Semi-final | Benson & Hedges Masters |
| | **v Mountjoy** | **5-3** | **Final** | **Benson & Hedges Irish Masters** |
| | v Mans | 8-13 | 1st round | Embassy World Championship |
| | v Andrewartha | 8-9 | 1st round | Coral UK Championship |
| **1979** | v Williams | 6-2 | Semi-final | Holsten Lager International |
| | **v Miles** | **11-7** | **Final** | **Holsten Lager International** |
| | v Mountjoy | 0-5 | Quarter-final | Benson & Hedges Masters |
| | v Werbeniuk | 11-13 | 1st round | Embassy World Championship |
| | v Werbeniuk | 8-9 | 3rd round | Coral UK Championship |
| **1980** | v Charlton | 5-2 | Quarter-final | Benson & Hedges Masters |
| | v Griffiths | 0-5 | Semi-final | Benson & Hedges Masters |
| | v Stevens | 8-13 | 2nd round | Embassy World Championship |
| | v Wildman | 7-9 | 1st round | Coral UK Championship |
| **1981** | v Dennis Taylor | 5-2 | 1st round | Benson & Hedges Masters |
| | v Reardon | 5-1 | Quarter-final | Benson & Hedges Masters |
| | v Griffiths | 5-6 | Semi-final | Benson & Hedges Masters |
| | v Houlihan | 9-1 | 1st round | John Courage English |
| | v S. Davis | 7-9 | 2nd round | John Courage English |
| | v Edmonds | 10-9 | 1st round | Embassy World Championship |
| | v Reardon | 11-13 | 2nd round | Embassy World Championship |
| | v Edmonds | 5-3 | 2nd round | Jameson International |
| | v Griffiths | 2-5 | 3rd round | Jameson International |
| | v Johnson | 5-9 | 2nd round | Coral UK Championship |
| **1982** | v S. Davis | 2-5 | 1st round | Lada Classic |
| | v Mountjoy | 4-5 | 1st round | Benson & Hedges Masters |
| | v Meo | 3-5 | 1st round | Benson & Hedges Irish Masters |
| | v Dunning | 10-4 | 1st round | Embassy World Championship |
| | v Thorne | 5-13 | 2nd round | Embassy World Championship |
| | v Edmonds | 5-2 | 1st round | Jameson International |
| | v Virgo | 4-5 | 2nd round | Jameson International |
| | v G. Foulds | 5-1 | 1st round | Professional Players Tournament |
| | v Martin | 5-3 | 2nd round | Professional Players Tournament |
| | v Virgo | 1-5 | 3rd round | Professional Players Tournament |
| | v Sinclair | 9-8 | 1st round | Coral UK Championship |
| | v Knowles | 9-6 | 2nd round | Coral UK Championship |
| | v Higgins | 5-9 | Quarter-final | Coral UK Championship |
| **1983** | v Reardon | 5-3 | 1st round | Lada Classic |
| | v David Taylor | 5-2 | Quarter-final | Lada Classic |
| | v S. Davis | 4-5 | Semi-final | Lada Classic |
| | v Hallett | 10-7 | 1st round | Embassy World Championship |
| | v Charlton | 11-13 | 2nd round | Embassy World Championship |
| | v Higgins | 2-3 | 1st round | Winfield Masters |
| | v Morgan | 5-1 | 1st round | Jameson International |
| | v Knowles | 5-4 | 2nd round | Jameson International |
| | v Griffiths | 4-5 | Quarter-final | Jameson International |
| | v Black | 5-2 | 1st round | Professional Players Tournament |
| | v Thorne | 1-5 | 2nd round | Professional Players Tournament |
| | v Dunning | 9-7 | 1st round | Coral UK Championship |
| | v Meo | 5-9 | 2nd round | Coral UK Championship |
| **1984** | v Johnson | 5-4 | Qualifying | Lada Classic |
| | v S. Davis | 1-5 | 1st round | Lada Classic |
| | v Thorburn | 5-4 | 1st round | Benson & Hedges Masters |
| | v Griffiths | 4-5 | Quarter-final | Benson & Hedges Masters |
| | v Miles | 10-3 | 1st round | Embassy World Championship |
| | v S. Davis | 5-13 | 2nd round | Embassy World Championship |
| | v S. Francisco | 2-5 | 1st round | Jameson International |
| | v P. Francisco | 2-5 | 1st round | Rothmans Grand Prix |
| | v Johnson | 6-9 | 1st round | Coral UK Open |
| **1985** | v King | 2-5 | 1st round | Mercantile Credit Classic |
| | v Charlton | 5-3 | 1st round | Benson & Hedges Masters |

| | | | | |
|---|---|---|---|---|
| | v White | 2-5 | Quarter-final | Benson & Hedges Masters |
| | v Medati | 4-9 | 1st round | Tolly Cobbold English Championship |
| | v Jonik | 6-0 | 1st round | Dulux British Open |
| | v Miles | 3-5 | 2nd round | Dulux British Open |
| | v Parrott | 3-10 | 1st round | Embassy World Championship |
| | v Foldvari | 5-4 | 3rd round | Goya Matchroom Trophy |
| | v Griffiths | 1-5 | 4th round | Goya Matchroom Trophy |
| | v B. Harris | 2-5 | 3rd round | Rothmans Grand Prix |
| | v V. Harris | 9-5 | 3rd round | Coral UK Open |
| | v Knowles | 7-9 | 4th round | Coral UK Open |
| | v S. Davis | 2-5 | 1st round | Kit Kat |
| **1986** | v Cripsey | 1-5 | 3rd round | Mercantile Credit Classic |
| | v Houlihan | 9-5 | 3rd round | Tolly Cobbold English Championship |
| | v Johnson | 7-9 | 4th round | Tolly Cobbold English Championship |
| | v Browne | 0-5 | 3rd round | Dulux British Open |
| | v Higgins | 7-10 | 1st round | Embassy World Championship |
| | v Williamson | 5-2 | 2nd round | BCE International |
| | v Knowles | 0-5 | 3rd round | BCE International |
| | v Burke | 5-3 | 2nd round | Rothmans Grand Prix |
| | v S. Francisco | 4-5 | 3rd round | Rothmans Grand Prix |
| | v Foldvari | 9-6 | 2nd round | Tennents UK Open |
| | v Wilson | 9-5 | 3rd round | Tennents UK Open |
| | v Stevens | 9-4 | 4th round | Tennents UK Open |
| | v Thorburn | 2-9 | 5th round | Tennents UK Open |
| **1987** | v D. Gilbert | 5-4 | 2nd round | Mercantile Credit Classic |
| | v Thorne | 5-3 | 3rd round | Mercantile Credit Classic |
| | v J. Campbell | 3-5 | 4th round | Mercantile Credit Classic |
| | v Wright | 6-1 | 2nd round | Tolly Ales English Championship |
| | v Martin | 5-6 | 3rd round | Tolly Ales English Championship |
| | v Whitthread | 5-2 | 2nd round | Dulux British Open |
| | v Meo | 5-1 | 3rd round | Dulux British Open |
| | v Martin | 5-2 | 4th round | Dulux British Open |
| | v Johnson | 5-3 | 5th round | Dulux British Open |
| | v White | 3-5 | Quarter-final | Dulux British Open |
| | v Bales | 10-3 | Qualifying | Embassy World Championship |
| | v Chaperon | 10-4 | Qualifying | Embassy World Championship |
| | v West | 5-10 | Qualifying | Embassy World Championship |
| | v Jack Rea | 5-0 | 3rd round | Fidelity International |
| | v Hallett | 2-5 | 4th round | Fidelity International |
| | v Chappel | 1-5 | 3rd round | Rothmans Grand Prix |
| | v Miles | 5-9 | 3rd round | Tennents UK Open |
| **1988** | v John Rea | 5-3 | 3rd round | Mercantile Credit Classic |
| | v White | 1-5 | 4th round | Mercantile Credit Classic |
| | v Fowler | 3-6 | 3rd round | English Championship |
| | v F. Davis | 5-0 | 3rd round | MIM Britannia British Open |
| | v Dennis Taylor | 5-0 | 4th round | MIM Britannia British Open |
| | v Williams | 4-5 | 5th round | MIM Britannia British Open |
| | v King | 7-10 | Qualifying | Embassy World Championship |
| | v Reardon | 5-4 | 3rd round | Fidelity International |
| | v Virgo | 5-1 | 4th round | Fidelity International |
| | v Reynolds | 2-5 | 5th round | Fidelity International |
| | v Johnston-Allen | 5-3 | 3rd round | Rothmans Grand Prix |
| | v J. McLaughlin | 3-5 | 4th round | Rothmans Grand Prix |
| | v Stevens | 5-3 | 3rd round | BCE Canadian Masters |
| | v Thorburn | 2-5 | 4th round | BCE Canadian Masters |
| | v N. Gilbert | 7-9 | 3rd round | Tennents UK Open |
| **1989** | v Clark | 2-5 | 3rd round | Mercantile Credit Classic |
| | v Edwards | 1-5 | 3rd round | English Championship |
| | v Robidoux | 1-5 | 3rd round | Anglian British Open |
| | v Duggan | 1-10 | Qualifying | Embassy World Championship |
| | v Sheehan | 5-4 | 2nd round | Hong Kong Open |
| | v Higgins | 2-5 | 3rd round | Hong Kong Open |
| | v Donnelly | 5-3 | 2nd round | 555 Asian Open |

| | | | | |
|---|---|---|---|---|
| | v S. Francisco | 1-5 | 3rd round | 555 Asian Open |
| | v Brumby | 1-5 | 2nd round | BCE International |
| | v Sinclair | 0-5 | 2nd round | Rothmans Grand Prix |
| | v B. Harris | 5-3 | 3rd round | Dubai Classic |
| | v Reynolds | 4-5 | 4th round | Dubai Classic |
| | v Cairns | 6-3 | 2nd round | Stormseal UK Open |
| | v Hendry | 1-9 | 3rd round | Stormseal UK Open |
| **1990** | v Brumby | 1-5 | 2nd round | Mercantile Credit Classic |
| | v S. Campbell | 5-3 | 2nd round | Pearl Assurance British Open |
| | v White | 4-5 | 3rd round | Pearl Assurance British Open |
| | v John Rea | 5-1 | 2nd round | European Open |
| | v Clark | 1-5 | 3rd round | European Open |
| | v Owers | 10-8 | Qualifying | Embassy World Championship |
| | v Wattana | 8-10 | Qualifying | Embassy World Championship |

## **KIRK STEVENS** (Canada)

**Born** 17.8.58. **Turned professional** 1978. **World ranking** 69 (50).

| | | | | |
|---|---|---|---|---|
| **1979** | v Amdor | 9-1 | Prelim | Embassy World Championship |
| | v Pulman | 9-0 | Qualifying | Embassy World Championship |
| | v F. Davis | 8-13 | 1st round | Embassy World Championship |
| **1980** | v Hallett | 9-3 | Qualifying | Embassy World Championship |
| | v Miles | 10-3 | 1st round | Embassy World Championship |
| | v Spencer | 13-8 | 2nd round | Embassy World Championship |
| | v Charlton | 13-7 | Quarter-final | Embassy World Championship |
| | v Higgins | 13-16 | Semi-final | Embassy World Championship |
| **1981** | v F. Davis | 4-5 | 1st round | Benson & Hedges Masters |
| | v David Taylor | 3-5 | Semi-final | Yamaha International Masters |
| | v Dunning | 10-4 | 1st round | Embassy World Championship |
| | v Dennis Taylor | 11-13 | 2nd round | Embassy World Championship |
| | v Thorburn | 1-5 | Quarter-final | Langs Supreme Scottish Masters |
| | v Meadowcroft | 5-1 | 2nd round | Jameson International |
| | v David Taylor | 0-5 | 3rd round | Jameson International |
| | v Griffiths | 0-5 | 1st round | Northern Ireland Classic |
| | v Hallett | 9-4 | 2nd round | Coral UK Championship |
| | v Werbeniuk | 7-9 | 3rd round | Coral UK Championship |
| **1982** | v Fitzmaurice | 10-4 | 1st round | Embassy World Championship |
| | v Fagan | 13-7 | 2nd round | Embassy World Championship |
| | v White | 9-13 | Quarter-final | Embassy World Championship |
| | v Watterson | 5-3 | 1st round | Jameson International |
| | v Mans | 5-2 | 2nd round | Jameson International |
| | v Griffiths | 5-3 | Quarter-final | Jameson International |
| | v Knowles | 3-9 | Semi-final | Jameson International |
| | v E. Hughes | 5-2 | 1st round | Professional Players Tournament |
| | v Johnson | 1-5 | 2nd round | Professional Players Tournament |
| **1983** | v Knowles | 5-0 | 1st round | Lada Classic |
| | v Thorburn | 5-3 | Quarter-final | Lada Classic |
| | v Werbeniuk | 2-5 | Semi-final | Lada Classic |
| | v Griffiths | 3-5 | 1st round | Benson & Hedges Masters |
| | v Fisher | 10-2 | 1st round | Embassy World Championship |
| | v Mans | 13-3 | 2nd round | Embassy World Championship |
| | v Thorburn | 12-13 | Quarter-final | Embassy World Championship |
| | v Thorburn | 2-5 | Semi-final | Winfield Masters |
| | v Caggianello | 9-0 | Quarter-final | Canadian Championship |
| | v Bear | 9-8 | Semi-final | Canadian Championship |
| | **v Jonik** | **9-8** | **Final** | **Canadian Championship** |
| | v Edmonds | 5-1 | 1st round | Professional Players Tournament |
| | v Murphy | 5-1 | 2nd round | Professional Players Tournament |
| | v Wildman | 5-0 | 3rd round | Professional Players Tournament |
| | v Meo | 3-5 | Quarter-final | Professional Players Tournament |
| **1984** | v E. McLaughlin | 5-4 | Qualifying | Lada Classic |

| | | | | |
|---|---|---|---|---|
| | v Macleod | 5-1 | 1st round | Lada Classic |
| | v Meo | 2-5 | Quarter-final | Lada Classic |
| | v David Taylor | 5-1 | 1st round | Benson & Hedges Masters |
| | v S. Davis | 5-3 | Quarter-final | Benson & Hedges Masters |
| | v White | 4-6 | Semi-final | Benson & Hedges Masters |
| | v Charlton | 5-3 | 1st round | Tolly Cobbold Classic |
| | v S. Davis | 4-5 | Semi-final | Tolly Cobbold Classic |
| | v Sinclair | 10-1 | 1st round | Embassy World Championship |
| | v David Taylor | 13-10 | 2nd round | Embassy World Championship |
| | v Reardon | 13-2 | Quarter-final | Embassy World Championship |
| | v White | 14-16 | Semi-final | Embassy World Championship |
| | v Meo | 1-5 | Quarter-final | Winfield Australian Masters |
| | v Higgins | 2-5 | 1st round | Langs Supreme Scottish Masters |
| | v White | 0-5 | 1st round | Carlsberg Challenge |
| | v Gauvreau | 1-5 | 1st round | Jameson International |
| | v Chappel | 5-3 | 1st round | Rothmans Grand Prix |
| | v Williams | 5-3 | 2nd round | Rothmans Grand Prix |
| | v Hallett | 5-3 | 3rd round | Rothmans Grand Prix |
| | v Dennis Taylor | 2-5 | Quarter-final | Rothmans Grand Prix |
| | v Chappel | 9-7 | 1st round | Coral UK Open |
| | v Johnson | 9-2 | 2nd round | Coral UK Open |
| | v Knowles | 9-7 | Quarter-final | Coral UK Open |
| | v S. Davis | 2-9 | Semi-final | Coral UK Open |
| **1985** | v Medati | 5-4 | 1st round | Mercantile Credit Classic |
| | v Thorne | 1-5 | 2nd round | Mercantile Credit Classic |
| | v Meo | 2-5 | 1st round | Benson & Hedges Masters |
| | v Gauvreau | 6-3 | 1st round | Dulux British Open |
| | v Wildman | 5-2 | 2nd round | Dulux British Open |
| | v Miles | 5-2 | 3rd round | Dulux British Open |
| | v Dennis Taylor | 5-2 | Quarter-final | Dulux British Open |
| | v S. Davis | 9-7 | Semi-final | Dulux British Open |
| | v S. Francisco | 9-12 | Final | Dulux British Open |
| | v Higgins | 3-5 | Quarter-final | Benson & Hedges Irish Masters |
| | v Edmonds | 10-8 | 1st round | Embassy World Championship |
| | v Parrott | 6-13 | 2nd round | Embassy World Championship |
| | v Chaperon | 4-6 | Quarter-final | Canadian Championship |
| | v Chappel | 3-5 | 3rd round | Goya Matchroom Trophy |
| | v Watson | 5-0 | 3rd round | Rothmans Grand Prix |
| | v Miles | 5-2 | 4th round | Rothmans Grand Prix |
| | v Longworth | 5-3 | 5th round | Rothmans Grand Prix |
| | v Knowles | 4-5 | Quarter-final | Rothmans Grand Prix |
| | v Newbury | 9-7 | 3rd round | Coral UK Open |
| | v Hallett | 9-5 | 4th round | Coral UK Open |
| | v Williams | 9-7 | 5th round | Coral UK Open |
| | v Dennis Taylor | 1-9 | Quarter-final | Coral UK Open |
| **1986** | v F. Davis | 2-5 | 3rd round | Mercantile Credit Classic |
| | v Reardon | 5-1 | 1st round | BCE Belgian Classic |
| | v Higgins | 5-4 | Semi-final | BCE Belgian Classic |
| | v Griffiths | 7-9 | Final | BCE Belgian Classic |
| | v Charlton | 4-5 | 1st round | Benson & Hedges Masters |
| | v Miles | 5-3 | 3rd round | Dulux British Open |
| | v Wilson | 5-0 | 4th round | Dulux British Open |
| | v Thorne | 4-5 | 5th round | Dulux British Open |
| | v Reynolds | 10-6 | 1st round | Embassy World Championship |
| | v Charlton | 13-12 | 2nd round | Embassy World Championship |
| | v Knowles | 9-13 | Quarter-final | Embassy World Championship |
| | v Thornley | 6-2 | 2nd round | Canadian Championship |
| | v Wych | 2-6 | Semi-final | Canadian Championship |
| | v Knowles | 5-3 | 1st round | Langs Scottish Masters |
| | v Higgins | 2-6 | Semi-final | Langs Scottish Masters |
| | v Bales | 3-5 | 3rd round | BCE International |
| | v Dodd | 4-5 | 3rd round | Rothmans Grand Prix |
| | v Scott | 9-2 | 3rd round | Tennents UK Open |

| | | | | |
|---|---|---|---|---|
| | v Spencer | 4-9 | 4th round | Tennents UK Open |
| **1987** | v Chaperon | 5-3 | 3rd round | Mercantile Credit Classic |
| | v West | 3-5 | 4th round | Mercantile Credit Classic |
| | v Thorne | 3-5 | 1st round | Benson & Hedges Masters |
| | v Chaperon | 5-4 | 3rd round | Dulux British Open |
| | v West | 5-4 | 4th round | Dulux British Open |
| | v David Taylor | 2-5 | 5th round | Dulux British Open |
| | v Thorne | 1-5 | 1st round | Benson & Hedges Irish Masters |
| | v Longworth | 4-10 | 1st round | Embassy World Championship |
| | v Caggianello | 6-0 | Quarter-final | Canadian Championship |
| | v Bear | 2-7 | Semi-final | Canadian Championship |
| | v O'Boye | 1-5 | 3rd round | Fidelity International |
| | v W. Jones | 5-1 | 3rd round | Rothmans Grand Prix |
| | v Parrott | 0-5 | 4th round | Rothmans Grand Prix |
| | v O'Boye | 9-8 | 3rd round | Tennents UK Open |
| | v Knowles | 8-9 | 4th round | Tennents UK Open |
| **1988** | v M. Bennett | 2-5 | 3rd round | Mercantile Credit Classic |
| | v M. Bennett | 10-7 | Qualifying | Embassy World Championship |
| | v Thorburn | 6-10 | 1st round | Embassy World Championship |
| | v Mikkelsen | 5-6 | Quarter-final | BCE Canadian Championship |
| | v D. Hughes | 5-2 | 2nd round | Fidelity International |
| | v J. Campbell | *scr* | 3rd round | Fidelity International |
| | v S. Campbell | 5-3 | 2nd round | Rothmans Grand Prix |
| | v Meo | 3-5 | 3rd round | Rothmans Grand Prix |
| | v Kelly | 5-1 | 2nd round | BCE Canadian Masters |
| | v Spencer | 3-5 | 3rd round | BCE Canadian Masters |
| | v Edwards | 9-4 | 2nd round | Tennents UK Open |
| | v Charlton | 9-7 | 3rd round | Tennents UK Open |
| | v Thorne | 3-9 | 4th round | Tennents UK Open |
| **1989** | v Edwards | 5-4 | 2nd round | Mercantile Credit Classic |
| | v Meo | 3-5 | 3rd round | Mercantile Credit Classic |
| | v Bear | 5-2 | 2nd round | European Open |
| | v Dennis Taylor | 0-5 | 3rd round | European Open |
| | v Marshall | 4-5 | 2nd round | Anglian British Open |
| | v Chambers | 10-8 | Qualifying | Embassy World Championship |
| | v T. Jones | 2-10 | Qualifying | Embassy World Championship |
| | v Gauvreau | 3-5 | 2nd round | Hong Kong Open |
| | v Marshall | 3-5 | 2nd round | 555 Asian Open |
| | v Kearney | 4-5 | 2nd round | BCE International |
| | v Meakin | 4-5 | 2nd round | Rothmans Grand Prix |
| | v Wattana | 4-5 | 2nd round | Dubai Classic |
| | v Dyson | 6-4 | 2nd round | Stormseal UK Open |
| | v Virgo | 9-7 | 3rd round | Stormseal UK Open |
| | v M. Bennett | 2-9 | 4th round | Stormseal UK Open |
| **1990** | v Rowswell | 3-5 | 2nd round | Mercantile Credit Classic |
| | v Meadowcroft | 5-4 | 2nd round | Pearl Assurance British Open |
| | v S. Davis | 2-5 | 3rd round | Pearl Assurance British Open |
| | v Pinches | 4-5 | 2nd round | European Open |
| | v Gollan | 6-10 | Qualifying | Embassy World Championship |

## DAVID TAYLOR (England)

**Born** 29.7.43. **Turned professional** 1968. **World ranking** 45 (33).

| | | | | |
|---|---|---|---|---|
| **1970** | v Bennett | 11-8 | 1st round | World Championship |
| | v Pulman | 22-39 | Quarter-final | World Championship |
| **1972** | v Charlton | 25-31 | Quarter-final | World Championship |
| **1973** | v Dunning | 9-4 | 1st round | World Championship |
| | v Spencer | 5-16 | 2nd round | World Championship |
| **1974** | v Dunning | 6-8 | 1st round | World Championship |
| **1975** | v King | 15-8 | 1st round | World Championship |
| | v Higgins | 2-15 | 2nd round | World Championship |

| | | | | |
|---|---|---|---|---|
| **1976** | v Greaves | 8-1 | Qualifying | Embassy World Championship |
| | v Jack Rea | 8-7 | Qualifying | Embassy World Championship |
| | v Spencer | 5-15 | 1st round | Embassy World Championship |
| **1977** | v Greaves | 11-0 | Qualifying | Embassy World Championship |
| | v Charlton | 5-13 | 1st round | Embassy World Championship |
| | v Greaves | 5-4 | 1st round | Super Crystalate UK Championship |
| | v Higgins | 4-5 | 2nd round | Super Crystalate UK Championship |
| **1978** | v Morgan | 9-7 | Qualifying | Embassy World Championship |
| | v Miles | 10-13 | 1st round | Embassy World Championship |
| | v Parkin | 9-2 | Qualifying | Coral UK Championship |
| | v Fagan | 9-7 | 1st round | Coral UK Championship |
| | v Virgo | 9-2 | Quarter-final | Coral UK Championship |
| | v Higgins | 9-5 | Semi-final | Coral UK Championship |
| | v Mountjoy | 9-15 | Final | Coral UK Championship |
| **1979** | v Fagan | 5-4 | 1st round | Benson & Hedges Masters |
| | v Reardon | 2-5 | Quarter-final | Benson & Hedges Masters |
| | v Dunning | 9-8 | Qualifying | Embassy World Championship |
| | v Higgins | 5-13 | 1st round | Embassy World Championship |
| | v Meo | 7-9 | 2nd round | Coral UK Championship |
| **1980** | v Edmonds | 10-3 | 1st round | Embassy World Championship |
| | v F. Davis | 13-5 | 2nd round | Embassy World Championship |
| | v Reardon | 13-11 | Quarter-final | Embassy World Championship |
| | v Thorburn | 7-16 | Semi-final | Embassy World Championship |
| | v Williams | 7-9 | 2nd round | Coral UK Championship |
| **1981** | v Stevens | 5-3 | Semi-final | Yamaha International Masters |
| | v S. Davis | 6-9 | Final | Yamaha International Masters |
| | v Dunning | 8-9 | 1st round | John Courage English |
| | v Wilson | 10-6 | 1st round | Embassy World Championship |
| | v F. Davis | 13-3 | 2nd round | Embassy World Championship |
| | v Thorburn | 6-13 | Quarter-final | Embassy World Championship |
| | v Stevens | 5-0 | 3rd round | Jameson International |
| | v S. Davis | 1-5 | Quarter-final | Jameson International |
| | v Higgins | 5-9 | 3rd round | Coral UK Championship |
| **1982** | v Reardon | 1-5 | 1st round | Lada Classic |
| | v Meo | 2-5 | 1st round | Benson & Hedges Masters |
| | v Fagan | 9-10 | 1st round | Embassy World Championship |
| | v Fisher | 5-1 | 1st round | Jameson International |
| | v Werbeniuk | 5-2 | 2nd round | Jameson International |
| | v S. Davis | 5-3 | Quarter-final | Jameson International |
| | v Virgo | 9-5 | Semi-final | Jameson International |
| | v Knowles | 6-9 | Final | Jameson International |
| | v Anderson | 5-1 | 1st round | Professional Players Tournament |
| | v Dennis Taylor | 1-5 | 2nd round | Professional Players Tournament |
| | v Dodd | 9-7 | 1st round | Coral UK Championship |
| | v Meo | 6-9 | 2nd round | Coral UK Championship |
| **1983** | v White | 5-3 | 1st round | Lada Classic |
| | v Spencer | 2-5 | Quarter-final | Lada Classic |
| | v White | 2-5 | 1st round | Benson & Hedges Masters |
| | v Charlton | 4-5 | 1st round | Benson & Hedges Irish Masters |
| | v Meadowcroft | 10-2 | 1st round | Embassy World Championship |
| | v Werbeniuk | 10-13 | 2nd round | Embassy World Championship |
| | v Donnelly | 3-5 | 1st round | Jameson International |
| | v Morgan | 5-3 | 1st round | Professional Players Tournament |
| | v Wildman | 3-5 | 2nd round | Professional Players Tournament |
| | v N. Foulds | 9-4 | 1st round | Coral UK Championship |
| | v Johnson | 3-9 | 2nd round | Coral UK Championship |
| **1984** | v Macleod | 4-5 | Qualifying | Lada Classic |
| | v Stevens | 1-5 | 1st round | Benson & Hedges Masters |
| | v Gauvreau | 10-5 | 1st round | Embassy World Championship |
| | v Stevens | 10-13 | 2nd round | Embassy World Championship |
| | v Charlton | 4-5 | Quarter-final | Winfield Australian Masters |
| | v W. Jones | 5-4 | 1st round | Jameson International |
| | v S. Davis | 1-5 | 2nd round | Jameson International |

| | | | | |
|---|---|---|---|---|
| | v O'Kane | 5-1 | 1st round | Rothmans Grand Prix |
| | v John Rea | 5-1 | 2nd round | Rothmans Grand Prix |
| | v S. Davis | 1-5 | 3rd round | Rothmans Grand Prix |
| | v Macleod | 9-6 | 1st round | Coral UK Open |
| | v Reardon | 4-9 | 2nd round | Coral UK Open |
| **1985** | v Longworth | 4-5 | 1st round | Mercantile Credit Classic |
| | v Reardon | 1-5 | 1st round | Benson & Hedges Masters |
| | v Cripsey | 9-5 | 1st round | Tolly Cobbold English Championship |
| | v Parrott | 9-6 | 2nd round | Tolly Cobbold English Championship |
| | v Knowles | 2-9 | Quarter-final | Tolly Cobbold English Championship |
| | v Bradley | 3-6 | 1st round | Dulux British Open |
| | v O'Kane | 10-4 | 1st round | Embassy World Championship |
| | v S. Davis | 4-13 | 2nd round | Embassy World Championship |
| | v White | 0-4 | 1st round | Winfield Australian Masters |
| | v T. Jones | 5-4 | 3rd round | Goya Matchroom Trophy |
| | v Werbeniuk | 5-4 | 4th round | Goya Matchroom Trophy |
| | v N. Foulds | 4-5 | 5th round | Goya Matchroom Trophy |
| | v Newbury | 5-2 | 3rd round | Rothmans Grand Prix |
| | v Longworth | 1-5 | 4th round | Rothmans Grand Prix |
| | v Mikkelsen | 9-6 | 3rd round | Coral UK Open |
| | v J. Campbell | 9-4 | 4th round | Coral UK Open |
| | v Knowles | 7-9 | 5th round | Coral UK Open |
| **1986** | v Gauvreau | 3-5 | 3rd round | Mercantile Credit Classic |
| | v S. Davis | 4-5 | 1st round | Benson & Hedges Masters |
| | v Edmonds | 6-9 | 3rd round | Tolly Cobbold English Championship |
| | v Medati | 1-5 | 3rd round | Dulux British Open |
| | v E. Hughes | 7-10 | 1st round | Embassy World Championship |
| | v Edmonds | 5-4 | 3rd round | BCE International |
| | v Johnson | 5-3 | 4th round | BCE International |
| | v Reynolds | 1-5 | 5th round | BCE International |
| | v W. Jones | 1-5 | 3rd round | Rothmans Grand Prix |
| | v Chaperon | 9-8 | 3rd round | Tennents UK Open |
| | v Thorburn | 4-9 | 4th round | Tennents UK Open |
| **1987** | v Bradley | 1-5 | 3rd round | Mercantile Credit Classic |
| | v Fitzmaurice | 6-1 | 3rd round | Tolly Ales English Championship |
| | v Williams | 2-6 | 4th round | Tolly Ales English Championship |
| | v Wilkinson | 5-4 | 3rd round | Dulux British Open |
| | v J. McLaughlin | 5-2 | 4th round | Dulux British Open |
| | v Stevens | 5-2 | 5th round | Dulux British Open |
| | v Thorburn | 3-5 | Quarter-final | Dulux British Open |
| | v Cripsey | 10-7 | Qualifying | Embassy World Championship |
| | v Mountjoy | 5-10 | 1st round | Embassy World Championship |
| | v Morra | 5-3 | 3rd round | Fidelity International |
| | v Knowles | 2-5 | 4th round | Fidelity International |
| | v Chaperon | 3-5 | 3rd round | Rothmans Grand Prix |
| | v Chaperon | 9-6 | 3rd round | Tennents UK Open |
| | v Higgins | 6-9 | 4th round | Tennents UK Open |
| **1988** | v M. Smith | 5-3 | 3rd round | Mercantile Credit Classic |
| | v Parrott | 0-5 | 4th round | Mercantile Credit Classic |
| | v Owers | 3-6 | 3rd round | English Championship |
| | v Medati | 4-5 | 3rd round | MIM Britannia British Open |
| | v Chaperon | 6-10 | Qualifying | Embassy World Championship |
| | v T. Wilson | 5-1 | 3rd round | Fidelity International |
| | v John Rea | 5-4 | 4th round | Fidelity International |
| | v S. Davis | 1-5 | 5th round | Fidelity International |
| | v Duggan | 1-5 | 3rd round | Rothmans Grand Prix |
| | v Dodd | 5-3 | 3rd round | BCE Canadian Masters |
| | v Roscoe | 5-1 | 4th round | BCE Canadian Masters |
| | v Dennis Taylor | 2-5 | 5th round | BCE Canadian Masters |
| | v M. Bennett | 4-9 | 3rd round | Tennents UK Open |
| **1989** | v Darrington | 5-2 | 3rd round | Mercantile Credit Classic |
| | v C. Wilson | 5-3 | 4th round | Mercantile Credit Classic |
| | v W. Jones | 3-5 | 5th round | Mercantile Credit Classic |

| | | | | |
|---|---|---|---|---|
| | v Gary Wilkinson | 2-5 | 3rd round | European Open |
| | v Price | 1-5 | 3rd round | English Championship |
| | v Clark | 2-5 | 3rd round | Anglian British Open |
| | v W. Jones | 7-10 | Qualifying | Embassy World Championship |
| | v B. Morgan | 4-5 | 3rd round | Hong Kong Open |
| | v Wattana | 1-5 | 3rd round | 555 Asian Open |
| | v Cairns | 4-5 | 2nd round | BCE International |
| | v V. Harris | 3-5 | 2nd round | Rothmans Grand Prix |
| | v King | 1-5 | 3rd round | Dubai Classic |
| | v Wright | 6-2 | 2nd round | Stormseal UK Open |
| | v West | 5-9 | 3rd round | Stormseal UK Open |
| **1990** | v P. Gibson | 5-1 | 2nd round | Mercantile Credit Classic |
| | v Thorne | 5-1 | 3rd round | Mercantile Credit Classic |
| | v B. Morgan | 4-5 | 4th round | Mercantile Credit Classic |
| | v Cairns | 5-0 | 2nd round | Pearl Assurance British Open |
| | v P. Francisco | 4-5 | 3rd round | Pearl Assurance British Open |
| | v Lawlor | 5-2 | 2nd round | European Open |
| | v E. Hughes | 5-4 | 3rd round | European Open |
| | v Chappel | 2-5 | 4th round | European Open |
| | v Wattana | 5-10 | Qualifying | Embassy World Championship |

## DENNIS TAYLOR (Northern Ireland)

**Born** 19.1.49. **Turned professional** 1971. **World ranking** 10 (8).

| | | | | |
|---|---|---|---|---|
| **1973** | v Thorburn | 8-9 | 1st round | World Championship |
| **1974** | v M. Owen | 1-8 | Qualifying | World Championship |
| **1975** | v Mans | 15-12 | 1st round | World Championship |
| | v F. Davis | 15-14 | 2nd round | World Championship |
| | v G. Owen | 19-9 | Quarter-final | World Championship |
| | v Charlton | 12-19 | Semi-final | World Championship |
| **1976** | v G. Owen | 15-9 | 1st round | Embassy World Championship |
| | v Reardon | 2-15 | Quarter-final | Embassy World Championship |
| **1977** | v Karnehm | 11-0 | Qualifying | Embassy World Championship |
| | v Mans | 13-11 | 1st round | Embassy World Championship |
| | v Mountjoy | 13-11 | Quarter-final | Embassy World Championship |
| | v Thorburn | 16-18 | Semi-final | Embassy World Championship |
| **1978** | v F. Davis | 9-13 | 1st round | Embassy World Championship |
| | v Mountjoy | 4-9 | 1st round | Coral UK Championship |
| **1979** | v S. Davis | 13-11 | 1st round | Embassy World Championship |
| | v Reardon | 13-8 | Quarter-final | Embassy World Championship |
| | v Virgo | 19-12 | Semi-final | Embassy World Championship |
| | v Griffiths | 16-24 | Final | Embassy World Championship |
| | v Thorne | 9-8 | 3rd round | Coral UK Championship |
| | v Fagan | 9-6 | Quarter-final | Coral UK Championship |
| | v Virgo | 4-9 | Semi-final | Coral UK Championship |
| **1980** | v Reardon | 3-5 | Quarter-final | Benson & Hedges Masters |
| | v Wych | 10-13 | 2nd round | Embassy World Championship |
| | v Sinclair | 9-6 | 2nd round | Coral UK Championship |
| | v Griffiths | 2-9 | Quarter-final | Coral UK Championship |
| **1981** | v Spencer | 2-5 | 1st round | Benson & Hedges Masters |
| | v S. Davis | 2-5 | Semi-final | Yamaha International Masters |
| | v Stevens | 13-11 | 2nd round | Embassy World Championship |
| | v Mountjoy | 8-13 | Quarter-final | Embassy World Championship |
| | v Williams | 5-1 | 3rd round | Jameson International |
| | v Virgo | 5-2 | Quarter-final | Jameson International |
| | v Martin | 9-1 | Semi-final | Jameson International |
| | v S. Davis | 0-9 | Final | Jameson International |
| | v Mountjoy | 4-5 | 1st round | Northern Ireland Classic |
| | v White | 5-9 | 3rd round | Coral UK Championship |
| **1982** | v Higgins | 1-5 | 1st round | Lada Classic |
| | v Reardon | 3-5 | 1st round | Benson & Hedges Masters |

| | | | | |
|---|---|---|---|---|
| | v Knowles | 5-2 | Semi-final | Tolly Cobbold Classic |
| | v S. Davis | 3-8 | Final | Tolly Cobbold Classic |
| | v Murphy | 6-0 | Semi-final | Irish Championship |
| | **v Higgins** | **16-13** | **Final** | **Irish Championship** |
| | v Sheehan | 5-3 | 1st round | Benson & Hedges Irish Masters |
| | v Reardon | 4-5 | Quarter-final | Benson & Hedges Irish Masters |
| | v S. Francisco | 7-10 | 1st round | Embassy World Championship |
| | v White | 5-4 | 1st round | Langs Supreme Scottish Masters |
| | v S. Davis | 1-6 | Semi-final | Langs Supreme Scottish Masters |
| | v Wildman | 5-2 | 1st round | Jameson International |
| | v Thorburn | 5-2 | 2nd round | Jameson International |
| | v Virgo | 3-5 | Quarter-final | Jameson International |
| | v Edmonds | 5-4 | 1st round | Professional Players Tournament |
| | v David Taylor | 5-1 | 2nd round | Professional Players Tournament |
| | v White | 3-5 | 3rd round | Professional Players Tournament |
| | v Meadowcroft | 9-7 | 1st round | Coral UK Championship |
| | v Griffiths | 7-9 | 2nd round | Coral UK Championship |
| **1983** | v S. Davis | 2-5 | 1st round | Lada Classic |
| | v S. Davis | 1-5 | Semi-final | Tolly Cobbold Classic |
| | v Kelly | 6-0 | Quarter-final | Irish Championship |
| | v Fagan | 6-1 | Semi-final | Irish Championship |
| | v Higgins | 11-16 | Final | Irish Championship |
| | v White | 4-5 | 1st round | Benson & Hedges Irish Masters |
| | v S. Francisco | 10-9 | 1st round | Embassy World Championship |
| | v S. Davis | 11-13 | 2nd round | Embassy World Championship |
| | v Reynolds | 5-3 | 1st round | Jameson International |
| | v Thorburn | 3-5 | 2nd round | Jameson International |
| | v Scott | 4-5 | 1st round | Professional Players Tournament |
| | v Murphy | 9-6 | 1st round | Coral UK Championship |
| | v White | 4-9 | 2nd round | Coral UK Championship |
| **1984** | v Hallett | 4-5 | Qualifying | Lada Classic |
| | v Knowles | 2-5 | 1st round | Benson & Hedges Masters |
| | v E. Hughes | 5-1 | 1st round | Benson & Hedges Irish Masters |
| | v Thorburn | 5-2 | Quarter-final | Benson & Hedges Irish Masters |
| | v Griffiths | 4-5 | Semi-final | Benson & Hedges Irish Masters |
| | v Johnson | 10-1 | 1st round | Embassy World Championship |
| | v Parrott | 13-11 | 2nd round | Embassy World Championship |
| | v Mountjoy | 13-8 | Quarter-final | Embassy World Championship |
| | v S. Davis | 9-16 | Semi-final | Embassy World Championship |
| | v Fowler | 5-0 | 1st round | Jameson International |
| | v Watchorn | 5-1 | 1st round | Rothmans Grand Prix |
| | v Virgo | 5-3 | 2nd round | Rothmans Grand Prix |
| | v Reardon | 5-3 | 3rd round | Rothmans Grand Prix |
| | v Stevens | 5-2 | Quarter-final | Rothmans Grand Prix |
| | v N. Foulds | 9-3 | Semi-final | Rothmans Grand Prix |
| | **v Thorburn** | **10-2** | **Final** | **Rothmans Grand Prix** |
| | v King | 9-5 | 1st round | Coral UK Open |
| | v Knowles | 2-9 | 2nd round | Coral UK Open |
| **1985** | v Williams | 3-5 | 1st round | Mercantile Credit Classic |
| | v Thorburn | 3-5 | 1st round | Benson & Hedges Masters |
| | v Scott | 6-2 | 1st round | Dulux British Open |
| | v Parrott | 5-2 | 2nd round | Dulux British Open |
| | v Newbury | 5-3 | 3rd round | Dulux British Open |
| | v Stevens | 2-5 | Quarter-final | Dulux British Open |
| | v Charlton | 4-5 | 1st round | Benson & Hedges Irish Masters |
| | v Jack Rea | 6-0 | Quarter-final | Irish Championship |
| | v E. Hughes | 6-5 | Semi-final | Irish Championship |
| | **v Higgins** | **10-5** | **Final** | **Irish Championship** |
| | v S. Francisco | 10-2 | 1st round | Embassy World Championship |
| | v Charlton | 13-6 | 2nd round | Embassy World Championship |
| | v Thorburn | 13-5 | Quarter-final | Embassy World Championship |
| | v Knowles | 16-5 | Semi-final | Embassy World Championship |
| | **v S. Davis** | **18-17** | **Final** | **Embassy World Championship** |

*Dennis Taylor*

| | | | | |
|---|---|---|---|---|
| | v Thorne | 3-5 | 1st round | Langs Scottish Masters |
| | v Cripsey | 5-1 | 3rd round | Goya Matchroom Trophy |
| | v B. Harris | 5-3 | 4th round | Goya Matchroom Trophy |
| | v Higgins | 5-1 | 5th round | Goya Matchroom Trophy |
| | v Parrott | 5-1 | Quarter-final | Goya Matchroom Trophy |
| | v Thorburn | 5-9 | Semi-final | Goya Matchroom Trophy |
| | v West | 5-1 | 3rd round | Rothmans Grand Prix |
| | v Williams | 5-2 | 4th round | Rothmans Grand Prix |
| | v Meo | 5-3 | 5th round | Rothmans Grand Prix |
| | v Wilson | 5-2 | Quarter-final | Rothmans Grand Prix |
| | v Knowles | 9-6 | Semi-final | Rothmans Grand Prix |
| | v S. Davis | 9-10 | Final | Rothmans Grand Prix |
| | v Parrott | 5-1 | 1st round | BCE Canadian Masters |
| | v Reardon | 8-3 | Semi-final | BCE Canadian Masters |
| | **v S. Davis** | **9-5** | **Final** | **BCE Canadian Masters** |
| | v Jim Bear | 9-3 | 3rd round | Coral UK Open |
| | v Cripsey | 9-2 | 4th round | Coral UK Open |
| | v N. Foulds | 9-5 | 5th round | Coral UK Open |
| | v Stevens | 9-1 | Quarter-final | Coral UK Open |
| | v Thorne | 7-9 | Semi-final | Coral UK Open |
| | v F. Davis | 5-0 | 1st round | Kit Kat |
| | v Griffiths | 6-4 | Semi-final | Kit Kat |
| | **v S. Davis** | **9-5** | **Final** | **Kit Kat** |
| **1986** | v Fitzmaurice | 5-1 | 3rd round | Mercantile Credit Classic |
| | v Reynolds | 5-4 | 4th round | Mercantile Credit Classic |
| | v Higgins | 4-5 | 5th round | Mercantile Credit Classic |
| | v Higgins | 1-5 | 1st round | BCE Belgian Classic |
| | v Mountjoy | 5-2 | 1st round | Benson & Hedges Masters |
| | v White | 3-5 | Quarter-final | Benson & Hedges Masters |
| | v Bales | 4-5 | 3rd round | Dulux British Open |
| | v Thorne | 2-5 | Quarter-final | Benson & Hedges Irish Masters |
| | v Hallett | 6-10 | 1st round | Embassy World Championship |
| | v Kelly | 6-1 | Quarter-final | Strongbow Irish Championship |
| | v Murphy | 6-3 | Semi-final | Strongbow Irish Championship |
| | **v Higgins** | **10-7** | **Final** | **Strongbow Irish Championship** |
| | v Griffiths | 5-4 | Semi-final | Camus Hong Kong Masters |
| | v Thorne | 3-8 | Final | Camus Hong Kong Masters |
| | v Johnson | 5-3 | 1st round | Carlsberg Challenge |
| | **v White** | **8-3** | **Final** | **Carlsberg Challenge** |
| | v Thorne | 5-6 | Semi-final | Matchroom Trophy |
| | v Foldvari | 5-1 | 3rd round | BCE International |
| | v Hendry | 5-3 | 4th round | BCE International |
| | v S. Francisco | 0-5 | 5th round | BCE International |
| | v Wright | 5-3 | 3rd round | Rothmans Grand Prix |
| | v Virgo | 5-3 | 4th round | Rothmans Grand Prix |
| | v Meo | 2-5 | 5th round | Rothmans Grand Prix |
| | v Thorne | 4-5 | 1st round | BCE Canadian Masters |
| | v Roe | 9-6 | 3rd round | Tennents UK Open |
| | v W. Jones | 2-9 | 4th round | Tennents UK Open |
| **1987** | v W. Jones | 2-5 | 3rd round | Mercantile Credit Classic |
| | v N. Foulds | 5-2 | 1st round | Benson & Hedges Masters |
| | v S. Francisco | 5-3 | Quarter-final | Benson & Hedges Masters |
| | v Thorburn | 6-5 | Semi-final | Benson & Hedges Masters |
| | **v Higgins** | **9-8** | **Final** | **Benson & Hedges Masters** |
| | v Roscoe | 5-1 | 3rd round | Dulux British Open |
| | v Charlton | 5-1 | 4th round | Dulux British Open |
| | v Griffiths | 5-4 | 5th round | Dulux British Open |
| | v Knowles | 4-5 | Quarter-final | Dulux British Open |
| | v E. Hughes | 5-4 | 1st round | Benson & Hedges Irish Masters |
| | v Thorburn | 5-1 | Quarter-final | Benson & Hedges Irish Masters |
| | v Thorne | 2-6 | Semi-final | Benson & Hedges Irish Masters |
| | v M. Bennett | 10-4 | 1st round | Embassy World Championship |
| | v N. Foulds | 10-13 | 2nd round | Embassy World Championship |

| | | | | |
|---|---|---|---|---|
| | v Sheehan | 6-3 | Quarter-final | Matchroom Irish Championship |
| | v Browne | 6-1 | Semi-final | Matchroom Irish Championship |
| | **v O'Boye** | **9-2** | **Final** | **Matchroom Irish Championship** |
| | **v Griffiths** | **6-3** | **Final** | **British Caledonian Tokyo Masters (WS)** |
| | v S. Davis | 4-5 | Semi-final | Riley Hong Kong Masters (WS) |
| | v Hendry | 5-3 | 1st round | Carling Champions |
| | **v Johnson** | **8-5** | **Final** | **Carling Champions** |
| | v Thorburn | 2-5 | 1st round | Langs Scottish Masters |
| | v Bradley | 5-0 | 3rd round | Fidelity International |
| | v Clark | 0-5 | 4th round | Fidelity International |
| | v Reardon | 5-1 | 3rd round | Rothmans Grand Prix |
| | v Werbeniuk | 5-3 | 4th round | Rothmans Grand Prix |
| | v Wilson | 5-2 | 5th round | Rothmans Grand Prix |
| | v Newbury | 5-2 | Quarter-final | Rothmans Grand Prix |
| | v P. Francisco | 9-4 | Semi-final | Rothmans Grand Prix |
| | v Hendry | 7-10 | Final | Rothmans Grand Prix |
| | v S. Davis | 5-1 | 1st round | Labatts Canadian Masters (WS) |
| | v Thorburn | 8-5 | Semi-final | Labatts Canadian Masters (WS) |
| | **v White** | **9-7** | **Final** | **Labatts Canadian Masters (WS)** |
| | v White | 6-2 | 1st round | Matchroom Trophy |
| | v S. Davis | 6-3 | Semi-final | Matchroom Trophy |
| | **v Thorne** | **10-3** | **Final** | **Matchroom Trophy** |
| | v Dodd | 9-8 | 3rd round | Tennents UK Open |
| | v O'Kane | 7-9 | 4th round | Tennents UK Open |
| **1988** | v Whitthread | 5-2 | 3rd round | Mercantile Credit Classic |
| | v Drago | 5-0 | 4th round | Mercantile Credit Classic |
| | v P. Francisco | 5-3 | 5th round | Mercantile Credit Classic |
| | v Parrott | 1-5 | Quarter-final | Mercantile Credit Classic |
| | v Hallett | 3-5 | 1st round | Benson & Hedges Masters |
| | v Kearney | 6-3 | Quarter-final | Irish Championship |
| | v Browne | 6-5 | Semi-final | Irish Championship |
| | v J. McLaughlin | 4-9 | Final | Irish Championship |
| | v Miles | 5-1 | 3rd round | MIM Britannia British Open |
| | v Spencer | 0-5 | 4th round | MIM Britannia British Open |
| | v Higgins | 3-5 | 1st round | Benson & Hedges Irish Masters |
| | v Werbeniuk | 10-8 | 1st round | Embassy World Championship |
| | v Drago | 5-13 | 2nd round | Embassy World Championship |
| | v White | 2-5 | Semi-final | LEP Hong Kong Masters |
| | v Chappel | 5-1 | 3rd round | Fidelity International |
| | v J. Campbell | 5-4 | 4th round | Fidelity International |
| | v Wych | 5-2 | 5th round | Fidelity International |
| | v S. Davis | 2-5 | Quarter-final | Fidelity International |
| | v Meo | 6-4 | 1st round | LEP Matchroom Championship |
| | v N. Foulds | 6-3 | Semi-final | LEP Matchroom Championship |
| | v S. Davis | 7-10 | Final | LEP Matchroom Championship |
| | v Ellis | 5-1 | 3rd round | Rothmans Grand Prix |
| | v Chaperon | 5-4 | 4th round | Rothmans Grand Prix |
| | v Hallett | 5-2 | 5th round | Rothmans Grand Prix |
| | v White | 5-2 | Quarter-final | Rothmans Grand Prix |
| | v S. Davis | 1-9 | Semi-final | Rothmans Grand Prix |
| | v Owers | 5-1 | 3rd round | BCE Canadian Masters |
| | v Clark | 5-4 | 4th round | BCE Canadian Masters |
| | v David Taylor | 5-2 | 5th round | BCE Canadian Masters |
| | v White | 3-5 | Quarter-final | BCE Canadian Masters |
| | v J. McLaughlin | 9-5 | 3rd round | Tennents UK Open |
| | v O'Boye | 9-4 | 4th round | Tennents UK Open |
| | v Parrott | 4-9 | 5th round | Tennents UK Open |
| | v Knowles | 9-7 | 1st round | Everest World Matchplay |
| | v Hendry | 7-9 | Quarter-final | Everest World Matchplay |
| **1989** | v Fowler | 5-3 | 3rd round | Mercantile Credit Classic |
| | v Newbury | 4-5 | 4th round | Mercantile Credit Classic |
| | v Parrott | 1-5 | 1st round | Benson and Hedges Masters |
| | v Stevens | 5-0 | 3rd round | European Open |

| | | | | |
|---|---|---|---|---|
| | v Mountjoy | 3-5 | 4th round | European Open |
| | v Roscoe | 4-5 | 3rd round | Anglian British Open |
| | v Parrott | 1-5 | 1st round | Benson and Hedges Irish Masters |
| | v E. Hughes | 10-3 | 1st round | Embassy World Championship |
| | v Parrott | 10-13 | 2nd round | Embassy World Championship |
| | v Thorne | 5-6 | 1st round | Lion Brown New Zealand Masters |
| | v Roscoe | 5-3 | 3rd round | Hong Kong Open |
| | v Gollan | 5-4 | 4th round | Hong Kong Open |
| | v Clark | 5-3 | 5th round | Hong Kong Open |
| | v Gary Wilkinson | 3-5 | Quarter-final | Hong Kong Open |
| | v D. Gilbert | 1-5 | 3rd round | 555 Asian Open |
| | v John Rea | 5-6 | 1st round | Regal Scottish Masters |
| | v Dyson | 5-1 | 3rd round | BCE International |
| | v Clark | 5-4 | 4th round | BCE International |
| | v B. Morgan | 4-5 | 5th round | BCE International |
| | v J. Campbell | 5-3 | 3rd round | Rothmans Grand Prix |
| | v Rowswell | 5-2 | 4th round | Rothmans Grand Prix |
| | v Newbury | 5-1 | 5th round | Rothmans Grand Prix |
| | v Reynolds | 3-5 | Quarter-final | Rothmans Grand Prix |
| | v D. Gilbert | 9-2 | 3rd round | Stormseal UK Open |
| | v Williams | 9-2 | 4th round | Stormseal UK Open |
| | v Hallett | 6-9 | 5th round | Stormseal UK Open |
| | v Hallett | 9-6 | 1st round | Everest World Matchplay |
| | v Parrott | 6-9 | Quarter-final | Everest World Matchplay |
| **1990** | v M. Bennett | 5-2 | 3rd round | Mercantile Credit Classic |
| | v Drago | 4-5 | 4th round | Mercantile Credit Classic |
| | v Thorne | 4-5 | 1st round | Benson and Hedges Masters |
| | v Fowler | 5-1 | 3rd round | Pearl Assurance British Open |
| | v Macleod | 5-2 | 4th round | Pearl Assurance British Open |
| | v Clark | 3-5 | 5th round | Pearl Assurance British Open |
| | v Dyson | 3-5 | 3rd round | European Open |
| | v Thorburn | 5-3 | 1st round | Benson and Hedges Irish Masters |
| | v Higgins | 5-2 | Quarter-final | Benson and Hedges Irish Masters |
| | v White | 6-5 | Semi-final | Benson and Hedges Irish Masters |
| | v S. Davis | 4-9 | Final | Benson and Hedges Irish Masters |
| | v N. Foulds | 8-10 | 1st round | Embassy World Championship |

## NICK TERRY (England)

**Born** 15.9.67. **Turned professional** 1988. **World ranking** 87 (72).

| | | | | |
|---|---|---|---|---|
| **1988** | v Roscoe | 2-5 | 1st round | Fidelity International |
| | v Sinclair | 5-3 | 1st round | Rothmans Grand Prix |
| | v Miles | 5-1 | 2nd round | Rothmans Grand Prix |
| | v N. Foulds | 4-5 | 3rd round | Rothmans Grand Prix |
| | v Donnelly | 5-1 | 1st round | BCE Canadian Masters |
| | v Gary Wilkinson | 3-5 | 2nd round | BCE Canadian Masters |
| | v Rigitano | 9-5 | 1st round | Tennents UK Open |
| | v King | 7-9 | 2nd round | Tennents UK Open |
| **1989** | v John Rea | 5-3 | 1st round | Mercantile Credit Classic |
| | v M. Bennett | 5-3 | 2nd round | Mercantile Credit Classic |
| | v P. Francisco | 5-4 | 3rd round | Mercantile Credit Classic |
| | v Mountjoy | 4-5 | 4th round | Mercantile Credit Classic |
| | v V. Harris | 2-5 | 1st round | European Open |
| | v Rowing | 5-1 | Prelim | English Championship |
| | v Marshall | 3-5 | 1st round | English Championship |
| | v Kearney | 5-3 | 1st round | Anglian British Open |
| | v Houlihan | 2-5 | 2nd round | Anglian British Open |
| | v Parkin | 10-0 | Qualifying | Embassy World Championship |
| | v Medati | 10-8 | Qualifying | Embassy World Championship |
| | v N. Gilbert | 5-10 | Qualifying | Embassy World Championship |
| | v Pinches | 1-5 | 1st round | Hong Kong Open |

| | | | | |
|---|---|---|---|---|
| | v Edmonds | 5-2 | 2nd round | 555 Asian Open |
| | v E. Hughes | 1-5 | 3rd round | 555 Asian Open |
| | v Meadowcroft | 5-1 | 1st round | BCE International |
| | v M. Bennett | 4-5 | 2nd round | BCE International |
| | v Sheehan | 5-4 | 1st round | Rothmans Grand Prix |
| | v Gary Wilkinson | 3-5 | 2nd round | Rothmans Grand Prix |
| | v Fitzmaurice | 5-3 | 2nd round | Dubai Classic |
| | v Wych | 2-5 | 3rd round | Dubai Classic |
| | v Watterson | 6-3 | 1st round | Stormseal UK Open |
| | v Reardon | 6-4 | 2nd round | Stormseal UK Open |
| | v Reynolds | 6-9 | 3rd round | Stormseal UK Open |
| **1990** | v D. Hughes | 5-0 | 1st round | Mercantile Credit Classic |
| | v Cripsey | 5-3 | 2nd round | Mercantile Credit Classic |
| | v Thorburn | 2-5 | 3rd round | Mercantile Credit Classic |
| | v Thornley | 5-1 | 1st round | Pearl Assurance British Open |
| | v J. Campbell | 5-1 | 2nd round | Pearl Assurance British Open |
| | v Mountjoy | 3-5 | 3rd round | Pearl Assurance British Open |
| | v Ellis | 3-5 | 1st round | European Open |
| | v S. Murphy | 10-4 | Qualifying | Embassy World Championship |
| | v Johnston-Allen | 1-10 | Qualifying | Embassy World Championship |

## CLIFF THORBURN C.M. (Canada)

**Born** 16.1.48. **Turned professional** 1973. **World ranking** 19 (7).

| | | | | |
|---|---|---|---|---|
| **1973** | v Dennis Taylor | 9-8 | 1st round | World Championship |
| | v Williams | 15-16 | 2nd round | World Championship |
| **1974** | v Morgan | 4-8 | 1st round | World Championship |
| **1975** | v Pulman | 3-5 | 1st round | Benson & Hedges Masters |
| | v Morgan | 15-6 | 1st round | World Championship |
| | v Miles | 15-2 | 2nd round | World Championship |
| | v Charlton | 12-19 | Quarter-final | World Championship |
| **1976** | v Higgins | 14-15 | 1st round | Embassy World Championship |
| **1977** | v Ross | 11-0 | Qualifying | Embassy World Championship |
| | v Williams | 13-6 | 1st round | Embassy World Championship |
| | v Charlton | 13-12 | Quarter-final | Embassy World Championship |
| | v Dennis Taylor | 18-16 | Semi-final | Embassy World Championship |
| | v Spencer | 21-25 | Final | Embassy World Championship |
| **1978** | v Mountjoy | 4-2 | Quarter-final | Benson & Hedges Masters |
| | v Spencer | 5-3 | Semi-final | Benson & Hedges Masters |
| | v Higgins | 5-7 | Final | Benson & Hedges Masters |
| | v Houlihan | 13-8 | 1st round | Embassy World Championship |
| | v Charlton | 12-13 | Quarter-final | Embassy World Championship |
| **1979** | v Mans | 4-5 | Quarter-final | Benson & Hedges Masters |
| | v Virgo | 10-13 | 1st round | Embassy World Championship |
| **1980** | v Virgo | 5-3 | 1st round | Benson & Hedges Masters |
| | v Griffiths | 3-5 | Quarter-final | Benson & Hedges Masters |
| | v Mountjoy | 13-10 | 2nd round | Embassy World Championship |
| | v Wych | 13-6 | Quarter-final | Embassy World Championship |
| | v David Taylor | 16-7 | Semi-final | Embassy World Championship |
| | **v Higgins** | **18-16** | **Final** | **Embassy World Championship** |
| **1981** | v Mans | 5-4 | Quarter-final | Benson & Hedges Masters |
| | v Higgins | 5-6 | Semi-final | Benson & Hedges Masters |
| | v Griffiths | 5-6 | Semi-final | Benson & Hedges Irish Masters |
| | v Miles | 13-2 | 2nd round | Embassy World Championship |
| | v David Taylor | 13-6 | Quarter-final | Embassy World Championship |
| | v S. Davis | 10-16 | Semi-final | Embassy World Championship |
| | v Stevens | 5-1 | Quarter-final | Langs Scottish Masters |
| | v Higgins | 6-2 | Semi-final | Langs Scottish Masters |
| | v White | 4-9 | Final | Langs Scottish Masters |
| | v Miles | 0-5 | 3rd round | Jameson International |
| | v White | 2-5 | 1st round | Northern Ireland Classic |

| | | | | |
|---|---|---|---|---|
| | v Meo | 6-9 | 3rd round | Coral UK Championship |
| **1982** | v Griffiths | 1-5 | 1st round | Lada Classic |
| | v Meo | 0-5 | Quarter-final | Benson & Hedges Masters |
| | v Higgins | 4-5 | Quarter-final | Benson & Hedges Irish Masters |
| | v White | 4-10 | 1st round | Embassy World Championship |
| | v Scott | 5-1 | 1st round | Jameson International |
| | v Dennis Taylor | 2-5 | 2nd round | Jameson International |
| | v Medati | 5-1 | 1st round | Professional Players Tournament |
| | v Everton | 5-2 | 2nd round | Professional Players Tournament |
| | v Werbeniuk | 2-5 | 3rd round | Professional Players Tournament |
| **1983** | v Wilson | 5-3 | 1st round | Lada Classic |
| | v Stevens | 3-5 | Quarter-final | Lada Classic |
| | v Johnson | 5-2 | 1st round | Benson & Hedges Masters |
| | v Griffiths | 5-3 | Quarter-final | Benson & Hedges Masters |
| | v Charlton | 6-5 | Semi-final | Benson & Hedges Masters |
| | **v Reardon** | **9-7** | **Final** | **Benson & Hedges Masters** |
| | v J. Campbell | 10-5 | 1st round | Embassy World Championship |
| | v Griffiths | 13-12 | 2nd round | Embassy World Championship |
| | v Stevens | 13-12 | Quarter-final | Embassy World Championship |
| | v Knowles | 16-15 | Semi-final | Embassy World Championship |
| | v S. Davis | 6-18 | Final | Embassy World Championship |
| | v Stevens | 5-2 | Semi-final | Winfield Masters |
| | **v Werbeniuk** | **7-3** | **Final** | **Winfield Masters** |
| | v Mikkelsen | 9-2 | Quarter-final | Canadian Championship |
| | v Jonik | 6-9 | Semi-final | Canadian Championship |
| | v Griffiths | 5-1 | 1st round | Langs Scottish Masters |
| | v Knowles | 2-6 | Semi-final | Langs Scottish Masters |
| | v Sinclair | 5-0 | 1st round | Jameson International |
| | v Dennis Taylor | 5-3 | 2nd round | Jameson International |
| | v Mountjoy | 5-2 | Quarter-final | Jameson International |
| | v Griffiths | 9-8 | Semi-final | Jameson International |
| | v S. Davis | 4-9 | Final | Jameson International |
| | v V. Harris | 5-1 | 1st round | Professional Players Tournament |
| | v Meadowcroft | 5-1 | 2nd round | Professional Players Tournament |
| | v Wilson | 5-3 | 3rd round | Professional Players Tournament |
| | v Johnson | 1-5 | Quarter-final | Professional Players Tournament |
| **1984** | v S. Francisco | 1-5 | Qualifying | Lada Classic |
| | v Spencer | 4-5 | 1st round | Benson & Hedges Masters |
| | v Dennis Taylor | 2-5 | Quarter-final | Benson & Hedges Irish Masters |
| | v Meo | 5-4 | 1st round | Tolly Cobbold Classic |
| | v Knowles | 3-5 | Semi-final | Tolly Cobbold Classic |
| | v Morra | 10-3 | 1st round | Embassy World Championship |
| | v Thorne | 13-11 | 2nd round | Embassy World Championship |
| | v White | 8-13 | Quarter-final | Embassy World Championship |
| | v S. Davis | 2-5 | 1st round | Langs Scottish Masters |
| | v Virgo | 0-5 | 1st round | Jameson International |
| | v Rigitano | 5-4 | 1st round | Rothmans Grand Prix |
| | v J. Campbell | 5-1 | 2nd round | Rothmans Grand Prix |
| | v Meo | 5-4 | 3rd round | Rothmans Grand Prix |
| | v Mountjoy | 5-3 | Quarter-final | Rothmans Grand Prix |
| | v S. Davis | 9-7 | Semi-final | Rothmans Grand Prix |
| | v Dennis Taylor | 2-10 | Final | Rothmans Grand Prix |
| | v J. McLaughlin | 9-4 | 1st round | Coral UK Open |
| | v Wilson | 9-3 | 2nd round | Coral UK Open |
| | v Reardon | 9-8 | Quarter-final | Coral UK Open |
| | v Higgins | 7-9 | Semi-final | Coral UK Open |
| **1985** | v Scott | 5-1 | 1st round | Mercantile Credit Classic |
| | v Longworth | 5-3 | 2nd round | Mercantile Credit Classic |
| | v Griffiths | 5-4 | Quarter-final | Mercantile Credit Classic |
| | v Johnson | 9-2 | Semi-final | Mercantile Credit Classic |
| | v Thorne | 8-13 | Final | Mercantile Credit Classic |
| | v Dennis Taylor | 5-3 | 1st round | Benson & Hedges Masters |
| | v Reardon | 5-0 | Quarter-final | Benson & Hedges Masters |

| | | | | |
|---|---|---|---|---|
| | v White | 6-4 | Semi-final | Benson & Hedges Masters |
| | **v Mountjoy** | **9-6** | **Final** | **Benson & Hedges Masters** |
| | v Rigitano | 6-3 | 1st round | Dulux British Open |
| | v Reynolds | 5-3 | 2nd round | Dulux British Open |
| | v Higgins | 2-5 | 3rd round | Dulux British Open |
| | v White | 3-5 | Quarter-final | Benson & Hedges Irish Masters |
| | v Hallett | 10-8 | 1st round | Embassy World Championship |
| | v Werbeniuk | 13-3 | 2nd round | Embassy World Championship |
| | v Dennis Taylor | 5-13 | Quarter-final | Embassy World Championship |
| | v Caggianello | 6-2 | Quarter-final | Canadian Championship |
| | v Wych | 6-5 | Semi-final | Canadian Championship |
| | **v Chaperon** | **6-4** | **Final** | **Canadian Championship** |
| | v Higgins | 4-5 | Semi-final | Carlsberg Trophy |
| | v Macleod | 5-1 | 1st round | Langs Scottish Masters |
| | v S. Francisco | 6-0 | Semi-final | Langs Scottish Masters |
| | **v Thorne** | **9-7** | **Final** | **Langs Scottish Masters** |
| | v Longworth | 5-3 | 3rd round | Goya Matchroom Trophy |
| | v Martin | 5-3 | 4th round | Goya Matchroom Trophy |
| | v J. Campbell | 5-0 | 5th round | Goya Matchroom Trophy |
| | v Duggan | 5-2 | Quarter-final | Goya Matchroom Trophy |
| | v Dennis Taylor | 9-5 | Semi-final | Goya Matchroom Trophy |
| | **v White** | **12-10** | **Final** | **Goya Matchroom Trophy** |
| | v Oliver | 5-0 | 3rd round | Rothmans Grand Prix |
| | v Wildman | 5-2 | 4th round | Rothmans Grand Prix |
| | v Johnson | 5-1 | 5th round | Rothmans Grand Prix |
| | v Griffiths | 5-1 | Quarter-final | Rothmans Grand Prix |
| | v S. Davis | 5-9 | Semi-final | Rothmans Grand Prix |
| | v White | 5-3 | 1st round | BCE Canadian Masters |
| | v S. Davis | 1-8 | Semi-final | BCE Canadian Masters |
| | v Dodd | 9-4 | 3rd round | Coral UK Open |
| | v Parrott | 9-6 | 4th round | Coral UK Open |
| | v Thorne | 7-9 | 5th round | Coral UK Open |
| | v Higgins | 4-5 | 1st round | Kit Kat |
| **1986** | v J. McLaughlin | 5-1 | 3rd round | Mercantile Credit Classic |
| | v Hallett | 5-3 | 4th round | Mercantile Credit Classic |
| | v Meo | 5-1 | 5th round | Mercantile Credit Classic |
| | v Johnson | 5-4 | Quarter-final | Mercantile Credit Classic |
| | v Mountjoy | 9-6 | Semi-final | Mercantile Credit Classic |
| | v White | 12-13 | Final | Mercantile Credit Classic |
| | v Johnson | 5-3 | 1st round | Benson & Hedges Masters |
| | v Griffiths | 5-2 | Quarter-final | Benson & Hedges Masters |
| | v Knowles | 6-4 | Semi-final | Benson & Hedges Masters |
| | **v White** | **9-5** | **Final** | **Benson & Hedges Masters** |
| | v Sheehan | 5-0 | 3rd round | Dulux British Open |
| | v Wildman | 5-1 | 4th round | Dulux British Open |
| | v Meo | 3-5 | 5th round | Dulux British Open |
| | v E. Hughes | 5-1 | Quarter-final | Benson & Hedges Irish Masters |
| | v Thorne | 4-6 | Semi-final | Benson & Hedges Irish Masters |
| | v Werbeniuk | 10-5 | 1st round | Embassy World Championship |
| | v E. Hughes | 13-6 | 2nd round | Embassy World Championship |
| | v Thorne | 13-6 | Quarter-final | Embassy World Championship |
| | v S. Davis | 12-16 | Semi-final | Embassy World Championship |
| | v Watson | 6-1 | Quarter-final | Canadian Championship |
| | v Jonik | 6-3 | Semi-final | Canadian Championship |
| | **v Wych** | **6-2** | **Final** | **Canadian Championship** |
| | v Parrott | 5-1 | 1st round | Langs Scottish Masters |
| | v White | 6-2 | Semi-final | Langs Scottish Masters |
| | **v Higgins** | **9-8** | **Final** | **Langs Scottish Masters** |
| | v Burke | 5-0 | 3rd round | BCE International |
| | v Wych | 5-3 | 4th round | BCE International |
| | v Griffiths | 5-4 | 5th round | BCE International |
| | v Wilson | 5-1 | Quarter-final | BCE International |
| | v P. Francisco | 9-7 | Semi-final | BCE International |

*Cliff Thorburn*

| | | | | |
|---|---|---|---|---|
| | v N. Foulds | 9-12 | Final | BCE International |
| | v O'Boye | 4-5 | 3rd round | Rothmans Grand Prix |
| | v Knowles | 1-5 | 1st round | BCE Canadian Masters |
| | v Fowler | 9-7 | 3rd round | Tennents UK Open |
| | v David Taylor | 9-4 | 4th round | Tennents UK Open |
| | v Spencer | 9-2 | 5th round | Tennents UK Open |
| | v N. Foulds | 2-9 | Quarter-final | Tennents UK Open |
| **1987** | v Cripsey | 5-0 | 3rd round | Mercantile Credit Classic |
| | v Reynolds | 4-5 | 4th round | Mercantile Credit Classic |
| | v Williams | 5-1 | 1st round | Benson & Hedges Masters |
| | v Thorne | 5-3 | Quarter-final | Benson & Hedges Masters |
| | v Dennis Taylor | 5-6 | Semi-final | Benson & Hedges Masters |
| | v Wildman | 5-3 | 3rd round | Dulux British Open |
| | v Cripsey | 5-2 | 4th round | Dulux British Open |
| | v Mountjoy | 5-4 | 5th round | Dulux British Open |
| | v David Taylor | 5-3 | Quarter-final | Dulux British Open |
| | v White | 5-9 | Semi-final | Dulux British Open |
| | v Dennis Taylor | 1-5 | Quarter-final | Benson & Hedges Irish Masters |
| | v O'Kane | 5-10 | 1st round | Embassy World Championship |
| | v Watson | 6-3 | Quarter-final | Canadian Championship |
| | v Morra | 7-4 | Semi-final | Canadian Championship |
| | **v Bear** | **8-4** | **Final** | **Canadian Championship** |
| | v Dennis Taylor | 5-2 | 1st round | Langs Scottish Masters |
| | v Johnson | 3-6 | Semi-final | Langs Scottish Masters |
| | v Grace | 5-1 | 3rd round | Fidelity International |
| | v Newbury | 5-3 | 4th round | Fidelity International |
| | v James | 5-0 | 5th round | Fidelity International |
| | v E. Hughes | 5-1 | Quarter-final | Fidelity International |
| | v Hendry | 9-1 | Semi-final | Fidelity International |
| | v S. Davis | 5-12 | Final | Fidelity International |
| | v T. Jones | 5-2 | 3rd round | Rothmans Grand Prix |
| | v Newbury | 0-5 | 4th round | Rothmans Grand Prix |
| | v Johnson | 5-3 | 1st round | Labatts Canadian Masters (WS) |
| | v Dennis Taylor | 5-8 | Semi-final | Labatts Canadian Masters (WS) |
| | v Cripsey | 9-6 | 3rd round | Tennents UK Open |
| | v Virgo | 9-6 | 4th round | Tennents UK Open |
| | v J. Campbell | 9-4 | 5th round | Tennents UK Open |
| | v Thorne | 8-9 | Quarter-final | Tennents UK Open |
| **1988** | v Reardon | 5-3 | 3rd round | Mercantile Credit Classic |
| | v Newbury | 3-5 | 4th round | Mercantile Credit Classic |
| | v Williams | 5-3 | 1st round | Benson and Hedges Masters |
| | v Parrott | 4-5 | Quarter-final | Benson and Hedges Masters |
| | v Newbury | 5-2 | 3rd round | MIM Britannia British Open |
| | v Medati | 5-2 | 4th round | MIM Britannia British Open |
| | v Thorne | 5-2 | 5th round | MIM Britannia British Open |
| | v Williams | 5-2 | Quarter-final | MIM Britannia British Open |
| | v Hendry | 5-9 | Semi-final | MIM Britannia British Open |
| | v Higgins | 3-5 | Quarter-final | Benson & Hedges Irish Masters |
| | v Stevens | 10-6 | 1st round | Embassy World Championship |
| | v Parrott | 13-10 | 2nd round | Embassy World Championship |
| | v James | 13-11 | Quarter-final | Embassy World Championship |
| | v S. Davis | 8-16 | Semi-final | Embassy World Championship |
| | v Jonik | 6-4 | Quarter-final | BCE Canadian Championship |
| | v Wych | 5-7 | Semi-final | BCE Canadian Championship |
| | v White | 4-6 | 1st round | LEP Matchroom Championship |
| | v Chappel | 5-1 | 3rd round | BCE Canadian Masters |
| | v Spencer | 5-2 | 4th round | BCE Canadian Masters |
| | v Graham | 5-4 | 5th round | BCE Canadian Masters |
| | v Hendry | 4-5 | Quarter-final | BCE Canadian Masters |
| | v Robidoux | 9-4 | 3rd round | Tennents UK Open |
| | v James | 9-6 | 4th round | Tennents UK Open |
| | v Roe | 9-8 | 5th round | Tennents UK Open |
| | v Hendry | 2-9 | Quarter-final | Tennents UK Open |

| | | | | |
|---|---|---|---|---|
| | v Johnson | 4-9 | 1st round | Everest World Matchplay |
| **1989** | v Glen Wilkinson | 5-2 | 3rd round | Mercantile Credit Classic |
| | v Cripsey | 5-1 | 4th round | Mercantile Credit Classic |
| | v Virgo | 5-3 | 5th round | Mercantile Credit Classic |
| | v Hendry | 5-4 | Quarter-final | Mercantile Credit Classic |
| | v Mountjoy | 5-9 | Semi-final | Mercantile Credit Classic |
| | v Johnson | 5-2 | 1st round | Benson and Hedges Masters |
| | v N. Foulds | 2-5 | Quarter-final | Benson and Hedges Masters |
| | v Edmonds | 5-2 | 3rd round | European Open |
| | v Macleod | 5-1 | 4th round | European Open |
| | v Mountjoy | 5-0 | 5th round | European Open |
| | v White | 3-5 | Quarter-final | European Open |
| | v Browne | 5-0 | 3rd round | Anglian British Open |
| | v D. Morgan | 5-4 | 4th round | Anglian British Open |
| | v Hallett | 4-5 | 5th round | Anglian British Open |
| | v Higgins | 4-5 | 1st round | Benson and Hedges Irish Masters |
| | v Charlton | 9-10 | 1st round | Embassy World Championship |
| | v T. Jones | 2-5 | 3rd round | Hong Kong Open |
| | v T. Jones | 2-5 | 3rd round | 555 Asian Open |
| | v Macleod | 6-2 | 1st round | Regal Scottish Masters |
| | v Parrott | 5-6 | Quarter-final | Regal Scottish Masters |
| | v Bond | 4-5 | 3rd round | BCE International |
| | v Meakin | 5-3 | 3rd round | Rothmans Grand Prix |
| | v T. Jones | 4-5 | 4th round | Rothmans Grand Prix |
| | v Rowing | 9-2 | 3rd round | Stormseal UK Open |
| | v P. Francisco | 5-9 | 4th round | Stormseal UK Open |
| | v Griffiths | 5-9 | 1st round | Everest World Matchplay |
| **1990** | v Terry | 5-2 | 3rd round | Mercantile Credit Classic |
| | v D. Morgan | 4-5 | 4th round | Mercantile Credit Classic |
| | v Mountjoy | 4-5 | 1st round | Benson and Hedges Masters |
| | v T. Murphy | 3-5 | 3rd round | Pearl Assurance British Open |
| | v Price | 0-5 | 3rd round | European Open |
| | v Dennis Taylor | 3-5 | 1st round | Benson and Hedges Irish Masters |
| | v C. Wilson | 10-6 | 1st round | Embassy World Championship |
| | v Mountjoy | 13-12 | 2nd round | Embassy World Championship |
| | v Parrott | 6-13 | Quarter-final | Embassy World Championship |

## **WILLIE THORNE** (England)

**Born** 4.3.54. **Turned professional** 1975. **World ranking** 11 (9).

| | | | | |
|---|---|---|---|---|
| **1976** | v Condo | 8-3 | Qualifying | Embassy World Championship |
| | v Meadowcroft | 5-8 | Qualifying | Embassy World Championship |
| **1977** | v Bennett | 11-4 | Qualifying | Embassy World Championship |
| | v Miles | 4-13 | 1st round | Embassy World Championship |
| | v Bennett | 5-1 | 1st round | Super Crystalate UK Championship |
| | v Williams | 5-4 | 2nd round | Super Crystalate UK Championship |
| | v Mountjoy | 4-5 | Quarter-final | Super Crystalate UK Championship |
| **1978** | v Williams | 9-3 | Qualifying | Embassy World Championship |
| | v Charlton | 12-13 | 1st round | Embassy World Championship |
| | v Bennett | 9-4 | Qualifying | Coral UK Championship |
| | v Reardon | 9-6 | 1st round | Coral UK Championship |
| | v Miles | 1-9 | Quarter-final | Coral UK Championship |
| **1979** | v Jim Charlton | 9-3 | Prelim | Embassy World Championship |
| | v Virgo | 8-9 | Qualifying | Embassy World Championship |
| | v Andrewartha | 9-4 | 2nd round | Coral UK Championship |
| | v Dennis Taylor | 8-9 | 3rd round | Coral UK Championship |
| **1980** | v Jack Rea | 9-1 | Qualifying | Embassy World Championship |
| | v Werbeniuk | 9-10 | 1st round | Embassy World Championship |
| | v Meadowcroft | 9-1 | 1st round | Coral UK Championship |
| | v Higgins | 7-9 | 2nd round | Coral UK Championship |
| **1981** | v Wildman | 9-2 | 1st round | John Courage English |

| | | | | |
|---|---|---|---|---|
| | v Dunning | 9-0 | 2nd round | John Courage English |
| | v Meo | 8-9 | Semi-final | John Courage English |
| | v Morra | 9-5 | Qualifying | Embassy World Championship |
| | v Greaves | 9-3 | Qualifying | Embassy World Championship |
| | v Mountjoy | 6-10 | 1st round | Embassy World Championship |
| | v Medati | 9-6 | Qualifying | Coral UK Championship |
| | v Edmonds | 9-4 | 2nd round | Coral UK Championship |
| | v S. Davis | 2-9 | 3rd round | Coral UK Championship |
| **1982** | v Roscoe | 9-1 | Qualifying | Embassy World Championship |
| | v Griffiths | 10-6 | 1st round | Embassy World Championship |
| | v Spencer | 13-5 | 2nd round | Embassy World Championship |
| | v Higgins | 10-13 | Quarter-final | Embassy World Championship |
| | v Reynolds | 3-5 | 1st round | Jameson International |
| | v Demarco | 5-3 | 1st round | Professional Players Tournament |
| | v Macleod | 4-5 | 2nd round | Professional Players Tournament |
| | v Wilson | 7-9 | 1st round | Coral UK Championship |
| | v Virgo | 10-3 | 1st round | Embassy World Championship |
| | v Higgins | 8-13 | 2nd round | Embassy World Championship |
| **1983** | v Murphy | 5-2 | Qualifying | Jameson International |
| | v Virgo | 5-2 | 1st round | Jameson International |
| | v Reardon | 5-0 | 2nd round | Jameson International |
| | v Charlton | 0-5 | Quarter-final | Jameson International |
| | v Everton | 5-1 | 1st round | Professional Players Tournament |
| | v Spencer | 5-1 | 2nd round | Professional Players Tournament |
| | v Reardon | 5-3 | 3rd round | Professional Players Tournament |
| | v E. Hughes | 5-1 | Quarter-final | Professional Players Tournament |
| | v Knowles | 7-9 | Semi-final | Professional Players Tournament |
| | v Wildman | 9-5 | 1st round | Coral UK Championship |
| | v S. Davis | 3-9 | 2nd round | Coral UK Championship |
| **1984** | v S. Davis | 2-5 | 1st round | Tolly Cobbold Classic |
| | v Mikkelsen | 10-3 | Qualifying | Embassy World Championship |
| | v Virgo | 10-9 | 1st round | Embassy World Championship |
| | v Thorburn | 11-13 | 2nd round | Embassy World Championship |
| | v Virgo | 3-5 | Quarter-final | Winfield Australian Masters |
| | v O'Kane | 5-3 | 1st round | Jameson International |
| | v Gauvreau | 5-3 | 2nd round | Jameson International |
| | v E. Hughes | 2-5 | Quarter-final | Jameson International |
| | v Newbury | 5-2 | 1st round | Rothmans Grand Prix |
| | v Macleod | 5-3 | 2nd round | Rothmans Grand Prix |
| | v N. Foulds | 1-5 | 3rd round | Rothmans Grand Prix |
| | v Parrot | 9-7 | 1st round | Coral UK Open |
| | v Charlton | 9-7 | 2nd round | Coral UK Open |
| | v Higgins | 5-9 | Quarter-final | Coral UK Open |
| **1985** | v Foldvari | 5-2 | 1st round | Mercantile Credit Classic |
| | v Stevens | 5-1 | 2nd round | Mercantile Credit Classic |
| | v Virgo | 5-1 | Quarter-final | Mercantile Credit Classic |
| | v S. Davis | 9-8 | Semi-final | Mercantile Credit Classic |
| | **v Thorburn** | **13-8** | **Final** | **Mercantile Credit Classic** |
| | v White | 2-5 | 1st round | Benson & Hedges Masters |
| | v Dodd | 9-1 | 1st round | Tolly Cobbold English Championship |
| | v Reynolds | 6-9 | 2nd round | Tolly Cobbold English Championship |
| | v Oliver | 6-3 | 1st round | Dulux British Open |
| | v Macleod | 0-5 | 2nd round | Dulux British Open |
| | v Fagan | 6-10 | 1st round | Embassy World Championship |
| | v Parrott | 0-5 | Quarter-final | Winfield Australian Masters |
| | v Dennis Taylor | 5-3 | 1st round | Langs Scottish Masters |
| | v White | 6-2 | Semi-final | Langs Scottish Masters |
| | v Thorburn | 7-9 | Final | Langs Scottish Masters |
| | v Fowler | 5-1 | 3rd round | Goya Matchroom Trophy |
| | v Scott | 5-1 | 4th round | Goya Matchroom Trophy |
| | v Duggan | 4-5 | 5th round | Goya Matchroom Trophy |
| | v W. Jones | 0-5 | 3rd round | Rothmans Grand Prix |
| | v Browne | 9-6 | 3rd round | Coral UK Open |

*Willie Thorne*

| | | | | |
|---|---|---|---|---|
| | v Virgo | 9-8 | 4th round | Coral UK Open |
| | v Thorburn | 9-7 | 5th round | Coral UK Open |
| | v Griffiths | 9-7 | Quarter-final | Coral UK Open |
| | v Dennis Taylor | 9-7 | Semi-final | Coral UK Open |
| | v S. Davis | 14-16 | Final | Coral UK Open |
| **1986** | v T. Jones | 3-5 | 3rd round | Mercantile Credit Classic |
| | v Reardon | 5-4 | 1st round | Benson & Hedges Masters |
| | v S. Davis | 4-5 | Quarter-final | Benson & Hedges Masters |
| | v Medati | 9-2 | 3rd round | Tolly Cobbold English Championship |
| | v Reynolds | 8-9 | 4th round | Tolly Cobbold English Championship |
| | v Dodd | 5-2 | 3rd round | Dulux British Open |
| | v Mans | 5-1 | 4th round | Dulux British Open |
| | v Stevens | 5-4 | 5th round | Dulux British Open |
| | v Griffiths | 5-4 | Quarter-final | Dulux British Open |
| | v Virgo | 9-4 | Semi-final | Dulux British Open |
| | v S. Davis | 7-12 | Final | Dulux British Open |
| | v Griffiths | 5-2 | 1st round | Benson & Hedges Irish Masters |
| | v Dennis Taylor | 5-2 | Quarter-final | Benson & Hedges Irish Masters |
| | v Thorburn | 6-4 | Semi-final | Benson & Hedges Irish Masters |
| | v White | 5-9 | Final | Benson & Hedges Irish Masters |
| | v Hendry | 10-8 | 1st round | Embassy World Championship |
| | v J. Campbell | 13-9 | 2nd round | Embassy World Championship |
| | v Thorburn | 6-13 | Quarter-final | Embassy World Championship |
| | v S. Davis | 5-2 | Semi-final | Camus Hong Kong Masters |
| | **v Dennis Taylor** | **8-3** | **Final** | **Camus Hong Kong Masters** |
| | v N. Foulds | 6-3 | 1st round | Matchroom Trophy |
| | v Dennis Taylor | 6-5 | Semi-final | Matchroom Trophy |
| | v **S. Davis** | **10-9** | **Final** | **Matchroom Trophy** |
| | v Drago | 2-5 | 3rd round | BCE International |
| | v Duggan | 5-0 | 3rd round | Rothmans Grand Prix |
| | v King | 5-2 | 4th round | Rothmans Grand Prix |
| | v N. Foulds | 3-5 | 5th round | Rothmans Grand Prix |
| | v Dennis Taylor | 5-4 | 1st round | BCE Canadian Masters |
| | v Knowles | 8-7 | Semi-final | BCE Canadian Masters |
| | v S. Davis | 3-9 | Final | BCE Canadian Masters |
| | v Murphy | 9-4 | 3rd round | Tennents UK Open |
| | v Grace | 9-1 | 4th round | Tennents UK Open |
| | v Drago | 5-9 | 5th round | Tennents UK Open |
| **1987** | v Spencer | 3-5 | 3rd round | Mercantile Credit Classic |
| | v Stevens | 5-3 | 1st round | Benson & Hedges Masters |
| | v Thorburn | 3-5 | Quarter-final | Benson & Hedges Masters |
| | v B. Harris | 6-2 | 3rd round | Tolly Ales English Championship |
| | v Martin | 6-3 | 4th round | Tolly Ales English Championship |
| | v Reynolds | 6-4 | Quarter-final | Tolly Ales English Championship |
| | v Meo | 3-9 | Semi-final | Tolly Ales English Championship |
| | v R. Harris | 5-1 | 3rd round | Dulux British Open |
| | v Duggan | 5-2 | 4th round | Dulux British Open |
| | v N. Foulds | 2-5 | 5th round | Dulux British Open |
| | v Stevens | 5-1 | 1st round | Benson & Hedges Irish Masters |
| | v White | 5-4 | Quarter-final | Benson & Hedges Irish Masters |
| | v Dennis Taylor | 6-2 | Semi-final | Benson & Hedges Irish Masters |
| | v S. Davis | 1-9 | Final | Benson & Hedges Irish Masters |
| | v Hendry | 7-10 | 1st round | Embassy World Championship |
| | v John Rea | 5-3 | 3rd round | Fidelity International |
| | v Virgo | 4-5 | 4th round | Fidelity International |
| | v Bear | 5-1 | 3rd round | Rothmans Grand Prix |
| | v Bales | 5-2 | 4th round | Rothmans Grand Prix |
| | v Drago | 5-2 | 5th round | Rothmans Grand Prix |
| | v P. Francisco | 3-5 | Quarter-final | Rothmans Grand Prix |
| | v N. Foulds | 6-5 | Semi-final | Matchroom Trophy |
| | v Dennis Taylor | 3-10 | Final | Matchroom Trophy |
| | v Oliver | 9-3 | 3rd round | Tennents UK Open |
| | v Murphy | 9-4 | 4th round | Tennents UK Open |

| | | | | |
|---|---|---|---|---|
| | v O'Kane | 9-7 | 5th round | Tennents UK Open |
| | v Thorburn | 9-8 | Quarter-final | Tennents UK Open |
| | v S. Davis | 2-9 | Semi-final | Tennents UK Open |
| **1988** | v Bradley | 5-1 | 3rd round | Mercantile Credit Classic |
| | v West | 2-5 | 4th round | Mercantile Credit Classic |
| | v Johnson | 4-5 | 1st round | Benson & Hedges Masters |
| | v Marshall | 6-3 | 3rd round | English Championship |
| | v Virgo | 6-0 | 4th round | English Championship |
| | v N. Foulds | 2-6 | Quarter-final | English Championship |
| | v Wych | 5-1 | 3rd round | MIM Britannia British Open |
| | v C. Wilson | 5-3 | 4th round | MIM Britannia British Open |
| | v Thorburn | 2-5 | 5th round | MIM Britannia British Open |
| | v Knowles | 3-5 | 1st round | Benson & Hedges Irish Masters |
| | v P. Francisco | 10-6 | 1st round | Embassy World Championship |
| | v Griffiths | 9-13 | 2nd round | Embassy World Championship |
| | v N. Foulds | 4-5 | Semi-final | LEP Hong Kong Masters |
| | v Chambers | 5-2 | 3rd round | Fidelity International |
| | v Drago | 5-2 | 4th round | Fidelity International |
| | v White | 4-5 | 5th round | Fidelity International |
| | v S. Davis | 2-5 | Semi-final | Dubai Duty Free Masters |
| | v S. Davis | 2-6 | 1st round | LEP Matchroom Championship |
| | v Gary Wilkinson | 3-5 | 3rd round | Rothmans Grand Prix |
| | v Fitzmaurice | 5-0 | 3rd round | BCE Canadian Masters |
| | v Mountjoy | 4-5 | 4th round | BCE Canadian Masters |
| | v D. Gilbert | 9-3 | 3rd round | Tennents UK Open |
| | v Stevens | 9-3 | 4th round | Tennents UK Open |
| | v Hendry | 4-9 | 5th round | Tennents UK Open |
| | v Hallett | 8-9 | 1st round | Everest World Matchplay |
| **1989** | v J. Smith | 5-1 | 3rd round | Mercantile Credit Classic |
| | v O'Kane | 5-3 | 4th round | Mercantile Credit Classic |
| | v Griffiths | 5-1 | 5th round | Mercantile Credit Classic |
| | v Clark | 5-4 | Quarter-final | Mercantile Credit Classic |
| | v W. Jones | 4-9 | Semi-final | Mercantile Credit Classic |
| | v Hendry | 2-5 | 1st round | Benson and Hedges Masters |
| | v Oliver | 5-0 | 3rd round | European Open |
| | v Higgins | 5-1 | 4th round | European Open |
| | v White | 3-5 | 5th round | European Open |
| | v Clark | 5-1 | 3rd round | English Championship |
| | v Roe | 5-1 | 4th round | English Championship |
| | v N. Foulds | 3-5 | Quarter-final | English Championship |
| | v Gary Wilkinson | 5-1 | 3rd round | Anglian British Open |
| | v Marshall | 5-1 | 4th round | Anglian British Open |
| | v S. Davis | 0-5 | 5th round | Anglian British Open |
| | v Browne | 10-5 | 1st round | Embassy World Championship |
| | v Hendry | 4-13 | 2nd round | Embassy World Championship |
| | v Dennis Taylor | 6-5 | 1st round | Lion Brown New Zealand Masters |
| | v Hendry | 6-5 | Semi-final | Lion Brown New Zealand Masters |
| | **v Johnson** | **7-4** | **Final** | **Lion Brown New Zealand Masters** |
| | v Brumby | 5-3 | 3rd round | Hong Kong Open |
| | v W. Jones | 5-1 | 4th round | Hong Kong Open |
| | v N. Foulds | 1-5 | 5th round | Hong Kong Open |
| | v Browne | 5-4 | 3rd round | 555 Asian Open |
| | v Gollan | 5-1 | 4th round | 555 Asian Open |
| | v Virgo | 5-2 | 5th round | 555 Asian Open |
| | v Hendry | 2-5 | Quarter-final | 555 Asian Open |
| | v T. Murphy | 5-2 | 3rd round | BCE International |
| | v West | 5-2 | 4th round | BCE International |
| | v White | 1-5 | 5th round | BCE International |
| | v J. McLaughlin | 5-2 | 3rd round | Rothmans Grand Prix |
| | v Wattana | 3-5 | 4th round | Rothmans Grand Prix |
| | v Medati | 9-3 | 3rd round | Stormseal UK Open |
| | v Higgins | 9-3 | 4th round | Stormseal UK Open |
| | v S. Davis | 4-9 | 5th round | Stormseal UK Open |

| | | | | |
|---|---|---|---|---|
| | v Mountjoy | 2-9 | 1st round | Everest World Matchplay |
| **1990** | v David Taylor | 1-5 | 3rd round | Mercantile Credit Classic |
| | v Dennis Taylor | 5-4 | 1st round | Benson and Hedges Masters |
| | v Hendry | 1-5 | Quarter-final | Benson and Hedges Masters |
| | v M. Bennett | 1-5 | 3rd round | Pearl Assurance British Open |
| | v Browne | 5-3 | 3rd round | European Open |
| | v N. Foulds | 3-5 | 4th round | European Open |
| | v Hallett | 5-1 | 1st round | Benson and Hedges Irish Masters |
| | v S. Davis | 3-5 | Quarter-final | Benson and Hedges Irish Masters |
| | v Drago | 10-4 | 1st round | Embassy World Championship |
| | v N. Foulds | 11-13 | 2nd round | Embassy World Championship |

## PAUL THORNLEY (Canada)

**Born** 15.4.44. **Turned professional** 1979. **World ranking** 124 (111).

| | | | | |
|---|---|---|---|---|
| **1983** | v Caggianello | 7-9 | 2nd round | Canadian Championship |
| **1984** | v Fisher | 8-10 | Qualifying | Embassy World Championship |
| | v Cripsey | 3-5 | Qualifying | Jameson International |
| | v Williamson | 2-5 | Qualifying | Rothmans Grand Prix |
| **1985** | v Chaperon | 1-5 | 1st round | Canadian Championship |
| | v Mienie | 10-3 | Qualifying | Embassy World Championship |
| | v Fagan | 10-7 | Qualifying | Embassy World Championship |
| | v Murphy | 3-10 | Qualifying | Embassy World Championship |
| **1986** | v Morra | 6-4 | 1st round | Canadian Championship |
| | v Stevens | 2-6 | 2nd round | Canadian Championship |
| **1987** | v Greaves | 6-10 | Qualifying | Embassy World Championship |
| | v Watson | 4-6 | 1st round | Canadian Championship |
| **1988** | v V. Harris | 5-4 | 1st round | MIM Britannia British Open |
| | v Wych | 1-5 | 2nd round | MIM Britannia British Open |
| | v Rowswell | 7-10 | Qualifying | Embassy World Championship |
| **1989** | v Demarco | 10-3 | Qualifying | Embassy World Championship |
| | v Bradley | 10-7 | Qualifying | Embassy World Championship |
| | v Werbeniuk | *wo* | Qualifying | Embassy World Championship |
| | v D. Gilbert | 4-10 | Qualifying | Embassy World Championship |
| | v Wright | 1-5 | 1st round | Hong Kong Open |
| | v M. Smith | 2-5 | 1st round | 555 Asian Open |
| | v Wright | 3-5 | 1st round | BCE International |
| | v Lawlor | 3-5 | 1st round | Rothmans Grand Prix |
| | v A. Harris | 1-5 | 1st round | Dubai Classic |
| | v Medati | 3-6 | 1st round | Stormseal UK Open |
| **1990** | v Morra | 3-5 | 1st round | Mercantile Credit Classic |
| | v Terry | 1-5 | 1st round | Pearl Assurance British Open |
| | v Sinclair | 2-5 | 1st round | European Open |
| | v Marshall | 0-10 | Qualifying | Embassy World Championship |

## JIMMY VAN RENSBERG (South Africa)

**Born** 24.10.31. **Turned professional** 1978. **World ranking** 115 (103).

| | | | | |
|---|---|---|---|---|
| **1979** | v Meadowcroft | 7-9 | Prelim | Embassy World Championship |
| **1980** | v Meo | 1-9 | Qualifying | Embassy World Championship |
| **1984** | v V. Harris | 10-7 | Qualifying | Embassy World Championship |
| | v Edmonds | 10-9 | Qualifying | Embassy World Championship |
| | v S. Francisco | 3-10 | Qualifying | Embassy World Championship |
| **1985** | v Longworth | 10-7 | Qualifying | Embassy World Championship |
| | v Gauvreau | 9-10 | Qualifying | Embassy World Championship |
| | v Scott | 4-5 | 2nd round | Goya Matchroom Trophy |
| | v E. McLaughlin | 5-4 | 2nd round | Rothmans Grand Prix |
| | v J. Campbell | 4-5 | 3rd round | Rothmans Grand Prix |
| | v Edmonds | 5-9 | 2nd round | Coral UK Open |

| | | | | |
|---|---|---|---|---|
| **1986** | v W. Jones | 5-4 | 2nd round | Mercantile Credit Classic |
| | v Parrott | 5-3 | 3rd round | Mercantile Credit Classic |
| | v S. Davis | 1-5 | 4th round | Mercantile Credit Classic |
| | v Wych | 0-5 | 2nd round | Dulux British Open |
| | v Williamson | 10-9 | Qualifying | Embassy World Championship |
| | v Sinclair | 10-2 | Qualifying | Embassy World Championship |
| | v J. Campbell | 6-10 | Qualifying | Embassy World Championship |
| | v Mienie | 7-1 | 2nd round | South African Championship |
| | v Ellis | 2-8 | Semi-final | South African Championship |
| | v Kearney | 5-3 | 2nd round | BCE International |
| | v West | 3-5 | 3rd round | BCE International |
| | v Roe | 3-5 | 2nd round | Rothmans Grand Prix |
| | v Roe | 6-9 | 2nd round | Tennents UK Open |
| **1987** | v N. Gilbert | 5-3 | 2nd round | Mercantile Credit Classic |
| | v S. Francisco | 4-5 | 3rd round | Mercantile Credit Classic |
| | v Morra | 1-5 | 2nd round | Dulux British Open |
| | v J. McLaughlin | 10-6 | Qualifying | Embassy World Championship |
| | v T. Jones | 0-10 | Qualifying | Embassy World Championship |
| | v O'Kane | 3-5 | 2nd round | Fidelity International |
| | v Murphy | 5-4 | 2nd round | Rothmans Grand Prix |
| | v Charlton | 1-5 | 3rd round | Rothmans Grand Prix |
| | v Whitthread | 9-5 | 1st round | Tennents UK Open |
| | v Reardon | 7-9 | 2nd round | Tennents UK Open |
| **1988** | v Grace | 5-3 | 2nd round | Mercantile Credit Classic |
| | v Griffiths | 2-5 | 3rd round | Mercantile Credit Classic |
| | v Reardon | 3-5 | 2nd round | MIM Britannia British Open |
| | v Meakin | 4-5 | 1st round | Fidelity International |
| | v Robidoux | 2-5 | 1st round | Rothmans Grand Prix |
| | v Fitzmaurice | 3-5 | 1st round | BCE Canadian Masters |
| | v Johnston-Allen | 4-9 | 1st round | Tennents UK Open |
| **1989** | v J. Smith | 4-5 | 1st round | Mercantile Credit Classic |
| | v Marshall | 1-5 | 1st round | European Open |
| | v Fowler | 1-5 | 2nd round | Anglian British Open |
| | v A. Harris | 7-10 | Qualifying | Embassy World Championship |
| | v T. Wilson | 5-4 | 1st round | Hong Kong Open |
| | v Robidoux | 1-5 | 2nd round | Hong Kong Open |
| | v A. Harris | 5-3 | 1st round | 555 Asian Open |
| | v Graham | 0-5 | 2nd round | 555 Asian Open |
| | v F. Davis | 4-5 | 1st round | BCE International |
| | v Oliver | 3-5 | 1st round | Rothmans Grand Prix |
| | v Jenkins | 5-2 | 1st round | Dubai Classic |
| | v Cripsey | 5-3 | 2nd round | Dubai Classic |
| | v Virgo | 4-5 | 3rd round | Dubai Classic |
| | v Marshall | 5-6 | 1st round | Stormseal UK Open |
| **1990** | v John Rea | 1-5 | 1st round | Mercantile Credit Classic |
| | v T. Wilson | 1-5 | 1st round | Pearl Assurance British Open |

## JOHN VIRGO (England)

**Born** 4.3.46. **Turned professional** 1976. **World ranking** 15 (13).

| | | | | |
|---|---|---|---|---|
| **1977** | v Andrewartha | 11-1 | Prelim | Embassy World Championship |
| | v Dunning | 11-6 | Qualifying | Embassy World Championship |
| | v Spencer | 9-13 | 1st round | Embassy World Championship |
| | v Dennis Taylor | 5-2 | 2nd round | Super Crystalate UK Championship |
| | v Miles | 5-2 | Quarter-final | Super Crystalate UK Championship |
| | v Fagan | 8-9 | Semi-final | Super Crystalate UK Championship |
| **1978** | v F. Davis | 8-9 | Qualifying | Embassy World Championship |
| | v Edmonds | 9-4 | Qualifying | Coral UK Championship |
| | v Pulman | 9-3 | 1st round | Coral UK Championship |
| | v David Taylor | 2-9 | Quarter-final | Coral UK Championship |
| **1979** | v Parkin | 9-0 | Prelim | Embassy World Championship |

*John Virgo*

| | | | | |
|---|---|---|---|---|
| | v Thorne | 9-8 | Qualifying | Embassy World Championship |
| | v Thorburn | 13-10 | 1st round | Embassy World Championship |
| | v Werbeniuk | 13-9 | Quarter-final | Embassy World Championship |
| | v Dennis Taylor | 12-19 | Semi-final | Embassy World Championship |
| | v Meo | 9-6 | 3rd round | Coral UK Championship |
| | v S. Davis | 9-7 | Quarter-final | Coral UK Championship |
| | v Dennis Taylor | 9-4 | Semi-final | Coral UK Championship |
| | **v Griffiths** | **14-13** | **Final** | **Coral UK Championship** |
| **1980** | v Thorburn | 3-5 | 1st round | Benson & Hedges Masters |
| | v Meadowcroft | 10-2 | 1st round | Embassy World Championship |
| | v Charlton | 12-13 | 2nd round | Embassy World Championship |
| | v Meo | 1-9 | 2nd round | Coral UK Championship |
| **1981** | v Meo | 6-9 | 1st round | John Courage English |
| | v Meo | 6-10 | 1st round | Embassy World Championship |
| | v Knowles | 5-2 | 2nd round | Jameson International |
| | v Reardon | 5-3 | 3rd round | Jameson International |
| | v Dennis Taylor | 2-5 | Quarter-final | Jameson International |
| | v White | 6-9 | 2nd round | Coral UK Championship |
| **1982** | v Hallett | 10-4 | 1st round | Embassy World Championship |
| | v Reardon | 8-13 | 2nd round | Embassy World Championship |
| | v V. Harris | 5-2 | Qualifying | Jameson International |
| | v Charlton | 5-4 | 1st round | Jameson International |
| | v Spencer | 5-4 | 2nd round | Jameson International |
| | v Dennis Taylor | 5-3 | Quarter-final | Jameson International |
| | v David Taylor | 5-9 | Semi-final | Jameson International |
| | v Black | 5-2 | 1st round | Professional Players Tournament |
| | v Hallett | 5-2 | 2nd round | Professional Players Tournament |
| | v Spencer | 5-1 | 3rd round | Professional Players Tournament |
| | v Johnson | 5-1 | Quarter-final | Professional Players Tournament |
| | v White | 4-10 | Semi-final | Professional Players Tournament |
| | v Kelly | 9-2 | 1st round | Coral UK Championship |
| | v Mountjoy | 9-5 | 2nd round | Coral UK Championship |
| | v Meo | 6-9 | Quarter-final | Coral UK Championship |
| **1983** | v Charlton | 2-5 | 1st round | Lada Classic |
| | v Mountjoy | 1-5 | 1st round | Benson & Hedges Masters |
| | v Murphy | 10-8 | Qualifying | Embassy World Championship |
| | v Thorne | 3-10 | 1st round | Embassy World Championship |
| | v Thorne | 2-5 | 1st round | Jameson International |
| | v French | 5-4 | 1st round | Professional Players Tournament |
| | v Wilson | 2-5 | 2nd round | Professional Players Tournament |
| | v Johnson | 6-9 | 1st round | Coral UK Championship |
| **1984** | v Wildman | 2-5 | Qualifying | Lada Classic |
| | v Reardon | 3-5 | 1st round | Benson & Hedges Masters |
| | v Thorburn | 9-10 | 1st round | Embassy World Championship |
| | v Thorne | 5-3 | Quarter-final | Winfield Australian Masters |
| | v Meo | 6-2 | Semi-final | Winfield Australian Masters |
| | v Knowles | 3-7 | Final | Winfield Australian Masters |
| | v F. Davis | 5-3 | Qualifying | Jameson International |
| | v Thorburn | 5-0 | 1st round | Jameson International |
| | v S. Francisco | 2-5 | 2nd round | Jameson International |
| | v Bradley | 5-0 | 1st round | Rothmans Grand Prix |
| | v Dennis Taylor | 3-5 | 2nd round | Rothmans Grand Prix |
| | v King | 4-9 | Qualifying | Coral UK Open |
| **1985** | v Bales | 5-1 | Qualifying | Mercantile Credit Classic |
| | v Werbeniuk | 5-2 | 1st round | Mercantile Credit Classic |
| | v Macleod | 5-0 | 2nd round | Mercantile Credit Classic |
| | v Thorne | 1-5 | Quarter-final | Mercantile Credit Classic |
| | v Darrington | 9-0 | 1st round | Tolly Cobbold English Championship |
| | v Johnson | 9-4 | 2nd round | Tolly Cobbold English Championship |
| | v S. Davis | 2-9 | Quarter-final | Tolly Cobbold English Championship |
| | v P. Francisco | 6-2 | 1st round | Dulux British Open |
| | v S. Davis | 2-5 | 2nd round | Dulux British Open |
| | v Wych | 10-4 | Qualifying | Embassy World Championship |

| | | | | |
|---|---|---|---|---|
| | v Meo | 6-10 | 1st round | Embassy World Championship |
| | v Meo | 3-5 | Quarter-final | Winfield Australian Masters |
| | v Miles | 5-2 | 3rd round | Goya Matchroom Trophy |
| | v S. Davis | 1-5 | 4th round | Goya Matchroom Trophy |
| | v P. Francisco | 4-5 | 3rd round | Rothmans Grand Prix |
| | v W. Jones | 9-7 | 3rd round | Coral UK Open |
| | v Thorne | 8-9 | 4th round | Coral UK Open |
| **1986** | v Gibson | 5-3 | 3rd round | Mercantile Credit Classic |
| | v White | 2-5 | 4th round | Mercantile Credit Classic |
| | v T. Jones | 9-7 | 3rd round | Tolly Cobbold English Championship |
| | v Parrott | 9-6 | 4th round | Tolly Cobbold English Championship |
| | v S. Davis | 2-9 | Quarter-final | Tolly Cobbold English Championship |
| | v Fowler | 5-1 | 3rd round | Dulux British Open |
| | v John Rea | 5-0 | 4th round | Dulux British Open |
| | v Charlton | 5-4 | 5th round | Dulux British Open |
| | v Meo | 5-3 | Quarter-final | Dulux British Open |
| | v Thorne | 4-9 | Semi-final | Dulux British Open |
| | v White | 7-10 | 1st round | Embassy World Championship |
| | v M. Bennett | 5-4 | 3rd round | BCE International |
| | v S. Francisco | 0-5 | 4th round | BCE International |
| | v Fagan | 5-2 | 3rd round | Rothmans Grand Prix |
| | v Dennis Taylor | 3-5 | 4th round | Rothmans Grand Prix |
| | v Miles | 9-7 | 3rd round | Tennents UK Open |
| | v Drago | 6-9 | 4th round | Tennents UK Open |
| **1987** | v M. Bennett | 5-3 | 3rd round | Mercantile Credit Classic |
| | v S. Davis | 2-5 | 4th round | Mercantile Credit Classic |
| | v Medati | 6-1 | 3rd round | Tolly Ales English Championship |
| | v Parrott | 2-6 | 4th round | Tolly Ales English Championship |
| | v Morra | 5-3 | 3rd round | Dulux British Open |
| | v S. Davis | 5-4 | 4th round | Dulux British Open |
| | v Wilson | 5-2 | 5th round | Dulux British Open |
| | v N. Foulds | 3-5 | Quarter-final | Dulux British Open |
| | v T. Jones | 10-9 | Qualifying | Embassy World Championship |
| | v N. Foulds | 4-10 | 1st round | Embassy World Championship |
| | v Murphy | 5-1 | 3rd round | Fidelity International |
| | v Thorne | 5-4 | 4th round | Fidelity International |
| | v Knowles | 5-2 | 5th round | Fidelity International |
| | v S. Davis | 2-5 | Quarter-final | Fidelity International |
| | v Gauvreau | 5-1 | 3rd round | Rothmans Grand Prix |
| | v Wilson | 3-5 | 4th round | Rothmans Grand Prix |
| | v F. Davis | 9-4 | 3rd round | Tennents UK Open |
| | v Thorburn | 6-9 | 4th round | Tennents UK Open |
| **1988** | v Rigitano | 5-2 | 3rd round | Mercantile Credit Classic |
| | v N. Foulds | 5-3 | 4th round | Mercantile Credit Classic |
| | v Parrott | 0-5 | 5th round | Mercantile Credit Classic |
| | v Dodd | 6-3 | 3rd round | English Championship |
| | v Thorne | 0-6 | 4th round | English Championship |
| | v Murphy | 5-1 | 3rd round | MIM Britannia British Open |
| | v Parrott | 1-5 | 4th round | MIM Britannia British Open |
| | v Duggan | 10-5 | Qualifying | Embassy World Championship |
| | v S. Davis | 8-10 | 1st round | Embassy World Championship |
| | v J. McLaughlin | 5-0 | 3rd round | Fidelity International |
| | v Spencer | 1-5 | 4th round | Fidelity International |
| | v Robidoux | 1-5 | 3rd round | Rothmans Grand Prix |
| | v Medati | 5-1 | 3rd round | BCE Canadian Masters |
| | v Newbury | 5-2 | 4th round | BCE Canadian Masters |
| | v Parrott | 4-5 | 5th round | BCE Canadian Masters |
| | v Rowswell | 9-3 | 3rd round | Tennents UK Open |
| | v O'Kane | 9-8 | 4th round | Tennents UK Open |
| | v Knowles | 9-3 | 5th round | Tennents UK Open |
| | v Mountjoy | 8-9 | Quarter-final | Tennents UK Open |
| **1989** | v Dodd | 5-2 | 3rd round | Mercantile Credit Classic |
| | v Chaperon | 5-1 | 4th round | Mercantile Credit Classic |

| | | | | |
|---|---|---|---|---|
| | v Thorburn | 3-5 | 5th round | Mercantile Credit Classic |
| | v White | 2-5 | 1st round | Benson and Hedges Masters |
| | v Reardon | 5-3 | 3rd round | European Open |
| | v Edwards | 5-3 | 4th round | European Open |
| | v Charlton | 4-5 | 5th round | European Open |
| | v Gary Wilkinson | 3-5 | 3rd round | English Championship |
| | v Fowler | 5-2 | 3rd round | Anglian British Open |
| | v Clark | 1-5 | 4th round | Anglian British Open |
| | v D. Morgan | 10-4 | 1st round | Embassy World Championship |
| | v White | 12-13 | 2nd round | Embassy World Championship |
| | v Wych | 5-4 | 3rd round | Hong Kong Open |
| | v Gauvreau | 5-2 | 4th round | Hong Kong Open |
| | v Hallett | 1-5 | 5th round | Hong Kong Open |
| | v B. Harris | 5-4 | 3rd round | 555 Asian Open |
| | v O'Kane | 5-3 | 4th round | 555 Asian Open |
| | v Thorne | 2-5 | 5th round | 555 Asian Open |
| | v T. Jones | 0-5 | 3rd round | BCE International |
| | v Longworth | 5-4 | 3rd round | Rothmans Grand Prix |
| | v Newbury | 0-5 | 4th round | Rothmans Grand Prix |
| | v Van Rensberg | 5-4 | 3rd round | Dubai Classic |
| | v Chappel | 5-4 | 4th round | Dubai Classic |
| | v J. McLaughlin | 4-5 | 5th round | Dubai Classic |
| | v Stevens | 7-9 | 3rd round | Stormseal UK Open |
| **1990** | v Wright | 5-2 | 3rd round | Mercantile Credit Classic |
| | v J. McLaughlin | 5-2 | 4th round | Mercantile Credit Classic |
| | v King | 1-5 | 5th round | Mercantile Credit Classic |
| | v White | 3-5 | 1st round | Benson and Hedges Masters |
| | v Browne | 1-5 | 3rd round | Pearl Assurance British Open |
| | v D. Campbell | 5-4 | 3rd round | European Open |
| | v Roscoe | 2-5 | 4th round | European Open |
| | v Gary Wilkinson | 10-6 | 1st round | Embassy World Championship |
| | v White | 6-13 | 2nd round | Embassy World Championship |

**PAUL WATCHORN** (Republic of Ireland)

**Born** 19.7.58. **Turned professional** 1982. **World ranking** 102 (114).

| | | | | |
|---|---|---|---|---|
| **1983** | v Johnson | 0-10 | Qualifying | Embassy World Championship |
| | v Morra | 3-5 | Qualifying | Jameson International |
| | v Parrott | 0-5 | Qualifying | Professional Players Tournament |
| **1984** | v Donnelly | 7-10 | Qualifying | Embassy World Championship |
| | v W. Jones | 0-5 | Qualifying | Jameson International |
| | v Dennis Taylor | 1-5 | 1st round | Rothmans Grand Prix |
| | v B. Harris | 9-7 | Qualifying | Coral UK Open |
| | v Everton | 9-6 | Qualifying | Coral UK Open |
| | v Fisher | 5-9 | Qualifying | Coral UK Open |
| **1985** | v D. Hughes | 5-0 | Prelim | Mercantile Credit Classic |
| | v Mikkelsen | 5-1 | Qualifying | Mercantile Credit Classic |
| | v Donnelly | 1-5 | Qualifying | Mercantile Credit Classic |
| | v Fitzmaurice | 6-1 | Qualifying | Dulux British Open |
| | v E. Hughes | 4-6 | 1st round | Dulux British Open |
| | v Kelly | 2-6 | Qualifying | Irish Championship |
| | v Hines | 4-10 | Qualifying | Embassy World Championship |
| | v Agrawal | 2-5 | 1st round | Goya Matchroom Trophy |
| | v Drago | 2-5 | 1st round | Rothmans Grand Prix |
| | v Sheehan | 9-7 | 1st round | Coral UK Open |
| **1986** | v Greaves | 4-5 | 1st round | Mercantile Credit Classic |
| | v Wilkinson | 4-5 | 1st round | Dulux British Open |
| | v Longworth | 7-10 | Qualifying | Embassy World Championship |
| | v J. McLaughlin | 0-5 | 1st round | Strongbow Irish Championship |
| | v Bear | 1-5 | 1st round | BCE International |
| | v Darrington | 5-2 | 1st round | Rothmans Grand Prix |

| | | | | |
|---|---|---|---|---|
| | v Drago | 3-5 | 2nd round | Rothmans Grand Prix |
| | v Kelly | 9-8 | 1st round | Tennents UK Open |
| | v Scott | 7-9 | 2nd round | Tennents UK Open |
| **1987** | v Donnelly | 5-0 | 1st round | Mercantile Credit Classic |
| | v Duggan | 1-5 | 2nd round | Mercantile Credit Classic |
| | v Dunning | 5-2 | 1st round | Dulux British Open |
| | v Cripsey | 4-5 | 2nd round | Dulux British Open |
| | v G. Foulds | 6-10 | Qualifying | Embassy World Championship |
| | v E. Hughes | 2-5 | 1st round | Matchroom Irish Championship |
| | v Oliver | 5-3 | 1st round | Fidelity International |
| | v Fowler | 1-5 | 2nd round | Fidelity International |
| | v Fisher | 4-5 | 1st round | Rothmans Grand Prix |
| | v Darrington | 9-2 | 1st round | Tennents UK Open |
| | v Bradley | 9-5 | 2nd round | Tennents UK Open |
| | v Meo | 1-9 | 3rd round | Tennents UK Open |
| **1988** | v Roscoe | 2-5 | 1st round | Mercantile Credit Classic |
| | v E. Hughes | 5-2 | 1st round | Irish Championship |
| | v J. McLaughlin | 5-6 | Quarter-final | Irish Championship |
| | v Morra | 1-5 | 1st round | MIM Britannia British Open |
| | v M. Gibson | 10-7 | Qualifying | Embassy World Championship |
| | v King | 4-10 | Qualifying | Embassy World Championship |
| | v B. Harris | 5-2 | 1st round | Fidelity International |
| | v Chappel | 4-5 | 2nd round | Fidelity International |
| | v Medati | 2-5 | 1st round | Rothmans Grand Prix |
| | v Miles | 5-2 | 1st round | BCE Canadian Masters |
| | v Macleod | 1-5 | 2nd round | BCE Canadian Masters |
| | v Miles | 6-9 | 1st round | Tennents UK Open |
| **1989** | v Glen Wilkinson | 3-5 | 1st round | Mercantile Credit Classic |
| | v B. Harris | 5-4 | 1st round | European Open |
| | v J. Campbell | 1-5 | 2nd round | European Open |
| | v Burke | 5-4 | 1st round | Irish Championship |
| | v Higgins | 2-5 | Quarter-final | Irish Championship |
| | v John Rea | 3-5 | 1st round | Anglian British Open |
| | v Grace | 10-6 | Qualifying | Embassy World Championship |
| | v Roe | 5-10 | Qualifying | Embassy World Championship |
| | v V. Harris | 4-5 | 1st round | Hong Kong Open |
| | v Miles | 3-5 | 1st round | 555 Asian Open |
| | v Marshall | 3-5 | 1st round | BCE International |
| | v Donnelly | 5-2 | 1st round | Rothmans Grand Prix |
| | v King | 3-5 | 2nd round | Rothmans Grand Prix |
| | v Miles | 3-5 | 1st round | Dubai Classic |
| | v P. Gibson | 6-3 | 1st round | Stormseal UK Open |
| | v King | 5-6 | 2nd round | Stormseal UK Open |
| **1990** | v Medati | 5-2 | 1st round | Mercantile Credit Classic |
| | v Fisher | 5-3 | 2nd round | Mercantile Credit Classic |
| | v Newbury | 2-5 | 3rd round | Mercantile Credit Classic |
| | v Wright | 1-5 | 1st round | Pearl Assurance British Open |
| | v Rowswell | 4-5 | 1st round | European Open |
| | v Kelly | 10-3 | Qualifying | Embassy World Championship |
| | v V. Harris | 10-6 | Qualifying | Embassy World Championship |
| | v Fisher | 10-7 | Qualifying | Embassy World Championship |
| | v Bond | 2-10 | Qualifying | Embassy World Championship |

## JAMES WATTANA (Thailand)

**Born** 17.1.70. **Turned professional** 1989. **World ranking** 33.

| | | | | |
|---|---|---|---|---|
| **1989** | v Owers | 5-2 | 1st round | Hong Kong Open |
| | v Graham | 4-5 | 2nd round | Hong Kong Open |
| | v Macleod | 5-2 | 2nd round | 555 Asian Open |
| | v David Taylor | 5-1 | 3rd round | 555 Asian Open |
| | v Hallett | 5-3 | 4th round | 555 Asian Open |

| | | | | |
|---|---|---|---|---|
| | v Mountjoy | 5-2 | 5th round | 555 Asian Open |
| | v S. Francisco | 5-2 | Quarter-final | 555 Asian Open |
| | v Griffiths | 5-0 | Semi-final | 555 Asian Open |
| | v Hendry | 6-9 | Final | 555 Asian Open |
| | v Edwards | 5-2 | 1st round | BCE International |
| | v Chappel | 5-3 | 2nd round | BCE International |
| | v P. Francisco | 5-0 | 3rd round | BCE International |
| | v Hendry | 3-5 | 4th round | BCE International |
| | v John Rea | 5-3 | 1st round | Rothmans Grand Prix |
| | v Macleod | 5-1 | 2nd round | Rothmans Grand Prix |
| | v S. Francisco | 5-2 | 3rd round | Rothmans Grand Prix |
| | v Thorne | 5-3 | 4th round | Rothmans Grand Prix |
| | v P. Gibson | 5-3 | 5th round | Rothmans Grand Prix |
| | v Mountjoy | 5-2 | Quarter-final | Rothmans Grand Prix |
| | v Reynolds | 8-9 | Semi-final | Rothmans Grand Prix |
| | v F. Davis | 5-1 | 1st round | Dubai Classic |
| | v Stevens | 5-4 | 2nd round | Dubai Classic |
| | v E. Hughes | 5-0 | 3rd round | Dubai Classic |
| | v Parrott | 3-5 | 4th round | Dubai Classic |
| | v Dodd | 6-2 | 1st round | Stormseal UK Open |
| | v Wych | 6-1 | 2nd round | Stormseal UK Open |
| | v Hallett | 7-9 | 3rd round | Stormseal UK Open |
| **1990** | v A. Harris | 5-3 | 1st round | Mercantile Credit Classic |
| | v D. Morgan | 1-5 | 2nd round | Mercantile Credit Classic |
| | v Reynolds | 5-4 | Play-offs | Benson and Hedges Masters |
| | v S. Davis | 2-5 | Quarter-final | Benson and Hedges Masters |
| | v Edwards | 5-2 | 1st round | Pearl Assurance British Open |
| | v Chambers | 5-3 | 2nd round | Pearl Assurance British Open |
| | v O'Kane | 5-1 | 3rd round | Pearl Assurance British Open |
| | v Knowles | 3-5 | 4th round | Pearl Assurance British Open |
| | v Medati | 5-1 | 1st round | European Open |
| | v Robidoux | 2-5 | 2nd round | European Open |
| | v Grech | 10-4 | Qualifying | Embassy World Championship |
| | v Dunning | 10-2 | Qualifying | Embassy World Championship |
| | v David Taylor | 10-5 | Qualifying | Embassy World Championship |
| | v Spencer | 10-8 | Qualifying | Embassy World Championship |
| | v Higgins | 6-10 | Qualifying | Embassy World Championship |

## MIKE WATTERSON (England)

**Born** 26.8.42. **Turned professional** 1981. **World ranking** 123 (110).

| | | | | |
|---|---|---|---|---|
| **1981** | v Medati | 5-3 | Qualifying | Jameson International |
| | v Everton | 5-4 | Qualifying | Jameson International |
| | v Fagan | 2-5 | Qualifying | Jameson International |
| | v Bennett | 9-4 | Qualifying | Coral UK Championship |
| | v Johnson | 3-9 | Qualifying | Coral UK Championship |
| **1982** | v Demarco | 9-6 | Qualifying | Embassy World Championship |
| | v Meadowcroft | 7-9 | Qualifying | Embassy World Championship |
| | v Everton | 5-1 | Qualifying | Jameson International |
| | v Fagan | 5-1 | Qualifying | Jameson International |
| | v Stevens | 3-5 | 1st round | Jameson International |
| | v Donnelly | 5-4 | 1st round | Professional Players Tournament |
| | v Griffiths | 2-5 | 2nd round | Professional Players Tournament |
| | v B. Harris | 3-9 | Qualifying | Coral UK Championship |
| **1983** | v J. Campbell | 6-10 | Qualifying | Embassy World Championship |
| | v Demarco | 5-3 | Qualifying | Jameson International |
| | v Mans | 5-4 | Qualifying | Jameson International |
| | v Meo | 5-3 | 1st round | Jameson International |
| | v S. Davis | 0-5 | 2nd round | Jameson International |
| | v Higgins | 5-2 | 1st round | Professional Players Tournament |
| | v Martin | 4-5 | 2nd round | Professional Players Tournament |

| | | | | |
|---|---|---|---|---|
| | v Everton | 9-6 | Qualifying | Coral UK Championship |
| | v F. Davis | 9-6 | Qualifying | Coral UK Championship |
| | v Mountjoy | 2-9 | 1st round | Coral UK Championship |
| **1984** | v Bennett | 10-5 | Qualifying | Embassy World Championship |
| | v King | 8-10 | Qualifying | Embassy World Championship |
| | v Black | 3-5 | Qualifying | Jameson International |
| | v W. Jones | 3-5 | Qualifying | Rothmans Grand Prix |
| | v Murphy | 4-9 | Qualifying | Coral UK Open |
| **1985** | v Edmonds | 2-5 | Qualifying | Mercantile Credit Classic |
| | v Kearney | 4-6 | Qualifying | Dulux British Open |
| | v W. Jones | 5-10 | Qualifying | Embassy World Championship |
| | v Fitzmaurice | 2-5 | 2nd round | Goya Matchroom Trophy |
| | v Caggianello | 5-1 | 2nd round | Rothmans Grand Prix |
| | v Williams | 2-5 | 3rd round | Rothmans Grand Prix |
| | v Jim Bear | 0-9 | 2nd round | Coral UK Open |
| **1986** | v Jenkins | 5-2 | 2nd round | Mercantile Credit Classic |
| | v Williams | 0-5 | 3rd round | Mercantile Credit Classic |
| | v G. Foulds | 1-9 | 2nd round | Tolly Cobbold English Championship |
| | v Mikkelsen | 10-2 | Qualifying | Embassy World Championship |
| | v Dodd | 1-10 | Qualifying | Embassy World Championship |
| | v Wright | 1-5 | 1st round | BCE International |
| | v M. Bennett | 1-5 | 1st round | Rothmans Grand Prix |
| | v Burke | 9-0 | 1st round | Tennents UK Open |
| | v Black | 9-3 | 2nd round | Tennents UK Open |
| | v P. Francisco | 4-9 | 3rd round | Tennents UK Open |
| **1987** | v Rowswell | 1-5 | 1st round | Mercantile Credit Classic |
| | v Roe | 3-5 | 1st round | Dulux British Open |
| | v James | 2-10 | Qualifying | Embassy World Championship |
| | v Anderson | 3-5 | 1st round | Fidelity International |
| | v Jack Rea | 6-9 | 1st round | Tennents UK Open |
| **1988** | v Chambers | 3-10 | Qualifying | Embassy World Championship |
| | v Kearney | 1-5 | 1st round | Fidelity International |
| | v Donnelly | 5-0 | 1st round | Rothmans Grand Prix |
| | v M. Bennett | 5-3 | 2nd round | Rothmans Grand Prix |
| | v Griffiths | 3-5 | 3rd round | Rothmans Grand Prix |
| | v Rigitano | 5-3 | 1st round | BCE Canadian Masters |
| | v Martin | 1-5 | 2nd round | BCE Canadian Masters |
| | v Kearney | 3-9 | 1st round | Tennents UK Open |
| **1989** | v Rigitano | 5-4 | 1st round | Mercantile Credit Classic |
| | v J. McLaughlin | 3-5 | 2nd round | Mercantile Credit Classic |
| | v Roscoe | 4-5 | 1st round | European Open |
| | v Edwards | 0-5 | 1st round | English Championship |
| | v Lawlor | 0-5 | 1st round | Anglian British Open |
| | v V. Harris | 5-10 | Qualifying | Embassy World Championship |
| | v S. Campbell | 0-5 | 1st round | Hong Kong Open |
| | v F. Davis | 2-5 | 1st round | 555 Asian Open |
| | v B. Harris | 3-5 | 1st round | BCE International |
| | v Houlihan | 4-5 | 1st round | Rothmans Grand Prix |
| | v Terry | 3-6 | 1st round | Stormseal UK Open |
| **1990** | v Rowswell | 4-5 | 1st round | Mercantile Credit Classic |
| | v Oliver | 0-5 | 1st round | Pearl Assurance British Open |
| | v Donnelly | 5-3 | 1st round | European Open |
| | v Chambers | 0-5 | 2nd round | European Open |
| | v Dodd | 3-10 | Qualifying | Embassy World Championship |

## BARRY WEST (England)

**Born** 24.10.58. **Turned professional** 1985. **World ranking** 28 (21).

| | | | | |
|---|---|---|---|---|
| **1985** | v Hendry | 4-5 | 1st round | Goya Matchroom Trophy |
| | v Meadowcroft | 5-2 | 2nd round | Rothmans Grand Prix |
| | v Dennis Taylor | 1-5 | 3rd round | Rothmans Grand Prix |

| | | | | |
|---|---|---|---|---|
| | v Roscoe | 9-5 | 2nd round | Coral UK Open |
| | v E. Hughes | 9-3 | 3rd round | Coral UK Open |
| | v Mountjoy | 9-4 | 4th round | Coral UK Open |
| | v Macleod | 9-4 | 5th round | Coral UK Open |
| | v S. Davis | 1-9 | Quarter-final | Coral UK Open |
| **1986** | v Darrington | 5-0 | 1st round | Mercantile Credit Classic |
| | v Meadowcroft | 5-0 | 2nd round | Mercantile Credit Classic |
| | v Wildman | 5-2 | 3rd round | Mercantile Credit Classic |
| | v Meo | 1-5 | 4th round | Mercantile Credit Classic |
| | v Gilbert | 8-9 | 1st round | Tolly Cobbold English Championship |
| | v Bennett | 5-1 | 1st round | Dulux British Open |
| | v E. McLaughlin | 5-3 | 2nd round | Dulux British Open |
| | v J. Campbell | 4-5 | 3rd round | Dulux British Open |
| | v Dunning | 10-3 | Qualifying | Embassy World Championship |
| | v Donnelly | 10-5 | Qualifying | Embassy World Championship |
| | v Werbeniuk | 8-10 | Qualifying | Embassy World Championship |
| | v Van Rensberg | 5-3 | 3rd round | BCE International |
| | v Griffiths | 1-5 | 4th round | BCE International |
| | v J. McLaughlin | 1-5 | 3rd round | Rothmans Grand Prix |
| | v T. Jones | 4-9 | 3rd round | Tennents UK Open |
| **1987** | v Jonik | 5-4 | 3rd round | Mercantile Credit Classic |
| | v Stevens | 5-3 | 4th round | Mercantile Credit Classic |
| | v Reynolds | 3-5 | 5th round | Mercantile Credit Classic |
| | v V. Harris | 6-3 | 3rd round | Tolly Ales English Championship |
| | v Dodd | 3-6 | 4th round | Tolly Ales English Championship |
| | v Grace | 5-2 | 3rd round | Dulux British Open |
| | v Stevens | 4-5 | 4th round | Dulux British Open |
| | v Spencer | 10-5 | Qualifying | Embassy World Championship |
| | v Reardon | 5-10 | 1st round | Embassy World Championship |
| | v Chaperon | 4-5 | 3rd round | Fidelity International |
| | v Cripsey | 3-5 | 3rd round | Rothmans Grand Prix |
| | v Gauvreau | 9-6 | 3rd round | Tennents UK Open |
| | v Johnson | 6-9 | 4th round | Tennents UK Open |
| **1988** | v Oliver | 5-3 | 3rd round | Mercantile Credit Classic |
| | v Thorne | 5-2 | 4th round | Mercantile Credit Classic |
| | v Griffiths | 2-5 | 5th round | Mercantile Credit Classic |
| | v Greaves | 6-5 | 3rd round | English Championship |
| | v White | 6-2 | 4th round | English Championship |
| | v Hallett | 6-5 | Quarter-final | English Championship |
| | v N. Foulds | 6-9 | Semi-final | English Championship |
| | v Dunning | 5-0 | 3rd round | MIM Britannia British Open |
| | v Williams | 0-5 | 4th round | MIM Britannia British Open |
| | v Newbury | 10-8 | Qualifying | Embassy World Championship |
| | v Mountjoy | 6-10 | 1st round | Embassy World Championship |
| | v King | 5-4 | 3rd round | Fidelity International |
| | v Dodd | 5-3 | 4th round | Fidelity International |
| | v Williams | 5-4 | 5th round | Fidelity International |
| | v White | 2-5 | Quarter-final | Fidelity International |
| | v Chambers | 5-3 | 3rd round | Rothmans Grand Prix |
| | v Griffiths | 1-5 | 4th round | Rothmans Grand Prix |
| | v Duggan | 3-5 | 3rd round | BCE Canadian Masters |
| | v T. Jones | 9-5 | 3rd round | Tennents UK Open |
| | v S. Francisco | 9-4 | 4th round | Tennents UK Open |
| | v M. Bennett | 9-4 | 5th round | Tennents UK Open |
| | v Griffiths | 5-9 | Quarter-final | Tennents UK Open |
| **1989** | v A. Harris | 4-5 | 3rd round | Mercantile Credit Classic |
| | v Macleod | 4-5 | 3rd round | European Open |
| | v Roe | 4-5 | 3rd round | English Championship |
| | v Graham | 5-1 | 3rd round | Anglian British Open |
| | v Knowles | 5-0 | 4th round | Anglian British Open |
| | v P. Francisco | 1-5 | 5th round | Anglian British Open |
| | v O'Boye | 7-10 | Qualifying | Embassy World Championship |
| | v John Rea | 5-4 | 3rd round | Hong Kong Open |

| | | | | |
|---|---|---|---|---|
| | v Hallett | 4-5 | 4th round | Hong Kong Open |
| | v Chambers | 5-3 | 3rd round | 555 Asian Open |
| | v D. Gilbert | 5-3 | 4th round | 555 Asian Open |
| | v Clark | 0-5 | 5th round | 555 Asian Open |
| | v Thorne | 2-5 | 4th round | BCE International |
| | v Chambers | 4-5 | 3rd round | Rothmans Grand Prix |
| | v W. Jones | 5-2 | 3rd round | Dubai Classic |
| | v Reynolds | 2-5 | 4th round | Dubai Classic |
| | v David Taylor | 9-5 | 3rd round | Stormseal UK Open |
| | v Hendry | 1-9 | 4th round | Stormseal UK Open |
| **1990** | v Rowing | 0-5 | 3rd round | Mercantile Credit Classic |
| | v Macleod | 0-5 | 3rd round | Pearl Assurance British Open |
| | v Fowler | 2-5 | 3rd round | European Open |
| | v Fowler | 9-10 | Qualifying | Embassy World Championship |

## JIMMY WHITE (England)

**Born** 2.5.62. **Turned professional** 1980. **World ranking** 4 (4).

| | | | | |
|---|---|---|---|---|
| **1981** | v Mikkelsen | 9-4 | Qualifying | Embassy World Championship |
| | v Meadowcroft | 9-8 | Qualifying | Embassy World Championship |
| | v S. Davis | 8-10 | 1st round | Embassy World Championship |
| | v Reardon | 5-4 | Quarter-final | Langs Supreme Scottish Masters |
| | v S. Davis | 6-5 | Semi-final | Langs Supreme Scottish Masters |
| | **v Thorburn** | **9-4** | **Final** | **Langs Supreme Scottish Masters** |
| | v Williams | 1-5 | 1st round | Jameson International |
| | v Thorburn | 5-2 | 1st round | Northern Ireland Classic |
| | v Mountjoy | 9-8 | Semi-final | Northern Ireland Classic |
| | **v S. Davis** | **11-9** | **Final** | **Northern Ireland Classic** |
| | v Everton | 9-4 | Qualifying | Coral UK Championship |
| | v Virgo | 9-6 | 2nd round | Coral UK Championship |
| | v Dennis Taylor | 9-5 | 3rd round | Coral UK Championship |
| | v Reardon | 9-8 | Quarter-final | Coral UK Championship |
| | v S. Davis | 0-9 | Semi-final | Coral UK Championship |
| **1982** | v Charlton | 4-5 | 1st round | Benson & Hedges Masters |
| | v Wildman | 9-4 | Qualifying | Embassy World Championship |
| | v Thorburn | 10-4 | 1st round | Embassy World Championship |
| | v Mans | 13-6 | 2nd round | Embassy World Championship |
| | v Stevens | 13-9 | Quarter-final | Embassy World Championship |
| | v Higgins | 15-16 | Semi-final | Embassy World Championship |
| | v Dennis Taylor | 4-5 | 1st round | Langs Supreme Scottish Masters |
| | v Meadowcroft | 5-1 | 1st round | Jameson International |
| | v Wilson | 2-5 | 2nd round | Jameson International |
| | v Wych | 5-0 | 2nd round | Professional Players Tournament |
| | v Dennis Taylor | 5-3 | 3rd round | Professional Players Tournament |
| | v Griffiths | 5-2 | Quarter-final | Professional Players Tournament |
| | v Virgo | 10-4 | Semi-final | Professional Players Tournament |
| | v Reardon | 5-10 | Final | Professional Players Tournament |
| | v Medati | 9-7 | 1st round | Coral UK Championship |
| | v Wilson | 9-5 | 2nd round | Coral UK Championship |
| | v Reardon | 8-9 | Quarter-final | Coral UK Championship |
| **1983** | v David Taylor | 3-5 | 1st round | Lada Classic |
| | v David Taylor | 5-2 | 1st round | Benson & Hedges Masters |
| | v Reardon | 2-5 | Quarter-final | Benson & Hedges Masters |
| | v Reardon | 6-9 | Final | Yamaha International Masters |
| | v Dennis Taylor | 5-4 | 1st round | Benson & Hedges Irish Masters |
| | v Higgins | 2-5 | Quarter-final | Benson & Hedges Irish Masters |
| | v Meo | 8-10 | 1st round | Embassy World Championship |
| | v Higgins | 3-5 | 1st round | Langs Supreme Scottish Masters |
| | v Morra | 3-5 | 1st round | Jameson International |
| | v Williamson | 5-2 | 1st round | Professional Players Tournament |
| | v Johnson | 3-5 | 2nd round | Professional Players Tournament |

| | | | | |
|---|---|---|---|---|
| | v Black | 9-1 | 1st round | Coral UK Championship |
| | v Dennis Taylor | 9-4 | 2nd round | Coral UK Championship |
| | v Reardon | 9-4 | Quarter-final | Coral UK Championship |
| | v S. Davis | 4-9 | Semi-final | Coral UK Championship |
| **1984** | v J. Campbell | 5-1 | Qualifying | Lada Classic |
| | v Charlton | 3-5 | 1st round | Lada Classic |
| | v Charlton | 5-2 | 1st round | Benson & Hedges Masters |
| | v Reardon | 5-3 | Quarter-final | Benson & Hedges Masters |
| | v Stevens | 6-4 | Semi-final | Benson & Hedges Masters |
| | **v Griffiths** | **9-5** | **Final** | **Benson & Hedges Masters** |
| | v Meo | 4-5 | 1st round | Benson & Hedges Irish Masters |
| | v Knowles | 1-5 | 1st round | Tolly Cobbold Classic |
| | v Williams | 10-6 | 1st round | Embassy World Championship |
| | v Charlton | 13-7 | 2nd round | Embassy World Championship |
| | v Thorburn | 13-8 | Quarter-final | Embassy World Championship |
| | v Stevens | 16-14 | Semi-final | Embassy World Championship |
| | v S. Davis | 16-18 | Final | Embassy World Championship |
| | v Knowles | 3-5 | Quarter-final | Winfield Australian Masters |
| | v Macleod | 5-0 | 1st round | Langs Supreme Scottish Masters |
| | v Knowles | 6-5 | Semi-final | Langs Supreme Scottish Masters |
| | v S. Davis | 4-9 | Final | Langs Supreme Scottish Masters |
| | v Stevens | 5-0 | 1st round | Carlsberg Challenge |
| | **v Knowles** | **9-7** | **Final** | **Carlsberg Challenge** |
| | v Williams | 5-3 | 1st round | Jameson International |
| | v Meo | 5-1 | 2nd round | Jameson International |
| | v Knowles | 4-5 | Quarter-final | Jameson International |
| | v Oliver | 5-1 | 1st round | Rothmans Grand Prix |
| | v S. Francisco | 1-5 | 2nd round | Rothmans Grand Prix |
| | v J. Campbell | 9-7 | 1st round | Coral UK Open |
| | v Mountjoy | 9-2 | 2nd round | Coral UK Open |
| | v S. Davis | 4-9 | Quarter-final | Coral UK Open |
| **1985** | v Browne | 5-2 | 1st round | Mercantile Credit Classic |
| | v King | 2-5 | 2nd round | Mercantile Credit Classic |
| | v Thorne | 5-2 | 1st round | Benson & Hedges Masters |
| | v Spencer | 5-2 | Quarter-final | Benson & Hedges Masters |
| | v Thorburn | 4-6 | Semi-final | Benson & Hedges Masters |
| | v Chalmers | 9-5 | 1st round | Tolly Cobbold English Championship |
| | v N. Foulds | 9-7 | 2nd round | Tolly Cobbold English Championship |
| | v Longworth | 5-9 | Quarter-final | Tolly Cobbold English Championship |
| | v T. Jones | 6-5 | 1st round | Dulux British Open |
| | v S. Francisco | 4-5 | 2nd round | Dulux British Open |
| | v Meo | 5-1 | 1st round | Benson & Hedges Irish Masters |
| | v Thorburn | 5-3 | Quarter-final | Benson & Hedges Irish Masters |
| | v Knowles | 6-4 | Semi-final | Benson & Hedges Irish Masters |
| | **v Higgins** | **9-5** | **Final** | **Benson & Hedges Irish Masters** |
| | v W. Jones | 10-4 | 1st round | Embassy World Championship |
| | v Meo | 13-11 | 2nd round | Embassy World Championship |
| | v Knowles | 10-13 | Quarter-final | Embassy World Championship |
| | v Johnson | 5-4 | Quarter-final | Winfield Australian Masters |
| | v Meo | 3-6 | Semi-final | Winfield Australian Masters |
| | v Higgins | 5-0 | 1st round | Langs Scottish Masters |
| | v Thorne | 2-6 | Semi-final | Langs Scottish Masters |
| | v Parrott | 5-3 | Semi-final | Carlsberg Challenge |
| | **v Higgins** | **8-3** | **Final** | **Carlsberg Challenge** |
| | v Fagan | 5-2 | 3rd round | Goya Matchroom Trophy |
| | v King | 5-2 | 4th round | Goya Matchroom Trophy |
| | v Reynolds | 5-1 | 5th round | Goya Matchroom Trophy |
| | v S. Davis | 5-3 | Quarter-final | Goya Matchroom Trophy |
| | v N. Foulds | 9-5 | Semi-final | Goya Matchroom Trophy |
| | v Thorburn | 10-12 | Final | Goya Matchroom Trophy |
| | v Fitzmaurice | 5-0 | 3rd round | Rothmans Grand Prix |
| | v O'Boye | 5-4 | 4th round | Rothmans Grand Prix |
| | v S. Francisco | 4-5 | 5th round | Rothmans Grand Prix |

| | | | | |
|---|---|---|---|---|
| | v Thorburn | 3-5 | 1st round | BCE Canadian Masters |
| | v Bradley | 9-4 | 3rd round | Coral UK Open |
| | v Chappel | 9-5 | 4th round | Coral UK Open |
| | v Higgins | 9-6 | 5th round | Coral UK Open |
| | v Knowles | 9-4 | Quarter-final | Coral UK Open |
| | v S. Davis | 5-9 | Semi-final | Coral UK Open |
| **1986** | v Fowler | 5-1 | 3rd round | Mercantile Credit Classic |
| | v Virgo | 5-2 | 4th round | Mercantile Credit Classic |
| | v Gauvreau | 5-2 | 5th round | Mercantile Credit Classic |
| | v S. Davis | 5-2 | Quarter-final | Mercantile Credit Classic |
| | v Williams | 9-7 | Semi-final | Mercantile Credit Classic |
| | **v Thorburn** | **13-12** | **Final** | **Mercantile Credit Classic** |
| | v Knowles | 3-5 | 1st round | BCE Belgian Classic |
| | v Meo | 5-4 | 1st round | Benson & Hedges Masters |
| | v Dennis Taylor | 5-3 | Quarter-final | Benson & Hedges Masters |
| | v S. Davis | 6-3 | Semi-final | Benson & Hedges Masters |
| | v Thorburn | 5-9 | Final | Benson & Hedges Masters |
| | v Williamson | 9-1 | 3rd round | Tolly Cobbold English Championship |
| | v Williams | 9-5 | 4th round | Tolly Cobbold English Championship |
| | v N. Foulds | 4-9 | Quarter-final | Tolly Cobbold English Championship |
| | v P. Francisco | 4-5 | 3rd round | Dulux British Open |
| | v Meo | 5-2 | Quarter-final | Benson & Hedges Irish Masters |
| | v Fagan | 6-0 | Semi-final | Benson & Hedges Irish Masters |
| | **v Thorne** | **9-5** | **Final** | **Benson & Hedges Irish Masters** |
| | v Virgo | 10-7 | 1st round | Embassy World Championship |
| | v Parrott | 13-8 | 2nd round | Embassy World Championship |
| | v S. Davis | 5-13 | Quarter-final | Embassy World Championship |
| | v Higgins | 5-1 | 1st round | Carlsberg Challenge |
| | v Dennis Taylor | 3-8 | Final | Carlsberg Challenge |
| | v Hendry | 5-1 | 1st round | Langs Scottish Masters |
| | v Thorburn | 2-6 | Semi-final | Langs Scottish Masters |
| | v Owers | 2-5 | 3rd round | BCE International |
| | v T. Jones | 5-0 | 3rd round | Rothmans Grand Prix |
| | v J. McLaughlin | 5-2 | 4th round | Rothmans Grand Prix |
| | v Hallett | 5-3 | 5th round | Rothmans Grand Prix |
| | v Hendry | 5-4 | Quarter-final | Rothmans Grand Prix |
| | v S. Francisco | 9-6 | Semi-final | Rothmans Grand Prix |
| | **v Williams** | **10-6** | **Final** | **Rothmans Grand Prix** |
| | v S. Davis | 2-5 | 1st round | BCE Canadian Masters |
| | v Edmonds | 9-4 | 3rd round | Tennents UK Open |
| | v P. Francisco | 9-5 | 4th round | Tennents UK Open |
| | v N. Foulds | 7-9 | 5th round | Tennents UK Open |
| **1987** | v Newbury | 5-4 | 3rd round | Mercantile Credit Classic |
| | v Bradley | 5-0 | 4th round | Mercantile Credit Classic |
| | v Duggan | 5-2 | 5th round | Mercantile Credit Classic |
| | v Griffiths | 5-3 | Quarter-final | Mercantile Credit Classic |
| | v Reynolds | 9-8 | Semi-final | Mercantile Credit Classic |
| | v S. Davis | 12-13 | Final | Mercantile Credit Classic |
| | v Meo | 4-5 | 1st round | Benson & Hedges Masters |
| | v Cripsey | 6-4 | 3rd round | Tolly Ales English Championship |
| | v Reynolds | 5-6 | 4th round | Tolly Ales English Championship |
| | v Chappel | 5-1 | 3rd round | Dulux British Open |
| | v Hallett | 5-2 | 4th round | Dulux British Open |
| | v Williams | 5-0 | 5th round | Dulux British Open |
| | v Spencer | 5-3 | Quarter-final | Dulux British Open |
| | v Thorburn | 9-5 | Semi-final | Dulux British Open |
| | **v N. Foulds** | **13-9** | **Final** | **Dulux British Open** |
| | v Thorne | 4-5 | Quarter-final | Benson & Hedges Irish Masters |
| | v Reynolds | 10-8 | 1st round | Embassy World Championship |
| | v Parrott | 13-11 | 2nd round | Embassy World Championship |
| | v O'Kane | 13-6 | Quarter-final | Embassy World Championship |
| | v S. Davis | 11-16 | Semi-final | Embassy World Championship |
| | v Hendry | 2-5 | Semi-final | Riley Hong Kong Masters (WS) |

*Jimmy White*

| | | | | |
|---|---|---|---|---|
| | v Higgins | 5-3 | 1st round | Langs Scottish Masters |
| | v Griffiths | 2-6 | Semi-final | Langs Scottish Masters |
| | v M. Bennett | 5-3 | 3rd round | Fidelity International |
| | v Longworth | 5-1 | 4th round | Fidelity International |
| | v Hallett | 4-5 | 5th round | Fidelity International |
| | v Wright | 5-4 | 3rd round | Rothmans Grand Prix |
| | v Drago | 3-5 | 4th round | Rothmans Grand Prix |
| | v Knowles | 5-1 | 1st round | Labatts Canadian Masters (WS) |
| | v N. Foulds | 8-7 | Semi-final | Labatts Canadian Masters (WS) |
| | v Dennis Taylor | 7-9 | Final | Labatts Canadian Masters (WS) |
| | v Dennis Taylor | 2-6 | 1st round | Matchroom Trophy |
| | v Dunning | 9-0 | 3rd round | Tennents UK Open |
| | v E. Hughes | 9-4 | 4th round | Tennents UK Open |
| | v Roe | 9-5 | 5th round | Tennents UK Open |
| | v Griffiths | 9-7 | Quarter-final | Tennents UK Open |
| | v Johnson | 9-4 | Semi-final | Tennents UK Open |
| | v S. Davis | 14-16 | Final | Tennents UK Open |
| **1988** | v James | 5-1 | 3rd round | Mercantile Credit Classic |
| | v Spencer | 5-1 | 4th round | Mercantile Credit Classic |
| | v Martin | 2-5 | 5th round | Mercantile Credit Classic |
| | v Mountjoy | 5-0 | 1st round | Benson & Hedges Masters |
| | v Johnson | 3-5 | Quarter-final | Benson & Hedges Masters |
| | v Clark | 6-5 | 3rd round | English Championship |
| | v West | 2-6 | 4th round | English Championship |
| | v Clark | 5-2 | 3rd round | MIM Britannia British Open |
| | v James | 5-1 | 4th round | MIM Britannia British Open |
| | v Gary Wilkinson | 5-1 | 5th round | MIM Britannia British Open |
| | v Hendry | 4-5 | Quarter-final | MIM Britannia British Open |
| | v Griffiths | 2-5 | Quarter-final | Benson & Hedges Irish Masters |
| | v J. Campbell | 10-3 | 1st round | Embassy World Championship |
| | v Hendry | 13-12 | 2nd round | Embassy World Championship |
| | v Knowles | 13-6 | Quarter-final | Embassy World Championship |
| | v Griffiths | 11-16 | Semi-final | Embassy World Championship |
| | v Dennis Taylor | 5-2 | Semi-final | LEP Hong Kong Masters |
| | **v N. Foulds** | **6-3** | **Final** | **LEP Hong Kong Masters** |
| | v Clark | 5-2 | 3rd round | Fidelity International |
| | v E. Hughes | 5-1 | 4th round | Fidelity International |
| | v Thorne | 5-4 | 5th round | Fidelity International |
| | v West | 5-2 | Quarter-final | Fidelity International |
| | v Reynolds | 9-5 | Semi-final | Fidelity International |
| | v S. Davis | 6-12 | Final | Fidelity International |
| | v Thorburn | 6-4 | 1st round | LEP Matchroom Championship |
| | v S. Davis | 4-6 | Semi-final | LEP Matchroom Championship |
| | v Fowler | 5-0 | 3rd round | Rothmans Grand Prix |
| | v W. Jones | 5-1 | 4th round | Rothmans Grand Prix |
| | v J. McLaughlin | 5-2 | 5th round | Rothmans Grand Prix |
| | v Dennis Taylor | 2-5 | Quarter-final | Rothmans Grand Prix |
| | v Roe | 5-3 | 3rd round | BCE Canadian Masters |
| | v M. Bennett | 5-3 | 4th round | BCE Canadian Masters |
| | v Longworth | 5-3 | 5th round | BCE Canadian Masters |
| | v Dennis Taylor | 5-3 | Quarter-final | BCE Canadian Masters |
| | v Hallett | 9-2 | Semi-final | BCE Canadian Masters |
| | **v S. Davis** | **9-4** | **Final** | **BCE Canadian Masters** |
| | v J. Campbell | 9-5 | 3rd round | Tennents UK Open |
| | v M. Bennett | 6-9 | 4th round | Tennents UK Open |
| | v Griffiths | 9-5 | Quarter-final | Everest World Matchplay |
| | v S. Davis | 5-9 | Semi-final | Everest World Matchplay |
| | v S. Davis | 4-5 | Final | Norwich Union European Grand Prix |
| **1989** | v W. Jones | 3-5 | 3rd round | Mercantile Credit Classic |
| | v Virgo | 5-2 | 1st round | Benson and Hedges Masters |
| | v Parrott | 4-5 | Quarter-final | Benson and Hedges Masters |
| | v Sinclair | 5-3 | 3rd round | European Open |
| | v Williams | 5-2 | 4th round | European Open |

| | | | | |
|---|---|---|---|---|
| | v Thorne | 5-3 | 5th round | European Open |
| | v Thorburn | 5-3 | Quarter-final | European Open |
| | v Griffiths | 4-5 | Semi-final | European Open |
| | v Houlihan | 5-3 | 3rd round | Anglian British Open |
| | v Reynolds | *scr* | 4th round | Anglian British Open |
| | v Parrott | 1-5 | Quarter-final | Benson and Hedges Irish Masters |
| | v O'Kane | 10-7 | 1st round | Embassy World Championship |
| | v Virgo | 13–12 | 2nd round | Embassy World Championship |
| | v Parrott | 7-13 | Quarter-final | Embassy World Championship |
| | v J. McLaughlin | 5-2 | 3rd round | Hong Kong Open |
| | v Charlton | 5-2 | 4th round | Hong Kong Open |
| | v Mountjoy | 5-3 | 5th round | Hong Kong Open |
| | v N. Foulds | 5-2 | Quarter-final | Hong Kong Open |
| | v Hallett | 2-5 | Semi-final | Hong Kong Open |
| | v Roscoe | 3-5 | 3rd round | 555 Asian Open |
| | v J. Smith | 5-3 | 3rd round | BCE International |
| | v Chaperon | 5-3 | 4th round | BCE International |
| | v Thorne | 5-1 | 5th round | BCE International |
| | v Robidoux | 4-5 | Quarter-final | BCE International |
| | v S. Campbell | 5-0 | 3rd round | Rothmans Grand Prix |
| | v Chambers | 5-1 | 4th round | Rothmans Grand Prix |
| | v Johnson | 0-5 | 5th round | Rothmans Grand Prix |
| | v Bond | 9-3 | 3rd round | Stormseal UK Open |
| | v N. Foulds | 9-5 | 4th round | Stormseal UK Open |
| | v Johnson | 9-6 | 5th round | Stormseal UK Open |
| | v Gary Wilkinson | 0-9 | Quarter-final | Stormseal UK Open |
| | v Mountjoy | 9-5 | Quarter-final | Everest World Matchplay |
| | v Reynolds | 9-8 | Semi-final | Everest World Matchplay |
| | **v Parrott** | **18-9** | **Final** | **Everest World Matchplay** |
| **1990** | v Virgo | 5-3 | 1st round | Benson and Hedges Masters |
| | v Knowles | 5-3 | Quarter-final | Benson and Hedges Masters |
| | v Hendry | 4-6 | Semi-final | Benson and Hedges Masters |
| | v Spencer | 5-4 | 3rd round | Pearl Assurance British Open |
| | v Meo | 5-2 | 4th round | Pearl Assurance British Open |
| | v James | 4-5 | 5th round | Pearl Assurance British Open |
| | v S. Murphy | 5-0 | 3rd round | European Open |
| | v Roe | 5-1 | 4th round | European Open |
| | v James | 4-5 | 5th round | European Open |
| | v Johnson | 5-4 | 1st round | Benson and Hedges Irish Masters |
| | v Hendry | 5-2 | Quarter-final | Benson and Hedges Irish Masters |
| | v Dennis Taylor | 5-6 | Semi-final | Benson and Hedges Irish Masters |
| | v Fowler | 10-4 | 1st round | Embassy World Championship |
| | v Virgo | 13-6 | 2nd round | Embassy World Championship |
| | v Griffiths | 13-5 | Quarter-final | Embassy World Championship |
| | v S. Davis | 16-14 | Semi-final | Embassy World Championship |
| | v Hendry | 12-18 | Final | Embassy World Championship |

## **TERRY WHITTHREAD** (England)

**Born** 7.7.64. **Turned professional** 1986. **World ranking** 118 (100).

| | | | | |
|---|---|---|---|---|
| **1986** | v Kelly | 1-5 | 1st round | BCE International |
| | v Duggan | 1-5 | 1st round | Rothmans Grand Prix |
| | v Darrington | 8-9 | 1st round | Tennents UK Open |
| **1987** | v Roscoe | 1-5 | 1st round | Mercantile Credit Classic |
| | v Fisher | 3-6 | 1st round | Tolly Ales English Championship |
| | v D. Hughes | 5-1 | 1st round | Dulux British Open |
| | v Spencer | 2-5 | 2nd round | Dulux British Open |
| | v Roscoe | 2-10 | Qualifying | Embassy World Championship |
| | v Jenkins | 1-5 | 1st round | Fidelity International |
| | v Roe | 1-5 | 1st round | Rothmans Grand Prix |
| | v Van Rensberg | 5-9 | 1st round | Tennents UK Open |

| | | | | |
|---|---|---|---|---|
| **1988** | v Fagan | 5-2 | 1st round | Mercantile Credit Classic |
| | v G. Foulds | 5-3 | 2nd round | Mercantile Credit Classic |
| | v Dennis Taylor | 2-5 | 3rd round | Mercantile Credit Classic |
| | v D. Gilbert | 1-6 | 1st round | English Championship |
| | v Glen Wilkinson | 5-4 | 1st round | MIM Britannia British Open |
| | v O'Kane | 2-5 | 2nd round | MIM Britannia British Open |
| | v Meadowcroft | 5-4 | 1st round | Fidelity International |
| | v O'Boye | 2-5 | 2nd round | Fidelity International |
| | v Grace | 5-4 | 1st round | Rothmans Grand Prix |
| | v Clark | 1-5 | 2nd round | Rothmans Grand Prix |
| | v Bear | 5-4 | 1st round | BCE Canadian Masters |
| | v Roe | 2-5 | 2nd round | BCE Canadian Masters |
| | v Donnelly | 9-8 | 1st round | Tennents UK Open |
| | v N. Gilbert | 5-9 | 2nd round | Tennents UK Open |
| **1989** | v Roscoe | 3-5 | 1st round | Mercantile Credit Classic |
| | v Sinclair | 4-5 | 1st round | European Open |
| | v D. Hughes | 5-1 | 1st round | English Championship |
| | v Cripsey | 2-5 | 2nd round | English Championship |
| | v Donnelly | 5-4 | 1st round | Anglian British Open |
| | v Murphy | 5-2 | 2nd round | Anglian British Open |
| | v Johnson | 2-5 | 3rd round | Anglian British Open |
| | v Donnelly | 10-7 | Qualifying | Embassy World Championship |
| | v Fowler | 6-10 | Qualifying | Embassy World Championship |
| | v Medati | 5-3 | 1st round | BCE International |
| | v D. Morgan | 0-5 | 2nd round | BCE International |
| **1990** | v M. Smith | 1-5 | 1st round | European Open |
| | v Price | 6-10 | Qualifying | Embassy World Championship |

## MARK WILDMAN (England)

**Born** 25.1.36. **Turned professional** 1979. **World ranking** 125 (97).

| | | | | |
|---|---|---|---|---|
| **1980** | v Jonik | 7-9 | Qualifying | Embassy World Championship |
| | v Wilson | 9-8 | Qualifying | Coral UK Championship |
| | v Spencer | 9-7 | 1st round | Coral UK Championship |
| | v F. Davis | 6-9 | 2nd round | Coral UK Championship |
| **1981** | v Bennett | 9-3 | Qualifying | John Courage English |
| | v Thorne | 2-9 | 1st round | John Courage English |
| | v Edmonds | 3-9 | Qualifying | Embassy World Championship |
| | v Morra | 5-3 | Qualifying | Jameson International |
| | v E. McLaughlin | 3-5 | Qualifying | Jameson International |
| | v Sinclair | 8-9 | Qualifying | Coral UK Championship |
| **1982** | v G. Foulds | 9-8 | Qualifying | Embassy World Championship |
| | v White | 4-9 | Qualifying | Embassy World Championship |
| | v Gibson | 5-1 | Qualifying | Jameson International |
| | v Hallett | 5-2 | Qualifying | Jameson International |
| | v Dennis Taylor | 2-5 | 1st round | Jameson International |
| | v Dunning | 5-4 | 1st round | Professional Players Tournament |
| | v Mans | 5-4 | 2nd round | Professional Players Tournament |
| | v Johnson | 4-5 | 3rd round | Professional Players Tournament |
| | v Roscoe | 9-4 | Qualifying | Coral UK Championship |
| | v Reardon | 5-9 | 1st round | Coral UK Championship |
| **1983** | v S. Davis | 2-5 | 1st round | Benson & Hedges Masters |
| | v B. Harris | 10-7 | Qualifying | Embassy World Championship |
| | v Griffiths | 8-10 | 1st round | Embassy World Championship |
| | v B. Harris | 5-2 | Qualifying | Jameson International |
| | v Mountjoy | 4-5 | 1st round | Jameson International |
| | v Jonik | 5-4 | 1st round | Professional Players Tournament |
| | v David Taylor | 5-3 | 2nd round | Professional Players Tournament |
| | v Stevens | 0-5 | 3rd round | Professional Players Tournament |
| | v Greaves | 9-5 | Qualifying | Coral UK Championship |
| | v Thorne | 5-9 | 1st round | Coral UK Championship |

| | | | | |
|---|---|---|---|---|
| **1984** | v Virgo | 5-2 | Qualifying | Lada Classic |
| | v S. Francisco | 5-1 | 1st round | Lada Classic |
| | v Charlton | 5-4 | Quarter-final | Lada Classic |
| | v Meo | 3-5 | Semi-final | Lada Classic |
| | v Andrewartha | 9-10 | Qualifying | Embassy World Championship |
| | v W. Jones | 0-5 | Qualifying | Jameson International |
| | v J. McLaughlin | 5-3 | 1st round | Rothmans Grand Prix |
| | v Mountjoy | 0-5 | 2nd round | Rothmans Grand Prix |
| | v T. Jones | 2-9 | Qualifying | Coral UK Open |
| **1985** | v Fagan | 3-5 | Qualifying | Mercantile Credit Classic |
| | v Longworth | 3-9 | 1st round | Tolly Cobbold English Championship |
| | v Gibson | 6-1 | 1st round | Dulux British Open |
| | v Stevens | 2-5 | 2nd round | Dulux British Open |
| | v Edmonds | 7-10 | Qualifying | Embassy World Championship |
| | v Scott | 1-5 | 3rd round | Goya Matchroom Trophy |
| | v Duggan | 5-4 | 3rd round | Rothmans Grand Prix |
| | v Thorburn | 2-5 | 4th round | Rothmans Grand Prix |
| | v Drago | 5-9 | 3rd round | Coral UK Open |
| **1986** | v West | 2-5 | 3rd round | Mercantile Credit Classic |
| | v Cripsey | 9-5 | 3rd round | Tolly Cobbold English Championship |
| | v Meo | 3-9 | 4th round | Tolly Cobbold English Championship |
| | v Jenkins | 5-4 | 3rd round | Dulux British Open |
| | v Thorburn | 1-5 | 4th round | Dulux British Open |
| | v Edmonds | 9-10 | Qualifying | Embassy World Championship |
| | v Rowswell | 5-2 | 2nd round | BCE International |
| | v P. Francisco | 2-5 | 3rd round | BCE International |
| | v Ellis | 5-1 | 2nd round | Rothmans Grand Prix |
| | v Longworth | 5-2 | 3rd round | Rothmans Grand Prix |
| | v Williams | 1-5 | 4th round | Rothmans Grand Prix |
| | v Roscoe | 6-9 | 2nd round | Tennents UK Open |
| **1987** | v Kearney | 3-5 | 2nd round | Mercantile Credit Classic |
| | v Parrott | 1-6 | 3rd round | Tolly Ales English Championship |
| | v Chalmers | 5-0 | 2nd round | Dulux British Open |
| | v Thorburn | 3-5 | 3rd round | Dulux British Open |
| | v Foldvari | 10-5 | Qualifying | Embassy World Championship |
| | v Wright | 0-10 | Qualifying | Embassy World Championship |
| | v Miles | 5-3 | 2nd round | Fidelity International |
| | v Griffiths | 1-5 | 3rd round | Fidelity International |
| | v Roe | 3-5 | 2nd round | Rothmans Grand Prix |
| | v Chambers | 5-9 | 2nd round | Tennents UK Open |
| **1988** | v Jonik | 5-4 | 2nd round | Mercantile Credit Classic |
| | v Parrott | 2-5 | 3rd round | Mercantile Credit Classic |
| | v D. Hughes | 0-6 | 2nd round | English Championship |
| | v Roscoe | 0-5 | 2nd round | MIM Britannia British Open |
| | v Mikkelsen | 10-5 | Qualifying | Embassy World Championship |
| | v Foldvari | 1-10 | Qualifying | Embassy World Championship |
| | v Jenkins | 1-5 | 1st round | Fidelity International |
| | v Fagan | 5-1 | 1st round | Rothmans Grand Prix |
| | v Martin | 1-5 | 2nd round | Rothmans Grand Prix |
| | v Jenkins | 5-1 | 1st round | BCE Canadian Masters |
| | v Duggan | 1-5 | 2nd round | BCE Canadian Masters |
| | v Mienie | 9-4 | 1st round | Tennents UK Open |
| | v Edmonds | 4-9 | 2nd round | Tennents UK Open |
| **1989** | v Morgan | 1-5 | 1st round | European Open |
| | v Medati | 4-5 | 1st round | English Championship |
| | v A. Harris | 4-5 | 1st round | Anglian British Open |
| | v Ellis | 7-10 | Qualifying | Embassy World Championship |
| | v J. McLaughlin | 1-5 | 2nd round | Hong Kong Open |
| | v Sheehan | 5-3 | 1st round | 555 Asian Open |
| | v Martin | 2-5 | 2nd round | 555 Asian Open |
| | v Meakin | 3-5 | 1st round | BCE International |
| | v Meakin | 2-5 | 1st round | Rothmans Grand Prix |
| | v Chappel | 1-5 | 2nd round | Dubai Classic |

| | | | | |
|---|---|---|---|---|
| | v Houlihan | 3-6 | 1st round | Stormseal UK Open |
| **1990** | v B. Harris | 2-5 | 1st round | Mercantile Credit Classic |
| | v Sinclair | 4-5 | 1st round | Pearl Assurance British Open |
| | v Meadowcroft | *wo* | 1st round | European Open |
| | v Roscoe | 3-5 | 2nd round | European Open |
| | v Sinclair | 5-10 | Qualifying | Embassy World Championship |

## GARY WILKINSON (England)

**Born** 7.4.66. **Turned professional** 1987. **World ranking** 20 (39).

| | | | | |
|---|---|---|---|---|
| **1987** | v Rigitano | 5-1 | 1st round | Fidelity International |
| | v Scott | 5-2 | 2nd round | Fidelity International |
| | v Hendry | 4-5 | 3rd round | Fidelity International |
| | v V. Harris | 5-0 | 1st round | Rothmans Grand Prix |
| | v O'Kane | 5-2 | 2nd round | Rothmans Grand Prix |
| | v Longworth | 5-4 | 3rd round | Rothmans Grand Prix |
| | v S. Francisco | 5-3 | 4th round | Rothmans Grand Prix |
| | v Newbury | 3-5 | 5th round | Rothmans Grand Prix |
| | v Jenkins | 9-3 | 1st round | Tennents UK Open |
| | v Grace | 9-5 | 2nd round | Tennents UK Open |
| | v Griffiths | 5-9 | 3rd round | Tennents UK Open |
| **1988** | v Reardon | 3-5 | 2nd round | Mercantile Credit Classic |
| | v Rowswell | 6-1 | 1st round | English Championship |
| | v Edmonds | 6-3 | 2nd round | English Championship |
| | v N. Foulds | 3-6 | 3rd round | English Championship |
| | v Black | 5-2 | 1st round | MIM Britannia British Open |
| | v Bales | 5-1 | 2nd round | MIM Britannia British Open |
| | v Meo | 5-2 | 3rd round | MIM Britannia British Open |
| | v S. Francisco | 5-3 | 4th round | MIM Britannia British Open |
| | v White | 1-5 | 5th round | MIM Britannia British Open |
| | v Medati | 9-10 | Qualifying | Embassy World Championship |
| | v Chambers | 4-5 | 2nd round | Fidelity International |
| | v D. Morgan | 5-1 | 2nd round | Rothmans Grand Prix |
| | v Thorne | 5-3 | 3rd round | Rothmans Grand Prix |
| | v Williams | 2-5 | 4th round | Rothmans Grand Prix |
| | v Terry | 5-3 | 2nd round | BCE Canadian Masters |
| | v C. Wilson | 2-5 | 3rd round | BCE Canadian Masters |
| | v Sheehan | 9-5 | 2nd round | Tennents UK Open |
| | v Chaperon | 9-0 | 3rd round | Tennents UK Open |
| | v S. Davis | 3-9 | 4th round | Tennents UK Open |
| **1989** | v Medati | 5-1 | 2nd round | Mercantile Credit Classic |
| | v James | 1-5 | 3rd round | Mercantile Credit Classic |
| | v Graham | 5-3 | 2nd round | European Open |
| | v David Taylor | 5-2 | 3rd round | European Open |
| | v Parrott | 2-5 | 4th round | European Open |
| | v J. Smith | 5-3 | 2nd round | English Championship |
| | v Virgo | 5-3 | 3rd round | English Championship |
| | v Graham | 5-1 | 4th round | English Championship |
| | v Rowswell | 5-1 | Quarter-final | English Championship |
| | v Hallett | 3-5 | Semi-final | English Championship |
| | v Miles | 5-2 | 2nd round | Anglian British Open |
| | v Thorne | 1-5 | 3rd round | Anglian British Open |
| | v V. Harris | 10-6 | Qualifying | Embassy World Championship |
| | v Reardon | 10-5 | Qualifying | Embassy World Championship |
| | v Drago | 10-9 | Qualifying | Embassy World Championship |
| | v Hendry | 9-10 | 1st round | Embassy World Championship |
| | v J. Smith | 5-1 | 2nd round | Hong Kong Open |
| | v Knowles | 5-2 | 3rd round | Hong Kong Open |
| | v Pinches | 5-4 | 4th round | Hong Kong Open |
| | v Newbury | 5-1 | 5th round | Hong Kong Open |
| | v Dennis Taylor | 5-3 | Quarter-final | Hong Kong Open |

*Gary Wilkinson*

| | | | | |
|---|---|---|---|---|
| | v O'Kane | 3-5 | Semi-final | Hong Kong Open |
| | v P. Gibson | 5-4 | 2nd round | 555 Asian Open |
| | v Charlton | 5-3 | 3rd round | 555 Asian Open |
| | v Meo | 5-2 | 4th round | 555 Asian Open |
| | v P. Francisco | 5-4 | 5th round | 555 Asian Open |
| | v Clark | 5-0 | Quarter-final | 555 Asian Open |
| | v Hendry | 4-5 | Semi-final | 555 Asian Open |
| | v B. Harris | 4-5 | 2nd round | BCE International |
| | v Terry | 5-3 | 2nd round | Rothmans Grand Prix |
| | v Drago | 5-1 | 3rd round | Rothmans Grand Prix |
| | v Parrott | 1-5 | 4th round | Rothmans Grand Prix |
| | v Dodd | 5-3 | 3rd round | Dubai Classic |
| | v Grech | 2-5 | 4th round | Dubai Classic |
| | v Sheehan | 6-2 | 2nd round | Stormseal UK Open |
| | v Roe | 9-2 | 3rd round | Stormseal UK Open |
| | v B. Morgan | 9-6 | 4th round | Stormseal UK Open |
| | v Parrott | 9-6 | 5th round | Stormseal UK Open |
| | v White | 9-0 | Quarter-final | Stormseal UK Open |
| | v S. Davis | 8-9 | Semi-final | Stormseal UK Open |
| **1990** | v Gauvreau | 5-1 | 2nd round | Mercantile Credit Classic |
| | v C. Wilson | 5-2 | 3rd round | Mercantile Credit Classic |
| | v J. Campbell | 5-4 | 4th round | Mercantile Credit Classic |
| | v W. Jones | 2-5 | 5th round | Mercantile Credit Classic |
| | v Fitzmaurice | 5-3 | 2nd round | Pearl Assurance British Open |
| | v Griffiths | 4-5 | 3rd round | Pearl Assurance British Open |
| | v Price | 4-5 | 2nd round | European Open |
| | v Gauvreau | 10-5 | Qualifying | Embassy World Championship |
| | v Marshall | 10-7 | Qualifying | Embassy World Championship |
| | v S. Francisco | 10-7 | Qualifying | Embassy World Championship |
| | v Virgo | 6-10 | 1st round | Embassy World Championship |

## GLEN WILKINSON (Australia)

**Born** 4.7.59. **Turned professional** 1985. **World ranking** 108 (91).

| | | | | |
|---|---|---|---|---|
| **1985** | v Jenkins | 6-2 | 1st round | Australian Championship |
| | v Heywood | 7-3 | 2nd round | Australian Championship |
| | v Charlton | 2-8 | Quarter-final | Australian Championship |
| | v Demarco | 5-2 | 1st round | Goya Matchroom Trophy |
| | v Longworth | 0-5 | 2nd round | Goya Matchroom Trophy |
| | v Gilbert | 4-5 | 1st round | Rothmans Grand Prix |
| | v Smith | 9-4 | 1st round | Coral UK Open |
| | v Fowler | 6-9 | 2nd round | Coral UK Open |
| **1986** | v O'Boye | 1-5 | 1st round | Mercantile Credit Classic |
| | v Watchorn | 5-4 | 1st round | Dulux British Open |
| | v Donnelly | 4-5 | 2nd round | Dulux British Open |
| | v Kearney | 5-10 | Qualifying | Embassy World Championship |
| | v Heywood | 6-0 | 2nd round | Australian Championship |
| | v J. Campbell | 1-6 | Quarter-final | Australian Championship |
| | v Bradley | 4-5 | 2nd round | BCE International |
| | v G. Foulds | 3-5 | 1st round | Rothmans Grand Prix |
| | v Jonik | 9-8 | 1st round | Tennents UK Open |
| | v Chappel | 2-9 | 2nd round | Tennents UK Open |
| **1987** | v Fitzmaurice | 5-2 | 1st round | Mercantile Credit Classic |
| | v Fowler | 1-5 | 2nd round | Mercantile Credit Classic |
| | v Fitzmaurice | 5-0 | 1st round | Dulux British Open |
| | v Mans | 5-2 | 2nd round | Dulux British Open |
| | v David Taylor | 4-5 | 3rd round | Dulux British Open |
| | v J. Campbell | 4-6 | Quarter-final | Australian Championship |
| | v P. Gibson | 3-5 | 1st round | Fidelity International |
| | v Owers | 5-4 | 2nd round | Rothmans Grand Prix |
| | v Wilson | 4-5 | 3rd round | Rothmans Grand Prix |

| | | | | |
|---|---|---|---|---|
| | v Meakin | 0-9 | 1st round | Tennents UK Open |
| **1988** | v Chalmers | 5-3 | 1st round | Mercantile Credit Classic |
| | v Werbeniuk | 2-5 | 2nd round | Mercantile Credit Classic |
| | v Whitthread | 4-5 | 1st round | MIM Britannia British Open |
| | v Everton | 10-2 | Qualifying | Embassy World Championship |
| | v W. Jones | 4-10 | Qualifying | Embassy World Championship |
| | v Potasznyk | 3-5 | 2nd round | Australian Championship |
| | v Mienie | 5-2 | 1st round | Fidelity International |
| | v Fisher | 4-5 | 2nd round | Fidelity International |
| | v Graham | 5-4 | 1st round | Rothmans Grand Prix |
| | v Macleod | 2-5 | 2nd round | Rothmans Grand Prix |
| | v Robidoux | 3-5 | 1st round | BCE Canadian Masters |
| | v Jack Rea | 9-0 | 1st round | Tennents UK Open |
| | v Dodd | 6-9 | 2nd round | Tennents UK Open |
| **1989** | v Watchorn | 5-3 | 1st round | Mercantile Credit Classic |
| | v Wych | 5-3 | 2nd round | Mercantile Credit Classic |
| | v Thorburn | 2-5 | 3rd round | Mercantile Credit Classic |
| | v A. Harris | 4-5 | 1st round | European Open |
| | v D. Morgan | 0-5 | 1st round | Anglian British Open |
| | v Kelly | 10-2 | Qualifying | Embassy World Championship |
| | v Bales | 10-1 | Qualifying | Embassy World Championship |
| | v Dodd | 4-10 | Qualifying | Embassy World Championship |
| | v Bond | 1-5 | 1st round | Hong Kong Open |
| | v Pinches | 4-5 | 1st round | 555 Asian Open |
| | v Dyson | 1-5 | 1st round | BCE International |
| | v Meadowcroft | 4-5 | 1st round | Rothmans Grand Prix |
| | v Black | 5-2 | 1st round | Dubai Classic |
| | v J. McLaughlin | 3-5 | 2nd round | Dubai Classic |
| | v S. Murphy | 1-6 | 1st round | Stormseal UK Open |
| **1990** | v Bond | 2-5 | 1st round | Mercantile Credit Classic |
| | v Brumby | 5-4 | 1st round | Pearl Assurance British Open |
| | v Fowler | 1-5 | 2nd round | Pearl Assurance British Open |
| | v Kelly | 3-5 | 1st round | European Open |
| | v S. Campbell | 2-10 | Qualifying | Embassy World Championship |

## REX WILLIAMS (England)

**Born** 20.7.33. **Turned professional** 1951. **World ranking** 38 (32).

| | | | | |
|---|---|---|---|---|
| **1969** | v Bennett | 38-11 | Quarter-final | World Championship |
| | v Spencer | 18-55 | Semi-final | World Championship |
| **1970** | v G. Owen | 11-31 | Quarter-final | World Championship (Apr) |
| **1972** | v Reardon | 25-23 | Quarter-final | World Championship |
| | v Higgins | 30-31 | Semi-final | World Championship |
| **1973** | v Thorburn | 16-15 | 2nd round | World Championship |
| | v Spencer | 7-16 | Quarter-final | World Championship |
| **1974** | v Pulman | 15-12 | 2nd round | World Championship |
| | v Mans | 15-4 | Quarter-final | World Championship |
| | v Miles | 7-15 | Semi-final | World Championship |
| **1975** | v Higgins | 5-3 | Quarter-final | Benson & Hedges Masters |
| | v Reardon | 4-5 | Semi-final | Benson & Hedges Masters |
| | v Anderson | 15-4 | 2nd round | World Championship |
| | v Higgins | 12-19 | Quarter-final | World Championship |
| **1976** | v Meadowcroft | 7-15 | 1st round | Embassy World Championship |
| **1977** | v Thorburn | 6-13 | 1st round | Embassy World Championship |
| **1978** | v Thorne | 3-9 | Qualifying | Embassy World Championship |
| | v Griffiths | 9-8 | Qualifying | Coral UK Championship |
| | v Miles | 8-9 | 1st round | Coral UK Championship |
| **1979** | v Spencer | 2-6 | Semi-final | Holsten Lager International |
| | v Greaves | 9-2 | Prelim | Embassy World Championship |

| | | | | |
|---|---|---|---|---|
| | v Miles | 5-9 | Qualifying | Embassy World Championship |
| **1980** | v Wych | 7-9 | Qualifying | Embassy World Championship |
| | v Barrie | 9-1 | Qualifying | Coral UK Championship |
| | v Mountjoy | 9-8 | 1st round | Coral UK Championship |
| | v David Taylor | 9-7 | 2nd round | Coral UK Championship |
| | v Reardon | 4-9 | Quarter-final | Coral UK Championship |
| **1981** | v Hood | 9-4 | Qualifying | Embassy World Championship |
| | v Edmonds | 7-9 | Qualifying | Embassy World Championship |
| | v French | 5-0 | Qualifying | Jameson International |
| | v White | 5-1 | 1st round | Jameson International |
| | v F. Davis | 5-0 | 2nd round | Jameson International |
| | v Dennis Taylor | 1-5 | 3rd round | Jameson International |
| | v French | 9-3 | Qualifying | Coral UK Championship |
| | v Roscoe | 9-4 | Qualifying | Coral UK Championship |
| | v Dunning | 9-4 | Qualifying | Coral UK Championship |
| | v Meo | 8-9 | 2nd round | Coral UK Championship |
| **1982** | v Black | 9-2 | Qualifying | Embassy World Championship |
| | v Mountjoy | 3-10 | 1st round | Embassy World Championship |
| | v Medati | 5-3 | Qualifying | Jameson International |
| | v E. McLaughlin | 5-1 | Qualifying | Jameson International |
| | v Griffiths | 2-5 | 1st round | Jameson International |
| | v Ross | 5-0 | 1st round | Professional Players Tournament |
| | v Charlton | 2-5 | 2nd round | Professional Players Tournament |
| | v G. Foulds | 9-7 | Qualifying | Coral UK Championship |
| | v S. Davis | 6-9 | 1st round | Coral UK Championship |
| | v Darrington | 10-0 | Qualifying | Embassy World Championship |
| | v F. Davis | 10-1 | Qualifying | Embassy World Championship |
| | v S. Davis | 4-10 | 1st round | Embassy World Championship |
| **1983** | v French | 5-1 | Qualifying | Jameson International |
| | v Reynolds | 3-5 | Qualifying | Jameson International |
| | v Sheehan | 5-1 | 1st round | Professional Players Tournament |
| | v Knowles | 4-5 | 2nd round | Professional Players Tournament |
| | v V. Harris | 9-6 | Qualifying | Coral UK Championship |
| | v Wilson | 4-9 | 1st round | Coral UK Championship |
| **1984** | v Reardon | 5-4 | Qualifying | Lada Classic |
| | v Meo | 3-5 | 1st round | Lada Classic |
| | v Oliver | 10-8 | Qualifying | Embassy World Championship |
| | v White | 6-10 | 1st round | Embassy World Championship |
| | v Meadowcroft | 5-4 | Qualifying | Jameson International |
| | v White | 3-5 | Qualifying | Jameson International |
| | v Chalmers | 5-0 | 1st round | Rothmans Grand Prix |
| | v Stevens | 3-5 | 2nd round | Rothmans Grand Prix |
| | v Fisher | 9-8 | Qualifying | Coral UK Open |
| | v Werbeniuk | 9-1 | 1st round | Coral UK Open |
| | v Higgins | 7-9 | 2nd round | Coral UK Open |
| **1985** | v Donnelly | 5-3 | Qualifying | Mercantile Credit Classic |
| | v Dennis Taylor | 5-3 | 1st round | Mercantile Credit Classic |
| | v Griffiths | 3-5 | 2nd round | Mercantile Credit Classic |
| | v T. Jones | 9-6 | 1st round | Tolly Cobbold English Championship |
| | v S. Davis | 2-9 | 2nd round | Tolly Cobbold English Championship |
| | v Fowler | 4-6 | 1st round | Dulux British Open |
| | v F. Davis | 10-6 | Qualifying | Embassy World Championship |
| | v Griffiths | 3-10 | 1st round | Embassy World Championship |
| | v King | 3-5 | 3rd round | Goya Matchroom Trophy |
| | v Watterson | 5-2 | 3rd round | Rothmans Grand Prix |
| | v Dennis Taylor | 2-5 | 4th round | Rothmans Grand Prix |
| | v King | 9-5 | 3rd round | Coral UK Open |
| | v P. Francisco | 9-7 | 4th round | Coral UK Open |
| | v Stevens | 7-9 | 5th round | Coral UK Open |
| **1986** | v Watterson | 5-0 | 3rd round | Mercantile Credit Classic |
| | v V. Harris | 5-1 | 4th round | Mercantile Credit Classic |
| | v Knowles | 5-2 | 5th round | Mercantile Credit Classic |
| | v Higgins | 5-2 | Quarter-final | Mercantile Credit Classic |

| | | | | |
|---|---|---|---|---|
| | v White | 7-9 | Semi-final | Mercantile Credit Classic |
| | v Miles | 9-6 | 3rd round | Tolly Cobbold English Championship |
| | v White | 5-9 | 4th round | Tolly Cobbold English Championship |
| | v Drago | 5-1 | 3rd round | Dulux British Open |
| | v Bales | 5-4 | 4th round | Dulux British Open |
| | v Werbeniuk | 3-5 | 5th round | Dulux British Open |
| | v S. Francisco | 4-10 | 1st round | Embassy World Championship |
| | v O'Boye | 5-0 | 3rd round | BCE International |
| | v Duggan | 5-4 | 4th round | BCE International |
| | v S. Davis | 4-5 | 5th round | BCE International |
| | v Bear | 5-2 | 3rd round | Rothmans Grand Prix |
| | v Wildman | 5-1 | 4th round | Rothmans Grand Prix |
| | v Higgins | 5-1 | 5th round | Rothmans Grand Prix |
| | v S. Davis | 5-1 | Quarter-final | Rothmans Grand Prix |
| | v N. Foulds | 9-8 | Semi-final | Rothmans Grand Prix |
| | v White | 6-10 | Final | Rothmans Grand Prix |
| | v Drago | 7-9 | 3rd round | Tennents UK Open |
| **1987** | v Morra | 5-2 | 3rd round | Mercantile Credit Classic |
| | v Charlton | 4-5 | 4th round | Mercantile Credit Classic |
| | v Thorburn | 1-5 | 1st round | Benson & Hedges Masters |
| | v T. Jones | 6-4 | 3rd round | Tolly Ales English Championship |
| | v David Taylor | 6-2 | 4th round | Tolly Ales English Championship |
| | v Johnson | 5-4 | Quarter-final | Tolly Ales English Championship |
| | v Foldvari | 5-4 | 3rd round | Dulux British Open |
| | v James | 5-2 | 4th round | Dulux British Open |
| | v White | 0-5 | 5th round | Dulux British Open |
| | v Macleod | 5-10 | 1st round | Embassy World Championship |
| | v Foldvari | 0-5 | 3rd round | Fidelity International |
| | v Edmonds | 3-5 | 3rd round | Rothmans Grand Prix |
| | v Roe | 7-9 | 3rd round | Tennents UK Open |
| **1988** | v Owers | 3-5 | 3rd round | Mercantile Credit Classic |
| | v Thorburn | 3-5 | 1st round | Benson & Hedges Masters |
| | v D. Hughes | 6-1 | 3rd round | English Championship |
| | v Hallett | 3-6 | 4th round | English Championship |
| | v N. Gilbert | 5-2 | 3rd round | MIM Britannia British Open |
| | v West | 5-0 | 4th round | MIM Britannia British Open |
| | v Spencer | 5-4 | 5th round | MIM Britannia British Open |
| | v Thorburn | 2-5 | Quarter-final | MIM Britannia British Open |
| | v Griffiths | 1-5 | 1st round | Benson & Hedges Irish Masters |
| | v James | 6-10 | 1st round | Embassy World Championship |
| | v Roe | 5-3 | 3rd round | Fidelity International |
| | v Duggan | 5-4 | 4th round | Fidelity International |
| | v West | 4-5 | 5th round | Fidelity International |
| | v Medati | 5-2 | 3rd round | Rothmans Grand Prix |
| | v Gary Wilkinson | 5-2 | 4th round | Rothmans Grand Prix |
| | v Edmonds | 5-3 | 5th round | Rothmans Grand Prix |
| | v Higgins | 4-5 | Quarter-final | Rothmans Grand Prix |
| | v Scott | 2-5 | 3rd round | BCE Canadian Masters |
| | v B. Harris | 9-4 | 3rd round | Tennents UK Open |
| | v Johnson | 7-9 | 4th round | Tennents UK Open |
| **1989** | v Wright | 0-5 | 3rd round | Mercantile Credit Classic |
| | v King | 5-2 | 3rd round | European Open |
| | v White | 2-5 | 4th round | European Open |
| | v Graham | 3-5 | 3rd round | English Championship |
| | v Roe | 2-5 | 3rd round | Anglian British Open |
| | v Roe | 3-10 | Qualifying | Embassy World Championship |
| | v Graham | 1-5 | 3rd round | Hong Kong Open |
| | v Oliver | 4-5 | 3rd round | 555 Asian Open |
| | v M. Smith | 4-5 | 3rd round | BCE International |
| | v Dodd | 3-5 | 3rd round | Rothmans Grand Prix |
| | v Chappel | 2-5 | 3rd round | Dubai Classic |
| | v T. Murphy | 9-6 | 3rd round | Stormseal UK Open |
| | v Dennis Taylor | 2-9 | 4th round | Stormseal UK Open |

| | | | | |
|---|---|---|---|---|
| **1990** | v Sinclair | 5-1 | 3rd round | Mercantile Credit Classic |
| | v S. Davis | 0-5 | 4th round | Mercantile Credit Classic |
| | v Sinclair | 5-3 | 3rd round | Pearl Assurance British Open |
| | v E. Hughes | 2-5 | 4th round | Pearl Assurance British Open |
| | v O'Boye | 5-2 | 3rd round | European Open |
| | v Mountjoy | 0-5 | 4th round | European Open |
| | v Bennett | 9-10 | Qualifying | Embassy World Championship |

## IAN WILLIAMSON (England)

**Born** 1.12.58. **Turned professional** 1982. **World ranking** 103 (92).

| | | | | |
|---|---|---|---|---|
| **1982** | v Donnelly | 5-3 | Qualifying | Jameson International |
| | v Kelly | 1-5 | Qualifying | Jameson International |
| | v Dodd | 1-9 | Qualifying | Coral UK Championship |
| **1983** | v French | 10-8 | Qualifying | Embassy World Championship |
| | v Dodd | 9-10 | Qualifying | Embassy World Championship |
| | v Darrington | 3-5 | Qualifying | Jameson International |
| | v White | 2-5 | 1st round | Professional Players Tournament |
| | v Hargreaves | 9-4 | Qualifying | Coral UK Championship |
| | v Black | 6-9 | Qualifying | Coral UK Championship |
| **1984** | v Houlihan | 10-5 | Qualifying | Embassy World Championship |
| | v Hines | 10-6 | Qualifying | Embassy World Championship |
| | v Miles | 6-10 | Qualifying | Embassy World Championship |
| | v V. Harris | 5-0 | Qualifying | Jameson International |
| | v G. Foulds | 4-5 | Qualifying | Jameson International |
| | v Thornley | 5-2 | Qualifying | Rothmans Grand Prix |
| | v Werbeniuk | 5-2 | 1st round | Rothmans Grand Prix |
| | v Johnson | 5-4 | 2nd round | Rothmans Grand Prix |
| | v Knowles | 2-5 | 3rd round | Rothmans Grand Prix |
| | v P. Francisco | 2-9 | Qualifying | Coral UK Open |
| **1985** | v Kearney | 5-3 | Qualifying | Mercantile Credit Classic |
| | v Fagan | 1-5 | Qualifying | Mercantile Credit Classic |
| | v Bradley | 8-9 | Qualifying | Tolly Cobbold English Championship |
| | v Chappel | 5-6 | Qualifying | Dulux British Open |
| | v Medati | 8-10 | Qualifying | Embassy World Championship |
| | v J. McLaughlin | 5-3 | 2nd round | Goya Matchroom Trophy |
| | v Werbeniuk | 2-5 | 3rd round | Goya Matchroom Trophy |
| | v Gilbert | 4-5 | 2nd round | Rothmans Grand Prix |
| | v Mikkelsen | 3-9 | 2nd round | Coral UK Championship |
| **1986** | v John Rea | 4-5 | 2nd round | Mercantile Credit Classic |
| | v Parkin | 9-4 | 2nd round | Tolly Cobbold English Championship |
| | v White | 1-9 | 3rd round | Tolly Cobbold English Championship |
| | v Cripsey | 5-4 | 2nd round | Dulux British Open |
| | v Knowles | 1-5 | 3rd round | Dulux British Open |
| | v Van Rensberg | 9-10 | Qualifying | Embassy World Championship |
| | v Spencer | 4-5 | 2nd round | BCE International |
| | v Hendry | 1-5 | 2nd round | Rothmans Grand Prix |
| | v Browne | 9-4 | 2nd round | Tennents UK Open |
| | v Martin | 5-9 | 3rd round | Tennents UK Open |
| **1987** | v Edmonds | 5-2 | 2nd round | Mercantile Credit Classic |
| | v Wilson | 4-5 | 3rd round | Mercantile Credit Classic |
| | v Roe | 6-4 | 2nd round | Tolly Ales English Championship |
| | v Hallett | 2-6 | 3rd round | Tolly Ales English Championship |
| | v King | 3-5 | 2nd round | Dulux British Open |
| | v Black | 8-10 | Qualifying | Embassy World Championship |
| | v Everton | 5-0 | 1st round | Fidelity International |
| | v Gauvreau | 5-1 | 2nd round | Fidelity International |
| | v Longworth | 4-5 | 3rd round | Fidelity International |
| | v Clark | 1-5 | 1st round | Rothmans Grand Prix |
| | v Kelly | 9-5 | 1st round | Tennents UK Open |
| | v Duggan | 7-9 | 2nd round | Tennents UK Open |

| | | | | |
|---|---|---|---|---|
| **1988** | v D. Hughes | 3-5 | 1st round | Mercantile Credit Classic |
| | v Dunning | 6-5 | 1st round | English Championship |
| | v Duggan | 2-6 | 2nd round | English Championship |
| | v Meakin | 5-1 | 1st round | MIM Britannia British Open |
| | v Bradley | 5-3 | 2nd round | MIM Britannia British Open |
| | v Hallett | 0-5 | 3rd round | MIM Britannia British Open |
| | v Bradley | 9-10 | Qualifying | Embassy World Championship |
| | v Darrington | 5-1 | 1st round | Fidelity International |
| | v Wright | 1-5 | 2nd round | Fidelity International |
| | v Everton | 5-0 | 1st round | Rothmans Grand Prix |
| | v Wych | 5-4 | 2nd round | Rothmans Grand Prix |
| | v Hendry | 2-5 | 3rd round | Rothmans Grand Prix |
| | v Chalmers | 5-2 | 1st round | BCE Canadian Masters |
| | v Gauvreau | 1-5 | 2nd round | BCE Canadian Masters |
| | v Everton | 9-1 | 1st round | Tennents UK Open |
| | v O'Boye | 4-9 | 2nd round | Tennents UK Open |
| **1989** | v Jenkins | 5-2 | 1st round | Mercantile Credit Classic |
| | v Browne | 3-5 | 2nd round | Mercantile Credit Classic |
| | v D. Hughes | 5-1 | 1st round | European Open |
| | v Reardon | 3-5 | 2nd round | European Open |
| | v Owers | 5-4 | 2nd round | English Championship |
| | v Knowles | 2-5 | 3rd round | English Championship |
| | v Graham | 4-5 | 1st round | Anglian British Open |
| | v Grech | 7-10 | Qualifying | Embassy World Championship |
| | v Darrington | 4-5 | 1st round | Hong Kong Open |
| | v Kelly | 5-4 | 1st round | 555 Asian Open |
| | v D. Gilbert | 1-5 | 2nd round | 555 Asian Open |
| | v Sheehan | 5-1 | 1st round | BCE International |
| | v Cripsey | 5-3 | 2nd round | BCE International |
| | v Chaperon | 4-5 | 3rd round | BCE International |
| | v D. Campbell | 0-5 | 1st round | Rothmans Grand Prix |
| | v D. Hughes | 5-1 | 1st round | Dubai Classic |
| | v Dodd | 0-5 | 2nd round | Dubai Classic |
| | v D. Hughes | 6-0 | 1st round | Stormseal UK Open |
| | v O'Boye | 4-6 | 2nd round | Stormseal UK Open |
| **1990** | v S. Campbell | 5-2 | 1st round | Mercantile Credit Classic |
| | v T. Murphy | 1-5 | 2nd round | Mercantile Credit Classic |
| | v G. Foulds | 5-0 | 1st round | Pearl Assurance British Open |
| | v Duggan | 3-5 | 2nd round | Pearl Assurance British Open |
| | v Dyson | 3-5 | 1st round | European Open |
| | v B. Morgan | 4-10 | Qualifying | Embassy World Championship |

## CLIFF WILSON (Wales)

**Born** 10.5.34. **Turned professional** 1979. **World ranking** 29 (18).

| | | | | |
|---|---|---|---|---|
| **1979** | v Pulman | 9-7 | 2nd round | Coral UK Championship |
| | v Griffiths | 4-9 | 3rd round | Coral UK Championship |
| | v Reardon | 3-9 | 1st round | Woodpecker Welsh Championship |
| **1980** | v Jonik | 9-6 | Qualifying | Embassy World Championship |
| | v Mountjoy | 6-10 | 1st round | Embassy World Championship |
| | v Wildman | 8-9 | Qualifying | Coral UK Championship |
| **1981** | v Andrewartha | 6-5 | Prelim | Woodpecker Welsh Championship |
| | v Mountjoy | 9-6 | Semi-final | Woodpecker Welsh Championship |
| | v Reardon | 6-9 | Final | Woodpecker Welsh Championship |
| | v Andrewartha | 9-4 | Qualifying | Embassy World Championship |
| | v Sinclair | 9-4 | Qualifying | Embassy World Championship |
| | v David Taylor | 6-10 | 1st round | Embassy World Championship |
| | v Meadowcroft | 4-5 | 1st round | Jameson International |
| | v Johnson | 5-9 | Qualifying | Coral UK Championship |
| **1982** | v M. Owen | 6-0 | 1st round | Welsh Championship |
| | v Griffiths | 6-9 | Semi-final | Welsh Championship |

| | | | | |
|---|---|---|---|---|
| | v Medati | 9-5 | Qualifying | Embassy World Championship |
| | v Charlton | 5-10 | 1st round | Embassy World Championship |
| | v Johnson | 5-4 | Qualifying | Jameson International |
| | v Mountjoy | 5-4 | 1st round | Jameson International |
| | v White | 5-2 | 2nd round | Jameson International |
| | v Knowles | 4-5 | Quarter-final | Jameson International |
| | v Morra | 5-2 | 1st round | Professional Players Tournament |
| | v Knowles | 5-4 | 2nd round | Professional Players Tournament |
| | v Reynolds | 1-5 | 3rd round | Professional Players Tournament |
| | v E. McLaughlin | 9-6 | Qualifying | Coral UK Championship |
| | v Thorne | 9-7 | 1st round | Coral UK Championship |
| | v White | 5-9 | 2nd round | Coral UK Championship |
| **1983** | v Thorburn | 3-5 | 1st round | Lada Classic |
| | v Roscoe | 6-4 | Quarter-final | Woodpecker Welsh Championship |
| | v Mountjoy | 3-9 | Semi-final | Woodpecker Welsh Championship |
| | v Everton | 10-1 | Qualifying | Embassy World Championship |
| | v Johnson | 10-8 | Qualifying | Embassy World Championship |
| | v Mountjoy | 2-10 | 1st round | Embassy World Championship |
| | v Donnelly | 1-5 | Qualifying | Jameson International |
| | v Bennett | 5-1 | 1st round | Professional Players Tournament |
| | v Virgo | 5-2 | 2nd round | Professional Players Tournament |
| | v Thorburn | 3-5 | 3rd round | Professional Players Tournament |
| | v Williams | 9-4 | 1st round | Coral UK Championship |
| | v Reardon | 4-9 | 2nd round | Coral UK Championship |
| **1984** | v Charlton | 0-5 | Qualifying | Lada Classic |
| | v Roscoe | 6-2 | 1st round | Strongbow Welsh Championship |
| | v Reardon | 9-4 | Semi-final | Strongbow Welsh Championship |
| | v Mountjoy | 3-9 | Final | Strongbow Welsh Championship |
| | v Mifsud | 8-10 | Qualifying | Embassy World Championship |
| | v Dodd | 1-5 | Qualifying | Jameson International |
| | v Donnelly | 5-2 | 1st round | Rothmans Grand Prix |
| | v Reardon | 4-5 | 2nd round | Rothmans Grand Prix |
| | v Dodd | 9-8 | Qualifying | Coral UK Open |
| | v Griffiths | 9-6 | 1st round | Coral UK Open |
| | v Thorburn | 3-9 | 2nd round | Coral UK Open |
| **1985** | v Fowler | 5-4 | Qualifying | Mercantile Credit Classic |
| | v Mountjoy | 5-4 | 1st round | Mercantile Credit Classic |
| | v Johnson | 0-5 | 2nd round | Mercantile Credit Classic |
| | v Longworth | 3-6 | 1st round | Dulux British Open |
| | v Fagan | 9-10 | Qualifying | Embassy World Championship |
| | v Roscoe | 6-3 | Quarter-final | BCE Welsh Championship |
| | v Mountjoy | 2-9 | Semi-final | BCE Welsh Championship |
| | v Roscoe | 5-1 | 3rd round | Goya Matchroom Trophy |
| | v Chappel | 5-0 | 4th round | Goya Matchroom Trophy |
| | v Johnson | 1-5 | 5th round | Goya Matchroom Trophy |
| | v Bales | 5-1 | 3rd round | Rothmans Grand Prix |
| | v Scott | 5-3 | 4th round | Rothmans Grand Prix |
| | v Drago | 5-2 | 5th round | Rothmans Grand Prix |
| | v Dennis Taylor | 2-5 | Quarter-final | Rothmans Grand Prix |
| | v Cripsey | 7-9 | 3rd round | Coral UK Open |
| **1986** | v Browne | 3-5 | 3rd round | Mercantile Credit Classic |
| | v Newbury | 6-4 | Quarter-final | Zetters Welsh Championship |
| | v Griffiths | 1-9 | Semi-final | Zetters Welsh Championship |
| | v Chaperon | 5-3 | 3rd round | Dulux British Open |
| | v Stevens | 0-5 | 4th round | Dulux British Open |
| | v Charlton | 6-10 | 1st round | Embassy World Championship |
| | v J. McLaughlin | 5-2 | 3rd round | BCE International |
| | v Bales | 5-1 | 4th round | BCE International |
| | v Knowles | 5-4 | 5th round | BCE International |
| | v Thorburn | 1-5 | Quarter-final | BCE International |
| | v Anderson | 5-4 | 3rd round | Rothmans Grand Prix |
| | v N. Foulds | 0-5 | 4th round | Rothmans Grand Prix |
| | v Spencer | 5-9 | 3rd round | Tennents UK Open |

| | | | | |
|---|---|---|---|---|
| **1987** | v Williamson | 5-4 | 3rd round | Mercantile Credit Classic |
| | v Dodd | 5-4 | 4th round | Mercantile Credit Classic |
| | v W. Jones | 5-3 | 5th round | Mercantile Credit Classic |
| | v Reynolds | 1-5 | Quarter-final | Mercantile Credit Classic |
| | v Newbury | 2-6 | Quarter-final | Matchroom Welsh Championship |
| | v G. Foulds | 5-3 | 3rd round | Dulux British Open |
| | v S. Francisco | 5-4 | 4th round | Dulux British Open |
| | v Virgo | 2-5 | 5th round | Dulux British Open |
| | v Wright | 4-10 | Qualifying | Embassy World Championship |
| | v Sinclair | 5-1 | 3rd round | Fidelity International |
| | v D. Gilbert | 1-5 | 4th round | Fidelity International |
| | v Glen Wilkinson | 5-4 | 3rd round | Rothmans Grand Prix |
| | v Virgo | 5-3 | 4th round | Rothmans Grand Prix |
| | v Dennis Taylor | 2-5 | 5th round | Rothmans Grand Prix |
| | v W. Jones | 9-6 | 3rd round | Tennents UK Open |
| | v S. Francisco | 1-9 | 4th round | Tennents UK Open |
| **1988** | v D. Gilbert | 5-3 | 3rd round | Mercantile Credit Classic |
| | v Griffiths | 2-5 | 4th round | Mercantile Credit Classic |
| | v Newbury | 6-3 | Quarter-final | Welsh Championship |
| | v Griffiths | 7-9 | Semi-final | Welsh Championship |
| | v Roscoe | 5-2 | 3rd round | MIM Britannia British Open |
| | v Thorne | 3-5 | 4th round | MIM Britannia British Open |
| | v Oliver | 10-6 | Qualifying | Embassy World Championship |
| | v Johnson | 7-10 | 1st round | Embassy World Championship |
| | v Duggan | 2-5 | 3rd round | Fidelity International |
| | v Chappel | 5-2 | 3rd round | Rothmans Grand Prix |
| | v Drago | 5-4 | 4th round | Rothmans Grand Prix |
| | v S. Davis | 1-5 | 5th round | Rothmans Grand Prix |
| | v Gary Wilkinson | 5-2 | 3rd round | BCE Canadian Masters |
| | v Reynolds | 5-4 | 4th round | BCE Canadian Masters |
| | v Hendry | 1-5 | 5th round | BCE Canadian Masters |
| | v Edmonds | 9-1 | 3rd round | Tennents UK Open |
| | v Reynolds | 3-9 | 4th round | Tennents UK Open |
| **1989** | v S. Campbell | 5-3 | 3rd round | Mercantile Credit Classic |
| | v David Taylor | 3-5 | 4th round | Mercantile Credit Classic |
| | v S. Davis | 2-5 | 1st round | Benson and Hedges Masters |
| | v T. Jones | 5-3 | 3rd round | European Open |
| | v Robidoux | 0-5 | 4th round | European Open |
| | v M. Bennett | 1-6 | Quarter-final | Senator Welsh Championship |
| | v John Rea | 5-2 | 3rd round | Anglian British Open |
| | v Chappel | 5-3 | 4th round | Anglian British Open |
| | v Reynolds | 0-5 | 5th round | Anglian British Open |
| | v Duggan | 1-10 | 1st round | Embassy World Championship |
| | v Duggan | 5-4 | 3rd round | Hong Kong Open |
| | v Mountjoy | *scr* | 4th round | Hong Kong Open |
| | v Gollan | 4-5 | 3rd round | 555 Asian Open |
| | v Wright | 5-2 | 3rd round | BCE International |
| | v Hallett | 5-4 | 4th round | BCE International |
| | v Marshall | 5-3 | 5th round | BCE International |
| | v Hendry | 2-5 | Quarter-final | BCE International |
| | v Rowswell | 4-5 | 3rd round | Rothmans Grand Prix |
| | v B. Morgan | 5-3 | 3rd round | Dubai Classic |
| | v Drago | 0-5 | 4th round | Dubai Classic |
| | v Browne | 9-7 | 3rd round | Stormseal UK Open |
| | v S. Davis | 3-9 | 4th round | Stormseal UK Open |
| **1990** | v Gary Wilkinson | 2-5 | 3rd round | Mercantile Credit Classic |
| | v Chappel | 4-6 | Quarter-final | Senator Welsh Championship |
| | v Dodd | 3-5 | 3rd round | Pearl Assurance British Open |
| | v J. Campbell | 0-5 | 3rd round | European Open |
| | v T. Wilson | 10-6 | Qualifying | Embassy World Championship |
| | v Thorburn | 6-10 | 1st round | Embassy World Championship |

## TONY WILSON (Isle of Man)

**Born** 12.2.64. **Turned professional** 1988. **World ranking** 71 (71).

| | | | | |
|---|---|---|---|---|
| **1988** | v M. Gibson | 5-1 | 1st round | Fidelity International |
| | v Browne | 5-3 | 2nd round | Fidelity International |
| | v David Taylor | 1-5 | 3rd round | Fidelity International |
| | v Scott | 5-3 | 1st round | Rothmans Grand Prix |
| | v Chappel | 1-5 | 2nd round | Rothmans Grand Prix |
| | v Grace | 5-2 | 1st round | BCE Canadian Masters |
| | v Clark | 3-5 | 2nd round | BCE Canadian Masters |
| | v Bradley | 7-9 | 1st round | Tennents UK Open |
| **1989** | v Foldvari | 4-5 | 1st round | Mercantile Credit Classic |
| | v M. Gibson | 5-3 | 1st round | European Open |
| | v Gauvreau | 5-3 | 2nd round | European Open |
| | v Spencer | *wo* | 3rd round | European Open |
| | v Fowler | 2-5 | 4th round | European Open |
| | v F. Davis | 5-1 | 1st round | Anglian British Open |
| | v N. Gilbert | 2-5 | 2nd round | Anglian British Open |
| | v M. Francisco | 10-5 | Qualifying | Embassy World Championship |
| | v Scott | 10-4 | Qualifying | Embassy World Championship |
| | v O'Boye | 8-10 | Qualifying | Embassy World Championship |
| | v Van Rensberg | 4-5 | 1st round | Hong Kong Open |
| | v Rigitano | 5-4 | 1st round | 555 Asian Open |
| | v D. Morgan | 1-5 | 2nd round | 555 Asian Open |
| | v Gollan | 2-5 | 1st round | BCE International |
| | v Kearney | 2-5 | 1st round | Rothmans Grand Prix |
| | v Lawlor | 2-5 | 2nd round | Dubai Classic |
| | v Fowler | 3-6 | 2nd round | Stormseal UK Open |
| **1990** | v S. Murphy | 1-5 | 1st round | Mercantile Credit Classic |
| | v Van Rensberg | 5-1 | 1st round | Pearl Assurance British Open |
| | v McLaughlin | 5-3 | 2nd round | Pearl Assurance British Open |
| | v S. Francisco | 5-4 | 3rd round | Pearl Assurance British Open |
| | v James | 0-5 | 4th round | Pearl Assurance British Open |
| | v Grace | 3-5 | 1st round | European Open |
| | v Meakin | 10-8 | Qualifying | Embassy World Championship |
| | v Cripsey | 10-6 | Qualifying | Embassy World Championship |
| | v Houlihan | 10-6 | Qualifying | Embassy World Championship |
| | v C. Wilson | 6-10 | Qualifying | Embassy World Championship |

## JON WRIGHT (England)

**Born** 10.8.62. **Turned professional** 1986. **World ranking** 85 (67).

| | | | | |
|---|---|---|---|---|
| **1986** | v Watterson | 5-1 | 1st round | BCE International |
| | v Black | 1-5 | 2nd round | BCE International |
| | v Fisher | 5-1 | 1st round | Rothmans Grand Prix |
| | v Bradley | 5-0 | 2nd round | Rothmans Grand Prix |
| | v Dennis Taylor | 3-5 | 3rd round | Rothmans Grand Prix |
| | v Smith | 9-7 | 1st round | Tennents UK Open |
| | v Fagan | 9-0 | 2nd round | Tennents UK Open |
| | v Johnson | 1-9 | 3rd round | Tennents UK Open |
| **1987** | v D. Hughes | 5-2 | 1st round | Mercantile Credit Classic |
| | v Chappel | 5-4 | 2nd round | Mercantile Credit Classic |
| | v E. Hughes | 5-4 | 3rd round | Mercantile Credit Classic |
| | v Hendry | 1-5 | 4th round | Mercantile Credit Classic |
| | v Chalmers | 6-5 | 1st round | Tolly Ales English Championship |
| | v Spencer | 1-6 | 2nd round | Tolly Ales English Championship |
| | v Sheehan | 2-5 | 1st round | Dulux British Open |
| | v Houlihan | 10-4 | Qualifying | Embassy World Championship |
| | v Browne | 10-6 | Qualifying | Embassy World Championship |
| | v Wildman | 10-0 | Qualifying | Embassy World Championship |

| | | | | |
|---|---|---|---|---|
| | v Wilson | 10-4 | Qualifying | Embassy World Championship |
| | v Higgins | 6-10 | 1st round | Embassy World Championship |
| | v Kelly | 5-2 | 2nd round | Fidelity International |
| | v Meo | 2-5 | 3rd round | Fidelity International |
| | v Rigitano | 5-0 | 2nd round | Rothmans Grand Prix |
| | v White | 4-5 | 3rd round | Rothmans Grand Prix |
| | v Lawlor | 7-9 | 2nd round | Tennents UK Open |
| **1988** | v Sinclair | 5-3 | 2nd round | Mercantile Credit Classic |
| | v Knowles | 1-5 | 3rd round | Mercantile Credit Classic |
| | v Fisher | 6-2 | 2nd round | English Championship |
| | v Knowles | 2-6 | 3rd round | English Championship |
| | v D. Gilbert | 2-5 | 2nd round | MIM Britannia British Open |
| | v Chambers | 10-2 | Qualifying | Embassy World Championship |
| | v Owers | 10-8 | Qualifying | Embassy World Championship |
| | v Hendry | 4-10 | Qualifying | Embassy World Championship |
| | v Williamson | 5-1 | 2nd round | Fidelity International |
| | v James | 3-5 | 3rd round | Fidelity International |
| | v Foldvari | 4-5 | 2nd round | Rothmans Grand Prix |
| | v Graham | 2-5 | 2nd round | BCE Canadian Masters |
| | v Rowing | 7-9 | 2nd round | Tennents UK Open |
| **1989** | v G. Foulds | 5-4 | 2nd round | Mercantile Credit Classic |
| | v Williams | 5-0 | 3rd round | Mercantile Credit Classic |
| | v S. Francisco | 2-5 | 4th round | Mercantile Credit Classic |
| | v Johnston-Allen | 4-5 | 2nd round | European Open |
| | v Rowswell | 2-5 | 2nd round | English Championship |
| | v Grace | 5-1 | 2nd round | Anglian British Open |
| | v Parrott | 1-5 | 3rd round | Anglian British Open |
| | v M. Smith | 7-10 | Qualifying | Embassy World Championship |
| | v Thornley | 5-1 | 1st round | Hong Kong Open |
| | v Fisher | 5-0 | 2nd round | Hong Kong Open |
| | v Hendry | 4-5 | 3rd round | Hong Kong Open |
| | v Jenkins | 5-3 | 1st round | 555 Asian Open |
| | v Browne | 3-5 | 2nd round | 555 Asian Open |
| | v Thornley | 5-3 | 1st round | BCE International |
| | v D. Gilbert | 5-1 | 2nd round | BCE International |
| | v C. Wilson | 2-5 | 3rd round | BCE International |
| | v J. Smith | 2-5 | 1st round | Rothmans Grand Prix |
| | v D. Campbell | 5-1 | 2nd round | Dubai Classic |
| | v James | 2-5 | 3rd round | Dubai Classic |
| | v G. Foulds | 6-1 | 1st round | Stormseal UK Open |
| | v David Taylor | 2-6 | 2nd round | Stormseal UK Open |
| **1990** | v G. Foulds | 5-4 | 1st round | Mercantile Credit Classic |
| | v Martin | 5-1 | 2nd round | Mercantile Credit Classic |
| | v Virgo | 2-5 | 3rd round | Mercantile Credit Classic |
| | v Watchorn | 5-1 | 1st round | Pearl Assurance British Open |
| | v Martin | 5-2 | 2nd round | Pearl Assurance British Open |
| | v Newbury | 3-5 | 3rd round | Pearl Assurance British Open |
| | v M. Gibson | 5-1 | 1st round | European Open |
| | v Edmonds | 5-4 | 2nd round | European Open |
| | v Parrott | 1-5 | 3rd round | European Open |
| | v D. Campbell | 6-10 | Qualifying | Embassy World Championship |

## JIM WYCH (Canada)

**Born** 11.1.55. **Turned professional** 1979. **World ranking** 53 (37).

| | | | | |
|---|---|---|---|---|
| **1980** | v John Bear | 9-5 | Qualifying | Embassy World Championship |
| | v Williams | 9-7 | Qualifying | Embassy World Championship |
| | v Pulman | 10-5 | 1st round | Embassy World Championship |
| | v Dennis Taylor | 13-10 | 2nd round | Embassy World Championship |
| | v Thorburn | 6-13 | Quarter-final | Embassy World Championship |
| **1981** | v Knowles | 3-9 | Qualifying | Embassy World Championship |

| | | | | |
|---|---|---|---|---|
| | v Johnson | 2-5 | 1st round | Jameson International |
| **1982** | v Higgins | 3-5 | 1st round | Benson & Hedges Irish Masters |
| | v John Bear | 4-9 | Qualifying | Embassy World Championship |
| | v Bennett | 5-0 | Qualifying | Jameson International |
| | v Werbeniuk | 3-5 | 1st round | Jameson International |
| | v Kelly | 5-0 | 1st round | Professional Players Tournament |
| | v White | 0-5 | 2nd round | Professional Players Tournament |
| **1983** | v Jonik | 5-9 | Quarter-final | Canadian Championship |
| **1984** | v Ganim | 10-1 | Qualifying | Embassy World Championship |
| | v Scott | 10-6 | Qualifying | Embassy World Championship |
| | v Fagan | 10-3 | Qualifying | Embassy World Championship |
| | v Reardon | 7-10 | 1st round | Embassy World Championship |
| **1985** | v Bradley | 10-7 | Qualifying | Embassy World Championship |
| | v Virgo | 4-10 | Qualifying | Embassy World Championship |
| | v Sanderson | 5-2 | 1st round | Canadian Championship |
| | v John Bear | 6-3 | Quarter-final | Canadian Championship |
| | v Thorburn | 5-6 | Semi-final | Canadian Championship |
| | v Rempe | 5-1 | 2nd round | Goya Matchroom Trophy |
| | v Mountjoy | 1-5 | 3rd round | Goya Matchroom Trophy |
| | v V. Harris | 3-5 | 2nd round | Rothmans Grand Prix |
| | v Duggan | 9-5 | 2nd round | Coral UK Open |
| | v S. Francisco | 8-9 | 3rd round | Coral UK Open |
| **1986** | v Demarco | 5-0 | 2nd round | Mercantile Credit Classic |
| | v E. Hughes | 2-5 | 3rd round | Mercantile Credit Classic |
| | v Van Rensberg | 5-0 | 2nd round | Dulux British Open |
| | v Reynolds | 5-3 | 3rd round | Dulux British Open |
| | v Knowles | 5-4 | 4th round | Dulux British Open |
| | v Parrott | 5-4 | 5th round | Dulux British Open |
| | v S. Davis | 2-5 | Quarter-final | Dulux British Open |
| | v Chappel | 10-6 | Qualifying | Embassy World Championship |
| | v Duggan | 10-5 | Qualifying | Embassy World Championship |
| | v Hallett | 7-10 | Qualifying | Embassy World Championship |
| | v Mikkelsen | 6-3 | 2nd round | Canadian Championship |
| | v Stevens | 6-2 | Semi-final | Canadian Championship |
| | v Thorburn | 2-6 | Final | Canadian Championship |
| | v Bradley | 5-2 | 3rd round | BCE International |
| | v Thorburn | 3-5 | 4th round | BCE International |
| | v John Rea | 5-2 | 3rd round | Rothmans Grand Prix |
| | v Mountjoy | 1-5 | 4th round | Rothmans Grand Prix |
| | v B. Harris | 9-6 | 3rd round | Tennents UK Open |
| | v N. Foulds | 3-9 | 4th round | Tennents UK Open |
| **1987** | v B. Harris | 3-5 | 3rd round | Mercantile Credit Classic |
| | v Murphy | 1-5 | 3rd round | Dulux British Open |
| | v Bradley | 10-7 | Qualifying | Embassy World Championship |
| | v Griffiths | 4-10 | 1st round | Embassy World Championship |
| | v Bear | 4-6 | Quarter-final | Canadian Championship |
| | v Jenkins | 5-4 | 2nd round | Fidelity International |
| | v Johnson | 5-4 | 3rd round | Fidelity International |
| | v E. Hughes | 4-5 | 4th round | Fidelity International |
| | v Marshall | 5-2 | 2nd round | Rothmans Grand Prix |
| | v Macleod | 5-4 | 3rd round | Rothmans Grand Prix |
| | v S. Davis | 1-5 | 4th round | Rothmans Grand Prix |
| | v Fisher | 9-6 | 2nd round | Tennents UK Open |
| | v Hendry | 9-7 | 3rd round | Tennents UK Open |
| | v Parrott | 6-9 | 4th round | Tennents UK Open |
| **1988** | v Clark | 2-5 | 2nd round | Mercantile Credit Classic |
| | v Thornley | 5-1 | 2nd round | MIM Britannia British Open |
| | v Thorne | 1-5 | 3rd round | MIM Britannia British Open |
| | v J. Smith | 10-3 | Qualifying | Embassy World Championship |
| | v M. Bennett | 5-10 | Qualifying | Embassy World Championship |
| | v Thornley | 6-5 | 1st round | BCE Canadian Championship |
| | v Morra | 6-5 | Quarter-final | BCE Canadian Championship |
| | v Thorburn | 7-5 | Semi-final | BCE Canadian Championship |

| | | | | |
|---|---|---|---|---|
| | v Robidoux | 4-8 | Final | BCE Canadian Championship |
| | v V. Harris | 5-3 | 2nd round | Fidelity International |
| | v Griffiths | 5-0 | 3rd round | Fidelity International |
| | v O'Kane | 5-4 | 4th round | Fidelity International |
| | v Dennis Taylor | 2-5 | 5th round | Fidelity International |
| | v Williamson | 4-5 | 2nd round | Rothmans Grand Prix |
| | v Foldvari | 5-2 | 2nd round | BCE Canadian Masters |
| | v Charlton | 4-5 | 3rd round | BCE Canadian Masters |
| | v Oliver | 9-6 | 2nd round | Tennents UK Open |
| | v Knowles | 4-9 | 3rd round | Tennents UK Open |
| **1989** | v Glen Wilkinson | 3-5 | 2nd round | Mercantile Credit Classic |
| | v G. Foulds | 5-0 | 2nd round | European Open |
| | v S. Francisco | 5-1 | 3rd round | European Open |
| | v Johnston-Allen | 5-4 | 4th round | European Open |
| | v Fowler | 5-4 | 5th round | European Open |
| | v Hallett | 3-5 | Quarter-final | European Open |
| | v A. Harris | 5-4 | 2nd round | Anglian British Open |
| | v Knowles | 2-5 | 3rd round | Anglian British Open |
| | v Johnston-Allen | 10-3 | Qualifying | Embassy World Championship |
| | v W. Jones | 9-10 | Qualifying | Embassy World Championship |
| | v Dunning | 5-1 | 2nd round | Hong Kong Open |
| | v Virgo | 4-5 | 3rd round | Hong Kong Open |
| | v M. Smith | 5-3 | 2nd round | 555 Asian Open |
| | v N. Foulds | 2-5 | 3rd round | 555 Asian Open |
| | v S. Murphy | 5-4 | 2nd round | BCE International |
| | v West | *scr* | 3rd round | BCE International |
| | v Price | 5-3 | 2nd round | Rothmans Grand Prix |
| | v Mountjoy | *scr* | 3rd round | Rothmans Grand Prix |
| | v Terry | 5-2 | 2nd round | Dubai Classic |
| | v Hendry | *scr* | 3rd round | Dubai Classic |
| | v Wattana | 1-6 | 2nd round | Stormseal UK Open |
| **1990** | v Foldvari | 5-2 | 2nd round | Mercantile Credit Classic |
| | v Reynolds | *scr* | 3rd round | Mercantile Credit Classic |
| | v M. Smith | 5-2 | 2nd round | Pearl Assurance British Open |
| | v Johnson | *scr* | 3rd round | Pearl Assurance British Open |

*At the end of the 1989–90 season, the following players became non-tournament playing members of the WPBSA:* Jim Bear (Canada), Mike Darrington (England), Dessie Sheehan (Republic of Ireland), Dennis Hughes (England), Mike Watterson (England), Paul Thornley (Canada), Mark Wildman (England), Jim Meadowcroft (England), Fred Davis (England), Geoff Foulds (England) and Jack Rea (Northern Ireland).

Other non-tournament playing members are: Billy Kelly (Republic of Ireland), Greg Jenkins (Australia), Bernie Mikkelsen (Canada), Ian Black (Scotland), Clive Everton (Wales), Derek Mienie (South Africa), Patsy Fagan (Republic of Ireland), Pascal Burke (Republic of Ireland), Jim Rempe (USA), Ian Anderson (Australia), Bernard Bennett (England), Derek Heaton (England), Joe Caggianello (Canada), Lou Condo (Australia), Bert Demarco (Scotland), Mannie Francisco (South Africa), Sam Frangie (Australia), James Giannaros (Australia), David Greaves (England), John Hargreaves (England),

Mike Hines (South Africa), Frank Jonik (Canada), Eddie McLaughlin (Scotland), Steve Mizerak (USA), Paddy Morgan (Australia), Maurice Parkin (England), Vladimir Potasznyk (Australia), Gerry Watson (Canada) and Bill Werbeniuk* (Canada).
**Werbeniuk was expelled from the association on 31 March 1989 for failing to pay a fine, but during the 1989–90 season was reinstated as a non-tournament member.*

Dave Chalmers (England) resigned from the WPBSA at the end of the 1989–90 season.

The ten amateurs who qualified for professional status for the 1990–91 season were: Ken Doherty (Republic of Ireland), Jon Birch (England), Gary Natale (Canada), Franky Chan (Hong Kong), Jason Whittaker (England), Alan McManus (Scotland), Rod Lawler (England), Jason Ferguson (England), Chris Cookson (England) and Jason Prince (Northern Ireland). Joe Grech (Malta), who started the 1989–90 season with non-tournament status, earned enough points during it to qualify for full tournament status.

## SNOOKER GREATS

**JOE DAVIS O.B.E.** (1901–1978)
Although only one of the 'Big Four' at billiards, Joe Davis was undoubtedly the number one at snooker. With his friend Bill Camkin, a Birmingham billiard trader, he promoted and won the first World Professional Snooker Championship in 1927. He went on to win the title every year until 1940. The Championship was suspended until 1946, at which point Davis beat Horace Lindrum 78–67 to take the title for the 15th time.

Davis then retired from Championship play. He continued to play in other tournaments and in the public's mind he was still the champion, whoever had won the World Championship in his absence.

His expertise at the three-ball game carried him to four World Professional Billiards titles but his name will always be synonymous with snooker. It was he who developed the modern break-making methods, using the black as the key colour, and it was he who brought the sport to the public's attention.

**WALTER DONALDSON** (1907–1973)
Consistent and steady, Walter Donaldson reached eight consecutive World Championship finals between 1948 and 1954. In 1947 and 1950 he beat Fred Davis to take the title.

As professional snooker's appeal dwindled in the mid-1950s, a disillusioned Donaldson turned his billiard room into a cowshed and broke up the slates of his table for crazy paving.

**JOHN PULMAN** (born 1926)
After winning the English Amateur Championship in 1946, John Pulman turned professional but was at his peak when the professional game was going through a period in the doldrums. He was never able to capitalise fully on his natural talent.

He won the world title in 1957 and then successfully withstood a series of challengers. When the influx of new professionals led to the Championship being restored to a tournament format, he once reached the final, losing to Ray Reardon.

An accident led to his retirement from playing in 1982 but he is still involved on the circuit as a member of ITV's commentary team.

# THE CIRCUIT

## LION BROWN NEW ZEALAND MASTERS

**First staged** 1988. **Sponsors** Lion Brown. **Venue** Wellington. **Initial prize-money** £40,000. **Prize-money last season** £43,270. **TV** TVNZ.

**1988**
**First round:** J. Johnson beat D. Reynolds 5-4; S. Hendry beat D. Morgan 5-2; M. Hallett beat D. O'Kane 5-1; A. Knowles beat W. King 5-4
**Semi-finals:** Hendry beat Johnson 5-2; Hallett beat Knowles 5-3
**Final:** Hendry beat Hallett 6-1
*Play-off for third place: Johnson beat Knowles 5-4*

**1989**
**First round:** A. Knowles beat J. Parrott 6-3; J. Johnson beat M. Hallett 6-5; W. Thorne beat Dennis Taylor 6-5; S. Hendry beat D. O'Kane 6-3
**Semi-finals:** Johnson beat Knowles 6-3; Thorne beat Hendry 6-5
**Final:** Thorne beat Johnson 7-4

## HONG KONG OPEN

**First staged** 1989. **Sponsors**—. **Venue** Hong Kong Exhibition and Convention Centre. **Initial prize-money** £200,000. **Prize-money last season** £200,000. **TV** Hong Kong and China.

**1989**
**First round:** M. Gibson beat R. Marshall 5-1; P. Gibson beat R. Grace 5-3; J. Smith beat B. Oliver 5-3; B. Pinches beat N. Terry 5-1; R. Foldvari beat G. Foulds 5-1; M. Darrington beat I. Williamson 5-4; S. Meakin beat J. Donnelly 5-4; B. Gollan beat Eddie Sinclair 5-3; N. Dyson beat F. Davis 5-1; M. Price beat F. Ellis 5-2; M. Rowing beat A. Harris 5-4; J. Wattana beat K. Owers 5-2; P. Houlihan beat A. Kearney 5-1; D. Sheehan beat M. Smith 5-4; G. Rigitano beat C. Edwards 5-3; W. Kelly beat M. Morra 5-2; M. Wildman *wo* T. Whitthread *scr*; J. Meadowcroft beat M. Bradley 5-2; S. Campbell beat M. Watterson 5-0; R. Rowswell beat A. Cairns 5-3; D. Hughes beat E. Lawlor 5-1; N. Bond beat Glen Wilkinson 5-1; I. Brumby beat G. Miles 5-3; G. Jenkins beat P. Medati 5-2; V. Harris beat P. Watchorn 5-4; J. Fitzmaurice *wo* Jim Bear *scr*; J. Dunning beat S. Murphy 5-3; M. Gauvreau beat Jack Rea 5-1; D. Campbell beat B. Harris 5-2; B. Morgan beat G. Scott 5-1; J. Wright beat P. Thornley 5-1; J. Van Rensberg beat T. Wilson 5-4
**Second round:** M. Gibson beat P. Browne 5-3; R. Edmonds beat P. Gibson 5-2; Gary Wilkinson beat J. Smith 5-1; Pinches beat M. Bennett 5-2; Foldvari beat J. O'Boye 5-0; M. Macleod beat Darrington 5-0; C. Roscoe beat Meakin 5-1; Gollan beat G. Cripsey 5-1; T. Jones beat Dyson 5-1; Price beat M. Johnston-Allen 5-1; Rowing beat S. Longworth 5-3; I. Graham beat Wattana 5-4; Houlihan beat J. Campbell 5-3; J. Spencer beat Sheehan 5-4; Rigitano beat N. Gilbert 5-3; D. Martin beat Kelly 5-2; J. McLaughlin beat Wildman 5-1; D. Gilbert beat Meadowcroft 5-3; R. Bales beat S. Campbell 5-2; S. Duggan beat Rowswell 5-3; J. Chambers beat D. Hughes 5-2; Bond beat D. Morgan 5-2; Brumby beat T. Murphy 5-0; W. King beat Jenkins 5-4; D. Fowler beat V. Harris 5-0; John Rea beat Fitzmaurice 5-4; J. Wych beat Dunning 5-1; Gauvreau beat K. Stevens 5-3; L. Dodd beat D. Campbell 5-4; B. Morgan beat T. Chappel 5-3;

Wright beat M. Fisher 5-0; A. Robidoux beat Van Rensberg 5-1
**Third round:** J. Parrott beat M. Gibson 5-3; S. Newbury beat Edmonds 5-4; Gary Wilkinson beat A. Knowles 5-2; Pinches beat S. Francisco 5-4; M. Clark beat Foldvari 5-4; R. Chaperon beat Macleod 5-3; Dennis Taylor beat Roscoe 5-3; Gollan beat E. Hughes 5-3; T. Jones beat C. Thorburn 5-2; D. Roe beat Price 5-4; S. James beat Rowing 5-1; Graham beat R. Williams 5-1; T. Meo beat Houlihan 5-0; A. Higgins beat Spencer 5-2; T. Griffiths beat Rigitano 5-3; D. O'Kane beat Martin 5-1; J. White beat J. McLaughlin 5-2; E. Charlton beat D. Gilbert 5-2; D. Mountjoy beat Bales 5-0; C. Wilson beat Duggan 5-4; Chambers beat D. Reynolds 5-4; N. Foulds beat Bond 5-2; W. Thorne beat Brumby 5-3; W. Jones beat King 5-1; M. Hallett beat Fowler 5-2; B. West beat John Rea 5-4; J. Virgo beat Wych 5-4; Gauvreau beat Drago 5-0; Dodd beat Johnson 5-0; B. Morgan beat David Taylor 5-4; S. Hendry beat Wright 5-4; Robidoux beat P. Francisco 5-3
**Fourth round:** Newbury beat Parrott 5-2; Gary Wilkinson beat Pinches 5-4; Clark beat Chaperon 5-2; Dennis Taylor beat Gollan 5-4; T. Jones beat Roe 5-1; Graham beat James 5-3; Higgins beat Meo 5-4; O'Kane beat Griffiths 5-4; White beat Charlton 5-2; Mountjoy *wo* C. Wilson *scr*; N. Foulds beat Chambers 5-0; Thorne beat W. Jones 5-1; Hallett beat West 5-4; Virgo beat Gauvreau 5-2; Dodd beat B. Morgan 5-2; Hendry beat Robidoux 5-4
**Fifth round:** Gary Wilkinson beat Newbury 5-1; Dennis Taylor beat Clark 5-3; Graham beat T. Jones 5-3; O'Kane beat Higgins 5-2; White beat Mountjoy 5-3; N. Foulds beat Thorne 5-1; Hallett beat Virgo 5-1; Hendry beat Dodd 5-3
**Quarter-finals:** Gary Wilkinson beat Dennis Taylor 5-3; O'Kane beat Graham 5-1; White beat N. Foulds 5-2; Hallett beat Hendry 5-4
**Semi-finals:** O'Kane beat Gary Wilkinson 5-4; Hallett beat White 5-2
**Final:** Hallett beat O'Kane 9-8

# 555 ASIAN OPEN

**First staged** 1989. **Sponsors** 555. **Venue** Studio 1, Channel 9, Bangkok. **Initial prize-money** £200,000. **Prize-money last season** £200,000. **TV** Thailand and China.

### 1989

**First round:** J. Van Rensberg beat A. Harris 5-3; J. Donnelly beat M. Rowing 5-4; G. Miles beat P. Watchorn 5-3; M. Smith beat P. Thornley 5-2; J. Smith beat G. Scott 5-0; N. Terry *wo* T. Whitthread *scr*; C. Edwards beat N. Bond 5-4; J. Wattana *wo* Jim Bear *scr*; N. Dyson beat K. Owers 5-1; B. Oliver beat A. Kearney 5-3; M. Morra beat F. Ellis 5-3; J. Fitzmaurice beat R. Foldvari 5-2; B. Rowswell beat R. Grace 5-0; M. Bradley beat Jack Rea 5-2; A. Cairns beat P. Houlihan 5-0; T. Wilson beat G. Rigitano 5-4; B. Pinches beat Glen Wilkinson 5-4; M. Gauvreau beat S. Murphy 5-4; D. Campbell beat E. Lawlor 5-4; P. Gibson beat M. Darrington 5-4; M. Price beat J. Meadowcroft 5-2; D. Hughes beat P. Medati 5-2; I. Williamson beat B. Kelly 5-4; F. Davis beat M. Watterson 5-2; J. Wright beat G. Jenkins 5-3; B. Gollan beat J. Dunning 5-1; B. Harris beat B. Morgan 5-3; R. Marshall beat I. Brumby 5-4; S. Meakin beat V. Harris 5-3; S. Campbell beat G. Foulds 5-4; E. Sinclair beat M. Gibson 5-2; M. Wildman beat D. Sheehan 5-3
**Second round:** I. Graham beat Van Rensberg 5-0; J. Spencer beat Donnelly 5-3; Miles beat R. Bales 5-4; J. Wych beat M. Smith 5-3; J. McLaughlin beat J. Smith 5-4; Terry beat R. Edmonds 5-2; Edwards beat M. Fisher 5-3; Wattana beat Macleod 5-2; T. Jones beat Dyson 5-3; Oliver beat J. Campbell 5-3; M. Bennett beat Morra 5-1; S. Duggan beat Fitzmaurice 5-1; D. Fowler beat Rowswell 5-3; J. O'Boye beat Bradley 5-3; Cairns beat S. Longworth 5-1; D. Morgan beat T. Wilson 5-1; C. Roscoe beat Pinches 5-2; G. Cripsey beat Gauvreau 5-4; John Rea beat D. Campbell 5-2; Gary Wilkinson beat P. Gibson 5-4; Price beat L. Dodd 5-1; W. King beat D. Hughes 5-0; D. Gilbert beat

Williamson 5-1; J. Chambers beat F. Davis 5-1; P. Browne beat Wright 5-3; Gollan beat N. Gilbert 5-2; B. Harris beat T. Murphy 5-3; Marshall beat K. Stevens 5-3; M. Johnston-Allen beat Meakin 5-1; S. Campbell beat Robidoux 5-2; T. Chappel beat Sinclair 5-0; D. Martin beat Wildman 5-2
**Third round:** Graham *wo* J. Parrott *scr*; S. Francisco beat Spencer 5-1; A. Knowles beat Miles 5-3; N. Foulds beat Wych 5-2; D. Mountjoy beat J. McLaughlin 5-3; E. Hughes beat Terry 5-1; M. Hallett beat Edwards 5-0; Wattana beat David Taylor 5-1; T. Jones beat C. Thorburn 5-2; Oliver beat R. Williams 5-4; S. James beat M. Bennett 5-3; Duggan beat S. Newbury 5-3; J. Johnson beat Fowler 5-4; T. Drago beat O'Boye 5-3; T. Griffiths beat Cairns 5-2; D. Roe beat D. Morgan 5-2; Roscoe beat J. White 5-3; P. Francisco beat Cripsey 5-1; Meo beat John Rea 5-2; Gary Wilkinson beat E. Charlton 5-3; M. Clark beat Price 5-2; King beat R. Chaperon 5-2; D. Gilbert beat Dennis Taylor 5-1; B. West beat Chambers 5-3; W. Thorne beat Browne 5-4; Gollan beat C. Wilson 5-4; J. Virgo beat B. Harris 5-4; D. O'Kane beat Marshall 5-1; D. Reynolds beat Johnston-Allen 5-2; W. Jones beat S. Campbell 5-3; S. Hendry beat Chappel 5-1; A. Higgins beat Martin 5-3
**Fourth round:** S. Francisco beat Graham 5-4; Knowles beat N. Foulds 5-3; Mountjoy beat E. Hughes 5-4; Wattana beat Hallett 5-3; T. Jones beat Oliver 5-1; Duggan beat James 5-3; Drago beat Johnson 5-2; Griffiths beat Roe 5-3; P. Francisco beat Roscoe 5-4; Gary Wilkinson beat Meo 5-2; Clark beat King 5-3; West beat D. Gilbert 5-3; Thorne beat Gollan 5-1; Virgo beat O'Kane 5-3; W. Jones beat Reynolds 5-2; Hendry beat Higgins 5-3
**Fifth round:** S. Francisco beat Knowles 5-2; Wattana beat Mountjoy 5-2; T. Jones beat Duggan 5-3; Griffiths beat Drago 5-3; Gary Wilkinson beat P. Francisco 5-4; Clark beat West 5-0; Thorne beat Virgo 5-2; Hendry beat W. Jones 5-0
**Quarter-finals:** Wattana beat S. Francisco 5-2; Griffiths beat T. Jones 5-3; Gary Wilkinson beat Clark 5-0; Hendry beat Thorne 5-2
**Semi-finals:** Wattana beat Griffiths 5-0; Hendry beat Gary Wilkinson 5-4
**Final:** Hendry beat Wattana 9-6

# REGAL SCOTTISH MASTERS

**First staged** 1981. **Sponsors** Langs (1981–87), Regal (1989– ). **Venue** Kelvin Hall, Glasgow (1981), Holiday Inn, Glasgow (1982), Skean Dhu Hotel (renamed Hospitality Inn), Glasgow (1983–87), Scottish Conference and Exhibition Centre, Glasgow (1989). **Initial prize-money** £20,500. **Prize-money this season** £86,000. **TV** BBC Scotland.

**1981** (*Langs*)
**Preliminary round:** V. Harris beat I. Black 4-0
**First round:** J. White beat R. Reardon 5-4; S. Davis beat D. Mountjoy 5-0; C. Thorburn beat K. Stevens 5-1; A. Higgins beat V. Harris 5-3
**Semi-finals:** White beat Davis 6-5; Thorburn beat Higgins 6-2
**Final:** White beat Thorburn 9-4

**1982** (*Langs*)
**First round:** Dennis Taylor beat J. White 5-4; S. Davis beat A. Knowles 5-4; T. Griffiths beat R. Reardon 5-3; A. Higgins beat E. Sinclair 5-1
**Semi-finals:** S. Davis beat Dennis Taylor 6-1; Higgins beat Griffiths 6-5
**Final:** S. Davis beat Higgins 9-4

**1983** (*Langs*)
**First round:** C. Thorburn beat T. Griffiths 5-1; S. Davis beat M. Macleod 5-1; A. Knowles beat T. Meo 5-4; A. Higgins beat J. White 5-3

**Semi-finals:** Knowles beat Thorburn 6-2; S. Davis beat Higgins 6-2
**Final:** S. Davis beat Knowles 9-6

**1984** (*Langs*)
**First round:** A. Knowles beat T. Griffiths 5-3; J. White beat M. Macleod 5-0; S. Davis beat C. Thorburn 5-2; A. Higgins beat K. Stevens 5-2
**Semi-finals:** White beat Knowles 6-5; S. Davis beat Higgins 6-4
**Final:** S. Davis beat White 9-4

**1985** (*Langs*)
**First round:** J. White beat A. Higgins 5-0; C. Thorburn beat M. Macleod 5-1; S. Francisco beat A. Knowles 5-4; W. Thorne beat Dennis Taylor 5-2
**Semi-finals:** Thorne beat White 6-2; Thorburn beat Francisco 6-0
**Final:** Thorburn beat Thorne 9-7

**1986** (*Langs*)
**First round:** C. Thorburn beat J. Parrott 5-1; J. White beat S. Hendry 5-1; K. Stevens beat A. Knowles 5-3; A. Higgins beat J. Johnson 5-2
**Semi-finals:** Thorburn beat White 6-2; Higgins beat Stevens 6-2
**Final:** Thorburn beat Higgins 9-8

**1987** (*Langs*)
**First round:** C. Thorburn beat Dennis Taylor 5-2; J. Johnson beat S. Hendry 5-2; T. Griffiths beat N. Foulds 5-4; J. White beat A. Higgins 5-3
**Semi-finals:** Johnson beat Thorburn 6-3; Griffiths beat White 6-2
**Final:** Johnson beat Griffiths 9-7

*The tournament was not held in 1988.*

**1989**
**First round:** John Rea beat Dennis Taylor 6-5; C. Thorburn beat M. Macleod 6-2
**Quarter-finals:** S. Davis beat Rea 6-2; T. Griffiths beat J. White 6-3; S. Hendry beat M. Hallett 6-1; J. Parrott beat C. Thorburn 6-5
**Semi-finals:** Griffiths beat S. Davis 6-2; Hendry beat Parrott 6-4
**Final:** Hendry beat Griffiths 10-1

## BCE INTERNATIONAL

**First staged** 1981. **Sponsors** Jameson (1981–84), Goya (1985), BCE (1986, 1989– ), Fidelity (1987–88). **Venue** Assembly Rooms, Derby (1981–82), Eldon Square Recreation Centre, Newcastle upon Tyne (1983–84), Trentham Gardens, Stoke (1985– ). **Initial prize-money** £66,000. **Prize-money last season** £200,000. **TV** ITV (1981–88), none 1989.

**1981** (*Jameson*)
**Qualifying groups**
1 M. Gibson beat S. Hood 5-3; Gibson beat M. Parkin 5-3; J. Dunning beat Gibson 5-3
2 C. Roscoe beat R. Andrewartha 5-2; D. Sheehan beat V. Harris 5-1; Roscoe beat Sheehan 5-1; J. Meadowcroft beat Roscoe 5-4
3 C. Everton beat K. Kennerley 5-4; M. Watterson beat P. Medati 5-3; Watterson beat Everton 5-4; P. Fagan beat Watterson 5-2
4 P. Houlihan *wo* J. Barrie *scr*; D. French beat G. Foulds 5-2; French beat Houlihan 5-3; R. Williams beat French 5-0
5 B. Demarco *wo* B. Mikkelsen *scr*; D. Hughes beat Jack Rea 5-4; Demarco beat Hughes 5-1; M. Hallett beat Demarco 5-4
6 E. Hughes beat M. Owen 5-1; J. Fitzmaurice beat B. Bennett 5-1; E. Hughes beat

Fitzmaurice 5-3; E. Hughes beat E. Sinclair 5-2

7 E. McLaughlin beat I. Black 5-3; M. Wildman beat M. Morra 5-3; E. McLaughlin beat Wildman 5-3; E. McLaughlin beat D. Greaves 5-1

8 M. Macleod beat B. Kelly 5-1; J. Johnson beat J. Donnelly 5-4; Johnson beat Macleod 5-1; Johnson *wo* J. Pulman *scr*

**First round:** J. Johnson beat J. Wych 5-2; D. Martin beat J. Dunning 5-2; R. Williams beat J. White 5-1; A. Knowles beat M. Hallett 5-2; R. Edmonds beat E. Hughes 5-4; J. Meadowcroft beat C. Wilson 5-4; T. Meo beat E. McLaughlin 5-2

**Second round:** G. Miles beat Johnson 5-3; Martin beat B. Werbeniuk 5-2; Williams beat F. Davis 5-0; A. Higgins beat P. Fagan 5-3; J. Spencer beat Edmonds 5-3; J. Virgo beat Knowles 5-2; K. Stevens beat Meadowcroft 5-1; P. Mans beat Meo 5-3

**Third round:** Miles beat C. Thorburn 5-0; Martin beat E. Charlton 5-2; Virgo beat R. Reardon 5-3; David Taylor beat Stevens 5-0; Dennis Taylor beat Williams 5-1; Higgins beat D. Mountjoy 5-1; T. Griffiths beat Spencer 5-2; S. Davis beat Mans 5-3

**Quarter-finals:** Martin beat Miles 5-1; Higgins beat Griffiths 5-2; Dennis Taylor beat Virgo 5-2; S. Davis beat David Taylor 5-1

**Semi-finals:** Dennis Taylor beat Martin 9-1; S. Davis beat Higgins 9-8

**Final:** S. Davis beat Dennis Taylor 9-0

**1982** (*Jameson*)

**Qualifying groups**

1 R. Edmonds beat D. Hughes 5-0; Edmonds beat G. Miles 5-1

2 V. Harris beat D. Sheehan 5-3; J. Virgo beat Harris 5-2

3 M. Fisher beat T. Murphy 5-1; Fisher beat F. Davis 5-3

4 B. Bennett beat M. Owen 5-2; J. Wych beat Bennett 5-0

5 M. Morra beat B. Demarco 5-2; D. Reynolds beat Morra 5-1

6 M. Watterson beat C. Everton 5-1; Watterson beat P. Fagan 5-1

7 E. Sinclair beat I. Anderson 5-2; Sinclair beat T. Meo 5-3

8 G. Scott beat B. Harris 5-4; Scott *wo* John Bear *scr*

9 J. Johnson *wo* J. Phillips *scr*; C. Wilson beat Johnson 5-4

10 E. Hughes beat M. Parkin 5-2; Hughes beat D. Martin 5-4

11 C. Ross *wo* D. Greaves *scr*; J. Meadowcroft beat Ross 5-0

12 I. Williamson beat J. Donnelly 5-3; B. Kelly beat G. Foulds 5-4; Kelly beat Williamson 5-1

13 C. Roscoe beat J. Dunning 5-2; D. French beat G. Cripsey 5-1; Roscoe beat French 5-2

14 M. Hallett beat F. Jonik 5-2; M. Wildman beat M. Gibson 5-1; Wildman beat Hallett 5-2

15 J. Fitzmaurice beat I. Black 5-3; L. Dodd beat M. Macleod 5-1; Dodd beat Fitzmaurice 5-3

16 R. Williams beat P. Medati 5-3; E. McLaughlin beat P. Houlihan 5-2; Williams beat McLaughlin 5-1

**First round:** A. Knowles beat Sinclair 5-2; Reynolds beat W. Thorne 5-3; S. Davis beat Roscoe 5-0; B. Werbeniuk beat Wych 5-3; David Taylor beat Fisher 5-1; K. Stevens beat Watterson 5-3; T. Griffiths beat Williams 5-2; J. Spencer beat Edmonds 5-2; Dennis Taylor beat Wildman 5-2; Virgo beat E. Charlton 5-4; P. Mans beat Dodd 5-3; J. White beat Meadowcroft 5-1; R. Reardon beat E. Hughes 5-3; C. Thorburn beat Scott 5-1; A. Higgins beat Kelly 5-3; Wilson beat D. Mountjoy 5-4

**Second round:** S. Davis beat Reynolds 5-0; David Taylor beat Werbeniuk 5-2; Stevens beat Mans 5-2; Griffiths beat Higgins 5-2; Dennis Taylor beat Thorburn 5-2; Wilson beat White 5-2; Virgo beat Spencer 5-4; Knowles beat Reardon 5-2

**Quarter-finals:** Virgo beat Dennis Taylor 5-3; David Taylor beat S. Davis 5-3; Knowles beat Wilson 5-4; Stevens beat Griffiths 5-3

**Semi-finals:** Knowles beat Stevens 9-3; David Taylor beat Virgo 9-5

**Final:** Knowles beat David Taylor 9-6

**1983** (*Jameson*)

**Qualifying groups**

1 M. Watterson beat B. Demarco 5-3; Watterson beat P. Mans 5-4
2 T. Murphy beat D. Sheehan 5-2; W. Thorne beat Murphy 5-2
3 R. Williams beat D. French 5-1; D. Reynolds beat Williams 5-3
4 J. Donnelly beat B. Bennett 5-1; Donnelly beat C. Wilson 5-1
5 M. Darrington beat I. Williamson 5-3; S. Francisco beat Darrington 5-2
6 W. King beat I. Black 5-3; G. Miles beat King 5-3
7 D. Hughes beat M. Parkin 5-0; J. Johnson beat Hughes 5-1
8 B. Harris beat J. Dunning 5-3; M. Wildman beat Harris 5-2
9 D. Martin beat D. Greaves 5-1; Martin beat P. Fagan 5-0
10 R. Andrewartha beat C. Everton 5-1; E. Sinclair beat Andrewartha 5-4
11 P. Medati beat V. Harris 5-0; M. Macleod beat Medati 5-3
12 F. Davis beat B. Kelly 5-1; P. Morgan beat J. Fitzmaurice 5-4; Morgan beat Davis 5-3
13 M. Hallett beat C. Roscoe 5-2; M. Morra beat P. Watchorn 5-3; Morra beat Hallett 5-3
14 G. Foulds beat P. Burke 5-2; E. Hughes beat M. Fisher 5-4; Hughes beat Foulds 5-1
15 M. Gibson beat L. Dodd 5-1; G. Scott beat P. Houlihan 5-0; Scott beat Gibson 5-3
16 E. McLaughlin beat J. Campbell 5-2; R. Edmonds beat Jack Rea 5-1; Edmonds beat McLaughlin 5-1

**First round:** Dennis Taylor beat Reynolds 5-3; R. Reardon beat Macleod 5-2; Thorne beat J. Virgo 5-2; Morra beat J. White 5-3; D. Mountjoy beat Wildman 5-4; Martin beat A. Higgins 5-2; Watterson beat T. Meo 5-3; Scott beat B. Werbeniuk 5-3; T. Griffiths beat Miles 5-2; S. Davis beat Hughes 5-1; Donnelly beat David Taylor 5-3; Francisco *wo* K. Stevens *scr*; E. Charlton beat Johnson 5-2; Thorburn beat Sinclair 5-0; J. Spencer beat Morgan 5-1; A. Knowles beat Edmonds 5-1

**Second round:** Griffiths beat Scott 5-0; Spencer beat Knowles 5-4; Thorburn beat Dennis Taylor 5-3; Mountjoy beat Martin 5-0; Charlton beat Morra 5-3; Thorne beat Reardon 5-0; S. Francisco beat Donnelly 5-1; S. Davis beat Watterson 5-0

**Quarter-finals:** Griffiths beat Spencer 5-4; Thorburn beat Mountjoy 5-2; Charlton beat Thorne 5-0; S. Davis beat S. Francisco 5-1

**Semi-finals:** Thorburn beat Griffiths 9-8; S. Davis beat Charlton 9-2

**Final:** S. Davis beat Thorburn 9-4

**1984** (*Jameson*)

**Qualifying groups**

1 G. Foulds beat P. Francisco 5-4; I. Williamson beat V. Harris 5-0; Foulds beat Williamson 5-4; Foulds beat J. Donnelly 5-3; J. Campbell beat Foulds 5-3
2 W. Jones beat P. Watchorn 5-0; M. Gibson beat P. Medati 5-3; Jones beat Gibson 5-2; Jones beat G. Scott 5-0; Jones beat M. Wildman 5-0
3 T. Jones beat D. French 5-1; S. Duggan beat Jones 5-2; E. Sinclair beat Duggan 5-0; Sinclair beat P. Mans 5-2
4 B. Bennett beat B. Demarco 5-1; Bennett *wo* P. Morgan *scr*; Bennett *wo* J. Wych *scr*; N. Foulds beat Bennett 5-0
5 R. Foldvari beat G. Rigitano 5-2; Foldvari beat R. Edmonds 5-1; L. Dodd beat Foldvari 5-3; Dodd beat C. Wilson 5-1
6 B. Mikkelsen beat T. Chappel 5-4; Mikkelsen beat C. Everton 5-0; C. Roscoe beat Mikkelsen 5-1; E. Hughes beat Roscoe 5-1
7 D. O'Kane beat M. Parkin 5-2; O'Kane beat E. McLaughlin 5-1; O'Kane beat J. Fitzmaurice 5-4; O'Kane beat M. Hallett 5-4
8 J. McLaughlin beat D. Greaves 5-3; F. Jonik beat McLaughlin 5-2; M. Gauvreau beat Jonik 5-1; Gauvreau beat J. Parrott 5-4
9 G. Cripsey beat P. Thornley 5-3; J. Dunning beat Cripsey 5-3; F. Davis beat Dunning 5-4; J. Virgo beat Davis 5-3
10 J. Hargreaves beat P. Houlihan 5-2; B. Kelly beat Hargreaves 5-2; Kelly beat

W. King 5-4; S. Francisco beat Kelly 5-3
11 D. Fowler beat R. Chaperon 5-0; Fowler *wo* P. Mifsud *scr*; Fowler beat R. Andrewartha 5-0; Fowler beat D. Martin 5-0
12 M. Bradley beat M. Darrington 5-3; Bradley beat Jack Rea 5-2; M. Morra beat Bradley 5-3; J. Johnson beat Morra 5-0
13 D. Chalmers *wo* Condo *scr*; W. Oliver beat D. Hughes 5-4; Chalmers beat Oliver 5-4; J. Meadowcroft beat Chalmers 5-1; R. Williams beat Meadowcroft 5-4
14 P. Browne beat John Rea 5-2; I. Black beat Browne 5-4; Black beat M. Watterson 5-3; M. Macleod beat Black 5-3
15 S. Newbury beat S. Longworth 5-4; P. Burke beat A. Kearney 5-4; Newbury beat Burke 5-0; Newbury beat P. Fagan 5-0; Newbury beat G. Miles 5-1
16 R. Bales beat D. Sheehan 5-2; Bales beat T. Murphy 5-4; Bales beat M. Fisher 5-3; D. Reynolds beat Bales 5-4

**First round:** S. Davis beat Campbell 5-1; A. Higgins beat Sinclair 5-1; T. Griffiths beat N. Foulds 5-3; R. Reardon beat Dodd 5-4; E. Hughes beat D. Mountjoy 5-1; W. Thorne beat O'Kane 5-3; Gauvreau beat K. Stevens 5-1; Virgo beat C. Thorburn 5-0; S. Francisco beat J. Spencer 5-2; Dennis Taylor beat Fowler 5-0; Johnson beat E. Charlton 5-1; J. White beat Williams 5-3; T. Meo beat Macleod 5-1; Newbury beat B. Werbeniuk 5-2; A. Knowles beat Reynolds 5-1; David Taylor beat W. Jones 5-4
**Second round:** S. Davis beat David Taylor 5-1; Higgins beat Griffiths 5-4; E. Hughes beat Reardon 5-1; Thorne beat Gauvreau 5-3; S. Francisco beat Virgo 5-2; Dennis Taylor beat Johnson 5-2; White beat Meo 5-1; Knowles beat Newbury 5-4
**Quarter-finals:** S. Davis beat Higgins 5-1; E. Hughes beat Thorne 5-2; S. Francisco *wo* Dennis Taylor *scr*; Knowles beat White 5-4
**Semi-finals:** S. Davis beat E. Hughes 9-3; Knowles beat S. Francisco 9-6
**Final:** S. Davis beat Knowles 9-2

**1985** (*Goya Matchroom*)
**First round:** M. Darrington beat D. Gilbert 5-2; O. Agrawal beat P. Watchorn 5-2; M. Smith beat D. Sheehan 5-2; S. Simngam beat D. Greaves 5-2; G. Wilkinson beat B. Demarco 5-2; J. Rempe beat P. Burke 5-3; S. Hendry beat B. West 5-4; Jim Bear beat P. Houlihan 5-2; J. Caggianello beat J. Hargreaves 5-2; D. Mienie *wo* G. Watson *scr*; J. O'Boye beat M. Parkin 5-3; R. Bales beat T. Drago 5-2; D. Hughes beat A. Kearney 5-1; G. Cripsey beat B. Bennett 5-3
**Second round:** B. Mikkelsen beat M. Fisher 5-3; M. Gibson beat P. Francisco 5-4; P. Fagan beat Mienie 5-4; W. King beat Caggianello 5-0; R. Chaperon beat D. Chalmers 5-2; Bales beat R. Edmonds 5-0; G. Miles beat O'Boye 5-2; J. Fitzmaurice beat M. Watterson 5-2; T. Chappel beat J. Meadowcraft 5-2; C. Roscoe beat G. Foulds 5-3; E. McLaughlin beat Hendry 5-3; Jim Bear beat J. Donnelly 5-2; T. Jones beat W. Kelly 5-3; M. Bradley beat John Rea 5-1; L. Dodd beat Simngam 5-4; Williamson beat J. McLaughlin 5-3; J. Dunning beat C. Everton 5-2; M. Morra beat B. Oliver 5-1; D. Fowler beat Agrawal 5-2; J. Wych beat Rempe 5-1; E. Sinclair beat Darrington 5-0; S. Longworth beat Wilkinson 5-0; Cripsey beat P. Medati 5-2; S. Newbury beat F. Jonik 5-4; S. Duggan beat F. Davis 5-1; I. Black beat G. Rigitano 5-4; R. Foldvari beat V. Harris 5-4; G. Scott beat J. Van Rensberg 5-4; T. Murphy beat Jack Rea 5-1; B. Harris beat P. Browne 5-3; W. Jones beat Smith 5-3; D. Hughes beat M. Gauvreau 5-4
**Third round:** S. Davis beat Bales 5-2; J. Virgo beat Miles 5-2; Chaperon beat S. Francisco 5-3; M. Macleod beat Fitzmaurice 5-1; Gibson beat E. Charlton 5-4; D. Reynolds beat Mikkelsen 5-0; J. White beat Fagan 5-2; King beat R. Williams 5-3; Chappel beat K. Stevens 5-3; C. Wilson beat Roscoe 5-1; J. Johnson beat Jim Bear 5-1; Bradley beat M. Hallett 5-4; David Taylor beat T. Jones 5-4; B. Werbeniuk beat Williamson 5-2; A. Knowles beat E. McLaughlin 5-1; N. Foulds beat Dodd 5-3; C. Thorburn beat Longworth 5-3; D. Martin beat Sinclair 5-1; D. Mountjoy beat Wych 5-1; J. Campbell beat Morra 5-2; W. Thorne beat Fowler 5-1; Scott beat M. Wildman 5-1; Duggan beat R. Reardon 5-4; Black beat P. Mans 5-4; T. Griffiths beat Newbury 5-2; J. Spencer beat Foldvari 5-4; T. Meo beat Dunning 5-0; J. Parrott beat W. Jones 5-3; A. Higgins beat

D. Hughes 5-1; Murphy beat E. Hughes 5-3; Dennis Taylor beat Cripsey 5-1; B. Harris beat D. O'Kane 5-3
**Fourth round:** S. Davis beat Virgo 5-1; Macleod beat Chaperon 5-4; Reynolds beat Gibson 5-0; White beat King 5-2; Wilson beat Chappel 5-0; Johnson beat Bradley 5-2; David Taylor beat Werbeniuk 5-4; N. Foulds beat Knowles 5-3; Thorburn beat Martin 5-3; Campbell beat Mountjoy 5-1; Thorne beat Scott 5-1; Duggan beat Black 5-1; Griffiths beat Spencer 5-1; Parrott beat Meo 5-4; Higgins beat Murphy 5-2; Dennis Taylor beat B. Harris 5-3
**Fifth round:** S. Davis beat Macleod 5-1; White beat Reynolds 5-1; Johnson beat Wilson 5-1; N. Foulds beat David Taylor 5-4; Thorburn beat Campbell 5-0; Duggan beat Thorne 5-4; Parrott beat Griffiths 5-1; Dennis Taylor beat Higgins 5-1
**Quarter-finals:** White beat S. Davis 5-3; N. Foulds beat Johnson 5-2; Thorburn beat Duggan 5-2; Dennis Taylor beat Parrott 5-1
**Semi-finals:** White beat N. Foulds 9-5; Thorburn beat Dennis Taylor 9-5
**Final:** Thorburn beat White 12-10

## 1986 (*BCE*)

**First round:** P. Burke beat J. Fitzmaurice 5-4; G. Wilkinson *wo* F. Jonik *scr*; A. Kearney *wo* S. Simngam *scr*; B. Kelly beat T. Whitthread 5-1; J. McLaughlin beat B. Bennett 5-0; J. Wright beat M. Watterson 5-1; B. Rowswell beat D. Sheehan 5-4; Jack Rea beat M. Darrington 5-4; G. Jenkins beat C. Everton 5-3; J. Dunning beat B. Demarco 5-4; M. Bennett beat M. Smith 5-4; P. Gibson beat J. Meadowcroft 5-2; I. Anderson *wo* E. McLaughlin *scr*; G. Rigitano beat D. Greaves 5-3; J. Bear beat P. Watchorn 5-1; P. Houlihan beat D. Chalmers 5-1; C. Roscoe beat M. Parkin 5-1; M. Morra beat F. Ellis 5-3; N. Gilbert beat O. Agrawal 5-0; K. Owers beat J. Hargreaves 5-3; B. Oliver beat D. Mienie 5-4; D. Roe beat D. Hughes 5-2; G. Foulds *wo* L. Heywood *scr*; M. Hines beat M. Fisher 5-2; J. Donnelly *wo* R. Grace *scr*; S. James beat D. Gilbert 5-2
**Second round:** Burke beat T. Jones 5-4; M. Bradley beat Wilkinson 5-4; P. Medati beat Kearney 5-3; J. Van Rensberg beat Kelly 5-1; R. Bales beat F. Davis 5-4; J. McLaughlin beat D. Fowler 5-2; J. Spencer beat I. Williamson 5-4; I. Black beat Wright 5-1; E. Sinclair beat P. Fagan 5-0; M. Wildman beat Rowswell 5-2; W. Jones beat Jack Rea 5-1; M. Gauvreau beat Jenkins 5-1; S. Newbury beat Dunning 5-4; M. Bennett beat P. Browne 5-1; R. Foldvari beat B. Harris 5-0; S. Hendry beat P. Gibson 5-2; John Rea beat Anderson 5-1; W. King beat Rigitano 5-0; J. O'Boye beat B. Mikkelsen 5-4; S. Duggan beat Bear 5-4; Houlihan beat G. Cripsey 5-1; T. Chappel beat Roscoe 5-3; J. Drago beat Morra 5-3; R. Chaperon beat N. Gilbert 5-3; Owers beat G. Scott 5-1; D. O'Kane beat Oliver 5-2; G. Miles beat Roe 5-1; G. Foulds beat V. Harris 5-4; M. Gibson beat Hines 5-1; L. Dodd *wo* P. Mans *scr*; T. Murphy beat Donnelly 5-2; R. Edmonds beat James 5-2
**Third round:** C. Thorburn beat Burke 5-0; J. Wych beat Bradley 5-2; T. Griffiths beat Medati 5-3; B. West beat Van Rensberg 5-3; Bales beat K. Stevens 5-3; C. Wilson beat J. McLaughlin 5-2; T. Knowles beat Spencer 5-0; E. Charlton beat Black 5-0; A. Higgins beat Sinclair 5-3; P. Francisco beat Wildman 5-2; R. Reardon beat W. Jones 5-4; Gauvreau beat M. Macleod 5-4; S. Francisco beat Newbury 5-4; J. Virgo beat M. Bennett 5-1; Dennis Taylor beat Foldvari 5-1; Hendry beat J. Parrott 5-3; S. Davis beat John Rea 5-1; King beat S. Longworth 5-0; R. Williams beat O'Boye 5-0; Duggan beat J. Campbell 5-3; Houlihan beat T. Meo 5-4; E. Hughes beat Chappel 5-4; Drago beat W. Thorne 5-2; Chaperon beat D. Martin 5-4; Owers beat J. White 5-2; O'Kane beat M. Hallet 5-1; N. Foulds beat Miles 5-2; G. Foulds beat B. Werbeniuk 5-2; D. Mountjoy beat M. Gibson 5-3; D. Reynolds beat Dodd 5-2; J. Johnson beat Murphy 5-4; David Taylor beat Edmonds 5-4
**Fourth round:** Thorburn beat Wych 5-3; Griffiths beat West 5-1; Wilson beat Bales 5-1; Knowles beat Charlton 5-1; P. Francisco beat Higgins 5-4; Gauvreau beat Reardon 5-2; S. Francisco beat Virgo 5-0; Dennis Taylor beat Hendry 5-3; S. Davis beat King 5-4; Williams beat Duggan 5-4; E. Hughes beat Houlihan 5-1; Chaperon beat Drago 5-1; Owers beat O'Kane 5-0; N. Foulds beat G. Foulds 5-0; Reynolds beat Mountjoy 5-2;

David Taylor beat Johnson 5-3
**Fifth round:** Thorburn beat Griffiths 5-4; Wilson beat Knowles 5-4; P. Francisco beat Gauvreau 5-2; S. Francisco beat Dennis Taylor 5-0; S. Davis beat Williams 5-4; E. Hughes beat Chaperon 5-0; N. Foulds beat Owers 5-1; Reynolds beat David Taylor 5-1
**Quarter-finals:** Thorburn beat Wilson 5-1; P. Francisco beat S. Francisco 5-3; E. Hughes beat S. Davis 5-4; N. Foulds beat Reynolds 5-2
**Semi-finals:** Thorburn beat P. Francisco 9-7; N. Foulds beat E. Hughes 9-8
**Final:** N. Foulds beat Thorburn 12-9

**1987** (*Fidelity*)
**First round:** P. Gibson beat Glen Wilkinson 5-3; Gary Wilkinson beat G. Rigitano 5-1; E. Sinclair beat D. Heaton 5-3; D. Gilbert beat A. Harris 5-4; R. Foldvari beat S. Meakin 5-3; P. Fagan *wo* E. McLaughlin *scr*; J. Smith *wo* F. Jonik *scr*; M. Clark beat J. Bear 5-2; G. Jenkins beat T. Whitthread 5-1; J. Meadowcroft beat D. Greaves 5-1; M. Smith beat J. Donnelly 5-3; I. Anderson beat M. Watterson 5-3; D. Roe beat F. Ellis 5-4; J. Chambers *wo* B. Mikkelsen *scr*; M. Fisher *wo* J. Rempe *scr*; D. Chalmers beat J. Fitzmaurice 5-4; I. Williamson beat C. Everton 5-0; C. Roscoe beat E. Lawler 5-4; Jack Rea beat P. Burke 5-1; J. Dunning beat D. Sheehan 5-1; N. Gilbert beat I. Black 5-3; R. Rowswell beat D. Hughes 5-1; P. Watchorn beat B. Oliver 5-3; M. Morra beat J. Hargreaves 5-4; V. Harris beat R. Marshall 5-1; B. Kelly beat M. Darrington 5-4
**Second round:** P. Gibson beat T. Jones 5-4; Gary Wilkinson beat G. Scott 5-2; Sinclair beat R. Edmonds 5-4; D. Gilbert beat P. Houlihan 5-3; Foldvari beat A. Kearney 5-1; J. O'Boye beat Fagan 5-1; M. Bradley beat J. Smith 5-1; Clark beat S. Duggan 5-2; J. Wych beat Jenkins 5-4; K. Owers beat Meadowcroft 5-3; W. King beat M. Smith 5-3; G. Cripsey beat Anderson 5-4; Roe beat F. Davis 5-3; S. James beat B. Harris 5-0; R. Grace beat Chambers 5-4; S. Newbury beat Fisher 5-0; M. Bennett beat Chambers 5-4; Williamson beat M. Gauvreau 5-1; Roscoe beat P. Browne 5-2; Jack Rea beat G. Foulds 5-4; W. Jones beat Dunning 5-1; N. Gilbert beat J. McLaughlin 5-4; M. Wildman beat Miles 5-3; R. Reardon beat Rowswell 5-4; D. Fowler beat Watchorn 5-1; Morra beat L. Dodd 5-3; John Rea beat R. Bales 5-2; T. Murphy beat P. Medati 5-3; T. Chappel beat M. Gibson 5-2; R. Chaperon beat V. Harris 5-4; D. O'Kane beat J. Van Rensberg 5-3; J. Wright beat Kelly 5-2
**Third round:** N. Foulds beat P. Gibson 5-2; S. Hendry beat Gary Wilkinson 5-4; C. Wilson beat Sinclair 5-1; D. Gilbert beat D. Martin 5-2; Foldvari beat R. Williams 5-0; O'Boye beat K. Stevens 5-1; Dennis Taylor beat Bradley 5-0; Clark beat T. Drago 5-2; Wych beat J. Johnson 5-4; E. Hughes beat Owers 5-4; S. Francisco beat King 5-2; B. Werbeniuk beat Cripsey 5-1; Roe beat D. Mountjoy 5-4; James beat J. Campbell 5-4; C. Thorburn beat Grace 5-1; Newbury beat P. Francisco 5-2; J. White beat M. Bennett 5-3; S. Longworth beat Williamson 5-4; M. Hallett beat Roscoe 5-3; J. Spencer beat Jack Rea 5-0; W. Jones beat D. Reynolds 5-4; N. Gilbert beat M. Macleod 5-1; T. Griffiths beat Wildman 5-1; E. Charlton beat Reardon 5-4; A. Knowles beat Fowler 5-4; David Taylor beat Morra 5-3; W. Thorne beat John Rea 5-3; J. Virgo beat Murphy 5-1; J. Parrott beat Chappel 5-1; Chaperon beat B. West 5-4; S. Davis beat O'Kane 5-2; T. Meo beat Wright 5-2
**Fourth round:** Hendry beat N. Foulds 5-2; D. Gilbert beat Wilson 5-1; O'Boye beat Foldvari 5-4; Clark beat Dennis Taylor 5-0; E. Hughes beat Wych 5-4; S. Francisco beat Werbeniuk 5-3; James beat Roe 5-3; Thorburn beat Newbury 5-3; White beat Longworth 5-1; Hallett beat Spencer 5-2; N. Gilbert beat W. Jones 5-4; Charlton beat Griffiths 5-2; Knowles beat David Taylor 5-2; Virgo beat Thorne 5-4; Parrott beat Chaperon 5-1; S. Davis beat Meo 5-3
**Fifth round:** Hendry beat D. Gilbert 5-0; O'Boye beat Clark 5-2; E. Hughes beat S. Francisco 5-4; Thorburn beat James 5-0; Hallett beat White 5-4; Charlton beat N. Gilbert 5-0; Virgo beat Knowles 5-2; S. Davis beat Parrott 5-2
**Quarter-finals:** Hendry beat O'Boye 5-2; Thorburn beat E. Hughes 5-1; Hallett beat Charlton 5-4; S. Davis beat Virgo 5-2
**Semi-finals:** Thorburn beat Hendry 9-1; S. Davis beat Hallett 9-3

**Final:** S. Davis beat Thorburn 12-5

**1988** (*Fidelity*)
**First round:** M. Smith beat D. Morgan 5-3; A. Robidoux beat I. Black 5-1; John Rea beat C. Edwards 5-2; T. Wilson beat M. Gibson 5-1; P. Watchorn beat B. Harris 5-2; D. Hughes beat G. Rigitano 5-4; V. Harris beat P. Burke 5-2; M. Johnston-Allen beat G. Scott 5-2; T. Whitthread beat J. Meadowcroft 5-4; J. Dunning beat B. Kelly 5-0; G. Jenkins beat M. Wildman 5-1; Glen Wilkinson beat D. Mienie 5-2; D. Sheehan beat M. Bradley 5-4; I. Williamson beat M. Darrington 5-1; Jim Bear beat D. Heaton 5-1; M. Price beat P. Medati 5-4; F. Davis beat S. Campbell 5-4; R. Foldvari beat A. Harris 5-1; E. Lawlor beat Jack Rea 5-2; J. Donnelly beat J. Smith 5-2; P. Gison *wo* F. Jonik *scr*; B. Mikkelsen beat J. Fitzmaurice 5-2; G. Foulds beat F. Ellis 5-2; R. Marshall beat B. Rowswell 5-4; C. Roscoe beat N. Terry 5-2; M. Morra beat C. Everton 5-2; B. Oliver beat P. Fagan 5-0; E. Sinclair beat M. Rowing 5-0; J. Chambers beat I. Graham 5-2; R. Grace *wo* D. Chalmers *scr*; T. Kearney beat M. Watterson 5-1; S. Meakin beat J. Van Rensberg 5-4
**Second round:** W. Jones beat M. Smith 5-2; Robidoux beat P. Houlihan 5-2; John Rea beat R. Bales 5-2; T. Wilson beat P. Browne 5-3; T. Chappel beat Watchorn 5-4; K. Stevens beat D. Hughes 5-2; J. Wych beat V. Harris 5-3; Johnston-Allen beat D. Gilbert 5-3; J. O'Boye beat Whitthread 5-2; N. Gilbert beat Dunning 5-0; K. Owers beat Jenkins 5-1; M. Fisher beat Glen Wilkinson 5-4; M. Macleod beat Sheehan 5-0; J. Wright beat Williamson 5-1; R. Edmonds beat Jim Bear 5-1; Price beat B. Werbeniuk 5-2; T. Murphy beat F. Davis 5-1; T. Jones beat Foldvari 5-4; J. McLaughlin beat Lawlor 5-3; R. Reardon beat Donnelly 5-1; G. Cripsey *wo* P. Gibson *scr*; D. Martin beat Mikkelsen 5-4; G. Miles beat G. Foulds 5-3; M. Bennett beat Marshall 5-1; L. Dodd beat Roscoe 5-1; W. King beat Morra 5-4; S. Duggan beat Oliver 5-3; D. Roe beat Sinclair 5-1; Chambers beat Gary Wilkinson 5-4; D. Fowler beat Grace 5-3; M. Clark beat Kearney 5-3; Meakin beat M. Gauvreau 5-3
**Third round:** S. Davis beat W. Jones 5-1; Robidoux beat E. Charlton 5-2; John Rea beat P. Francisco 5-0; David Taylor beat T. Wilson 5-1; Dennis Taylor beat Chappel 5-1; J. Campbell *wo* K. Stevens *scr*; Wych beat T. Griffiths 5-0; D. O'Kane beat Johnston-Allen 5-3; M. Hallett beat O'Boye 5-3; T. Meo beat N. Gilbert 5-1; S. Francisco beat Owers 5-1; R. Chaperon beat Fisher 5-3; Macleod beat A. Higgins 5-2; S. James beat Wright 5-3; S. Hendry beat Edmonds 5-1; S. Longworth beat Price 5-4; N. Foulds beat Murphy 5-3; D. Reynolds beat T. Jones 5-4; J. Virgo beat J. McLaughlin 5-0; J. Spencer beat Reardon 5-4; J. Johnson beat Cripsey 5-3; D. Mountjoy beat Martin 5-1; A. Knowles beat Miles 5-4; S. Newbury beat M. Bennett 5-0; Dodd beat J. Parrott 5-4; B. West beat King 5-4; Duggan beat C. Wilson 5-2; R. Williams beat Roe 5-3; W. Thorne beat Chambers 5-2; T. Drago beat Fowler 5-3; J. White beat Clark 5-2; E. Hughes beat Meakin 5-0
**Fourth round:** S. Davis beat Robidoux 5-4; David Taylor beat John Rea 5-4; Dennis Taylor beat J. Campbell 5-4; Wych beat O'Kane 5-4; Meo beat Hallett 5-3; Chaperon beat S. Francisco 5-2; James beat Macleod 5-2; Hendry beat Longworth 5-3; Reynolds beat N. Foulds 5-3; Spencer beat Virgo 5-1; Johnson beat Mountjoy 5-4; Newbury beat Knowles 5-4; West beat Dodd 5-3; Williams beat Duggan 5-4; Thorne beat Drago 5-2; White beat E. Hughes 5-1
**Fifth round:** S. Davis beat David Taylor 5-1; Dennis Taylor beat Wych 5-2; Meo beat Chaperon 5-4; James beat Hendry 5-2; Reynolds beat Spencer 5-2; Johnson beat Newbury 5-2; West beat Williams 5-4; White beat Thorne 5-4
**Quarter-finals:** S. Davis beat Dennis Taylor 5-2; James beat Meo 5-1; Reynolds beat Johnson 5-1; White beat West 5-2
**Semi-finals:** S. Davis beat James 9-1; White beat Reynolds 9-5
**Final:** S. Davis beat White 12-6

**1989**
**First round:** A. Kearney beat M. Gauvreau 5-3; P. Houlihan beat Jack Rea 5-4; N. Terry

beat J. Meadowcroft 5-1; M. Darrington beat V. Harris 5-2; B. Morgan beat G. Miles 5-0; T. Whitthread beat P. Medati 5-3; N. Dyson beat Glen Wilkinson 5-1; B. Kelly beat M. Morra 5-3; B. Gollan beat T. Wilson 5-2; F. Davis beat J. Van Rensberg 5-4; M. Bradley beat G. Foulds 5-1; S. Campbell beat John Rea 5-4; F. Ellis beat E. Sinclair 5-2; S. Murphy beat M. Price 5-4; J. Smith beat J. Donnelly 5-4; I. Williamson beat D. Sheehan 5-1; B. Pinches beat G. Scott 5-4; J. Wattana beat C. Edwards 5-2; B. Oliver beat G. Rigitano 5-1; R. Grace beat E. Lawlor 5-4; R. Marshall beat P. Watchorn 5-3; I. Brumby beat K. Owers 5-4; A. Harris beat M. Gibson 5-4; T. Wright beat P. Thornley 5-3; N. Bond *wo* Jim Bear *scr*; J. Fitzmaurice beat M. Rowswell 5-4; D. Campbell beat P. Gibson 5-1; M. Smith beat D. Hughes 5-0; B. Harris beat M. Watterson 5-3; A. Cairns beat R. Foldvari 5-4; M. Rowing beat J. Dunning 5-0; S. Meakin beat M. Wildman 5-3
**Second round:** Kearney beat K. Stevens 5-4; Houlihan beat R. Edmonds 5-2; M. Bennett beat Terry 5-4; J. O'Boye beat Darrington 5-3; B. Morgan beat D. Fowler 5-4; D. Morgan beat T. Whitthread 5-0; Dyson beat J. Chambers 5-3; W. King beat Kelly 5-0; Gollan beat S. Longworth 5-0; S. Duggan beat F. Davis 5-1; Robidoux beat Bradley 5-2; R. Bales beat S. Campbell 5-3; T. Murphy beat Ellis 5-4; J. Wych beat S. Murphy 5-4; J. Smith beat N. Gilbert 5-2; Williamson beat G. Cripsey 5-3; I. Graham beat Pinches 5-0; Wattana beat T. Chappel 5-3; T. Jones beat Oliver 5-1; M. Johnston-Allen beat Grace 5-0; Marshall beat C. Roscoe 5-4; Brumby beat J. Spencer 5-1; L. Dodd beat A. Harris 5-3; Wright beat D. Gilbert 5-1; Bond beat P. Browne 5-0; J. Campbell beat Fitzmaurice 5-3; J. McLaughlin beat D. Campbell 5-0; M. Smith beat D. Martin 5-3; B. Harris beat Gary Wilkinson 5-4; Cairns beat David Taylor 5-4; M. Fisher beat Rowing 5-4; M. Macleod beat Meakin 5-4
**Third round:** S. Davis beat Kearney 5-1; W. Jones beat Houlihan 5-2; M. Bennett beat T. Meo 5-2; N. Foulds beat O'Boye 5-0; B. Morgan beat J. Johnson 5-2; E. Hughes beat D. Morgan 5-4; Dennis Taylor beat Dyson 5-1; M. Clark beat King 5-4; T. Griffiths beat Gollan 5-4; S. Newbury beat Duggan 5-2; Robidoux beat Mountjoy 5-4; Bales beat D. Roe 5-4; W. Thorne beat T. Murphy 5-2; B. West *wo* Wych *scr*; J. White beat J. Smith 5-3; R. Chaperon beat Williamson 5-4; S. Hendry beat Graham 5-0; Wattana beat P. Francisco 5-0; J. Jones beat J. Virgo 5-0; Johnston-Allen beat Higgins 5-1; Marshall beat D. Reynolds 5-3; E. Charlton beat Brumby 5-4; M. Hallett beat Dodd 5-4; C. Wilson beat Wright 5-2; Bond beat C. Thorburn 5-4; S. Francisco beat J. Campbell 5-4; S. James beat J. McLaughlin 5-3; M. Smith beat R. Williams 5-4; A. Knowles beat B. Harris 5-1; Cairns beat D. O'Kane 5-2; J. Parrott beat Fisher 5-2; T. Drago beat Macleod 5-4
**Fourth round:** S. Davis beat W. Jones 5-2; N. Foulds beat M. Bennett 5-2; B. Morgan beat E. Hughes 5-3; Dennis Taylor beat Clark 5-4; Newbury beat Griffiths 5-2; Robidoux beat Bales 5-1; Thorne beat West 5-2; White beat Chaperon 5-3; Hendry beat Wattana 5-3; T. Jones beat Johnston-Allen 5-2; Marshall beat Charlton 5-2; C. Wilson beat Hallett 5-4; Bond beat S. Francisco 5-3; James beat M. Smith 5-3; Knowles beat Cairns 5-2; Parrott beat Drago 5-3
**Fifth round:** S. Davis beat N. Foulds 5-3; B. Morgan beat Dennis Taylor 5-4; Robidoux beat Newbury 5-2; White beat Thorne 5-1; Hendry beat T. Jones 5-4; C. Wilson beat Marshall 5-3; Bond beat James 5-0; Parrott beat Knowles 5-2
**Quarter-finals:** S. Davis beat B. Morgan 5-2; Robidoux beat White 5-4; Hendry beat C. Wilson 5-2; Bond beat Parrott 5-2
**Semi-finals:** S. Davis beat Robidoux 6-3; Hendry beat Bond 6-5
**Final:** S. Davis beat Hendry 9-4

# ROTHMANS GRAND PRIX

**First staged** 1982. **Sponsors** WPBSA (1982–83 when entitled Professional Players Tournament), Rothmans (1984– ). **Venue** La Reserve, Sutton Coldfield & International Snooker Club, Aston, Birmingham (1982), Redwood Lodge Country Club (1983), Hexagon, Reading (1984– ). **Initial prize-money** £32,000. **Prize-money last season** £350,000. **TV** BBC.

**1982** (*Professional Players Tournament*)
**First round:** E. Sinclair beat F. Davis 5-2; J. Meadowcroft beat B. Bennett 5-4; M. Watterson beat J. Donnelly 5-4; T. Griffiths beat C. Roscoe 5-1; A. Higgins beat D. French 5-3; R. Reardon beat T. Murphy 5-0; B. Werbeniuk beat P. Morgan 5-3; C. Everton beat P. Fagan 5-2; C. Thorburn beat P. Medati 5-1; David Taylor beat I. Anderson 5-1; Dennis Taylor beat R. Edmonds 5-4; J. Wych beat B. Kelly 5-0; R. Williams beat C. Ross 5-0; P. Mans beat E. McLaughlin 5-2; W. Thorne beat B. Demarco 5-3; M. Wildman beat J. Dunning 5-4; J. Johnson beat G. Miles 5-1; E. Charlton beat D. Hughes 5-2; F. Jonik beat D. Mountjoy 5-3; K. Stevens beat E. Hughes 5-2; T. Meo beat M. Owen 5-4; C. Wilson beat M. Morra 5-2; A. Knowles beat P Houlihan 5-4; J. Virgo beat I. Black 5-2; M. Hallett beat V. Harris 5-3; D. Martin beat M. Gibson 5-2; J. Fitzmaurice beat D. Sheehan 5-1; J. Spencer beat G. Foulds 5-1
**Second round:** Werbeniuk beat Jack Rea 5-2; Sinclair beat Meadowcroft 5-3; Thorburn beat Everton 5-2; Griffiths beat Watterson 5-2; Reardon beat Higgins 5-2; Dennis Taylor beat David Taylor 5-1; Wildman beat Mans 5-4; Charlton beat Williams 5-2; M. Macleod beat Thorne 5-4; White beat Wych 5-0; Johnson beat Stevens 5-1; Meo beat Jonik 5-0; Wilson beat Knowles 5-4; Virgo beat Hallett 5-2; Spencer beat Martin 5-3; Reynolds beat Fitzmaurice 5-0
**Third round:** Werbeniuk beat Thorburn 5-2; Johnson beat Wildman 5-4; Reynolds beat Wilson 5-1; Virgo beat Spencer 5-1; Charlton beat Meo 5-3; White beat Dennis Taylor 5-3; Griffiths beat Sinclair 5-3; Reardon beat Macleod 5-2
**Quarter-finals:** White beat Griffiths 5-2; Virgo beat Johnson 5-1; Reardon beat Werbeniuk 5-3; Charlton beat Reynolds 5-1
**Semi-finals:** White beat Virgo 10-4; Reardon beat Charlton 10-7
**Final:** Reardon beat White 10-5

**1983** (*Professional Players Tournament*)
**Qualifying:** G. Ganim Jr beat G. Cripsey 5-4; S. Duggan beat M. Darrington 5-4; T. Jones beat W. Oliver 5-2; D. French beat N. Foulds 5-2; B. Bennett beat B. Demarco 5-4; P. Burke beat G. Foulds 5-4; V. Harris *wo* P. Mifsud *scr*; P. Medati beat D. Hughes 5-1; T. Murphy beat P. Browne 5-2; J. Parrott beat P. Watchorn 5-0; D. Sheehan beat P. Houlihan 5-2; M. Morra beat J. Hargreaves 5-0; D. Greaves beat R. Andrewartha 5-2; W. King beat B. Harris 5-3; P. Morgan beat M. Gibson 5-4
**First round:** R. Reardon beat Ganim 5-4; C. Thorburn beat V. Harris 5-1; J. Meadowcroft beat C. Roscoe 5-4; Duggan beat J. Dunning 5-2; J. Virgo beat French 5-4; J. Spencer beat I. Black 5-2; W. Thorne beat C. Everton 5-1; C. Wilson beat Bennett 5-1; T. Griffiths beat L. Dodd 5-3; J. White beat I. Williamson 5-2; Parrott beat P. Fagan 5-2; J. Johnson beat Burke 5-3; E. Hughes beat E. Sinclair 5-4; M. Fisher beat F. Davis 5-4; B. Werbeniuk beat T. Jones 5-4; E. Charlton beat E. McLaughlin 5-0; M. Watterson beat A. Higgins 5-2; K. Stevens beat R. Edmonds 5-1; D. Martin beat J. Fitzmaurice 5-0; T. Murphy beat M. Macleod 5-0; J. Campbell beat D. Mountjoy 5-3; David Taylor beat P. Morgan 5-3; G. Miles beat M. Gauvreau 5-3; M. Wildman beat F. Jonik 5-4; G. Scott beat Dennis Taylor 5-4; T. Meo beat W. King 5-2; S. Francisco beat M. Morra 5-3; D. Reynolds beat D. Greaves 5-1; R. Williams beat D. Sheehan 5-1; M. Hallett beat B. Kelly 5-0; A. Knowles beat P. Medati 5-1; S. Davis beat J. Donnelly 5-1
**Second round:** Reardon beat Duggan 5-2; Thorburn beat Meadowcroft 5-1; Thorne beat

Spencer 5-1; Wilson beat Virgo 5-2; Griffiths beat Parrott 5-1; Johnson beat White 5-3; E. Hughes beat Werbeniuk 5-0; Charlton beat Fisher 5-4; Stevens beat Murphy 5-1; Martin beat Watterson 5-4; Wildman beat David Taylor 5-3; Campbell beat Miles 5-2; Meo beat Reynolds 5-0; S. Francisco beat Scott 5-1; Knowles beat Williams 5-4; Hallett beat S. Davis 5-2
**Third round:** Thorne beat Reardon 5-3; Thorburn beat Wilson 5-3; E. Hughes beat Griffiths 5-2; Johnson beat Charlton 5-0; Stevens beat Wildman 5-0; Campbell beat Martin 5-0; Knowles beat S. Francisco 5-0; Meo beat Hallett 5-3
**Quarter-finals:** Johnson beat Thorburn 5-1; Thorne beat E. Hughes 5-1; Meo beat Stevens 5-3; Knowles beat Campbell 5-3
**Semi-finals:** Knowles beat Thorne 9-7; Johnson beat Meo 9-6
**Final:** Knowles beat Johnson 9-8

**1984**
**Qualifying:** I. Williamson beat P. Thornley 5-2; Donnelly beat J. Hargreaves 5-4; B. Demarco *wo* P. Fagan *scr*; V. Harris beat F. Davis 5-1; J. Dunning beat D. Hughes 5-0; D. O'Kane beat B. Kelly 5-4; M. Gauvreau beat R. Foldvari 5-2; E. McLaughlin beat S. Longworth 5-2; M. Morra beat G. Cripsey 5-3; S. Duggan beat P. Browne 5-2; D. Sheehan *wo* L. Condo *scr*; Sheehan beat B. Mikkelsen 5-3; P. Burke beat M. Darrington 5-3; D. Chalmers beat R. Andrewartha 5-2; W. King beat D. Greaves 5-0; P. Medati beat L. Dodd 5-4; R. Chaperon beat A. Kearney 5-1; Chaperon beat M. Gibson 5-4; P. Francisco beat I. Black 5-4; G. Rigitano beat R. Edmonds 5-3; M. Bradley beat F. Jonik 5-1; W. Jones beat M. Watterson 5-3; John Rea beat J. Fitzmaurice 5-2; R. Bales *wo* J. Wych *scr*; S. Newbury beat M. Fisher 5-0; W. Oliver beat B. Bennett 5-3; C. Everton beat P. Houlihan 5-3; J. McLaughlin beat J. Meadowcroft 5-1; T. Chappel beat G. Scott 5-1; T. Murphy beat G. Foulds 5-1; T. Jones beat E. Sinclair 5-4; C. Roscoe beat D. French 5-0; P. Watchorn *wo* P. Morgan *scr*; D. Fowler *wo* P. Mifsud *scr*
**First round:** A. Knowles beat V. Harris 5-1; Dunning beat P. Mans 5-4; Williamson beat B. Werbeniuk 5-2; J. Johnson beat Medati 5-1; W. Thorne beat Newbury 5-2; M. Macleod beat King 5-4; N. Foulds beat Demarco 5-2; T. Jones beat T. Griffiths 5-3; R. Reardon beat Roscoe 5-1; C. Wilson beat Donnelly 5-2; Dennis Taylor beat Watchorn 5-1; J. Virgo beat Bradley 5-0; A. Higgins beat Bales 5-1; M. Hallett beat Sheehan 5-1; R. Williams beat Chalmers 5-0; K. Stevens beat Chappel 5-3; C. Thorburn beat Rigitano 5-4; J. Campbell beat W. Jones 5-4; T. Meo beat Burke 5-1; D. Martin beat Chaperon 5-4; D. Mountjoy beat E. McLaughlin 5-4; M. Wildman beat J. McLaughlin 5-3; J. Parrott beat Gauvreau 5-3; E. Charlton beat Everton 5-1; J. White beat Oliver 5-1; S. Francisco beat Duggan 5-3; P. Francisco beat J. Spencer 5-2; D. Reynolds beat Fowler 5-2; David Taylor beat O'Kane 5-1; John Rea beat E. Hughes 5-4; G. Miles beat Murphy 5-3; S. Davis beat Morra 5-2
**Second round:** Knowles beat Dunning 5-1; Williamson beat Johnson 5-4; Thorne beat Macleod 5-3; N. Foulds beat T. Jones 5-0; Reardon beat Wilson 5-4; Dennis Taylor beat Virgo 5-3; Hallett beat Higgins 5-3; Stevens beat Williams 5-3; Thorburn beat Campbell 5-1; Meo beat Martin 5-4; Mountjoy beat Wildman 5-0; Charlton beat Parrott 5-1; S. Francisco beat White 5-1; David Taylor beat John Rea 5-1; S. Davis beat Miles 5-0; Reynolds beat P. Francisco 5-4
**Third round:** Knowles beat Williamson 5-2; N. Foulds beat Thorne 5-1; Dennis Taylor beat Reardon 5-3; Stevens beat Hallett 5-3; Thorburn beat Meo 5-4; Mountjoy beat Charlton 5-4; Reynolds beat S. Francisco 5-1; S. Davis beat David Taylor 5-1
**Quarter-finals:** N. Foulds beat Knowles 5-2; Dennis Taylor beat Stevens 5-2; Thorburn beat Mountjoy 5-3; S. Davis beat Reynolds 5-0
**Semi-finals:** Dennis Taylor beat N. Foulds 9-3; Thorburn beat S. Davis 9-7
**Final:** Dennis Taylor beat Thorburn 10-2

**1985**
**First round:** B. West beat B. Demarco 5-2; P. Houlihan *wo* G. Robinson *scr*; S. Simngam

beat D. Mienie 5-3; T. Drago beat P. Watchorn 5-2; R. Bales beat M. Smith 5-1; G. Watson beat D. Sheehan 5-1; J. Hargreaves beat G. Cripsey 5-1; A. Kearney beat Jim Bear 5-3; D. Gilbert beat G. Wilkinson 5-4; J. O'Boye beat S. Hendry 5-4; D. Hughes beat B. Bennett 5-4; M. Darrington beat D. Greaves 5-2; O. Agrawal beat J. Rempe 5-2
**Second round:** West beat J. Meadowcroft 5-2; M. Watterson beat J. Caggianello 5-1; T. Jones beat Houlihan 5-4; Simngam beat F. Davis 5-3; G. Foulds beat Black 5-3; Drago beat W. King 5-4; G. Scott beat D. Chalmers 5-2; Bales beat M. Fisher 5-3; Watson beat C. Roscoe 5-2; G. Miles beat Rigitano 5-4; S. Newbury beat P. Burke 5-3; S. Longworth beat Hargreaves 5-2; T. Chappel beat L. Dodd 5-2; J. Van Rensberg beat E. McLaughlin 5-4; M. Gibson beat M. Bradley 5-4; R. Edmonds beat Kearney 5-2; B. Oliver beat P. Fagan 5-4; S. Duggan beat M. Gauvreau 5-4; Gilbert beat I. Williams 5-4; B. Mikkelsen beat T. Murphy 5-4; W. Jones beat John Rea 5-0; P. Francisco beat C. Everton 5-0; J. McLaughlin beat P. Medati 5-2; B. Harris beat P. Browne 5-3; J. Fitzmaurice beat E. Sinclair 5-3; O'Boye beat R. Chaperon 5-3; B. Kelly beat J. Donnelly 5-4; M. Morra beat D. Hughes 5-2; V. Harris beat J. Wych 5-3; Darrington beat R. Foldvari 5-3; Agrawal *wo* J. Dunning *scr*; D. Fowler beat F. Jonik 5-4
**Third round:** Dennis Taylor beat West 5-1; R. Williams beat Watterson 5-2; T. Meo beat T. Jones 5-2; E. Hughes beat Simngam 5-1; E. Charlton beat G. Foulds 5-1; Drago beat M. Macleod 5-3; Scott beat R. Reardon 5-4; C. Wilson beat Bales 5-1; K. Stevens beat Watson 5-0; Miles beat D. Reynolds 5-3; David Taylor beat Newbury 5-2; Longworth beat J. Parrott 5-2; D. Mountjoy beat Chappel 5-1; J. Campbell beat Van Rensberg 5-4; A. Knowles beat Gibson 5-1; Edmonds beat D. O'Kane 5-2; C. Thorburn beat Oliver 5-0; M. Wildman beat Duggan 5-4; J. Johnson beat Gilbert 5-2; M. Hallett beat Mikkelsen 5-3; W. Jones beat W. Thorne 5-0; P. Francisco beat J. Virgo 5-4; T. Griffiths beat J. McLaughlin 5-4; B. Harris beat J. Spencer 5-2; J. White beat Fitzmaurice 5-0; O'Boye beat P. Mans 5-3; S. Francisco beat Kelly 5-2; D. Martin beat Morra 5-2; A. Higgins beat V. Harris 5-1; N. Foulds beat Darrington 5-0; S. Davis beat Agrawal 5-0; Fowler beat B. Werbeniuk 5-1
**Fourth round:** Dennis Taylor beat Williams 5-2; Meo beat E. Hughes 5-3; Drago beat Charlton 5-3; Wilson beat Scott 5-3; Stevens beat Miles 5-2; Longworth beat David Taylor 5-1; Campbell beat Mountjoy 5-2; Knowles beat Edmonds 5-3; Thorburn beat Wildman 5-2; Johnson beat Hallett 5-4; P. Francisco beat W. Jones 5-3; Griffiths beat B. Harris 5-3; White beat O'Boye 5-4; S. Francisco beat Martin 5-3; Higgins beat N. Foulds 5-3; S. Davis beat Fowler 5-1
**Fifth round:** Dennis Taylor beat Meo 5-3; Wilson beat Drago 5-2; Stevens beat Longworth 5-3; Knowles beat Campbell 5-4; Thorburn beat Johnson 5-1; Griffiths beat P. Francisco 5-2; S. Francisco beat White 5-4; S. Davis beat Higgins 5-0
**Quarter-finals:** Dennis Taylor beat Wilson 5-2; Knowles beat Stevens 5-4; Thorburn beat Griffiths 5-1; S. Davis beat S. Francisco 5-2
**Semi-finals:** Dennis Taylor beat Knowles 9-6; S. Davis beat Thorburn 9-5
**Final:** S. Davis beat Dennis Taylor 10-9

## 1986

**First round:** D. Mienie beat J. Fitzmaurice 5-2; Watchorn beat M. Darrington 5-2; M. Morra beat S. James 5-3; G. Foulds beat G. Wilkinson 5-3; J. Bear beat B. Bennett 5-2; F. Ellis *wo* E. McLaughlin *scr*; J. Meadowcroft beat D. Greaves 5-2; T. Whitthread *wo* S. Simngam *scr*; J. Donnelly beat N. Gilbert 5-1; F. Jonik *wo* L. Heywood *scr*; I. Anderson beat B. Oliver 5-4; A. Kearney beat G. Jenkins 5-3; P. Gibson beat J. Dunning 5-1; J. Wright beat M. Fisher 5-1; R. Grace beat P. Houlihan 5-1; D. Gilbert beat B. Rowswell 5-1; P. Burke beat C. Roscoe 5-3; Jack Rea beat D. Hughes 5-2; D. Roe beat J. Hargreaves 5-1; G. Rigitano beat C. Everton 5-1; M. Smith beat M. Hines 5-2; J. McLaughlin beat K. Owers 5-2; B. Kelly beat M. Parkin 5-2; D. Chalmers beat O. Agrawal 5-1; D. Sheehan beat B. Demarco 5-1; M. Bennett beat M. Watterson 5-1
**Second round:** M. Gibson beat Mienie 5-4; T. Drago beat Watchorn 5-3; Morra beat I. Black 5-4; G. Foulds beat B. Mikkelsen 5-1; Bear beat D. Fowler 5-2; M. Wildman beat Ellis 5-1; F. Davis beat R. Bales 5-4; Meadowcroft *wo* P. Mans *scr*; S. Duggan beat

Whitthread 5-1; W. King beat Donnelly 5-2; G. Miles beat Jonik 5-1; Anderson beat T. Murphy 5-4; T. Chappel beat Kearney 5-1; G. Cripsey beat P. Gibson 5-3; Wright beat M. Bradley 5-0; P. Fagan beat Grace 5-3; J. O'Boye beat R. Edmonds 5-2; S. Newbury beat D. Gilbert 5-1; J. Spencer beat Burke 5-3; W. Jones beat R. Foldvari 5-3; B. Harris beat Jack Rea 5-0; John Rea beat E. Sinclair 5-4; Roe beat J. Van Rensberg 5-3; P. Medati beat Rigitano 5-1; T. Jones beat Smith 5-0; J. McLaughlin beat M. Gauvreau 5-3; L. Dodd beat G. Scott 5-2; V. Harris beat Kelly 5-3; R. Chaperon beat Chalmers 5-2; S. Hendry beat I. Williamson 5-1; P. Browne beat Sheehan 5-4; M. Bennett beat D. O'Kane 5-2

**Third round:** S. Davis beat M. Gibson 5-1; Drago beat E. Charlton 5-4; T. Griffiths beat Morra 5-3; J. Campbell beat G. Foulds 5-0; R. Williams beat Bear 5-2; Wildman beat S. Longworth 5-2; A. Higgins beat F. Davis 5-0; D. Martin *wo* Meadowcroft *scr*; W. Thorne beat Duggan 5-0; King beat B. Werbeniuk 5-2; N. Foulds beat Miles 5-1; C. Wilson beat Anderson 5-4; T. Meo beat Chappel 5-1; J. Parrott beat Cripsey 5-4; Dennis Taylor beat Wright 5-3; J. Virgo beat Fagan 5-2; O'Boye beat C. Thorburn 5-4; Newbury beat D. Reynolds 5-0; S. Francisco beat Spencer 5-4; W. Jones beat David Taylor 5-1; D. Mountjoy beat B. Harris 5-2; J. Wych beat John Rea 5-2; A. Knowles beat Roe 5-3; P. Francisco beat Medati 5-1; J. White beat T. Jones 5-0; J. McLaughlin beat B. West 5-1; Dodd beat K. Stevens 5-4; M. Hallett beat V. Harris 5-2; Chaperon beat R. Reardon 5-3; Hendry beat E. Hughes 5-1; Browne beat J. Johnson 5-2; M. Bennett beat M. Macleod 5-1

**Fourth round:** S. Davis beat Drago 5-1; Griffiths beat Campbell 5-1; Williams beat Wildman 5-1; Higgins beat Martin 5-2; Thorne beat King 5-2; N. Foulds beat Wilson 5-0; Meo beat Parrott 5-3; Dennis Taylor beat Virgo 5-3; Newbury beat O'Boye 5-2; S. Francisco beat W. Jones 5-4; Mountjoy beat Wych 5-1; Knowles beat P. Francisco 5-3; White beat J. McLaughlin 5-2; Hallett beat Dodd 5-2; Hendry beat Chaperon 5-2; Browne beat M. Bennett 5-0

**Fifth round:** S. Davis beat Griffiths 5-2; Williams beat Higgins 5-1; N. Foulds beat Thorne 5-3; Meo beat Dennis Taylor 5-2; S. Francisco beat Newbury 5-2; Knowles beat Mountjoy 5-1; White beat Hallett 5-3; Hendry beat Browne 5-3

**Quarter-finals:** Williams beat S. Davis 5-1; N. Foulds beat Meo 5-3; S. Francisco beat Knowles 5-2; White beat Hendry 5-4

**Semi-finals:** Williams beat N. Foulds 9-8; White beat S. Francisco 9-6

**Final:** White beat Williams 10-6

### 1987

**First round:** G. Rigitano beat Jack Rea 5-4; J. Meadowcroft beat A. Harris 5-3; J. Bear beat D. Greaves 5-0; I. Anderson beat G. Jenkins 5-2; P. Gibson beat P. Fagan 5-0; P. Burke beat C. Everton 5-1; R. Foldvari beat J. Dunning 5-0; Glen Wilkinson *wo* J. Rempe *scr*; M. Smith beat I. Black 5-0; D. Gilbert beat E. Lawlor 5-2; Gary Wilkinson beat B. Harris 5-0; C. Roscoe *wo* J. Hargreaves *scr*; S. Meakin beat M. Morra 5-2; M. Clark beat I. Williamson 5-1; M. Fisher beat P. Watchorn 5-4; D. Heaton *wo* M. Watterson *scr*; B. Rowswell beat J. Smith 5-3; B. Kelly *wo* B. Mikkelsen *scr*; J. Donnelly beat D. Hughes 5-1; M. Darrington beat D. Chalmers 5-2; F. Jonik beat N. Gilbert 5-3; B. Oliver *wo* E. McLaughlin *scr*; D. Roe beat T. Whitthread 5-1; E. Sinclair beat F. Ellis 5-4; J. Chambers beat J. Fitzmaurice 5-2; R. Marshall beat D. Sheehan 5-1

**Second round:** J. Wright beat Rigitano 5-0; Meadowcroft beat P. Browne 5-3; Bear beat B. Harris 5-3; R. Bales beat Anderson 5-1; P. Gibson beat S. Duggan 5-4; G. Cripsey beat M. Gibson 5-2; S. James beat G. Foulds 5-0; John Rea beat M. Bradley 5-1; R. Reardon beat Burke 5-2; Foldvari beat W. King 5-4; Glen Wilkinson beat K. Owers 5-4; M. Gauvreau beat M. Smith 5-3; D. Fowler beat D. Gilbert 5-1; Gary Wilkinson beat D. O'Kane 5-2; T. Jones beat Roscoe 5-1; S. Newbury beat Meakin 5-1; Clark beat R. Grace 5-1; Fisher beat F. Davis 5-0; P. Houlihan beat Heaton 5-0; R. Chaperon beat Rowswell 5-4; L. Dodd beat Kelly 5-2; W. Jones beat Donnelly 5-3; A. Kearney beat Darrington 5-0; T. Chappel beat Jonik 5-4; J. McLaughlin beat Oliver 5-2; Roe beat

M. Wildman 5-3; R. Edmonds beat Sinclair 5-2; J. Van Rensberg beat T. Murphy 5-4; Chambers beat J. O'Boye 5-3; M. Bennett beat R. Medati 5-4; G. Miles beat G. Scott 5-2; J. Wych beat Marshall 5-2
**Third round:** J. White beat Wright 5-4; T. Drago beat Meadowcroft 5-1; W. Thorne beat Bear 5-1; Bales beat J. Campbell 5-3; P. Gibson beat M. Hallett 5-4; Cripsey beat B. West 5-3; J. Johnson beat James 5-4; P. Francisco beat John Rea 5-3; Dennis Taylor beat Reardon 5-1; B. Werbeniuk beat Foldvari 5-1; C. Wilson beat Glen Wilkinson 5-4; J. Virgo beat Gauvreau 5-1; S. Francisco beat Fowler 5-1; Gary Wilkinson beat S. Longworth 5-4; C. Thorburn beat T. Jones 5-2; Newbury beat T. Meo 5-0; Clark beat N. Foulds 5-4; Fisher beat E. Hughes 5-4; Houlihan beat D. Reynolds 5-4; Chaperon beat David Taylor 5-3; J. Parrott beat Dodd 5-1; K. Stevens beat W. Jones 5-1; T. Griffiths beat Kearney 5-0; Chappel beat J. Spencer 5-1; T. Knowles beat J. McLaughlin 5-0; Roe beat D. Martin 5-4; Edmonds beat R. Williams 5-3; E. Charlton beat Van Rensberg 5-3; Chambers beat D. Mountjoy 5-2; S. Hendry beat M. Bennett 5-1; S. Davis beat Miles 5-1; Wych beat M. Macleod 5-4
**Fourth round:** Drago beat White 5-3; Thorne beat Bales 5-2; Cripsey beat P. Gibson 5-4; P. Francisco beat Johnson 5-2; Dennis Taylor beat Werbeniuk 5-3; Wilson beat Virgo 5-3; Gary Wilkinson beat S. Francisco 5-3; Newbury beat Thorburn 5-0; Fisher beat Clark 5-4; Chaperon beat Houlihan 5-0; Parrott beat Stevens 5-0; Griffiths beat Chappel 5-3; Knowles beat Roe 5-2; Charlton beat Edmonds 5-3; Hendry beat Chambers 5-1; S. Davis beat Wych 5-1
**Fifth round:** Thorne beat Drago 5-2; P. Francisco beat Cripsey 5-1; Dennis Taylor beat Wilson 5-2; Newbury beat Gary Wilkinson 5-3; Chaperon beat Fisher 5-2; Parrott beat Griffiths 5-4; Knowles beat Charlton 5-0; Hendry beat S. Davis 5-2
**Quarter-finals:** P. Francisco beat Thorne 5-3; Dennis Taylor beat Newbury 5-2; Parrott beat Chaperon 5-2; Hendry beat Knowles 5-2
**Semi-finals:** Dennis Taylor beat P. Francisco 9-4; Hendry beat Parrott 9-7
**Final:** Hendry beat Dennis Taylor 10-7

## 1988

**First round:** I. Williamson beat C. Everton 5-0; J. Smith beat G. Foulds 5-3; A. Robidoux beat J. Van Rensberg 5-2; S. Campbell beat I. Black 5-1; B. Oliver beat J. Fitzmaurice 5-3; John Rea beat M. Darrington 5-4; G. Jenkins beat Jim Bear 5-4; M. Gibson beat P. Burke 5-4; M. Morra *wo* D. Chalmers *scr*; J. Dunning beat D. Heaton 5-1; D. Morgan beat B. Rowswell 5-0; P. Medati beat P. Watchorn 5-2; B. Harris beat Jack Rea 5-2; D. Mienie *wo* J. Meadowcroft *scr*; N. Terry beat E. Sinclair 5-3; C. Edwards *wo* P. Gibson *scr*; B. Kelly beat F. Davis 5-3; G. Rigitano *wo* F. Jonik *scr*; V. Harris beat R. Marshall 5-3; M. Johnston-Allen beat C. Roscoe 5-1; F. Ellis beat E. Lawlor 5-4; M. Wildman beat P. Fagan 5-1; B. Mikkelsen beat D. Hughes 5-4; M. Smith beat D. Sheehan 5-4; M. Watterson beat J. Donnelly 5-0; J. Chambers beat S. Meakin 5-0; M. Bradley beat M. Rowing 5-3; T. Whitthread beat R. Grace 5-4; T. Wilson beat G. Scott 5-3; R. Foldvari beat M. Price 5-1; A. Harris beat T. Kearney 5-2; Glen Wilkinson beat I. Graham 5-4
**Second round:** Williamson beat J. Wych 5-4; M. Fisher beat J. Smith 5-3; Robidoux beat R. Bales 5-1; K. Stevens beat S. Campbell 5-3; N. Gilbert beat Oliver 5-4; P. Houlihan beat John Rea 5-1; J. O'Boye beat Jenkins 5-1; L. Dodd beat M. Gibson 5-1; Morra beat R. Reardon 5-4; R. Edmonds beat Dunning 5-3; Gary Wilkinson beat Morgan 5-1; Medati beat W. King 5-1; D. Roe beat B. Harris 5-2; D. Gilbert beat Mienie 5-0; Terry beat G. Miles 5-1; S. Duggan beat Edwards 5-4; D. Fowler beat Kelly 5-4; W. Jones beat Rigitano 5-3; J. McLaughlin beat V. Harris 5-4; Johnston-Allen beat P. Browne 5-2; Ellis beat M. Gauvreau 5-2; D. Martin beat Wildman 5-1; T. Jones beat Mikkelsen 5-3; M. Smith beat G. Cripsey 5-0; Watterson beat M. Bennett 5-3; Chambers beat K. Owers 5-3; Bradley beat T. Murphy 5-3; M. Clark beat Whitthread 5-1; T. Chappel beat T. Wilson 5-4; R. Foldvari beat Wright 5-4; B. Werbeniuk beat A. Harris 5-1; M. Macleod beat Glen Wilkinson 5-3
**Third round:** S. Hendry beat Williamson 5-2; D. Mountjoy beat Fisher 5-1; Robidoux

beat J. Virgo 5-1; T. Meo beat Stevens 5-3; N. Gilbert beat S. Francisco 5-4; E. Charlton beat Houlihan 5-3; A. Knowles beat O'Boye 5-4; D. Reynolds beat Dodd 5-3; J. Parrott beat Morra 5-3; Edmonds beat S. Longworth 5-3; Gary Wilkinson beat W. Thorne 5-3; R. Williams beat Medati 5-2; A. Higgins beat Roe 5-4; D. O'Kane beat D. Gilbert 5-4; N. Foulds beat Terry 5-4; S. Duggan beat David Taylor 5-1; White beat Fowler 5-0; W. Jones beat J. Campbell 5-2; J. McLaughlin beat P. Francisco 5-2; J. Spencer beat Johnston-Allen 5-3; Dennis Taylor beat Ellis 5-1; R. Chaperon beat Martin 5-0; M. Hallett beat T. Jones 5-2; S. James beat M. Smith 5-3; T. Griffiths beat Watterson 5-3; B. West beat Chambers 5-3; J. Johnson beat Bradley 5-2; E. Hughes beat Clark 5-3; C. Wilson beat Chappel 5-2; T. Drago beat Foldvari 5-3; S. Davis *wo* Werbeniuk *suspended*; S. Newbury beat Macleod 5-3
**Fourth round:** Mountjoy beat Hendry 5-1; Robidoux beat Meo 5-0; N. Gilbert beat Charlton 5-0; Knowles beat Reynolds 5-3; Edmonds beat Parrott 5-3; Williams beat Gary Wilkinson 5-2; Higgins beat O'Kane 5-0; N. Foulds beat Duggan 5-4; White beat W. Jones 5-1; J. McLaughlin beat Spencer 5-3; Dennis Taylor beat Chaperon 5-4; Hallett beat James 5-2; Griffiths beat West 5-1; E. Hughes beat Johnson 5-2; Wilson beat Drago 5-4; S. Davis beat Newbury 5-1
**Fifth round:** Robidoux beat Mountjoy 5-4; N. Gilbert beat Knowles 5-4; Williams beat Edmonds 5-3; Higgins beat N. Foulds 5-3; White beat J. McLaughlin 5-2; Dennis Taylor beat Hallett 5-2; Griffiths beat E. Hughes 5-2; S. Davis beat Wilson 5-1
**Quarter-finals:** Robidoux beat N. Gilbert 5-4; Higgins beat Williams 5-4; Dennis Taylor beat White 5-2; S. Davis beat Griffiths 5-3.
**Semi-finals:** Higgins beat Robidoux 9-7; S. Davis beat Dennis Taylor 9-1
**Final:** S. Davis beat Higgins 10-6

## 1989

**First round:** J. Meadowcroft beat Glen Wilkinson 5-4; A. Harris beat F. Ellis 5-2; E. Sinclair *wo* T. Whitthread *scr*; J. Smith beat J. Wright 5-2; I. Brumby *wo* Jim Bear *scr*; R. Marshall beat R. Grace 5-2; S. Meakin beat M. Wildman 5-2; P. Houlihan beat M. Watterson 5-4; B. Kelly beat F. Davis 5-4; G. Rigitano beat G. Miles 5-3; M. Rowing beat M. Bradley 5-4; P. Medati beat N. Dyson 5-4; E. Lawlor beat P. Thornley 5-3; J. Dunning beat J. Fitzmaurice 5-3; S. Campbell beat R. Foldvari 5-4; G. Foulds beat K. Owers 5-1; M. Smith beat B. Pinches 5-2; N. Bond beat G. Scott 5-0; M. Price beat M. Gibson 5-4; M. Morra beat A. Cairns 5-4; M. Gauvreau beat Jack Rea 5-2; J. Wattana beat John Rea 5-3; P. Gibson beat B. Gollan 5-4; A. Kearney beat T. Wilson 5-2; D. Campbell beat I. Williamson 5-0; B. Rowswell beat M. Darrington 5-2; B. Harris beat B. Morgan 5-2; B. Oliver beat J. Van Rensberg 5-3; V. Harris beat D. Hughes 5-4; P. Watchorn beat J. Donnelly 5-2; S. Murphy beat C. Edwards 5-4; N. Terry beat D. Sheehan 5-4
**Second round:** S. Duggan beat Meadowcroft 5-1; N. Gilbert beat A. Harris 5-2; Sinclair beat J. Spencer 5-0; J. Smith beat J. O'Boye 5-4; R. Edmonds beat Brumby 5-2; C. Roscoe beat Marshall 5-4; Meakin beat K. Stevens 5-4; T. Jones beat Houlihan 5-0; M. Johnston-Allen beat Kelly 5-1; D. Fowler beat Rigitano 5-4; A. Robidoux beat Rowing 5-4; M. Bennett beat Medati 5-2; D. Morgan beat Lawlor 5-3; D. Gilbert beat Dunning 5-1; S. Campbell beat R. Bales 5-2; J. Chambers beat G. Foulds 5-2; G. Cripsey beat M. Smith 5-4; Bond beat T. Chappel 5-2; J. Wych beat Price 5-3; Morra beat I. Graham 5-0; J. McLaughlin beat Gauvreau 5-3; Wattana beat M. Macleod 5-1; P. Gibson beat Fisher 5-3; L. Dodd beat Kearney 5-1; J. Campbell beat D. Campbell 5-3; Rowswell beat T. Murphy 5-1; S. Longworth beat B. Harris 5-2; Oliver beat D. Martin 5-3; V. Harris beat David Taylor 5-3; W. King beat Watchorn 5-3; S. Murphy beat P. Browne 5-3; Gary Wilkinson beat Terry 5-3
**Third round:** S. Davis beat Duggan 5-1; N. Foulds beat N. Gilbert 5-1; T. Meo beat Sinclair 5-2; J. Smith beat P. Francisco 5-3; A. Knowles beat Edmonds 5-4; M. Clark beat Roscoe 5-3; C. Thorburn beat Meakin 5-3; T. Jones beat O'Kane 5-2; M. Hallett beat Johnston-Allen 5-1; Fowler beat D. Roe 5-4; Robidoux beat S. James 5-2; E. Hughes beat M. Bennett 5-2; J. Johnson beat D. Morgan 5-2; A. Higgins beat

D. Gilbert 5-3; J. White beat S. Campbell 5-0; Chambers beat B. West 5-4; S. Hendry beat Cripsey 5-2; Bond beat R. Chaperon 5-4; D. Mountjoy *wo* Wych *scr*; Morra beat W. Jones 5-4; W. Thorne beat J. McLaughlin 5-2; Wattana beat S. Francisco 5-2; P. Gibson beat T. Griffiths 5-2; Dodd beat R. Williams 5-3; Dennis Taylor beat J. Campbell 5-3; Rowswell beat C. Wilson 5-4; J. Virgo beat Longworth 5-4; S. Newbury beat Oliver 5-4; D. Reynolds beat V. Harris 5-0; King beat E. Charlton 5-0; J. Parrott beat S. Murphy 5-1; Gary Wilkinson beat Drago 5-1
**Fourth round:** S. Davis beat N. Foulds 5-4; J. Smith beat Meo 5-3; Knowles beat Clark 5-2; T. Jones beat Thorburn 5-4; Fowler beat Hallett 5-3; Robidoux beat E. Hughes 5-1; Johnson beat Higgins 5-2; White beat Chambers 5-1; Hendry beat Bond 5-1; Mountjoy beat Morra 5-0; Wattana beat Thorne 5-3; P. Gibson beat Dodd 5-4; Dennis Taylor beat Rowswell 5-2; Newbury beat Virgo 5-0; Reynolds beat King 5-3; Parrott beat Gary Wilkinson 5-1
**Fifth round:** S. Davis beat J. Smith 5-1; Knowles beat T. Jones 5-4; Fowler beat Robidoux 5-4; Johnson beat White 5-0; Mountjoy beat Hendry 5-3; Wattana beat P. Gibson 5-3; Dennis Taylor beat Newbury 5-1; Reynolds beat Parrott 5-2
**Quarter-finals:** S. Davis beat Knowles 5-2; Fowler beat Johnson 5-4; Wattana beat Mountjoy 5-2; Reynolds beat Dennis Taylor 5-3
**Semi-finals:** S. Davis beat Fowler 9-2; Reynolds beat Wattana 9-8
**Final:** S. Davis beat Reynolds 10-0

## BCE CANADIAN MASTERS

**First staged** 1985. **Sponsors** BCE. **Venue** CBC Studios, Toronto (1985–87), Minkler Auditorium, North York (1988). **Initial prize-money** £50,000. **Prize-money last season** £200,000. **TV** CBC.

### 1985

**First round:** Dennis Taylor beat J. Parrott 5-1; R. Reardon beat A. Knowles 5-2; C. Thorburn beat J. White 5-3; S. Davis beat T. Griffiths 5-4
**Semi-finals:** Taylor beat Reardon 8-3; S. Davis beat Thorburn 8-1
**Final:** Taylor beat S. Davis 9-5

### 1986

**First round:** W. Thorne beat Dennis Taylor 5-4; A. Knowles beat C. Thorburn 5-1; S. Davis beat J. White 5-2; A. Higgins beat J. Johnson 5-3
**Semi-finals:** Thorne beat Knowles 8-7; S. Davis beat Higgins 8-2
**Final:** S. Davis beat Thorne 9-3

### 1987

**First round:** N. Foulds beat T. Griffiths 5-4; J. White beat A. Knowles 5-1; C. Thorburn beat J. Johnson 5-3; Dennis Taylor beat S. Davis 5-1
**Semi-finals:** White beat N. Foulds 8-7; Dennis Taylor beat Thorburn 8-5
**Final:** Dennis Taylor beat White 9-7

### 1988

**First round:** M. Smith beat Jack Rea 5-1; G. Scott beat C. Everton 5-0; A. Robidoux beat Glen Wilkinson 5-3; J. Chambers beat P. Fagan 5-2; J. Fitzmaurice beat J. Van Rensberg 5-3; M. Prize beat J. Meadowcroft 5-0; B. Oliver beat J. Rempe 5-3; J. Smith beat G. Foulds 5-1; M. Darrington beat V. Harris 5-0; B. Kelly *wo* P. Gibson *scr*; I. Graham beat E. Sinclair 5-3; R. Foldvari beat P. Burke 5-2; N. Terry beat J. Donnelly 5-1; M. Watterson beat G. Rigitano 5-3; S. Campbell beat A. Kearney 5-2; B. Rowswell beat F. Ellis 5-1; M Gibson beat D. Hughes 5-1; M. Wildman beat G. Jenkins 5-1; A. Harris beat M. Morra 5-3; I. Williamson beat D. Chalmers 5-2; P. Medati beat C. Edwards 5-3; M. Johnston-Allen beat B. Harris 5-4; J. Dunning beat D. Sheehan 5-3; D. Morgan beat F. Davis 5-2; C. Roscoe *wo* F. Jonik *scr*; R. Marshall

beat I. Black 5-1; E. Lawlor beat B. Mikkelsen 5-2; T. Wilson beat R. Grace 5-2; P. Watchorn beat G. Miles 5-2; M. Bradley beat S. Meakin 5-0; T. Whitthread beat Jim Bear 5-4; John Rea beat M. Rowing 5-2
**Second round:** M. Smith beat P. Houlihan 5-2; Scott beat R. Edmonds 5-2; Robidoux beat M. Fisher 5-0; T. Murphy beat J. Chambers 5-3; Fitzmaurice beat J. McLaughlin 5-2; Price beat D. Gilbert 5-4; Oliver beat J. Campbell 5-3; R. Reardon beat J. Smith 5-2; T. Chappel beat Darrington 5-1; K. Stevens beat Kelly 5-1; Graham beat J. Wright 5-2; J. Wych beat Foldvari 5-2; Gary Wilkinson beat Terry 5-3; D. Martin beat Watterson 5-1; S. Campbell beat R. Bales 5-2; D. Fowler beat Rowswell 5-4; W. King beat M. Gibson 5-3; S. Duggan beat Wildman 5-1; J. O'Boye beat A. Harris 5-3; M. Gauvreau beat Williamson 5-1; Medati beat G. Cripsey 5-0; N. Gilbert beat Johnston-Allen 5-4; B. Werbeniuk beat Dunning 5-3; D. Morgan beat T. Jones 5-0; Roscoe beat W. Jones 5-4; L. Dodd beat Marshall 5-3; K. Owers beat Lawlor 5-2; M. Clark beat T.Wilson 5-3; M. Macleod beat Watchorn 5-1; P. Browne beat Bradley 5-2; D. Roe beat Whitthread 5-2; M. Bennett beat John Rea 5-4
**Third round:** S. Davis beat M. Smith 5-0; Scott beat R. Williams 5-2; J. Johnson beat Robidoux 5-1; S. James beat Murphy 5-3; W. Thorne beat Fitzmaurice 5-0; D. Mountjoy beat Price 5-2; T. Griffiths beat Oliver 5-4; Reardon beat R. Chaperon 5-4; C. Thorburn beat Chappel 5-1; J. Spencer beat Stevens 5-3; Graham beat P. Francisco 5-3; E. Charlton beat Wych 5-4; C. Wilson beat Gary Wilkinson 5-2; D. Reynolds beat Martin 5-0; S. Hendry beat S. Campbell 5-2; Fowler beat T. Drago 5-1; King beat N. Foulds 5-3; Duggan beat B. West 5-3; M. Hallett beat O'Boye 5-0; Gauvreau beat T. Meo 5-0; J. Virgo beat Medati 5-1; S. Newbury beat N. Gilbert 5-3; J. Parrott beat Dunning 5-2; D. Morgan beat D. O'Kane 5-3; Roscoe beat A. Knowles 5-2; David Taylor beat Dodd 5-3; Dennis Taylor beat Owers 5-1; Clark beat A. Higgins 5-3; Macleod beat S. Francisco 5-4; S. Longworth beat Browne 5-4; J. White beat Roe 5-3; M. Bennett beat E. Hughes 5-2
**Fourth round:** S. Davis beat Scott 5-1; James beat Johnson 5-4; Mountjoy beat Thorne 5-4; Griffiths beat Reardon 5-2; Thorburn beat Spencer 5-2; Graham beat Charlton 5-2; C. Wilson beat Reynolds 5-4; Hendry beat Fowler 5-2; King beat Duggan 5-4; Hallett beat Gauvreau 5-3; Virgo beat Newbury 5-2; Parrott beat D. Morgan 5-3; David Taylor beat Roscoe 5-1; Dennis Taylor beat Clark 5-4; Longworth beat Macleod 5-3; White beat M. Bennett 5-3
**Fifth round:** S. Davis beat James 5-0; Griffiths beat Mountjoy 5-4; Thorburn beat Graham 5-4; Hendry beat Wilson 5-1; Hallett beat King 5-2; Parrott beat Virgo 5-4; Dennis Taylor beat David Taylor 5-2; White beat Longworth 5-0
**Quarter-finals:** S. Davis beat Griffiths 5-3; Hendry beat Thorburn 5-4; Hallett beat Parrott 5-3; White beat Dennis Taylor 5-3
**Semi-finals:** S. Davis beat Hendry 9-5; White beat Hallett 9-2
**Final:** White beat S. Davis 9-4

*Not staged in 1989.*

# DUBAI CLASSIC

**First staged** 1989. **Sponsors** Dubai Duty Free and Emirates. **Venue** Al Nasr Stadium, Dubai. **Initial prize-money** £200,000. **Prize-money last season** £200,000. **TV** Dubai and satellite.

### 1989

**First round:** P. Gibson beat J. Meadowcroft 5-4; J. Wattana beat F. Davis 5-1; D. Campbell beat R. Foldvari 5-2; C. Everton *wo* T. Whitthread *scr*; P. Medati beat R. Grace 5-3; A. Kearney beat A. Cairns 5-1; N. Bond beat K. Owers 5-1; M. Morra beat B. Mikkelsen 5-2; J. Grech beat F. Ellis 5-1; I. Williamson beat D. Hughes 5-1; E. Sinclair beat D. Heaton 5-1; G. Rigitano beat J. Donnelly 5-1; E. Lawlor beat Jack Rea 5-3; M. Gibson beat V. Harris 5-3; G. Miles beat P. Watchorn 5-3; A. Harris beat

P. Thornley 5-1; J. Dunning beat P. Fagan 5-2; M. Smith beat S. Murphy 5-1; M. Bradley beat N. Dyson 5-4; B. Rowswell beat B. Kelly 5-0; S. Meakin beat J. Smith 5-4; Glen Wilkinson beat I. Black 5-2; J. Van Rensberg beat G. Jenkins 5-3; M. Wildman *wo* M. Watterson *scr*; M. Price beat P. Burke 5-0; B. Harris beat D. Sheehan 5-3; P. Houlihan beat B. Pinches 5-1; I. Brumby beat S. Campbell 5-4; B. Morgan beat M. Darrington 5-2; B. Gollan *wo* Jim Bear *scr*; G. Foulds beat M. Rowing 5-4; J. Fitzmaurice beat B. Oliver 5-4
**Second round:** P. Gibson beat M. Johnston-Allen 5-0; Wattana beat K. Stevens 5-4; J. Wright beat D. Campbell 5-1; J. Chambers beat Everton 5-1; Medati beat D. Gilbert 5-3; M. Fisher beat Kearney 5-3; Bond beat T. Murphy 5-0; Morra beat N. Gilbert 5-4; Grech beat C. Roscoe 5-1; L. Dodd beat Williamson 5-0; Sinclair beat I. Graham 5-4; M. Bennett beat Rigitano 5-2; Lawlor beat T. Wilson 5-2; R. Bales beat M. Gibson 5-4; Miles beat C. Edwards 5-4; W. King beat A. Harris 5-3; T. Jones beat Dunning 5-2; P. Browne beat M. Smith 5-1; M. Gauvreau beat Bradley 5-4; Rowswell beat John Rea 5-4; J. Campbell beat Meakin 5-0; J. McLaughlin beat Glen Wilkinson 5-3; Van Rensberg beat G. Cripsey 5-3; T. Chappel beat Wildman 5-1; D. Martin beat Price 5-3; B. Harris beat S. Duggan 5-3; D. Morgan beat Houlihan 5-2; G. Scott beat Brumby 5-4; B. Morgan beat Edmonds 5-0; R. Marshall beat Gollan 5-2; M. Macleod beat G. Foulds 5-1; N. Terry beat Fitzmaurice 5-3
**Third round:** J. Parrott beat P. Gibson 5-2; Wattana beat E. Hughes 5-0; S. James beat Wright 5-2; Chambers beat J. O'Boye 5-4; Medati beat S. Francisco 5-4; P. Francisco beat Fisher 5-0; Bond beat J. Johnson 5-3; A. Robidoux beat Morra 5-1; Grech beat A. Knowles 5-3; Gary Wilkinson beat Dodd 5-3; A. Higgins beat Sinclair 5-2; D. O'Kane beat M. Bennett 5-2; E. Charlton beat Lawlor 5-3; D. Roe beat Miles 5-3; D. Mountjoy beat Miles 5-2; King beat David Taylor 5-1; T. Jones beat M. Hallett 5-4; D. Fowler beat Browne 5-4; M. Clark beat Gauvreau 5-1; Rowswell beat R. Chaperon 5-4; J. Campbell beat S. Newbury 5-1; J. McLaughlin beat S. Longworth 5-1; J. Virgo beat Van Rensberg 5-4; Chappel beat R. Williams 5-2; D. Reynolds beat Martin 5-2; Spencer beat B. Harris 5-3; B. West beat D. Morgan 5-1; W. Jones beat Scott 5-3; C. Wilson beat B. Morgan 5-3; T. Drago beat Marshall 5-0; S. Hendry beat Macleod 5-3; J. Wych beat Terry 5-2
**Fourth round:** Parrott beat Wattana 5-3; James beat Chambers 5-4; P. Francisco beat Medati 5-1; Bond beat Robidoux 5-4; Grech beat Gary Wilkinson 5-2; Higgins beat O'Kane 5-3; Roe beat Charlton 5-3; Mountjoy beat King 5-2; Fowler beat T. Jones 5-4; Clark beat Rowswell 5-4; J. McLaughlin beat J. Campbell 5-1; Virgo beat Chappel 5-4; Reynolds beat Spencer 5-4; West beat W. Jones 5-2; Drago beat C. Wilson 5-0; Hendry *wo* Wych *scr*
**Fifth round:** Parrott beat James 5-3; P. Francisco beat Bond 5-4; Higgins beat Grech 5-4; Mountjoy beat Roe 5-4; Fowler beat Clark 5-2; J. McLaughlin beat Virgo 5-4; Reynolds beat West 5-2; Hendry beat Drago 5-3
**Quarter-finals:** Parrott beat P. Francisco 5-1; Mountjoy beat Higgins 5-2; Fowler beat J. McLaughlin 5-1; Hendry beat Reynolds 5-3
**Semi-finals:** Mountjoy beat Parrott 5-4; Hendry beat Fowler 5-4
**Final:** Hendry beat Mountjoy 9-2

## STORMSEAL UK OPEN

**First staged** 1977. **Sponsors** Super Crystalate (1977), Coral (1979–85), Tennents (1986–88), Stormseal (1989– ). **Venue** Blackpool Tower Circus (1977), Guild Hall, Preston (1978– ). **Initial prize-money** £7,000. **Prize-money last season** £420,000. **TV** BBC.

**1977** (*Super Crystalate UK Championship*)
**First round:** J. Virgo *wo* J. Barrie *scr*; C. Ross beat J. Karnehm 5-4; P. Fagan beat Jack Rea 5-1; J. Meadowcroft beat P. Houlihan 5-1; D. Mountjoy beat R. Andrewartha 5-2; W. Thorne beat B. Bennett 5-1; J. Dunning beat M. Parkin 5-4;

David Taylor beat D. Greaves 5-4
**Second round:** Virgo beat Dennis Taylor 5-2; G. Miles beat Ross 5-1; Fagan beat F. Davis 5-0; Meadowcroft beat R. Reardon 5-4; Mountjoy beat J. Spencer 5-3; Thorne beat R. Williams 5-4; Dunning *wo* J. Pulman *scr*; A. Higgins beat David Taylor 5-4
**Quarter-finals:** Virgo beat Miles 5-2; Fagan beat Meadowcroft 5-4; Mountjoy beat Thorne 5-4; Higgins beat Dunning 5-0
**Semi-finals:** Fagan beat Virgo 9-8; Mountjoy beat Higgins 9-2
**Final:** Fagan beat Mountjoy 12-9

**1978** (*Coral UK Championship*)
**Qualifying:** W. Thorne beat B. Bennett 9-4; R. Andrewartha beat P. Houlihan 9-3; D. Mountjoy beat J. Barrie 9-5; R. Williams beat T. Griffiths 9-8; J. Dunning beat D. Greaves 9-3; J. Virgo beat R. Edmonds 9-4; David Taylor beat M. Parkin 9-2; J. Meadowcroft beat Jack Rea 9-5
**First round:** David Taylor beat Fagan 9-7; Virgo beat J. Pulman 9-3; F. Davis beat Dunning 9-2; A. Higgins beat Meadowcroft 9-6; Thorne beat R. Reardon 9-6; G. Miles beat Williams 9-8; Mountjoy beat Dennis Taylor 9-4; Andrewartha beat J. Spencer 9-8
**Quarter-finals:** David Taylor beat Virgo 9-2; Higgins beat F. Davis 9-4; Miles beat Thorne 9-1; Mountjoy beat Andrewartha 9-4
**Semi-finals:** David Taylor beat Higgins 9-5; Mountjoy beat Miles 9-1
**Final:** Mountjoy beat David Taylor 15-9

**1979** (*Coral UK Championship*)
**Qualifying:** Jack Rea beat B. Bennett 9-8; M. Hallett beat M. Parkin 9-1; J. Dunning beat D. Greaves 9-8
**First round:** W. Thorne beat R. Andrewartha 9-4; P. Houlihan beat Jack Rea 9-3; S. Davis beat Dunning 9-3; P. Fagan beat Hallett 9-4; B. Werbeniuk beat J. Johnson 9-3; R. Edmonds beat J. Meadowcroft 9-3; T. Meo beat David Taylor 9-7; C. Wilson beat J. Pulman 9-7
**Second round:** S. Davis beat D. Mountjoy 9-5; T. Griffiths beat Wilson 9-4; A. Higgins beat Houlihan 9-3; Fagan beat G. Miles 9-5; Werbeniuk beat J. Spencer 9-8; Dennis Taylor beat Thorne 9-8; J. Virgo beat Meo 9-6; Edmonds beat F. Davis 9-6
**Quarter-finals:** Werbeniuk beat Edmonds 9-8; Dennis Taylor beat Fagan 9-6; Virgo beat S. Davis 9-7; Griffiths beat Higgins 9-7
**Semi-finals:** Virgo beat Dennis Taylor 9-4; Griffiths beat Werbeniuk 9-3
**Final:** Virgo beat Griffiths 14-13

**1980** (*Coral UK Championship*)
**Preliminary round:** M. Hallett beat B. Bennett 9-4; S. Hood beat C. Ross 9-3
**Qualifying:** Hallett beat R. Edmonds 9-8; E. Sinclair beat K. Kennerley 9-1; M. Wildman beat C. Wilson 9-8; J. Meadowcroft beat D. Greaves 9-1; R. Andrewartha beat A. Knowles 9-8; R. Williams beat J. Barrie 9-1; J. Johnson beat J. Dunning 9-6; T. Meo beat Hood 9-5
**First round:** Meo beat P. Houlihan 9-1; S. Davis beat Hallett 9-1; P. Fagan beat Johnson 9-4; Sinclair beat G. Miles 9-5; Thorne beat Meadowcroft 9-1; Wildman beat J. Spencer 9-7; Williams beat D. Mountjoy 9-8; Andrewartha beat J. Pulman 9-6
**Second round:** Meo beat J. Virgo 9-1; S. Davis beat B. Werbeniuk 9-3; Dennis Taylor beat Sinclair 9-6; T. Griffiths beat Fagan 9-8; A. Higgins beat Thorne 9-7; F. Davis beat Wildman 9-6; R. Reardon beat Andrewartha 9-3; Williams beat David Taylor 9-7
**Quarter-finals:** S. Davis beat Meo 9-5; Griffiths beat Dennis Taylor 9-2; Higgins beat F. Davis 9-6; Reardon beat Williams 9-4
**Semi-finals:** S. Davis beat Griffiths 9-0; Higgins beat Reardon 9-7
**Final:** S. Davis beat Higgins 16-6

**1981** (*Coral UK Championship*)
**Qualifying groups**
1 P. Medati beat E. McLaughlin 9-5; Medati beat J. Donnelly 9-7; W. Thorne beat

Medati 9-6

2 M. Hallett beat V. Harris 9-4; Hallett beat D. Hughes 9-6; Hallett beat P. Fagan 9-5

3 M. Gibson beat J. Fitzmaurice 9-6; C. Everton beat Gibson 9-7; J. White beat Everton 9-4

4 J. Johnson beat T. Murphy 9-1; M. Watterson beat B. Bennett 9-4; Johnson beat Watterson 9-3; Johnson beat C. Wilson 9-5

5 P. Houlihan beat K. Kennerley 9-1; Houlihan beat I. Black 9-4; Houlihan beat J. Meadowcroft 9-4

6 G. Foulds beat B. Kelly 9-7; A. Knowles beat Foulds 9-1

7 E. Sinclair beat M. Wildman 9-8; Sinclair beat S. Hood 9-0; D. Martin beat Sinclair 9-7

8 R. Williams beat D. French 9-3; C. Roscoe beat M. Macleod 9-7; Williams beat Roscoe 9-4; Williams beat J. Dunning 9-4

**First round:** Thorne beat R. Edmonds 9-4; K. Stevens beat Hallet 9-4; White beat J. Virgo 9-6; Johnson beat J. Spencer 9-5; G. Miles beat Houlihan 9-5; Knowles beat F. Davis 9-6; A. Higgins beat Martin 9-7; T. Meo beat Williams 9-8

**Second round:** S. Davis beat Thorne 9-2; B. Werbeniuk beat Stevens 9-7; White beat Dennis Taylor 9-5; R. Reardon beat Johnson 9-7; T. Griffiths beat Miles 9-4; Knowles beat D. Mountjoy 9-6; Higgins beat David Taylor 9-5; Meo beat C. Thorburn 9-6

**Quarter-finals:** S. Davis beat Werbeniuk 9-5; White beat Reardon 9-8; Griffiths beat Knowles 9-5; Meo beat Higgins 9-4

**Semi-finals:** S. Davis beat White 9-0; Griffiths beat Meo 9-3

**Final:** S. Davis beat Griffiths 16-3

**1982** (*Coral UK Championship*)

**Qualifying groups**

1 T. Meo beat G. Scott 9-5

2 C. Wilson beat E. McLaughlin 9-6

3 D. Martin beat M. Macleod 9-6

4 J. Meadowcroft beat D. Hughes 9-8

5 J. Donnelly beat C. Ross 9-5

6 P. Houlihan *wo* J. Dunning *scr*

7 M. Hallett beat B. Demarco 9-1

8 B. Kelly beat J. Fitzmaurice 9-0

9 G. Foulds beat M. Gibson 9-2; R. Williams beat Foulds 9-7

10 V. Harris beat M. Owen 9-4; J. Johnson beat Harris 9-8

11 T. Murphy beat C. Everton 9-4; E. Sinclair beat Murphy 9-5

12 B. Harris beat G. Cripsey 9-6; Harris beat M. Watterson 9-3

13 M. Fisher beat I. Black 9-3; Fisher beat R. Edmonds 9-8

14 L. Dodd beat I. Williamson 9-1; Dodd beat D. French 9-7

15 B. Bennett *wo* J. Phillips *scr*; P. Medati beat Bennett 9-1

16 C. Roscoe beat Jack Rea 9-6; M. Wildman beat Roscoe 9-4

**First round:** S. Davis beat Williams 9-6; P. Fagan beat B. Harris 9-6; T. Griffiths beat Johnson 9-1; Dennis Taylor beat Meadowcroft 9-7; David Taylor beat Dodd 9-7; Meo beat G. Miles 9-4; J. Virgo beat Kelly 9-2; D. Mountjoy beat Houlihan 9-3; R. Reardon beat Wildman 9-5; Hallett beat F. Davis 9-7; Wilson beat W. Thorne 9-7; J. White beat Medati 9-7; J. Spencer beat Sinclair 9-8; A. Knowles beat Donnelly 9-6; D. Reynolds beat Fisher 9-6; A. Higgins beat Martin 9-7

**Second round:** S. Davis beat Fagan 9-3; Griffiths beat Dennis Taylor 9-7; Meo beat David Taylor 9-6; Virgo beat Mountjoy 9-5; Reardon beat Hallett 9-8; White beat Wilson 9-5; Spencer beat Knowles 9-6; Higgins beat Reynolds 9-8

**Quarter-finals:** Griffiths beat S. Davis 9-6; Meo beat Virgo 9-6; Reardon beat White 9-8; Higgins beat Spencer 9-5

**Semi-finals:** Griffiths beat Meo 9-7; Higgins beat Reardon 9-6

**Final:** Griffiths beat Higgins 16-15

**1983** (*Coral UK Championship*)
**Qualifying groups**
1 J. Johnson beat M. Gibson 9-6
2 T. Jones beat E. Sinclair 9-3
3 M. Wildman beat D. Greaves 9-5
4 M. Macleod beat B. Bennett 9-0
5 M. Watterson beat C. Everton 9-6; Watterson beat F. Davis 9-6
6 M. Darrington beat G. Cripsey 9-3; M. Hallett beat Darrington 9-1
7 N. Foulds beat C. Roscoe 9-2; Foulds beat J. Meadowcroft 9-2
8 V. Harris beat P. Houlihan 9-6; R. Williams beat Harris 9-6
9 D. French beat Jack Rea 9-5; D. Martin beat French 9-3
10 G. Foulds beat S. Duggan 9-8; Foulds beat L. Dodd 9-7
11 J. Parrott beat G. Scott 9-7; Parrott beat M. Fisher 9-0
12 R. Andrewartha beat W. Oliver 9-1; J. Dunning beat Andrewartha 9-2
13 T. Murphy beat B. Demarco 9-4; Murphy beat Donnelly 9-4
14 P. Medati beat D. Hughes 9-3; Medati beat R. Edmonds 9-7
15 B. Harris beat E. McLaughlin 9-8; Harris beat J. Fitzmaurice 9-3
16 I. Williamson beat J. Hargreaves 9-4; I. Black beat Williamson 9-6

**First round:** T. Griffiths beat Martin 9-4; Hallett beat G. Miles 9-4; Johnson beat J. Virgo 9-6; David Taylor beat N. Foulds 9-4; A. Knowles beat J. Jones 9-5; D. Mountjoy beat Watterson 9-2; A. Higgins beat Macleod 9-6; Medati beat D. Reynolds 9-3; C. Wilson beat Williams 9-4; R. Reardon beat B. Harris 9-7; Dennis Taylor beat Murphy 9-6; J. White beat Black 9-1; J. Spencer beat Dunning 9-7; T. Meo beat Parrott 9-7; W. Thorne beat Wildman 9-5; S. Davis beat G. Foulds 9-1
**Second round:** Griffiths beat Hallett 9-5; Johnson beat David Taylor 9-3; Knowles beat Mountjoy 9-5; Higgins beat Medati 9-1; Reardon beat Wilson 9-4; White beat Dennis Taylor 9-4; Meo beat Spencer 9-5; S. Davis beat Thorne 9-3
**Quarter-finals:** White beat Reardon 9-4; Griffiths beat Johnson 9-2; Higgins beat Knowles 9-5; S. Davis beat Meo 9-4
**Semi-finals:** Higgins beat Griffiths 9-4; S. Davis beat White 9-4
**Final:** Higgins beat S. Davis 16-15

**1984** (*Coral UK Open*)
**Qualifying rounds**
1 T. Jones beat R. Chaperon 9-1; Jones beat P. Fagan 9-2; Jones beat M. Wildman 9-2
2 P. Watchorn beat B. Harris 9-7; Watchorn beat C. Everton 9-6; M. Fisher beat Watchorn 9-5; R. Williams beat Fisher 9-8
3 R. Foldvari beat D. Greaves 9-5; G. Cripsey beat Foldvari 9-7; J. Fitzmaurice beat Cripsey 9-8; J. Parrott beat Fitzmaurice 9-6
4 P. Francisco beat D. Sheehan 9-5; P. Francisco beat I. Williamson 9-2; E. Sinclair beat P. Francisco 9-8; S. Francisco beat Sinclair 9-4
5 D. Fowler beat B. Demarco 9-3; Fowler beat W. Oliver 9-3; Fowler beat F. Davis 9-4; Fowler beat N. Foulds 9-6
6 D. O'Kane beat W. Jones 9-7; O'Kane beat S. Duggan 9-6; G. Scott beat O'Kane 9-7; M. Macleod beat Scott 9-5
7 S. Newbury beat G. Rigitano 9-6; Newbury beat F. Jonik 9-3; L. Dodd beat Newbury 9-6; C. Wilson beat Dodd 9-8
8 J. McLaughlin beat D. French 9-3; McLaughlin *wo* P. Morgan *scr*; McLaughlin beat C. Roscoe 9-8; McLaughlin beat G. Miles 9-8
9 R. Bales beat D. Chalmers 9-2; Bales beat E. McLaughlin 9-4; M. Gauvreau beat Bales 9-8; Gauvreau beat P. Mans 9-6
10 G. Foulds beat D. Hughes 9-7; P. Browne beat Foulds 9-5; W. King beat Browne 9-5; King beat J. Virgo 9-4
11 John Rea beat B. Bennett 9-5; Rea beat F. Dunning 9-3; Rea beat R. Edmonds 9-6; J. Johnson beat Rea 9-6
12 T. Chappel beat P. Houlihan 9-3; Chappel beat I. Black 9-3; Chappel *wo*

R. Andrewartha *scr*; Chappel beat D. Reynolds 9-6
13 J. Hargreaves beat P. Medati 9-6; M. Gibson beat Hargreaves 9-8; J. Donnelly beat Gibson 9-6; J. Campbell beat Donnelly 9-6
14 M. Bradley beat V. Harris 9-8; Bradley beat B. Kelly 9-6; Bradley beat J. Meadowcroft 9-7; M. Hallett beat Bradley 9-8
15 S. Longworth beat M. Darrington 9-5; Longworth beat P. Burke 9-4; M. Morra beat Longworth 9-1; E. Hughes beat Morra 9-8
16 T. Murphy beat A. Kearney 9-2; Murphy beat M. Watterson 9-4; Murphy beat D. Martin 9-8

**First round:** A. Higgins beat T. Jones 9-7; S. Davis beat Murphy 9-1; J. White beat Campbell 9-7; Williams beat B. Werbeniuk 9-1; W. Thorne beat Parrott 9-7; E. Charlton beat S. Francisco 9-4; D. Mountjoy beat Hallett 9-2; T. Meo beat E. Hughes 9-4; R. Reardon beat Fowler 9-2; K. Stevens beat Chappel 9-7; Dennis Taylor beat King 9-5; Wilson beat T. Griffiths 9-6; Johnson beat J. Spencer 9-6; David Taylor beat Macleod 9-6; A. Knowles beat Gauvreau 9-5; C. Thorburn beat J. McLaughlin 9-4
**Second round:** Thorne beat Charlton 9-7; White beat Mountjoy 9-2; Higgins beat Williams 9-7; Stevens beat Johnson 9-2; Reardon beat David Taylor 9-4; Thorburn beat Wilson 9-3; Knowles beat Dennis Taylor 9-2; S. Davis beat Meo 9-7
**Quarter-finals:** Higgins beat Thorne 9-5; S. Davis beat White 9-4; Thorburn beat Reardon 9-8; Stevens beat Knowles 9-7
**Semi-finals:** Higgins beat Thorburn 9-7; S. Davis beat Stevens 9-2
**Final:** S. Davis beat Higgins 16-8

**1985** (*Coral UK Open*)
**First round:** D. Sheehan beat P. Watchorn 9-7; T. Drago beat D. Gilbert 9-5; G. Wilkinson beat M. Smith 9-4; O. Agrawal beat S. Hendry 9-2; B. West *wo* G. Robinson *scr*; G. Jenkins beat P. Burke 9-5; J. O'Boye beat B. Bennett 9-3; M. Darrington *wo* M. Parkin *scr*; P. Houlihan beat G. Watson 9-4; J. Hargreaves beat D. Mienie 9-7; D. Hughes beat A. Kearney 9-8; S. Simngam beat R. Bales 9-2; Jim Bear beat B. Demarco 9-1; G. Cripsey beat D. Greaves 9-4
**Second round:** Sheehan beat G. Scott 9-6; Drago beat J. Donnelly 9-8; S. Longworth beat M. Gibson 9-2; D. Fowler beat Wilkinson 9-6; M. Morra beat Agrawal 9-8; West beat C. Roscoe 9-5; G. Miles beat B. Oliver 9-4; T. Murphy beat C. Everton 9-4; M. Bradley beat Jenkins 9-3; T. Chappell *wo* J. McLaughlin *scr*; R. Edmonds beat J. Van Rensberg 9-5; F. Davis beat John Rea 9-8; B. Mikkelsen beat I. Williamson 9-3; P. Medati beat W. Kelly 9-1; O'Boye beat M. Gauvreau 9-5; V. Harris beat I. Black 9-3; L. Dodd *wo* Jack Rea *scr*; E. Sinclair beat G. Foulds 9-4; P. Browne beat D. Chalmers 9-4; W. Jones beat J. Fitzmaurice 9-3; J. Wych beat S. Duggan 9-5; Darrington beat R. Foldvari 9-6; T. Jones beat F. Jonik 9-4; J. McLaughlin beat R. Chaperon 9-5; S. Newbury beat Houlihan 9-3; J. Meadowcroft beat Hargreaves 9-8; P. Francisco *wo* G. Rigitano *scr*; W. King beat D. Hughes 9-0; Simngam beat M. Fisher 9-4; P. Fagan beat B. Harris 9-2; Jim Bear beat M. Watterson 9-0; Cripsey *wo* J. Dunning *scr*
**Third round:** S. Davis beat Sheehan 9-1; Drago beat M. Wildman 9-5; T. Meo beat Longworth 9-5; Fowler beat P. Mans 9-2; D. Mountjoy beat Morra 9-2; West beat E. Hughes 9-3; R. Reardon beat Miles 9-4; M. Macleod beat Murphy 9-7; J. White beat Bradley 9-4; Chappel beat D. O'Kane 9-5; A. Higgins beat Edmonds 9-8; F. Davis beat B. Werbeniuk 9-7; David Taylor beat Mikkelsen 9-6; J. Campbell beat Medati 9-7; A. Knowles beat O'Boye 9-5; J. Spencer beat V. Harris 9-5; C. Thorburn beat Dodd 9-4; J. Parrott beat Sinclair 9-2; W. Thorne beat Browne 9-6; J. Virgo beat W. Jones 9-7; S. Francisco beat Wych 9-8; D. Martin beat Darrington 9-3; T. Griffiths beat T. Jones 9-5; D. Reynolds beat J. McLaughlin 9-7; K. Stevens beat Newbury 9-7; M. Hallett beat Meadowcroft 9-1; P. Francisco beat E. Charlton 9-5; R. Williams beat King 9-5; J. Johnson beat Simngam 9-4; N. Foulds beat Fagan 9-5; Dennis Taylor beat Jim Bear 9-3; Cripsey beat C. Wilson 9-7
**Fourth round:** S. Davis beat Drago 9-2; Meo beat Fowler 9-2; West beat Mountjoy 9-4; Macleod beat Reardon 9-5; White beat Chappel 9-5; Higgins beat F. Davis 9-2; David

Taylor beat Campbell 9-4; Knowles beat Spencer 9-7; Thorburn beat Parrott 9-6; Thorne beat Virgo 9-8; S. Francisco beat Martin 9-6; Griffiths beat Reynolds 9-7; Stevens beat Hallett 9-5; Williams beat P. Francisco 9-7; N. Foulds beat Johnson 9-8; Dennis Taylor beat Cripsey 9-2
**Fifth round:** S. Davis beat Meo 9-5; West beat Macleod 9-4; White beat Higgins 9-6; Knowles beat David Taylor 9-7; Thorne beat Thorburn 9-7; Griffiths beat S. Francisco 9-5; Stevens beat Williams 9-7; Dennis Taylor beat N. Foulds 9-5
**Quarter-finals:** S. Davis beat West 9-1; White beat Knowles 9-4; Thorne beat Griffiths 9-7; Dennis Taylor beat Stevens 9-1
**Semi-finals:** S. Davis beat White 9-5; Thorne beat Dennis Taylor 9-7
**Final:** S. Davis beat Thorne 16-14

**1986** (*Tennents UK Open*)
**First round:** G. Wilkinson beat F. Jonik 9-8; M. Fisher beat D. Greaves 9-4; K. Owers beat D. Gilbert 9-8; M. Morra beat B. Bennett 9-3; D. Sheehan beat M. Bennett 9-8; D. Hughes beat F. Ellis 9-6; R. Grace beat P. Houlihan 9-6; B. Oliver beat D. Chalmers 9-6; S. James beat G. Rigitano 9-5; J. Dunning beat A. Kearney 9-6; C. Roscoe beat M. Parkin 9-1; D. Roe beat G. Foulds 7-1 (*retd*); J. Hargreaves *wo* L. Heywood *scr*; M. Darrington beat T. Whitthread 9-8; P. Watchorn beat B. Kelly 9-8; Jack Rea *wo* S. Simngam *scr*; J. Bear beat C. Everton 9-1; M. Watterson beat P. Burke 9-0; N. Gilbert beat J. Donnelly 9-8; J. Fitzmaurice beat M. Hines 9-4; P. Gibson beat O. Agrawal 9-6; G. Jenkins beat D. Mienie 9-6; B. Rowswell *wo* E. McLaughlin *scr*; J. Wright beat M. Smith 9-7; J. Meadowcroft beat B. Demarco 9-2
**Second round:** T. Chappel beat Wilkinson 9-2; V. Harris beat Fisher 9-4; Owers beat S. Newbury 9-8; B. Mikkelsen beat E. Sinclair 9-8; T. Drago beat Morra 9-6; G. Miles beat Sheehan 9-8; T. Murphy beat D. Hughes 9-0; Grace beat P. Medati 9-5; S. Hendry beat Oliver 9-1; I. Williamson beat P. Browne 9-4; J. O'Boye beat S. Duggan 9-4; W. King beat James 9-8; M. Gibson beat Dunning 9-2; Roscoe beat M. Wildman 9-6; Roe beat J. Van Rensberg 9-6; W. Jones beat Hargreaves 9-0; D. Fowler beat Darrington 9-6; R. Chaperon beat Dodd 9-4; G. Scott beat Watchorn 9-7; J. Spencer beat R. Foldvari 9-6; G. Cripsey beat R. Bales 9-6; B. Harris beat Jack Rea 9-5; R. Edmonds beat Bear 9-6; Watterson beat I. Black 9-3; John Rea beat N. Gilbert 9-8; T. Jones beat Fitzmaurice 9-0; P. Gibson *wo* P. Mans *scr*; D. O'Kane beat Jenkins 9-5; J. McLaughlin beat Gauvreau 9-8; Rowswell beat F. Davis 9-4; Wright beat P. Fagan 9-0; M. Bradley beat Meadowcroft 9-2
**Third round:** S. Davis beat Chappel 9-7; E. Charlton beat V. Harris 9-2; S. Francisco beat Owers 9-3; D. Reynolds beat Mikkelsen 9-6; Drago beat R. Williams 9-7; J. Virgo beat Miles 9-7; W. Thorne beat Murphy 9-4; Grace beat M. Macleod 9-6; A. Higgins beat Hendry 9-8; D. Martin beat Williamson 9-5; T. Meo beat O'Boye 9-3; M. Hallett beat King 9-5; R. Reardon beat M. Gibson 9-6; E. Hughes beat Roscoe 9-8; Dennis Taylor beat Roe 9-6; W. Jones beat J. Campbell 9-3; C. Thorburn beat Fowler 9-7; David Taylor beat Chaperon 9-8; K. Stevens beat Scott 9-2; Spencer beat C. Wilson 9-5; N. Foulds beat Cripsey 9-7; J. Wych beat B. Harris 9-6; J. White beat Edmonds 9-4; P. Francisco beat Watterson 9-4; A. Knowles beat John Rea 9-4; T. Jones beat B. West 9-4; T. Griffiths beat P. Gibson 9-3; O'Kane beat B. Werbeniuk 9-5; D. Mountjoy beat J. McLaughlin 9-6; S. Longworth beat Rowswell 9-3; J. Johnson beat Wright 9-1; J. Parrott beat Bradley 9-4
**Fourth round:** S. Davis beat Charlton 9-6; Reynolds beat S. Francisco 9-8; Drago beat Virgo 9-6; Thorne beat Grace 9-1; Higgins beat Martin 9-6; Hallett beat Meo 9-4; E. Hughes beat Reardon 9-5; W. Jones beat Dennis Taylor 9-2; Thorburn beat David Taylor 9-4; Spencer beat Stevens 9-4; N. Foulds beat Wych 9-3; White beat P. Francisco 9-5; Knowles beat T. Jones 9-2; Griffiths beat O'Kane 9-0; Longworth beat Mountjoy 9-1; Parrott beat Johnson 9-1
**Fifth round:** S. Davis beat Reynolds 9-5; Drago beat Thorne 9-5; Higgins beat Hallet 9-7; W. Jones beat E. Hughes 9-5; Thorburn beat Spencer 9-2; N. Foulds beat White 9-7; Knowles beat Griffiths 9-6; Parrott beat Longworth 9-6

**Quarter-finals:** S. Davis beat Drago 9-8; Higgins beat W. Jones 9-5; N. Foulds beat Thorburn 9-2; Parrott beat Knowles 9-4
**Semi-finals:** S. Davis beat Higgins 9-3; N. Foulds beat Parrott 9-3
**Final:** S. Davis beat N. Foulds 16-7

**1987** (*Tennents UK Open*)
**First round:** J. Meadowcroft *wo* E. McLaughlin *scr*; E. Lawlor beat J. Fitzmaurice 9-0; I. Williamson beat B. Kelly 9-5; Jack Rea beat M. Watterson 9-6; R. Foldvari beat M. Clark 9-8; M. Fisher *wo* J. Hargreaves *scr*; J. Donnelly beat I. Anderson 9-4; B. Rowswell beat C. Everton 9-4; B. Oliver beat P. Burke 9-1; M. Smith beat F. Jonik 9-5; J. Chambers beat C. Roscoe 9-4; P. Gibson beat G. Rigitano 9-5; F. Ellis beat D. Sheehan 9-8; P. Watchorn beat M. Darrington 9-2; D. Gilbert beat D. Heaton 9-5; I. Black beat J. Smith 9-8; J. Bear beat D. Chalmers 9-5; A. Harris beat M. Morra 9-8; Gary Wilkinson beat G. Jenkins 9-3; D. Hughes *wo* B. Mikkelsen *scr*; J. Van Rensberg beat T. Whitthread 9-5; S. Meakin beat Glen Wilkinson 9-0; D. Roe beat R. Marshall 9-3; V. Harris beat D. Greaves 9-1; J. Dunning beat P. Fagan 9-4; N. Gilbert beat E. Sinclair 9-8
**Second round:** W. King beat Meadowcroft 9-4; Lawlor beat J. Wright 9-7; S. Duggan beat Williamson 9-7; R. Chaperon beat Jack Rea 9-6; S. Newbury beat Foldvari 9-5; J. Wych beat Fisher 9-6; John Rea beat J. McLaughlin 9-5; J. O'Boye beat Donnelly 9-2; L. Dodd beat Medati 9-6; D. O'Kane beat Rowswell 9-2; Oliver beat G. Scott 9-4; T. Murphy beat M. Gibson 9-0; M. Smith beat P. Browne 9-4; Chambers beat M. Wildman 9-5; G. Cripsey beat P. Gibson 9-6; F. Davis beat Ellis 9-6; D. Fowler beat Kearney 9-7; Miles beat P. Houlihan 9-3; T. Jones beat S. James 9-6; Watchorn beat M. Bradley 9-5; T. Chappel beat D. Gilbert 9-2; B. Werbeniuk beat Black 9-5; Bear beat B. Harris 9-4; M. Gauvreau beat A. Harris 9-3; Gary Wilkinson beat R. Grace 9-5; R. Edmonds beat D. Hughes 9-4; R. Reardon beat Van Rensberg 9-7; W. Jones beat Meakin 9-1; Roe beat K. Owers 9-7; V. Harris beat M. Bennett 9-7; Dunning beat R. Bales 9-8; N. Gilbert beat G. Foulds 9-4
**Third round:** S. Davis beat King 9-2; P. Francisco beat Lawlor 9-4; A. Higgins beat Duggan 9-4; David Taylor beat Chaperon 9-6; J. Parrott beat Newbury 9-5; Wych beat S. Hendry 9-7; T. Knowles beat John Rea 9-6; K. Stevens beat O'Boye 9-8; Dennis Taylor beat Dodd 9-8; O'Kane beat E. Charlton 9-8; Thorne beat Oliver 9-3; Murphy beat T. Drago 9-7; M. Smith beat Mountjoy 9-7; J. Campbell beat Chambers 9-7; C. Thorburn beat Cripsey 9-6; J. Virgo beat F. Davis 9-4; Fowler beat N. Foulds 9-5; Miles beat J. Spencer 9-5; M. Hallett beat T. Jones 9-2; T. Meo beat Watchorn 9-1; Chappel beat D. Reynolds 9-5; S. Longworth beat Werbeniuk 9-5; J. Johnson beat Bear 9-5; B. West beat Gauvreau 9-6; T. Griffiths beat Gary Wilkinson 9-5; Edmonds beat M. Macleod 9-4; S. Francisco beat Reardon 9-3; C. Wilson beat W. Jones 9-6; Roe beat R. Williams 9-7; V. Harris beat D. Martin 9-7; J. White beat Dunning 9-0; E. Hughes beat N. Gilbert 9-7
**Fourth round:** S. Davis beat P. Francisco 9-6; Higgins beat David Taylor 9-6; Parrott beat Wych 9-6; Knowles beat Stevens 9-8; O'Kane beat Dennis Taylor 9-7; Thorne beat Murphy 9-4; Campbell beat M. Smith 9-8; Thorburn beat Virgo 9-6; Fowler beat Miles 9-4; Hallett beat Meo 9-5; Chappel beat Longworth 9-6; Johnson beat West 9-6; Griffiths beat Edmonds 9-5; S. Francisco beat Wilson 9-1; Roe beat V. Harris 9-5; White beat E. Hughes 9-4
**Fifth round:** S. Davis beat Higgins 9-2; Parrott beat Knowles 9-4; Thorne beat O'Kane 9-7; Thorburn beat Campbell 9-4; Hallett beat Fowler 9-4; Johnson beat Chappel 9-4; Griffiths beat S. Francisco 9-3; White beat Roe 9-5
**Quarter-finals:** S. Davis beat Parrott 9-5; Thorne beat Thorburn 9-8; Johnson beat Hallett 9-7; White beat Griffiths 9-7
**Semi-finals:** S. Davis beat Thorne 9-2; White beat Johnson 9-4
**Final:** S. Davis beat White 16-14

**1988** (*Tennents UK Open*)
**First round:** N. Terry beat G. Rigitano 9-5; D. Sheehan beat F. Davis 9-7; S. Campbell beat J. Dunning 9-5; F. Ellis beat Jim Bear 9-7; M. Bradley beat T. Wilson 9-7; I. Williamson beat C. Everton 9-1; G. Miles beat P. Watchorn 9-6; T. Whitthread beat J. Donnelly 9-8; A. Robidoux beat I. Black 9-2; T. Kearney beat M. Watterson 9-3; John Rea beat S. Meakin 9-6; M. Gibson beat A. Harris 9-8; E. Lawlor beat J. Fitzmaurice 9-1; C. Edwards beat E. Sinclair 9-8; M. Price beat R. Grace 9-3; C. Roscoe beat M. Darrington 9-7; M. Rowing beat G. Foulds 9-4; M. Johnston-Allen beat J. Van Rensberg 9-4; M. Smith beat R. Marshall 9-6; B. Harris beat I. Graham 9-4; B. Rowswell beat G. Jenkins 9-4; D. Morgan *wo* P. Gibson *scr*; B. Oliver beat B. Kelly 9-2; Glen Wilkinson beat Jack Rea 9-0; J. Chambers *wo* D. Chalmers *scr*; M. Morra beat D. Hughes 9-2; M. Wildman beat D. Mienie 9-4; J. Smith beat J. Meadowcroft 9-7; P. Medati *wo* F. Jonik *scr*; G. Scott beat P. Fagan 9-2; R. Foldvari beat P. Burke 9-0; V. Harris beat B. Mikkelsen 9-3
**Second round:** W. King beat Terry 9-7; Gary Wilkinson beat Sheehan 9-5; M. Clark beat S. Campbell 9-3; D. Fowler beat Ellis 9-3; J. McLaughlin beat Bradley 9-3; J. O'Boye beat Williamson 9-4; D. Martin beat Miles 9-7; N. Gilbert beat Whitthread 9-5; Robidoux beat R. Bales 9-4; Kearney beat P. Browne 9-6; John Rea beat G. Cripsey 9-2; D. Roe beat M. Gibson 9-3; D. Gilbert beat Lawlor 9-2; K. Stevens beat Edwards 9-4; T. Murphy beat Price 9-6; Roscoe beat P. Houlihan 9-8; Rowing beat J. Wright 9-7; W. Jones beat M. Johnston-Allen 9-8; M. Smith beat B. Werbeniuk 9-5; B. Harris beat M. Macleod 9-8; Rowswell beat M. Gauvreau 9-7; R. Reardon beat Morgan 9-5; J. Wych beat Oliver 9-6; L. Dodd beat Glen Wilkinson 9-6; K. Owers beat Chambers 9-4; S. Duggan beat Morra 9-8; R. Edmonds beat Wildman 9-4; T. Chappel beat J. Smith 9-6; Medati beat M. Fisher 9-3; T. Jones beat Scott 9-5; J. Campbell beat Foldvari 9-7; M. Bennett beat V. Harris 9-7
**Third round:** S. Davis beat King 9-7; Gary Wilkinson beat R. Chaperon 9-0; Clark beat M. Hallett 9-6; Fowler beat S. Longworth 9-8; Dennis Taylor beat J. McLaughlin 9-5; O'Boye beat E. Hughes 9-8; J. Parrott beat Martin 9-6; N. Gilbert beat J. Spencer 9-7; C. Thorburn beat Robidoux 9-4; S. James beat Kearney 9-1; P. Francisco beat John Rea 9-2; Roe beat T. Meo 9-6; W. Thorne beat D. Gilbert 9-3; Stevens beat E. Charlton 9-7; S. Hendry beat Murphy 9-4; Roscoe beat S. Newbury 9-7; N. Foulds beat Rowing 9-4; D. Mountjoy beat W. Jones 9-7; J. Johnson beat M. Smith 9-2; R. Williams beat B. Harris 9-4; J. Virgo beat Rowswell 9-3; D. O'Kane beat Reardon 9-8; A. Knowles beat Wych 9-4; T. Griffiths beat Owers 9-2; Duggan beat T. Drago 9-7; C. Wilson beat Edmonds 9-1; D. Reynolds beat Chappel 9-4; S. Francisco beat Medati 9-8; B. West beat T. Jones 9-5; J. White beat J. Campbell 9-5; M. Bennett beat David Taylor 9-4
**Fourth round:** S. Davis beat Gary Wilkinson 9-3; Fowler beat Clark 9-6; Dennis Taylor beat O'Boye 9-4; Parrott beat N. Gilbert 9-8; Thorburn beat James 9-6; Roe beat P. Francisco 9-7; Thorne beat Stevens 9-3; Hendry beat Roscoe 9-3; Mountjoy beat N. Foulds 9-4; Johnson beat Williams 9-7; Virgo beat O'Kane 9-8; Knowles beat Higgins 9-6; Griffiths beat Duggan 9-2; Reynolds beat C. Wilson 9-3; West beat S. Francisco 9-4; M. Bennett beat White 9-6
**Fifth round:** S. Davis beat Fowler 9-6; Parrott beat Dennis Taylor 9-4; Thorburn beat Roe 9-8; Hendry beat Thorne 9-4; Mountjoy beat Johnson 9-5; Virgo beat Knowles 9-3; Griffiths beat Reynolds 9-6; West beat Bennett 9-4
**Quarter-finals:** S. Davis beat Parrott 9-4; Hendry beat Thorburn 9-2; Mountjoy beat Virgo 9-8; Griffiths beat West 9-5
**Semi-finals:** Hendry beat S. Davis 9-3; Mountjoy beat Griffiths 9-4
**Final:** Mountjoy beat Hendry 16-12

**1989**
**First round:** M. Rowing beat F. Davis 6-5; E. Lawlor beat I. Brumby 6-5; M. Morra beat G. Rigitano 6-4; B. Gollan beat J. Dunning 6-4; J. Wright beat G. Foulds 6-1; S. Meakin beat A. Harris 6-2; B. Rowswell beat M. Darrington 6-2; B. Pinches beat M. Smith 6-4; N. Bond beat E. Sinclair 6-5; P. Medati beat P. Thornley 6-3; J. Bear beat Jack Rea 6-0;

T. Wilson *wo* T. Whitthread *scr*; J. Donnelly beat J. Fitzmaurice 6-2; A. Cairns beat G. Miles 6-2; P. Watchorn beat P. Gibson 6-3; S. Campbell beat R. Foldvari 6-5; N. Dyson beat John Rea 6-4; I. Williamson beat D. Hughes 6-0; M. Price beat T. Kearney 6-1; B. Morgan beat V. Harris 6-3; N. Terry beat M. Watterson 6-3; M. Gibson beat C. Edwards 6-0; D. Sheehan beat G. Scott 6-1; B. Harris beat D. Campbell 6-2; P. Houlihan beat M. Wildman 6-3; B. Oliver beat F. Ellis 6-5; S. Murphy beat Glen Wilkinson 6-1; R. Marshall beat J. Van Rensberg 6-5; M. Gauvreau beat J. Meadowcroft 6-1; J. Wattana beat L. Dodd 6-2; R. Grace beat M. Bradley 6-4; J. Smith beat K. Owers 6-5
**Second round:** Rowing beat R. Edmonds 6-4; J. McLaughlin beat Lawlor 6-3; T. Jones beat Morra 6-3; Gollan beat D. Martin 6-0; David Taylor beat Wright 6-2; Meakin beat N. Gilbert 6-5; Rowswell beat M. Fisher 6-5; M. Johnston-Allen beat Pinches 6-1; Bond beat M. Macleod 6-3; Medati beat C. Roscoe 6-5; M. Bennett beat Bear 6-5; D. Fowler beat T. Wilson 6-3; S. Duggan beat Donnelly 6-1; J. Spencer beat Cairns 6-3; W. King beat Watchorn 6-5; S.Campbell beat D. Morgan 6-5; K. Stevens beat Dyson 6-4; J. O'Boye beat Williamson 6-4; Price beat R. Bales 6-2; B. Morgan beat G. Cripsey 6-2; Terry beat R. Reardon 6-4; S. Longworth beat M. Gibson 6-4; Gary Wilkinson beat Sheehan 6-2; D. Gilbert beat B. Harris 6-2; I. Graham beat Houlihan 6-0; P. Browne beat Oliver 6-2; T. Chappel beat S. Murphy 6-1; Marshall beat J. Campbell 6-4; J. Chambers beat Gauvreau 6-2; Wattana beat J. Wych 6-1; T. Murphy beat Grace 6-0; A. Robidoux beat J. Smith 6-0
**Third round:** O'Boye beat D. Mountjoy 9-8; Gollan beat E. Charlton 9-2; Robidoux beat Meo 9-5; S. Francisco beat Longworth 9-7; A. Knowles beat Marshall 9-2; T. Drago beat Johnston-Allen 9-7; T. Griffiths beat King 9-4; T. Jones beat S. Newbury 9-7; C. Thorburn beat Rowing 9-2; P. Francisco beat S. Campbell 9-5; K. Stevens beat J. Virgo 9-7; Bennett beat E. Hughes 9-3; D. Reynolds beat Terry 9-6; W. Jones beat Fowler 9-7; S. Hendry beat Spencer 9-1; B. West beat David Taylor 9-5; J. Parrott beat J. McLaughlin 9-2; B. Chaperon beat Price 9-6; B. Morgan beat S. James 9-4; Gary Wilkinson beat Roe 9-2; J. Johnson beat Chambers 9-7; M. Clark beat Rowswell 9-1; J. White beat Bond 9-3; N. Foulds beat Meakin 9-1; M. Hallett beat Wattana 9-7; D. O'Kane beat Graham 9-7; Dennis Taylor beat D. Gilbert 9-2; R. Williams beat T. Murphy 9-6; W. Thorne beat Medati 9-3; A. Higgins beat Duggan 9-7; S. Davis beat Chappel 9-3
**Fourth round:** Gollan beat O'Boye 9-5; Robidoux beat S. Francisco 9-3; Knowles beat Drago 9-7; Griffiths beat T. Jones 9-8; P. Francisco beat Thorburn 9-5; Bennett beat Stevens 9-2; Reynolds beat W. Jones 9-8; Hendry beat West 9-1; Parrott beat Chaperon 9-8; Gary Wilkinson beat B. Morgan 9-6; Johnson beat Clark 9-6; White beat N. Foulds 9-5; Hallett beat O'Kane 9-0; Dennis Taylor beat Williams 9-2; Thorne beat Higgins 9-3; Davis beat C. Wilson 9-3
**Fifth round:** Robidoux beat Gollan 9-5; Griffiths beat Knowles 9-7; Bennett beat P. Francisco 9-3; Hendry beat Reynolds 9-8; Gary Wilkinson beat Parrott 9-6; White beat Johnson 9-6; Hallett beat Dennis Taylor 9-6; Davis beat Thorne 9-4
**Quarter-finals:** Griffiths beat Robidoux 9-2; Hendry beat Bennett 9-2; Gary Wilkinson beat White 9-0; Davis beat Hallett 9-5
**Semi-finals:** Davis beat Wilkinson 9-8; Hendry beat Griffiths 9-7
**Final:** Hendry beat Davis 16-12

## EVEREST WORLD MATCHPLAY

**First staged** 1988. **Sponsors** Everest. **Venue** Brentwood Centre. **Initial prize-money** £250,000. **Prize-money last season** £250,000. **TV** ITV.

### 1988

**First round:** M. Hallett beat W. Thorne 9-8; T. Griffiths beat P. Francisco 9-7; J. Johnson beat C. Thorburn 9-4; Dennis Taylor beat A. Knowles 9-7

**Quarter-finals:** S. Davis beat Hallett 9-2; J. White beat Griffiths 9-5; J. Parrott beat Johnson 9-7; S. Hendry beat Dennis Taylor 9-7
**Semi-finals:** S. Davis beat White 9-5; Parrott beat Hendry 9-6
**Final:** S. Davis beat Parrott 9-5

**1989**
**First round:** D. Reynolds beat T. Meo 9-7; D. Mountjoy beat W. Thorne 9-2; T. Griffiths beat C. Thorburn 9-5; Dennis Taylor beat M. Hallett 9-6
**Quarter-finals:** Reynolds beat S. Davis 9-7; S. Hendry beat Griffiths 9-3; J. White beat Mountjoy 9-5; J. Parrott beat Taylor 9-6
**Semi-finals:** White beat Reynolds 9-8; Parrott beat Hendry 9-8
**Final:** White beat Parrott 18-9

## NORWICH UNION EUROPEAN GRAND PRIX

**First staged** 1988. **Sponsors** Norwich Union. **Venue** Final–Monte Carlo*. **Initial prize-money** £135,000. **Prize-money last season** £50,000. **TV** Canal Plus.
**Matches at various European venues produced four qualifiers for the final leg.*

**1988**
**Final:** S. Davis beat J. White 5-4

**1989**
**Final:** J. Johnson beat S. Hendry 5-3

## MERCANTILE CREDIT CLASSIC

**First staged** 1980*. **Sponsors** Wilsons (1980–82), Lada (1983–84), Mercantile Credit (1985– ). **Venue** Civic Centre, Oldham (1982), Spectrum Arena, Warrington (1983–86), Norbreck Castle Hotel, Blackpool (1987– ). **Initial prize-money** £15,000 (1982). **Prize-money last season** £300,000. **TV** ITV.
**The first two events, both in 1980, were small invitation events which do not meet the conditions required for full inclusion in this book.*

**1982** (*Wilsons*)
**First round:** T. Griffiths beat C. Thorburn 5-1; A. Higgins beat Dennis Taylor 5-1; R. Reardon beat David Taylor 5-1; S. Davis beat J. Spencer 5-2
**Semi-finals:** Griffiths beat Higgins 5-1; S. Davis beat Reardon 5-4
**Final:** Griffiths beat S. Davis 9-8

**1983** (*Lada Classic*)
**First round:** E. Charlton beat J. Virgo 5-2; J. Spencer beat R. Reardon 5-3; C. Thorburn beat C. Wilson 5-3; D. Mountjoy beat T. Griffiths 5-1; David Taylor beat J. White 5-3; B. Werbeniuk beat A. Higgins 5-4; K. Stevens beat A. Knowles 5-0; S. Davis beat Dennis Taylor 5-2
**Quarter-finals:** Spencer beat David Taylor 5-2; Werbeniuk beat Mountjoy 5-2; Stevens beat Thorburn 5-3; S. Davis beat Charlton 5-4
**Semi-finals:** S. Davis beat Spencer 5-4; Werbeniuk beat Stevens 5-2
**Final:** S. Davis beat Werbeniuk 9-5

**1984** (*Lada Classic*)
**First qualifying round:** G. Foulds beat M. Gauvreau 5-2; B. Demarco beat M. Gibson 5-2;

N. Foulds beat P. Houlihan 5-3; M. Morra beat P. Burke 5-2; G. Ganim beat D. Hughes 5-2; I. Williamson beat D. French 5-1; J. Hargreaves beat W. King 5-3; W. Oliver beat D. Sheehan 5-3; T. Jones beat P. Mifsud 5-3; P. Morgan beat M. Darrington 5-3; G. Cripsey beat V. Harris 5-4; J. Parrott beat B. Bennett 5-0; P. Browne beat D. Greaves 5-2; P. Watchorn beat R. Andrewartha 5-2; S. Duggan beat B. Harris 5-2; P. Medati beat T. Murphy 5-4
**Second qualifying round:** E. McLaughlin beat G. Foulds 5-1; G. Scott beat Demarco 5-2; N. Foulds beat Jack Rea 5-1; Morra beat C. Everton 5-0; C. Roscoe beat Ganim 5-3; F. Jonik beat Williamson 5-1; Hargreaves beat B. Kelly 5-4; Oliver beat J. Donnelly 5-4; Morgan beat M. Watterson 5-3; T. Jones beat I. Black 5-0; J. Campbell beat Cripsey 5-3; Parrott beat J. Fitzmaurice 5-2; R. Edmonds beat Browne 5-1; M. Fisher beat Watchorn 5-4; L. Dodd beat Duggan 5-2; E. Hughes beat Medati 5-1
**Third qualifying round:** E. McLaughlin beat W. Thorne 5-3; D. Reynolds beat Scott 5-3; C. Wilson beat N. Foulds 5-4; S. Francisco beat Morra 5-1; Roscoe beat G. Miles 5-2; J. Johnson beat Jonik 5-2; M. Wildman beat Hargreaves 5-1; P. Fagan beat Oliver 5-1; E. Sinclair beat Morgan 5-2; M. Macleod beat T. Jones 5-2; Campbell beat F. Davis 5-0; Parrott beat D. Martin 5-1; R. Williams beat Edmonds 5-1; J. Meadowcroft beat Fisher 5-0; M. Hallett beat Dodd 5-1; E. Hughes beat J. Dunning 5-4
**First round:** K. Stevens beat E. McLaughlin 5-4; T. Griffiths beat Reynolds 5-2; E. Charlton beat Wilson 5-0; S. Francisco beat C. Thorburn 5-1; Roscoe beat B. Werbeniuk 5-4; J. Spencer beat Johnson 5-4; Wildman beat J. Virgo 5-2; A. Higgins beat Fagan 5-3; S. Davis beat Sinclair 5-2; Macleod beat David Taylor 5-4; J. White beat Campbell 5-1; Parrott beat D. Mountjoy 5-4; Williams beat R. Reardon 5-4; T. Meo beat Meadowcroft 5-1; Hallett beat Dennis Taylor 5-4; A. Knowles beat E. Hughes 5-1
**Second round:** S. Davis beat Spencer 5-1; Charlton beat White 5-2; Wildman beat S. Francisco 5-1; Knowles beat Hallett 5-3; Stevens beat Macleod 5-1; Griffiths beat Roscoe 5-2; Meo beat Williams 5-3; Parrott beat Higgins 5-2
**Quarter-finals:** Wildman beat Charlton 5-4; S. Davis beat Griffiths 5-4; Meo beat Stevens 5-2; Parrott beat Knowles 5-1
**Semi-finals:** Meo beat Wildman 5-3; S. Davis beat Parrott 5-4
**Final:** S. Davis beat Meo 9-8

## 1985

**Preliminary round:** P. Watchorn beat D. Hughes 5-0; B. Mikkelsen beat D. Chalmers 5-1
**First qualifying round:** T. Jones beat D. Greaves 5-2; J. Giannaros beat T. Chappel 5-2; S. Newbury beat V. Harris 5-3; G. Foulds beat R. Chaperon 5-3; D. Sheehan beat John Rea 5-2; R. Bales beat B. Bennett 5-1; R. Foldvari beat P. Houlihan 5-1; P. Medati beat G. Cripsey 5-4; J. McLaughlin beat B. Demarco 5-1; S. Longworth beat P. Francisco 5-4; A. Kearney beat D. French 5-1; P. Browne beat M. Bradley 5-3; W. Jones beat D. O'Kane 5-0; D. Fowler beat Rigitano 5-0; J. Hargreaves beat Darrington 5-2
**Second qualifying round:** T. Jones beat M. Gibson 5-0; Newbury beat P. Burke 5-1; G. Foulds beat F. Jonik 5-2; E. McLaughlin beat Sheehan 5-2; Bales beat B. Kelly 5-3; Foldvari beat Jack Rea 5-4; J. McLaughlin beat I. Black 5-0; Longworth beat B. Oliver 5-1; Watchorn beat Mikkelsen 5-1; I. Williamson beat Kearney 5-3; Browne beat C. Everton 5-0; S. Duggan beat W. Jones 5-0; Fowler beat T. Murphy 5-0; R. Edmonds beat Hargreaves 5-2
**Third qualifying round:** T. Jones beat L. Dodd 5-1; M. Gauvreau beat Giannaros 5-3; Newbury beat M. Morra 5-2; G. Foulds beat J. Fitzmaurice 5-1; E. McLaughlin beat F. Davis 5-1; Medati beat C. Roscoe 5-4; G. Scott beat J. McLaughlin 5-4; Longworth beat M. Fisher 5-1; J. Donnelly beat Watchorn 5-1; P. Fagan beat Williamson 5-1; W. King beat Duggan 5-4; Fowler beat J. Meadowcroft 5-2; Edmonds beat M. Watterson 5-2
**Fourth qualifying round:** S. Francisco beat T. Jones 5-1; Fagan beat M. Wildman 5-3; M. Hallett beat G. Foulds 5-4; M. Macleod beat E. McLaughlin 5-4; Medati beat J. Parrott 5-3; C. Wilson beat Fowler 5-4; Gauvreau beat E. Sinclair 5-1; J. Johnson beat Edmonds 5-4; Scott beat J. Campbell 5-4; E. Hughes beat Newbury 5-3; King beat

D. Reynolds 5-2; R. Williams beat Donnelly 5-3; J. Virgo beat Bales 5-1; Longworth beat N. Foulds 5-3; Foldvari beat D. Martin 5-2; Browne beat G. Miles 5-3
**First round:** Longworth beat David Taylor 5-4; Johnson beat A. Knowles 5-1; C. Thorburn beat Scott 5-1; King beat J. Spencer 5-2; T. Griffiths beat Fagan 5-0; J. White beat Browne 5-2; E. Hughes beat T. Meo 5-4; Macleod beat Charlton 5-1; A. Higgins beat Gauvreau 5-3; Virgo beat B. Werbeniuk 5-2; Wilson beat D. Mountjoy 5-4; Williams beat Dennis Taylor 5-3; R. Reardon beat Hallett 5-3; S. Davis beat S. Francisco 5-0; W. Thorne beat Foldvari 5-2; K. Stevens beat Medati 5-4
**Second round:** Reardon beat E. Hughes 5-1; S. Davis beat Higgins 5-2; Virgo beat Macleod 5-0; Thorne beat Stevens 5-1; Thorburn beat Longworth 5-3; Griffiths beat Williams 5-3; Johnson beat Wilson 5-0; King beat White 5-2
**Quarter-finals:** S. Davis beat Reardon 5-1; Thorburn beat Griffiths 5-4; Johnson beat King 5-3; Thorne beat Virgo 5-1
**Semi-finals:** Thorne beat S. Davis 9-8; Thorburn beat Johnson 9-2
**Final:** Thorne beat Thorburn 13-8

## 1986

**First round:** D. Gilbert beat G. Watson 5-4; A. Kearney beat Jim Bear 5-0; S. Hendry beat D. Sheehan 5-2; B. Demarco beat O. Agrawal 5-4; M. Smith beat D. Mienie 5-1; J. O'Boye beat G. Wilkinson 5-1; B. West beat M. Darrington 5-0; P. Burke beat D. Hughes 5-3; S. Simngam beat J. Hargreaves 5-1; R. Bales beat M. Parkin 5-0; D. Greaves beat P. Watchorn 5-4; G. Jenkins *wo* G. Robinson *scr*; G. Cripsey beat T. Drago 5-4; P. Houlihan beat B. Bennett 5-0
**Second round:** T. Jones beat Gilbert 5-3; G. Foulds beat I. Black 5-2; W. King beat S. Duggan 5-2; P. Medati beat Kearney 5-2; Hendry beat G. Miles 5-1; M. Bradley beat B. Oliver 5-3; B. Mikkelsen beat G. Scott 5-1; J. Donnelly beat D. Chalmers 5-0; F. Davis beat B. Kelly 5-3; J. Wych beat Demarco 5-0; B. Harris beat M. Morra 5-3; Smith beat R. Edmonds 5-2; O'Boye beat S. Longworth 5-1; West beat J. Meadowcroft 5-0; J. McLaughlin beat E. McLaughlin 5-2; John Rea beat I. Williamson 5-4; R. Chaperon beat Burke 5-2; J. Van Rensberg beat W. Jones 5-4; P. Francisco beat F. Jonik 5-2; T. Murphy beat T. Chappel 5-4; M. Gauvreau beat Simngam 5-1; M. Gibson *wo* J. Dunning *scr*; P. Browne beat C. Everton 5-0; D. Fowler beat Bales 5-4; G. Rigitano beat L. Dodd 5-3; E. Sinclair beat Greaves 5-1; V. Harris beat C. Roscoe 5-1; M. Watterson beat Jenkins 5-2; M. Fisher beat Jack Rea 5-3; Cripsey beat S. Newbury 5-4; J. Fitzmaurice beat P. Fagan 5-3; Houlihan beat R. Foldvari 5-4
**Third round:** T. Jones beat W. Thorne 5-3; B. Werbeniuk beat G. Foulds 5-3; D. Mountjoy beat King 5-4; D. O'Kane beat Medati 5-0; Hendry beat S. Francisco 5-4; N. Foulds beat Bradley 5-3; Mikkelsen beat R. Reardon 5-3; J. Campbell beat Donnelly 5-2; F. Davis beat K. Stevens 5-2; E. Hughes beat Wych 5-2; J. Johnson beat B. Harris 5-4; P. Mans beat Smith 5-4; T. Meo beat O'Boye 5-3; West beat M. Wildman 5-2; C. Thorburn beat J. McLaughlin 5-1; M. Hallett beat John Rea 5-2; S. Davis beat Chaperon 5-1; Van Rensberg beat J. Parrott 5-3; P. Francisco beat E. Charlton 5-1; D. Martin beat Murphy 5-3; Gauvreau beat David Taylor 5-3; Browne beat C. Wilson 5-3; J. White beat Fowler 5-1; J. Virgo beat Gibson 5-3; A. Knowles beat Rigitano 5-4; M. Macleod beat Sinclair 5-2; V. Harris beat T. Griffiths 5-3; R. Williams beat Watterson 5-0; A. Higgins beat Fisher 5-0; Cripsey beat J. Spencer 5-1; Dennis Taylor beat Fitzmaurice 5-1; D. Reynolds beat Houlihan 5-1
**Fourth round:** Werbeniuk beat T. Jones 5-3; Mountjoy beat O'Kane 5-3; N. Foulds beat Hendry 5-4; Campbell beat Mikkelsen 5-2; E. Hughes beat F. Davis 5-3; Johnson beat Mans 5-2; Meo beat West 5-1; Thorburn beat Hallett 5-3; S. Davis beat Van Rensberg 5-1; P. Francisco beat Martin 5-2; Gauvreau beat Browne 5-3; White beat Virgo 5-2; Knowles beat Macleod 5-4; Williams beat V. Harris 5-1; Higgins beat Cripsey 5-2; Dennis Taylor beat Reynolds 5-4
**Fifth round:** Mountjoy beat Werbeniuk 5-3; N. Foulds beat Campbell 5-1; Johnson beat E. Hughes 5-1; Thorburn beat Meo 5-1; S. Davis beat P. Francisco 5-0; White beat Gauvreau 5-2; Williams beat Knowles 5-2; Higgins beat Dennis Taylor 5-4

**Quarter-finals:** Mountjoy beat N. Foulds 5-3; Thorburn beat Johnson 5-4; White beat S. Davis 5-2; Williams beat Higgins 5-2
**Semi-finals:** Thorburn beat Mountjoy 9-6; White beat Williams 9-7
**Final:** White beat Thorburn 13-12

## 1987

**First round:** J. Meadowcroft *wo* L. Heywood *scr*; B. Rowswell beat M. Watterson 5-1; P. Watchorn beat J. Donnelly 5-0; G. Foulds beat B. Bennett 5-2; C. Everton *wo* E. McLaughlin *scr*; A. Kearney beat O. Agrawal 5-0; D. Roe beat M. Darrington 5-0; F. Jonik beat S. James 5-4; D. Mienie *wo* J. Hargreaves *scr*; P. Burke *wo* J. Bear *scr*; G. Jenkins beat M. Parkin 5-2; M. Bennett beat D. Sheehan 5-3; K. Owers beat P. Houlihan 5-1; M. Morra beat F. Ellis 5-1; M. Fisher beat B. Demarco 5-0; C. Roscoe beat T. Whitthread 5-1; B. Oliver beat D. Greaves 5-4; G. Wilkinson beat J. Fitzmaurice 5-2; Jack Rea beat B. Kelly 5-3; J. Wright beat D. Hughes 5-2; N. Gilbert beat M. Smith 5-0; P. Gibson *wo* S. Simngam *scr*; G. Rigitano beat R. Grace 5-4
**Second round:** S. Newbury beat Meadowcroft 5-1; M. Bradley beat Rowswell 5-4; S. Duggan beat Watchorn 5-1; J. McLaughlin beat M. Gibson 5-3; J. O'Boye beat V. Harris 5-1; G. Foulds beat D. O'Kane 5-4; J. Spencer beat D. Gilbert 5-4; P. Browne beat Dunning 5-1; W. Jones beat Everton 5-0; Kearney beat M. Wildman 5-3; L. Dodd beat Medati 5-4; I. Williamson beat R. Edmonds 5-2; R. Chaperon beat Roe 5-4; Jonik beat T. Drago 5-2; G. Cripsey beat Mienie 5-0; W. King beat Burke 5-0; Jenkins beat G. Scott 5-4; M. Bennett beat I. Black 5-3; John Rea beat Owers 5-2; T. Murphy beat R. Bales 5-2; Morra *wo* P. Mans *scr*; Fisher beat F. Davis 5-2; Roscoe *wo* P. Fagan *scr*; T. Jones beat Oliver 5-0; D. Fowler beat Wilkinson 5-1; B. Mikkelsen beat R. Foldvari 5-1; S. Hendry beat Jack Rea 5-1; Wright beat T. Chappel 5-4; J. Van Rensberg beat N. Gilbert 5-3; R. Harris beat P. Gibson 5-3; E. Sinclair beat G. Miles 5-1; M. Gauvreau beat Rigitano 5-0
**Third round:** J. White beat Newbury 5-4; Bradley beat David Taylor 5-1; Duggan beat N. Foulds 5-3; B. Werbeniuk beat J. McLaughlin 5-1; T. Griffiths beat O'Boye 5-1; D. Martin beat G. Foulds 5-4; Spencer beat W. Thorne 5-3; J. Campbell beat Browne 5-2; W. Jones beat Dennis Taylor 5-2; Kearney beat M. Macleod 5-0; Dodd beat D. Mountjoy 5-4; C. Wilson beat Williamson 5-4; K. Stevens beat Chaperon 5-3; B. West beat Jonik 5-4; C. Thorburn beat Cripsey 5-0; D. Reynolds beat King 5-4; S. Davis beat Jenkins 5-0; J. Virgo beat M. Bennett 5-3; T. Meo beat John Rea 5-4; S. Longworth beat Murphy 5-3; R. Williams beat Morra 5-2; E. Charlton beat Fisher 5-0; A. Higgins beat Roscoe 5-2; J. Parrott beat T. Jones 5-2; Fowler beat A. Knowles 5-4; M. Hallett beat Mikkelsen 5-3; Hendry beat R. Reardon 5-3; Wright beat E. Hughes 5-4; S. Francisco beat Van Rensberg 5-4; B. Harris beat J. Wych 5-3; J. Johnson beat Sinclair 5-0; P. Francisco beat Gauvreau 5-3
**Fourth round:** White beat Bradley 5-0; Duggan beat Werbeniuk 5-0; Griffiths beat Martin 5-4; Campbell beat Spencer 5-3; W. Jones beat Kearney 5-1; Wilson beat Dodd 5-4; West beat Stevens 5-3; Reynolds beat Thorburn 5-4; S. Davis beat Virgo 5-2; Meo beat Longworth 5-0; Charlton beat Williams 5-4; Parrott beat Higgins 5-2; Fowler beat Hallett 5-4; Hendry beat Wright 5-1; S. Francisco beat N. Harris 5-3; P. Francisco beat Johnson 5-3
**Fifth round:** White beat Duggan 5-2; Griffiths beat Campbell 5-3; Wilson beat W. Jones 5-3; Reynolds beat West 5-3; S. Davis beat Meo 5-2; Parrott beat Charlton 5-4; Hendry beat Fowler 5-4; S. Francisco beat P. Francisco 5-1
**Quarter-finals:** White beat Griffiths 5-3; Reynolds beat Wilson 5-1; S. Davis beat Parrott 5-4; Hendry beat S. Francisco 5-0
**Semi-finals:** White beat Reynolds 9-8; S. Davis beat Hendry 9-3
**Final:** S. Davis beat White 13-12

## 1988

**First round:** D. Roe beat W. Kelly 5-1; J. Donnelly beat N. Gilbert 5-2; A. Harris beat G. Jenkins 5-4; M. Morra beat R. Marshall 5-0; B. Rowswell beat J. Chambers 5-2;

R. Foldvari beat D. Greaves 5-3; D. Hughes beat I. Williamson 5-3; Glen Wilkinson beat D. Chalmers 5-3; D. Gilbert beat Jack Rea 5-2; C. Everton beat J. Meadowcroft 5-3; B. Oliver beat P. Burke 5-2; M. Clark *wo* B. Mikkelsen *scr*; Gary Wilkinson *wo* M. Watterson *scr*; G. Rigitano *wo* J. Hargreaves *scr*; F. Jonik beat J. Dunning 5-2; M. Smith beat J. Fitzmaurice 5-2; M. Fisher *wo* E. McLaughlin *scr*; T. Whitthread beat P. Fagan 5-2; J. Bear beat J. Smith 5-3; E. Sinclair beat E. Lawlor 5-3; C. Roscoe beat P. Watchorn 5-2; D. Sheehan beat D. Heaton 5-2; V. Harris beat F. Ellis 5-1; S. Meakin beat M. Darrington 5-4; P. Gibson beat I. Black 5-2
**Second round:** L. Dodd beat Roe 5-2; Donnelly beat S. Duggan 5-4; T. Jones beat A. Harris 5-2; Morra beat M. Gauvreau 5-4; Rowswell beat D. O'Kane 5-4; R. Edmonds beat Foldvari 5-4; T. Chappel beat D. Hughes 5-3; B. Werbeniuk beat Glen Wilkinson 5-2; J. Van Rensberg beat R. Grace 5-3; D. Gilbert beat B. Harris 5-4; M. Bradley beat Everton 5-2; Oliver beat W. King 5-3; Clark beat J. Wych 5-2; M. Bennett beat Miles 5-1; R. Reardon beat Gary Wilkinson 5-3; S. Newbury beat A. Kearney 5-1; R. Chaperon beat P. Medati 5-3; Rigitano beat D. Fowler 5-2; M. Wildman beat Jonik 5-4; M. Smith beat P. Browne 5-1; K. Owers beat Fisher 5-0; G. Cripsey beat M. Gibson 5-4; Whitthread beat G. Foulds 5-3; G. Scott beat Bear 5-3; J. Wright beat Sinclair 5-3; Roscoe beat W. Jones 5-4; J. O'Boye beat Sheehan 5-3; T. Murphy beat V. Harris 5-2; F. Davis beat Meakin 5-4; J. McLaughlin beat P. Gibson 5-4; S. James beat P. Houlihan 5-2; John Rea beat R. Bales 5-0
**Third round:** S. Davis beat Dodd 5-0; Donnelly beat M. Macleod 5-4; A. Higgins beat T. Jones 5-0; T. Meo beat Morra 5-1; S. Francisco beat Rowswell 5-3; S. Longworth beat Edmonds 5-3; J. Johnson beat Chappel 5-2; S. Hendry beat Werbeniuk 5-2; T. Griffiths beat Van Rensberg 5-2; C. Wilson beat D. Gilbert 5-3; W. Thorne beat Bradley 5-1; B. West beat Oliver 5-3; Clark beat M. Hallett 5-4; M. Bennett beat K. Stevens 5-2; C. Thorburn beat Reardon 5-3; Newbury beat E. Hughes 5-1; N. Foulds beat Chaperon 5-1; J. Virgo beat Rigitano 5-2; J. Parrott beat Wildman 5-2; David Taylor beat M. Smith 5-3; Owers beat R. Williams 5-3; P. Francisco beat Cripsey 5-2; Dennis Taylor beat Whitthread 5-2; T. Drago beat Scott 5-3; A. Knowles beat Wright 5-1; Roscoe beat E. Charlton 5-3; D. Reynolds beat O'Boye 5-3; Murphy beat J. Campbell 5-3; D. Mountjoy beat F. Davis 5-0; D. Martin beat J. McLaughlin 5-2; J. White beat James 5-1; J. Spencer beat John Rea 5-3
**Fourth round:** S. Davis beat Donnelly 5-0; Higgins beat Meo 5-3; S. Francisco beat Longworth 5-2; Hendry beat Johnson 5-2; Griffiths beat Wilson 5-2; West beat Thorne 5-2; Clark beat M. Bennett 5-2; Newbury beat Thorburn 5-3; Virgo beat N. Foulds 5-3; Parrott beat David Taylor 5-0; P. Francisco beat Owers 5-0; Dennis Taylor beat Drago 5-0; Knowles beat Roscoe 5-0; Murphy beat Reynolds 5-4; Martin beat Mountjoy 5-4; White beat Spencer 5-1
**Fifth round:** S. Davis beat Higgins 5-0; Hendry beat S. Francisco 5-3; Griffiths beat West 5-2; Newbury beat Clark 5-2; Parrott beat Virgo 5-0; Dennis Taylor beat P. Francisco 5-3; Knowles beat Murphy 5-3; Martin beat White 5-2
**Quarter-finals:** S. Davis beat Hendry 5-3; Newbury beat Griffiths 5-4; Parrott beat Dennis Taylor 5-1; Knowles beat Martin 5-1
**Semi-finals:** S. Davis beat Newbury 9-2; Parrott beat Knowles 9-4
**Final:** S. Davis beat Parrott 13-11

## 1989

**First round:** M. Johnston-Allen beat G. Scott 5-0; A. Harris beat Jim Bear 5-3; I. Williamson beat G. Jenkins 5-2; P. Medati *wo* D. Chalmers *scr*; N. Terry beat John Rea 5-3; D. Hughes *wo* P. Gibson *scr*; C. Roscoe beat T. Whitthread 5-3; J. Dunning beat M. Price 5-3; Glen Wilkinson beat P. Watchorn 5-3; A. Kearney beat B. Kelly 5-3; E. Sinclair beat S. Meakin 5-1; M. Watterson beat G. Rigitano 5-4; M. Wildman *wo* F. Jonik *scr*; M. Bradley beat P. Fagan 5-3; Jack Rea beat M. Gibson 5-3; J. Chambers beat D. Mienie 5-2; R. Foldvari beat T. Wilson 5-4; D. Morgan beat V. Harris 5-3; D. Sheehan *wo* F. Davis *scr*; I. Graham beat R. Grace 5-4; J. Smith beat J. Van Rensberg 5-4; J. Fitzmaurice beat J. Meadowcroft 5-2; M. Rowing beat M. Smith

5-3; R. Marshall beat I. Black 5-0; F. Ellis beat J. Donnelly 5-0; G. Foulds beat C. Everton 5-0; A. Robidoux beat B. Harris 5-1; C. Edwards beat E. Lawlor 5-1; S. Campbell beat B. Oliver 5-4; M. Darrington beat M. Morra 5-2; B. Rowswell beat P. Burke 5-2; G. Miles beat B. Mikkelsen 5-3

**Second round:** T. Chappel beat Johnston-Allen 5-2; A. Harris beat D. Gilbert 5-4; P. Browne beat Williamson 5-3; Gary Wilkinson beat Medati 5-1; Terry beat M. Bennett 5-3; D. Hughes beat J. O'Boye 5-1; Roscoe beat K. Owers 5-3; S. Duggan beat Dunning 5-2; Glen Wilkinson beat J. Wych 5-3; G. Cripsey beat Kearney 5-2; L. Dodd beat Sinclair 5-3; J. McLaughlin beat Watterson 5-3; D. Fowler *wo* Wildman *scr*; Bradley beat T. Jones 5-4; T. Murphy beat Jack Rea 5-0; R. Reardon beat Chambers 5-4; D. Martin beat Foldvari 5-2; M. Clark beat Morgan 5-1; Sheehan beat M. Fisher 5-3; M. Macleod beat Graham 5-4; J. Smith beat R. Bales 5-1; N. Gilbert beat Fitzmaurice 5-3; W. King beat Rowing 5-4; Marshall beat R. Edmonds 5-2; D. Roe beat Ellis 5-0; J. Wright beat G. Foulds 5-4; B. Werbeniuk beat Robidoux 5-4; K. Stevens beat Edwards 5-4; S. Campbell beat J. Campbell 5-2; Darrington beat P. Houlihan 5-4; W. Jones beat Rowswell 5-3; Miles beat M. Gauvreau 5-3

**Third round:** Chappel beat S. Davis 5-3; A. Harris beat B. West 5-4; Browne beat M. Hallett 5-2; S. James beat Gary Wilkinson 5-1; Terry beat P. Francisco 5-4; D. Mountjoy beat D. Hughes 5-0; A. Knowles beat Roscoe 5-4; D. Reynolds beat Duggan 5-1; C. Thorburn beat Glen Wilkinson 5-2; Cripsey beat S. Longworth 5-3; J. Virgo beat Dodd 5-2; R. Chaperon beat J. McLaughlin 5-3; Dennis Taylor beat Fowler 5-3; S. Newbury beat Bradley 5-3; S. Hendry beat Murphy 5-2; Reardon beat E. Charlton 5-1; N. Foulds beat Martin 5-1; Clark beat J. Spencer 5-2; J. Johnson beat Sheehan 5-2; A. Higgins beat Macleod 5-2; W. Thorne beat J. Smith 5-1; D. O'Kane beat N. Gilbert 5-2; T. Griffiths beat King 5-2; T. Drago beat Marshall 5-1; J. Parrott beat Roe 5-2; Wright beat R. Williams 5-0; S. Francisco *wo* Werbeniuk *scr*; T. Meo beat Stevens 5-3; C. Wilson beat S. Campbell 5-3; David Taylor beat Darrington 5-2; W. Jones beat J. White 5-3; E. Hughes beat Miles 5-2

**Fourth round:** Chappel beat A. Harris 5-1; Browne beat James 5-4; Mountjoy beat Terry 5-4; Knowles beat Reynolds 5-4; Thorburn beat Cripsey 5-1; Virgo beat Chaperon 5-1; Newbury beat Dennis Taylor 5-4; Hendry beat Reardon 5-4; Clark beat N. Foulds 5-4; Johnson beat Higgins 5-0; Thorne beat O'Kane 5-3; Griffiths beat Drago 5-0; Parrott beat Wright 5-2; S. Francisco beat Meo 5-1; David Taylor beat C. Wilson 5-3; W. Jones beat E. Hughes 5-1

**Fifth round:** Browne beat Chappel 5-1; Mountjoy beat Knowles 5-4; Thorburn beat Virgo 5-3; Hendry beat Newbury 5-1; Clark beat Johnson 5-3; Thorne beat Griffiths 5-1; Parrott beat S. Francisco 5-1; W. Jones beat David Taylor 5-3

**Quarter-finals:** Mountjoy beat Browne 5-3; Thorburn beat Hendry 5-4; Thorne beat Clark 5-4; W. Jones beat Parrott 5-4

**Semi-finals:** Mountjoy beat Thorburn 9-5; W. Jones beat Thorne 9-4

**Final:** Mountjoy beat W. Jones 13-11

## 1990

**First round:** J. Meadowcroft beat B. Oliver 5-3; B. Pinches beat G. Scott 5-0; I. Williamson beat S. Campbell 5-2; P. Watchorn beat Medati 5-2; J. Wright beat G. Foulds 5-4; J. Smith beat J. Donnelly 5-2; M. Morra beat P. Thornley 5-3; B. Harris beat M. Wildman 5-2; I. Brumby beat E. Lawlor 5-4; N. Bond beat Glen Wilkinson 5-2; R. Foldvari *wo* T. Whitthread *scr*; M. Rowing beat J. Bear 5-3; M. Bradley beat J. Fitzmaurice 5-4; A. Cairns beat M. Smith 5-2; A. Kearney *wo* V. Harris *scr*; R. Marshall beat Jack Rea 5-2; C. Edwards beat S. Meakin 5-4; John Rea beat J. Van Rensberg 5-1; G. Miles beat M. Gibson 5-3; B. Rowswell beat M. Watterson 5-4; K. Owers beat B. Gollan 5-2; M. Gauvreau beat D. Sheehan 5-0; S. Murphy beat T. Wilson 5-1; D. Campbell beat J. Dunning 5-2; N. Terry beat D. Hughes 5-0; J. Wattana beat A. Harris 5-3; P. Gibson beat F. Ellis 5-3; B. Morgan beat F. Davis 5-0; G. Rigitano beat M. Price 5-2; N. Dyson beat L. Dodd 5-3; P. Houlihan beat R. Grace 5-2; E. Sinclair beat M. Darrington 5-3

**Second round:** S. Duggan beat J. Meadowcroft 5-3; M. Macleod beat Pinches 5-4; T. Murphy beat Williamson 5-1; Watchorn beat M. Fisher 5-3; Wright beat D. Martin 5-1; J. McLaughlin beat J. Smith 5-1; W. King beat Morra 5-3; B. Harris beat P. Browne 5-3; Brumby beat J. Spencer 5-1; C. Roscoe beat Bond 5-4; J. Wych beat Foldvari 5-2; Rowing beat D. Gilbert 5-1; N. Gilbert beat Bradley 5-1; Cairns beat A. Robidoux 5-4; T. Jones beat Kearney 5-1; D. Fowler beat Marshall 5-2; Edwards beat S. Longworth 5-4; M. Johnston-Allen beat John Rea 5-4; J. Chambers beat Miles 5-3; Rowswell beat K. Stevens 5-3; J. Campbell beat Owers 5-3; Gary Wilkinson beat Gauvreau 5-1; S. Murphy beat O'Boye 5-0; R. Edmonds beat D. Campbell 5-3; Terry beat G. Cripsey 5-3; D. Morgan beat Wattana 5-1; David Taylor beat P. Gibson 5-1; B. Morgan beat R. Bales 5-3; M. Bennett beat Rigitano 5-2; Dyson beat I. Graham 5-3; T. Chappel beat Houlihan 5-0; Sinclair beat R. Reardon 5-4
**Third round:** Duggan beat D. Mountjoy 5-4; P. Francisco beat Macleod 5-2; T. Meo beat T. Murphy 5-2; S. Newbury beat Watchorn 5-2; J. Virgo beat Wright 5-2; J. McLaughlin beat D. Roe 5-2; King beat T. Griffiths 5-1; E. Charlton beat B. Harris 5-2; Brumby *wo* J. White *scr*; S. Francisco beat Roscoe 5-1; D. Reynolds *wo* Wych *scr*; Rowing beat B. West 5-0; N. Gilbert beat J. Johnson 5-0; M. Clark beat Cairns 5-2; S. Hendry beat T. Jones 5-3; D. O'Kane beat Fowler 5-4; J. Parrott beat Edwards 5-2; A. Higgins beat Johnston-Allen 5-0; S. James beat Chambers 5-4; R. Chaperon beat Rowswell 5-1; J. Campbell beat A. Knowles 5-4; Gary Wilkinson beat C. Wilson 5-2; M. Hallett beat S. Murphy 5-1; W. Jones beat Edmonds 5-1; C. Thorburn beat Terry 5-2; D. Morgan beat N. Foulds 5-4; David Taylor beat W. Thorne 5-1; B. Morgan beat E. Hughes 5-1; Dennis Taylor beat M. Bennett 5-2; T. Drago beat Dyson 5-3; S. Davis beat Chappel 5-4; R. Williams beat Sinclair 5-1
**Fourth round:** P. Francisco beat Duggan 5-2; Newbury beat Meo 5-4; Virgo beat J. McLaughlin 5-2; King beat Charlton 5-2; S. Francisco beat Brumby 5-0; Rowing beat Reynolds 5-4; Clark beat N. Gilbert 5-2; O'Kane beat Hendry 5-2; Parrott beat Higgins 5-4; James beat Chaperon 5-2; Gary Wilkinson beat J. Campbell 5-4; W. Jones beat Hallett 5-3; D. Morgan beat Thorburn 5-4; B. Morgan beat David Taylor 5-4; Drago beat Dennis Taylor 5-4; S. Davis beat Williams 5-0
**Fifth round:** Newbury beat P. Francisco 5-3; King beat Virgo 5-1; S. Francisco beat Rowing 5-1; O'Kane beat Clark 5-1; James beat Parrott 5-3; W. Jones beat Gary Wilkinson 5-2; B. Morgan beat D. Morgan 5-1; S. Davis beat Drago 5-3
**Quarter-finals:** King beat Newbury 5-3; S. Francisco beat O'Kane 5-4; James beat W. Jones 5-2; S. Davis beat B. Morgan 5-1
**Semi-finals:** King beat S. Francisco 6-5; James beat S. Davis 6-4
**Final:** James beat King 10-6

# BENSON AND HEDGES MASTERS

**First staged** 1975. **Sponsors** Benson and Hedges. **Venue** West Centre Hotel (1975), New London Theatre (1976–78), Wembley Conference Centre (1979– ). **Initial prize-money** £5,000. **Prize-money last season** £275,000. **TV** BBC.

## 1975

**First round:** J. Pulman beat C. Thorburn 5-3; A. Higgins beat B. Werbeniuk 5-0
**Quarter-finals:** E. Charlton beat F. Davis 5-3; J. Spencer beat Pulman 5-3; R. Reardon beat G. Miles 5-3; R. Williams beat Higgins 5-3
**Semi-finals:** Spencer beat Charlton 5-2; Reardon beat Williams 5-4
**Final:** Spencer beat Reardon 9-8

## 1976

**First round:** F. Davis beat C. Thorburn 4-2; J. Pulman beat Dennis Taylor 4-2
**Quarter-finals:** G. Miles beat A. Higgins 4-1; R. Reardon beat Pulman 4-1; J. Spencer beat F. Davis 4-0; E. Charlton beat R. Williams 4-1

**Semi-finals:** Miles beat Spencer 5-4; Reardon beat Charlton 5-4
**Final:** Reardon beat Miles 7-3

**1977**
**First round:** D. Mountjoy beat J. Pulman 4-2; J. Spencer beat Dennis Taylor 4-2
**Quarter-finals:** R. Reardon beat R. Williams 4-1; G. Miles beat Spencer 4-1; A. Higgins beat P. Mans 4-2; Mountjoy beat F. Davis 4-2
**Semi-finals:** Mountjoy beat Higgins 5-3; Reardon beat Miles 5-2
**Final:** Mountjoy beat Reardon 7-6

**1978**
**First round:** J. Pulman beat P. Fagan 4-2; G. Miles beat F. Davis 4-3
**Quarter-finals:** J. Spencer beat Pulman 4-2; A. Higgins beat Dennis Taylor 4-3; C. Thorburn beat D. Mountjoy 4-2; R. Reardon beat Miles 4-1
**Semi-finals:** Higgins beat Reardon 5-1; Thorburn beat Spencer 5-3
**Final:** Higgins beat Thorburn 7-5

**1979**
**First round:** D. Mountjoy beat F. Davis 5-2; David Taylor beat P. Fagan 5-4
**Quarter-finals:** A. Higgins beat E. Charlton 5-2; P. Mans beat C. Thorburn 5-4; Mountjoy beat Spencer 5-0; R. Reardon beat Taylor 5-2
**Semi-finals:** Higgins beat Mountjoy 5-1; Mans beat Reardon 5-3
**Final:** Mans beat Higgins 8-4

**1980**
**First round:** C. Thorburn beat J. Virgo 5-3; A. Higgins beat F. Davis 5-1
**Quarter-finals:** R. Reardon beat Dennis Taylor 5-3; T. Griffiths beat Thorburn 5-3; J. Spencer beat E. Charlton 5-2; Higgins beat P. Mans 5-1
**Semi-finals:** Griffiths beat Spencer 5-0; Higgins beat Reardon 5-2
**Final:** Griffiths beat Higgins 9-5

**1981**
**First round:** P. Mans beat S. Davis 5-3; D. Mountjoy beat E. Charlton 5-0; F. Davis beat K. Stevens 5-4; J. Spencer beat Dennis Taylor 5-2
**Quarter-finals:** A. Higgins beat Mountjoy 5-1; C. Thorburn beat Mans 5-4; Spencer beat R. Reardon 5-1; T. Griffiths beat F. Davis 5-2
**Semi-finals:** Higgins beat Thorburn 6-5; Griffiths beat Spencer 6-5
**Final:** Higgins beat Griffiths 9-6

**1982**
**First round:** R. Reardon beat Dennis Taylor 5-3; D. Mountjoy beat J. Spencer 5-4; T. Meo beat David Taylor 5-2; E. Charlton beat J. White 5-4
**Quarter-finals:** Meo beat C. Thorburn 5-0; S. Davis beat Mountjoy 5-2; A. Higgins beat Charlton 5-1; T. Griffiths beat Reardon 5-3
**Semi-finals:** S. Davis beat Meo 6-4; Griffiths beat Higgins 6-5
**Final:** S. Davis beat Griffiths 9-5

**1983**
**First round:** B. Werbeniuk beat A. Higgins 5-4; E. Charlton beat T. Meo 5-3; T. Griffiths beat K. Stevens 5-3; C. Thorburn beat J. Johnson 5-2; R. Reardon beat D. Reynolds 5-1; D. Mountjoy beat J. Virgo 5-1; S. Davis beat M. Wildman 5-2; J. White beat David Taylor 5-2
**Quarter-finals:** Charlton beat Werbeniuk 5-3; Thorburn beat Griffiths 5-3; Reardon beat White 5-2; Mountjoy beat S. Davis 5-4
**Semi-finals:** Thorburn beat Charlton 6-5; Reardon beat Mountjoy 6-3
**Final:** Thorburn beat Reardon 9-7

**1984**
**First round:** A. Knowles beat Dennis Taylor 5-2; R. Reardon beat J. Virgo 5-3;

J. Spencer beat C. Thorburn 5-4; T. Griffiths beat B. Werbeniuk 5-1; J. White beat E. Charlton 5-2; A. Higgins beat D. Mountjoy 5-2; K. Stevens beat David Taylor 5-1; S. Davis beat T. Meo 5-0
**Quarter-finals:** Griffiths beat Spencer 5-4; Knowles beat Higgins 5-1; White beat Reardon 5-3; Stevens beat S. Davis 5-3
**Semi-finals:** Griffiths beat Knowles 6-4; White beat Stevens 6-4
**Final:** White beat Griffiths 9-5

**1985**
**First round:** J. White beat W. Thorne 5-2; J. Spencer beat E. Charlton 5-3; R. Reardon beat David Taylor 5-1; C. Thorburn beat Dennis Taylor 5-3; D. Mountjoy beat A. Knowles 5-3; T. Meo beat K. Stevens 5-2; T. Griffiths beat B. Werbeniuk 5-2; A. Higgins beat S. Davis 5-4
**Quarter-finals:** White beat Spencer 5-2; Thorburn beat Reardon 5-0; Mountjoy beat Meo 5-4; Griffiths beat Higgins 5-1
**Semi-finals:** Thorburn beat White 6-4; Mountjoy beat Griffiths 6-2
**Final:** Thorburn beat Mountjoy 9-6

**1986**
**First round:** C. Thorburn beat J. Johnson 5-3; T. Griffiths beat A. Higgins 5-4; E. Charlton beat K. Stevens 5-4; A. Knowles beat S. Francisco 5-1; S. Davis beat David Taylor 5-4; W. Thorne beat R. Reardon 5-4; J. White beat T. Meo 5-4; Dennis Taylor beat D. Mountjoy 5-2
**Quarter-finals:** Thorburn beat Griffiths 5-2; Knowles beat Charlton 5-4; S. Davis beat Thorne 5-4; White beat Dennis Taylor 5-3
**Semi-finals:** Thorburn beat Knowles 6-4; White beat S. Davis 6-3
**Final:** Thorburn beat White 9-5

**1987**
**First round:** C. Thorburn beat R. Williams 5-1; W. Thorne beat K. Stevens 5-3; S. Francisco beat A. Knowles 5-2; Dennis Taylor beat N. Foulds 5-2; D. Mountjoy beat S. Davis 5-2; T. Meo beat J. White 5-4; A. Higgins beat T. Griffiths 5-4; J. Johnson beat R. Reardon 5-2
**Quarter-finals:** Thorburn beat Thorne 5-3; Taylor beat S. Francisco 5-3; Meo beat Mountjoy 5-4; Higgins beat Johnson 5-1
**Semi-finals:** Taylor beat Thorburn 6-5; Higgins beat Meo 6-2
**Final:** Taylor beat Higgins 9-8

**1988**
**First round:** M. Hallett beat Dennis Taylor 5-3; A. Higgins beat A. Knowles 5-4; C. Thorburn beat R. Williams 5-3; J. Parrott beat N. Foulds 5-4; J. White beat D. Mountjoy 5-0; J. Johnson beat W. Thorne 5-4; T. Griffiths beat S. Francisco 5-3; S. Davis beat D. Reynolds 5-2
**Quarter-finals:** Hallett beat Higgins 5-2; Parrott beat Thorburn 5-4; Johnson beat White 5-3; S. Davis beat Griffiths 5-0
**Semi-finals:** Hallett beat Parrott 6-5; S. Davis beat Johnson 6-3
**Final:** S. Davis beat M. Hallett 9-0

**1989**
**First round:** S. Davis beat C. Wilson 5-2; A. Knowles beat M. Hallett 5-3; T. Griffiths beat S. Francisco 5-1; S. Hendry beat W. Thorne 5-2; N. Foulds beat P. Francisco 5-2; C. Thorburn beat J. Johnson 5-2; J. Parrott beat Dennis Taylor 5-1; J. White beat J. Virgo 5-2

**Quarter-finals:** S. Davis beat Knowles 5-0; Hendry beat Griffiths 5-3; N. Foulds beat Thorburn 5-2; Parrott beat White 5-4
**Semi-finals:** Hendry beat S. Davis 6-3; Parrott beat N. Foulds 6-5
**Final:** Hendry beat Parrott 9-6

**1990**
**Play-offs:** S. James beat A. Higgins 5-2; J. Wattana beat D. Reynolds 5-4
**First round:** S. Hendry beat James 5-2; W. Thorne beat Dennis Taylor 5-4; A. Knowles beat T. Griffiths 5-4; J. White beat J. Virgo 5-3; J. Parrott beat T. Meo 5-3; J. Johnson beat M. Hallett 5-4; D. Mountjoy beat C. Thorburn 5-4; S. Davis beat Wattana 5-2
**Quarter-finals:** Hendry beat Thorne 5-1; White beat Knowles 5-3; Parrott beat Johnson 5-3; S. Davis beat Mountjoy 5-0
**Semi-finals:** Hendry beat White 5-4; Parrott beat S. Davis 6-2
**Final:** Hendry beat Parrott 9-4

## PEARL ASSURANCE BRITISH OPEN

**First staged** 1985. **Sponsors** Dulux (1985–87), MIM Britannia (1988), Anglian (1989), Pearl Assurance (1990– ). **Venue** Assembly Rooms, Derby. **Initial prize-money** £250,000. **Prize-money last season** £375,000. **TV** ITV.

**1985** *(Dulux)*
**Qualifying:** T. Chappel beat I. Williamson 6-5; D. Chalmers beat P. Burke 6-5; John Rea beat M. Fisher 6-0; W. King beat P. Medati 6-4; D. Fowler beat C. Everton 6-1; T. Murphy beat D. Sheehan 6-3; R. Foldvari beat S. Duggan 6-4; V. Harris beat L. Dodd 6-1; T. Jones beat G. Foulds 6-0; P. Francisco beat B. Kelly 6-3; D. O'Kane beat G. Cripsey 6-4; S. Newbury beat P. Browne 6-0; M. Bradley beat M. Morra 6-2; A. Kearney beat M. Watterson 6-4; D. French beat E. McLaughlin 6-0; R. Chaperon beat P. Fagan 6-5; B. Harris beat J. Meadowcroft 6-1; S. Longworth beat F. Davis 6-1; B. Mikkelsen beat D. Hughes 6-0; G. Scott beat M. Darrington 6-3; J. Giannaros beat C. Roscoe 6-1; F. Jonik beat J. McLaughlin 6-2; W. Jones beat J. Donnelly 6-1; P. Watchorn beat J. Fitzmaurice 6-1; R. Bales beat I. Black 6-4; M. Gauvreau beat D. Greaves 6-3; M. Gibson beat B. Demarco 6-1; R. Edmonds beat D. Mienie 6-1
**First round:** D. Reynolds beat Giannaros 6-3; M. Macleod beat Murphy 6-5; E. Hughes beat Watchorn 6-4; Longworth beat C. Wilson 6-3; W. Jones beat J. Johnson 6-5; M. Hallett *wo* Mikkelsen *scr*; C. Thorburn beat G. Rigitano 6-3; A. Higgins beat Bales 6-3; Chaperon beat B. Werbeniuk 6-1; S. Francisco beat Kearney 6-4; T. Meo beat Foldvari 6-0; W. Thorne beat W. Oliver 6-3; B. Harris beat E. Charlton 6-3; J. White beat T. Jones 6-5; A. Knowles beat French 6-2; N. Foulds beat J. Hargreaves 6-1; Newbury beat E. Sinclair 6-3; M. Wildman beat Gibson 6-1; J. Spencer beat Jonik 6-0; V. Harris beat D. Mountjoy 6-5; O'Kane beat J. Campbell 6-4; G. Miles beat Edmonds 6-1; T. Griffiths beat Chalmers 6-0; R. Reardon beat King 6-5; J. Parrott beat John Rea 6-4; Bradley beat David Taylor 6-3; K. Stevens beat Gauvreau 6-3; J. Virgo beat P. Francisco 6-2; Fowler beat R. Williams 6-4; D. Martin beat B. Bennett 6-0; S. Davis beat Chappel 6-5; Dennis Taylor beat Scott 6-2
**Second round:** Newbury beat Griffiths 5-3; Bradley beat Fowler 5-4; S. Davis beat Virgo 5-2; Knowles beat Longworth 5-2; O'Kane beat V. Harris 5-3; Thorburn beat Reynolds 5-3; Higgins beat N. Foulds 5-1; Dennis Taylor beat Parrott 5-2; Macleod beat Thorne 5-0; Martin beat Reardon 5-4; Miles beat Spencer 5-3; S. Francisco beat White 5-4; Meo beat Hallett 5-4; E. Hughes beat B. Harris 5-4; Stevens beat Wildman 5-2; Chaperon beat W. Jones 5-2
**Third round:** Meo beat Knowles 5-2; S. Davis beat Bradley 5-2; O'Kane beat Martin 5-4; S. Francisco beat Chaperon 5-2; Dennis Taylor beat Newbury 5-3; E. Hughes beat Macleod 5-2; Stevens beat Miles 5-2; Higgins beat Thorburn 5-2
**Quarter-finals:** Stevens beat Dennis Taylor 5-2; S. Davis beat O'Kane 5-1; S. Francisco beat Meo 5-4; Higgins beat E. Hughes 5-2

**Semi-finals:** Stevens beat S. Davis 9-7; S. Francisco beat Higgins 9-6
**Final:** S. Francisco beat Stevens 12-9

**1986** (*Dulux*)
**First round:** J. O'Boye beat Jim Bear 5-1; J. Hargreaves *wo* G. Watson *scr*; O. Agrawal beat D. Greaves 5-3; D. Gilbert beat P. Burke 5-1; S. Hendry beat D. Hughes 5-1; G. Wilkinson beat P. Watchorn 5-4; D. Sheehan beat S. Simngam 5-2; G. Jenkins beat B. Demarco 5-1; B. West beat B. Bennett 5-1; G. Cripsey beat M. Darrington 5-4; P. Houlihan *wo* G. Robinson *scr*; A. Kearney beat M. Smith 5-2; R. Bales beat M. Parkin 5-1; T. Drago *wo* D. Mienie *scr*
**Second round:** T. Jones beat O'Boye 5-2; F. Davis beat W. Kelly 5-4; G. Scott beat D. Chalmers 5-1; Hargreaves beat R. Edmonds 5-3; L. Dodd beat F. Jonik 5-4; W. Jones beat G. Rigitano 5-1; G. Miles beat Agrawal 5-4; R. Chaperon beat V. Harris 5-0; John Rea beat W. King 5-1; D. Fowler beat T. Chappel 5-4; Gilbert beat M. Morra 5-4; P. Browne beat Hendry 5-0; J. Donnelly beat Wilkinson 5-4; S. Newbury beat W. Oliver 5-2; Sheehan *wo* M. Watterson *scr*; Jenkins beat J. Meadowcroft 5-2; I. Black beat M. Gibson 5-0; B. Harris beat E. Sinclair 5-3; P. Medati beat C. Everton 5-1; West beat E. McLaughlin 5-3; P. Fagan beat J. Fitzmaurice 5-4; C. Roscoe beat B. Mikkelsen 5-4; I. Williamson beat Cripsey 5-4; J. Wych beat J. Van Rensberg 5-0; P. Francisco beat G. Foulds 5-2; S. Longworth beat Houlihan 5-3; M. Bradley beat Jack Rea 5-1; S. Duggan beat T. Murphy 5-1; J. McLaughlin beat M. Fisher 5-3; R. Foldvari beat Kearney 5-2; Bales *wo* J. Dunning *scr*; Drago beat M. Gauvreau 5-3
**Third round:** S. Francisco beat T. Jones 5-2; M. Macleod beat F. Davis 5-4; T. Griffiths beat Scott 5-3; N. Foulds beat Hargreaves 5-4; W. Thorne beat Dodd 5-2; P. Mans beat W. Jones 5-2; K. Stevens beat Miles 5-3; C. Wilson beat Chaperon 5-3; John Rea beat R. Reardon 5-3; J. Virgo beat Fowler 5-1; E. Charlton beat Gilbert 5-2; Browne beat J. Spencer 5-0; T. Meo beat Donnelly 5-3; Newbury beat D. O'Kane 5-3; C. Thorburn beat Sheehan 5-0; M. Wildman beat Jenkins 5-4; S. Davis beat Black 5-2; D. Martin beat B. Harris 5-1; Medati beat David Taylor 5-1; J. Campbell beat West 5-4; Fagan beat D. Mountjoy 5-1; J. Parrott beat Roscoe 5-2; A. Knowles beat Williamson 5-1; Wych beat D. Reynolds 5-3; P. Francisco beat J. White 5-4; Longworth beat E. Hughes 5-4; A. Higgins beat Bradley 5-3; M. Hallett beat Duggan 5-3; J. Johnson beat J. McLaughlin 5-2; B. Werbeniuk beat Foldvari 5-4; Bales beat Dennis Taylor 5-4; R. Williams beat Drago 5-1
**Fourth round:** Macleod beat S. Francisco 5-1; Griffiths beat N. Foulds 5-3; Thorne beat Mans 5-1; Stevens beat Wilson 5-0; Virgo beat John Rea 5-0; Charlton beat Browne 5-1; Meo beat Newbury 5-0; Thorne beat Wildman 5-1; S. Davis beat Martin 5-1; Campbell beat Medati 5-4; Parrott beat Fagan 5-0; Wych beat Knowles 5-4; P. Francisco beat Longworth 5-2; Higgins beat Hallett 5-1; Werbeniuk beat Johnson 5-3; Williams beat Bales 5-4
**Fifth round:** Griffiths beat Macleod 5-2; Thorne beat Stevens 5-4; Virgo beat Charlton 5-4; Meo beat Thorburn 5-3; S. Davis beat Campbell 5-0; Wych beat Parrott 5-4; Higgins beat P. Francisco 5-2; Werbeniuk beat Williams 5-3
**Quarter-finals:** Thorne beat Griffiths 5-4; Virgo beat Meo 5-3; S. Davis beat Wych 5-2; Higgins beat Werbeniuk 5-1
**Semi-finals:** Thorne beat Virgo 9-4; S. Davis beat Higgins 9-3
**Final:** S. Davis beat Thorne 12-7

**1987** (*Dulux*)
**First round:** M. Morra beat M. Bennett 5-4; B. Rowswell beat G. Jenkins 5-1; G. Foulds beat D. Greaves 5-3; D. Roe beat M. Watterson 5-3; B. Kelly beat B. Bennett 5-2; P. Gibson beat O. Agrawal 5-0; N. Gilbert beat P. Houlihan 5-4; J. Hargreaves beat M. Parkin 5-4; J. Donnelly *wo* L. Heywood *scr*; C. Roscoe beat D. Mienie 5-2; F. Ellis beat M. Smith 5-2; D. Chalmers *wo* S. Simngam *scr*; P. Watchorn beat J. Dunning 5-2; K. Owers beat F. Jonik 5-4; M. Fisher *wo* C. Everton *scr*; R. Grace beat J. Meadowcroft 5-4; G. Wilkinson beat J. Fitzmaurice 5-0; T. Kearney *wo* Jim Bear *scr*; G. Rigitano beat

B. Demarco 5-1; S. James beat M. Darrington 5-3; T. Whitthread beat D. Hughes 5-1; P. Burke *wo* E. McLaughlin *scr*; B. Oliver beat Jack Rea 5-1; D. Sheehan beat J. Wright 5-2

**Second round:** M. Gauvreau beat R. Bales 5-0; Morra beat J. Van Rensberg 5-1; Rowswell beat D. O'Kane 5-4; G. Foulds beat R. Edmonds 5-3; Roe beat I. Black 5-0; W. King beat Williamson 5-3; B. Harris beat Kelly 5-2; S. Duggan beat Gibson 5-3; D. Fowler beat Dodd 5-1; N. Gilbert beat W. Jones 5-3; J. O'Boye beat M. Bradley 5-1; T. Murphy beat D. Gilbert 5-4; Hargreaves beat John Rea 5-3; T. Jones beat Donnelly 5-2; Roscoe beat S. Newbury 5-3; P. Medati beat Ellis 5-0; M. Wildman beat Chalmers 5-0; G. Cripsey beat Watchorn 5-4; Owers beat F. Davis 5-3; E. Sinclair beat S. Hendry 5-2; R. Chaperon beat Fisher 5-2; Grace beat P. Fagan 5-3; J. McLaughlin beat M. Gibson 5-1; Wilkinson beat Mans 5-2; T. Chappel beat Kearney 5-3; Rigitano beat P. Browne 5-4; R. Foldvari beat B. Mikkelsen 5-3; James beat G. Miles 5-2; J. Spencer beat Whitthread 5-2; G. Scott beat Burke 5-2; T. Drago beat Oliver 5-1; V. Harris beat Sheehan 5-4

**Third round:** S. Davis beat Gauvreau 5-0; J. Virgo beat Morra 5-3; S. Francisco beat Rowswell 5-0; C. Wilson beat G. Foulds 5-3; N. Foulds beat Roe 5-1; King beat J. Parrott 5-1; W. Thorne beat B. Harris 5-1; Duggan beat S. Longworth 5-2; A. Knowles beat Fowler 5-4; D. Reynolds beat N. Gilbert 5-2; R. Reardon beat O'Boye 5-4; Murphy beat J. Wych 5-1; T. Griffiths beat John Rea 5-2; T. Jones beat M. Macleod 5-4; Dennis Taylor beat Roscoe 5-1; E. Charlton beat Medati 5-4; C. Thorburn beat Wildman 5-3; Cripsey beat B. Werbeniuk 5-2; D. Mountjoy beat Owers 5-1; P. Francisco beat Sinclair 5-3; K. Stevens beat Chaperon 5-4; B. West beat Grace 5-2; J. McLaughlin beat A. Higgins 5-4; David Taylor beat Wilkinson 5-4; J. White beat Chappel 5-1; M. Hallett beat Rigitano 5-1; R. Williams beat Foldvari 5-4; James beat J. Campbell 5-1; Spencer beat T. Meo 5-1; D. Martin beat Scott 5-3; J. Johnson beat Drago 5-0; E. Hughes beat V. Harris 5-1

**Fourth round:** Virgo beat S. Davis 5-4; Wilson beat S. Francisco 5-4; N. Foulds beat King 5-4; Thorne beat Duggan 5-2; Knowles beat Reynolds 5-0; Murphy beat Reardon 5-4; Griffiths beat T. Jones 5-3; Dennis Taylor beat Charlton 5-1; Thorburn beat Cripsey 5-2; Mountjoy beat P. Francisco 5-3; Stevens beat West 5-4; David Taylor beat J. McLaughlin 5-2; White beat Hallett 5-2; Williams beat James 5-2; Spencer beat Martin 5-2; Johnson beat E. Hughes 5-3

**Fifth round:** Virgo beat Wilson 5-2; N. Foulds beat Thorne 5-2; Knowles beat Murphy 5-3; Dennis Taylor beat Griffiths 5-4; Thorburn beat Mountjoy 5-4; David Taylor beat Stevens 5-2; White beat Williams 5-0; Spencer beat Johnson 5-3

**Quarter-finals:** N. Foulds beat Virgo 5-3; Knowles beat Dennis Taylor 5-4; Thorburn beat David Taylor 5-3; White beat Spencer 5-3

**Semi-finals:** N. Foulds beat Knowles 9-2; White beat Thorburn 9-5

**Final:** White beat N. Foulds 13-9

**1988** (*MIM Britannia*)

**First round:** M. Clark beat M. Fisher 5-1; J. Bear beat A. Harris 5-2; Gary Wilkinson beat I. Black 5-2; J. Fitzmaurice *wo* C. Everton *scr*; G. Rigitano beat R. Marshall 5-2; M. Morra beat P. Watchorn 5-1; F. Ellis *wo* M. Watterson *scr*; D. Hughes beat P. Fagan 5-4; N. Gilbert beat D. Sheehan 5-3; J. Dunning beat F. Jonik 5-3; P. Thornley beat V. Harris 5-4; C. Roscoe beat P. Gibson 5-4; B. Oliver beat M. Smith 5-0; M. Darrington beat P. Burke 5-4; R. Foldvari beat D. Heaton 5-1; J. Meadowcroft beat B. Kelly 5-1; T. Whitthread beat Glen Wilkinson 5-4; D. Chalmers *wo* B. Mikkelsen *scr*; E. Lawlor beat E. Sinclair 5-3; B. Rowswell beat Jack Rea 5-1; D. Gilbert *wo* E. McLaughlin *scr*; I. Williamson beat S. Meakin 5-1; J. Donnelly beat D. Greaves 5-4; G. Jenkins beat J. Smith 5-3; J. Van Rensberg *wo* J. Hargreaves *scr*; D. Roe beat J. Chambers 5-3

**Second round:** Clark beat R. Grace 5-0; S. James beat W. King 5-2; Bear beat P. Houlihan 5-0; Gary Wilkinson beat R. Bales 5-1; T. Jones beat Fitzmaurice 5-3; R. Chaperon beat Rigitano 5-2; Morra beat M. Bennett 5-2; T. Chappel beat Ellis 5-0; G. Miles beat K. Owers 5-2; F. Davis beat D. Hughes 5-2; N. Gilbert beat Werbeniuk

5-1; Dunning beat G. Scott 5-3; J. Wych beat Thornley 5-1; Roscoe beat M. Wildman 5-0; S. Newbury beat Oliver 5-3; P. Medati beat M. Gauvreau 5-1; D. Fowler beat A. Kearney 5-1; Darrington beat L. Dodd 5-4; Foldvari beat G. Foulds 5-3; T. Murphy beat Meadowcroft 5-4; D. O'Kane beat Whitthread 5-2; P. Browne beat Chalmers 5-2; Lawlor beat B. Harris 5-2; Rowswell beat J. McLaughlin 5-2; M. Gibson beat S. Duggan 5-2; D. Gilbert beat J. Wright 5-2; Williamson beat M. Bradley 5-3; G. Cripsey beat Donnelly 5-4; J. O'Boye beat Jenkins 5-1; W. Jones beat John Rea 5-3; R. Reardon beat Van Rensberg 5-3; Roe beat R. Edmonds 5-1

**Third round:** J. White beat Clark 5-2; James beat E. Charlton 5-2; S. Francisco beat Bear 5-0; Gary Wilkinson beat T. Meo 5-2; T. Jones beat A. Higgins 5-3; Chaperon *wo* K. Stevens *scr*; T. Griffiths beat Morra 5-1; S. Hendry beat Chappel 5-1; Dennis Taylor beat Miles 5-1; J. Spencer beat F. Davis 5-0; R. Williams beat N. Gilbert 5-2; B. West beat Dunning 5-0; W. Thorne beat Wych 5-1; C. Wilson beat Roscoe 5-2; C. Thorburn beat Newbury 5-2; Medati beat David Taylor 5-4; N. Foulds beat Fowler 5-3; P. Francisco beat Darrington 5-1; J. Parrott beat Foldvari 5-1; J. Virgo beat Murphy 5-1; O'Kane beat Mountjoy 5-3; Browne beat D. Martin 5-4; J. Johnson beat Lawlor 5-1; Rowswell beat S. Longworth 5-4; A. Knowles beat M. Gibson 5-4; M. Macleod beat D. Gilbert 5-4; M. Hallett beat Williamson 5-0; Cripsey beat E. Hughes 5-3; O'Boye beat Reynolds 5-2; J. Campbell beat W. Jones 5-3; Reardon beat S. Davis 5-0; Roe beat T. Drago 5-3

**Fourth round:** White beat James 5-1; Gary Wilkinson beat S. Francisco 5-3; T. Jones beat Chaperon 5-4; Hendry beat Griffiths 5-1; Spencer beat Dennis Taylor 5-0; Williams beat West 5-0; Thorne beat Wilson 5-3; Thorburn beat Medati 5-2; N. Foulds beat P. Francisco 5-3; Parrott beat Virgo 5-1; O'Kane beat Browne 5-2; Johnson beat Rowswell 5-2; Macleod beat Knowles 5-4; Hallett beat Cripsey 5-2; O'Boye beat Campbell 5-1; Roe beat Reardon 5-2

**Fifth round:** White beat Gary Wilkinson 5-1; Hendry beat T. Jones 5-3; Williams beat Spencer 5-4; Thorburn beat Thorne 5-2; Parrott beat N. Foulds 5-0; O'Kane beat Johnson 5-2; Hallett beat Macleod 5-2; O'Boye beat Roe 5-1

**Quarter-finals:** Hendry beat White 5-4; Thorburn beat Williams 5-2; Parrott beat O'Kane 5-2; Hallett beat O'Boye 5-4

**Semi-finals:** Hendry beat Thorburn 9-5; Hallett beat Parrott 9-8

**Final:** Hendry beat Hallett 13-2

**1989** (*Anglian*)

**First round:** C. Edwards beat I. Black 5-3; J. Meadowcroft beat G. Jenkins 5-4; C. Roscoe beat S. Meakin 5-1; J. Smith beat G. Foulds 5-3; M. Gibson beat M. Rowing 5-0; M. Price beat G. Rigitano 5-0; A. Harris beat M. Wildman 5-4; I. Graham beat I. Williamson 5-4; E. Sinclair beat M. Mikkelsen 5-3; D. Morgan beat Glen Wilkinson 5-0; T. Wilson beat F. Davis 5-1; J. Fitzmaurice beat J. Dunning 5-1; J. Van Rensberg *wo* F. Jonik *scr*; M. Darrington beat G. Scott 5-4; S. Campbell beat P. Medati 5-3; A. Robidoux beat B. Harris 5-0; N. Terry beat A. Kearney 5-3; J. Rempe beat M. Morra 5-1; John Rea beat P. Watchorn 5-3; E. Lawlor beat M. Watterson 5-0; T. Whitthread beat J. Donnelly 5-4; Jim Bear beat Jack Rea 5-4; M. Johnston-Allen beat V. Harris 5-1; B. Rowswell beat F. Ellis 5-1; R. Grace beat P. Fagan 5-2; P. Burke *wo* P. Gibson *scr*; M. Smith beat D. Hughes 5-1; B. Kelly beat B. Oliver 5-4; G. Miles beat D. Chalmers 5-4; R. Marshall beat J. Chambers 5-2; M. Bradley beat C. Everton 5-0; R. Foldvari beat D. Sheehan 5-1

**Second round:** Edwards beat J. O'Boye 5-4; T. Jones beat Meadowcroft 5-1; Roscoe *wo* B. Werbeniuk *scr*; M. Bennett beat J. Smith 5-4; J. Campbell beat M. Gibson 5-2; D. Roe beat Price 5-2; J. Wych beat A. Harris 5-4; Graham beat S. Duggan 5-2; P. Browne beat Sinclair 5-2; D. Morgan beat J. McLaughlin 5-0; N. Gilbert beat T. Wilson 5-2; R. Bales beat Fitzmaurice 5-1; D. Fowler beat Van Rensberg 5-1; M. Clark beat Darrington 5-2; R. Reardon beat S. Campbell 5-4; Robidoux beat W. King 5-2; P. Houlihan beat Terry 5-2; L. Dodd beat Rempe 5-0; John Rea beat D. Gilbert 5-3; T. Chappel beat Lawlor 5-2; Whitthread beat T. Murphy 5-2; Jim Bear

beat D. Martin 5-2; Johnston-Allen beat R. Edmonds 5-4; W. Jones beat Rowswell 5-0; J. Wright beat Grace 5-1; K. Owers beat Burke 5-2; M. Macleod beat M. Smith 5-4; M. Gauvreau beat Kelly 5-0; Gary Wilkinson beat Miles 5-2; Marshall beat K. Stevens 5-4; G. Cripsey beat Bradley 5-4; Foldvari beat M. Fisher 5-0
**Third round:** S. Hendry beat Edwards 5-0; D. O'Kane beat T. Jones 5-4; Roscoe beat Dennis Taylor 5-4; T. Meo beat M. Bennett 5-1; P. Francisco beat J. Campbell 5-2; Roe beat R. Williams 5-2; T. Knowles beat Wych 5-2; B. West beat Graham 5-1; C. Thorburn beat Browne 5-0; D. Morgan beat E. Charlton 5-3; M. Hallett beat N. Gilbert 5-3; R. Bales beat S. Newbury 5-3; J. Virgo beat Fowler 5-2; Clark beat David Taylor 5-2; N. Foulds beat Reardon 5-1; Robidoux beat J. Spencer 5-1; J. White beat Houlihan 5-3; D. Reynolds beat Dodd 5-2; C. Wilson beat John Rea 5-2; Chappel beat S. James 5-3; J. Johnson beat Whitthread 5-2; T. Drago beat Jim Bear 5-2; Johnston-Allen beat T. Griffiths 5-1; E. Hughes beat W. Jones 5-2; J. Parrott beat Wright 5-1; S. Longworth beat Owers 5-1; Macleod beat S. Francisco 5-4; D. Mountjoy beat Gauvreau 5-0; W. Thorne beat Gary Wilkinson 5-1; Marshall beat R. Chaperon 5-2; S. Davis beat Cripsey 5-1; A. Higgins beat Foldvari 5-1
**Fourth round:** Hendry beat O'Kane 5-2; Meo beat Roscoe 5-3; P. Francisco beat Roe 5-3; West beat Knowles 5-0; Thorburn beat D. Morgan 5-4; Hallett beat Bales 5-0; Clark beat Virgo 5-1; N. Foulds beat Robidoux 5-1; Reynolds *wo* White *scr*; C. Wilson beat Chappel 5-3; Johnson beat Drago 5-3; Johnston-Allen beat E. Hughes 5-2; Parrott beat Longworth 5-1; Mountjoy beat Macleod 5-0; Thorne beat Marshall 5-1; S. Davis beat Higgins 5-0
**Fifth round:** Meo beat Hendry 5-3; P. Francisco beat West 5-1; Hallett beat Thorburn 5-4; Clark beat Foulds 5-4; Reynolds beat C. Wilson 5-0; Johnson beat Johnston-Allen 5-2; Parrott beat Mountjoy 5-2; S. Davis beat Thorne 5-0
**Quarter-finals:** Meo beat P. Francisco 5-3; Hallett beat Clark 5-3; Reynolds beat Johnson 5-4; Parrott beat S. Davis 5-1
**Semi-finals:** Meo beat Hallett 9-8; Reynolds beat Parrott 9-8
**Final:** Meo beat Reynolds 13-6

**1990**

**First round:** M. Gauvreau beat B. Pinches 5-4; B. Morgan beat G. Scott 5-1; B. Gollan beat P. Gibson 5-1; J. Dunning beat M. Gibson 5-4; M. Bradley beat R. Grace 5-1; L. Dodd *wo* T. Whitthread *scr*; J. Bear beat J. Smith 5-4; R. Marshall beat S. Meakin 5-2; G. Miles beat N. Dyson 5-3; S. Murphy beat R. Foldvari 5-3; N. Terry beat P. Thornley 5-1; J. Wright beat P. Watchorn 5-1; M. Smith beat M. Darrington 5-4; J. Donnelly beat D. Hughes 5-2; A. Harris beat F. Ellis 5-3; E. Sinclair beat M. Wildman 5-4; W. Williamson beat G. Foulds 5-0; P. Medati beat D. Sheehan 5-2; Glen Wilkinson beat I. Brumby 5-4; M. Rowing beat F. Davis 5-2; V. Harris beat Jack Rea 5-2; J. Wattana beat C. Edwards 5-2; S. Campbell beat M. Price 5-3; A. Kearney beat P. Houlihan 5-2; J. Fitzmaurice beat M. Morra 5-2; T. Wilson beat J. Van Rensberg 5-1; B. Oliver beat M. Watterson 5-0; K. Owers beat G. Rigitano 5-3; N. Bond beat B. Rowswell 5-3; A. Cairns beat John Rea 5-1; J. Meadowcroft beat E. Lawlor 5-2; B. Harris beat D. Campbell 5-2
**Second round:** R. Bales beat Gauvreau 5-1; S. Longworth beat B. Morgan 5-3; Gollan beat T. Jones 5-1; M. Macleod beat Dunning 5-1; P. Browne beat Bradley 5-2; Dodd beat W. King 5-2; T. Murphy beat Bear 5-2; Marshall beat N. Gilbert 5-2; Miles beat G. Cripsey 5-2; S. Murphy beat J. O'Boye 5-3; Terry beat J. Campbell 5-1; Wright beat D. Martin 5-2; J. Wych beat M. Smith 5-2; Donnelly beat D. Gilbert 5-4; D. Morgan beat A. Harris 5-3; Sinclair beat R. Edmonds 5-3; S. Duggan beat Williamson 5-3; A. Robidoux beat Medati 5-1; D. Fowler beat Glen Wilkinson 5-1; Rowing beat R. Reardon 5-4; M. Bennett beat V. Harris 5-0; Wattana beat J. Chambers 5-3; J. Spencer beat S. Campbell 5-3; I. Graham beat Kearney 5-4; Gary Wilkinson beat Fitzmaurice 5-3; T. Wilson beat J. McLaughlin 5-3; Oliver beat C. Roscoe 5-4; M. Johnston-Allen beat Owers 5-4; T. Chappel beat Bond 5-4; David Taylor beat Cairns 5-0; K. Stevens beat Meadowcroft 5-4; B. Harris beat M. Fisher 5-1

**Third round:** T. Meo beat Bales 5-2; T. Drago beat Longworth 5-0; A. Knowles beat Gollan 5-2; Macleod beat B. West 5-0; Browne beat J. Virgo 5-1; Dodd beat C. Wilson 5-3; T. Murphy beat C. Thorburn 5-3; Marshall beat D. Roe 5-3; M. Hallett beat Miles 5-1; M. Clark beat S. Murphy 5-2; D. Mountjoy beat Terry 5-3; S. Newbury beat Wright 5-3; J. Johnson *wo* Wych *scr*; R. Chaperon beat Donnelly 5-0; D. Morgan beat Hendry 5-4; R. Williams beat Sinclair 5-3; Duggan beat Parrott 5-1; Robidoux beat E. Charlton 5-3; Dennis Taylor beat Fowler 5-1; Rowing beat W. Jones 5-4; M. Bennett beat W. Thorne 5-1; Wattana beat O'Kane 5-1; J. White beat Spencer 5-4; N. Foulds beat Graham 5-2; T. Griffiths beat Gary Wilkinson 5-4; T. Wilson beat S. Francisco 5-4; S. James beat Oliver 5-1; E. Hughes beat Johnston-Allen 5-1; D. Reynolds beat Chappel 5-2; P. Francisco beat David Taylor 5-4; S. Davis beat Stevens 5-2; A. Higgins beat B. Harris 5-3
**Fourth round:** E. Hughes beat Williams 5-2; Marshall beat Johnson 5-4; Newbury beat T. Murphy 5-2; Clark beat Browne 5-2; Higgins beat M. Bennett 5-2; Robidoux beat Duggan 5-4; Mountjoy beat Reynolds 5-2; Knowles beat Wattana 5-3; N. Foulds beat Drago 5-0; Chaperon beat Hallett 5-3; S. Davis beat D. Morgan 5-4; P. Francisco beat Griffiths 5-1; James beat T. Wilson 5-0; Dennis Taylor beat Macleod 5-2; White beat Meo 5-0; Dodd beat Rowing 5-2
**Fifth round:** Marshall beat E. Hughes 5-0; Clark beat Dennis Taylor 5-3; Chaperon beat Robidoux 5-4; Higgins beat Mountjoy 5-3; Dodd beat Knowles 5-4; Newbury beat S. Davis 5-2; N. Foulds beat P. Francisco 5-3; James beat White 5-4
**Quarter-finals:** Marshall beat Newbury 5-4; James beat Dodd 5-2; Chaperon beat N. Foulds 5-3; Higgins beat Clark 5-3
**Semi-finals:** Chaperon beat Marshall 9-5; Higgins beat James 9-3
**Final:** Chaperon beat Higgins 10-8

# EUROPEAN OPEN

**First staged** 1989. **Sponsors** ICI (quarter-finals onward) (1989). **Venue** Deauville Casino, France (1989), Maison du Judo, Lyon, France (1990). **Initial prize-money** £200,000. **Prize-money last season** £200,000. **TV** Eurosport.

## 1989

**First round:** J. Chambers beat M. Mikkelsen 5-3; D. Morgan beat W. Wildman 5-1; I. Williamson beat D. Hughes 5-1; C. Edwards beat M. Smith 5-4; P. Watchorn beat M. Harris 5-4; F. Davis beat C. Everton 5-0; E. Lawlor beat J. Fitzmaurice 5-0; I. Graham beat G. Scott 5-1; A. Harris beat Glen Wilkinson 5-4; T. Wilson beat M. Gibson 5-3; G. Foulds beat Jack Rea 5-4; M. Johnston-Allen beat J. Donnelly 5-3; F. Ellis beat A. Kearney 5-4; J. Smith beat B. Rowswell 5-2; M. Bradley beat J. Rempe 5-4; G. Rigitano beat P. Burke 5-2; M. Rowing beat R. Foldvari 5-4; M. Morra beat S. Campbell 5-3; C. Roscoe beat M. Watterson 5-4; V. Harris beat N. Terry 5-2; P. Medati beat D. Sheehan 5-1; A. Robidoux beat J. Meadowcroft 5-0; M. Price beat John Rea 5-4; M. Darrington beat J. Dunning 5-4; R. Grace beat S. Meakin 5-4; I. Black beat P. Fagan 5-1; Jim Bear beat B. Kelly 5-0; R. Marshall beat J. Van Rensberg 5-1; B. Oliver beat D. Chalmers 5-4; E. Sinclair beat T. Whitthread 5-4; G. Miles beat G. Jenkins 5-3
**Second round:** Chambers beat R. Bales 5-1; S. Duggan beat Morgan 5-4; R. Reardon beat Williamson 5-3; Edwards *wo* B. Werbeniuk *scr*; J. Campbell beat Watchorn 5-1; M. Bennett beat F. Davis 5-2; Lawlor beat K. Owers 5-4; Gary Wilkinson beat Graham 5-3; D. Fowler beat A. Harris 5-1; T. Wilson beat M. Gauvreau 5-3; J. Wych beat G. Foulds 5-0; Johnston-Allen beat J. Wright 5-4; D. Gilbert beat Ellis 5-2; P. Browne beat J. Smith 5-4; J. O'Boye beat Bradley 5-3; W. Jones beat Rigitano 5-4; M. Clark beat Rowing 5-0; Morra beat N. Gilbert 5-1; G. Cripsey beat Roscoe 5-4; D. Roe beat V. Harris 5-1; T. Jones beat Medati 5-2; Robidoux beat M. Fisher 5-1; J. McLaughlin beat Price 5-3; T. Chappel beat Darrington 5-0; R. Edmonds beat Grace 5-1; Macleod

beat Black 5-1; K. Stevens beat Bear 5-2; T. Murphy beat Marshall 5-4; Oliver beat D. Martin 5-4; L. Dodd *wo* both P. Gibson & F. Jonik *scr*; Sinclair beat P. Houlihan 5-1; King beat Miles 5-2
**Third round:** Chambers *wo* S. Davis *scr*; E. Charlton beat Duggan 5-2; J. Virgo beat Reardon 5-3; Edwards beat R. Chaperon 5-3; J. Campbell beat P. Francisco 5-0; M. Bennett beat T. Drago 5-1; J. Parrott *wo* E. Lawlor *scr*; Gary Wilkinson beat David Taylor 5-2; Fowler beat A. Knowles 5-2; T. Wilson *wo* J. Spencer *scr*; Wych beat S. Francisco 5-1; Johnston-Allen beat S. James 5-1; M. Hallett beat D. Gilbert 5-3; Browne *wo* D. Reynolds *scr*; S. Hendry beat O'Boye 5-2; S. Longworth *wo* W. Jones *scr*; Clark beat N. Foulds 5-3; E. Hughes beat Morra 5-1; J. Johnson beat Cripsey 5-2; Roe beat T. Meo 5-1; C. Wilson beat T. Jones 5-3; Robidoux beat S. Newbury 5-0; T. Griffiths beat J. McLaughlin 5-3; Chappel beat D. O'Kane 5-0; C. Thorburn beat Edmonds 5-2; Macleod beat B. West 5-4; Dennis Taylor beat Stevens 5-0; D. Mountjoy beat Murphy 5-1; W. Thorne beat Oliver 5-0; A. Higgins beat Dodd 5-2; J. White beat Sinclair 5-3; R. Williams beat King 5-2
**Fourth round:** Charlton beat Chambers 5-2; Virgo beat Edwards 5-3; J. Campbell beat M. Bennett 5-3; Parrott beat Gary Wilkinson 5-2; Fowler beat T. Wilson 5-2; Wych beat Johnston-Allen 5-4; Hallett beat Browne 5-4; Hendry beat Longworth 5-0; Clark beat E. Hughes 5-1; Johnson beat Roe 5-2; Robidoux beat C. Wilson 5-0; Griffiths beat Chapel 5-2; Thorburn beat Macleod 5-1; Mountjoy beat Dennis Taylor 5-3; Thorne beat Higgins 5-1; White beat Williams 5-2
**Fifth round:** Charlton beat Virgo 5-4; Parrott beat J. Campbell 5-0; Wych beat Fowler 5-4; Hallett beat Hendry 5-3; Clark beat Johnson 5-4; Griffiths beat Robidoux 5-3; Thorburn beat Mountjoy 5-0; White beat Thorne 5-3
**Quarter-finals:** Parrott beat Charlton 5-1; Hallett beat Wych 5-3; Griffiths beat Clark 5-1; White beat Thorburn 5-3
**Semi-finals:** Parrott beat Hallett 5-4; Griffiths beat White 5-4
**Final:** Parrott beat Griffiths 9-8

## 1990

**First round:** J. Wright beat M. Gibson 5-1; M. Bradley *wo* J. Van Rensberg *scr*; A. Cairns beat J. Bear 5-4; B. Harris beat J. Fitzmaurice 5-3; B. Rowswell beat P. Watchorn 5-4; N. Bond beat J. Dunning 5-0; J. Wattana beat P. Medati 5-1; B. Gollan beat V. Harris 5-2; N. Dyson beat I. Williamson 5-3; John Rea beat G. Rigitano 5-4; D. Campbell beat P. Houlihan 5-4; M. Wildman *wo* J. Meadowcroft *scr*; B. Pinches beat R. Marshall 5-4; K. Owers beat G. Foulds 5-1; S. Murphy beat F. Davis 5-0; M. Gauvreau beat S. Meakin 5-3; R. Foldvari beat D. Hughes 5-1; M. Morra beat J. Smith 5-4; Jack Rea beat A. Harris 5-4; E. Lawlor beat D. Sheehan 5-3; B. Kelly beat Glen Wilkinson 5-3; S. Campbell beat G. Scott 5-2; M. Smith beat T. Whitthread 5-1; B. Oliver beat M. Rowing 5-4; M. Price beat I. Brumby 5-1; F. Ellis beat N. Terry 5-3; M. Watterson beat J. Donnelly 5-3; G. Miles beat M. Darrington 5-2; C. Edwards beat B. Morgan 5-2; E. Sinclair beat P. Thornley 5-2; A. Kearney beat P. Gibson 5-1; R. Grace beat T. Wilson 5-3
**Second round:** Wright beat R. Edmonds 5-4; I. Graham beat Bradley 5-0; N. Gilbert beat Cairns 5-3; D. Fowler beat B. Harris 5-3; D. Morgan beat Rowswell 5-2; Bond beat M. Fisher 5-2; A. Robidoux beat Wattana 5-2; J. Campbell beat Gollan 5-3; Dyson beat S. Longworth 5-3; J. Spencer beat John Rea 5-1; D. Campbell beat D. Gilbert 5-2; C. Roscoe beat Wildman 5-3; Pinches beat K. Stevens 5-4; Owers beat T. Murphy 5-2; S. Murphy beat G. Cripsey 5-2; D. Martin beat Gauvreau 5-4; Foldvari beat M. Macleod 5-4; J. McLaughlin beat Morra 5-0; T. Chappel beat Jack Rea 5-1; David Taylor beat Lawlor 5-2; P. Browne beat Kelly 5-4; M. Johnston-Allen beat S. Campbell 5-0; M. Bennett beat M. Smith 5-3; Oliver *wo* J. Wych *scr*; Price beat Gary Wilkinson 5-4; Ellis beat W. King 5-4; J. Chambers beat Watterson 5-0; J. O'Boye beat Miles 5-1; Edwards beat T. Jones 5-4; Sinclair beat S. Duggan 5-3; R. Bales beat Kearney 5-3; Grace beat L. Dodd 5-3
**Third round:** J. Parrott beat Wright 5-1; W. Jones beat Graham 5-1; J. Johnson beat

N. Gilbert 5-2; Fowler beat B. West 5-2; D. Reynolds beat D. Morgan 5-3; Bond beat T. Drago 5-2; Robidoux beat M. Hallett 5-1; J. Campbell beat C. Wilson 5-0; Dyson beat Dennis Taylor 5-3; M. Clark beat Spencer 5-1; J. Virgo beat D. Campbell 5-4; Roscoe beat P. Francisco 5-3; S. James beat Pinches 5-2; A. Higgins beat Owers 5-2; J. White beat S. Murphy 5-0; D. Roe beat Martin 5-1; S. Hendry beat Foldvari 5-1; S. Newbury beat J. McLaughlin 5-2; Chappel beat A. Knowles 5-3; David Taylor beat E. Hughes 5-4; W. Thorne beat Browne 5-3; N. Foulds beat Johnston-Allen 5-2; M. Bennett beat T. Griffiths 5-2; S. Francisco beat Oliver 5-2; Price beat C. Thorburn 5-0; E. Charlton beat Ellis 5-3; D. Mountjoy beat Chambers 5-4; R. Williams beat O'Boye 5-2; Edwards beat Meo 5-4; O'Kane beat Sinclair 5-4; S. Davis beat Bales 5-2; R. Chaperon beat Grace 5-2

**Fourth round:** Parrott beat W. Jones 5-0; Johnson beat Fowler 5-1; Bond beat Reynolds 5-4; J. Campbell beat Robidoux 5-4; Dyson beat Clark 5-2; Roscoe beat Virgo 5-2; James beat Higgins 5-2; White beat Roe 5-1; Hendry beat Newbury 5-1; Chappel beat David Taylor 5-2; N. Foulds beat Thorne 5-3; M. Bennett beat S. Francisco 5-3; Charlton beat Price 5-4; Mountjoy beat Williams 5-0; Edwards beat O'Kane 5-2; S. Davis beat Chaperon 5-0

**Fifth round:** Parrott beat Johnson 5-2; Bond beat J. Campbell 5-4; Roscoe beat Dyson 5-2; James beat White 5-4; Hendry beat Chappel 5-2; Foulds beat M. Bennett 5-2; Mountjoy beat Charlton 5-2; S. Davis beat Edwards 5-4

**Quarter-finals:** Parrott beat Bond 5-3; James beat Roscoe 5-2; Hendry beat N. Foulds 5-3; S. Davis beat Mountjoy 5-0

**Semi-finals:** Parrott beat James 6-3; Hendry beat S. Davis 6-3

**Final:** Parrott beat Hendry 10-6

## BRITISH CAR RENTAL WORLD CUP

**First staged** 1979. **Sponsors** State Express (1979–83), Guinness (1985), Car Care Plan (1986), Tuborg (1987), Fersina Windows (1988–89), British Car Rental (1990– ). **Venue** The Hexagon, Reading (1979–83), Bournemouth International Centre (1985– ). **Initial prize-money** £27,500. **Prize-money last season** £150,000. **TV** BBC.

**1979** (*State Express World Team Classic*)

**Group A**

England (F. Davis, G. Miles, J. Spencer) beat Rest of World (P. Mans, J. Van Rensberg, P. Fagan) 8-7; England beat Northern Ireland (Jack Rea, A. Higgins, Dennis Taylor) 8-7; Northern Ireland beat Rest of World 8-7

**Group B**

Wales (R. Reardon, T. Griffiths, D. Mountjoy) beat Canada (C. Thorburn, K. Stevens, B. Werbeniuk) 9-6; Australia (E. Charlton, G. Owen, P. Morgan) beat Canada 8-7; Wales beat Australia 9-6

**Final:** Wales beat England 14-3

**1980** (*State Express World Team Classic*)

**Group A**

Wales (R. Reardon, T. Griffiths, D. Mountjoy) beat Canada (C. Thorburn, K. Stevens, B. Werbeniuk) 10-5; Canada beat Rest of World (J. Rempe, E. Sinclair, P. Mans) 9-6; Wales beat Rest of World 13-2

**Group B**

England (F. Davis, J. Virgo, David Taylor) beat Ireland (A. Higgins, Dennis Taylor, P. Fagan) 11-4; Australia (E. Charlton, I. Anderson, P. Morgan) beat England 8-7; Ireland beat Australia 10-5

**Semi-finals:** Wales beat Ireland 8-7; Canada beat England 8-5

**Final:** Wales beat Canada 8-5

**1981** (*State Express World Team Classic*)
**Preliminary match:** Republic of Ireland (E. Hughes, P. Fagan, D. Sheehan) beat Scotland (I. Black, M. Macleod, E. Sinclair) 4-2
**Group A**
England (S. Davis, J. Spencer, David Taylor) beat Australia (I. Anderson, E. Charlton, P. Morgan) 4-3; Northern Ireland (T. Murphy, Dennis Taylor, A. Higgins) beat Australia 4-1; England beat Northern Ireland 4-3
**Group B**
Wales (R. Reardon, D. Mountjoy, T. Griffiths) beat Canada (K. Stevens, C. Thorburn, B. Werbeniuk) 4-2; Wales beat Republic of Ireland 4-0; Canada beat Republic of Ireland 4-2
**Semi-finals:** England beat Canada 4-2; Wales beat Northern Ireland 4-3
**Final:** England beat Wales 4-3

**1982** (*State Express World Team Classic*)
**Preliminary match:** Scotland (E. Sinclair, J. Donnelly, I. Black) beat Republic of Ireland (E. Hughes, P. Fagan, D. Sheehan) 4-2
**Group A**
England (A. Knowles, S. Davis, J. White) beat Northern Ireland (A. Higgins, T. Murphy, Dennis Taylor) 4-3; Scotland beat Northern Ireland 4-1; England beat Scotland 4-1
**Group B**
Canada (C. Thorburn, B. Werbeniuk, K. Stevens) beat Wales (T. Griffiths, D. Mountjoy, R. Reardon) 4-3; Canada beat Australia (E. Charlton, P. Morgan, I. Anderson) 4-0; Wales beat Australia 4-1
**Semi-finals:** England beat Wales 4-2; Canada beat Scotland 4-0
**Final:** Canada beat England 4-2

**1983** (*State Express World Team Classic*)
**Preliminary match:** Scotland (E. Sinclair, M. Macleod, I. Black) beat Republic of Ireland (B. Kelly, E. Hughes, P. Fagan) 4-2
**Group A**
Wales (D. Mountjoy, R. Reardon, T. Griffiths) beat Canada (C. Thorburn, B. Werbeniuk, K. Stevens) 4-3; Canada beat Australia (E. Charlton, W. King, J. Campbell) 4-2; Wales beat Australia 4-0
**Group B**
England (S. Davis, A. Knowles, T. Meo) beat Northern Ireland (A. Higgins, T. Murphy, Dennis Taylor) 4-1; Northern Ireland beat Scotland 4-3; England beat Scotland 4-0
**Semi-finals:** Wales beat Northern Ireland 4-1; England beat Canada 4-2
**Final:** England beat Wales 4-2

**1985** (*Guinness World Cup*)
**First round:** Wales beat Australia 5-4 (T. Griffiths drew with E. Charlton 1-1; D. Mountjoy beat J. Campbell 2-0; R. Reardon lost to W. King 0-2; Mountjoy drew with Charlton 1-1; Griffiths beat King 1-0); England A beat Scotland 5-4 (S. Davis lost to E. Sinclair 0-2; A. Knowles drew with M. Macleod 1-1; T. Meo beat J. Donnelly 2-0; S. Davis drew with Sinclair 1-1; Knowles beat Macleod 1-0); England B beat Rest of World 5-2 (J. White beat S. Francisco 2-0; W. Thorne drew with J. Rempe 1-1; J. Spencer drew with D. O'Kane 1-1; White beat Francisco 1-0); Ireland beat Canada 5-2 (Dennis Taylor beat K. Stevens 2-0; E. Hughes drew with C. Thorburn 1-1; A. Higgins drew with B. Werbeniuk 1-1; Higgins beat Thorburn 1-0)
**Semi-finals:** Ireland beat Wales 5-3 (Dennis Taylor drew with Mountjoy 1-1; E. Hughes lost to Griffiths 0-2; Higgins beat Reardon 2-0; Higgins beat Mountjoy 2-0); England A beat England B 5-2 (S. Davis beat Spencer 2-0; Knowles drew with Thorne 1-1; Meo drew with White 1-1; S. Davis beat White 1-0)
**Final:** Ireland beat England A 9-7 (Dennis Taylor drew with Knowles 1-1; E. Hughes lost to S. Davis 0-2; Higgins drew with Meo 1-1; Dennis Taylor drew with Knowles 1-1;

Dennis Taylor drew with S. Davis 1-1; E. Hughes drew with Knowles 1-1; Higgins beat Meo 2-0; Higgins beat S. Davis 2-0)

**1986** (*Car Care Plan World Cup*)
**First round:** Ireland A beat Ireland B 5-0 (A. Higgins beat P. Fagan 2-0; E. Hughes beat T. Murphy 2-0; Dennis Taylor beat P. Browne 1-0); Wales beat Scotland 5-1 (D. Mountjoy beat M. Macleod 2-0; R. Reardon drew with E. Sinclair 1-1; T. Griffiths beat J. Donnelly 2-0); Canada beat Rest of World 5-0 (C. Thorburn beat T. Drago 2-0; K. Stevens beat O. Agrawal 2-0; B. Werbeniuk beat S. Simngam 1-0); England beat Australia 5-2 (A. Knowles drew with J. Campbell 1-1; J. White drew with E. Charlton 1-1; S. Davis beat W. King 2-0; S. Davis beat Campbell 1-0)
**Semi-finals:** Ireland A beat Wales 5-2 (Higgins beat Mountjoy 2-0; Hughes lost to Reardon 0-2; Dennis Taylor beat Griffiths 2-0; Taylor beat Griffiths 1-0); Canada beat England 5-3 (Thorburn drew with Knowles 1-1; Stevens beat White 2-0; Werbeniuk drew with S. Davis 1-1; Thorburn drew with S. Davis 1-1)
**Final:** Ireland A beat Canada 9-7 (Dennis Taylor drew with Thorburn 1-1; Hughes lost to Stevens 0-2; Higgins beat Werbeniuk 2-0; Higgins drew with Stevens 1-1; Higgins drew with Thorburn 1-1; Hughes drew with Stevens 1-1; Taylor beat Werbeniuk 2-0; Taylor drew with Thorburn 1-1)

**1987** (*Tuborg World Cup*)
**First round:** Wales beat Australia 5-1 (R. Reardon drew with E. Charlton 1-1; D. Mountjoy beat W. King 2-0; T. Griffiths beat J. Campbell 2-0); Ireland A beat Ireland B 5-1 (E. Hughes beat P. Browne 2-0; A. Higgins beat P. Fagan 2-0; Dennis Taylor drew with T. Murphy 1-1); Canada beat Rest of World 5-4 (K. Stevens beat S. Francisco 2-0; C. Thorburn drew with T. Drago 1-1; B. Werbeniuk lost to D. O'Kane 0-2; Stevens drew with Drago 1-1; Thorburn beat Francisco 1-0); England beat Scotland 5-1 (J. Johnson drew with S. Hendry 1-1; S. Davis beat M. Gibson 2-0; T. Meo beat M. Macleod 2-0)
**Semi-finals:** Ireland A beat Wales 5-2 (Taylor lost to Griffiths 0-2; Hughes beat Reardon 2-0; Higgins beat Mountjoy 2-0; Higgins beat Griffiths 1-0); Canada beat England 5-4 (Stevens drew with Johnson 1-1; Thorburn beat Davis 2-0; Werbeniuk drew with Meo 1-1; Stevens lost to Davis 0-2; Thorburn beat Johnson 1-0)
**Final:** Ireland A beat Canada 9-2 (Hughes drew with Stevens 1-1; Higgins beat Thorburn 2-0; Taylor beat Werbeniuk 2-0; Taylor beat Stevens 2-0; Hughes drew with Stevens 1-1; Taylor beat Thorburn 1-0)

**1988** (*Fersina*)
**First round:** England beat Republic of Ireland 5-1 (S. Davis beat J. O'Boye 2-0; J. White beat E. Hughes 2-0; N. Foulds drew with P. Browne 1-1); Rest of World beat Northern Ireland 5-3 (D. O'Kane lost to D. Taylor 0-2; T. Drago beat A. Higgins 2-0; Drago drew with Taylor 1-1); Australia beat Canada 5-0 (J. Campbell beat J. Wych 2-0; W. King beat B. Werbeniuk 2-0; E. Charlton beat C. Thorburn 1-0); Scotland beat Wales 5-4 (M. Macleod beat D. Mountjoy 2-0; J. Rea drew with T. Griffiths 1-1; S. Hendry drew with C. Wilson 1-1; Hendry lost to Griffiths 0-2; Macleod beat Wilson 1-0)
**Semi-finals:** England beat Rest of World 5-3 (Davis drew with Drago 1-1; Foulds drew with O'Kane 1-1; White drew with Francisco 1-1; White beat Francisco 2-0); Australia beat Scotland 5-1 (Campbell beat Macleod 2-0; King beat Rea 2-0; Charlton drew with Hendry 1-1)
**Final:** England beat Australia 9-7 (Davis drew with Campbell 1-1; Foulds drew with King 1-1; White lost to Charlton 0-2; White drew with Charlton 1-1; White drew with King 1-1; Foulds drew with Campbell 1-1; Davis beat Charlton 2-0; Davis beat King 2-0)

**1989** (*Fersina*)
**First round:** England beat Republic of Ireland 5-1 (S. Davis beat E. Hughes 2-0; N. Foulds beat T. Kearney 2-0; J. White drew with P. Browne 1-1); Canada beat

Northern Ireland 5-1 (C. Thorburn beat A. Higgins 2-0; K. Stevens beat T. Murphy 2-0; R. Chaperon drew with Dennis Taylor 1-1); Rest of World beat Australia 5-2 (T. Drago beat J. Campbell 2-0; S. Francisco lost to E. Charlton 0-2; D. O'Kane beat W. King 2-0; Drago beat Charlton 1-0); Wales beat Scotland 5-3 (T. Griffiths drew with S. Hendry 1-1; C. Wilson beat M. Macleod 2-0; D. Mountjoy drew with J. Donnelly 1-1; Mountjoy drew with Hendry 1-1)
**Semi-finals:** England beat Canada 5-2 (Davis beat Thorburn 2-0; White drew with Stevens 1-1; Foulds drew with Chaperon 1-1; Foulds beat Thorburn 1-0); Rest of World beat Wales 5-3 (O'Kane lost to Mountjoy 0-2; Drago beat Griffiths 2-0; Francisco drew with Wilson 1-1; Drago beat Mountjoy 2-0)
**Final:** England beat Rest of World 9-8 (Davis drew with Drago 1-1; Foulds beat O'Kane 2-0; White lost to Francisco 1-3; White drew with Drago 1-1; Davis beat O'Kane 2-0; Foulds drew with Francisco 1-1; Foulds lost to Drago 0-2; Davis beat O'Kane 1-0)

**1990**
**First round:** Canada beat Scotland 5-3 (R. Chaperon drew with John Rea 1-1; C. Thorburn drew with M. Macleod 1-1; A. Robidoux drew with S. Hendry 1-1; Robidoux beat Hendry 2-0); Australia beat Wales 5-3 (J. Campbell drew with D. Mountjoy 1-1; W. King beat C. Wilson 2-0; E. Charlton drew with T. Griffiths 1-1; Charlton drew with Mountjoy 1-1); Northern Ireland beat Rest of the World 5-2 (Dennis Taylor drew with S. Francisco 1-1; T. Murphy drew with D. O'Kane 1-1; A. Higgins beat T. Drago 2-0; Higgins beat Drago 1-0); Republic of Ireland beat England 5-4 (A. Kearney drew with S. Davis 1-1; P. Browne lost to J. White 0-2; E. Hughes drew with J. Parrott 1-1; Hughes beat Parrott 2-0; Browne beat Davis 1-0)
**Semi-finals:** Canada beat Australia 5-1 (Chaperon beat Campbell 2-0; Thorburn drew with King 1-1; Robidoux beat Charlton 2-0); Northern Ireland beat Republic of Ireland 5-2 (Taylor beat Browne 2-0; Murphy lost to Hughes 0-2; Higgins beat Kearney 2-0; Higgins beat Hughes 1-0)
**Final:** Canada beat Northern Ireland 9-5 (Chaperon drew with Taylor 1-1; Thorburn beat Murphy 2-0; Robidoux drew with Higgins 1-1; Robidoux beat Higgins 2-0; Chaperon drew with Taylor 1-1; Thorburn lost to Higgins 0-2; Robidoux beat Murphy 2-0)

## BENSON AND HEDGES IRISH MASTERS

**First staged** 1978. **Sponsors** Benson and Hedges. **Venue** Goffs, Kill, Co Kildare. **Initial prize-money** £3,000. **Prize-money last season** £150,000. **TV** RTE.

**1978**
**Final:** J. Spencer beat D. Mountjoy 5-3

**1979**
**Final:** D. Mountjoy beat R. Reardon 6-5

**1980**
**Final:** T. Griffiths beat D. Mountjoy 9-8

**1981**
**First round:** Dennis Taylor beat J. Spencer 4-2; S. Davis beat J. Virgo 4-3
**Quarter-finals:** T. Griffiths beat K. Stevens 4-0; Thorburn beat D. Mountjoy 4-0; R. Reardon beat S. Davis 4-2; A. Higgins beat Dennis Taylor 4-2
**Semi-finals:** Griffiths beat Thorburn 6-5; Reardon beat Higgins 6-5
**Final:** Griffiths beat Reardon 9-7

**1982**
**First round:** Dennis Taylor beat D. Sheehan 5-3; T. Meo beat J. Spencer 5-3; A. Higgins beat J. Wych 5-3; D. Mountjoy beat E. Hughes 5-4

**Quarter-finals:** T. Griffiths beat T. Meo 5-3; R. Reardon beat Dennis Taylor 5-4; S. Davis beat Mountjoy 5-2; Higgins beat C. Thorburn 5-4
**Semi-finals:** Griffiths beat Reardon 6-3; S. Davis beat Higgins 6-2
**Final:** Griffiths beat S. Davis 9-5

**1983**
**First round:** J. White beat Dennis Taylor 5-4; T. Meo beat P. Burke 5-0; D. Mountjoy beat A. Knowles 5-1; E. Charlton beat David Taylor 5-4
**Quarter-finals:** R. Reardon beat Meo 5-4; A. Higgins beat White 5-2; S. Davis beat Charlton 5-1; T. Griffiths beat Mountjoy 5-4
**Semi-finals:** Reardon beat Higgins 6-3; S. Davis beat Griffiths 6-2
**Final:** S. Davis beat Reardon 9-2

**1984**
**First round:** T. Griffiths beat B. Werbeniuk 5-2; Dennis Taylor beat E. Hughes 5-1; T. Meo beat J. White 5-4; A. Higgins beat E. Charlton 5-2
**Quarter-finals:** Dennis Taylor beat C. Thorburn 5-2; Griffiths beat A. Knowles 5-0; Higgins beat R. Reardon 5-2; S. Davis beat Meo 5-4
**Semi-finals:** Griffiths beat Dennis Taylor 6-5; S. Davis beat Higgins 6-4
**Final:** S. Davis beat Griffiths 9-1

**1985**
**First round:** E. Charlton beat Dennis Taylor 5-4; J. White beat T. Meo 5-1; E. Hughes beat R. Reardon 5-0; A. Higgins beat T. Griffiths 5-2
**Quarter-finals:** A. Knowles beat Charlton 5-3; White beat C. Thorburn 5-3; S. Davis beat Hughes 5-4; Higgins beat K. Stevens 5-3
**Semi-finals:** White beat Knowles 6-4; Higgins beat S. Davis 6-2
**Final:** White beat Higgins 9-5

**1986**
**First round:** E. Hughes beat R. Reardon 5-2; W. Thorne beat T. Griffiths 5-2; T. Meo beat A. Higgins 5-4; P. Fagan *wo* K. Stevens *scr*
**Quarter-finals:** C. Thorburn beat Hughes 5-1; Thorne beat Dennis Taylor 5-2; J. White beat Meo 5-2; Fagan beat A. Knowles 5-4
**Semi-finals:** Thorne beat Thorburn 6-4; White beat Fagan 6-0
**Final:** White beat Thorne 9-5

**1987**
**First round:** W. Thorne beat K. Stevens 5-1; Dennis Taylor beat E. Hughes 5-4; T. Meo beat A. Knowles 5-2; T. Griffiths beat A. Higgins 5-1
**Quarter-finals:** Thorne beat J. White 5-4; Taylor beat C. Thorburn 5-1; S. Davis beat Meo 5-2; Griffiths beat J. Johnson 5-0
**Semi-finals:** Thorne beat Taylor 6-2; Davis beat Griffiths 6-2
**Final:** Davis beat Thorne 9-1

**1988**
**First round:** T. Griffiths beat R. Williams 5-1; T. Knowles beat W. Thorne 5-3; A. Higgins beat Dennis Taylor 5-3; J. Johnson beat E. Hughes 5-4
**Quarter-finals:** Griffiths beat J. White 5-2; N. Foulds beat Knowles 5-3; Higgins beat C. Thorburn 5-3; S. Davis beat Johnson 5-0
**Semi-finals:** Foulds beat Griffiths 6-4; Davis beat Higgins 6-2
**Final:** Davis beat Foulds 9-4

**1989**
**First round:** M. Hallett beat A. Knowles 5-0; T. Griffiths beat J. McLaughlin 5-4; A. Higgins beat C. Thorburn 5-4; J. Parrott beat Dennis Taylor 5-1
**Quarter-finals:** S. Hendry beat Griffiths 5-2; S. Davis beat Hallett 5-4; Parrott beat J. White 5-1; Higgins beat N. Foulds 5-2

**Semi-finals:** Higgins beat Parrott 6-4; Hendry beat Davis 6-4
**Final:** Higgins beat Hendry 9-8

**1990**
**First round:** Dennis Taylor beat C. Thorburn 5-3; J. White beat J. Johnson 5-4; T. Griffiths beat D. Mountjoy 5-1; W. Thorne beat M. Hallett 5-1
**Quarter-finals:** Taylor beat A. Higgins 5-2; White beat S. Hendry 5-2; Griffiths beat J. Parrott 5-3; S. Davis beat Thorne 5-3
**Semi-finals:** Taylor beat White 6-5; Davis beat Griffiths 6-3
**Final:** Davis beat Taylor 9-4

# EMBASSY WORLD PROFESSIONAL CHAMPIONSHIP

**First staged** 1927. **Sponsors** Embassy (1976– ). **Venue** Crucible Theatre, Sheffield (1977– ). **Initial prize-money** £15,300. **Prize-money last season** £620,800. **TV** BBC.

**1927**
**First round:** M. Inman beat T. Newman 8-5; T. Carpenter beat N. Butler 8-3
**Second round:** T. A. Dennis beat F. Lawrence 8-7; A. Cope beat A. Mann 8-6; J. Davis beat J. Brady 10-5; Carpenter beat Inman 8-3
**Semi-finals:** J. Davis beat Cope 16-7; Dennis beat Carpenter 12-10
**Final:** J. Davis beat Dennis 20-11

**1928**
**First round:** T. Newman beat F. Smith 12-6; A. Mann beat A. Cope 14-9
**Second round:** Newman beat T. A. Dennis 12-5; F. Lawrence beat Mann 12-11
**Third round:** Lawrence beat Newman 12-7
**Final:** J. Davis beat Lawrence 16-13

**1929**
**First round:** F. Lawrence beat A. Mann 13-12
**Semi-finals:** J. Davis beat Lawrence 13-10; T. A. Dennis beat K. Prince 14-6
**Final:** J. Davis beat Dennis 19-14

**1930**
**First round:** F. Lawrence beat A. Mann 13-11; N. Butler beat T. Newman 13-11
**Semi-finals:** J. Davis beat Lawrence 13-2; T. A. Dennis beat Butler 13-11
**Final:** J. Davis beat Dennis 25-12

**1931**
**Final:** J. Davis beat T. A. Dennis 25-21

**1932**
**First round:** C. McConachy beat T. A. Dennis 13-11
**Final:** J. Davis beat McConachy 30-19

**1933**
**First round:** W. Donaldson beat W. Leigh 13-11
**Semi-finals:** J. Davis beat Donaldson 13-1; W. Smith beat T. A. Dennis 16-9
**Final:** J. Davis beat Smith 25-18

**1934**
**Final:** J. Davis beat T. Newman 25-23

**1935**
**First round:** W. Smith beat C. Stanbury 13-12

**Semi-finals:** Smith beat A. Mann 13-4; J. Davis beat T. Newman 15-10
**Final:** J. Davis beat Smith 25-20

**1936**
**First round:** C. O'Donnell beat S. Lee 16-15; H. Lindrum beat H. Terry 20-11; J. Davis beat T. Newman 29-2; W. Smith beat S. Smith 16-15; C. Stanbury beat A. Mann 22-9
**Second round:** Alec Brown beat Stanbury 16-15; Lindrum beat O'Donnell 19-6 (*retd*); J. Davis beat W. Smith 22-9; S. Newman *wo*
**Semi-finals:** J. Davis beat Alec Brown 21-10; Lindrum beat S. Newman 29-2
**Final:** J. Davis beat Lindrum 34-27

**1937**
**First round:** W. A. Withers beat F. Davis 17-14
**Second round:** J. Davis beat Withers 30-1; H. Lindrum beat S. Lee 20-11; W. Smith beat T. Newman 16-15; S. Smith beat Alec Brown 18-13
**Semi-finals:** Lindrum beat W. Smith 20-11; J. Davis beat S. Smith 18-13
**Final:** J. Davis beat Lindrum 32-29

**1938**
**First qualifying round:** H. Holt beat C. W. Read 21-10
**Second qualifying round:** F. Davis beat Holt 23-8
**First round:** F. Davis beat Alec Brown 14-6 (*retd ill*); S. Smith beat C. Stanbury 27-4; J. Davis beat S. Lee 24-7; W. Smith beat T. Newman 16-15
**Semi-finals:** J. Davis beat W. Smith (*nrs*); S. Smith beat F. Davis (*nrs*)
**Final:** J. Davis beat S. Smith 37-24

**1939**
**First qualifying round:** W. Donaldson beat H. Holt 18-13; H. W. Laws beat S. Newman 19-12
**Second qualifying round:** Donaldson beat Laws 18-13
**First round:** S. Smith beat S. Lee 21-10; W. Donaldson beat C. Falkiner 21-10; T. Newman beat A. Mann 19-12; F. Davis beat C. Stanbury 19-12
**Second round:** J. Davis beat W. Smith 19-12; F. Davis beat T. Newman 20-11; Alec Brown beat H. Lindrum 17-14; S. Smith beat Donaldson 16-15
**Semi-finals:** J. Davis beat F. Davis 17-14; S. Smith beat Alec Brown 20-11
**Final:** J. Davis beat S. Smith 43-30

**1940**
**Qualifying round:** H. Holt beat C. Stanbury 18-13
**First round:** W. Donaldson beat Holt 24-7; J. Davis beat Alec Brown 20-11; F. Davis beat S. Lee 20-11; S. Smith beat T. Newman 22-9
**Semi-finals:** J. Davis beat Donaldson 22-9; F. Davis beat S. Smith 17-14
**Final:** J. Davis beat F. Davis 37-36

**1946**
**First qualifying round:** K. Kennerley beat F. Lawrence 22-9; C. Stanbury beat J. Barrie 18-13; S. Newman beat W. Leigh 16-15
**Second qualifying round:** Kennerley beat T. Reece 8-2 (*retd*); S. Newman beat Stanbury 17-14
**Third qualifying round:** S. Newman beat Kennerley 21-10
**First round:** J. Davis beat W. Donaldson 21-10; S. Newman beat S. Lee 19-12; F. Davis beat Alec Brown 24-7; H. Lindrum beat H. Holt 17-14
**Semi-finals:** J. Davis beat S. Newman 21-10; Lindrum beat F. Davis 16-12
**Final:** J. Davis beat Lindrum 78-67

**1947**
**First qualifying round:** Albert Brown beat J. Pulman 21-14; W. Leigh beat H. F. Francis 19-16; S. Lee beat J. Lees 19-16; K. Kennerley beat C. Stanbury 23-12; E. Newman *wo*

H. Holt *scr*
**Second qualifying round:** J. Barrie beat F. Lawrence 25-10; Albert Brown beat Newman 28-7; Kennerley beat A. Mann 23-12; Leigh beat Lee 25-10
**Third qualifying round:** Albert Brown beat Barrie 24-11; Kennerley beat Leigh 21-14
**Fourth qualifying round:** Albert Brown beat Kennerley 21-14
**First round:** H. Lindrum beat Albert Brown 39-34; S. Smith beat Alec Brown 43-28; W. Donaldson beat S. Newman 46-25; F. Davis beat C. McConachy 53-20
**Semi-finals:** Donaldson beat Lindrum 39-32; F. Davis beat Smith 39-32
**Final:** Donaldson beat F. Davis 82-63

**1948**
**First qualifying round:** C. Stanbury beat E. Newman 26-9; W. Leigh beat H. Holt 18-17; J. Barrie beat H. F. Francis 19-16; J. Pulman *wo* S. Lee *scr*
**Second qualifying round:** Leigh beat Barrie 21-14; Pulman beat Stanbury 19-16
**Third qualifying round:** Pulman beat Leigh 18-17
**First round:** F. Davis beat Alec Brown 43-28; C. McConachy beat J. Pulman 42-29; Albert Brown beat S. Smith 36-35; W. Donaldson beat K. Kennerley 46-25
**Semi-finals:** F. Davis beat McConachy 43-28; Donaldson beat Alec Brown 40-31
**Final:** F. Davis beat Donaldson 84-61

**1949**
**First qualifying round:** C. Stanbury beat H. F. Francis 18-17
**Second qualifying round:** Stanbury beat Jack Rea 18-17
**Third qualifying round:** Stanbury beat H. Holt 18-17
**First round:** W. Donaldson beat Stanbury 58-13; J. Pulman beat Albert Brown 42-29; S. Smith beat Alec Brown 41-30; F. Davis beat K. Kennerley 50-21
**Semi-finals:** Donaldson beat Pulman 49-22; F. Davis beat Smith 42-29
**Final:** F. Davis beat Donaldson 80-65

**1950**
**First qualifying round:** W. Smith beat W. A. Withers 28-7; H. Holt beat H. W. Laws 26-9; S. Lee beat C. Stanbury 20-15; K. Kennerley beat J. Barrie 21-14
**Second qualifying round:** Kennerley beat Smith 22-13; Lee beat Holt 16-8 (*retd ill*)
**Third qualifying round:** Kennerley beat Lee 21-14
**First round:** Albert Brown beat J. Pulman 37-34; W. Donaldson beat K. Kennerley 42-29; G. Chenier beat P. Mans 37-34; F. Davis beat Alec Brown 44-27
**Semi-finals:** Donaldson beat Albert Brown 37-34; F. Davis beat Chenier 43-28
**Final:** Donaldson beat F. Davis 51-46

**1951**
**First qualifying round:** J. Barrie beat S. Lee 23-12
**Second qualifying round:** Barrie beat H. W. Laws 28-7
**First round:** F. Davis beat Barrie 42-29; H. Lindrum beat Albert Brown 43-28; W. Donaldson beat K. Kennerley 41-30; J. Pulman beat S. Smith 38-33
**Semi-finals:** Donaldson beat Lindrum 41-30; F. Davis beat Pulman 22-14 (*retd ill*)
**Final:** F. Davis beat Donaldson 58-39

**1952**
**First round:** Alec Brown beat R. Williams 39-22; Jack Rea beat J. Lees 38-32; Albert Brown beat J. Pulman 32-27 (*records incomplete*)
**Semi-finals:** W. Donaldson beat Albert Brown 31-30
**Final:** F. Davis beat Donaldson 38-35

**1953**
**First qualifying round:** W. Smith beat J. Lees 21-14; K. Kennerley beat R. Williams 25-12
**Second qualifying round:** Kennerley beat Smith 42-29
**First round:** Albert Brown beat Alec Brown 35-26; J. Pulman beat Jack Rea 36-25; W. Donaldson beat Kennerley 42-19; F. Davis beat J. Barrie 32-29

**Semi-finals:** Donaldson beat Brown (*nrs*); F. Davis beat Pulman 36-25
**Final:** F. Davis beat Donaldson 37-34

**1954**
**First round:** J. Pulman beat Jack Rea 31-30
**Semi-finals:** W. Donaldson beat Alec Brown 36-25; F. Davis beat Pulman 32-29
**Final:** F. Davis beat Donaldson 39-21

**1955**
**First round:** J. Pulman beat R. Williams 22-15; Jack Rea beat H. Stokes (*nrs*)
**Semi-finals:** F. Davis beat Rea 36-25; Pulman beat Alec Brown (*nrs*)
**Final:** F. Davis beat Pulman 37-34

**1956**
**Semi-finals:** J. Pulman beat Jack Rea 36-25; F. Davis beat R. Williams 35-26
**Final:** F. Davis beat Pulman 38-35

**1957**
**Semi-finals:** J. Pulman beat R. Williams 21-16; Jack Rea beat K. Kennerley 25-12
**Final:** Pulman beat Rea 39-34

Through lack of public support no Championship was organised between 1957 and 1964. After a truce with the BA and CC a new system was adopted whereby the champion defended his title against a series of single challengers. These matches resulted as follows:

**1964**
J. Pulman beat F. Davis 19-16; J. Pulman beat R. Williams 40-33

**1965**
J. Pulman beat F. Davis 37-36; J. Pulman beat R. Williams 25-22 (*matches*); J. Pulman beat F. Van Rensberg 39-12

**1966**
J. Pulman beat F. Davis 5-2 (*matches*)

**1968**
J. Pulman beat E. Charlton 39-34

**1969** (*Players No. 6*)
**First round:** J. Spencer beat J. Pulman 25-18; R. Williams beat B. Bennett 25-4; G. Owen beat Jack Rea 25-17; F. Davis beat R. Reardon 25-24
**Semi-finals:** Spencer beat Williams 37-12; G. Owen beat Davis 37-24
**Final:** Spencer beat Owen 37-24

**1970 (April)** (*Players No. 6*)
**First round:** David Taylor beat B. Bennett 11-8
**Quarter-finals:** J. Pulman beat David Taylor 31-20; G. Owen beat R. Williams 31-11; R. Reardon beat F. Davis 31-26; J. Spencer beat Jack Rea 31-15
**Semi-finals:** Pulman beat G. Owen 37-12; Reardon beat Spencer 37-33
**Final:** Reardon beat Pulman 37-33

**1970 (November)**
**Round robin:** J. Spencer beat P. Mans 20-17; beat N. Squire 27-10; beat J. Pulman 23-14
R. Reardon beat Mans 22-15; beat E. Charlton 21-16; beat Spencer 21-16
W. Simpson beat G. Owen 19-18; beat Pulman 21-16; beat Mans 19-18
Charlton beat Squire 27-10; beat Mans 26-11; beat Owen 23-14
Owen beat P. Morgan 26-11; beat Squire 26-11; Morgan beat Simpson 21-16
**Semi-finals:** Spencer beat Reardon 34-15; Simpson beat Charlton 27-22

**Final:** Spencer beat Simpson 37-29

**1972**

**First qualifying round:** A. Higgins beat R. Gross 15-6; M. Parkin beat G. Thompson 11-10; G. Miles beat B. Bennett 15-6; J. Dunning beat P. Houlihan 11-10
**Second qualifying round:** Higgins beat Parkin 11-3; Dunning beat Miles 11-5
**First round:** J. Pulman beat Dunning 19-7; Higgins beat Jack Rea 19-11
**Quarter-finals:** J. Spencer beat F. Davis 31-21; E. Charlton beat David Taylor 31-25; Higgins beat Pulman 31-23; R. Williams beat R. Reardon 25-23
**Semi-finals:** Higgins beat Williams 31-30; Spencer beat Charlton 37-32
**Final:** Higgins beat Spencer 37-32

**1973** (*Park Drive*)

**First round:** P. Houlihan beat Jack Rea 9-2; D. Greaves beat B. Bennett 9-8; G. Miles beat G. Thompson 9-5; P. Mans beat R. Gross 9-2; W. Simpson beat M. Parkin 9-3; C. Thorburn beat Dennis Taylor 9-8; David Taylor beat J. Dunning 9-4; J. Meadowcroft *wo* K. Kennerley *scr*
**Second round:** F. Davis beat Greaves 16-1; Miles beat J. Pulman 16-10; E. Charlton beat Mans 16-8; G. Owen beat Simpson 16-14; R. Reardon beat Meadowcroft 16-10; R. Williams beat Thorburn 16-15; J. Spencer beat David Taylor 16-5; A. Higgins beat Houlihan 16-3
**Quarter-finals:** Higgins beat F. Davis 16-14; Spencer beat Williams 16-7; Charlton beat Miles 16-6; Reardon beat G. Owen 16-6
**Semi-finals:** Charlton beat Higgins 23-9; Reardon beat Spencer 23-22
**Final:** Reardon beat Charlton 38-32

**1974** (*Park Drive*)

**Qualifying:** J. Dunning beat D. Greaves 8-2; W. Simpson beat Jack Rea 8-3; J. Meadowcroft beat P. Houlihan 8-5; C. Thorburn beat A. McDonald 8-3; J. Pulman beat J. Karnehm 8-0; David Taylor beat R. Gross 8-7; M. Owen beat Dennis Taylor 8-1
**First round:** B. Bennett beat Simpson 8-2; B. Werbeniuk beat G. Thompson 8-3; Meadowcroft beat K. Kennerley 8-5; M. Owen beat M. Parkin 8-5; P. Mans beat I. Anderson 8-1; Pulman beat S. Lee 8-0; Dunning beat David Taylor 8-6; P. Morgan beat Thorburn 8-4
**Second round:** Mans beat J. Spencer 15-13; Dunning beat E. Charlton 15-13; M. Owen beat G. Owen 15-8; A. Higgins beat Bennett 15-4; G. Miles beat Morgan 15-7; R. Williams beat Pulman 15-12; F. Davis beat Werbeniuk 15-5; R. Reardon beat Meadowcroft 15-3
**Quarter-finals:** Williams beat Mans 15-4; Reardon beat M. Owen 15-11; Miles beat Dunning 15-13; F. Davis beat Higgins 15-14
**Semi-finals:** Miles beat Williams 15-7; Reardon beat F. Davis 15-3
**Final:** Reardon beat Miles 22-12

**1975**

**Qualifying:** P. Tarrant beat B. Bennett 15-8; L. Condo beat M. Parkin 15-8; D. Greaves beat J. Charlton 15-14
**First round:** W. Simpson beat R. Mares 15-5; J. Pulman beat Tarrant 15-5; David Taylor beat R. King 15-8; I. Anderson beat Condo 15-8; Dennis Taylor beat P. Mans 15-12; G. Owen beat Greaves 15-3; B. Werbeniuk beat J. Meadowcroft 15-9; C. Thorburn beat P. Morgan 15-6
**Second round:** R. Reardon beat Simpson 15-11; J. Spencer beat Pulman 15-10; A. Higgins beat David Taylor 15-2; R. Williams beat Anderson 15-4; Dennis Taylor beat F. Davis 15-14; G. Owen beat J. Dunning 15-8; E. Charlton beat Werbeniuk 15-11; Thorburn beat G. Miles 15-2
**Quarter-finals:** Reardon beat Spencer 19-17; Higgins beat Williams 19-12; Dennis Taylor beat G. Owen 19-9; Charlton beat Thorburn 19-12
**Semi-finals:** Charlton beat Dennis Taylor 19-12; Reardon beat Higgins 19-14

**Final:** Reardon beat Charlton 31-30

### 1976

*Qualifying Group A:* **First round** J. Meadowcroft beat D. Wheelwright 8-1; R. Gross beat M. Parkin 8-5; L. Condo beat M. Owen 8-6. **Second round** Meadowcroft beat Gross 8-6; W. Thorne beat Condo 8-3. **Third round** Meadowcroft beat Thorne 8-5
*Qualifying Group B:* **First round** Jack Rea beat I. Anderson 8-5; D. Greaves beat J. Charlton 8-5. **Second round** Rea beat B. Bennett 8-5; David Taylor beat Greaves 8-5. **Third round** David Taylor beat Rea 8-7
**First round:** R. Reardon beat J. Dunning 15-7; Dennis Taylor beat G. Owen 15-9; P. Mans beat G. Miles 15-10; Meadowcroft beat R. Williams 15-7; E. Charlton beat J. Pulman 15-9; F. Davis beat B. Werbeniuk 15-12; A. Higgins beat C. Thorburn 15-14; J. Spencer beat David Taylor 15-5
**Quarter-finals:** Reardon beat Dennis Taylor 15-2; Mans beat Meadowcroft 15-8; Charlton beat F. Davis 15-13; Higgins beat Spencer 15-14
**Semi-finals:** Reardon beat Mans 20-10; Higgins beat Charlton 20-18
**Final:** Reardon beat Higgins 27-16

### 1977

**First qualifying round:** J. Virgo beat R. Andrewartha 11-1
**Second qualifying round:** P. Fagan beat J. Meadowcroft 11-9; Virgo beat J. Dunning 11-6; W. Thorne beat B. Bennett 11-4; J. Pulman *wo*; David Taylor beat D. Greaves 11-0; C. Thorburn beat C. Ross 11-0; Dennis Taylor beat J. Karnehm 11-0; D. Mountjoy beat Jack Rea 11-9
**First round:** R. Reardon beat Fagan 13-7; J. Spencer beat Virgo 13-9; G. Miles beat Thorne 13-4; Pulman beat F. Davis 13-12; E. Charlton beat David Taylor 13-5; Thorburn beat R. Williams 13-6; Dennis Taylor beat P. Mans 13-11; Mountjoy beat A. Higgins 13-12
**Quarter-finals:** Spencer beat Reardon 13-6; Pulman beat Miles 13-10; Thorburn beat Charlton 13-12; Dennis Taylor beat Mountjoy 13-11
**Semi-finals:** Spencer beat Pulman 18-16; Thorburn beat Dennis Taylor 18-16
**Final:** Spencer beat Thorburn 25-21

### 1978

**First qualifying round:** M. Parkin beat B. Bennett 9-4; R. Andrewartha beat J. Karnehm 9-0; J. Barrie beat D. Greaves 9-3; P. Houlihan beat C. Ross 9-1
**Second qualifying round:** D. Mountjoy beat Andrewartha 9-3; P. Fagan beat J. Dunning 9-5; W. Thorne beat R. Williams 9-3; B. Werbeniuk beat M. Parkin 9-2; P. Mans beat Barrie 9-6; David Taylor beat P. Morgan 9-7; Houlihan beat J. Meadowcroft 9-6; F. Davis beat J. Virgo 9-8
**First round:** Mans beat J. Spencer 13-8; G. Miles beat David Taylor 13-10; Fagan beat A. Higgins 13-12; F. Davis beat Dennis Taylor 13-9; E. Charlton beat Thorne 13-12; C. Thorburn beat Houlihan 13-8; Werbeniuk beat J. Pulman 13-4; R. Reardon beat Mountjoy 13-9
**Quarter-finals:** Mans beat Miles 13-7; F. Davis beat Fagan 13-10; Charlton beat Thorburn 13-12; Reardon beat Werbeniuk 13-6
**Semi-finals:** Mans beat F. Davis 18-16; Reardon beat Charlton 18-14
**Final:** Reardon beat Mans 25-18

### 1979

**First qualifying round:** D. Mountjoy beat D. Mienie 9-1; T. Griffiths beat B. Bennett 9-2; P. Houlihan beat J. Barrie 9-5; W. Thorne beat J. Charlton 9-3; J. Virgo beat M. Parkin 9-0; J. Dunning beat Jack Rea 9-5; R. Williams beat D. Greaves 9-2; J. Meadowcroft beat J. Van Rensberg 9-7; R. Andrewartha beat R. Edmonds 9-8; S. Davis beat I. Anderson 9-1; K. Stevens beat R. Amdor 9-1
**Second qualifying round:** Virgo beat Thorne 9-8; B. Werbeniuk beat Andrewartha 9-2; David Taylor beat Dunning 9-8; Mountjoy beat Houlihan 9-6; S. Davis beat P. Fagan

9-2; Griffiths beat Meadowcroft 9-6; Stevens beat J. Pulman 9-0; G. Miles beat Williams 9-5

**First round:** E. Charlton beat Mountjoy 13-6; Werbeniuk beat J. Spencer 13-11; Virgo beat C. Thorburn 13-10; F. Davis beat Stevens 13-8; Dennis Taylor beat S. Davis 13-11; A. Higgins beat David Taylor 13-5; Griffiths beat P. Mans 13-8; R. Reardon beat Miles 13-8

**Quarter-finals:** Charlton beat F. Davis 13-4; Dennis Taylor beat Reardon 13-8; Virgo beat Werbeniuk 13-9; Griffiths beat Higgins 13-12

**Semi-finals:** Griffiths beat Charlton 19-17; Dennis Taylor beat Virgo 19-12

**Final:** Griffiths beat Dennis Taylor 24-16

## 1980

**Qualifying groups**

1 Jack Rea beat B. Bennett 9-1; W. Thorne beat K. Robitaille 9-4; Thorne beat Rea 9-1

2 S. Davis beat C. Ross 9-3; P. Morgan beat P. Thornley 9-4; Davis beat Morgan 9-0

3 M. Hallett beat K. Kennerley 9-2; K. Stevens beat D. Greaves 9-3; Stevens beat Hallett 9-3

4 J. Johnson beat R. Andrewartha 9-5; P. Houlihan beat Johnson 9-6; T. Meo beat J. Van Rensberg 9-1; Meo beat Houlihan 9-1

5 R. Amdor beat B. Mikkelsen 9-7; R. Williams beat Amdor 9-4; J. Wych beat John Bear 9-5; Wych beat Williams 9-7

6 F. Jonik beat M. Wildman 9-7; C. Wilson beat Jonik 9-6

7 R. Edmonds beat M. Parkin 9-2; S. Hood beat J. Dunning 16-7; Edmonds beat Hood 9-6

8 E. Sinclair beat M. Morra 9-5; Sinclair beat D. Mienie 9-7; J. Meadowcroft beat Sinclair 9-1

**First round:** S. Davis beat P. Fagan 10-6; A. Higgins beat Meo 10-9; D. Mountjoy beat Wilson 10-6; Wych beat J. Pulman 10-5; J. Virgo beat Meadowcroft 10-2; Stevens beat G. Miles 10-3; David Taylor beat Edmonds 10-3; B. Werbeniuk beat Thorne 10-9

**Second round:** S. Davis beat T. Griffiths 13-10; Higgins beat P. Mans 13-6; Stevens beat J. Spencer 13-8; E. Charlton beat Virgo 13-12; C. Thorburn beat Mountjoy 13-10; Wych beat Dennis Taylor 13-10; R. Reardon beat Werbeniuk 13-6; David Taylor beat F. Davis 13-5

**Quarter-finals:** David Taylor beat Reardon 13-11; Thorburn beat Wych 13-6; Stevens beat Charlton 13-7; Higgins beat S. Davis 13-9

**Semi-finals:** Thorburn beat David Taylor 16-7; Higgins beat Stevens 16-13

**Final:** Thorburn beat Higgins 18-16

## 1981

**Qualifying groups**

1 W. Thorne beat M. Morra 9-5; D. Greaves beat M. Parkin 9-5; Thorne beat Greaves 9-3

2 J. White beat B. Mikkelsen 9-4; White beat J. Meadowcroft 9-8

3 R. Edmonds beat M. Wildman 9-3; R. Williams beat S. Hood 9-4; Edmonds beat Williams 9-7

4 T. Meo beat J. Johnson 9-8; M. Hallett beat F. Jonik 9-1; Meo beat Hallett 9-4

5 J. Dunning beat B. Bennett 9-6; Dunning beat P. Fagan 9-7

6 D. Martin beat I. Anderson 9-3; Martin beat J. Pulman 9-2

7 C. Wilson beat R. Andrewartha 9-4; E. Sinclair beat P. Morgan 9-8; Wilson beat Sinclair 9-4

8 A. Knowles beat C. Ross 7-0 (*retd*); Knowles beat J. Wych 9-3

**First round:** G. Miles beat Knowles 10-8; David Taylor beat Wilson 10-6; D. Mountjoy beat Thorne 10-6; K. Stevens beat Dunning 10-4; Meo beat J. Virgo 10-6; S. Davis beat White 10-8; B. Werbeniuk beat Martin 10-4; J. Spencer beat Edmonds 10-9

**Second round:** C. Thorburn beat Miles 13-2; David Taylor beat F. Davis 13-3; T. Griffiths beat Meo 13-6; S. Davis beat Alex Higgins 13-8; Mountjoy beat E. Charlton

13-7; Dennis Taylor beat Stevens 13-11; Werbeniuk beat P. Mans 13-5; R. Reardon beat Spencer 13-11

**Quarter-finals:** Thorburn beat David Taylor 13-6; S. Davis beat Griffiths 13-9; Mountjoy beat Dennis Taylor 13-8; Reardon beat Werbeniuk 13-10

**Semi-finals:** S. Davis beat Thorburn 16-10; Mountjoy beat Reardon 16-10

**Final:** S. Davis beat Mountjoy 18-12

### 1982

**Qualifying groups**

1 John Bear beat F. Jonik 9-4; Bear beat J. Wych 9-4
2 D. Hughes beat C. Everton 9-4; T. Meo beat Hughes 9-4
3 D. Reynolds beat D. Sheehan 9-5; Reynolds beat R. Edmonds 9-6
4 E. Hughes *wo* D. Mienie *scr*; A. Knowles beat Hughes 9-7
5 M. Wildman beat G. Foulds 9-8; J. White beat Wildman 9-4
6 C. Roscoe beat B. Mikkelsen 9-6; W. Thorne beat Roscoe 9-1
7 P. Medati beat J. Phillips 9-3; C. Wilson beat Medati 9-5
8 P. Houlihan beat I. Anderson 9-5; D. Martin beat Houlihan 9-3
9 M. Macleod beat E. McLaughlin 9-8; J. Dunning beat Macleod 9-4
10 M. Watterson beat B. Demarco 9-6; J. Meadowcroft beat Watterson 9-7
11 D. French beat B. Bennett 9-3; P. Fagan beat French 9-6
12 I. Black beat M. Parkin 9-6; R. Williams beat Black 9-2
13 J. Johnson beat V. Harris 9-4; M. Hallett beat Johnson 9-8
14 J. Donnelly beat M. Gibson 9-8; E. Sinclair beat B. Kelly 9-8; Donnelly beat Sinclair 9-8
15 P. Morgan beat D. Greaves 9-2; S. Francisco beat C. Ross 9-0; Francisco beat Morgan 9-1
16 M. Morra beat T. Murphy 9-5; J. Fitzmaurice *wo* J. Pulman *scr*; Fitzmaurice beat Morra 9-7

**First round:** Knowles beat S. Davis 10-1; G. Miles beat Martin 10-5; B. Werbeniuk beat Bear 10-7; E. Charlton beat Wilson 10-5; S. Francisco beat Dennis Taylor 10-7; Reynolds beat F. Davis 10-7; J. Virgo beat Hallett 10-4; R. Reardon beat Donnelly 10-5; A. Higgins beat Meadowcroft 10-5; D. Mountjoy beat Williams 10-3; Fagan beat David Taylor 10-9; K. Stevens beat Fitzmaurice 10-4; P. Mans beat Meo 10-8; White beat C. Thorburn 10-4

**Second round:** Knowles beat Miles 13-7; Charlton beat Werbeniuk 13-5; S. Francisco beat Reynolds 13-8; Reardon beat Virgo 13-8; Thorne beat Spencer 13-5; Higgins beat Mountjoy 13-12; Stevens beat Fagan 13-7; White beat Mans 13-6

**Quarter-finals:** Charlton beat Knowles 13-11; Reardon beat S. Francisco 13-8; Higgins beat Thorne 13-10; White beat Stevens 13-9

**Semi-finals:** Reardon beat Charlton 16-11; Higgins beat White 16-15

**Final:** Higgins beat Reardon 18-15

### 1983

**Qualifying groups**

1 B. Kelly beat B. Demarco 10-4; S. Francisco beat Kelly 10-5
2 P. Morgan beat P. Burke 10-9; G. Miles beat Morgan 10-6
3 T. Murphy beat P. Houlihan 10-9; J. Virgo beat Murphy 10-8
4 R. Williams beat M. Darrington 10-0; Williams beat F. Davis 10-1
5 M. Wildman beat B. Harris 10-7; Wildman *wo* J. Wych *scr*
6 R. Edmonds beat F. Jonik 10-4; D. Reynolds beat Edmonds 10-6
7 M. Fisher beat P. Fagan 10-8; E. McLaughlin beat D. Greaves 10-7; Fisher beat McLaughlin 10-9
8 T. Meo beat V. Harris 10-0; G. Foulds beat M. Gibson 10-6; Meo beat Foulds 10-4
9 I. Black beat M. Morra 10-9; P. Medati beat John Bear 10-7; Black beat Medati 10-4
10 C. Wilson beat C. Everton 10-1; J. Johnson beat P. Watchorn 10-0; Wilson beat

Johnson 10-8
11 M. Macleod beat M. Owen 10-5; D. Martin beat M. Parkin 10-1; Martin beat Macleod 10-7
12 J. Meadowcroft beat B. Bennett 10-3; G. Cripsey beat D. Hughes 10-2; Meadowcroft beat Cripsey 10-6
13 J. Donnelly beat D. Sheehan 10-6; J. Campbell beat M. Watterson 10-6; Campbell beat Donnelly 10-2
14 L. Dodd *wo* J. Dunning *scr*; I. Williamson beat D. French 10-8; Dodd beat Williamson 10-9
15 M. Hallett beat R. Andrewartha 10-7; W. King beat I. Anderson 10-6; Hallett beat King 10-6
16 E. Hughes beat J. Fitzmaurice 10-7; E. Sinclair beat C. Roscoe 10-2; Hughes beat Sinclair 10-8

**First round:** A. Higgins beat Reynolds 10-4; W. Thorne beat Virgo 10-3; B. Werbeniuk beat Martin 10-4; David Taylor beat Meadowcroft 10-2; E. Charlton beat Dodd 10-7; J. Spencer beat Hallett 10-7; Dennis Taylor beat S. Francisco 10-9; S. Davis beat Williams 10-4; C. Thorburn beat Campbell 10-5; T. Griffiths beat Wildman 10-8; P. Mans beat Black 10-3; K. Stevens beat Fisher 10-2; D. Mountjoy beat Wilson 10-2; Meo beat J. White 10-8; A. Knowles beat Miles 10-3; R. Reardon beat E. Hughes 10-7
**Second round:** Higgins beat Thorne 13-8; Werbeniuk beat David Taylor 13-10; Charlton beat Spencer 13-11; S. Davis beat Dennis Taylor 13-11; Thorburn beat Griffiths 13-12; Meo beat Mountjoy 13-11; Knowles beat Reardon 13-12; Stevens beat Mans 13-3
**Quarter-finals:** Higgins beat Werbeniuk 13-11; S. Davis beat Charlton 13-5; Thorburn beat Stevens 13-12; Knowles beat Meo 13-9
**Semi-finals:** Thorburn beat Knowles 16-15; S. Davis beat Higgins 16-5
**Final:** S. Davis beat Thorburn 18-6

**1984**

**Qualifying groups**
1 J. Parrott beat D. Hughes 10-3; Parrott beat C. Everton 10-2; Parrott beat P. Mans 10-0
2 B. Mikkelsen beat P. Medati 10-8; Mikkelsen beat F. Jonik 10-9; W. Thorne beat Mikkelsen 10-3
3 M. Morra beat G. Foulds 10-2; T. Murphy beat J. Fitzmaurice 10-8; Morra beat Murphy 10-5; Morra beat D. Reynolds 10-7
4 W. Sanderson beat P. Morgan 10-8; P. Mifsud beat E. Hughes 10-5; Mifsud beat Sanderson 10-5; Mifsud beat C. Wilson 10-8
5 J. Van Rensberg beat V. Harris 10-7; R. Edmonds beat D. Greaves 10-0; Van Rensberg beat Edmonds 10-9; S. Francisco beat Van Rensberg 10-3
6 I. Williamson beat P. Houlihan 10-5; M. Hines beat I. Black 10-5; Williamson beat Hines 10-6; G. Miles beat Williamson 10-6
7 M. Gibson beat G. Rigitano 10-7; M. Fisher beat P. Thornley 10-8; Gibson beat Fisher 10-7; J. Johnson beat Gibson 10-3
8 E. McLaughlin beat J. Hargreaves 10-5; R. Andrewartha *wo* John Bear *scr*; Andrewartha beat McLaughlin 10-8; Andrewartha beat M. Wildman 10-9
9 J. Wych beat G. Ganim Jr 10-1; G. Scott beat L. Heywood 10-7; Wych beat Scott 10-6; Wych beat P. Fagan 10-3
10 P. Browne beat S. Duggan 10-9; C. Roscoe beat B. Demarco 10-7; Browne beat Roscoe 10-4; E. Sinclair beat Browne 10-1
11 M. Gauvreau beat J. Campbell 10-7; G. Cripsey beat M. Parkin 10-4; Gauvreau beat Cripsey 10-1; Gauvreau beat M. Macleod 10-6
12 I. Anderson beat G. Watson 10-4; J. Donnelly beat P. Watchorn 10-7; Donnelly beat Anderson 10-6; F. Davis beat Donnelly 10-5
13 W. King beat T. Jones 10-9; M. Watterson beat B. Bennett 10-5; King beat Watterson 10-8; King beat Dave Martin 10-8
14 J. Caggianello beat M. Darrington 10-7; W. Oliver beat J. Dunning 10-3; Oliver beat

Caggianello 10-7; R. Williams beat Oliver 10-8
15 N. Foulds beat D. French 10-5; L. Dodd beat J. Giannaros 10-1; Foulds beat Dodd 10-4; Foulds beat J. Meadowcroft 10-2
16 B. Harris beat D. Sheehan 10-3; P. Burke beat B. Kelly 10-7; Burke beat Harris 10-4; M. Hallett beat Burke 10-5

**First round:** S. Davis beat King 10-3; J. Spencer beat Miles 10-3; T. Griffiths beat Mifsud 10-2; B. Werbeniuk beat F. Davis 10-4; N. Foulds beat A. Higgins 10-9; D. Mountjoy beat Hallett 10-4; Dennis Taylor beat Johnson 10-1; Parrott beat A. Knowles 10-7; C. Thorburn beat Morra 10-3; Thorne beat J. Virgo 10-9; J. White beat Williams 10-6; E. Charlton beat Andrewartha 10-4; K. Stevens beat Sinclair 10-1; David Taylor beat Gauvreau 10-5; S. Francisco beat T. Meo 10-5; R. Reardon beat Wych 10-7
**Second round:** S. Davis beat Spencer 13-5; Griffiths beat Werbeniuk 13-5; Mountjoy beat N. Foulds 13-6; Dennis Taylor beat Parrott 13-11; Thorburn beat Thorne 13-11; White beat Charlton 13-7; Stevens beat David Taylor 13-10; Reardon beat S. Francisco 13-8
**Quarter-finals:** S. Davis beat Griffiths 13-10; Dennis Taylor beat Mountjoy 13-8; White beat Thorburn 13-8; Stevens beat Reardon 13-2
**Semi-finals:** S. Davis beat Dennis Taylor 16-9; White beat Stevens 16-14
**Final:** S. Davis beat White 18-16

## 1985

**Qualifying groups**

1 G. Rigitano beat D. Sheehan 10-9; Rigitano beat B. Harris 10-4; Rigitano beat B. Kelly 10-6; Rigitano beat M. Fisher 10-2; N. Foulds beat Rigitano 10-8
2 D. O'Kane *wo* J. McLaughlin *scr*; O'Kane beat V. Harris 10-5; O'Kane beat F. Jonik 10-5; O'Kane beat L. Dodd 10-7; O'Kane beat D. Martin 10-8
3 S. Longworth beat J. Giannaros 10-1; Longworth beat G. Cripsey 10-8; J. Van Rensberg beat Longworth 10-7; M. Gauvreau beat Van Rensberg 10-9; D. Reynolds beat Gauvreau 10-1
4 R. Chaperon beat R. Bales 10-7; Chaperon beat L. Heywood 10-1; Chaperon beat P. Morgan 10-3; F. Davis beat Chaperon 10-9; R. Williams beat F. Davis 10-6
5 D. Hughes beat D. French 10-5; S. Newbury beat Hughes 10-9; Newbury beat P. Burke 10-3; Newbury beat G. Scott 10-2; E. Hughes beat Newbury 10-6
6 M. Hines beat T. Chappel 10-8; Hines beat P. Watchorn 10-4; M. Gibson beat Hines 10-7; P. Fagan beat Gibson 10-8; Fagan beat C. Wilson 10-9
7 D. Fowler beat J. Hargreaves 10-0; Fowler *wo* G. Watson *scr*; Fowler *wo* J. Caggianello *scr*; Fowler beat J. Donnelly 10-0; J. Parrott beat Fowler 10-2
8 R. Foldvari *wo* P. Thornley *scr*; Foldvari beat B. Oliver 10-3; R. Edmonds beat Foldvari 10-3; Edmonds beat M. Wildman 10-7
9 D. Chalmers beat D. Greaves 10-3; Chalmers beat E. McLaughlin 10-9; Chalmers beat I. Black 10-4; M. Hallett beat Chalmers 10-1
10 G. Foulds beat M. Parkin 10-6; Foulds beat C. Everton 10-2; Foulds beat C. Roscoe 10-7; J. Johnson beat Foulds 10-6
11 P. Medati beat B. Bennett 10-4; Medati beat I. Williamson 10-8; Medati beat W. King 10-9; S. Francisco beat Medati 10-7
12 I. Anderson beat A. Kearney 10-8; P. Browne beat Anderson 10-5; M. Morra beat Browne 10-6; J. Campbell beat Morra 10-9
13 W. Jones beat John Rea 10-3; Jones beat J. Dunning 10-6; Jones beat M. Watterson 10-5; Jones beat G. Miles 10-8
14 M. Bradley beat D. Mienie 10-4; Bradley beat B. Mikkelsen 10-9; J. Wych beat Bradley 10-7; J. Virgo beat Wych 10-4
15 P. Francisco beat B. Demarco 10-4; Francisco beat T Murphy 10-4; Francisco beat J. Meadowcroft 10-5; M. Macleod beat Francisco 10-7
16 T. Jones beat M. Darrington 10-2; Jones beat S. Duggan 10-8; Jones beat J. Fitzmaurice 10-4; Jones beat E. Sinclair 10-2

**First round:** S. Davis beat N. Foulds 10-8; David Taylor beat O'Kane 10-4; A. Higgins beat Reynolds 10-4; T. Griffiths beat Williams 10-3; R. Reardon beat E. Hughes 10-9;

Fagan beat W. Thorne 10-6; Parrott beat J. Spencer 10-3; K. Stevens beat Edmonds 10-8; C. Thorburn beat Hallett 10-8; B. Werbeniuk beat Johnson 10-8; Dennis Taylor beat S. Francisco 10-2; E. Charlton beat Campbell 10-3; J. White beat W. Jones 10-4; T. Meo beat Virgo 10-6; D. Mountjoy beat Macleod 10-5; A. Knowles beat T. Jones 10-8
**Second round:** S. Davis beat David Taylor 13-4; Griffiths beat Higgins 13-7; Reardon beat Fagan 13-9; Parrott beat Stevens 13-6; Thorburn beat Werbeniuk 13-3; Dennis Taylor beat Charlton 13-6; White beat Meo 13-11; Knowles beat Mountjoy 13-6
**Quarter-finals:** S. Davis beat Griffiths 13-6; Reardon beat Parrott 13-12; Dennis Taylor beat Thorburn 13-5; Knowles beat White 13-10
**Semi-finals:** S. Davis beat Reardon 16-5; Dennis Taylor beat Knowles 16-5
**Final:** Dennis Taylor beat S. Davis 18-17

**1986**

**First qualifying round:** D. Gilbert beat R. Bales 10-7; O. Agrawal beat D. Hughes 10-6; A. Kearney beat G. Wilkinson 10-5; B. Oliver beat J. O'Boye 10-8; D. Sheehan beat P. Houlihan 10-7; M. Gibson beat G. Jenkins 10-4; S. Simngam beat B. Bennett 10-0; Jim Bear beat P. Burke 10-8; T. Drago beat G. Cripsey 10-4; M. Smith beat D. Greaves 10-4; B. West *wo* J. Giannaros *scr*; P. Thornley beat D. Mienie 10-3; R. Grace beat M. Parkin 10-8; S. Hendry beat B. Demarco 10-7; P. Watchorn *wo* J. Rempe *scr*; B. Mikkelsen beat J. Hargreaves 10-7; M. Darrington *wo* W. Sanderson *scr*
**Second qualifying round:** J. Wych beat T. Chappel 10-6; S. Duggan beat M. Fisher 10-3; T. Jones beat V. Harris 10-7; Gilbert beat M. Bradley 10-7; S. Newbury beat Agrawal 10-5; I. Black beat B. Harris 10-8; G. Scott beat Kearney 10-8; D. Fowler beat Oliver 10-8; C. Roscoe beat G. Foulds 10-3; W. King beat Sheehan 10-4; Gibson beat M. Morra 10-9; P. Medati beat Simngam 10-9; R. Chaperon beat F. Jonik 10-8; M. Gauvreau beat Jim Bear 10-5; F. Davis beat D. Chalmers 10-6; P. Francisco beat Drago 10-4; J. Donnelly beat Smith 10-6; West beat J. Dunning 10-3; T. Murphy beat J. McLaughlin 10-7; Thornley beat P. Fagan 10-7; W. Jones beat Grace 10-3; Hendry beat P. Browne 10-9; E. Sinclair beat P. Morgan 10-8; J. Van Rensberg beat I. Williamson 10-9; John Rea beat E. McLaughlin 10-6; S. Longworth beat Watchorn 10-7; G. Miles beat C. Everton 10-3; R. Foldvari beat G. Rigitano 10-6; M. Watterson beat Mikkelsen 10-2; L. Dodd beat J. Fitzmaurice 10-6; Darrington beat J. Meadowcroft 10-6; R. Edmonds beat B. Kelly 10-0
**Third qualifying round:** Wych beat Duggan 10-5; Gilbert beat T. Jones 10-7; Newbury beat Black 10-2; Fowler beat Scott 10-7; King beat Roscoe 10-5; Medati beat Gibson 10-6; Gauvreau beat Chaperon 10-8; P. Francisco beat F. Davis 10-1; West beat Donnelly 10-5; Murphy beat Thornley 10-3; Hendry beat W. Jones 10-8; Van Rensberg beat Sinclair 10-2; Longworth beat John Rea 10-4; Foldvari beat Miles 10-7; Dodd beat Watterson 10-1; Edmonds beat Darrington 10-5
**Fourth qualifying round:** M. Hallett beat Wych 10-7; D. Martin beat Gilbert 10-5; J. Spencer beat Newbury 10-7; Fowler beat M. Macleod 10-6; D. Reynolds beat King 10-7; C. Wilson beat Medati 10-6; R. Williams beat Gauvreau 10-3; N. Foulds beat P. Francisco 10-9; B. Werbeniuk beat West 10-8; E. Hughes beat Murphy 10-7; Hendry beat O'Kane 10-9; J. Campbell beat Van Rensberg 10-6; J. Virgo beat Longworth 10-8; J. Parrott beat Foldvari 10-6; P. Mans beat Dodd 10-7; Edmonds beat M. Wildman 10-9
**First round:** Hallett beat Dennis Taylor 10-6; J. Johnson beat Martin 10-3; A. Higgins beat J. Spencer 10-7; T. Griffiths beat Fowler 10-2; K. Stevens beat Reynolds 10-6; E. Charlton beat Wilson 10-6; S. Francisco beat Williams 10-4; A. Knowles beat N. Foulds 10-9; C. Thorburn beat Werbeniuk 10-5; E. Hughes beat David Taylor 10-7; W. Thorne beat Hendry 10-8; Campbell beat R. Reardon 10-8; J. White beat Virgo 10-7; Parrott beat T. Meo 10-4; D. Mountjoy beat Mans 10-3; S. Davis beat Edmonds 10-4
**Second round:** Johnson beat Hallett 13-6; Griffiths beat Higgins 13-12; Stevens beat Charlton 13-12; Knowles beat S. Francisco 13-10; Thorburn beat E. Hughes 13-6; Thorne beat Campbell 13-9; White beat Parrott 13-8; S. Davis beat Mountjoy 13-5

**Quarter-finals:** Johnson beat Griffiths 13-12; Knowles beat Stevens 13-9; Thorburn beat Thorne 13-6; S. Davis beat White 13-5
**Final:** Johnson beat S. Davis 18-12

## 1987

**First qualifying round:** J. Bear beat Jack Rea 10-5; A. Kearney *wo* F. Jonik *scr*; S. James beat M. Watterson 10-2; G. Jenkins beat R. Grace 10-9; D. Greaves beat P. Thornley 10-6; M. Darrington beat B. Demarco 10-6; J. Rempe beat M. Smith 10-9; G. Rigitano beat P. Morgan 4-0; C. Roscoe beat T. Whitthread 10-2; M. Morra beat P. Gibson 10-6; D. Chalmers *wo* E. McLaughlin *scr*; M. Bennett beat J. Hargreaves 10-6; B. Kelly beat B. Bennett 10-0; J. Meadowcroft beat D. Mienie 10-3; G. Foulds beat P. Watchorn 10-6; D. Hughes beat M. Parkin 10-5; B. Oliver beat P. Burke 10-5; J. Dunning beat J. Caggianello 10-7; J. Wright beat P. Houlihan 10-4; B. Rowswell *wo* S. Simngam *scr*; J. Fitzmaurice beat C. Everton 10-2; D. Roe *wo* O. Agrawal *scr*; K. Owers beat M. Fisher 10-5
**Second qualifying round:** M. Gauvreau beat Bear 10-3; P. Medati beat Kearney 10-8; E. Sinclair beat T. Drago 10-9; R. Edmonds beat James 10-1; T. Murphy beat Jenkins 10-4; G. Miles beat Greaves 10-7; S. Hendry beat Darrington 10-7; Rempe beat John Rea 10-9; Rigitano beat V. Harris 10-6; S. Newbury beat L. Dodd 10-7; S. Duggan beat Roscoe 10-7; T. Chappel beat Morra 10-8; T. Jones beat Chalmers 10-1; J. Van Rensberg beat J. McLaughlin 10-6; M. Bennett beat B. Mikkelsen 10-4; W. Jones beat J. Donnelly 10-3; I. Black beat I. Williamson 10-8; D. O'Kane beat D. Gilbert 10-2; M. Gibson beat Kelly 10-9; G. Cripsey beat Meadowcroft 10-9; D. Fowler beat G. Foulds 10-6; B. Harris beat D. Hughes 10-2; Oliver beat P. Fagan 10-2; G. Scott beat Dunning 10-7; M. Wildman beat Foldvari 10-5; Wright beat Browne 10-6; M. Bradley beat Rowswell 10-6; J. O'Boye beat N. Gilbert 10-5; J. Spencer beat R. Bales 10-2; R. Chaperon beat Fitzmaurice 10-2; W. King beat Roe 10-4; Owers beat F. Davis 10-5
**Third qualifying round:** Medati beat Gauvreau 10-3; Edmonds beat Sinclair 10-6; Murphy beat Miles 10-7; Hendry beat Rempe 10-4; Newbury beat Rigitano 10-4; Chappel beat Duggan 10-3; T. Jones beat Van Rensberg 10-0; M. Bennett beat W. Jones 10-3; O'Kane beat Black 10-2; Cripsey beat M. Gibson 10-4; Fowler beat B. Harris 10-5; Oliver beat Scott 10-5; Wright beat Wildman 10-0; Bradley beat O'Boye 10-7; Spencer beat Chaperon 10-4; King beat Owers 10-4
**Fourth qualifying round:** E. Hughes beat Medati 10-2; M. Macleod beat Edmonds 10-7; S. Longworth beat Murphy 10-2; Hendry beat D. Martin 10-7; M. Hallett beat Newbury 10-4; J. Campbell beat Chappel 10-6; J. Virgo beat T. Jones 10-9; M. Bennett beat W. Jones 10-3; O'Kane beat P. Francisco 10-5; David Taylor beat Cripsey 10-7; J. Parrott beat Fowler 10-3; D. Reynolds beat Oliver 10-7; Wright beat C. Wilson 10-4; J. Wych beat Bradley 10-7; B. West beat Spencer 10-5; King beat E. Charlton 10-4
**First round:** J. Johnson beat E. Hughes 10-9; Macleod beat R. Williams 10-5; Longworth beat K. Stevens 10-4; Hendry beat W. Thorne 10-7; Hallett beat A. Knowles 10-6; S. Francisco beat Campbell 10-3; N. Foulds beat Virgo 10-4; Dennis Taylor beat M. Bennett 10-4; O'Kane beat Thorburn 10-5; D. Mountjoy beat David Taylor 10-5; Parrott beat T. Meo 10-8; J. White beat Reynolds 10-8; A. Higgins beat Wright 10-6; T. Griffiths beat Wych 10-4; R. Reardon beat West 10-5; S. Davis beat King 10-7
**Second round:** Johnson beat Macleod 13-7; Hendry beat Longworth 10-7; Hallett beat S. Francisco 13-9; N. Foulds beat Dennis Taylor 13-10; O'Kane beat Mountjoy 13-5; White beat Parrott 13-11; Griffiths beat Higgins 13-10; S. Davis beat Reardon 13-4
**Quarter-finals:** Johnson beat Hendry 13-12; N. Foulds beat Hallett 13-9; White beat O'Kane 13-6; S. Davis beat Griffiths 13-5
**Semi-finals:** Johnson beat N. Foulds 16-9; S. Davis beat White 16-11
**Final:** S. Davis beat Johnson 18-14

## 1988

**Preliminary round:** A. Harris beat S. Mizerak 10-2
**First qualifying round:** P. Gibson beat D. Sheehan 10-9; A. Harris beat M. Fisher 10-4;

C. Roscoe beat E. McLaughlin 10-1; G. Miles beat D. Hughes 10-3; N. Gilbert beat John Rea 10-5; I. Williamson *wo* J. Caggianello *scr*; B. Rowswell beat P. Thornley 10-7; B. Oliver beat D. Chalmers 10-9; A. Robidoux *wo* F. Jonik *scr*; B. Kelly beat A. Kearney 10-4; S. James *wo* T. Whitthread *scr*; P. Watchorn beat M. Gibson 10-7; M. Clark beat M. Darrington 10-5; G. Rigitano beat J. Dunning 10-7; J. Smith beat J. Donnelly 10-4; Glen Wilkinson beat C. Everton 10-2; M. Morra beat S. Meakin 10-5; M. Smith beat V. Harris 10-6; E. Lawlor *wo* J. Van Rensberg *scr*; B. Mikkelsen beat Jack Rea 10-3; R. Foldvari beat J. Rempe 10-4; J. Meadowcroft beat B. Bennett 10-5; D. Gilbert beat D. Heaton 10-2; P. Medati beat Gary Wilkinson 10-9; I. Black *wo* J. Hargreaves *scr*; P. Fagan beat D. Greaves 10-3; E. Sinclair beat P. Burke 10-2; D. Roe beat B. Demarco 10-2; J. Chambers beat M. Watterson 10-3; J. Bear beat D. Mienie 10-4; J. Fitzmaurice beat M. Parkin 10-6

**Second qualifying round:** P. Gibson beat M. Gauvreau 10-9; S. Duggan beat A. Harris 10-4; T. Murphy beat Roscoe 10-8; R. Chaperon beat Marshall 10-3; Miles beat R. Bales 10-7; T. Chappel beat N. Gilbert 10-8; M. Bradley beat Williamson 10-9; B. Werbeniuk beat Rowswell 10-6; Oliver beat R. Reardon 10-6; Robidoux *wo* R. Grace *scr*; P. Browne beat Kelly 10-8; James beat J. O'Boye 10-7; W. King beat Watchorn 10-4; Clark beat G. Scott 10-4; M. Bennett beat Rigitano 10-4; J. Wych beat J. Smith 10-3; W. Jones beat Glen Wilkinson 10-4; Morra beat R. Edmonds 10-8; M. Smith beat J. McLaughlin 10-3; S. Newbury beat E. Lawlor 10-3; M. Wildman beat Mikkelsen 10-5; Foldvari beat T. Jones 10-9; G. Cripsey beat Meadowcroft 10-3; P. Houlihan *wo* D. Gilbert *scr*; L. Dodd beat Medati 10-6; D. Fowler beat Black 10-1; B. Harris beat Fagan 10-1; Sinclair beat D. O'Kane 10-9; K. Owers beat Roe 10-7; J. Wright beat Chambers 10-2; Bear beat G. Foulds 10-2; F. Davis beat Fitzmaurice 10-8

**Third qualifying round:** Duggan beat P. Gibson 10-9; Chaperon beat Murphy 10-5; Chappel beat Miles 10-7; Werbeniuk beat Bradley 10-8; Oliver beat Robidoux 10-2; James beat Browne 10-1; King beat Clark 10-9; M. Bennett beat Wych 10-5; W. Jones beat Morra 10-8; Newbury beat M. Smith 10-9; Foldvari beat Wildman 10-1; Cripsey beat Houlihan 10-4; Fowler beat Dodd 10-8; B. Harris beat Sinclair 10-0; Wright beat Owers 10-8; F. Davis beat Bear 10-4

**Fourth qualifying round:** J. Virgo beat Duggan 10-5; Chaperon beat David Taylor 10-6; T. Drago beat Chappel 10-7; Werbeniuk beat T. Meo 10-4; C. Wilson beat Oliver 10-6; James beat E. Hughes 10-6; King beat J. Spencer 10-7; K. Stevens beat M. Bennett 10-7; W. Jones beat D. Martin 10-5; B. West beat Newbury 10-8; P. Francisco beat Foldvari 10-5; S. Longworth beat Cripsey 10-2; Fowler beat M. Macleod 10-3; E. Charlton beat B. Harris 10-4; S. Hendry beat Wright 10-4; J. Campbell beat F. Davis 10-3

**First round:** S. Davis beat Virgo 10-8; M. Hallett beat Chaperon 10-2; Drago beat A. Higgins 10-2; Dennis Taylor beat Werbeniuk 10-8; J. Johnson beat Wilson 10-7; James beat R. Williams 10-6; J. Parrott beat King 10-4; C. Thorburn beat Stevens 10-6; N. Foulds beat W. Jones 10-7; D. Mountjoy beat West 10-6; W. Thorne beat P. Francisco 10-6; T. Griffiths beat Longworth 10-1; T. Knowles beat Fowler 10-8; Charlton beat S. Francisco 10-7; Hendry beat D. Reynolds 10-6; J. White beat Campbell 10-3

**Second round:** S. Davis beat Hallett 13-1; Drago beat Dennis Taylor 13-5; James beat Johnson 13-9; Thorburn beat Parrott 13-10; N. Foulds beat Mountjoy 13-1; Griffiths beat Thorne 13-9; Knowles beat Charlton 13-7; White beat Hendry 13-12

**Quarter-finals:** S. Davis beat Drago 13-4; Thorburn beat James 13-11; Griffiths beat Foulds 13-9; White beat Knowles 13-6

**Semi-finals:** S. Davis beat Thorburn 16-8; Griffiths beat White 16-11

**Final:** S. Davis beat Griffiths 18-11

## 1989

**First qualifying round:** N. Terry beat M. Parkin 10-0; C. Edwards beat J. Giannaros 10-4; M. Rowing beat S. Mizerak 10-1; B. Bennett beat C. Everton 10-4; P. Thornley beat B. Demarco 10-3; T. Wilson beat M. Francisco 10-5; D. Mienie beat V. Potasnik 10-6; M. Johnston-Allen beat E. McLaughlin 10-3; I. Graham beat D. Greaves 10-0;

S. Campbell *wo* G. Watson *scr*; J. Grech beat D. Heaton 10-6; M. Price *wo* P. Morgan *scr*; R. Marshall beat M. Hines 10-1; D. Morgan beat S. Frangie 10-5

**Second qualifying round:** Terry beat P. Medati 10-8; Edwards beat Jim Bear 10-7; Rowing beat J. Dunning 10-9; F. Davis beat B. Bennett 10-4; Thornley beat M. Bradley 10-7; P. Fagan beat G. Foulds 10-6; B. Oliver beat J. Rempe 10-5; P. Watchorn beat R. Grace 10-6; M. Morra beat B. Mikkelsen 10-4; M. Gibson beat M. Darrington 10-0; T. Whitthread beat J. Donnelly 10-7; T. Wilson beat G. Scott 10-4; J. Meadowcroft beat Mieni 10-7; S. Meakin beat A. Kearney 10-3; J. Fitzmaurice beat C. Roscoe 10-9; V. Harris beat M. Watterson 10-5; A. Harris beat J. Van Rensberg 10-7; Johnston-Allen beat G. Rigitano 10-3; Graham *wo* B. Harris *scr*; M. Smith beat S. Campbell 10-9; J. Smith beat R. Foldvari 10-4; J. Chambers beat I. Anderson 10-7; Grech beat I. Williamson 10-7; Glen Wilkinson beat B. Kelly 10-2; John Rea beat D. Hughes 10-3; I. Black beat D. Sheehan 10-8; Price beat E. Sinclair 10-9; B. Rowswell beat P. Burke 10-0; P. Gibson beat Marshall 10-3; D. Morgan beat E. Lawlor 10-2; F. Ellis beat M. Wildman 10-7; A. Robidoux beat G. Miles 10-8

**Third qualifying round:** N. Gilbert beat Terry 10-5; Edwards beat T. Chappel 10-7; Rowing beat W. King 10-7; S. Duggan beat F. Davis 10-3; Thornley *wo* B. Werbeniuk *scr*; D. Gilbert beat Fagan 10-4; T. Murphy beat Oliver 10-8; D. Roe beat Watchorn 10-5; M. Clark beat Morra 10-6; D. Martin beat M. Gibson 10-7; D. Fowler beat Whitthread 10-6; J. O'Boye beat T. Wilson 10-8; M. Macleod beat Meadowcroft 10-9; P. Browne beat Meakin 10-9; R. Reardon beat Fitzmaurice 10-5; Gary Wilkinson beat V. Harris 10-6; W. Jones beat A. Harris 10-4; J. Wych beat Johnston-Allen 10-3; Graham beat G. Cripsey 10-2; M. Smith beat J. Wright 10-7; T. Jones beat J. Smith 10-7; K. Stevens beat Chambers 10-8; L. Dodd beat Grech 10-9; Glen Wilkinson beat R. Bales 10-1; John Rea beat P. Houlihan 10-5; R. Edmonds beat Black 10-3; Price beat M. Bennett 10-9; Rowswell beat M. Gauvreau 10-7; K. Owers beat P. Gibson 10-8; D. Morgan beat J. Campbell 10-4; J. McLaughlin beat Ellis 10-9; Robidoux beat M. Fisher 10-2

**Fourth qualifying round:** N. Gilbert beat Edwards 10-8; Duggan beat Rowing 10-6; D. Gilbert beat Thornley 10-4; Roe beat Murphy 10-7; Clark beat Martin 10-2; O'Boye beat Fowler 10-6; Browne beat Macleod 10-6; Gary Wilkinson beat Reardon 10-5; W. Jones beat Wych 10-9; Graham beat M. Smith 10-6; T. Jones beat Stevens 10-2; Dodd beat Glen Wilkinson 10-4; John Rea beat Edmonds 10-7; Rowswell beat Price 10-6; D. Morgan beat Owers 10-8; Robidoux beat J. McLaughlin 10-2

**Fifth qualifying round:** S. Newbury beat N. Gilbert 10-7; Duggan beat J. Spencer 10-1; D. Mountjoy beat D. Gilbert 10-7; Roe beat R. Williams 10-3; R. Chaperon beat Clark 10-4; O'Boye beat B. West 10-7; Browne beat S. Longworth 10-0; Gary Wilkinson beat T. Drago 10-9; W. Jones beat David Taylor 10-7; D. Reynolds beat Graham 10-5; T. Meo beat T. Jones 10-7; E. Charlton beat Dodd 10-6; S. James beat John Rea 10-7; E. Hughes beat Rowswell 10-9; D. Morgan beat A. Higgins 10-8; D. O'Kane beat Robidoux 10-5

**First round:** S. Davis beat Newbury 10-5; Duggan beat C. Wilson 10-1; M. Hallett beat Mountjoy 10-7; Roe beat A. Knowles 10-6; T. Griffiths beat Chaperon 10-6; S. Francisco beat O'Boye 10-6; W. Thorne beat Browne 10-5; S. Hendry beat Gary Wilkinson 10-9; W. Jones beat N. Foulds 10-9; Reynolds beat P. Francisco 10-7; Meo beat J. Johnson 10-5; Charlton beat C. Thorburn 10-9; J. Parrott beat James 10-9; Dennis Taylor beat E. Hughes 10-3; J. Virgo beat D. Morgan 10-4; J. White beat O'Kane 19-7

**Second round:** S. Davis beat Duggan 13-3; Hallett beat Roe 13-12; Griffiths beat S. Francisco 13-9; Hendry beat Thorne 13-4; Reynolds beat W. Jones 13-3; Meo beat Charlton 13-8; Parrott beat Dennis Taylor 13-10; White beat Virgo 13-12

**Quarter-finals:** S. Davis beat Hallett 13-3; Hendry beat Griffiths 13-5; Meo beat Reynolds 13-9; Parrott beat White 13-7

**Semi-finals:** S. Davis beat Hendry 16-9; Parrott beat Meo 16-7

**Final:** S. Davis beat Parrott 18-3

**1990**

**First qualifying round:** G. Jenkins beat G. Foulds 10-5; J. Wattana beat J. Grech 10-4; A. Cairns beat B. Bennett 10-4; S. Murphy beat B. Mikkelsen 10-7; I. Brumby beat B. Demarco 10-6; B. Gollan beat C. Everton 10-2; B. Morgan beat D. Heaton 10-1; P. Watchorn beat B. Kelly 10-3; N. Bond beat B. Werbeniuk 10-1; Jack Rea beat P. Burke 10-4; B. Pinches beat M. Parkin 10-0; N. Dyson beat I. Black 10-5; D. Campbell beat D. Greaves 10-3; G. Rigitano *wo* E. McLaughlin *scr*; D. Mienie beat J. Meadowcroft 10-1

**Second qualifying round:** John Rea beat J. Smith 10-4; M. Smith beat F. Ellis 10-6; C. Edwards beat D. Sheehan 10-8; B. Harris beat Jenkins 10-4; L. Dodd beat M. Watterson 10-3; S. Campbell beat Glen Wilkinson 10-2; K. Owers beat M. Darrington 10-1; Wattana beat J. Dunning 10-2; Cairns beat G. Scott 10-3; A. Kearney beat P. Medati 10-7; N. Terry beat S. Murphy 10-4; Brumby beat F. Davis 10-6; Gollan beat P. Gibson 10-5; B. Morgan beat I. Williamson 10-4; Watchorn beat V. Harris 10-6; Bond beat B. Rowswell 10-1; M. Gauvreau beat Jack Rea 10-9; R. Marshall beat P. Thornley 10-0; Pinches beat B. Oliver 10-8; M. Morra *wo* J. Van Rensberg *scr*; E. Lawlor beat M. Gibson 10-6; Dyson beat Bradley 10-6; M. Price beat T. Whitthread 10-6; D. Campbell beat J. Wright 10-6; E. Sinclair beat M. Wildman 10-5; M. Rowing beat R. Foldvari 10-9; Rigitano beat J. Donnelly 10-6; R. Grace beat A. Harris 10-8; J. Bear beat J. Fitzmaurice 10-5; G. Miles beat D. Hughes 10-5; P. Houlihan beat Mienie 10-5; T. Wilson beat S. Meakin 10-8

**Third qualifying round:** John Rea beat T. Murphy 10-7; D. Morgan beat M. Smith 10-6; A. Robidoux beat Edwards 10-3; R. Edmonds beat B. Harris 10-4; Dodd beat W. King 10-8; S. Campbell beat S. Longworth 10-6; J. Spencer beat Owers 10-8; Wattana beat David Taylor 10-5; Cairns beat R. Reardon 10-8; N. Gilbert beat Kearney 10-6; M. Johnston-Allen beat Terry 10-1; P. Browne beat Brumby 10-6; Gollan beat K. Stevens 10-6; B. Morgan beat J. O'Boye 10-2; Watchorn beat M. Fisher 10-7; Bond beat T. Jones 10-2; Gary Wilkinson beat Gauvreau 10-5; Marshall beat D. Martin 10-6; Pinches beat C. Roscoe 10-6; T. Chappel beat Morra 10-8; M. Bennett beat Lawlor 10-3; M. Macleod beat Dyson 10-9; Price beat S. Duggan 10-9; J. Campbell beat D. Campbell 10-5; I. Graham beat Sinclair 10-3; Rowing *wo* J. Wych *scr*; D. Fowler beat Rigitano 10-6; D. Gilbert beat Crace 10-9; J. Chambers beat Bear 10-3; Miles beat R. Bales 10-7; Houlihan beat J. McLaughlin 10-5; T. Wilson beat G. Cripsey 10-6

**Fourth qualifying round:** D. Morgan beat John Rea 10-7; Robidoux beat Edmonds 10-6; S. Campbell beat Dodd 10-7; Wattana beat Spencer 10-8; N. Gilbert beat Cairns 10-6; Johnston-Allen beat Browne 10-2; Gollan beat B. Morgan 10-6; Bond beat Watchorn 10-2; Gary Wilkinson beat Marshall 10-7; Chappel beat Pinches 10-3; M. Bennett beat Macleod 10-1; Price beat J. Campbell 10-6; Graham beat Rowing 10-8; Fowler beat D. Gilbert 10-3; Chambers beat Miles 10-5; T. Wilson beat Houlihan 10-6

**Fifth qualifying round:** D. Morgan beat R. Chaperon 10-9; Robidoux beat D. O'Kane 10-2; N. Foulds beat S. Campbell 10-7; A. Higgins beat Wattana 10-6; N. Gilbert beat D. Roe 10-6; P. Francisco beat Johnston-Allen 10-7; Gollan beat E. Hughes 10-7; S. Newbury beat Bond 10-6; Gary Wilkinson beat S. Francisco 10-7; Chappel beat M. Clark 10-9; M. Bennett beat R. Williams 10-9; E. Charlton beat Price 10-5; T. Drago beat Graham 10-7; Fowler beat B. West 10-9; W. Jones beat Chambers 10-6; C. Wilson beat T. Wilson 10-6

**First round:** S. Davis beat Charlton 10-1; S. James beat Higgins 10-5; W. Thorne beat Drago 10-4; N. Foulds beat Dennis Taylor 10-8; T. Griffiths beat N. Gilbert 10-4; A. Knowles beat Chappel 10-4; J. Virgo beat Gary Wilkinson 10-6; J. White beat Fowler 10-4; S. Hendry beat Robidoux 10-7; T. Meo beat W. Jones 10-8; D. Morgan beat J. Johnson 10-8; M. Hallett beat Newbury 10-9; C. Thorburn beat C. Wilson 10-6; D. Mountjoy beat Gollan 10-8; D. Reynolds beat P. Francisco 10-7; J. Parrott beat M. Bennett 10-9

**Second round:** S. Davis beat James 13-7; N. Foulds beat Thorne 13-11; Griffiths beat Knowles 13-6; White beat Virgo 13-6; Hendry beat Meo 13-7; D. Morgan beat Hallett 13-8; Thorburn beat Mountjoy 13-12; Parrott beat Reynolds 13-11

**Quarter-finals:** S. Davis beat N. Foulds 13-8; White beat Griffiths 13-5; Hendry beat D. Morgan 13-6; Parrott beat Thorburn 13-6
**Semi-finals:** White beat S. Davis 16-14; Hendry beat Parrott 16-11
**Final:** Hendry beat White 18-12

## WPBSA NON-RANKING EVENTS

In 1988 the WPBSA instituted three non-ranking events for players knocked out in the early rounds of specific tournaments. Each carried prize-money of £25,000 with the winner taking £5,000. The three finals resulted:

**Marcos Leisure Centre, Glasgow**
Gary Wilkinson beat A. Higgins 5-4
**Pontins, Brixham**
P. Browne beat P. Francisco 5-1
**Excelsior Snooker Centre, Leeds**
David Taylor beat S. Meakin 9-1

In 1989–90, two more events were staged with the same prize-money. The two finals resulted:

**Clacton Snooker Centre**
R. Foldvari beat D. Morgan 8-1
**Marcos Leisure Centre, Glasgow**
K. Owers beat D. Gilbert 9-6

# STORMSEAL MATCHROOM LEAGUE

Steve Davis won his fourth consecutive Matchroom League with a match to spare to collect the £70,000 first prize. Cliff Thorburn and John Parrott, the bottom two finishers, were relegated. Steve James and James Wattana will replace them in the 1991 league. The 1990 league was sponsored by Stormseal.

## LEAGUE SCORECARD

| *Match* | | | | |
|---|---|---|---|---|
| 1 | Stephen Hendry | 5 | Willie Thorne | 3 |
| 2 | Neal Foulds | 5 | Cliff Thorburn | 3 |
| 3 | Doug Mountjoy | 5 | Tony Meo | 3 |
| 4 | Tony Meo | 5 | Neal Foulds | 3 |
| 5 | Steve Davis | 7 | Willie Thorne | 1 |
| 6 | Stephen Hendry | 4 | Dennis Taylor | 4 |
| 7 | Dennis Taylor | 6 | Tony Meo | 2 |
| 8 | Stephen Hendry | 6 | Cliff Thorburn | 2 |
| 9 | Jimmy White | 4 | Willie Thorne | 4 |
| 10 | Cliff Thorburn | 5 | John Parrott | 3 |
| 11 | Neal Foulds | 7 | John Parrott | 1 |
| 12 | Steve Davis | 4 | Jimmy White | 4 |
| 13 | Willie Thorne | 6 | Tony Meo | 2 |
| 14 | Willie Thorne | 4 | Doug Mountjoy | 4 |
| 15 | Jimmy White | 5 | John Parrott | 3 |
| 16 | Steve Davis | 6 | Cliff Thorburn | 2 |
| 17 | Stephen Hendry | 6 | Neal Foulds | 2 |
| 18 | Neal Foulds | 8 | Dennis Taylor | 0 |
| 19 | Stephen Hendry | 5 | Doug Mountjoy | 3 |
| 20 | Willie Thorne | 6 | Cliff Thorburn | 2 |
| 21 | John Parrott | 4 | Dennis Taylor | 4 |
| 22 | Steve Davis | 5 | Doug Mountjoy | 3 |
| 23 | Steve Davis | 5 | Neal Foulds | 3 |
| 24 | John Parrott | 5 | Stephen Hendry | 3 |
| 25 | Willie Thorne | 5 | Neal Foulds | 3 |
| 26 | Steve Davis | 5 | Tony Meo | 3 |
| 27 | Tony Meo | 5 | Cliff Thorburn | 3 |
| 28 | Steve Davis | 4 | John Parrott | 4 |
| 29 | John Parrott | 4 | Willie Thorne | 4 |
| 30 | Cliff Thorburn | 7 | Jimmy White | 1 |
| 31 | Dennis Taylor | 4 | Doug Mountjoy | 4 |
| 32 | Jimmy White | 4 | Neal Foulds | 4 |
| 33 | Doug Mountjoy | 5 | Jimmy White | 3 |
| 34 | Doug Mountjoy | 6 | Neal Foulds | 2 |
| 35 | Tony Meo | 5 | Stephen Hendry | 3 |
| 36 | Doug Mountjoy | 5 | John Parrott | 3 |
| 37 | Steve Davis | 6 | Dennis Taylor | 2 |
| 38 | Jimmy White | 5 | Stephen Hendry | 3 |
| 39 | Dennis Taylor | 6 | Jimmy White | 2 |
| 40 | Willie Thorne | 5 | Dennis Taylor | 3 |

| *Match* | | | | |
|---|---|---|---|---|
| 41 | Dennis Taylor | 5 | Cliff Thorburn | 3 |
| 42 | Cliff Thorburn | 6 | Doug Mountjoy | 2 |
| 43 | Jimmy White | 4 | Tony Meo | 4 |
| 44 | John Parrott | 6 | Tony Meo | 2 |
| 45 | Stephen Hendry | 6 | Steve Davis | 2 |

## LEAGUE TABLE

| *Player* | *Prize-money* | *P* | *W* | *D* | *L* | *F* | *A* | *Pts* |
|---|---|---|---|---|---|---|---|---|
| Steve Davis | (£70,000) | 9 | 6 | 2 | 1 | 44 | 28 | 20 |
| Stephen Hendry | (£30,000) | 9 | 5 | 1 | 3 | 41 | 31 | 16 |
| Willie Thorne | (£25,000) | 9 | 4 | 3 | 2 | 38 | 34 | 15 |
| Doug Mountjoy | (£20,000) | 9 | 4 | 2 | 3 | 37 | 35 | 14 |
| Dennis Taylor | (£17,000) | 9 | 3 | 3 | 3 | 34 | 38 | 12 |
| Neal Foulds | (£15,000) | 9 | 3 | 1 | 5 | 37 | 35 | 10 |
| Jimmy White | (£13,000) | 9 | 2 | 4 | 3 | 32 | 40 | 10 |
| Tony Meo | (£11,000) | 9 | 3 | 1 | 5 | 31 | 41 | 10 |
| Cliff Thorburn | (£9,000) | 9 | 3 | 0 | 6 | 33 | 39 | 9 |
| John Parrott | (£5,000) | 9 | 2 | 3 | 4 | 33 | 39 | 9 |

**Highest break 142 points John Parrott** (£5,000 prize-money)

# MATCHROOM INTERNATIONAL LEAGUE

## LEAGUE SCORECARD

| *Fixtures 1990* | | | | |
|---|---|---|---|---|
| 16 January (*France*) | Steve Davis | 3 | Jimmy White | 5 |
| 24 January (*Germany*) | Steve Davis | 3 | Tony Meo | 5 |
| 31 January (*Iceland*) | Steve Davis | 4 | Alex Higgins | 4 |
| 16 February (*Finland*) | Tony Meo | 5 | Alex Higgins | 3 |
| 18 March (*Holland*) | Terry Griffiths | 7 | Alex Higgins | 1 |
| 6 April (*Belgium*) | Steve Davis | 4 | Terry Griffiths | 4 |
| 7 April (*Belgium*) | Jimmy White | 5 | Alex Higgins | 3 |
| 3 May (*Germany*) | Jimmy White | 6 | Mike Hallett | 2 |
| 12 May (*Austria*) | Jimmy White | 4 | Terry Griffiths | 4 |
| 14 May (*Portugal*) | Steve Davis | 6 | Mike Hallett | 2 |
| 18 May (*Spain*) | Mike Hallett | 2 | Terry Griffiths | 6 |
| 14 June (*Spain*) | Jimmy White | 3 | Tony Meo | 5 |
| 15 June (*Spain*) | Terry Griffiths | 4 | Tony Meo | 4 |
| 16 June (*Spain*) | Mike Hallett | 0 | Tony Meo | 8 |
| 17 June (*Spain*) | Mike Hallett | 6 | Alex Higgins | 2 |

## LEAGUE TABLE

| *Player* | *Prize-money* | *P* | *W* | *D* | *L* | *F* | *A* | *Pts* |
|---|---|---|---|---|---|---|---|---|
| Tony Meo | (£25,000) | 5 | 4 | 1 | 0 | 27 | 13 | 13 |
| Jimmy White | (£12,000) | 5 | 3 | 1 | 1 | 23 | 17 | 10 |
| Terry Griffiths | (£10,000) | 5 | 2 | 3 | 0 | 25 | 15 | 9 |
| Steve Davis | (£8,000) | 5 | 1 | 2 | 2 | 20 | 20 | 5 |
| Mike Hallett | (£6,000) | 5 | 1 | 0 | 4 | 12 | 28 | 3 |
| Alex Higgins | (£4,000) | 5 | 0 | 1 | 4 | 13 | 27 | 1 |

**Highest break 135 points Jimmy White** (*France*) (£4,000 prize-money)

# NATIONAL PROFESSIONAL CHAMPIONSHIPS

From 1985 until the end of the 1988–89 season, the WPBSA's prize fund subsidy of £1,000 per player enabled the national professional championships to be staged annually. However, when the subsidy was withdrawn only the Welsh championship survived as it was the only one with both sponsorship and television contracts.

## ENGLISH CHAMPIONSHIP

**1981** (*John Courage*)
**Qualifying:** R. Edmonds beat M. Hallett 9-3; J. Johnson beat A. Knowles 9-2; M. Wildman beat B. Bennett 9-3; J. Dunning beat D. Greaves 9-4; J. Meadowcroft beat J. Barrie 9-3
**First round:** Edmonds beat F. Davis 9-6; T. Meo beat J. Virgo 9-6; G. Miles beat S. Hood 9-1; S. Davis beat Meadowcroft 9-2; J. Spencer beat P. Houlihan 9-1; W. Thorne beat Wildman 9-2; Johnson *wo*; Dunning beat David Taylor 9-8
**Quarter-finals:** S. Davis beat Spencer 9-7; Meo beat Miles 9-7; Thorne beat Dunning 9-0; Edmonds beat Johnson 9-5
**Semi-finals:** S. Davis beat Edmonds 9-0; Meo beat Thorne 9-8
**Final:** S. Davis beat Meo 9-3

**1985** (*Tolly Cobbold*)
**Qualifying:** D. Fowler beat W. Oliver 9-7; M. Bradley beat I. Williamson 9-8; T. Jones beat P. Houlihan 9-1; L. Dodd beat R. Bales 9-5; J. Fitzmaurice beat D. Greaves 9-3; M. Fisher beat D. French 9-8; S. Duggan beat B. Harris 9-8; D. Hughes beat M. Watterson 9-5; D. Chalmers beat J. Meadowcroft 9-3; S. Longworth beat R. Edmonds 9-4; P. Medati beat J. Hargreaves 9-8; G. Foulds beat F. Davis 9-2; G. Cripsey beat B. Bennett 9-0; G. Scott beat V. Harris 9-7
**First round:** S. Davis beat Fowler 9-3; M. Hallett beat Duggan 9-4; J. Johnson beat Scott 9-1; T. Meo beat Fisher 9-3; J. Virgo beat M. Darrington 9-0; D. Reynolds beat Fitzmaurice 9-2; R. Williams beat T. Jones 9-6; W. Thorne beat Dodd 9-1; Longworth beat M. Wildman 9-3; J. White beat Chalmers 9-5; Medati beat J. Spencer 9-4; N. Foulds beat D. Hughes 9-3; David Taylor beat Cripsey 9-5; J. Parrott beat G. Foulds 9-4; D. Martin beat G. Miles 9-7; A. Knowles beat Bradley 9-8
**Second round:** Virgo beat Johnson 9-4; Reynolds beat Thorne 9-6; S. Davis beat Williams 9-2; Meo beat Hallett 9-4; Knowles beat Martin 9-3; David Taylor beat Parrott 9-7; White beat N. Foulds 9-7; Longworth beat Medati 9-7
**Quarter-finals:** Meo beat Reynolds 9-4; Longworth beat White 9-5; Knowles beat David Taylor 9-2; S. Davis beat Virgo 9-2
**Semi-finals:** Knowles beat Longworth 9-6; S. Davis beat Meo 9-8
**Final:** S. Davis beat Knowles 9-2

**1986** (*Tolly Cobbold*)
**First round:** D. Gilbert beat B. West 9-8; P. Houlihan beat J. Hargreaves 9-5
**Second round:** M. Bradley beat Gilbert 9-5; F. Davis beat D. Hughes 9-6; T. Jones beat B. Harris 9-5; W. Oliver beat L. Dodd 9-5; P. Medati beat D. Greaves 9-4; S. Longworth

beat S. Duggan 9-4; G. Cripsey beat J. Meadowcroft 9-1; G. Scott beat B. Bennett 9-1; I. Williamson beat M. Watterson 9-1; R. Edmonds beat M. Smith 9-8; D. Fowler beat M. Darrington 9-3; Houlihan *wo* J. Dunning *scr*; D. Chalmers beat Fisher 9-2; R. Bales beat V. Harris 9-7

**Third round:** S. Davis beat Bradley 9-3; D. Martin beat F. Davis 9-8; J. Virgo beat T. Jones 9-7; J. Parrott beat Oliver 9-0; W. Thorne beat Medati 9-2; D. Reynolds beat Longworth 9-5; M. Wildman beat Cripsey 9-5; T. Meo beat Scott 9-1; J. White beat Williamson 9-1; R. Williams beat Miles 9-6; N. Foulds beat G. Foulds 9-4; Edmonds beat David Taylor 9-6; J. Johnson beat Fowler 9-7; J. Spencer beat Houlihan 9-5; M. Hallett beat Chalmers 9-1; A. Knowles beat Bales 9-4

**Fourth round:** S. Davis beat Martin 9-4; Virgo beat Parrott 9-6; Reynolds beat Thorne 9-8; Meo beat Wildman 9-3; White beat Williams 9-5; N. Foulds beat Edmonds 9-4; Johnson beat Spencer 9-7; Hallett beat Knowles 9-5

**Quarter-finals:** S. Davis beat Virgo 9-2; Meo beat Reynolds 9-4; N. Foulds beat White 9-4; Hallett beat Johnson 9-6

**Semi-finals:** Meo beat S. Davis 9-7; N. Foulds beat Hallett 9-8

**Final:** Meo beat Foulds 9-7

**1987** (*Tolly Ales*)

**First round:** M. Fisher beat T. Whitthread 6-3; P. Gibson beat D. Hughes 6-3; J. Wright beat D. Chalmers 6-5; B. Bennett beat N. Gilbert 6-5; D. Roe beat D. Greaves 6-1; K. Owers *wo* P. Houlihan *scr*; S. James beat J. Hargeaves 6-5

**Second round:** S. Duggan beat Fisher 6-0; M. Bradley beat D. Gilbert 6-3; P. Medati beat Gibson 6-2; M. Wildman *wo* M. Watterson *scr*; B. Harris beat G. Foulds 6-1; J. Spencer beat Wright 6-1; R. Edmonds beat Bennett 6-1; G. Cripsey beat J. Dunning 6-1; L. Dodd beat Smith 6-3; V. Harris beat M. Darrington 6-3; I. Williamson beat Roe 6-4; Owers beat R. Bales 6-5; T. Jones beat B. Oliver 6-1; J. Fitzmaurice beat G. Scott 6-2; James beat F. Davis 6-2; G. Miles *wo* J. Meadowcroft *scr*

**Third round:** T. Meo beat Duggan 6-3; D. Fowler beat Bradley 6-3; J. Virgo beat Medati 6-1; J. Parrott beat Wildman 6-1; W. Thorne beat B. Harris 6-2; D. Martin beat Spencer 6-5; D. Reynolds beat Edmonds 6-3; J. White beat Cripsey 6-4; Dodd beat A. Knowles 6-2; B. West beat V. Harris 6-3; M. Hallett beat Williamson 6-2; Owers beat N. Foulds 6-3; R. Williams beat Jones 6-4; David Taylor beat Fitzmaurice 6-1; James beat S. Longworth 6-2; J. Johnson beat Miles 6-3

**Fourth round:** Meo beat Fowler 6-0; Parrott beat Virgo 6-2; Thorne beat Martin 6-3; Reynolds beat White 6-5; Dodd beat West 6-3; Hallett beat Owers 6-2; Williams beat David Taylor 6-2; Johnson beat James 6-3

**Quarter-finals:** Meo beat Parrott 6-3; Thorne beat Reynolds 6-4; Dodd beat Hallett 6-5; Johnson beat Williams 6-5

**Semi-finals:** Meo beat Thorne 9-3; Dodd beat Johnson 9-5

**Final:** Meo beat Dodd 9-5

**1988**

**First round:** N. Gilbert beat A. Harris 6-3; J. Chambers beat P. Gibson 6-0; D. Gilbert beat T. Whitthread 6-1; E. Lawlor beat D. Roe 6-5; D. Chalmers *wo* M. Fisher *scr*; S. Meakin beat M. Darrington 6-3; M. Smith beat G. Miles 6-1; J. Smith beat V. Harris 6-3; Gary Wilkinson beat B. Rowswell 6-1; P. Medati beat N. Bennett 6-0; D. Heaton beat J. Meadowcroft 6-0; R. Marshall beat B. Oliver 6-3; D. Hughes beat J. Fitzmaurice 6-3; I. Williamson beat J. Dunning 6-5; D. Greaves beat S. James 6-5; M. Clark *wo* M. Watterson *scr*

**Second round:** F. Davis beat N. Gilbert 6-5; Chambers beat G. Scott 6-3; D. Gilbert beat R. Bales 6-2; Lawlor beat M. Bradley 6-5; J. Wright beat Fisher 6-2; K. Owers beat Meakin 6-2; M. Smith beat B. Harris 6-4; J. Smith beat T. Jones 6-5; Gary Wilkinson beat R. Edmonds 6-3; L. Dodd beat Heaton 6-0; Marshall beat P. Houlihan 6-4; D. Hughes beat M. Wildman 6-0; S. Duggan beat Williamson 6-2; Greaves beat G. Cripsey 6-4; Clark beat G. Foulds 6-0

**Third round:** T. Meo beat F. Davis 6-3; S. Longworth beat Chambers 6-4; D. Reynolds beat D. Gilbert 6-3; J. Parrott beat Lawlor 6-3; A. Knowles beat Wright 6-2; Owers beat David Taylor 6-3; D. Martin beat M. Smith 6-5; J. Johnson beat J. Smith 6-5; N. Foulds beat Gary Wilkinson 6-3; Fowler beat J. Spencer 6-3; J. Virgo beat Dodd 6-3; W. Thorne beat Marshall 6-3; R. Williams beat D. Hughes 6-1; M. Hallett beat Duggan 6-3; B. West beat Greaves 6-5; J. White beat Clark 6-5
**Fourth round:** Meo beat Longworth 6-4; Reynolds beat Parrott 6-2; Knowles beat Owers 6-4; Johnson beat Martin 6-4; N. Foulds beat Fowler 6-1; Thorne beat Virgo 6-0; Hallett beat Williams 6-3; West beat White 6-2
**Quarter-finals:** Reynolds beat Meo 6-4; Johnson beat Knowles 6-3; N. Foulds beat Thorne 6-2; West beat Hallett 6-5
**Semi-finals:** Reynolds beat Johnson 9-8; N. Foulds beat West 9-6
**Final:** Reynolds beat N. Foulds 9-5

### 1989

**Preliminary:** I. Graham beat D. Heaton 5-1; M. Johnston-Allen beat B. Bennett 5-2; N. Terry beat M. Rowing 5-1; C. Edwards *wo* D. Greaves *scr*
**First round:** A. Harris *wo* G. Scott *scr*; B. Rowswell beat V. Harris 5-3; Graham beat M. Darrington 5-3; J. Smith *wo* P. Gibson *scr*; J. Fitzmaurice beat B. Harris 5-4; M Price beat Johnston-Allen 5-4; R. Marshall beat Terry 5-3; I. Williamson *wo* S. Meakin *scr*; G. Miles beat M. Smith 5-4; S. Campbell beat J. Dunning 5-3; Edwards beat M. Watterson 5-0; M. Bradley beat J. Chambers 5-2; B. Oliver beat G. Foulds 5-1; E. Lawlor beat F. Davis 5-2; T. Whitthread beat D. Hughes 5-1; P. Medati beat M. Wildman 5-4
**Second round:** A. Harris beat T. Jones 5-3; Rowswell beat J. Wright 5-2; Graham beat S. Duggan 5-2; Gary Wilkinson beat J. Smith 5-3; P. Houlihan beat Fitzmaurice 5-4; Price beat R. Edmonds 5-4; Marshall beat N. Gilbert 5-4; Williamson beat Owers 5-4; Miles beat M. Fisher 5-4; D. Fowler beat Campbell 5-1; Edwards beat Dodd 5-1; D. Gilbert beat Bradley 5-4; M. Clark beat Oliver 5-2; D. Roe beat Lawlor 5-1; G. Cripsey beat Whitthread 5-0; Medati beat R. Bales 5-3
**Third round:** D. Reynolds beat A. Harris 5-1; Rowswell beat D. Martin 5-2; Graham beat R. Williams 5-3; Wilkinson beat J. Virgo 5-3; M. hallett beat Houlihan 5-2; Price beat David Taylor 5-1; S. Longworth beat Marshall 5-3; T. Knowles beat Williamson 5-2; J. Parrott beat Miles 5-3; Fowler beat T. Meo 5-3; Edwards beat J. Spencer 5-1; J. Johnson beat D. Gilbert 5-2; W. Thorne beat Clark 5-1; Roe beat B. West 5-4; Cripsey beat S. James 5-3; N. Foulds beat Medati 5-3
**Fourth round:** Rowswell beat Reynolds 5-4; Wilkinson beat Graham 5-1; Hallett beat Price 5-4; Longworth beat Knowles 5-4; Parrott beat Fowler 5-4; Johnson beat Edwards 5-0; Thorne beat Roe 5-1; N. Foulds beat Cripsey 5-1
**Quarter-finals:** Wilkinson beat Rowswell 5-1; Hallett beat Longworth 5-1; Parrott beat Johnson 5-4; N. Foulds beat Thorne 5-3
**Semi-finals:** Hallett beat Wilkinson 5-3; Parrott beat N. Foulds 5-4
**Final:** Hallett beat Parrott 9-7

## IRISH CHAMPIONSHIP

### 1972

**Challenge:** A. Higgins beat Jack Rea 28-12

### 1978

**Challenge:** A. Higgins beat Dennis Taylor 21-7

### 1979

**Challenge:** A. Higgins beat P. Fagan 21-13

**1980**
**Challenge:** Dennis Taylor beat A. Higgins 21-15

**1981**
**Challenge:** Dennis Taylor beat P. Fagan 22-21

**1982**
**First round:** E. Hughes beat D. Sheehan 6-1
**Quarter-finals:** E. Hughes beat Jack Rea 6-0; T. Murphy beat P. Fagan 6-2
**Semi-finals:** Dennis Taylor beat Murphy 6-0; A. Higgins beat E. Hughes 6-2
**Final:** Taylor beat Higgins 16-13

**1983**
**First round:** Dennis Taylor beat B. Kelly 6-0; P. Fagan beat T. Murphy 6-4; A. Higgins beat Jack Rea 6-3; E. Hughes beat P. Burke 6-2
**Semi-finals:** Higgins beat E. Hughes 6-2; Taylor beat Fagan 6-1
**Final:** Higgins beat Taylor 16-11

**1985** (*Strongbow*)
**Preliminary:** J. McLaughlin beat D. Sheehan 6-3
**Qualifying:** P. Burke beat A. Kearney 6-4; T. Murphy beat P. Browne 6-3; B. Kelly beat P. Watchorn 6-2; Jack Rea beat McLaughlin 6-5
**Quarter-finals:** P. Fagan beat Murphy 6-2; Dennis Taylor beat Jack Rea 6-0; A. Higgins beat Burke 6-0; E. Hughes beat Kelly 6-2
**Semi-finals:** Taylor beat Hughes 6-5; Higgins beat Fagan 6-3
**Final:** Taylor beat Higgins 10-5

**1986** (*Strongbow*)
**First round:** B. Kelly beat Jack Rea 5-0; T. Murphy beat J. O'Boye 5-0; E. Hughes beat D. Sheehan 5-0; A. Kearney beat P. Fagan 5-0; J. McLaughlin beat P. Watchorn 5-0; P. Burke beat P. Browne 5-4
**Quarter-finals:** Dennis Taylor beat Kelly 6-1; Murphy beat Kearney 6-2; A. Higgins beat McLaughlin 6-2; Hughes beat Burke 6-3
**Semi-finals:** Taylor beat Murphy 6-3; Higgins beat Hughes 6-2
**Final:** Taylor beat Higgins 10-7

**1987** (*Matchroom*)
**First round:** D. Sheehan beat J. McLaughlin 5-4; P. Browne beat Jack Rea 5-3; T. Kearney beat T. Murphy 5-1; J. O'Boye beat B. Kelly 5-0; P. Burke beat P. Fagan 5-3; E. Hughes beat P. Watchorn 5-2
**Quarter-finals:** Dennis Taylor beat Sheehan 6-3; Hughes beat Kearney 6-1; Browne beat Burke 6-2; O'Boye *wo* Higgins *scr*
**Semi-finals:** Taylor beat Browne 6-1; O'Boye beat Hughes 6-3
**Final:** Taylor beat O'Boye 9-2

**1988**
**First round:** A. Kearney beat P. Fagan 5-3; T. Murphy beat B. Kelly 5-1; P. Browne beat Jack Rea 5-0; P. Watchorn beat E. Hughes 5-2; J. McLaughlin beat P. Burke 5-3; J. O'Boye beat D. Sheehan 5-0
**Quarter-finals:** Dennis Taylor beat Kearney 6-3; Browne beat Murphy 6-5; McLaughlin beat Watchorn 6-5; O'Boye beat A. Higgins 6-4
**Semi-finals:** Taylor beat Browne 6-5; McLaughlin beat O'Boye 6-4
**Final:** McLaughlin beat Taylor 9-4

**1989**
**First round:** Jack Rae *wo* P. Fagan *scr*; P. Browne beat D. Sheehan 5-2; A. Kearney beat B. Kelly 5-2; P. Watchorn beat B. Burke 5-4
**Quarter-finals:** J. McLaughlin beat Rea 5-0; Browne beat T. Murphy 5-3; E. Hughes beat Kearney 5-1; A. Higgins beat Watchorn 5-2

**Semi-finals:** McLaughlin beat Browne 6-3; Higgins beat Hughes 6-2
**Final:** Higgins beat McLaughlin 9-7

# SCOTTISH CHAMPIONSHIP

**1980**
**Challenge:** E. Sinclair beat C. Ross 11-6

**1981**
**First round:** M. Gibson beat B. Demarco 5-3; J. Donnelly beat E. Sinclair 5-0; E. McLaughlin beat C. Ross 5-3; I. Black beat M. Macleod 5-4
**Semi-finals:** Gibson beat Donnelly 6-4; Black beat E. McLaughlin 6-3
**Final:** Black beat Gibson 11-7

**1982**
**First round:** M. Macleod beat J. Donnelly 6-5
**Quarter-finals:** C. Ross beat B. Demarco 6-5; M. Gibson beat E. McLaughlin 6-3; I. Black beat Macleod 6-0; E. Sinclair beat J. Phillips 6-3
**Semi-finals:** Black beat Ross 6-4; Sinclair beat Gibson 6-2
**Final:** Sinclair beat Black 11-7

**1983**
**First round:** J. Donnelly beat B. Demarco 6-4; I. Black beat E. McLaughlin 6-4; M. Macleod beat M. Gibson 6-5
**Semi-finals:** E. Sinclair beat Donnelly 6-5; Macleod beat Black 6-2
**Final:** Macleod beat Sinclair 11-9

**1985**
**First round:** M. Macleod beat E. McLaughlin 6-4; M. Gibson beat I. Black 6-2; John Rea beat J. Donnelly 6-2; E. Sinclair beat B. Demarco 6-3
**Semi-final:** Macleod beat Gibson 6-4; Sinclair beat John Rea 6-2
**Final:** Macleod beat Sinclair 10-2

**1986** (*Canada Dry*)
**First round:** S. Hendry beat B. Demarco 6-1
**Quarter-finals:** Hendry beat M. Macleod 6-5; I. Black beat E. McLaughlin 6-4; John Rea beat J. Donnelly 6-1; M.Gibson beat E. Sinclair 6-4
**Semi-finals:** Hendry beat Black 6-2; Gibson beat John Rea 6-0
**Final:** Hendry beat Gibson 10-5

**1987**
**First round:** S. Hendry beat B. Demarco 6-2; John Rea beat I. Black 6-1; E. Sinclair beat M. Gibson 6-2; J. Donnelly beat M. Macleod 6-2
**Semi-finals:** Hendry beat Rea 6-0; Donnelly beat Sinclair 6-4
**Final:** Hendry beat Donnelly 10-7

**1988** (*Swish*)
**First round:** B. Demarco beat E. McLaughlin 6-0
**Quarter-finals:** S. Hendry beat Demarco 6-0; M. Gibson beat I. Black 6-2; John Rea beat E. Sinclair 6-5; M. Macleod beat J. Donnelly 6-5
**Semi-finals:** Hendry beat Gibson 6-1; Macleod beat Rea 6-5
**Final:** Hendry beat Macleod 10-4

**1989**
**First round:** M. Macleod beat E. McLaughlin 5-0; M. Gibson beat E. Sinclair 5-4; John Rea beat I. Black 5-3; J. Donnelly beat B. Demarco 5-1

**Semi-finals:** Macleod beat Gibson 5-1; Rea beat Donnelly 5-1
**Final:** Rea beat Macleod 9-7

# WELSH CHAMPIONSHIP

**1977** (*William Hill*)
**Challenge:** R. Reardon beat D. Mountjoy 12-8

**1980** (*Woodpecker*)
**First round:** D. Mountjoy beat T. Griffiths 9-6; R. Reardon beat C. Wilson 9-3
**Final:** Mountjoy beat Reardon 9-6

**1981** (*Woodpecker*)
**Qualifying:** C. Wilson beat R. Andrewartha 6-5
**First round:** Wilson beat D. Mountjoy 9-6; R. Reardon beat T. Griffiths 9-6
**Final:** Reardon beat Wilson 9-6

**1982** (*Woodpecker*)
**First round:** C. Wilson beat M. Owen 6-0; T. Griffiths beat C. Roscoe 6-2; R. Reardon beat C. Everton 6-1; D. Mountjoy beat R. Andrewartha 6-3
**Semi-finals:** Griffiths beat Wilson 9-6; Mountjoy beat Reardon 9-7
**Final:** Mountjoy beat Griffiths 9-8

**1983** (*Woodpecker*)
**First round:** T. Griffiths beat C. Everton 6-1; R. Reardon beat R. Andrewartha 6-2; C. Wilson beat C. Roscoe 6-4; D. Mountjoy beat M. Owen 6-0
**Semi-finals:** Reardon beat Griffiths 9-4; Mountjoy beat Wilson 9-3
**Final:** Reardon beat Mountjoy 9-1

**1984** (*Strongbow*)
**First round:** D. Mountjoy beat C. Everton 6-1; T. Griffiths beat R. Andrewartha 6-1; R. Reardon beat M. Owen 6-1; C. Wilson beat C. Roscoe 6-2
**Semi-finals:** Mountjoy beat Griffiths 9-5; Wilson beat Reardon 9-4
**Final:** Mountjoy beat Wilson 9-3

**1985** (*BCE*)
**First round:** S. Newbury beat W. Jones 6-2; T. Chappel beat M. Owen 6-0
**Quarter finals:** R. Reardon beat C. Everton 6-2; D. Mountjoy beat Newbury 6-5; C. Wilson beat C. Roscoe 6-3; T. Griffiths beat Chappel 6-0
**Semi-finals:** Griffiths beat Reardon 9-3; Mountjoy beat Wilson 9-2
**Final:** Griffiths beat Mountjoy 9-4

**1986** (*Zetters*)
**First round:** T. Chappel *wo* M. Owen *scr*; W. Jones beat C. Everton 6-2
**Quarter-finals:** T. Griffiths beat Chappel 6-4; C. Wilson beat S. Newbury 6-4; D. Mountjoy beat C. Roscoe 6-4; W. Jones beat Reardon 6-4
**Semi-finals:** Griffiths beat Wilson 9-1; Mountjoy beat W. Jones 9-7
**Final:** Griffiths beat Mountjoy 9-3

**1987** (*Matchroom*)
**First round:** W. Jones beat M. Bennett 6-3; C. Roscoe beat C. Everton 6-2
**Quarter-finals:** T. Griffiths beat Jones 6-2; S. Newbury beat C. Wilson 6-2; T. Chappel beat R. Reardon 6-4; D. Mountjoy beat Roscoe 6-2
**Semi-finals:** Newbury beat Griffiths 9-6; Mountjoy beat Chappel 9-2
**Final:** Mountjoy beat Newbury 9-7

**1988** (*Senator*)
**First round:** M. Bennett beat C. Everton 6-0; T. Chappel beat C. Roscoe 6-4
**Quarter-finals:** D. Mountjoy beat Bennett 6-3; W. Jones beat R. Reardon 6-5; C. Wilson beat S. Newbury 6-3; T. Griffiths beat Chappel 6-4
**Semi-finals:** Jones beat Mountjoy 9-5; Griffiths beat Wilson 9-7
**Final:** Griffiths beat Jones 9-3

**1989** (*Senator*)
**First round:** D. Morgan beat T. Chappel 6-5; M. Bennett beat C. Roscoe 6-3
**Quarter-finals:** T. Griffiths beat Morgan 6-5; S. Newbury beat W. Jones 6-5; D. Mountjoy beat R. Reardon 6-3; Bennett beat C. Wilson 6-1
**Semi-finals:** Griffiths beat Newbury 9-7; Mountjoy beat Bennet 9-5
**Final:** Mountjoy beat Griffiths 9-6

**1990** (*Senator*)
**First round:** R. Reardon beat M. Bennett 6-2; D. Morgan beat C. Roscoe 6-4
**Quarter-finals:** D. Mountjoy beat Reardon 6-3; W. Jones beat S. Newbury 6-3; T. Chappel beat C. Wilson 6-4; D. Morgan beat T. Griffiths 6-4
**Semi-finals:** Mountjoy beat W. Jones 9-7; D. Morgan beat Chappel 9-8
**Final:** D. Morgan beat Mountjoy 9-7

## AUSTRALIAN CHAMPIONSHIP

**1985**
**First round:** G. Wilkinson beat G. Jenkins 6-2; G. Robinson beat J. Charlton* 6-0; L. Condo beat E. Charlton* 6-2
**Second round:** Wilkinson beat L. Heywood 7-3; R. Foldvari beat Robinson 7-2; J. Giannaros beat Condo 7-2; I. Anderson *wo* G. Ganim *scr*
**Quarter-finals:** E. Charlton beat Wilkinson 8-2; P. Morgan beat Giannaros 8-4; W. King beat Anderson 8-2; J. Campbell beat Foldvari 8-5
**Semi-finals:** Charlton beat Morgan 9-3; Campbell beat King 9-6
**Final:** Campbell beat Charlton 10-7

**1986**
**First-round:** G. Jenkins beat G. Ganim** 6-2; L. Condo** beat E. Charlton Jr* 6-0; J. Charlton* beat G. Robinson* 6-4
**Second round:** Condo beat J. Giannaros 6-4; I. Anderson beat J. Charlton 6-2; G. Wilkinson beat L. Heywood 6-0; R. Foldvari beat Jenkins 6-3
**Quarter-finals:** J. Campbell beat Wilkinson 6-1; Foldvari beat P. Morgan 6-2; W. King beat Condo 6-3; E. Charlton beat Anderson 6-2
**Semi-finals:** Campbell beat Foldvari 8-3; King beat Charlton 8-6
**Final:** King beat Campbell 10-3

**1987**
**Qualifying round:** S. Frangie* beat W. Potasnyk* 6-4
**First round:** G. Jenkins beat L. Condo** 6-1; I. Anderson beat L. Heywood* 6-4; G. Wilkinson beat J. Charlton* 6-0; Frangie beat P. Morgan** 6-5
**Quarter-finals:** W. King beat Jenkins 6-4; R. Foldvari beat Frangie 6-2; E. Charlton beat Anderson 6-2; J. Campbell beat Wilkinson 6-4
**Semi-finals:** King beat Foldvari 8-1; Charlton beat Campbell 8-6
**Final:** King beat Charlton 10-7

**1988**
**Qualifying round:** W. Potasznyk* beat Edward Charlton* 5-1
**Second round:** S. Frangie* beat L. Condo** 5-2; G. Jenkins beat P. Morgan** 5-3;

I. Anderson beat J. Giannaros** 5-2; Potasznyk beat Glen Wilkinson 5-3
**Quarter-finals:** Eddie Charlton beat Jenkins 5-0; W. King beat Frangie 5-4; R. Foldvari beat Potasznyk 5-3; J. Campbell beat Anderson 5-0
**Semi-finals:** Foldvari beat King 8-4; Campbell beat Charlton 8-6
**Final:** Campbell beat Foldvari 9-7

* Member of Australian Professional Association only
** Non-tournament playing member of WPBSA

*Eddie Charlton won the Australian Championship for the first time in 1964 and was beaten only in 1968 until he lost to John Campbell in 1985.*

# CANADIAN CHAMPIONSHIP

### 1983

**First round:** G. Rigitano beat M. Gauvreau 9-6; R. Chaperon beat G. Watson 9-5; J. Caggianello beat W. Sanderson 9-5
**Second round:** B. Mikkelsen beat Rigitano 9-4; F. Jonik beat Chaperon 9-4; Jim Bear beat M. Morra 9-8; Caggianello beat P. Thornley 9-7
**Quarter-finals:** C. Thorburn beat Mikkelsen 9-2; Jonik beat J. Wych 9-5; Jim Bear beat John Bear 9-5; K. Stevens beat Caggianello 9-0
**Semi-finals:** Jonik beat Thorburn 9-6; Stevens beat Jim Bear 9-8
**Final:** Stevens beat Jonik 9-8

### 1985

**First round:** J. Caggianello beat Jim Bear 5-4; R. Chaperon beat P. Thornley 5-1; B. Mikkelsen beat G. Watson 5-3; John Bear beat M. Morra 5-4; J. Wych beat W. Sanderson 5-2
**Quarter-finals:** Chaperon beat K. Stevens 6-4; F. Jonik beat Mikkelsen 6-4; C. Thorburn beat Caggianello 6-2; Wych beat John Bear 6-3
**Semi-finals:** Chaperon beat Jonik 6-3; Thorburn beat Wych 6-5
**Final:** Thorburn beat Chaperon 6-4

### 1986

**First round:** G. Watson beat J. Caggianello 6-1; F. Jonik beat G. Rigitano 6-1; R. Chaperon beat J. Bear 6-3; B. Mikkelsen beat W. Sanderson 6-1; P. Thornley beat M. Morra 6-4
**Second round:** C. Thorburn beat Watson 6-1; Jonik beat Chaperon 6-3; J. Wych beat Mikkelsen 6-3; K. Stevens beat Thornley 6-2
**Semi-finals:** Thorburn beat Jonik 6-3; Wych beat Stevens 6-2
**Final:** Thorburn beat Wych 6-2

### 1987 (*BCE*)

**First round:** G. Watson beat P. Thornley 6-4; F. Jonik beat W. Sanderson 6-0; M. Morra beat R. Chaperon 6-5; J. Wych beat G. Rigitano 6-4; Jim Bear beat B. Mikkelsen 6-0; J. Caggianello beat M. Gauvreau 6-3
**Quarter-finals:** Morra beat Jonik 6-2; C. Thorburn beat Watson 6-3; Bear beat Wych 6-4; K. Stevens beat Caggianello 6-0
**Semi-finals:** Bear beat Stevens 7-2; Thorburn beat Morra 7-4
**Final:** Thorburn beat Bear 8-4

### 1988 (*BCE*)

**First round:** F. Jonik *wo* G. Rigitano *scr*; M. Morra beat G. Watson 6-2; J. Wych beat P. Thornley 6-5; A. Robidoux beat R. Chaperon 6-3; J. Caggianello beat Jim Bear 6-3; B. Mikkelsen beat M. Gauvreau 6-2
**Quarter-finals:** C. Thorburn beat Jonik 6-4; Wych beat Morra 6-4; Robidoux beat Caggianello 6-4; Mikkelsen beat K. Stevens 6-5

**Semi-finals:** Wych beat Thorburn 7-5; Robidoux beat Mikkelsen 7-3
**Final:** Robidoux beat Wych 8-4

# SOUTH AFRICAN CHAMPIONSHIP

### 1986

**First round:** P. Francisco beat V. Blignaut* 6-3; D. Mienie beat M. Hines 6-5; F. Ellis beat R. Amdor* 6-2
**Second round:** S. Francisco beat G. Johnston* 7-0; P. Francisco beat R. Grace 7-1; J. Van Rensberg beat Mienie 7-1; Ellis beat P. Mans 7-6
**Semi-finals:** S. Francisco beat P. Francisco 8-3; Ellis beat Van Rensberg 8-2
**Final:** S. Francisco beat Ellis 9-1

### 1987

**Semi-finals:** F. Ellis beat R. Grace 9-8; J. Van Rensberg beat P. Mans* 9-4
**Final:** Ellis beat Van Rensberg 9-4

* Member of the South African Professional Association but not the WPBSA

# PROFESSIONAL BILLIARDS

## THE WORLD PROFESSIONAL BILLIARDS CHAMPIONSHIP

Founded in 1870, the World Professional Billiards Championship is the oldest of all the game's events but since snooker has become by far the most popular of the billiard table games it has declined steadily in public appeal.

The problems started in the 1930s when the four best players in the world, Walter Lindrum, Joe Davis, Tom Newman and Clark McConachy, mastered all aspects of the game so completely that they effectively killed it as a public entertainment. They did such a thorough job that there was only one Championship between 1934 and 1968 that they did not claim – when Rex Williams travelled to New Zealand and beat McConachy, then 73 and suffering from Parkinson's disease.

Williams successfully defended the title three times against various challengers but lost it in June 1980 to Joe's younger brother Fred, who thus became only the second player to have held world titles at both billiards and snooker – the first, of course, was Joe.

In November 1980, the event reverted to a tournament format and a variety of playing systems was tried: time-limit games, points-up games and, for the first time last season, the best of five games of 400-up. This formula gave frequent climaxes, as in frames of snooker, and also eliminated the possibility of very large breaks.

1985 also saw Channel 4 attempt a 'Pot Black'-style billiards event, the Blue Arrow Masters. Viewing figures for this were encouraging and the BBC agreed to televise the final of the 1986 World Professional Championship which was again played over the best of five games of 400-up.

In 1987, from the Albert Hall, Bolton, both the semi-finals and final were televised. Norman Dagley, who had earlier in the season won the UK Championship, added the professional title to his two world amateur victories by beating Robby Foldvari 3-1 in the final.

For the 1987–88 season, the format of the World and UK Championships was altered to the best of seven games (except for finals) of 150-up. This format was also adopted for two new events, the European Championship and the Yorkshire Bank Open. Dagley retained the 1988 world title at Bolton but the 1989 Championship, which was held at Leura, New South Wales, Australia under the more traditional time limit system, was won by Mike Russell who thus became the youngest ever champion.

## World Professional Billiards Championship (1870–1920)

| | | | |
|---|---|---|---|
| **1870** (Feb) | W. Cook | J. Roberts Sr | 1,200-1,083 |
| (Apr) | J. Roberts Jr | W. Cook | 1,000- 522 |
| (June) | J. Roberts Jr | A. Bowles | 1,000- 759 |
| (Nov) | J. Bennett | J. Roberts Jr | 1,000- 905 |
| **1871** (Jan) | J. Roberts Jr | J. Bennett | 1,000- 637 |
| (May) | W. Cook | J. Roberts Jr | 1,000- 985 |
| (Nov) | W. Cook | J. Bennett | 1,000- 942 |
| **1872** (Mar) | W. Cook | J. Roberts Jr | 1,000- 799 |
| **1874** (Feb) | W. Cook | J. Roberts Jr | 1,000- 784 |
| **1875** (May) | J. Roberts Jr | W. Cook | 1,000- 837 |
| (Dec) | J. Roberts Jr | W. Cook | 1,000- 865 |
| **1877** (May) | J. Roberts Jr | W. Cook | 1,000- 779 |
| **1880** (Nov) | J. Bennett | W. Cook | 1,000- 949 |
| **1881** (Jan) | J. Bennett | T. Taylor | 1,000- 910 |
| **1885** (Apr) | J. Roberts Jr | W. Cook | 3,000-2,908 |
| (June) | J. Roberts Jr | J. Bennett | 3,000-1,360 |
| **1899** | C. Dawson | J. North | 9,000-4,715 |
| **1900** | C. Dawson | H. W. Stevenson | 9,000-6,775 |
| **1901** | H. W. Stevenson | C. Dawson | 9,000-6,406 |
| | C. Dawson | H. W. Stevenson | 9,000-5,796 |
| | H. W. Stevenson (*declared champion – no contest*) | | |
| **1903** | C. Dawson | H. W. Stevenson | 9,000-8,700 |
| **1908** | M. Inman (*declared champion – no contest*) | | |
| **1909** | M. Inman | A. Williams | 9,000-7,662 |
| *Under Billiards Control Club Rules* | | | |
| **1909** | H. W. Stevenson (*declared champion – no contest*) | | |
| **1910** | H. W. Stevenson | M. Inman (*match abandoned*) | 13,370-13,212 |
| | H. W. Stevenson | M. Inman | 18,000-16,907 |
| **1911** | H. W. Stevenson | M. Inman | 18,000-16,914 |
| **1912** | M. Inman | T. Reece | 18,000- 9,675 |
| **1913** | M. Inman | T. Reece | 18,000-16,627 |
| **1914** | M. Inman | T. Reece | 18,000-12,826 |
| **1919** | M. Inman | H. W. Stevenson | 16,000- 9,468 |
| **1920** | W. Smith | C. Falkiner | 16,000-14,500 |

## World Professional Billiards Championship (1921–89)

### 1921

**First round:** C. Falkiner beat H. W. Stevenson 7,334-5,084; T. Newman beat T. Tothill 8,000-3,267
**Semi-finals:** Newman beat Falkiner 8,000-6,627; T. Reece beat F. Lawrence nrs
**Final:** Newman beat Reece 16,000-10,744

### 1922

**First round:** T. Reece beat M. McConachy 8,000-6,767
**Semi-finals:** T. Newman beat J. Davis 8,000-5,181; C. Falkiner beat Reece 8,000-7,289
**Final:** Newman beat Falkiner 16,000-15,167

**1923**

**First round:** M. Inman beat A. Peall 16,000-11,758; C. Falkiner beat T. Reece 16,000-14,952
**Semi-finals:** T. Newman beat Inman 16,000-14,506; W. Smith beat Falkiner 16,000-8,695
**Final:** Smith beat Newman 16,000-15,180

**1924**

**First round:** T. Newman beat C. McConachy 16,000-8,703
**Final:** Newman beat T. Reece 16,000-14,845

**1925**

T. Newman beat T. Reece 16,000-10,092

**1926**

T. Newman beat J. Davis 16,000-9,505

**1927**

**First round:** M. Inman beat T. Reece 8,000-5,527
**Second round:** J. Davis beat Inman 8,000-6,895
**Challenge round:** T. Newman beat Davis 16,000-14,763

**1928**

**First round:** T. Carpenter beat T. Reece 8,000-7,283
**Second round:** J. Davis beat Carpenter 8,000-5,602
**Challenge round:** Davis beat T. Newman 16,000-14,874

**1929**

**First round:** T. Newman beat T. Carpenter 8,000-5,984
**Final:** J. Davis beat Newman 18,000-17,219

**1930**

**First round:** T. Newman beat M. Inman 24,001-10,104; J. Davis beat C. Falkiner 21,975-19,815
**Final:** Davis beat Newman 20,918-20,117

**1932**

**First round:** J. Davis beat C. McConachy 25,161-19,259

**1933**

**First round:** W. Lindrum beat T. Newman 21,470-20,252
**Final:** Lindrum beat Davis 21,815-21,121

**1934**

**First round:** W. Lindrum beat C. McConachy 21,903-20,795
**Final:** Lindrum beat J. Davis 23,533-22,678

**1951**

C. McConachy beat J. Barrie 6,681-5,057

**1968**

R. Williams beat C. McConachy 5,499-5,234

**1971**

R. Williams beat B. Bennett 9,250-4,058

**1973**

R. Williams beat J. Karnehm 8,360-4,336

**1974**

R. Williams beat E. Charlton 7,017-4,916

**1976**

R. Williams beat E. Charlton 9,105-5,149

**1980** (*May*)

F. Davis beat R. Williams 5,978-4,452

**1980** (*Nov*)

**Qualifying:** P. Morgan beat J. Dunning 1,655-1,107; M. Wildman beat B. Bennett 1,968-678; S. Davis beat K. Kennerley 1,809-965

**Quarter-finals:** J. Barrie beat S. Davis 2,186-870; F. Davis beat Morgan 1,907-978; R. Edmonds beat J. Karnehm 1,513-1,306; Wildman beat R. Williams 1,476-1,415

**Semi-finals:** F. Davis beat Barrie 1,253-1,153; Wildman beat Edmonds 1,629-955

**Final:** F. Davis beat Wildman 3,037-2,064

**1982**

**First round:** C. Everton beat B. Bennett 1,500-556

**Quarter-finals:** F. Davis beat Everton 1,500-652; R. Williams beat J. Karnehm 1,500-569; R. Edmonds beat K. Kennerley 1,500-753; M. Wildman beat J. Fitzmaurice 1,500-721

**Semi-finals:** Williams beat Davis 1,500-1494; Wildman beat Edmonds 1500-765

**Final:** Williams beat Wildman 3,000-1,785

**1983**

**Qualifying:** I. Williamson beat D. Martin 1,000-710; B. Bennett beat G 1,000-683

**First round:** J. Karnehm beat M. Darrington 1,500-1,199; Bennett beat J. Fitzmaurice 1,500-1,396; C. Everton beat Williamson 1,500-1,085; E. Charlton beat T. Murphy 1,500-1,105

**Quarter-finals:** R. Williams beat Bennett 1,500-443; F. Davis beat Everton 1,500-477; R. Edmonds beat Karnehm 1,500-1,075; Charlton beat M. Wildman 1,500-778

**Semi-finals:** Davis beat Charlton 1,500-956; Williams beat Edmonds 1,500-671

**Final:** Williams beat Davis 1,500-605

**1984**

**Qualifying:** T. Murphy beat M. Darrington 1,021-861

**First round:** P. Morgan beat B. Bennett 1,021-639; I. Williamson beat C. Everton 746-496; J. Karnehm beat G. Ganim jnr 1,270-733; Murphy beat J. Fitzmaurice 1,050-868

**Quarter-finals:** F. Davis beat Murphy 1,242-852; E. Charlton beat Karnehm 944-931; Williamson beat R. Edmonds 918-805; M. Wildman beat Morgan 1,347-759

**Semi-finals:** Charlton beat Davis 1,436-829; Wildman beat Williamson 1,501-849

**Final:** Wildman beat Charlton 1,045-1,012

**1985**

**First round:** P. Francisco beat M. Darrington 3-0; I. Williamson beat B. Bennett 3-0; J. Karnehm beat E. Charlton 3-0; R. Edmonds beat A. Higgins 3-0; M. Wildman beat T. Jones 3-0; N. Dagley beat J. Fitzmaurice 3-0; R. Foldvari *wo* B. Oliver *scr*; F. Davis beat C. Everton 3-1

**Quarter-finals:** Dagley beat Karnehm 3-0; Foldvari beat Davis 3-0; Wildman beat Francisco 3-0; Edmonds beat Williamson 3-1

**Semi-finals:** Edmonds beat Wildman 3-0; Dagley beat Foldvari 3-0

**Final:** Edmonds beat Dagley 3-1

**1986**

**Qualifying:** R. Close beat E. Hughes 3-1; G. Scott beat B. Oliver 3-0
**First round:** E. Charlton beat T. Jones 3-0; I. Williamson beat Scott 3-0; R. Foldvari beat J. Fitzmaurice 3-0; N. Dagley beat B. Bennett 3-0; Close beat F. Davis 3-0; P. Francisco beat C. Everton 3-0; M. Wildman beat G. Thompson 3-0
**Quarter-finals:** Edmonds beat Francisco 3-0; Dagley beat Charlton 3-0; Foldvari beat Close 3-0; Wildman beat Williamson 3-2
**Semi-finals:** Dagley beat Edmonds 3-1; Foldvari beat Wildman 3-1
**Final:** Foldvari beat Dagley 3-1

**1987**

**First round:** G. Thompson beat J. Fitzmaurice 2-0; G. Miles *wo* L. Dielis *scr*; T. Jones *wo* R. Ceulemans *scr*; C. Everton beat H. Griffiths 2-1
**Second round:** R. Foldvari beat E. Hughes 3-0; F. Davis beat Thompson 3-0; P. Francisco beat Miles 3-0; R. Edmonds beat B. Bennett 3-0; N. Dagley beat R. Close 3-0; I. Williamson *wo* Jones *scr*; E. Charlton beat J. Karnehm 3-1; M. Wildman beat Everton 3-0
**Quarter-finals:** Foldvari beat Davis 3-1; Edmonds beat Francisco 3-0; Dagley beat Williamson 3-1; Wildman beat Charlton 3-1
**Semi-finals:** Foldvari beat Edmands 3-1; Dagley beat Wildman 3-0
**Final:** Dagley beat Foldvari 3-1

**1988**

**Preliminary round:** H. Griffiths beat G. Cripsey 4-2; M. Ferreira beat J. Fitzmaurice 4-1; T. Murphy beat C. Everton 4-2; H. Nimmo beat G. Thompson 4-3; D. Heaton beat B. Bennett 4-2; E. Hughes *wo* G. Scott *scr*
**First round:** N. Dagley beat M. Russell 4-0; Griffiths beat J. Karnehm 4-2; I. Williamson beat R. Close 4-2; Ferreira beat M. Wildman 4-2; R. Edmonds beat Hughes 4-0; E. Charlton beat Murphy 4-1; Nimmo beat F. Davis 4-2; R. Foldvari beat Heaton 4-0
**Quarter-finals:** Dagley beat Griffiths 4-1; Williamson beat Ferreira 4-2; Charlton beat Edmonds 4-3; Foldvari beat Nimmo 4-2
**Semi-finals:** Dagley beat Williamson 4-1; Charlton beat Foldvari 4-1
**Final:** Dagley beat Charlton 7-4

**1989**

**Qualifying Group A:** J. Karnehm beat E. Hughes 745-271; Karnehm beat J. Murphy 819-300; Hughes beat Murphy 553-531
**Qualifying Group B:** P. Gilchrist beat G. Thompson 966-535; G. Sethi beat J. Campbell 963-399; Campbell beat Thompson 507-452; Sethi beat Gilchrist 792-754; Sethi beat Thompson 1377-446; Gilchrist beat Campbell 627-392
**Qualifying Group C:** H. Griffiths beat P. Burke 678-298; C. Everton beat S. Naisby 505-253; Naisby beat Burke 773-282; Griffiths beat Everton 416-404; Everton beat Burke 482-215; Naisby beat Griffiths 717-338
**First round:** N. Dagley beat H. Nimmo 1422-866; B. Close beat Sethi 1477-984; M. Russell beat Griffiths 2108-826; I. Williamson beat M. Ferreira 999-998; R. Edmonds beat Karnehm 1209-973; E. Charlton beat Naisby 889-844; Gilchrist beat M. Wildman 1493-851; Hughes beat R. Foldvari 990-932
**Quarter-finals:** Dagley beat Close 1547-893; Russell beat Williamson 1155-857; Charlton beat Edmonds 1143-766; Gilchrist beat Hughes 1577-874
**Semi-finals:** Russell beat Dagley 1685-1001; Gilchrist beat Charlton 1336-743
**Final:** Russell beat Gilchrist 2242-1347

## United Kingdom Professional Billiards Championship (1934–90)

**1934**

J. Davis beat T. Newman 18,745-18,301

**1935**

J. Davis beat T. Newman 21,733-19,919

**1936**

**First round:** W. Smith beat S. Lee 10,373-7,212
**Semi-finals:** T. Newman beat S. Smith 9,561-7,792; J. Davis beat W. Smith 10,965-9,566
**Final:** Davis beat Newman 21,710-19,790

**1937**

**First round:** S. Smith beat S. Lee 8,135-4,209
**Semi-finals:** T. Newman *wo* W. Smith *scr*; J. Davis beat S. Smith 12,046-8,516
**Final:** Davis beat Newman 22,601-18,321

**1938**

**Semi-finals:** T. Newman beat S. Smith 8,959-7,227; J. Davis beat S. Lee 15,238-6,048
**Final:** Davis beat Newman 20,933-19,542

**1946**

J. Barrie beat W. Leigh 8,972-6,782

**1950**

**First round:** J. Barrie beat S. Lee 7,645-5,593
**Semi-finals:** Barrie beat W. Smith 7,009-5,941; K. Kennerley *wo*
**Final:** Barrie beat Kennerley 9,046-5,069

**1951**

F. Davis beat K. Kennerley 8,120-6,011

**1979** (*Super Crystalate*)

**Quarter-finals:** J. Karnehm beat J. Dunning 2,041-760; R. Williams beat R. Edmonds 1,537-1,350; J. Barrie beat S. Davis 2,292-629; F. Davis beat B. Bennett 1,953-679
**Semi-finals:** Williams beat Karnehm 1,539-1,182; Barrie beat F. Davis 1,548-1,031
**Final:** Williams beat Barrie 2,952-2,116

**1980**

**First round:** S. Davis beat S. Hood 1,670-1,029; B. Bennett beat C. Ross 1,093-933
**Quarter-finals:** J. Barrie beat M. Wildman 2,001-815; J. Karnehm beat Kennerley 1,990-842; R. Edmonds beat Bennett 1,380-914; R. Williams beat S. Davis 1,871-862
**Semi-finals:** Karnehm beat Barrie 1,755-1,085; Williams beat Edmonds 2,159-789
**Final:** Karnehm beat Williams 2,518-2,423

**1981**

**Qualifying:** S. Davis beat N. Bennett 980-770; R. Edmonds beat G. Miles 1,881-473; J. Pulman beat K. Kennerley 1,078-879
**Quarter-finals:** J. Karnehm beat Edmonds 1,307-935; J. Barrie beat Pulman 1,743-509; R. Williams beat S. Davis 1,575-579; F. Davis beat M. Wildman 1,304-805
**Semi-finals:** Karnehm beat Barrie 1,338-074; Williams beat F. Davis 2,003-999
**Final:** Williams beat Karnehm 1,592-1,112

**1983**

**First round:** B. Bennett beat D. Greaves 750-280; C. Everton beat M. Darrington 750-177;

I. Williamson beat T. Murphy 750-625; R. Edmonds beat J. Fitzmaurice 750-505
**Quarter-finals:** Edmonds beat J. Karnehm 1,500-1,194; M. Wildman beat Everton 1,500-1,170; F. Davis beat Williamson 1,500-604; R. Williams beat Bennett 1,500-230
**Semi-finals:** Wildman beat Williams 1,500-1,272; F. Davis beat Edmonds 1,500-936
**Final:** Wildman beat Davis 1,500-1,032

**1987**

**First round:** C. Everton beat J. Fitzmaurice 2-1; H. Griffiths beat G. Thompson 2-1; B. Bennett beat D. Greaves 2-0
**Second round:** M. Wildman *wo* G. Miles *scr*; R. Close *wo* T. Jones *scr*; E. Hughes *wo* P. Francisco *scr*; R. Edmonds beat M. Darrington 3-0; N. Dagley *wo* J. Karnehm *scr*; I. Williamson beat Everton 3-1; F. Davis beat Griffiths 3-0; R. Foldvari beat Bennet 3-0
**Quarter-finals:** Wildman beat Close 3-1; Edmonds beat Hughes 3-2; Dagley beat Williamson 3-1; Foldvari beat Davis 3-2
**Semi-finals:** Edmonds beat Wildman 3-0; Dagley beat Foldvari 3-2
**Final:** Dagley beat Edmonds 3-1

**1988** (*Strachan*)

**Preliminary round:** C. Everton beat T. Murphy 4-2; M. Russell beat G. Scott 4-0; G. Cripsey beat H. Griffiths 4-2; H. Nimmo beat B. Bennett 4-0
**First round:** N. Dagley beat Everton 4-1; I. Williamson beat E. Hughes 4-0; E. Charlton beat G. Thompson 4-2; Russell beat M. Wildman 4-3; R. Close beat R. Edmonds 4-3; F. Davis beat Cripsey 4-0; Nimmo beat J. Karnehm 4-2; R. Foldvari beat M. Ferreira 4-1
**Quarter-finals:** Williamson beat Dagley 4-2; Russell beat Charlton 4-2; Close beat Davis 4-0; Foldvari beat Nimmo 4-0
**Semi-finals:** Williamson beat Russell 4-2; Foldvari beat Close 4-1
**Final:** Williamson beat Foldvari 7-3

**1988** (*Strachan*) (*Nov*)

**Qualifying:** C. Everton beat J. Dunning 4-0; P. Gilchrist beat B. Bennett 4-0
**First round:** I. Williamson beat F. Davis 4-1; R. Close beat H. Griffiths 4-0; M. Ferreira beat M. Wildman 4-2; Everton *wo* R. Edmonds *scr*; R. Foldvari beat G. Thompson 4-0; M. Russell beat H. Nimmo 4-0; Gilchrist beat E. Charlton 4-1; N. Dagley beat J. Karnehm 4-0
**Quarter-finals:** Close beat Williamson 4-0; Ferreira beat Everton 4-1; Russell beat Foldvari 4-1; Dagley beat Gilchrist 4-3
**Semi-finals:** Close beat Ferreira 4-1; Russell beat Dagley 4-0
**Final:** Russell beat Close 7-0

**1990**

**Preliminary round:** E. Hughes *wo* B. Bennett *scr*; G. Thompson beat G. Sethi 679-365; F. Davis beat J. Dunning 744-228; D. Edwards beat H. Griffiths 743-407; J. Murphy beat J. Karnehm 638-630
**First round:** M. Russell beat M. Wildman 679-511; E. Charlton beat Hughes 633-235; P. Gilchrist beat Thompson 640-487; C. Everton beat R. Foldvari 365-337; I. Williamson beat Davis 533-252; R. Edmonds beat H. Nimmo 673-463; B. Close beat Edwards 680-455; Murphy beat N. Dagley 693-531
**Quarter-finals:** Edmonds beat Williamson 457-390; Murphy beat Close 492-455; Gilchrist beat Everton 863-264; Russell beat Charlton 750-417
**Semi-finals:** Russell beat Gilchrist 1973-1014; Murphy beat Edmonds 1149-1073
**Final:** Russell beat Murphy 1478-1058

*Mike Russell*

# EUROPEAN BILLIARDS CHAMPIONSHIP

**1987**

**First round:** Robbie Foldvari (Australia) beat Clive Everton (Wales) 4-0; Mike Russell (England) beat Bob Close (England) 4-2; Jack Karnehm (England) beat Howard Griffiths (Wales) 4-1; Michael Ferreira (India) beat Ray Edmonds (England) 4-3; Norman Dagley (England) beat Graham Cripsey (England) 4-0; Ian Williamson (England) beat Eugene Hughes (Republic of Ireland) 4-3; Eddie Charlton (Australia) beat Bernard Bennett (England) 4-0; Mark Wildman (England) beat Geoff Thompson (England) 4-1
**Quarter-finals:** Foldvari beat Russell 4-1; Karnehm beat Ferreira 4-3; Dagley beat Williamson 4-2; Wildman beat Charlton 4-1
**Semi-finals:** Foldvari beat Karnehm 4-2; Dagley beat Wildman 4-2
**Final:** Dagley beat Foldvari 7-5

**1988**

**Group A:** M. Ferreira beat H. Nimmo 4-0; N. Dagley beat B. Close 4-1; Close beat Nimmo 4-1; Dagley beat Ferreira 4-1; Close beat Ferreira 4-1; Dagley beat Nimmo 4-1
**Group B:** I. Williamson beat C. Everton 4-0
**Group C:** G. Cripsey beat H. Griffiths 4-1; R. Edmonds beat Griffiths 4-0; Edmonds beat Cripsey 4-0
**Group D:** M. Russell beat G. Thompson 4-0; R. Foldvari beat J. Karnehm 4-2; Thompson beat Karnehm 4-2; Foldvari beat Russell 4-0; Russell beat Karnehm 4-0; Foldvari beat Thompson 4-1
**Semi-final Group A:** Close beat Williamson 4-3; Dagley beat Everton 4-3; Close beat Everton 4-1; Dagley beat Williamson 4-0; Dagley beat Close 4-2; Williamson beat Everton 4-0
**Semi-final Group B:** Foldvari beat Cripsey 4-0; Russell beat Edmonds 4-0; Edmonds beat Foldvari 4-3; Russell beat Cripsey 4-0; Edmonds beat Cripsey 4-0; Russell beat Foldvari 4-3
**Semi-finals:** Dagley beat Edmonds 4-1; Russell beat Close 4-3
**Final:** Russell beat Dagley 7-4

# YORKSHIRE BANK OPEN

**1988**

**Preliminary round:** H. Nimmo beat B. Bennett 4-0; H. Griffiths beat D. Heaton 4-0; C. Everton beat G. Cripsey 4-2; M. Russell *wo* G. Scott *scr*
**First round:** N. Dagley beat E. Hughes 4-1; R. Close beat F. Davis 4-3; Nimmo beat I. Williamson 4-3; M. Ferreira beat M. Wildman 4-3; R. Edmonds beat Griffiths 4-0; G. Thompson beat J. Karnehm 4-0; E. Charlton beat Everton 4-0; Russell beat R. Foldvari 4-2
**Quarter finals:** Dagley beat Close 4-1; Ferreira beat Nimmo 4-0; Edmonds beat Thompson 4-2; Russell beat Charlton 4-3
**Semi-finals:** Ferreira beat Dagley 4-2; Edmonds beat Russell 4-0
**Final:** Edmonds beat Ferreira 7-3

**1989**

**Qualifying:** T. Jones beat B. Bennett 4-1

**First round:** M. Russell beat H. Nimmo 4-0; I. Williamson beat H. Griffiths 4-0; N. Dagley beat M. Ferreira 4-1; P. Gilchrist beat R. Close 4-3; R. Foldvari beat J. Dunning 4-0; M. Wildman beat G. Thompson 4-0; R. Edmonds beat Jones 4-0; E. Charlton beat C. Everton 4-0
**Quarter-finals:** Gilchrist beat Edmonds 4-2; Williamson beat Wildman 4-1; Russell beat Foldvari 4-1; Dagley beat Charlton 4-1
**Semi-finals:** Williamson beat Gilchrist 4-2; Russell beat Dagley 4-1
**Final:** Russell beat Williamson 7-2

## BRITISH OPEN

*Two-and-a-half-hour matches except for final, five hours.*

**1989**
**Qualifying:** E. Hughes beat P. Burke 641-521; P. Gilchrist beat G. Thompson 784-495; J. Karnehm beat V. Potasnik 832-423; C. Everton beat J. Dunning 481-451; H. Griffiths *wo* T. Jones *scr*
**First round:** Gilchrist beat R. Edmonds 702-583; N. Dagley beat Hughes 756-541; Everton beat R. Foldvari 466-314; I. Williamson beat Griffiths 765-239; H. Nimmo beat M. Wildman 647-473; R. Close beat F. Davis 576-467; M. Russell beat Karnehm 888-726; M. Ferreira beat E. Charlton 716-461
**Quarter-finals:** Russell beat Williamson 709-549; Nimmo beat Everton 449-416; Gilchrist beat Ferreira 782-632; Close beat Dagley 622-561
**Semi-finals:** Gilchrist beat Nimmo 946-518; Russell beat Close 1,054-576
**Final:** Gilchrist beat Russell 1,489-974

**1989**
**Preliminary round:** C. Everton beat G. Cripsey 429-225; F. Davis beat B. Bennett 491-211; E. Hughes beat J. Dunning 664-646; J. Murphy *wo* J. Karnehm *scr*; S. Naisby beat H. Griffiths 908-264; G. Sethi beat G. Thompson 825-367
**First round:** N. Dagley beat H. Nimmo 615-368; Everton *wo* M. Ferreira *scr*; Davis beat R. Edmonds 493-409; Hughes beat R. Foldvari 400-390; I. Williamson beat Murphy 566-305; B. Close *wo* M. Wildman *scr*; P. Gilchrist beat Naisby 639-510; Sethi beat M. Russell 1073-557
**Quarter-finals:** Dagley beat Everton 685-332; Hughes beat Davis 638-473; Williamson beat Close 501-329; Gilchrist beat Sethi 650-423
**Semi-finals:** Gilchrist beat Williamson 935-827; Dagley beat Hughes 1505-903
**Final:** Gilchrist beat Dagley 1166-1008

## ROTHMANS WORLD MATCHPLAY CHAMPIONSHIP

**1989**
**Qualifying:** J. McLaughlin *wo* T. Jones *scr*
**First round:** N. Dagley beat H. Griffiths 4-0; J. Karnehm beat H. Nimmo 4-1; M. Wildman beat McLaughlin 4-1; M. Russell beat B. Bennett 4-0; I. Williamson beat C. Everton 4-1; R. Close beat J. Dunning 4-0; M. Ferreira beat P. Burke 4-0; R. Foldvari beat P. Gilchrist 4-0
**Quarter-finals:** Dagley beat Karnehm 4-0; Russell beat Wildman 4-1; Williamson beat Close 4-1; Ferreira beat Foldvari 4-1
**Semi-finals:** Russell beat Dagley 4-3; Williamson beat Ferreira 4-2
**Final:** Russell beat Williamson 6-1

## BILLIARDS PROFESSIONALS

Some snooker players also play billiards but some specialise in the three ball game. Two young Tees-siders, Mike Russell and Peter Gilchrist, contested the 1989 World Professional final in Leura, New South Wales with Russell winning 2242-1347. Russell also retained the Strachan UK title and Gilchrist retained the British Open title.

Norman Dagley, who won two world and fifteen English amateur titles before turning professional in 1984 (the first time he could envisage a significant financial return from professional billiards status), has won two world professional titles and one UK.

The European Championship, the Yorkshire Bank Open and the Rothmans World Matchplay Championship, all of which are held by Russell, were not played in the 1989–90 season.

The 1990 World Professional Championship was due to be played in Australia in August.

### RANKING LIST

All snooker members of the WPBSA are entitled to play in the WPBSA's billiards events. The WPBSA also has a number of billiards-only members who are entitled to play only in billiards events. These are: Bob Close (England), Norman Dagley (England), David Edwards (Wales), Michael Ferreira (India), Peter Gilchrist (England), Howard Griffiths (Wales), Jack Karnehm (England), John Murphy (England), Hugh Nimmo (Scotland), Mike Russell (England), Geet Sethi (India) and Geoff Thompson (England).

*Ranking List for the 1989–90 season with the World Championship still to be added:*

1. Mike Russell (31 pts); 2. Norman Dagley (22); 3. Ian Williamson (19); 4. Peter Gilchrist (16); 5. Bob Close (14); 6. Ray Edmonds (11); 7. Eddie Charlton (9); 8. Michael Ferreira (9); 9. Robby Foldvari (9); 10. Clive Everton (5); 11. Hugh Nimmo (5); 12. John Murphy (3); 13. Eugene Hughes (3); 14. Fred Davis (2); 15. Mark Wildman (2); 16 Geet Sethi (1); 17. Jack Karnehm (1); 18. Howard Griffiths (1); 19. Geoff Thompson (1); 20. Graham Cripsey (1).

# THE WOMEN'S GAME

Allison Fisher, 22, won the Women's World Championship for the third time by beating Ann-Marie Farren, the 1987 champion, 6-5 in a marathon final at Pontins, Brixham and regained the women's UK title by beating Stacey Hillyard 5-0 at the Willie Thorne Snooker Centre, Leicester. Fisher and Hillyard each won one Women's World Amateur title before all distinctions between professionals and amateurs were abolished in the women's game.

Fisher's career seems likely to blossom through signing a management contract with Barry Hearn, who manages Steve Davis, Jimmy White and other leading players. Hearn had, for two seasons, employed her as the warm-up act in his Matchroom League and supported the suggestion that she should be awarded membership of the World Professional Billiards and Snooker Association — and thus a place on the professional tournament circuit — as a special case. However, the package of proposals which included this suggestion was narrowly defeated.

Hillyard became the first woman to make a century in competition with 114 in the Bournemouth League in January 1985. Fisher and Kim Shaw have also made century breaks in competition and players like Farren, Karen Corr and Tessa Davidson have all emphasised improving standards at the top of the women's game.

Hearn has guaranteed £50,000 in prize money over the next five years for the Women's World Championship which he will stage, promote and offer to satellite television.

## WOMEN'S WORLD CHAMPIONSHIP

**1986**

**Last 16:** A. Fisher (England) beat L. Horsbrough (England) 3-0; G. Aplin (England) beat C. Wälch (England) 3-1; M. Fisher (England) beat S. Newbury (Wales) 3-0; A. Jones (England) beat S. Martin (Australia) 3-0; S. Hillyard (England) beat J. Dowen (England) 3-1; S. LeMaich (Canada) beat A. Davies (Wales) 3-1; K. Shaw (England) beat S. Sinanan (England) 3-1; M. Tart (England) beat H. Isitt (Wales) 3-0
**Quarter-finals:** A. Fisher beat Aplin 4-0; Jones beat M. Fisher 4-1; LeMaich beat Hillyard 4-3; Shaw beat Tart 4-0
**Semi-finals:** A. Fisher beat Jones 4-1; LeMaich beat Shaw 4-3
**Final:** A. Fisher beat LeMaich 5-0

**1987**

**Last 16:** A-M. Farren (England) beat A. Davies (Wales) 3-1; A. Jones (England) beat L. Horsburgh (England) 3-1; J. Banks (England) beat M. O'Driscoll (Republic of Ireland) 3-2; M. Fisher (England) beat R. Clements (England) 3-1; S. Hillyard (England) beat J. Heyhurst (England) 3-1; G. Aplin (England) beat J. Dowen (England) 3-0; K. Leech (England) beat M. Tart (England) 3-0; A. Fisher (England) beat L. Gordon (England) 3-0
**Quarter-finals:** Farren beat Jones 4-1; M. Fisher beat Banks 4-1; Hillyard beat Aplin 4-1; A. Fisher beat Leech 4-0
**Semi-finals:** Farren beat M. Fisher 4-0; Hillyard beat A. Fisher 4-3
**Final:** Farren beat Hillyard 5-1

**1988**

**Last 16:** A-M. Farren (England) beat T. Davidson (England) 4-3; K. Corr (England) beat M. O'Driscoll (Rep. of Ireland) 4-3; L. Gordon (England) beat J. Bedford (England) 4-0; M. Fisher (England) beat M. Brown (England) 4-0; S. Hillyard (England) beat A. Ratcliffe (England) 4-1; L. Horsburgh (England) beat K. Shaw (England) 4-3; L. Jones (Denmark) beat C. Walch (England) 4-1; A. Fisher (England) beat R. Abbot (England) 4-0
**Quarter-finals:** Farren beat Corr 4-0; M. Fisher beat Gordon 4-2; Hillyard beat Horsburgh 4-3; A. Fisher beat Jones 4-0
**Semi-finals:** Farren beat M. Fisher 5-4; A. Fisher beat Hillyard 5-0
**Final:** A. Fisher beat Farren 6-1

**1989**

**Last 16:** A. Fisher (England) beat S. Smith (England) 4-1; T. Davidson (England) beat K. Shaw (England) 4-2; K. Corr (England) beat A. Jones (England) 4-2; M. Fisher (England) beat D. Dale (Australia) 4-3; A-M. Farren (England) beat L. Gordon (England) 4-0; G. Aplin (England) beat M. Simmons (Australia) 4-1; L. Horsburgh (England) beat C. Walch (England) 4-3; S. Hillyard (England) beat M. O'Driscoll (Rep. of Ireland) 4-0
**Quarter-finals:** A. Fisher beat Davidson 4-0; Corr beat M. Fisher 4-1; Hillyard beat Horsburgh 4-2; Farren beat Aplin 4-3
**Semi-finals:** Fisher beat Corr 5-0; Farren beat Hillyard 5-3
**Final:** Fisher beat Farren 6-5

## TUBORG WOMEN'S UK CHAMPIONSHIP

**1987**

**Quarter-finals:** A. Fisher (England) beat M. Tart (England) 4-0; A-M. Farren (England) beat S. Hillyard (England) 4-3; G. Aplin (England) beat K. Shaw (England) 4-1; M. Fisher (England) beat R. Clements (England) 4-1
**Semi-finals:** A. Fisher beat Farren 4-0; M. Fisher beat Aplin 4-0
**Finals:** A. Fisher beat M. Fisher 5-1

**1988**

**Quarter-finals:** A-M. Farren (England) beat C. Walch (England) 4-3; S. Hillyard (England) beat L. Gordon (England) 4-0; J. Dowen (England) beat

M. Fisher (England) 4-3; A. Fisher (England) beat K. Corr (England) 4-0
**Semi-finals:** Hillyard beat Farren 4-1; A. Fisher beat Dowen 4-0
**Final:** A. Fisher beat Hillyard 5-2

**1989**
**Last 16:** S. Hillyard (England) beat S. Dick (Wales) 3-0; L. Horsburgh (England) beat L. Gordon (England) 3-0; K. Corr (England) beat J. Banks (England) 3-0; G. Aplin (England) beat M. O'Driscoll (Rep. of Ireland) 3-0; M. Fisher (England) beat G. Jones (England) 3-0; K. Shaw (England) beat J. Dowen (England) 3-0; T. Davidson (England) beat C. Walch (England) 3-0; A-M. Farren (England) beat R. Abbott (England) 3-2
**Quarter-finals:** Hillyard beat Horsburgh 4-0; Corr beat Aplin 4-2; Shaw beat Fisher 4-1; Davidson beat Farren 4-1
**Semi-finals:** Hillyard beat Corr 4-2; Davidson beat Shaw 4-1
**Final:** Davidson beat Hillyard 4-1

**1990**
**Last 16:** A. Fisher (England) beat G. Jones (England) 4-0; K. Shaw (England) beat C. Walch (England) 4-3; S. Dick (Wales) beat M. Fisher (England) 4-1; M. Tart (England) beat K. Corr (England) 4-1; A-M. Farren (England) beat J. Banks (England) 4-0; M. O'Driscoll (Rep. of Ireland) beat L. Horsburgh (England) 4-0; G. Aplin (England) beat L. Gordon (England) 4-1; S. Hillyard (England) beat S. Smith (England) 4-0
**Quarter-finals:** Fisher beat Shaw 4-0; Dick beat Tart 4-1; Farren beat O'Driscoll 4-0; Hillyard beat Aplin 4-0
**Semi-finals:** Fisher beat Dick 4-0; Hillyard beat Farren 4-3
**Final:** Fisher beat Hillyard 5-0

# THE AMATEUR GAME

## THE WORLD AMATEUR SNOOKER CHAMPIONSHIP

The English Amateur Billiards Championship is the oldest domestic amateur title. It was started in 1888 and was followed in 1916 by the English Amateur Snooker Championship. It was not until 1926 that the first World Amateur Billiards Championship, then called the British Empire Championship, was staged, and in 1963, the inaugural World Amateur Snocker Championship was held in Calcutta.

The two events then took place in alternate years until it was decided that from 1985 the snooker would become an annual event. For that first Championship in 1963 there were only five entries from four countries – England, Australia, India and Ceylon (now Sri Lanka). The 1987 Championship in Bangalore, India, attracted 47 players representing 26 countries – an indication of just how fast the game is developing all over the world.

Before India's Omprakesh Agrawal captured the title in Dublin, the event had been dominated by British players. Gary Owen (England) won it in 1963 and 1966 and another Englishman, David Taylor, in 1968. Jonathan Barron gave England their fourth title in 1970 and Ray Edmonds made it six in a row when he won both in 1972 and 1974.

Welshman Doug Mountjoy broke the stranglehold by taking the 1976 title and his fellow countryman Cliff Wilson won it in 1978 before England gave the Championship its youngest ever titleholder when Jimmy White won in 1980 at the age of 18. The title went back to Wales with Terry Parsons in 1982 and Parsons again reached the final in 1984 only to lose to Agrawal.

Each country affiliated to the International Billiards and Snooker Federation is entitled to send two competitors who are initially split into round robin groups with the quarter-finals onwards being knockout.

The biggest innovation in amateur snooker came in 1972 when the then world governing body, the Billiards and Snooker Control Council (now effectively the English body), lifted all restrictions on amateurs accepting prize-money or fees for exhibitions. This brought about a new breed of full-time amateur players who capitalise fully on a variety of privately organised tournaments which carry thousands of pounds in prize-money.

However, the money available in the 'amateur' game pales into insignificance when compared to the prosperity at the top of the professional game. Consequently, there is a high turnover of top amateurs who, as soon as they become eligible, join the professional ranks.

## World Amateur Snooker Championships

| | *Wins* | *For* | *Agst* |
|---|---|---|---|
| **1963** (*Calcutta*) | | | |
| G. Owen (England) | 4 | 23 | 7 |
| F. Harris (Australia) | 3 | 21 | 17 |
| M. J. M. Lafir (Ceylon) | 2 | 19 | 18 |
| T. Monteiro (India) | 1 | 14 | 19 |
| W. Jones (India) | 0 | 7 | 24 |
| **1966** (*Karachi*) | | | |
| G. Owen (England) | 5 | 30 | 7 |
| J. Spencer (England) | 4 | 26 | 14 |
| W. Barrie (Australia) | 3 | 23 | 22 |
| M. J. M. Lafir (Ceylon) | 2 | 22 | 20 |
| L. U. Demarco (Scotland) | 1 | 14 | 28 |
| H. Karim (Pakistan) | 0 | 6 | 30 |
| **1968** (*Sydney*) | | | |
| *Group A* | | | |
| David Taylor (England) | 4 | 24 | 13 |
| J. Van Rensberg (S. Africa) | 3 | 22 | 14 |
| H. Andrews (Australia) | 2 | 17 | 16 |
| T. Monteiro (India) | 1 | 17 | 22 |
| L. Napper (N. Zealand) | 0 | 9 | 24 |
| *Group B* | | | |
| M. Williams (Australia) | 3 | 22 | 14 |
| P. Morgan (Ireland) | 3 | 19 | 14 |
| M. J. M. Lafir (Ceylon) | 2 | 19 | 16 |
| S. Shroff (India) | 2 | 20 | 19 |
| R. Flutey (N. Zealand) | 0 | 7 | 24 |

*Play-offs*
*Semi-finals*: Williams beat Van Rensberg 8-7; David Taylor beat Morgan 8-3
*Final*: David Taylor beat Williams 8-7

| | *Wins* | *For* | *Agst* |
|---|---|---|---|
| **1970** (*Edinburgh*) | | | |
| *Group A* | | | |
| S. Hood (England) | 5 | 20 | 9 |
| P. Mifsud (Malta) | 4 | 22 | 11 |
| M. J. M. Lafir (Sri Lanka) | 4 | 20 | 16 |
| J. Phillips (Scotland) | 4 | 19 | 18 |
| D. Sneddon (Scotland) | 2 | 17 | 17 |
| L. Glozier (N. Zealand) | 2 | 10 | 21 |
| J. Clint (N. Ireland) | 0 | 8 | 24 |
| *Group B* | | | |
| J. Barron (England) | 5 | 21 | 13 |
| D. May (Wales) | 4 | 22 | 18 |
| S. Shroff (India) | 3 | 18 | 14 |
| E. Sinclair (Scotland) | 3 | 16 | 16 |
| J. Rogers (Ireland) | 3 | 16 | 19 |
| L. U. Demarco (Scotland) | 2 | 15 | 19 |

| | *Wins* | *For* | *Agst* |
|---|---|---|---|
| H. Andrews (Australia) | 1 | 13 | 22 |

*Final*: Barron beat Hood 11-7

**1972** (*Cardiff*)

| | *Wins* | *For* | *Agst* |
|---|---|---|---|
| *Group A* | | | |
| J. Van Rensberg (S. Africa) | 3 | 12 | 6 |
| K. Tristram (N. Zealand) | 1 | 8 | 8 |
| G. Thomas (Wales) | 1 | 6 | 8 |
| L. U. Demarco (Scotland) | 1 | 6 | 10 |
| *Group B* | | | |
| M. Francisco (S. Africa) | 3 | 15 | 5 |
| J. Barron (England) | 3 | 15 | 10 |
| A. Borg (Malta) | 2 | 12 | 11 |
| A. Lloyd (Wales) | 2 | 11 | 14 |
| T. Monteiro (India) | 0 | 3 | 16 |
| *Group C* | | | |
| P. Mifsud (Malta) | 4 | 16 | 5 |
| R. Edmonds (England) | 3 | 14 | 7 |
| J. Rogers (Ireland) | 2 | 8 | 8 |
| M. Berni (Wales) | 1 | 7 | 12 |
| B. Bennett (N. Zealand) | 0 | 3 | 16 |
| *Group D* | | | |
| A. Savur (India) | 2 | 10 | 6 |
| M. Williams (Australia) | 2 | 9 | 7 |
| D. Sneddon (Scotland) | 2 | 9 | 9 |
| D. May (Wales) | 0 | 6 | 12 |
| *Semi-final groups* | | | |
| *Group A* | | | |
| Barron | 3 | 12 | 4 |
| Savur | 2 | 10 | 8 |
| Tristram | 1 | 6 | 8 |
| Mifsud | 0 | 6 | 12 |
| *Group B* | | | |
| M. Francisco | 2 | 11 | 9 |
| Edmonds | 2 | 11 | 9 |
| Van Rensberg | 1 | 8 | 10 |
| Williams | 1 | 9 | 11 |

*Semi-finals*: Edmonds beat Barron 8-6; M. Francisco beat Savur 8-7(51, 72)

*Final*: Edmonds beat M. Francisco 11-10

**1974** (*Dublin*)

| | *Wins* | *For* | *Agst* |
|---|---|---|---|
| *Group A* | | | |
| R. Edmonds (England) | 7 | 31 | 11 |
| M. J. M. Lafir (Sri Lanka) | 6 | 30 | 19 |
| E. Sinclair (Scotland) | 6 | 28 | 21 |
| G. Thomas (Wales) | 4 | 24 | 22 |
| D. Sheehan (Ireland) | 4 | 25 | 24 |
| P. Donnelly (N. Ireland) | 3 | 21 | 28 |
| S. Shroff (India) | 3 | 16 | 26 |
| N. Stockman (N. Zealand) | 2 | 18 | 29 |
| J. Sklazeski (Canada) | 1 | 18 | 31 |

| | *Wins* | *For* | *Agst* |
|---|---|---|---|
| *Group B* | | | |
| A. Lloyd (Wales) | 8 | 32 | 14 |
| W. Hill (N. Zealand) | 5 | 26 | 21 |
| P. Burke (Ireland) | 4 | 26 | 20 |
| L. Condo (Australia) | 4 | 26 | 21 |
| A. Borg (Malta) | 4 | 27 | 23 |
| D. Sneddon (Scotland) | 4 | 23 | 21 |
| A. Savur (India) | 4 | 24 | 23 |
| R. Cowley (Isle of Man) | 3 | 16 | 27 |
| N. J. Rahim (Sri Lanka) | 0 | 2 | 32 |

*Quarter-finals*: Edmonds beat Condo 4(60)-3; Sinclair beat Hill 4-2; Burke beat Lafir 4-3; Thomas beat Lloyd 4-2
*Semi-finals*: Edmonds beat Sinclair 8(54)-4(79); Thomas beat Burke 8-2
*Final*: Edmonds beat Thomas 11-9

**1976** (*Johannesburg*)

| | | | |
|---|---|---|---|
| *Group A* | | | |
| D. Mountjoy (Wales) | 7 | 28 | 9 |
| J. Van Rensberg (S. Africa) | 5 | 24 | 16 |
| R. Edmonds (England) | 4 | 20 | 18 |
| N. Stockman (N. Zealand) | 4 | 21 | 19 |
| E. Sinclair (Scotland) | 4 | 21 | 21 |
| P. Burke (Ireland) | 2 | 17 | 25 |
| J. Van Niekerk (S. Africa) | 1 | 17 | 27 |
| P. Reynolds (Isle of Man) | 1 | 14 | 27 |
| *Group B* | | | |
| P. Mifsud (Malta) | 6 | 25 | 9 |
| S. Francisco (S. Africa) | 6 | 27 | 12 |
| T. Griffiths (Wales) | 5 | 23 | 14 |
| C. Ross (England) | 4 | 19 | 17 |
| R. Paquette (Canada) | 4 | 22 | 22 |
| E. Swaffield (N. Ireland) | 1 | 16 | 26 |
| L. Heywood (Australia) | 1 | 13 | 27 |
| L. Watson (Ireland) | 1 | 9 | 27 |
| *Group C* | | | |
| M. Francisco (S. Africa) | 6 | 27 | 12 |
| R. Atkins (Australia) | 6 | 25 | 12 |
| R. Andrewartha (England) | 5 | 25 | 14 |
| J. Clint (N. Ireland) | 4 | 17 | 18 |
| L. U. Demarco (Scotland) | 3 | 21 | 21 |
| B. Mikkelsen (Canada) | 3 | 19 | 22 |
| K. Tristram (N. Zealand) | 1 | 9 | 27 |
| R. Cowley (Isle of Man) | 0 | 11 | 28 |

*Elimination match*: Griffiths beat Andrewartha 4(51)-0
*Quarter-finals*: Mountjoy beat Atkins 5(80)-1; Van Rensberg beat Griffiths 5-3(52); S. Francisco beat M. Francisco 5-1; Mifsud beat Edmonds 5-1
*Semi-finals*: Mountjoy beat S. Francisco 8(51)-2; Mifsud beat Van Rensberg 8(50)-4
*Final*: Mountjoy beat Mifsud 11(62, 79)-1

| | Wins | For | Agst |
|---|---|---|---|
| **1978** (*Malta*) | | | |
| *Group A* | | | |
| K. Burles (Australia) | 6 | 26 | 10 |
| P. Mifsud (Malta) | 6 | 26 | 10 |
| J. Johnson (England) | 5 | 23 | 9 |
| J. Donnelly (Scotland) | 5 | 20 | 13 |
| D. McVeigh (N. Ireland) | 2 | 15 | 20 |
| P. Reynolds (Isle of Man) | 2 | 10 | 22 |
| V. Cremona (Malta) | 2 | 9 | 25 |
| M. Mohideen (Sri Lanka) | 0 | 8 | 28 |
| *Group B* | | | |
| A. Lloyd (Wales) | 6 | 26 | 12 |
| K. Stevens (Canada) | 5 | 23 | 16 |
| J. Grech (Malta) | 4 | 23 | 16 |
| E. Hughes (Ireland) | 4 | 23 | 21 |
| M. J. M. Lafir (Sri Lanka) | 3 | 19 | 20 |
| D. Meredith (N. Zealand) | 3 | 18 | 20 |
| S. Shroff (India) | 2 | 14 | 23 |
| L. McCann (N. Ireland) | 1 | 10 | 27 |
| *Group C* | | | |
| C. Wilson (Wales) | 8 | 32 | 10 |
| R. Paquette (Canada) | 5 | 24 | 14 |
| D. Kwok (N. Zealand) | 5 | 23 | 20 |
| A. Savur (India) | 5 | 26 | 22 |
| I. Williamson (England) | 3 | 22 | 24 |
| R. Atkins (Australia) | 3 | 21 | 24 |
| R. Miller (Scotland) | 3 | 18 | 24 |
| A. Borg (Malta) | 2 | 15 | 27 |
| C. Cooper (Isle of Man) | 2 | 13 | 29 |

*Elimination match*: Grech beat Kwok 4-0
*Quarter-finals*: Burles beat Paquette 5-4; Stevens beat Mifsud 5-0; Johnson beat Lloyd 5(72)-0; Wilson beat Grech 5-4
*Semi-finals*: Johnson beat Burles 8(85)-4; Wilson beat Stevens 8(64)-2(81)
*Final*: Wilson beat Johnson 11(87)-5(66)

| | Wins | For | Agst |
|---|---|---|---|
| **1980** (*Launceston*) | | | |
| *Group A* | | | |
| J. White (England) | 6 | 24 | 9 |
| A. Savur (India) | 4 | 20 | 11 |
| E. Hughes (Ireland) | 4 | 21 | 13 |
| J. Grech (Malta) | 3 | 19 | 18 |
| L. Adams (N. Zealand) | 3 | 15 | 18 |
| Loo Yap Long (Singapore) | 1 | 6 | 23 |
| R. Burke (N. Ireland) | 0 | 11 | 24 |
| *Group B* | | | |
| J. Giannaros (Australia) | 6 | 24 | 11 |
| S. Newbury (Wales) | 4 | 20 | 14 |
| R. Paquette (Canada) | 4 | 20 | 15 |
| D. Meredith (N. Zealand) | 4 | 20 | 16 |
| G. Parikh (India) | 2 | 17 | 18 |

| | *Wins* | *For* | *Agst* |
|---|---|---|---|
| S. Clarke (N. Ireland) | 1 | 10 | 22 |
| Lau Weng Yew (Singapore) | 0 | 8 | 24 |
| J. Bonner (Australia) | 4 | 17 | 17 |
| W. King (Australia) | 3 | 19 | 15 |
| E. McLaughlin (Scotland) | 3 | 16 | 16 |
| J. O'Boye (England) | 1 | 14 | 21 |
| S. Padayachi (Fiji) | 0 | 2 | 24 |
| *Group D* | | | |
| A. Lloyd (Wales) | 6 | 24 | 4 |
| J. Campbell (Australia) | 5 | 22 | 8 |
| D. Sheehan (Ireland) | 4 | 17 | 14 |
| M. Gibson (Scotland) | 3 | 16 | 20 |
| H. Boteju (Sri Lanka) | 2 | 16 | 20 |
| P. Reynolds (Isle of Man) | 1 | 11 | 23 |
| W. Barrie (Australia) | 0 | 7 | 24 |

*Quarter-finals*: Savur beat Lloyd 5(54)-3; Atkins beat Giannaros 5(53)-3(82); Mifsud beat Campbell 5(63)-3; White beat Newbury 5(70)-4
*Semi-finals*: Atkins beat Savur 8-6; White beat Mifsud 8(100)-6(83)
*Final*: White beat Atkins 11(80, 101)-2(60)

**1982** (*Calgary*)

*Group A*

| | Wins | For | Agst |
|---|---|---|---|
| J. Grech (Malta) | 6 | 28 | 13 |
| A. Kearney (Ireland) | 6 | 26 | 15 |
| D. O'Kane (N. Zealand) | 6 | 28 | 18 |
| B. McConnell (Canada) | 5 | 26 | 19 |
| P. Kippie (Scotland) | 5 | 23 | 16 |
| S. Habib (India) | 4 | 22 | 21 |
| V. Saengthong (Thailand) | 3 | 20 | 28 |
| Lui Yew Keong (Singapore) | 1 | 13 | 30 |
| J. A. Wahid (Sri Lanka) | 0 | 6 | 32 |
| *Group B* | | | |
| T. Parsons (Wales) | 7 | 31 | 7 |
| P. Browne (Ireland) | 7 | 31 | 12 |
| G. Kwok Kwan Shing (Hong Kong) | 7 | 28 | 12 |
| G. Parikh (India) | 5 | 27 | 21 |
| A. Thomson (Zimbabwe) | 4 | 17 | 23 |
| G. Kwok (N. Zealand) | 3 | 17 | 26 |
| H. Boteju (Sri Lanka) | 2 | 15 | 28 |
| W. Craig (Isle of Man) | 1 | 14 | 29 |
| T. Dada (Pakistan) | 0 | 10 | 32 |
| *Group C* | | | |
| J. Bear (Canada) | 7 | 30 | 12 |
| M. Bradley (England) | 7 | 30 | 12 |
| J. Jorgensen (Canada) | 6 | 25 | 17 |
| W. Mills (N. Ireland) | 5 | 26 | 17 |
| J. Giannaros (Australia) | 5 | 25 | 21 |
| P. Reynolds (Isle of Man) | 3 | 23 | 23 |
| Cheung Che-Ming (Hong Kong) | 2 | 17 | 25 |

| | *Wins* | *For* | *Agst* |
|---|---|---|---|
| E. Amro (Egypt) | 1 | 11 | 31 |
| V. Yassa (Sudan) | 0 | 3 | 32 |
| *Group D* | | | |
| W. Jones (Wales) | 6 | 27 | 13 |
| P. Mifsud (Malta) | 6 | 29 | 15 |
| W. King (Australia) | 6 | 29 | 17 |
| R. Chaperon (Canada) | 5 | 24 | 18 |
| D. Chalmers (England) | 5 | 25 | 24 |
| R. Lane (Scotland) | 3 | 23 | 23 |
| S. Pavis (N. Ireland) | 3 | 19 | 27 |
| Lau Weng Yew (Singapore) | 2 | 15 | 29 |
| S. Sherif (Egypt) | 0 | 7 | 32 |

*Quarter-finals*: W. Jones beat Kearney 5-1; Parsons beat Bradley 5(69, 54)-0; Grech beat Browne 5(55)-3; Bear beat Mifsud 5-2
*Semi-finals*: Parsons beat Jones 8(103, 87)-5(54); Bear beat Grech 8-7
*Final*: Parsons beat Bear 11(61, 58, 58)-8(57, 69)

**1984** (*Dublin*)

| | | | |
|---|---|---|---|
| *Group A* | | | |
| A. Micallef (Malta) | 9 | 38 | 16 |
| T. Parsons (Wales) | 8 | 37 | 11 |
| P. Ennis (Ireland) | 8 | 34 | 28 |
| V. Saengthong (Thailand) | 7 | 34 | 19 |
| J. Sigurossonn (Iceland) | 6 | 29 | 29 |
| T. Finstad (Canada) | 4 | 28 | 28 |
| B. Bjorkman (Sweden) | 4 | 26 | 27 |
| A. Thomson (Zimbabwe) | 3 | 24 | 34 |
| D. Feeney (U.S.A.) | 3 | 21 | 35 |
| K. Sirisoma (Sri Lanka) | 3 | 16 | 33 |
| L. Talman (Belgium) | 0 | 11 | 40 |
| *Group B* | | | |
| D. John (Wales) | 9 | 37 | 10 |
| T. Drago (Malta) | 8 | 35 | 15 |
| A. Robidou (Canada) | 8 | 36 | 20 |
| S. Simngam (Thailand) | 7 | 33 | 20 |
| J. Long (Ireland) | 6 | 30 | 24 |
| M. G. Jayaram (India) | 5 | 30 | 23 |
| A. Campbell (Australia) | 4 | 25 | 29 |
| J. McIntyre (N. Ireland) | 4 | 21 | 30 |
| R. Cowley (Isle of Man) | 3 | 20 | 30 |
| M. Sedupathi (Sri Lanka) | 1 | 6 | 36 |
| C. D'Avoine (Mauritius) | 0 | 3 | 40 |
| *Group C* | | | |
| G. Wilkinson (Australia) | 8 | 30 | 13 |
| J. Wright (England) | 7 | 27 | 14 |
| H. Haenga (N. Zealand) | 7 | 26 | 14 |
| H. Bakahati (Egypt) | 6 | 26 | 21 |
| M. Colquitt (Isle of Man) | 5 | 24 | 20 |
| S. Hendry (Scotland) | 5 | 23 | 22 |
| T. Kollins (U.S.A.) | 3 | 16 | 27 |

| | *Wins* | *For* | *Agst* |
|---|---|---|---|
| K. Friopjofssonn (Iceland) | 3 | 15 | 28 |
| H. Thwaites (Belgium) | 1 | 3 | 32 |
| Lui Yew Keong (Singapore) | *scr* | | |
| *Group D* | | | |
| C. Archer (England) | 9 | 32 | 15 |
| O. Agrawal (India) | 7 | 33 | 16 |
| D. Kwok (N. Zealand) | 5 | 27 | 21 |
| G. Kwok Kwan Shing (Hong Kong) | 5 | 26 | 23 |
| H. Morgan (N. Ireland) | 5 | 27 | 27 |
| J. Selby (Wales) | 4 | 24 | 23 |
| L. Yew (Singapore) | 3 | 25 | 28 |
| G. Carnegie (Scotland) | 3 | 22 | 32 |
| M. Hallgren (Sweden) | 2 | 17 | 32 |
| M. Sadek (Egypt) | 2 | 15 | 31 |

*Quarter-finals*: Agrawal beat John 5-4; Wright beat A. Micallef 5(69, 70)-1; Archer beat Drago 5-4; Parsons beat Wilkinson 5(66)-2

*Semi-finals*: Agrawal beat Wright 8(75)-5; Parsons beat Archer 8(58, 78, 52)-3

*Final*: Agrawal beat Parsons 11(69, 74, 62, 54)-7

**1985** (*Blackpool*)

| | | | |
|---|---|---|---|
| *Group A* | | | |
| P. Mifsud (Malta) | 8 | 37 | 16 |
| R. Marshall (England) | 7 | 33 | 21 |
| G. Lackenby (Australia) | 7 | 35 | 23 |
| S. Robertson (N. Zealand) | 7 | 33 | 24 |
| J. Long (Ireland) | 6 | 31 | 28 |
| A. Essam (Egypt) | 5 | 28 | 25 |
| K. Erwin (Ireland) | 5 | 28 | 27 |
| J. Allan (Scotland) | 5 | 27 | 29 |
| M. Lennoye (Belgium) | 3 | 22 | 35 |
| M. Hallgren (Sweden) | 2 | 23 | 32 |
| I. Adam (Mauritius) | 0 | 3 | 40 |
| *Group B* | | | |
| J. McNellan (Scotland) | 10 | 40 | 11 |
| T. Whitthread (England) | 8 | 34 | 11 |
| T. Saelim (Thailand) | 8 | 37 | 18 |
| D. Kwok (N. Zealand) | 6 | 28 | 22 |
| S. Sawant (India) | 6 | 28 | 22 |
| L. K. Guan (Singapore) | 5 | 25 | 27 |
| T. Dada (Pakistan) | 4 | 27 | 27 |
| A. Thomson (Zimbabwe) | 3 | 20 | 31 |
| H. Boteju (Sri Lanka) | 3 | 17 | 32 |
| P. Reynolds (Isle of Man) | 2 | 18 | 35 |
| P. Rivet (Mauritius) | 0 | 2 | 40 |
| *Group C* | | | |
| J. Grech (Malta) | 9 | 39 | 12 |
| D. John (Wales) | 8 | 37 | 14 |
| J. Bonner (Australia) | 8 | 35 | 20 |
| G. Kwok Kwan Shing (Hong Kong) | 7 | 35 | 22 |
| W. Pu-Ob-Orm (Thailand) | 6 | 29 | 23 |

| | Wins | For | Agst |
|---|---|---|---|
| M. Sobala (Canada) | 5 | 29 | 27 |
| L. A. Bux (Pakistan) | 5 | 24 | 28 |
| H. Bakhaty (Egypt) | 3 | 23 | 31 |
| K. Sirisoma (Sri Lanka) | 2 | 14 | 33 |
| H. Ramj (Kenya) | 1 | 13 | 37 |
| A. Agustsson (Iceland) | 1 | 10 | 38 |
| *Group D* | | | |
| M. Bennett (Wales) | 11 | 40 | 16 |
| G. Sethi (India) | 9 | 34 | 15 |
| A. Robidoux (Canada) | 8 | 34 | 22 |
| G. Burns (Ireland) | 8 | 30 | 23 |
| J. Wright (England) | 6 | 25 | 19 |
| S. Pavis (N. Ireland) | 5 | 28 | 27 |
| B. Bjorkman (Sweden) | 5 | 26 | 30 |
| M. Colquitt (Isle of Man) | 5 | 25 | 30 |
| K. Fridthjofsson (Iceland) | 3 | 14 | 32 |
| L. Nazarali (Kenya) | 3 | 15 | 34 |
| D. Barron (Zimbabwe) | 3 | 22 | 35 |

*Quarter-finals*: Marshall beat McNellan 5(50)-1; John beat Bennett 5(44, 37)-2(30); Mifsud beat Whitthread 5(32, 39, 39)-2; Grech beat Sethi 5(42, 59, 50)-2(41, 30)
*Semi-finals*: John beat Marshall 8(37, 30, 40, 30, 46, 40, 32, 31)-4; Mifsud beat Grech 8(41, 58, 35)-4(56, 82, 40)
*Final:* Mifsud beat John 11(68, 32, 34, 59, 31, 39)-6(31, 47, 31, 48)

**1986** (*New Zealand*)

| | Wins | For | Agst |
|---|---|---|---|
| *Group A* | | | |
| G. Burns (Ireland) | 9 | 36 | 15 |
| J. Griffiths (Wales) | 7 | 29 | 20 |
| B. Lui (Singapore) | 6 | 26 | 21 |
| A. Harris (England) | 6 | 31 | 22 |
| N. Nopachorn (Thailand) | 6 | 30 | 22 |
| P. Hawkes (Australia) | 4 | 27 | 23 |
| M. Lannoye (Belgium) | 3 | 23 | 26 |
| B. Bjorkman (Sweden) | 2 | 15 | 30 |
| P. De Groot (N. Zealand) | 1 | 19 | 33 |
| A. Thomson (Zimbabwe) | 1 | 11 | 35 |
| *Group B* | | | |
| K. Jones (Wales) | 7 | 29 | 9 |
| M. Colquitt (Isle of Man) | 6 | 24 | 12 |
| M. Haenga (N. Zealand) | 4 | 25 | 20 |
| L. Amir Bux (Pakistan) | 4 | 20 | 20 |
| G. Sethi (India) | 3 | 23 | 19 |
| C. Sewell (N. Ireland) | 3 | 20 | 19 |
| M. Raibin (Sri Lanka) | 1 | 10 | 24 |
| A. Verny (Mauritius) | 0 | 1 | 28 |
| *Group C* | | | |
| G. Grennan (England) | 9 | 36 | 17 |
| S. Sawant (India) | 6 | 31 | 15 |
| J. Allan (Scotland) | 5 | 28 | 22 |
| W. Pu-Ob-Orm (Thailand) | 5 | 26 | 22 |

| | *Wins* | *For* | *Agst* |
|---|---|---|---|
| K. Doherty (Rep. of Ireland) | 5 | 26 | 27 |
| R. Johansson (Sweden) | 4 | 23 | 27 |
| G. Natale (Canada) | 4 | 22 | 31 |
| G. Campbell (N. Ireland) | 3 | 23 | 31 |
| F. Chan (Hong Kong) | 2 | 23 | 33 |
| H. Bakhaty (Egypt) | 2 | 20 | 33 |
| *Group D* | | | |
| P. Mifsud (Malta) | 9 | 36 | 10 |
| B. Gollan (Canada) | 8 | 34 | 8 |
| G. Miller (Australia) | 6 | 29 | 17 |
| S. Leung (Hong Kong) | 5 | 25 | 19 |
| L. Weng Yew (Singapore) | 5 | 26 | 24 |
| T. Dada (Pakistan) | 3 | 20 | 28 |
| R. Young (N. Zealand) | 3 | 16 | 29 |
| L. Cameron (Scotland) | 2 | 15 | 29 |
| H. Boteju (Sri Lanka) | 2 | 14 | 34 |
| Y. Van Velthoven (Belgium) | 1 | 15 | 32 |

*Quarter-finals*: Grennan beat Griffiths 5(38, 91)-2(39, 88, 39, 48); Jones beat Gollan 5(64)-1; Burns beat Colquitt 5(60)-0; Mifsud beat Sawant 5(66, 81)-2
*Semi-finals*: Mifsud beat Burns 8(52, 56)-5(57, 60); Jones beat Grennan 8(37, 41, 51, 83, 40)-7(45, 38, 48, 36)
*Final*: Mifsud beat Jones 11(41, 55, 60, 34, 43, 42)-9(99, 57, 63, 45, 43, 44, 52, 45, 66)

**1987** (*Bangalore*)

| | | | |
|---|---|---|---|
| *Group A* | | | |
| J. Allan (Scotland) | 5 | 20 | 7 |
| P. Mifsud (Malta) | 4 | 19 | 6 |
| B. Bjorkman (Sweden) | 3 | 15 | 14 |
| B. Lui (Singapore) | 2 | 14 | 16 |
| R. Karaitiana (N.Z.) | 1 | 8 | 16 |
| S. Mahboob (Bangladesh) | 0 | 3 | 20 |
| *Group B* | | | |
| J. Wattana (Thailand) | 5 | 20 | 9 |
| J. White (Canada) | 3 | 17 | 14 |
| S. Tong (Hong Kong) | 3 | 14 | 13 |
| Y. Mirza (India) | 3 | 13 | 12 |
| M. Rowing (England) | 1 | 14 | 17 |
| M. Loon Hong (Malaysia) | 0 | 7 | 20 |
| *Group C* | | | |
| D. Morgan (Wales) | 5 | 20 | 3 |
| S. McClarey (N. Ireland) | 3 | 15 | 10 |
| S. Lannigan (England) | 3 | 15 | 10 |
| P. Su Liang (Malaysia) | 3 | 13 | 11 |
| M. Yousef (Pakistan) | 1 | 3 | 16 |
| *Group D* | | | |
| A. Robidoux (Canada) | 5 | 20 | 2 |
| J. Long (Rep. of Ireland) | 3 | 14 | 9 |
| F. Chan (Hong Kong) | 3 | 14 | 11 |
| H. Boteju (Sri Lanka) | 3 | 13 | 12 |
| P. Houke (Netherlands) | 1 | 10 | 16 |

| | Wins | For | Agst |
|---|---|---|---|
| *Group E* | | | |
| G. Sethi (India) | 4 | 19 | 11 |
| M. Henson (W. Germany) | 4 | 17 | 12 |
| K. Doherty (Rep. of Ireland) | 3 | 18 | 8 |
| R. Farebrother (Australia) | 3 | 13 | 12 |
| T. Dada (Pakistan) | 1 | 10 | 18 |
| A. Borg (Malta) | 0 | 4 | 20 |
| *Group F* | | | |
| J. Swail (N. Ireland) | 5 | 20 | 4 |
| P. Hawkes (Australia) | 4 | 17 | 8 |
| D. Barron (Zimbabwe) | 2 | 13 | 15 |
| S. Agrawal (India) | 2 | 13 | 16 |
| S. Lemmens (Belgium) | 1 | 8 | 14 |
| R. Ameen (Bangladesh) | 0 | 6 | 20 |
| *Group G* | | | |
| J. Grech (Malta) | 6 | 24 | 9 |
| B. L'Orange (Norway) | 4 | 22 | 13 |
| S. Nivison (Scotland) | 4 | 19 | 14 |
| J. Herbert (Wales) | 3 | 19 | 15 |
| Lim Koon Guan (Singapore) | 2 | 16 | 19 |
| A. A. Aziz (Egypt) | 2 | 10 | 17 |
| K. Hossen (Mauritius) | 0 | 1 | 24 |
| *Group H* | | | |
| U. Kaimuk (Thailand) | 5 | 20 | 5 |
| M. Lennoye (Belgium) | 3 | 14 | 14 |
| D. Meredith (N.Z.) | 2 | 15 | 14 |
| R. Dikstra (Netherlands) | 2 | 12 | 13 |
| P. Reynolds (Isle of Man) | 2 | 12 | 17 |
| K. Sirisoma (Sri Lanka) | 1 | 9 | 18 |

*Pre-quarter finals:* Darren Morgan beat B. L'Orange 5-0: 69(40)-45(34), 64(44)-30, 67(50)-28, 70(61)-2, 108(89)-0; J. Wattana beat M. Lennoye 5-3: 96(44, 39)-8, 13-71, 18-56, 72(52)-50, 72-15, 16-64(40), 86(45)-5, 68(50)-41; A. Robidoux beat M. Henson 5-1: 27-76(38), 49-34, 67(54)-61(36), 84(55)-10, 66(39)-41, 86(32)-36; J. Allan beat P. Hawkes 5-3: 45-72(32), 67-55, 31-88(38, 35), 40-62, 80(41)-38, 88(42)-29, 61-28, 88-31; P. Mifsud beat J. Swail 5-3: 0-102(102), 23-79(59), 73(36)-16, 55-18, 62-8, 63-64(42), 57-50, 60-19; G. Sethi beat J. White: 65(36)-17, 97(55)-5, 33-74(30, 31), 75(31, 36)-58(43), 77(36)-5, 24-67(32), 54-52; J. Grech beat S. McClarey 5-0: 66-28, 60(38)-22, 69(30, 33)-21, 56-24, 76(35, 32); U. Kaimuk beat J. Long 5-3: 13-73, 72(36)-30, 92(34)-17, 92(32)-28, 41-64, 8-82(65), 64-20, 65(37)-10

*Quarter-finals*: D. Morgan beat J. Wattana 5-3: 95(36, 35)-2, 67(37)-23, 20-114(71), 78(77)-0, 5-66(60), 29-76(60), 73-35, 84(80)-47(45); A. Robidoux beat J. Allan 5-4: 84(67)-34, 78(36)-14, 64(32)-42, 45-78(37), 1-74(67), 38-61, 13-93(68), 51-31, 63-34; G. Sethi beat P. Mifsud 5-4: 104(40)-48, 22-70(38), 89(48)-31, 61(33)-39, 8-71, 6-71(69), 75(58)-1, 7-61, 80(49)-42; J. Grech beat U. Kaimuk 5-4: 26-81(30), 71(31)-63, 63(40)-67(67), 84(32)-35, 69(40)-56, 9-90(71), 55-62, 84(31)-28, 59-56(44)

*Semi-finals*: D. Morgan beat A. Robidoux 8-5: 72(38)-14, 83(82)-43, 94(64)-8, 87(53)-24, 72(40)-9, 64(37)-49, 21-79(44, 35); 39-71(48), 47-86(56), 39(34)-75, 19-73(59), 102(69, 33)-23, 63-52(30); J. Grech beat G. Sethi 8-3: 72-29, 72-45(40), 46-71, 69-44(35), 71(63)-17, 26-86(60), 101(45, 56)-45(3); 116(86)-13, 6-58(36), 55-35, 70(31)-13

*Match for 3rd and 4th place*: A. Robidoux beat G. Sethi 4-1: 55-67, 136(81, 42)-0, 81(52)-46(38), 84(84)-5, 64(31, 33)-62
*Final:* D. Morgan beat J. Grech 11-4: 86(30)-11, 92(60)-28, 62(37)-51, 18-94(52), 89(68)-31, 73(42)-30, 98(90)-0; 22-71(50), 31-73(49), 69-29, 84(66)-15, 78(50)-20, 33-73(38), 84(39)-7, 73(40)-59

| | *Wins* | *For* | *Agst* |
|---|---|---|---|
| **1988** (*Sydney*) | | | |
| *Group A* | | | |
| J. Wattana (Thailand) | 5 | 20 | 2 |
| B. Gollan (Canada) | 4 | 19 | 9 |
| H. Bakhaty (Egypt) | 3 | 12 | 11 |
| Y. Merchant (India) | 2 | 13 | 12 |
| W. Braam (Netherlands) | 1 | 7 | 16 |
| M. Gutowski (W. Germany) | 0 | 0 | 20 |
| *Group B* | | | |
| B. Pinches (England) | 6 | 24 | 6 |
| M. Colquitt (Isle of Man) | 5 | 22 | 10 |
| N. O'Neill (N. Ireland) | 3 | 19 | 14 |
| F. Chan (Hong Kong) | 3 | 16 | 14 |
| B. Choo (Malaysia) | 3 | 15 | 14 |
| A. Helmy (Egypt) | 1 | 5 | 21 |
| Mahboob Syed (Bangladesh) | 0 | 2 | 24 |
| *Group C* | | | |
| P. Mifsud (Malta) | 4 | 19 | 6 |
| K. G. Lim (Singapore) | 4 | 18 | 7 |
| G. Burns (Rep. of Ireland) | 3 | 15 | 14 |
| D. Collins (Australia) | 2 | 10 | 13 |
| H. Boteju (Sri Lanka) | 2 | 11 | 15 |
| S. Hamdan (Brunei) | 0 | 2 | 20 |
| *Group D* | | | |
| J. Allan (Scotland) | 6 | 24 | 8 |
| J. Buckley (Rep. of Ireland) | 6 | 24 | 8 |
| B. Anderson (New Zealand) | 5 | 21 | 12 |
| M. Y. Mirad (Pakistan) | 4 | 20 | 14 |
| E. Van Der Linden (Belgium) | 3 | 19 | 26 |
| M. Mansoor (Sri Lanka) | 2 | 15 | 21 |
| S. Lal (Fiji) | 2 | 13 | 23 |
| H. H. J. Tengah (Brunei) | 0 | 1 | 28 |
| *Group E* | | | |
| J. Peplow (Malta) | 5 | 20 | 9 |
| N. Nopachorn (Thailand) | 3 | 16 | 10 |
| S. Robertson (New Zealand) | 3 | 17 | 11 |
| L. Weng Yew (Singapore) | 2 | 13 | 12 |
| A. Thomson (Zimbabwe) | 2 | 11 | 15 |
| A. Verny (Mauritius) | 0 | 0 | 20 |
| *Group F* | | | |
| P. Doran (N. Ireland) | 4 | 17 | 8 |
| B. L'Orange (Norway) | 4 | 19 | 11 |
| S. Gorski (Australia) | 3 | 16 | 11 |
| G. Sethi (India) | 3 | 16 | 12 |

| | *Wins* | *For* | *Agst* |
|---|---|---|---|
| D. Barron (Zimbabwe) | 1 | 8 | 18 |
| R. Ameen (Bangladesh) | 0 | 4 | 20 |
| *Group G* | | | |
| R. Jones (Wales) | 4 | 19 | 6 |
| S. Ventham (England) | 4 | 17 | 10 |
| J. Bonner (Australia) | 3 | 16 | 10 |
| R. Dikstra (Netherlands) | 3 | 13 | 10 |
| N. Bohling (Sweden) | 1 | 5 | 16 |
| D. Nanji (Fiji) | 0 | 2 | 20 |
| *Group H* | | | |
| P. Dawkins (Wales) | 5 | 23 | 10 |
| D. Henry (Scotland) | 4 | 21 | 10 |
| K. Kwok (Hong Kong) | 4 | 17 | 12 |
| J. Bear (Canada) | 4 | 18 | 16 |
| R. Johansson (Sweden) | 2 | 14 | 16 |
| M. Lannoye (Belgium) | 2 | 13 | 21 |
| H. Yoshida (Japan) | 0 | 3 | 24 |

*Pre-quarter-finals:* R. Jones beat B. L'Orange 5-0: 64-39, 57(31)-45, 69-37, 65-40, 56-37; D. Henry beat P. Mifsud 5-3: 54-23, 17-60(39), 91(33)-20, 20-85, 73(49)-26, 74(34)-28, 3-66(40), 69(44)-40(40); B. Gollan beat P. Doran 5-0: 54-46(40), 93(68)-16, 105(105)-0, 88(87)-31(31), 69(39)-11; J. Allan beat N. Nopachorn 5-2: 53-34, 34-49, 82(31, 52)-1, 80(39, 30)-5, 58-41, 22-62, 75(53)-5; J. Wattana beat M. Colquitt 5-0: 99(47)-17, 102(31, 40)-7, 100(46, 46)-29, 78(78)-17, 76(45, 30)-0; J. Peplow beat K. G. Lim 5-0: 67(42)-34, 82(65)-13, 60-30, 61-60, 56-35; P. Dawkins beat J. Buckley 5-1: 15-84, 52(31)-42, 62-51, 74(40)-18, 68(54)-36, 64(32)-5; B. Pinches beat S. Ventham 5-0: 64-54, 60-48, 68(55)-13, 71(35)-49(39), 69(60)-39

*Quarter-finals:* Pinches beat Gollan 5-0: 125(91, 33)-11, 80(54)-51(33), 74(32)-10, 66(42)-15, 123(107)-1; Peplow beat Dawkins 5-4: 82-28, 83(67)-48(32), 49-41, 36-77, 77(32)-20, 7-78, 30-75(52), 36-57, 91(67)-29; Henry beat Allan 5-1: 22-73, 70(34)-51, 79(50)-1, 74-14, 76(48)-1, 91(32)-47(34); Wattana beat Jones 5-0: 68-33, 62-24, 84(39)-18, 67(67)-19, 63(31)-52(30)

*Semi-finals:* Wattana beat Peplow 8-2: 107(77)-17, 70(49)-53(38), 34-68(35), 56-44, 49-60, 87-17, 81(49)-17, 64-38, 87(60)-21, 77(44)-0; Pinches beat Henry 8-5: 75-33, 61(60)-54(37), 0-99(50, 31), 66(37)-41, 10-76(52), 29-101(53, 40), 7-83(56), 64-46, 100(53, 47)-20, 75(34, 41)-53(53), 89(89)-19, 8-80, 85-19

*Final:* Wattana beat Pinches 11-8: 55-43, 47-65(31), 76-30, 67-54(31), 17-78(34, 32), 49-84(38), 71-48, 60(33)-74(61), 59-34, 22-77(56), 0-140(35, 105), 79-23, 143(78, 65)-0, 73(32)-40, 119(99)-1, 62-69(30), 99(69)-9, 15-95(41), 96(96)-0

**1989** (*Singapore*)

| | *Wins* | *For* | *Agst* |
|---|---|---|---|
| *Group A* | | | |
| J. Birch (England) | 7 | 28 | 3 |
| T. Chuchart (Thailand) | 6 | 24 | 9 |
| M. Colquitt (Isle of Man) | 5 | 25 | 12 |
| S. Jagtiani (India) | 3 | 19 | 20 |
| M. Sadek (Egypt) | 3 | 15 | 16 |
| S. Tulabing (Philippines) | 2 | 11 | 22 |
| S. Verbeck (Belgium) | 2 | 10 | 25 |
| Y. Shimura (Japan) | 0 | 3 | 28 |

| | Wins | For | Agst |
|---|---|---|---|
| *Group B* | | | |
| G. Natale (Canada) | 7 | 28 | 6 |
| P. Mifsud (Malta) | 6 | 27 | 11 |
| S. Robertson (New Zealand) | 4 | 21 | 11 |
| M. H. Raibin (Sri Lanka) | 4 | 18 | 21 |
| M. Drude (West Germany) | 3 | 21 | 18 |
| D. Barron (Zimbabwe) | 3 | 14 | 22 |
| R. Waweru (Kenya) | 1 | 9 | 24 |
| S. Padyachi (Fiji) | 0 | 7 | 28 |
| *Group C* | | | |
| K. Doherty (Rep. of Ireland) | 7 | 28 | 4 |
| A. Sharpe (N. Ireland) | 5 | 24 | 14 |
| K. Kwok (Hong Kong) | 5 | 20 | 11 |
| T. Dada (Pakistan) | 4 | 19 | 17 |
| L. K. Guan (Singapore) | 4 | 20 | 19 |
| G. Yoshida (Japan) | 2 | 13 | 23 |
| G. Hayward (New Zealand) | 1 | 16 | 24 |
| G. Lebret (France) | 0 | 0 | 28 |
| *Group D* | | | |
| N. Jones (Wales) | 5 | 21 | 13 |
| D. Clarke (England) | 4 | 19 | 9 |
| P. Houke (Netherlands) | 4 | 19 | 12 |
| R. Chew (Singapore) | 4 | 19 | 13 |
| M. Hallgren (Sweden) | 2 | 15 | 18 |
| A. Thomson (Zimbabwe) | 2 | 13 | 17 |
| A. Gonsalves (Bangladesh) | 0 | 0 | 24 |
| *Group E* | | | |
| F. Chan (Hong Kong) | 7 | 28 | 9 |
| P. Dawkins (Wales) | 5 | 23 | 12 |
| B. L'Orange (Norway) | 4 | 22 | 16 |
| T. Ang (Singapore) | 4 | 19 | 15 |
| B. Valdimarsson (Iceland) | 4 | 21 | 18 |
| M. McGuire (Isle of Man) | 3 | 17 | 19 |
| S. Lal (Fiji) | 1 | 10 | 24 |
| A. Hamdan (Dar es Salaam) | 0 | 1 | 28 |
| *Group F* | | | |
| T. Finstad (Canada) | 6 | 26 | 16 |
| A. O'Connor (Rep. of Ireland) | 5 | 25 | 14 |
| A. Borg (Malta) | 5 | 25 | 14 |
| H. Morgan (N. Ireland) | 5 | 23 | 16 |
| M. Yousuf (Pakistan) | 3 | 18 | 22 |
| H. Boteju (Sri Lanka) | 2 | 15 | 26 |
| H. Bakhaty (Egypt) | 1 | 15 | 26 |
| F. Yue (Malaysia) | 1 | 14 | 27 |
| *Group G* | | | |
| S. Gorski (Australia) | 6 | 24 | 10 |
| E. Henderson (Scotland) | 5 | 22 | 7 |
| M. Henson (West Germany) | 4 | 20 | 12 |
| U. Khaimuk (Thailand) | 3 | 16 | 14 |

| | *Wins* | *For* | *Agst* |
|---|---|---|---|
| Y. Van Velthoven (Belgium) | 2 | 17 | 16 |
| C. Jaunboccus (Mauritius) | 1 | 4 | 22 |
| H. B. Jafarudin (Dar es Salaam) | 0 | 2 | 24 |
| *Group H* | | | |
| M. Campbell (Scotland) | 6 | 24 | 8 |
| Y. Merchant (India) | 5 | 23 | 6 |
| S. Chong (Malaysia) | 4 | 21 | 12 |
| J. Erlingsson (Iceland) | 3 | 15 | 15 |
| B. Saxon (Australia) | 2 | 13 | 17 |
| S. Timol (Mauritius) | 1 | 4 | 24 |
| M. Syed (Bangladesh) | 0 | 3 | 24 |

*Pre-quarter-finals:* J. Birch beat A. Sharpe 5-4: 107-14, 86(39,38)-9, 38-65, 60(43)-65, 72-55, 72(43)-61, 37-71, 14-74(51), 67-65; G. Natale beat Y. Merchant 5-4: 58-53, 68-28, 47-77(42), 47-54, 62-34, 62-25, 38-57, 18-98(54), 63-54; T. Finstad beat D. Clarke 5-4: 72(30)-39, 35-70, 29-60, 9-84(34), 58(35)-40(32), 71-51, 9-80(35), 70(33,32)-15, 63-43; P. Dawkins beat S. Gorski 5-4: 55-26, 6-65, 71(34)-58(37), 43-73, 41-68, 91(86)-5, 54(31)-50, 23-75(57), 72-36; Ken Doherty beat A. O'Connor 5-2: 60(44)-51(31), 67-26, 45-61, 80-28, 8-94(42,37), 56-54, 63(41)-22; M. Campbell beat P. Mifsud 5-4: 75(32)-43, 73(35)-9, 12-82(56), 44(40)-68(32,36), 32-66(39), 70(30)-43, 71(31)-32, 40-68(38), 56-36; F. Chan beat E. Henderson 5-3: 55-36, 1-92, 6-80(49), 87(63)-7, 62-59, 92-41, 54-59(32), 70(46)-32; N. Jones beat T. Chuchart 5-3: 58-55, 67-0, 66(33)-27, 68-8, 36-74(43), 24-74(33), 39-60, 69(51)-27

*Quarter-finals:* Doherty beat Jones 5-0: 94(30)-31, 93-23, 100(42,36)-17, 75(43)-47, 64-39; Finstad beat Dawkins 5-2: 71(42)-67(49), 35-53, 92(77)-5, 45-73, 76(40)-55, 57(51)-49, 75(35,40)-52; Chan beat Campbell 5-2: 53-69(42), 9-84(51), 76(62)-8, 63(31)-59, 81(63)-5, 78(70)-26, 84-32; Birch beat Natale 5-2: 58-48, 73-14, 55(52)-63(32), 72(63)-37(36), 29-76(31), 71-20, 62-39

*Semi-finals:* Birch beat Finstad 8-1: 78(43)-48, 74(36)-20, 83(32,31)-26, 105(33)-53(45), 84(31,37)-44, 91(90)-15, 22-89(46), 112(63)-0, 91(39)-40(40); Doherty beat Chan 8-2: 39-69, 75(45)-25, 66-57, 60-34, 58-52, 40-67(64), 111(31,80)-4, 87-6, 84(77)-52, 67-66(37)

*Final:* Doherty beat Birch 11-2: 107(44,35)-10, 69-47(39), 99(52,42)-24, 79(68)-30, 76(36)-21, 58(32)-90(38), 74(31)-19, 6-84(63), 70(68)-24, 74(42)-30(30), 65(41)-47, 75(48)-41, 72(53)-29

## World Amateur Billiards Championships

| | *Won* | *Score (average)* | *Highest break* | *No of centuries* |
|---|---|---|---|---|
| **1926** (*London*) | | | | |
| J. Earlham (England) | 4 | 8,000 (25.6) | 282 | 18 |
| G. Shailer (Australia) | 3 | 7,394 (16.8) | 203 | 13 |
| M. Smith (Scotland) | 2 | 6,569 (12.7) | 130 | 4 |
| P. Rutledge (S. Africa) | 1 | 5,902 (12.5) | 142 | 2 |
| T. McCluney (N. Ireland) | 0 | 5,617 (11.9) | 144 | 4 |
| **1927** (*London*) | | | | |
| A. Prior (S. Africa) | 3 | 6,000 (16.6) | 184 | 9 |
| H. F. Coles (Wales) | 2 | 5,533 (12.2) | 164 | 2 |
| L. Steeples (England) | 1 | 5,506 (14.8) | 236 | 9 |
| M. Smith (Scotland) | 0 | 4,499 (12.6) | 158 | 1 |
| **1929** (*Johannesburg*) | | | | |
| L. Hayes (Australia) | 3 | 6,000 (15.5) | 136 | 6 |

| | *Won* | *Score (average)* | *Highest break* | *No of centuries* |
|---|---|---|---|---|
| A. Prior (S. Africa) | 2 | 5,512 (16.0) | 226 | 7 |
| H. F. Coles (England) | 1 | 5,592 (14.7) | 170 | 7 |
| P. Rutledge (S. Africa) | 0 | 2,882 (10.9) | 164 | 1 |
| **1931** (*Sydney*) | | | | |
| L. Steeples (England) | 4 | 8,000 (37.3) | 461 | 24 |
| S. Lee (England) | 3 | 7,126 (22.1) | 433 | 18 |
| L. Hayes (Australia) | 2 | 6,113 (15.3) | 167 | 6 |
| H. Goldsmith (Australia) | 1 | 4,995 (13.0) | 179 | 4 |
| W. Hackett (N. Zealand) | 0 | 3,549 (7.7) | 97 | 0 |
| **1933** (*London*) | | | | |
| S. Lee (England) | 4 | 12,402 (28.0) | 394 | 31 |
| T. Jones (Wales) | 3 | 9,883 (18.7) | 144 | 8 |
| A. Prior (S. Africa) | 2 | 9,113 (18.3) | 235 | 13 |
| M. Smith (Scotland) | 1 | 8,292 (17.5) | 166 | 5 |
| J. Blackburn (N. Ireland) | 0 | 6,362 (12.5) | 94 | 0 |
| **1935** (*London*) | | | | |
| H. F. Coles (England) | 4 | 13,665 (28.4) | 267 | 33 |
| J. McGhie (Scotland) | 3 | 9,359 (19.4) | 207 | 11 |
| I. Edwards (Wales) | 2 | 9,814 (18.1) | 196 | 11 |
| S. Fenning (Ireland) | 1 | 9,068 (17.4) | 161 | 6 |
| P. Deb (India) | 0 | 7,461 (13.1) | 123 | 5 |
| **1936** (*Johannesburg*) | | | | |
| R. Marshall (Australia) | 3 | 8,526 (22.0) | 248 | 24 |
| A. Prior (S. Africa) | 2 | 7,014 (17.7) | 197 | 11 |
| J. Thompson (England) | 1 | 7,705 (21.2) | 245 | 15 |
| A. Bowlly (S. Africa) | 0 | 4,548 (9.0) | 93 | 0 |
| *Three 2 hour sessions* | | | | |
| **1938** (*Melbourne*) | | | | |
| R. Marshall (Australia) | 6 | 17,626 (39.0) | 427 | 59 |
| K. Kennerley (England) | 5 | 14,528 (30.1) | 472 | 45 |
| T. Cleary (Australia) | 4 | 8,535 (19.7) | 322 | 17 |
| S. Moses (N. Zealand) | 2 | 6,727 (13.1) | 129 | 4 |
| M. M. Begg (India) | 2 | 6,685 (13.4) | 111 | 2 |
| A. Burke (S. Africa) | 1 | 5,993 (12.0) | 119 | 1 |
| A. Albertson (N. Zealand) | 1 | 5,805 (12.4) | 107 | 1 |
| **1951** (*London*) | | | | |
| R. Marshall (Australia) | 6 | 14,735 (38.1) | 423 | 42 |
| F. Edwards (England) | 5 | 13,459 (26.7) | 345 | 36 |
| T. Cleary (Australia) | 4 | 12,373 (25.5) | 330 | 31 |
| W. Ramage (Scotland) | 3 | 7,638 (19.1) | 151 | 8 |
| W. Pierce (Wales) | 2 | 6,029 (13.6) | 225 | 3 |
| W. Jones (India) | 1 | 7,202 (16.6) | 138 | 10 |
| E. Haslem (N. Ireland) | 0 | 5,896 (14.1) | 125 | 3 |
| **1952** (*Calcutta*) | | | | |
| L. Driffield (England) | 5 | 8,529 (34.5) | 278 | 31 |
| R. Marshall (Australia) | 3 | 9,237 (37.3) | 351 | 27 |
| C. Hirjee (India) | 3 | 7,701 (22.7) | 230 | 14 |

| | *Won* | *Score (average)* | *Highest break* | *No of centuries* |
|---|---|---|---|---|
| W. Ramage (Scotland) | 3 | 6,525 (20.8) | 211 | 10 |
| W. Jones (India) | 1 | 6,731 (23.3) | 253 | 6 |
| A. Yunoos (Burma) | 0 | 3,768 (11.0) | 79 | 0 |
| **1954** (*Sydney*) | | | | |
| T. Cleary (Australia) | 4 | 11,496 (33.5) | 682 | 35 |
| R. Marshall (Australia) | 3 | 11,488 (36.0) | 407 | 35 |
| F. Edwards (England) | 2 | 9,053 (24.7) | 328 | 26 |
| W. Jones (India) | 1 | 8,523 (20.5) | 209 | 17 |
| T. G. Rees (S. Africa) | 0 | 6,271 (16.9) | 207 | 6 |
| **1958** (*Calcutta*) | | | | |
| W. Jones (India) | 5 | 16,493 | 501 | 56 |
| L. Driffield (England) | 4 | 14,370 | 499 | 48 |
| T. Cleary (Australia) | 3 | 13,626 | 431 | 52 |
| C. Hirjee (India) | 2 | 12,853 | 226 | 38 |
| W. Asciak (Malta) | 1 | 6,329 | 154 | 7 |
| M. Hman (Burma) | 0 | 5,633 | 215 | 8 |
| **1960** (*Edinburgh*) | | | | |
| J. H. Beetham (England) | 7 | 9,351 | 277 | 29 |
| J. Long (Australia) | 6 | 10,634 | 353 | 26 |
| W. Jones (India) | 5 | 12,397 | 589 | 30 |
| M. Francisco (S. Africa) | 4 | 7,773 | 148 | 11 |
| W. Ramage (Scotland) | 3 | 7,938 | 283 | 12 |
| W. Asciak (Malta) | 2 | 8,408 | 194 | 11 |
| W. Dennison (N. Ireland) | 1 | 6,231 | 155 | 4 |
| A. Ramage (Scotland) | 0 | 5,706 | 101 | 2 |
| **1962** (*Perth*) | | | | |
| R. Marshall (Australia) | 5 | 12,367 (35.6) | 348 | 57 |
| W. Jones (India) | 5 | 10,805 (26.9) | 489 | 34 |
| T. Cleary (Australia) | 4 | 9,808 (27.0) | 315 | 27 |
| J. H. Beetham (England) | 3 | 7,626 (22.9) | 283 | 18 |
| S. Benajee (India) | 3 | 8,332 (17.2) | 219 | 9 |
| R. A. Karim (Pakistan) | 1 | 5,657 (11.9) | 130 | 3 |
| W. Harcourt (N. Zealand) | 0 | 5,623 (14.3) | 123 | 5 |
| *Play off:* Marshall beat Jones 3,623-2,891 | | | | |
| **1964** (*Pukekohe*) | | | | |
| W. Jones (India) | 9 | 16,628 (24.5) | 294 | 49 |
| J. Karnehm (England) | 8 | 12,953 (21.8) | 390 | 28 |
| M. Ferreira (India) | 7 | 13,345 (19.0) | 182 | 29 |
| M. Francisco (S. Africa) | 6 | 12,957 (22.0) | 518 | 38 |
| A. Nolan (England) | 5 | 12,126 (19.9) | 259 | 26 |
| T. Cleary (Australia) | 4 | 10,781 (13.9) | 241 | 19 |
| H. Robinson (N. Zealand) | 3 | 7,643 (10.5) | 85 | 0 |
| T. Yesberg (N. Zealand) | 2 | 7,528 (10.4) | 80 | 0 |
| M. Mavalwala (Pakistan) | 1 | 8,404 (11.3) | 174 | 1 |
| A. E. Redmond (S. Africa) | 0 | 6,914 (9.0) | 107 | 1 |
| **1967** (*Colombo*) | | | | |
| L. Driffield (England) | 8 | 13,556 (30.5) | 421 | 53 |
| M. J. M. Lafir (Ceylon) | 7 | 12,562 (18.4) | 218 | 31 |

| | *Won* | *Score (average)* | *Highest break* | *No of centuries* |
|---|---|---|---|---|
| M. Francisco (S. Africa) | 6 | 12,477 (20.4) | 301 | 32 |
| M. Ferreira (India) | 5 | 11,140 (19.5) | 507 | 22 |
| J. Long (Australia) | 4 | 11,068 (17.5) | 261 | 27 |
| T. Cleary (Australia) | 3 | 9,252 (11.6) | 322 | 15 |
| N. J. Rahim (Ceylon) | 2 | 6,895 (8.8) | 116 | 3 |
| M. S. M. Marzuq (Ceylon) | 1 | 7,153 (7.9) | 88 | 0 |
| F. Holz (N. Zealand) | 0 | 5,350 (7.1) | 68 | 0 |
| **1969** (*London*) | | | | |
| J. Karnehm (England) | 9 | 12,902 | 232 | 27 |
| M. Ferreira (India) | 7 | 14,115 | 629 | 34 |
| M. Francisco (S. Africa) | 7 | 13,760 | 335 | 35 |
| M. J. M. Lafir (Ceylon) | 7 | 12,934 | 296 | 28 |
| R. Marshall (Australia) | 6 | 13,033 | 216 | 33 |
| M. Wildman (England) | 6 | 11,739 | 274 | 22 |
| R. Oriel (Wales) | 5 | 13,306 | 297 | 30 |
| S. Mohan (India) | 5 | 13,407 | 219 | 24 |
| P. Mifsud (Malta) | 2 | 10,410 | 173 | 8 |
| A. Twohill (N. Zealand) | 1 | 10,016 | 146 | 12 |
| F. Holz (N. Zealand) | 0 | 6,061 | 65 | 0 |
| **1971** (*Malta*) | | | | |
| *Group A* | | | | |
| M. Francisco (S. Africa) | 4 | 6,450 | 321 | 15 |
| M. J. M. Lafir (Ceylon) | 3 | 4,757 | 233 | 4 |
| P. Mifsud (Malta) | 2 | 4,142 | 134 | 2 |
| D. Sneddon (Scotland) | 1 | 3,160 | 121 | 2 |
| L. Napper (N. Zealand) | 0 | 3,798 | 87 | 0 |
| *Group B* | | | | |
| S. Mohan (India) | 4 | 5,839 | 188 | 11 |
| N. Dagley (England) | 3 | 5,454 | 330 | 11 |
| M. Ferreira (India) | 2 | 4,423 | 227 | 4 |
| C. Everton (Wales) | 1 | 3,893 | 205 | 5 |
| W. Asciak (Malta) | 0 | 4,511 | 188 | 7 |
| *Play-offs:* | | | | |
| Dagley | 3 | 6,041 | 348 | 17 |
| M. Francisco | 2 | 3,981 | 353 | 11 |
| Mohan | 1 | 3,822 | 327 | 11 |
| Lafir | 0 | 2,514 | 211 | 5 |
| **1973** (*Bombay*) | | | | |
| M. J. M. Lafir (Sri Lanka) | 9 | 16,956 (34.1) | 859 | 43 |
| S. Mohan (India) | 7 | 17,016 (30.8) | 468 | 53 |
| M. Ferreira (India) | 7 | 15,639 (25.4) | 421 | 41 |
| P. Tarrant (Australia) | 6 | 13,200 (24.4) | 373 | 36 |
| C. Everton (Wales) | 5 | 9,921 (18.2) | 240 | 17 |
| A. Nolan (England) | 4 | 12,709 (20.8) | 265 | 31 |
| P. Mifsud (Malta) | 4 | 12,253 (18.8) | 203 | 23 |
| E. Simons (N. Zealand) | 2 | 8,521 (12.4) | 94 | 0 |
| B. Kirkness (N. Zealand) | 1 | 8,464 (13.5) | 195 | 7 |
| L. U. Demarco (Scotland) | 0 | 7,488 (10.4) | 87 | 0 |

| | *Won* | *Score (average)* | *Highest break* | *No of centuries* |
|---|---|---|---|---|
| **1975** (*Auckland*) | | | | |
| *Group A* | | | | |
| N. Dagley (England) | 5 | 9,257 | 477 | 24 |
| D. Sneddon (Scotland) | 4 | 6,272 | 124 | 4 |
| G. Parikh (India) | 3 | 6,471 | 197 | 16 |
| J. Reece (Australia) | 2 | 4,058 | 125 | 4 |
| H. Robinson (N. Zealand) | 1 | 4,529 | 123 | 2 |
| M. Shaharwardi (Sri Lanka) | 0 | 4,032 | 121 | 1 |
| *Group B* | | | | |
| M. Ferreira (India) | 5 | 9,022 | 411 | 26 |
| C. Everton (Wales) | 4 | 6,043 | 272 | 13 |
| R. Close (England) | 3 | 5,449 | 164 | 10 |
| T. Yesberg (N. Zealand) | 2 | 4,373 | 131 | 3 |
| J. Long (Australia) | 1 | 4,598 | 157 | 5 |
| B. Bennett (N. Zealand) | 0 | 3,684 | 95 | 0 |

*Play-offs*
*Semi-finals*: Dagley beat Everton 1,293(222)-775; Ferreira beat Sneddon 2,470(211)-681
*Final*: Dagley beat Ferreira 3,385(200, 228, 202, 314)-2,268(281)

| | *Won* | *Score (average)* | *Highest break* | *No of centuries* |
|---|---|---|---|---|
| **1977** (*Melbourne*) | | | | |
| *Group A* | | | | |
| N. Dagley (England) | 5 | 7,546 | 272 | 16 |
| C. Everton (Wales) | 4 | 4,962 | 170 | 7 |
| S. Aleem (India) | 3 | 7,028 | 263 | 11 |
| G. Ganim Sr (Australia) | 2 | 6,322 | 231 | 6 |
| H. Robinson (N. Zealand) | 1 | 4,133 | 93 | 0 |
| J. Nugent (Scotland) | 0 | 4,131 | 68 | 0 |
| *Group B* | | | | |
| M. Ferreira (India) | 5 | 12,554 | 519 | 33 |
| R. Close (England) | 4 | 7,252 | 207 | 15 |
| G. Ganim Jr (Australia) | 3 | 6,424 | 192 | 9 |
| T. Yesberg (N. Zealand) | 2 | 4,349 | 109 | 1 |
| W. Weerasinghe (Sri Lanka) | 1 | 4,364 | 97 | 0 |
| D. Pratt (Scotland) | 0 | 4,316 | 108 | 1 |

*Play-offs*
*Semi-finals*: Ferreira beat Everton 2,155-1,310; Close beat Dagley 1,912(234)-1,781(236)
*Final*: Ferreira beat Close 2,683-2,564(231)

| | *Won* | *Score (average)* | *Highest break* | *No of centuries* |
|---|---|---|---|---|
| **1979** (*Colombo*) | | | | |
| *Group A* | | | | |
| M. Ferreira (India) | 7 | 14,695 | 467 | 40 |
| M. J. M. Lafir (Sri Lanka) | 5 | 12,456 | 370 | 30 |
| K. Shirley (England) | 5 | 10,656 | 195 | 13 |
| W. Barrie (Australia) | 4 | 8,255 | 128 | 2 |
| B. Kirkness (N. Zealand) | 4 | 7,283 | 214 | 8 |
| H. Nimmo (Scotland) | 2 | 7,022 | 105 | 2 |
| M. S. U. Mohideen (Sri Lanka) | 1 | 6,408 | 76 | 0 |
| R. Lim Sin Foo (Singapore) | 0 | 6,433 | 97 | 0 |
| *Group B* | | | | |
| N. Dagley (England) | 6 | 12,539 | 466 | 39 |

| | Won | Score (average) | Highest break | No of centuries |
|---|---|---|---|---|
| P. Mifsud (Malta) | 6 | 12,193 | 325 | 31 |
| S. Agrawal (India) | 6 | 11,924 | 355 | 30 |
| G. Ganim Jr (Australia) | 3 | 8,486 | 267 | 15 |
| C. Everton (Wales) | 3 | 6,905 | 211 | 11 |
| W. A. J. Weerasinghe (Sri Lanka) | 3 | 7,883 | 202 | 7 |
| B. Bennett (N. Zealand) | 1 | 6,083 | 101 | 1 |
| E. Fisher (Canada) | 0 | 4,198 | 88 | 0 |

*Play-offs*
*Semi-finals*: Mifsud beat Ferreira 2,489(338, 285)-1,856; Dagley beat Lafir 2,694(266, 444, 289)-1,692(240)
*Final*: Mifsud beat Dagley 2,943(361)-2,152

**1981** (*New Delhi*)

*Group A*

| | Won | Score (average) | Highest break | No of centuries |
|---|---|---|---|---|
| N. Dagley (England) | 6 | 11,982 | 416 | 42 |
| S. Agrawal (India) | 5 | 12,967 | 384 | 39 |
| G. Ganim Jr (Australia) | 4 | 7,934 | 178 | 13 |
| A. K. B. Giles (N. Zealand) | 3 | 6,895 | 162 | 5 |
| D. Sneddon (Scotland) | 2 | 7,071 | 123 | 6 |
| J. W. H. Boteju (Sri Lanka) | 1 | 6,312 | 107 | 1 |
| A. A. Essam (Egypt) | 0 | 3,948 | 59 | – |

*Group B*

| | Won | Score (average) | Highest break | No of centuries |
|---|---|---|---|---|
| M. Ferreira (India) | 6 | 13,862 | 630 | 58 |
| L. A. Bux (Pakistan) | 5 | 8,712 | 257 | 21 |
| R. Close (England) | 3 | 7,161 | 217 | 15 |
| J. Grech (Malta) | 3 | 7,388 | 402 | 9 |
| D. Meredith (N. Zealand) | 3 | 6,507 | 154 | 7 |
| H. Roberts-Thomson (Australia) | 2 | 6,535 | 151 | 5 |
| S. M. Shahawardi (Sri Lanka) | 0 | 5,111 | 77 | – |

*Semi-finals*: Dagley beat Bux 2,890(229, 277, 218)-1,505(257); Ferreira beat Agrawal 3,272(213, 532, 327, 527, 630)-1,964(233, 253)
*Final*: Ferreira beat Dagley 2,725(208, 349, 245, 244)-2,631(223, 296, 281)

**1983** (*Malta*)

*Group A*

| | Won | Score (average) | Highest break | No of centuries |
|---|---|---|---|---|
| M. Ferreira (India) | 6 | | 463 | 31 |
| R. Foldvari (Australia) | 5 | | 302 | 30 |
| L. A. Bux (Pakistan) | 4 | | 177 | 9 |
| H. Nimmo (Scotland) | 3 | | 224 | 6 |
| D. Meredith (N. Zealand) | 2 | | 157 | 7 |
| H. Griffiths (Wales) | 1 | | 112 | 1 |
| A. Micallef (Malta) | 0 | | 122 | 6 |

*Group B*

| | Won | Score (average) | Highest break | No of centuries |
|---|---|---|---|---|
| S. Agrawal (India) | 5 | | 635 | 42 |
| N. Dagley (England) | 5 | | 368 | 30 |
| J. Grech (Malta) | 5 | | 286 | 31 |
| V. Ellul (Malta) | 2 | | 145 | 2 |
| R. Lim (Singapore) | 2 | | 96 | – |
| W. Loughan (N. Ireland) | 2 | | 198 | 5 |
| H. Boteju (Sri Lanka) | 0 | | 120 | 2 |

*Semi-finals*: Agrawal beat Foldvari 2,047(240, 503)-1,900(302, 225, 231); Ferreira beat Dagley 1,983(463)-1,919(258)
*Final*: Ferreira beat Agrawal 3,933(353, 398, 201, 254)-2,744(242, 212)

| | *Won* | *Score (average)* | *Highest break* | *No of centuries* |
|---|---|---|---|---|
| **1985** (*Malta*) | | | | |
| *Group A* | | | | |
| R. Marshall (Australia) | 7 | | 396* | |
| M. Ferreira (India) | 6 | | 341 | |
| L. A. Bux (Pakistan) | 5 | | 229 | |
| R. Robinson (N. Zealand) | 4 | | 100 | |
| D. Sneddon (Scotland) | 3 | | 190 | |
| T. Ward (England) | 2 | | 106 | |
| Lau Weng Yew (Singapore) | 1 | | 92 | |
| S. Clarke (N. Ireland) | 0 | | 101 | |
| *Group B* | | | | |
| G. Sethi (India) | 7 | | 604 | |
| S. Agrawal (India) | 6 | | 599 | |
| R. Close (England) | 5 | | 182 | |
| H. Nimmo (Scotland) | 3 | | 146 | |
| D. Meredith (N. Zealand) | 3 | | 263 | |
| K. Sirisoma (Sri Lanka) | 2 | | 118 | |
| F. Humphries | 1 | | 131 | |
| A. Micallef (Malta) | 1 | | 138 | |

**unfinished*

*Semi-finals*: Sethi beat Ferreira 2,513(201, 303)-2,379; Marshall beat Agrawal 2,782(300, 204)-1,872
*Final*: Sethi beat Marshall 3,809(546, 235, 348, 232, 257)-2,453(201)

| | *Won* | *Score (average)* | *Highest break* | *No of centuries* |
|---|---|---|---|---|
| **1987** (*Belfast*) | | | | |
| *Group A* | | | | |
| G. Sethi (India) | 8 | | 364 | 51 |
| D. Edwards (Wales) | 7 | | 215 | 19 |
| D. Elliott (Northern Ireland) | 6 | | 192 | 9 |
| T. Ward (England) | 5 | | 130 | 5 |
| B. Kirkness (New Zealand) | 4 | | 196 | 8 |
| D. Collins (Australia) | 3 | | 183 | 18 |
| J. McIntyre (Northern Ireland) | 2 | | 132 | 1 |
| M. Spoormans (Belgium) | 1 | | 77 | – |
| R. Brennan (Republic of Ireland) | 0 | | 88 | – |
| *Group B* | | | | |
| J. Grech (Malta) | 7 | | 447 | 43 |
| S. Agrawal (India) | 7 | | 491 | 50 |
| P. Gilchrist (England) | 7 | | 242 | 23 |
| D. Meredith (New Zealand) | 5 | | 243 | 21 |
| B. Kelly (Scotland) | 4 | | 218 | 1 |
| S. McClarey (Northern Ireland) | 3 | | 136 | 4 |
| J. Millen (Australia) | 2 | | 112 | 2 |
| T. Martin (Republic of Ireland) | 1 | | 95 | – |
| M. De Sutter (Belgium) | 0 | | 174 | 1 |

*Semi-finals:* Grech beat Edwards 2971(271, 236, 480)-1748(212); Sethi beat Agrawal 2959(242, 288, 366, 221)-2456
*Final:* Sethi beat Grech 4846(760, 206, 202, 224, 248, 460)-3256(200, 244, 360, 253, 358, 238)

## World Amateur Championship Records

**Snooker**

| | | |
|---|---|---|
| B. Gollan (Canada) | 135 | 1988 |

**Billiards**

| | | |
|---|---|---|
| T. Cleary (Australia) | 682 (2 pots) | 1954 |
| M. J. M. Lafir (Sri Lanka) | 859 (5 pots) | 1973 |
| M. Ferreira (India) | 467 (3 pots) | 1979 |

# NATIONAL AMATEUR CHAMPIONSHIPS

## ENGLAND

### Snooker

| | |
|---|---|
| **1916** | C. N. Jacques |
| **1917** | C. N. Jacques |
| **1918** | T. N. Palmer |
| **1919** | S. H. Fry |
| **1920** | A. R. Wisdom |
| **1921** | M. J. Vaughan |
| **1922** | J. McGlynn |
| **1923** | W. Coupe |
| **1924** | W. Coupe |
| **1925** | J. McGlynn |
| **1926** | W. Nash |
| **1927** | O. T. Jackson |
| **1928** | P. H. Matthews |
| **1929** | L. Steeples |
| **1930** | L. Steeples |
| **1931** | P. H. Matthews |
| **1932** | W. E. Bach |
| **1933** | E. Bedford |
| **1934** | C. H. Beavis |
| **1935** | C. H. Beavis |
| **1936** | P. H. Matthews |
| **1937** | K. Kennerley |
| **1938** | P. H. Matthews |
| **1939** | P. Bendon |
| **1940** | K. Kennerley |
| *1941–45* | *No contests* |
| **1946** | H. J. Pulman |
| **1947** | H. Morris |
| **1948** | S. Battye |
| **1949** | T. C. Gordon |
| **1950** | A. Nolan |
| **1951** | R. Williams |
| **1952** | C. Downey |
| **1953** | T. C. Gordon |
| **1954** | G. Thompson |
| **1955** | M. Parkin |
| **1956** | T. C. Gordon |
| **1957** | R. Gross |
| **1958** | M. Owen |
| **1959** | M. Owen |
| **1960** | R. Gross |
| **1961** | A. Barnett |
| **1962** | R. Gross |
| **1963** | G. Owen |
| **1964** | R. Reardon |
| **1965** | P. Houlihan |
| **1966** | J. Spencer |
| **1967** | M. Owen |
| **1968** | David Taylor |
| **1969** | R. Edmonds |
| **1970** | J. Barron |
| **1971** | J. Barron |
| **1972** | J. Barron |
| **1973** | M. Owen |
| **1974** | R. Edmonds |
| **1975** | S. Hood |
| **1976** | C. Ross |
| **1977** | T. Griffiths |
| **1978** | T. Griffiths |
| **1979** | J. White |
| **1980** | J. O'Boye |
| **1981** | V. Harris |
| **1982** | D. Chalmers |
| **1983** | T. Jones |
| **1984** | S. Longworth |
| **1985** | T. Whitthread |
| **1986** | A. Harris |
| **1987** | M. Rowing |
| **1988** | B. Pincher |
| **1989** | N. Bond |
| **1990** | J. Swail |

### Billiards

| | |
|---|---|
| **1888** | H. A. O. Lonsdale |
| | A. P. Gaskell |
| **1889** | A. P. Gaskell |
| | A. P. Gaskell |
| **1890** | A. P. Gaskell |
| | A. P. Gaskell |
| | W. D. Courtney |
| **1891** | W. D. Courtney |
| | A. P. Gaskell |
| **1892** | A. R. Wisdom |
| | S. S. Christey |
| **1893** | A. R. Wisdom |
| | S. H. Fry |
| | A. H. Vahid |
| **1894** | H. Mitchell |
| | W. T. Maughan |
| *1895* | *No contest* |
| **1896** | S. H. Fry |
| *1897–98* | *No contests* |
| **1899** | A. R. Wisdom |
| **1900** | S. H. Fry |
| **1901** | S. S. Christey |
| **1902** | A. W. T. Good |
| | A. W. T. Good |
| **1903** | A. R. Wisdom |
| | S. S. Christey |
| **1904** | W. A. Lovejoy |
| **1905** | A. W. T. Good |
| **1906** | E. C. Breed |
| **1907** | H. C. Virr |
| **1908** | H. C. Virr |
| **1909** | Major Fleming |
| **1910** | H. A. O Lonsdale |
| **1911** | H. C. Virr |
| **1912** | H. C. Virr |
| **1913** | H. C. Virr |
| **1914** | H. C. Virr |
| **1915** | A. W. T. Good |
| **1916** | S. H. Fry |
| **1917** | J. Graham-Symes |
| **1918** | J. Graham-Symes |
| **1919** | S. H. Fry |
| **1920** | S. H. Fry |
| **1921** | S. H. Fry |
| **1922** | J. Graham-Symes |
| **1923** | W. P. McLeod |
| **1924** | W. P. McLeod |
| **1925** | S. H. Fry |
| **1926** | J. Earlam |
| **1927** | L. Steeples |
| **1928** | A. Wardle |
| **1929** | H. F. E Coles |
| **1930** | L. Steeples |
| **1931** | S. Lee |
| **1932** | S. Lee |
| **1933** | S. Lee |
| **1934** | S. Lee |
| **1935** | H. F. E. Coles |
| **1936** | J. Thompson |
| **1937** | K. Kennerley |
| **1938** | K. Kennerley |
| **1939** | K. Kennerley |
| **1940** | K. Kennerley |

| | | | | | |
|---|---|---|---|---|---|
| *1941–45* | *No contests* | **1961** | J. H. Beetham | **1977** | R. Close |
| **1946** | M. Showman | **1962** | A. L. Driffield | **1978** | N. Dagley |
| **1947** | J. Thompson | **1963** | J. H. Beetham | **1979** | N. Dagley |
| **1948** | J. Thompson | **1964** | A. Nolan | **1980** | N. Dagley |
| **1949** | F. Edwards | **1965** | N. Dagley | **1981** | N. Dagley |
| **1950** | F. Edwards | **1966** | N. Dagley | **1982** | N. Dagley |
| **1951** | F. Edwards | **1967** | A. L. Driffield | **1983** | N. Dagley |
| **1952** | A. L. Driffield | **1968** | M. Wildman | **1984** | N. Dagley |
| **1953** | A. L. Driffield | **1969** | J. Karnehm | **1985** | R. Close |
| **1954** | A. L. Driffield | **1970** | N. Dagley | **1986** | K. Shirley |
| **1955** | F. Edwards | **1971** | N. Dagley | **1987** | D. Edwards |
| **1956** | F. Edwards | **1972** | N. Dagley | **1988** | P. Gilchrist |
| **1957** | A. L. Driffield | **1973** | N. Dagley | **1989** | D. Edwards |
| **1958** | A. L. Driffield | **1974** | N. Dagley | **1990** | M. Goodwill |
| **1959** | A. L. Driffield | **1975** | N. Dagley | | |
| **1960** | J. H. Beetham | **1976** | R. Close | | |

## NORTHERN IRELAND

### Snooker

| | | | | | |
|---|---|---|---|---|---|
| **1927** | G. Barron | **1950** | J. Bates | **1971** | S. Crothers |
| **1928** | J. Perry | **1951** | J. Stevenson | **1972** | P. Donnelly |
| **1929** | W. Lyttle | **1952** | J. Stevenson | **1973** | J. Clint |
| **1930** | J. Luney | **1953** | J. Stevenson | **1974** | P. Donnelly |
| **1931** | J. McNally | **1954** | W. Seeds | **1975** | J. Clint |
| **1932** | Capt. J. Ross | **1955** | J. Stevenson | **1976** | E. Swaffield |
| **1933** | J. French | **1956** | S. Brooks | **1977** | D. McVeigh |
| **1934** | Capt. J. Ross | **1957** | M. Gill | **1978** | D. McVeigh |
| **1935** | W. Agnew | **1958** | W. Agnew | **1979** | R. Burke |
| **1936** | W. Lowe | **1959** | W. Hanna | **1980** | S. Clarke |
| **1937** | J. Chambers | **1960** | M. Gill | **1981** | T. Murphy |
| **1938** | J. McNally | **1961** | D. Anderson | **1982** | S. Pavis |
| **1939** | J. McNally | **1962** | S. McMahon | **1983** | J. McLaughlin Jr |
| *1940* | *No contest* | **1963** | D. Anderson | **1984** | J. McLaughlin Jr |
| **1941** | J. McNally | **1964** | P. Morgan | **1985** | S. Pavis |
| *1942–44* | *No contests* | **1965** | M. Gill | **1986** | C. Sewell |
| **1945** | J. McNally | **1966** | S. Crothers | **1987** | S. McClarey |
| **1946** | J. McNally | **1967** | D. Anderson | **1988** | P. Doran |
| **1947** | J. Rea | **1968** | A. Higgins | **1989** | H. Morgan |
| **1948** | J. Bates | **1969** | D. Anderson | **1990** | K. McAlinden |
| **1949** | J. Bates | **1970** | J. Clint | | |

### Billiards

| | | | | | |
|---|---|---|---|---|---|
| **1925** | T. McCluney | **1948** | J. Bates | **1968** | D. Anderson |
| **1926** | T. McCluney | **1949** | J. Bates | **1969** | W. Loughan |
| **1927** | J. Sloan | **1950** | J. Bates | **1970** | S. Crothers |
| **1928** | A. Davison | **1951** | E. Haslem | **1971** | J. Bates |
| **1929** | J. Blackburn | **1952** | R. Taylor | *1972–73* | *No contests* |
| **1930** | J. Blackburn | **1953** | W. Scanlon | **1974** | P. Donnelly |
| **1931** | J. Blackburn | **1954** | W. Scanlon | **1975** | P. Donnelly |
| **1932** | W. Lowe | **1955** | D. Turley | **1976** | P. Donnelly |
| **1933** | W. Mills | **1956** | J. Stevenson | **1977** | T. Taylor |
| **1934** | W. Lowe | **1957** | W. Scanlon | **1978** | W. Loughan |
| **1935** | W. Morrison | **1958** | W. Hanna | **1979** | J. Bates |
| **1936** | J. Blackburn | **1959** | W. Hanna | **1980** | S. Clarke |
| **1937** | J. Blackburn | **1960** | W. Dennison | **1981** | W. Loughan |
| **1938** | W. Lowe | **1961** | R. Hanna | **1982** | P. Donnelly |
| **1939** | W. Lowe | **1962** | N. McQuay | **1983** | F. Clarke |
| *1940* | *No contest* | **1963** | W. Hanna | **1984** | D. Elliott |
| **1941** | E. Haslem | **1964** | D. Anderson / D. Turley | **1985** | S. Clarke |
| *1942–44* | *No contests* | | | **1986** | D. Elliott |
| **1945** | E. Haslem | **1965** | W. Ashe | **1987** | D. Elliott |
| **1946** | J. Holness | **1966** | D. Anderson | **1988** | D. Elliott |
| **1947** | J. Bates | **1967** | W. Loughan | **1989** | J. McIntyre |

## REPUBLIC OF IRELAND

### Snooker

|  |  |
|---|---|
| **1931** | J. Ayres |
| *1932* | *No contest* |
| **1933** | S. Fenning |
| *1934* | *No contest* |
| **1935** | S. Fenning |
| *1936* | *No contest* |
| **1937** | P. J. O'Connor |
| *1938–39* | *No contests* |
| **1940** | P. Merrigan |
| *1941* | *No contest* |
| **1942** | P. J. O'Connor |
| *1943* | *No contest* |
| **1944** | S. Fenning |
| *1945–46* | *No contests* |
| **1947** | C. Downey |
| **1948** | P. Merrigan |
| **1949** | S. Fenning |
| *1950–51* | *No contests* |
| **1952** | W. Brown |
| **1953** | S. Brooks |
| **1954** | S. Fenning |
| **1955** | S. Fenning |
| **1956** | W. Brown |
| **1957** | J. Connolly |
| **1958** | G. Gibson |
| *1959–60* | *No contests* |
| **1961** | W. Brown |
| **1962** | J. Weber |
| **1963** | J. Rogers |
| **1964** | J. Rogers |
| **1965** | W. Fields |
| **1966** | G. Hanway |
| **1967** | P. Morgan |
| **1968** | G. Hanway |
| **1969** | D. Dally |
| **1970** | D. Sheehan |
| **1971** | D. Sheehan |
| **1972** | J. Rogers |
| **1973** | F. Murphy |
| **1974** | P. Burke |
| **1975** | F. Nathan |
| **1976** | P. Burke |
| **1977** | J. Clusker |
| **1978** | E. Hughes |
| **1979** | E. Hughes |
| **1980** | D. Sheehan |
| **1981** | A. Kearney |
| **1982** | P. Browne |
| **1983** | J. Long |
| **1984** | P. Ennis |
| **1985** | G. Burns |
| **1986** | G. Burns |
| **1987** | K. Doherty |
| **1988** | J. Buckley |
| **1989** | K. Doherty |
| **1990** | S. O'Connor |

### Billiards

|  |  |
|---|---|
| **1931** | J. Ayres |
| *1932* | *No contest* |
| **1933** | J. Ayres |
| **1934** | S. Fenning |
| **1935** | S. Fenning |
| **1936** | S. Fenning |
| **1937** | T. O'Brien |
| *1938–41* | *No contests* |
| **1942** | S. Fenning |
| *1943* | *No contest* |
| **1944** | S. Fenning |
| *1945–47* | *No contests* |
| **1948** | W. Brown |
| **1949** | S. Fenning |
| *1950–51* | *No contests* |
| **1952** | M. Nolan |
| **1953** | D. Turley |
| **1954** | M. Nolan |
| **1955** | M. Nolan |
| **1956** | M. Nolan |
| **1957** | M. Nolan |
| **1958** | W. Dennison |
| *1959–60* | *No contests* |
| **1961** | K. Smyth |
| **1962** | K. Smyth |
| **1963** | J. Bates |
| **1964** | J. Bates |
| **1965** | L. Codd |
| **1966** | L. Codd |
| **1967** | P. Morgan |
| **1968** | P. Morgan |
| **1969** | J. Rogers |
| **1970** | L. Drennan |
| **1971** | L. Codd |
| **1972** | L. Codd |
| **1973** | T. Martin |
| **1974** | T. Doyle |
| **1975** | P. Fenelon |
| **1976** | J. Rogers |
| **1977** | E. Hughes |
| **1978** | E. Hughes |
| **1979** | L. Drennan |
| **1980** | P. Burke |
| **1981** | P. Burke |
| **1982** | D. Elliott |
| **1984** | A. Murphy |
| **1985** | A. Roche |
| **1987** | L. Drennan |

## SCOTLAND

### Snooker

|  |  |
|---|---|
| **1931** | G. Brown |
| *1932–45* | *No contests* |
| **1946** | J. Levey |
| **1947** | J. Levey |
| **1948** | I. Wexelstein |
| **1949** | W. Ramage |
| **1950** | W. Ramage |
| **1951** | A. Wilson |
| **1952** | D. Emerson |
| **1953** | P. Spence |
| **1954** | D. Edmond |
| **1955** | L. U. Demarco |
| **1956** | W. Barrie |
| **1957** | T. Paul |
| **1958** | J. Phillips |
| **1959** | J. Phillips |
| **1960** | E. Sinclair |
| **1961** | J. Phillips |
| **1962** | A. Kennedy |
| **1963** | E. Sinclair |
| **1964** | J. Phillips |
| **1965** | L. U. Demarco |
| **1966** | L. U. Demarco |
| **1967** | E. Sinclair |
| **1968** | E. Sinclair |
| **1969** | A. Kennedy |
| **1970** | D. Sneddon |
| **1971** | J. Phillips |
| **1972** | D. Sneddon |
| **1973** | E. Sinclair |
| **1974** | D. Sneddon |
| **1975** | E. Sinclair |
| **1976** | E. Sinclair |
| **1977** | R. Miller |
| **1978** | J. Donnelly |
| **1979** | S. Nivison |
| **1980** | M. Gibson |
| **1981** | R. Lane |
| **1982** | P. Kippie |
| **1983** | G. Carnegie |
| **1984** | S. Hendry |
| **1985** | S. Hendry |
| **1986** | S. Muir |
| **1987** | S. Nivison |
| **1988** | D. Henry |
| **1989** | M. Campbell |
| **1990** | A. McManus |

### Billiards

|  |  |
|---|---|
| **1913** | Capt. Croneen |
| *1914–21* | *No contests* |
| **1922** | H. L. Fleming |
| **1923** | M. Smith |
| *1924* | *No contest* |
| **1925** | W. D. Greenlees |
| **1926** | M. Smith |
| **1927** | M. Smith |

| | |
|---|---|
| **1928** | M. Smith |
| **1929** | J. McGhee |
| **1930** | M. Smith |
| **1933** | A. Ramage |
| **1934** | N. Canney |
| **1935** | H. King |
| **1936** | N. Canney |
| **1937** | J. McGhee |
| **1938** | J. McGhee |
| *1939* | *No contest* |
| **1940** | W. McCann |
| *1941–45* | *No contests* |
| **1946** | J. Levey |
| **1947** | A. Ramage |
| **1948** | W. Ramage |
| **1949** | W. Ramage |
| **1950** | A. Ramage |
| **1951** | W. Ramage |
| **1952** | J. Murray |
| **1953** | J. Bates |
| **1954** | J. Bates |
| **1955** | W. Ramage |
| **1956** | W. Ramage |
| **1957** | W. Ramage |
| **1958** | W. Ramage |
| **1959** | W. Ramage |
| **1960** | A. Ramage |
| **1961** | P. Spence |
| **1962** | W. Ramage |
| **1963** | W. Ramage |
| **1964** | W. Ramage |
| **1965** | W. Ramage |
| **1966** | W. Ramage |
| **1967** | W. Ramage |
| **1968** | A. Kennedy |
| **1969** | A. Kennedy |
| **1970** | D. Sneddon |
| **1971** | D. Sneddon |
| **1972** | L. U. Demarco |
| **1973** | D. Sneddon |
| **1974** | D. Sneddon |
| **1975** | D. Sneddon |
| **1976** | D. Sneddon |
| **1977** | J. Nugent |
| **1978** | D. Sneddon |
| **1979** | H. Nimmo |
| **1980** | D. Sneddon |
| **1981** | D. Sneddon |
| **1982** | W. Kelly |
| **1983** | H. Nimmo |
| **1984** | D. Sneddon |
| **1987** | W. Kelly |

## WALES

### Snooker

| | |
|---|---|
| **1930** | T. Jones |
| **1931** | T. Jones |
| **1932** | T. Jones |
| **1933** | T. Jones |
| **1934** | T. Jones |
| **1935** | T. Jones |
| **1936** | T. Jones |
| **1937** | G. Howells |
| **1938** | B. Gravenor |
| **1939** | W. E. James |
| *1940–46* | *No contests* |
| **1947** | T. Jones |
| **1948** | R. Smith |
| **1949** | A. J. Ford |
| **1950** | R. Reardon |
| **1951** | R. Reardon |
| **1952** | R. Reardon |
| **1953** | R. Reardon |
| **1954** | R. Reardon |
| **1955** | R. Reardon |
| **1956** | C. Wilson |
| **1957** | R. D. Meredith |
| **1958** | A. Kemp |
| **1959** | J. R. Price |
| **1960** | L. Luker |
| **1961** | T. Parsons |
| **1962** | A. J. Ford |
| **1963** | R. D. Meredith |
| **1964** | M. L. Berni |
| **1965** | T. Parsons |
| **1966** | L. L. O'Neill |
| **1967** | L. L. O'Neill |
| **1968** | D. Mountjoy |
| **1969** | T. Parsons |
| **1970** | D. T. May |
| **1971** | D. T. May |
| **1972** | G. Thomas |
| **1973** | A. Lloyd |
| **1974** | A. Lloyd |
| **1975** | T. Griffiths |
| **1976** | D. Mountjoy |
| **1977** | C. Wilson |
| **1978** | A. Lloyd |
| **1979** | C. Wilson |
| **1980** | S. Newbury |
| **1981** | C. Roscoe |
| **1982** | T. Parsons |
| **1983** | W. Jones |
| **1984** | T. Parsons |
| **1985** | M. Bennett |
| **1986** | K. Jones |
| **1987** | D. Morgan |
| **1988** | P. Dawkins |
| **1989** | P. Dawkins |

### Billiards

| | |
|---|---|
| **1920** | H. F. E. Coles |
| **1921** | H. F. E. Coles |
| **1922** | H. F. E. Coles |
| **1923** | H. F. E. Coles |
| **1924** | H. F. E. Coles |
| **1925** | Unknown |
| **1926** | Unknown |
| **1927** | Unknown |
| **1928** | G. Moore |
| **1929** | J. Tregoning |
| **1930** | Unknown |
| **1931** | L. Prosser |
| **1932** | T. Jones |
| **1933** | T. Jones |
| **1934** | Unknown |
| **1935** | I. Edwards |
| **1936** | J. Tregoning |
| **1937** | B. Gravenor |
| **1938** | J. Tregoning |
| **1939** | B. Gravenor |
| *1940–45* | *No contests* |
| **1946** | T. G. Rees |
| **1947** | T. C. Morse |
| **1948** | J. Tregoning |
| **1949** | I. Edwards |
| **1950** | W. Pierce |
| **1951** | W. Pierce |
| **1952** | J. Tregoning |
| **1953** | B. Sainsbury |
| **1954** | R. Smith |
| **1955** | J. Tregoning |
| **1956** | A. J. Ford |
| **1957** | R. Smith |
| **1958** | R. W. Oriel |
| **1959** | A. J. Ford |
| **1960** | C. Everton |
| **1961** | R. W. Oriel |
| **1962** | R. W. Oriel |
| **1963** | R. W. Oriel |
| **1964** | R. W. Oriel |
| **1965** | R. W. Oriel |
| **1966** | R. W. Oriel |
| **1967** | R. W. Oriel |
| **1968** | D. E. Edwards |
| **1969** | R. W. Oriel |
| **1970** | R. W. Oriel |
| **1971** | R. W. Oriel |
| **1972** | C. Everton |
| **1973** | C. Everton |
| **1974** | R. W. Oriel |
| **1975** | R. W. Oriel |
| **1976** | C. Everton |
| **1977** | C. Everton |
| **1978** | R. W. Oriel |
| **1979** | R. W. Oriel |
| | *No further contests* |

# AUSTRALIA

## Snooker

|  |  |
|---|---|
| **1953** | W. Simpson |
| **1954** | W. Simpson |
| **1955** | E. Pickett |
| **1956** | R. Marshall |
| **1957** | W. Simpson |
| **1958** | F. Harris |
| **1959** | K. Burles |
| **1960** | K. Burles |
| **1961** | M. Williams |
| **1962** | W. Barrie |
| **1963** | F. Harris |
| **1964** | W. Barrie |
| **1965** | W. Barrie |
| **1966** | M. Williams |
| **1967** | M. Williams |
| **1968** | M. Williams |
| **1969** | W. Barrie |
| **1970** | M. Williams |
| **1971** | M. Williams |
| **1972** | M. Williams |
| **1973** | M. Williams |
| **1974** | L. Condo |
| **1975** | R. Atkins |
| **1976** | R. Atkins |
| **1977** | R. Atkins |
| **1978** | K. Burles |
| **1979** | J. Campbell |
| **1980** | W. King |
| **1981** | W. King |
| **1982** | J. Giannaros |
| **1983** | G. Lackenby |
| **1984** | G. Wilkinson |
| **1985** | J. Bonner |
| **1986** | G. Miller |
| **1987** | P. Hawkes |
| **1988** | J. Bonner |
| **1989** | S. Gorski |

## Billiards

|  |  |
|---|---|
| **1913** | G. B. Shailer |
| *1914–19* | *No contests* |
| **1920** | J. R. Hooper |
| **1921** | G. B. Shailer |
| **1922** | G. B. Shailer |
| **1923** | G. B. Shailer |
| **1924** | E. Eccles |
| **1925** | G. B. Shailer |
| **1926** | L. W. Hayes |
| **1927** | L. W. Hayes |
| **1928** | L. W. Hayes |
| **1929** | A. H. Hearndon |
| **1930** | S. Ryan |
| **1931** | H. L. Goldsmith |
| **1932** | A. Sakzewski |
| **1933** | L. W. Hayes |
| **1934** | L. W. Hayes |
| **1935** | L. W. Hayes |
| **1936** | R. Marshall |
| **1937** | R. Marshall |
| **1938** | R. Marshall |
| **1939** | R. Marshall |
| *1940–45* | *No contests* |
| **1946** | R. Marshall |
| **1947** | T. Cleary |
| **1948** | R. Marshall |
| **1949** | R. Marshall |
| **1950** | T. Cleary |
| **1951** | R. Marshall |
| **1952** | R. Marshall |
| **1953** | R. Marshall |
| **1954** | R. Marshall |
| **1955** | R. Marshall |
| **1956** | J. Long |
| **1957** | R. Marshall |
| **1958** | T. Cleary |
| **1959** | R. Marshall |
| **1960** | J. Long |
| **1961** | R. Marshall |
| **1962** | R. Marshall |
| **1963** | R. Marshall |
| **1964** | J. Long |
| **1965** | T. Cleary |
| **1966** | T. Cleary |
| **1967** | J. Long |
| **1968** | J. Long |
| **1969** | R. Marshall |
| **1970** | R. Marshall |
| **1971** | M. Williams |
| **1972** | P. Tarrant |
| **1973** | P. Tarrant |
| **1974** | J. Reece |
| **1975** | J. Long |
| **1976** | G. Ganim Jr |
| **1977** | G. Ganim Jr |
| **1978** | G. Ganim Jr |
| **1979** | G. Ganim Jr |
| **1980** | G. Ganim Jr |
| **1981** | G. Ganim Jr |
| **1982** | R. Foldvari |
| **1983** | R. Foldvari |
| **1984** | F. Humphreys |
| **1985** | R. Marshall |
| **1986** | R. Marshall |
| **1987** | P. Tarrant |
| **1988** | P. Tarrant |
| **1989** | P. Tarrant |

# CANADA

## Snooker

|  |  |
|---|---|
| **1979** | J. Wych |
| **1980** | Jim Bear |
| **1981** | R. Chaperon |
| **1983** | A. Robidoux |
| **1984** | T. Finstad |
| **1985** | A. Robidoux |

## Billiards

|  |  |
|---|---|
| **1979** | E. Fisher |
| **1980** | S. Holden |
| **1981** | R. Chaperon |
| **1982** | R. Chaperon |

# INDIA

## Snooker

|  |  |
|---|---|
| **1939** | P. K. Deb |
| **1940** | P. K. Deb |
| **1941** | V. R. Freer |
| **1942** | P. K. Deb |
| *1943–45* | *No contests* |
| **1946** | T. A. Selvaraj |
| **1947** | T. Sadler |
| **1948** | W. Jones |
| **1949** | T. A. Selvaraj |
| **1950** | F. Edwards (Eng) |
| **1951** | T. A. Selvaraj |
| **1952** | W. Jones |
| **1953** | A. L. Driffield (Eng) |
| **1954** | W. Jones |
| **1955** | T. A. Selvaraj |
| **1956** | M. J. M. Lafir |
| **1957** | M. J. M. Lafir |
| **1958** | W. Jones |
| **1959** | M. J. M. Lafir |
| **1960** | W. Jones |
| **1961** | M. J. M. Lafir |
| **1962** | R. Marshall (Aust) |
| **1963** | M. J. M. Lafir |
| **1964** | S. Shroff |
| **1965** | S. Shroff |
| **1966** | T. Monteiro |
| **1967** | S. Shroff |
| **1968** | S. Mohan |
| **1969** | S. Shroff |
| **1970** | S. Shroff |
| **1971** | T. Monteiro |
| **1972** | S. Shroff |
| **1973** | S. Shroff |
| **1974** | M. J. M. Lafir |
| **1975** | M. J. M. Lafir |
| **1976** | A. Savur |
| **1977** | M. J. M. Lafir |
| **1978** | A. Savur |
| **1979** | A. Savur |
| **1980** | J. White (Eng) |
| **1981** | G. Parikh |
| **1984** | G. Sethi |
| **1985** | G. Sethi |
| **1986** | G. Sethi |
| **1987** | G. Sethi |
| **1988** | G. Sethi |

## Billiards

| | | | | | |
|---|---|---|---|---|---|
| **1935** | P. K. Deb | **1955** | W. Jones | **1973** | S. Mohan |
| **1936** | P. K. Deb | **1956** | C. Hirjee | **1974** | M. Ferreira |
| **1937** | M. M. Begg | **1957** | W. Jones | **1975** | G. C. Parikh |
| **1938** | P. K. Deb | **1958** | C. Hirjee | **1976** | M. Ferreira |
| **1939** | P. K. Deb | **1959** | T. Cleary (Aust) | **1977** | M. J. M. Lafir |
| **1940** | S. H. Lyth | **1960** | W. Jones | **1978** | M. Ferreira |
| **1941** | V. R. Freer | **1961** | W. Jones | **1979** | M. Ferreira |
| **1942** | V. R. Freer | **1962** | R. Marshall (Aust) | **1980** | M. Ferreira |
| *1943–45* | *No contests* | **1963** | W. Jones | **1981** | G. Sethi |
| **1946** | C. Hirjee | **1964** | W. Jones | **1982** | M. Ferreira |
| **1947** | C. Hirjee | **1965** | W. Jones | **1983** | S. Agrawal |
| **1948** | V. R. Freer | **1966** | W. Jones | **1984** | G. Sethi |
| **1949** | T. A. Selvaraj | **1967** | A. Savur | **1985** | M. Ferreira |
| **1950** | W. Jones | **1968** | S. Mohan | **1986** | G. Sethi |
| **1951** | W. Jones | **1969** | M. Ferreira | **1987** | G. Sethi |
| **1952** | W. Jones | **1970** | S. Mohan | **1988** | G. Sethi |
| **1953** | L. Driffield (Eng) | **1971** | S. Mohan | | |
| **1954** | W. Jones | **1972** | S. Mohan | | |

# MALTA

## Snooker

| | | | | | |
|---|---|---|---|---|---|
| **1947** | L. Galea | **1961** | A. Borg | **1975** | P. Mifsud |
| **1948** | T. B. Oliver | **1962** | A. Borg | **1976** | P. Mifsud |
| **1949** | L. Galea | **1963** | M. Tonna | **1977** | A. Borg |
| **1950** | W. Asciak | **1964** | A. Borg | **1978** | P. Mifsud |
| **1951** | W. Asciak | **1965** | A. Borg | **1979** | P. Mifsud |
| **1952** | A. Borg | **1966** | A. Borg | **1980** | J. Grech |
| **1953** | A. Borg | **1967** | A. Borg | **1981** | J. Grech |
| **1954** | W. Asciak | **1968** | P. Mifsud | **1982** | P. Mifsud |
| **1955** | A. Borg | **1969** | P. Mifsud | **1983** | P. Mifsud |
| **1956** | W. Asciak | **1970** | P. Mifsud | **1984** | T. Drago |
| **1957** | W. Asciak | **1971** | P. Mifsud | **1985** | P. Mifsud |
| **1958** | W. Asciak | **1972** | P. Mifsud | **1988** | P. Mifsud |
| **1959** | A. Borg | **1973** | A. Borg | | |
| **1960** | A. Borg | **1974** | A. Borg | | |

## Billiards

| | | | | | |
|---|---|---|---|---|---|
| **1947** | V. Micallef | **1959** | A. Asciak | **1972** | W. Asciak |
| *1948* | *No contests* | **1960** | A. Asciak | **1973** | P. Mifsud |
| **1949** | E. Bartolo | **1961** | A. Borg | **1974** | P. Mifsud |
| **1950** | W. Asciak | **1962** | J. Bartolo | **1975** | P. Mifsud |
| **1951** | W. Asciak | **1963** | J. Bartolo | **1976** | P. Mifsud |
| **1952** | W. Asciak | **1964** | W. Asciak | **1977** | P. Mifsud |
| **1953** | W. Asciak | **1965** | A. Asciak | **1978** | J. Grech |
| **1954** | W. Asciak | **1966** | A. Asciak | **1979** | P. Mifsud |
| **1955** | W. Asciak | **1967** | A. Asciak | **1980** | J. Grech |
| **1956** | W. Asciak | **1969** | P. Mifsud | *1981* | *No contest* |
| **1957** | W. Asciak | **1970** | W. Asciak | **1982** | V. Ellul |
| **1958** | A. Asciak | **1971** | P. Mifsud | **1983** | J. Grech |

# NEW ZEALAND

## Snooker

| | | | | | |
|---|---|---|---|---|---|
| **1945** | S. Moses | **1958** | W. Harcourt | **1971** | B. J. Bennett |
| **1946** | J. Munro | **1959** | W. Thomas | **1972** | N. Stockman |
| **1947** | W. Thompson | **1960** | T. Yesberg | **1973** | W. Hill |
| **1948** | L. Stout | **1961** | F. Franks | **1974** | K. Tristram |
| **1949** | L. Stout | **1962** | K. Murphy | **1975** | K. Tristram |
| **1950** | L. Stout | **1963** | W. Harcourt | **1976** | D. Kwok |
| **1951** | N. Lewis | **1964** | T. Yesberg | **1977** | D. Meredith |
| **1952** | L. Stout | **1965** | L. Napper | **1978** | D. Meredith |
| **1953** | L. Stout | **1966** | L. Napper | **1979** | D. Meredith |
| **1954** | R. Franks | **1967** | R. Flutey | **1980** | D. O'Kane |
| **1955** | L. Stout | **1968** | L. Napper | **1981** | D. Kwok |
| **1956** | L. Stout | **1969** | L. Glozier | **1982** | D. Kwok |
| **1957** | W. Harcourt | **1970** | K. Tristram | **1983** | D. Kwok |

| | |
|---|---|
| **1984** | D. Kwok |
| **1985** | P. de Groot |
| **1986** | D. Meredith |
| **1987** | S. Robertson |
| **1988** | S. Robertson |
| **1989** | S. Robertson |

## Billiards

| | |
|---|---|
| **1908** | J. Ryan |
| *1909* | *No contests* |
| **1910** | F. Lovelock |
| **1911** | F. Lovelock |
| **1912** | H. Valentine |
| **1913** | H. Valentine |
| **1914** | N. Lynch |
| **1915** | W. E. Warren |
| **1916** | H. Siedeberg |
| **1917** | H. Siedeberg |
| **1918** | W. E. Warren |
| **1919** | H. Siedeberg |
| **1920** | W. E. Warren |
| **1921** | H. Siedeberg |
| **1922** | E. V. Roberts |
| **1923** | E. V. Roberts |
| **1924** | R. Fredotovich |
| **1925** | C. Mason |
| **1926** | E. V. Roberts |
| **1927** | E. V. Roberts |
| **1928** | A. Bowie |
| **1929** | L. Stout |
| **1930** | W. E. Hackett |
| **1931** | A. Duncan |
| **1932** | C. Mason |
| **1933** | A. Albertson |
| **1934** | H. McLean |
| **1935** | L. Holdsworth |
| **1936** | S. Moses |
| **1937** | S. Moses |
| **1938** | L. Holdsworth |
| **1939** | R. Carrick |
| **1940** | S. Moses |
| **1941** | R. Carrick |
| **1942** | R. Carrick |
| **1943** | A. Albertson |
| **1944** | S. Moses |
| **1945** | J. Shepherd |
| **1946** | R. Carrick |
| **1947** | C. Peek |
| **1948** | R. Carrick |
| **1949** | R. Carrick |
| **1950** | R. Carrick |
| **1951** | R. Carrick |
| **1952** | L. Stout |
| **1953** | A. Twohill |
| **1954** | A. Twohill |
| **1955** | A. Twohill |
| **1956** | A. Twohill |
| **1957** | A. Twohill |
| **1958** | A. Albertson |
| **1959** | A. Twohill |
| **1960** | W. Harcourt |
| **1961** | A. Albertson |
| **1962** | W. Harcourt |
| **1963** | H. C. Robinson |
| **1964** | T. Yesberg |
| **1965** | L. Napper |
| **1966** | A. Twohill |
| **1967** | A. Twohill |
| **1968** | A. Twohill |
| **1969** | E. Simmons |
| **1970** | L. Napper |
| **1971** | W. Harcourt |
| **1972** | B. Kirkness |
| **1973** | H. C. Robinson |
| **1974** | H. C. Robinson |
| **1975** | T. Yesberg |
| **1976** | H. C. Robinson |
| **1977** | B. Kirkness |
| **1978** | B. Kirkness |
| **1979** | R. Adams |
| **1980** | D. Meredith |
| **1981** | D. Meredith |
| **1982** | D. Meredith |
| **1983** | D. Meredith |
| **1984** | D. Meredith |
| **1985** | D. Meredith |
| **1986** | B. Kirkness |
| **1987** | D. Meredith |
| **1988** | K. Giles |
| **1989** | D. Meredith |

# SOUTH AFRICA

## Snooker

| | |
|---|---|
| **1937** | A. Prior |
| **1938** | A. H. Ashby |
| **1939** | A. Prior |
| *1940–45* | *No contests* |
| **1946** | F. Walker |
| *1947* | *No contest* |
| **1948** | F. Walker |
| **1949** | E. Kerr |
| **1950** | T. G. Rees |
| **1951** | T. G. Rees |
| **1952** | T. G. Rees |
| **1953** | J. Van Rensberg |
| **1954** | J. Van Rensberg |
| **1955** | J. Van Rensberg |
| **1956** | F. Walker |
| **1957** | J. Van Rensberg |
| **1958** | R. Walker |
| **1959** | M. Fancisco |
| **1960** | P. Mans Jr |
| **1961** | J. Van Rensberg |
| **1962** | J. Van Rensberg |
| **1963** | J. Van Rensberg |
| **1964** | M. Francisco |
| **1965** | M. Francisco |
| **1966** | M. Francisco |
| **1967** | J. Van Rensberg |
| **1968** | S. Francisco |
| **1969** | S. Francisco |
| **1970** | J. Van Rensberg |
| **1971** | M. Francisco |
| **1972** | J. Van Rensberg |
| **1973** | J. Van Rensberg |
| **1974** | S. Francisco |
| **1975** | M. Francisco |
| *1976* | *No contest* |
| **1977** | S. Francisco |
| **1978** | J. van Niekerk |
| **1979** | F. Ellis |
| **1980** | F. Ellis |
| **1981** | P. Francisco |
| **1982** | P. Francisco |
| **1983** | P. Francisco |
| **1984** | N. van Niekerk |
| **1985** | P. Smallshaw |
| **1986** | S. Mouton |

## Billiards

| | |
|---|---|
| **1920** | Sgt Bruyns |
| **1921** | A. Prior |
| **1922** | A. Prior |
| *1923* | *No contest* |
| **1924** | A. Prior |
| **1925** | P. Rutledge |
| **1926** | A. Prior |
| **1927** | A. Percival |
| **1928** | P. Rutledge |
| *1929–30* | *No contests* |
| **1931** | A. Prior |
| *1932–36* | *No contests* |
| **1937** | A. M. Burke |
| **1938** | A. Prior |
| **1939** | A. Prior |
| *1940–45* | *No contests* |
| **1946** | P. G. Kempen |
| *1947* | *No contest* |
| **1948** | P. G. Kempen |
| **1949** | T. G. Rees |
| **1950** | T. G. Rees |
| **1951** | I. Drapin |
| **1952** | T. G. Rees |
| **1953** | T. G. Rees |
| **1954** | F. Walker |
| **1955** | F. Walker |
| **1956** | G. Povall |
| **1957** | F. Walker |
| **1958** | F. Walker |
| **1959** | M. Francisco |
| **1960** | R. Walker |
| **1961** | M. Francisco |
| **1962** | M. Francisco |
| **1963** | M. Francisco |
| **1964** | M. Francisco |
| **1965** | M. Francisco |
| **1966** | M. Francisco |
| **1967** | J. Van Rensberg |
| **1968** | M. Francisco |
| **1969** | M. Francisco |
| **1970** | M. Francisco |
| **1971** | M. Francisco |
| **1972** | S. Francisco |
| **1973** | S. Francisco |
| **1974** | M. Francisco |

| | | | | | |
|---|---|---|---|---|---|
| **1975** | S. Francisco | **1979** | C. van Dijk | **1983** | C. van Dijk |
| *1976* | *No contests* | **1980** | C. van Dijk | **1984** | C. van Dijk |
| **1977** | M. Francisco | **1981** | P. Spence | **1985** | C. van Dijk |
| **1978** | C. van Dijk | **1982** | P. Francisco | **1986** | C. van Dijk |

## SRI LANKA

### Snooker

| | | | | | |
|---|---|---|---|---|---|
| **1951** | M. S. A. Hassan | **1963** | M. J. M. Izzath | **1975** | N. A. Rahim |
| **1952** | M. J. M Lafir | **1964** | M. J. M. Lafir | **1976** | M. S. U. Mohideen |
| **1953** | M. J. M. Lafir | **1965** | M. J. M. Lafir | **1977** | M. S. U. Mohideen |
| **1954** | M. J. M Lafir | **1966** | M. J. M. Lafir | **1978** | N. A. Rahim |
| **1955** | M. J. M. Lafir | **1967** | N. J. Rahim | **1981** | J. W. H. Boteju |
| **1956** | M. J. M. Lafir | *1968* | *No contest* | **1982** | J. A. Wahid |
| **1957** | M. J. M. Lafir | **1969** | M. J. M. Lafir | **1983** | J. W. H. Boteju |
| **1958** | M. J. M. Lafir | **1970** | N. J. Rahim | **1984** | K. Scrisoma |
| **1959** | M. J. M. Lafir | *1971* | *No contest* | **1985** | J. W. H. Boteju |
| **1960** | M. J. M. Lafir | **1972** | N. J. Rahim | **1986** | J. W. H. Boteju |
| **1961** | M. J. M. Lafir | **1973** | M. J. M. Lafir | **1987** | J. W. H. Boteju |
| **1962** | M. J. M. Lafir | **1974** | *Abandoned* | | |

### Billiards

| | | | | | |
|---|---|---|---|---|---|
| **1951** | M. J. M. Lafir | **1962** | M. J. M. Lafir | **1976** | W. Weerasinghe |
| **1952** | M. J. M. Lafir | **1963** | M. H. M. Mujahid | **1977** | W. Weerasinghe |
| **1953** | M. J. M. Lafir | **1964** | M. J. M. Lafir | **1978** | J. W. H Boteju |
| **1954** | A. C. Cambal | **1966** | M. J. M. Lafir | **1979** | W. Weerasinghe |
| **1955** | T. A. Selvaraj | **1967** | J. K. Bakshani | **1981** | J. W. H Boteju |
| **1956** | T. A. Selvaraj | **1969** | M. J. M. Lafir | **1982** | J. W. H Boteju |
| **1957** | M. J. M. Lafir | **1970** | M. J. M. Lafir | **1983** | W. Weerasinghe |
| **1958** | M. J. M. Lafir | **1972** | M. J. M. Lafir | **1984** | J. W. H Boteju |
| **1959** | M. J. M. Lafir | **1973** | M. J. M. Lafir | **1985** | K. Scrisoma |
| **1960** | M. J. M. Lafir | **1974** | S. Shaharwardi | **1986** | J. W. H. Boteju |
| **1961** | M. J. M. Lafir | **1975** | M. S. U. Mohideen | | |

## FIXTURES 1990–91

| | |
|---|---|
| **September 12–16** | REGAL SCOTTISH MASTERS<br>at Motherwell Civic Centre<br>Box office: (0698) 66166 |
| **October 8–21** | ROTHMANS GRAND PRIX<br>at Hexagon, Reading<br>Box office: (0734) 591591 |
| **October 29–<br>November 3** | ASIAN OPEN |
| **November 5–11** | DUBAI CLASSIC<br>at Al Nasr Stadium, Dubai |
| **November 16–<br>December 2** | STORMSEAL UK OPEN<br>at Guild Hall, Preston<br>Box office: (0772) 21721 |
| **December 6–15** | WORLD MATCHPLAY<br>at International Hall, Brentwood<br>Box office: (0277) 229621 |
| **January 1–12** | MERCANTILE CREDIT CLASSIC<br>at Bournemouth International Centre<br>Box office: (0202) 297297 |
| **February 3–10** | BENSON AND HEDGES MASTERS<br>at Wembley Conference Centre<br>Box office: (071) 901 1234 |
| **February 17–<br>March 3** | PEARL ASSURANCE BRITISH OPEN<br>at Assembly Rooms, Derby<br>Box office: (0332) 369311 |

| | |
|---|---|
| **March 9–17** | EUROPEAN OPEN |
| **April 2–7** | BENSON AND HEDGES IRISH MASTERS<br>at Goffs, Kill, Co Kildare |
| **April 20–<br>May 6** | EMBASSY WORLD CHAMPIONSHIP<br>at Crucible Theatre, Sheffield<br>Box office (by post):<br>Crucible Theatre, Norfolk Street,<br>Sheffield SA 1DA |

*Note:* These dates are subject to amendment.